BUSINESS MANAGEMENT OF
TELECOMMUNICATIONS

HEINRICH M. SCHOENING

Upper Saddle River, New Jersey
Columbus, Ohio

Library of Congress Cataloging in Publication Data

Schoening, Heinrich M.
    Business management of telecommunications/by Heinrich M. Schoening.
        p. cm.
    Includes bibliographical references and index.
    ISBN 0-13-098388-8
    1. Telecommunication—Management. I. Title.

HE7661.S36 2004
384'.068—dc22   2003062449

Editor in Chief: Stephen Helba
Editor: Charles E. Stewart, Jr.
Assistant Editor: Mayda Bosco
Production Editor: Kevin Happell
Design Coordinator: Diane Ernsberger
Cover Designer: Thomas Borah
Cover Art: PhotoDisc
Production Manager: Matthew Ottenweller
Marketing Manager: Ben Leonard

This book was set in Times Roman by Carlisle Communications Ltd. It was printed and bound by Courier Kendallville, Inc. The cover was printed by Phoenix Color Corp.

Excel, Microsoft, MS-DOS, Outlook, PowerPoint, Project, Visio, Visual Basic, Windows, and Word are either registered trademarks or trademarks of Microsoft Corporation in the United States and/or other countries. Microsoft products are the intellectual property of Microsoft Corporation and are protected by copyright laws and one or more U.S. and foreign patents and patent applications.

Pearson Education Ltd.
Pearson Education Singapore Pte. Ltd.
Pearson Education Canada, Ltd.
Pearson Education—Japan

Pearson Education Australia Pty. Limited
Pearson Education North Asia Ltd.
Pearson Educación de Mexico, S.A. de C.V.
Pearson Education Malaysia Pte. Ltd.

10 9 8 7 6 5 4 3 2
ISBN 0-13-098388-8

This book is dedicated to
the memory of my father and mother.
Max and Mina Schoening

BRIEF CONTENTS

CONTENTS

3 WHAT IS TELECOMMUNICATIONS MANAGEMENT?   49

4 CRITERIA FOR MANAGERIAL SUCCESS   65

5 TELECOMMUNICATIONS MANAGER SKILL REQUIREMENTS   85

PART 2
TELECOMMUNICATIONS
PLANNING 105

9 TECHNOLOGY MANAGEMENT SKILLS 181

10 TELECOMMUNICATIONS PLANNING—A CASE STUDY 225

PART 3 PROJECT MANAGEMENT 267

PREFACE

WHAT IS TELECOMMUNICATIONS MANAGEMENT?

Telecommunications technology—LANs, WANs, internetworks, telephone systems, and the World Wide Web—has been one of the fastest growing technology fields since the deregulation of U.S. telecommunications services in 1984. Since 1984, telecommunications technology has become an integral part of the basic information infrastructure used by businesses, governments, and individuals. The growth in telecommunications technology has been matched by the number of individuals seeking to benefit from the promise of high salaries and long term careers in a dynamic field. Today, owning computers without having access to a strong telecommunications infrastructure is equivalent to owning an automobile in a nation that does not have highways. It just doesn't make sense!

Fortunately, there is no shortage of the telecommunications technology needed to build and maintain a telecommunications highway that allows a more effective use of computer technologies. However, the down side associated with an overabundance of technology options is that an extremely complex technology environment, which must be managed effectively if its potential benefits are to be realized, is created.

The text's underlying philosophy is that telecommunications managers need strong managerial skills in two areas:

1. business management
2. technology management

Business management utilizes the skill set needed to operate effectively as a manager within a business. Technology management skills include the ability to effectively select, design, implement, and operate telecommunications technology. A prerequisite for understanding the text's technology management discussion is to have a good technical knowledge of telecommunications technologies, because it is difficult—if not impossible—to effectively manage technology without understanding the underlying technical concepts. Readers who do not have a good technical understanding of telecommunications may find that the information contained in Parts 2, 3, 4, and 5 will be very difficult to understand.

WHY ARE MANAGERS NEEDED?

During the 1700s, a new generation of machines ushered in the industrial revolution in Western Europe. A new breed of business entrepreneurs emerged to build factories to house these wonderful machines that didn't need to sleep and didn't require work breaks. The machines needed workers to feed them raw materials, to direct the machine's processing cycle, and to remove finished product, which was produced at an astounding rate compared to the creation of artisan products. Factory owners found that they had to employ hundreds of workers to "care for and feed" a relatively small number of machines, and they also found that their ability to generate high profits was directly dependent upon the effective use of the large factory worker population.

By the 1900s, a new profession had emerged in the machine-driven factory environment of the industrial revolution: the professional factory manager. The role of a factory manager was to coordinate the efforts of workers and machines, optimize the machines' output, and maximize the owner's profits. Factory owners found that, without competent managers to direct people and technology (machines), they could not survive in an increasingly competitive factory business environment.

The basic theme of this text is that businesses need to manage their telecommunications machines effectively to derive the benefits of telecommunications technology. Effectively using the telecommunications machine requires the use of skilled managers who have strong managerial and technology skills. This idea is best illustrated by an old Arabian proverb: "An army of sheep led by a lion will defeat an army of lions led by a sheep." The text's purpose is to assist in the development of lion leaders who can effectively manage telecommunications departments.

The text examines the managerial tools and techniques that have been introduced since professional managers arrived on the business scene, and it will apply these basic principles to solve some telecommunications management problems found within a business. While the text's focus is on telecommunications management, the managerial topics presented in the text are also applicable for managing other nontelecommunications technologies.

THE PROBLEM WITH TECHNICALLY TRAINED EMPLOYEES IS ...

A common complaint of employers about newly hired personnel is that new hires have academic knowledge but don't know how to effectively apply their knowledge in a business environment. Normally, new hires must gain organizational experience before they are able to generate useful business results.

The major problem encountered by technically trained personnel when entering the business world is that they don't know how to translate their "good technology stuff" into terms that business managers can understand. When this communication gap occurs, the technical individual is either relegated to carrying out mundane operational tasks or becomes a potential candidate for outsourcing. To be successful in performing a technical function within a business, the benefits of using telecommunications products and services must be explained in nontechnical terms and must utilize an accounting format—you must use the language of business managers.

TEXT STRUCTURE

The text has been written for: (1) learning business telecommunications management topics as part of an academic program and (2) as a reference book for individuals in the telecommunications field. For this reason, it contains a blend of reference information, self-assessment questions and answers, case studies, and generic problem solution methods and processes. An intentional level of redundancy has been included between Part 1 and the other parts of the text, because Part 1 is intended to be an introduction to telecommunications management. Parts 2, 3, 4,

and 5 are intended to integrate telecommunications technology and managerial concepts.

The text is divided into five parts:

Part 1: Telecommunications Management Basics

Part 2: Telecommunications Planning

Part 3: Project Management

Part 4: Operations Management

Part 5: Acquisition Management

Part 1, *Telecommunications Management Basics,* describes the nature of the telecommunications management department and reviews skills that aspiring managers should have prior to proceeding to Parts 2, 3, 4, and 5 of the text. Part 1 uses the following discussion points as the forum for organizing information:

1. What do telecommunications managers do?
2. What is telecommunications (technology)?
3. What is management?
4. How is telecommunications "managerial success" measured?
5. What skills do telecommunications managers need?

If the reader does not have the basic telecommunications management knowledge and skills outlined in Part 1, one of two situations may exist: (1) the reader may be a student, and Part 1 is being used to introduce telecommunications management requirements; or (2) the reader may have to acquire additional knowledge and skills before proceeding on to Parts 2, 3, 4, and 5.

Part 2, *Telecommunications Planning,* builds provides a top-down discussion of the telecommunications planning process. It describes the relationship between business and telecommunications strategic planning and the conversion of strategic plans into practical results, then reviews the specific tools and techniques that are used in business and technology management planning processes.

Financial annual planning cycle concepts are discussed, and their relationships to the strategic, tactical, and operational planning processes found in businesses are explained. Different options are discussed for both businesses and telecommunications departments. Various problem-solving and decision-making techniques commonly used for business management purposes are introduced. A case study is used to illustrate the application of managerial planning tools and techniques to develop a business's telecommunications strategic plan.

Part 3, *Project Management,* describes the project management tools and techniques that are available to a telecommunications manager for carrying out administrative and technology project responsibilities. A manual CPM process is used to provide readers with a conceptual understanding of CP planning benefits that can be applied as common sense judgment criteria. CPM is primarily used with large, complex, technology projects, but telecommunications managers also must handle many administrative (nontechnology) projects. Therefore, technology and administrative project processes are reviewed.

A case study is provided to illustrate the use of project management tools and techniques for both technology and nontechnology (administrative) projects. While a manual project management solution is provided for Part 3's technical projects, Appendix B also illustrates the application of project management software (Microsoft Project) to provide a computer-based case study solution.

Part 4, *Operations Management,* describes a telecommunications manager's responsibilities when managing the day-to-day operations of an operations-oriented technology infrastructure. The focus is on managing operating expenses—a key concern of upper business management—and the BVA control process is examined in detail.

A case study demonstrates the development and application of the BVA control process, and the ISO X.700 Network Management framework is referenced as a technology management tool.

Part 5, *Acquisition Management,* describes selection and evaluation processes for acquiring telecommunications systems and networks. It includes a discussion of RFIs, RFQs, and RFPs, and their appropriate use in the acquisition process. The selection process is based on applying a decision-making process that addresses both business and technology. A LCA/NPV format is used to document financial information.

A case study illustrates the application of acquisition tools and techniques for purchasing telecommunications products and services.

Episodic Knowledge

The study of management is episodic in nature—management knowledge and skills consist of many closely connected but independent knowledge areas that must be understood. Unless all the concepts that comprise the whole is understood, individual topics may appear to digress from the main theme of management, even though they are important elements. By the same reasoning, unless the individual concepts are understood, a knowledge gap will exist regarding the composition of the whole. As a result, the managerial education process is one where islands of knowledge are acquired in episodes and learners must be able to consolidate and integrate the information found in many islands of knowledge to acquire new knowledge.

To minimize the need for backtracking to review previously covered material, condensed versions of ancillary topics will be inserted at appropriate points in the text. While this results in some repetition of text information, it helps to cover the relevant information needed to understand the chapter topic. This approach also provides a degree of modularity between sections and, hopefully, avoids the trap of requiring someone to know all topics in great detail to understand one section of the text.

Using the Text

When the text is used as part of a telecommunications degree program, Part 1, *Telecommunications Management,* should be incorporated into an introductory telecommunications course to provide an overview of telecommunications management—a viewpoint that is not found in most telecommunications management texts. Once the student has obtained a basic education in the technical and business topics typically included in a telecommunications program, Parts 2, 3, 4, and 5 are intended for use as a one-semester intermediate or upper-level course. The text content demonstrates the translation of telecommunications information into a nontechnical format, which is useful in academic or business settings.

For individuals who are already working in the telecommunications field and are using the text as a reference, Part 1 is intended to provide self-assessment to determine whether or not they are ready to proceed to Parts 2, 3, 4, and 5. If readers are comfortable with their knowledge of Part 1 topics, they should be ready to proceed to the remaining sections.

Because the text CD contains case study examples, the "do-it-yourself" reader will be able to see the basic logic used to solve problems in Parts 2, 3, 4, and 5.

TEXT FEATURES

Parts

Each of the text's five parts is preceded by an overview of the chapters that will be presented. After Part 1, the overviews also describe the relationship of the new material to previously discussed material.

Chapters

Each chapter begins with a business-oriented summary of chapter contents, including a list of learning objectives for the chapter.

Illustrations

The text contains graphics and tables to help teach new concepts and document the solutions to case study problems.

Managerial Focus

The criteria for (telecommunications) managerial success is to: (1) achieve business success and (2) achieve personal success. The theme of the text is that this is only possible if a real-world perspective is continually applied to managing telecommunications. This underlying theme will be evident throughout the text.

Examples and Applications

There are many examples that illustrate the managerial concepts, methods, and processes introduced in the text. Detailed case studies are provided to illustrate the application of managerial concepts within a hypothetical real-world, business environment.

Chapter Summaries

Chapter summaries are provided to correspond with the learning objectives provided at the beginning of each chapter. A series of open-ended questions are also introduced to provide self-assessment for readers.

Key Terms

Each chapter (excluding case study chapters) contains a list of key terms used throughout the chapter. Definitions of these terms are included in a glossary prepared specifically for the text.

Practice Problems

Multiple choice questions are provided at the end of most chapters. However, more complex concepts require a more sophisticated appraisal mechanism, and practice problems are provided in these cases. In addition, short case studies are provided at the end of a few choice chapters.

Appendixes

Four appendixes are provided to supplement the material covered in the text:

1. Appendix A: Personal Computing for Managers
2. Appendix B: Microsoft Project—Another Personal Computing Tool
3. Appendix C: Job Descriptions and Performance Appraisals
4. Appendix D: Present Value of a $1

These appendixes have been written as learning/self-teaching materials, and the principles provided in Appendix A and B have been used throughout the text to solve managerial problems. Appendix C provides additional information to answer the question raised by many aspiring telecommunications managers: "What do telecommunications managers do?"

Glossary

An extensive glossary is included with the text.

Instructor Materials

A detailed Instructor's Manual is available for text instructors. It provides presentation slides, a multiple choice question database, additional practice problems, case studies for lab assignments, and guidelines for teaching each chapter.

ACKNOWLEDGMENTS

In many ways, writing a textbook is like writing a history book from a personal perspective. While I may provide an interpretation of my experience, the story is incomplete unless it is placed within the context of the past.

Business Management of Telecommunications provides a view of telecommunications management based on my business experience and academic background. I have selected and interpreted telecommunications management topics, based on the experience gained during my life. Therefore, heartfelt thanks are given to Johnson & Johnson—my employer for thirty years—for providing the opportunity to meet many talented individuals and gain firsthand experience in managing a business's computer and telecommunications departments. Thanks are also given to DeVry University in North Brunswick, NJ, for giving me the opportunity to teach telecommunications topics and supporting my efforts in writing the text.

Special thanks are extended to Kevin Happell, Pearson Education/Prentice Hall Production Editor, and Tricia Rawnsley, Copy Editor, for their diligence and patience in guiding me through the formidable task of converting a conceptual text into one suitable for publication.

Finally, I would like to thank the following people who reviewed this manuscript:

Professor Sam Guccione, Eastern Illinois University

Professor David P. Beach, Indiana State University

Professor Phillip Davis, Del Mar College

Professor Fred Seals, Blinn College

Professor Tim Staley, DeVry University

Professor K.R. Kirkendall, Boise State University

TRADEMARK NOTICES

Trademark names have been used throughout the text and, rather than inserting a trademark symbol with each occurrence, the use of the trademark names are acknowledged here. There is no intention to infringe upon them. The product names, trademarks, and registered trademarks are the property of their respective owners. Microsoft software products are referenced continually in the text. Microsoft is a registered trademark. Office, Word, Excel, PowerPoint, and Visio are reigistered product names of Microsoft Corporation.

ABOUT THE AUTHOR

Heinrich M. Schoening was employed by Johnson & Johnson, the world's most comprehensive and broadly based manufacturer of health care products, for thirty years. His experience at Johnson & Johnson included over twenty years of managerial experience in various engineering, information services, and telecommunications positions. He retired in 1993 from his position as director of corporate telecommunications—the top telecommunications management position in the company. In 1996, he began teaching telecommunications courses; the text is based on both his practical managerial experience and his teaching experience.

While the author was teaching telecommunications management courses, he found that the existing text options were either handbooks that provided a broad range of information but had limited in-depth explanations of key topics or were teaching texts that focused narrowly on specific subjects such as accounting, business management, project management, business, or telecommunications. This text is written with the intent to provide a macroview of telecommunications management problems. Individual subjects are pieces of a puzzle that must be assembled to provide a total picture of management problem solutions.

1

TELECOMMUNICATIONS MANAGEMENT BASICS

Telecommunications managers are not born; they are products of education and experience. Becoming a professional telecommunications manager requires a long-term commitment to developing a broad range of managerial and technical skills, and demonstrating the ability to manage people and telecommunications technology in real-world situations. A telecommunications manager must understand technology concepts and must have the necessary business and people skills to direct the efforts of others to use technology effectively.

Writing a text used to teach telecommunications management is analogous to writing a text on how to build a bridge that will span a 1,000 yard stretch of open water and support 6 lanes of bumper-to-bumper automobile traffic. In both cases, it is not possible to cover the entire topic in a single text. However, if the bridge text is written for someone who has a civil engineering degree and fifteen years of diversified engineering design experience, the text can focus on the technical topics that are unique to bridge building without covering the prerequisite basic engineering topics necessary for an understanding of the bridge-building discussion.

The same analogy exists for a text written about telecommunications management. The management of telecommunications—or any complex technology—requires a manager to have a broad knowledge base of mathematics, human communications, technology, computer software, and business skills. This text will assume that the reader has the basic skills needed to understand the concepts and applications presented in the text.

Managerial competence is demonstrated by the selection and application of the appropriate basic skills needed to successfully complete an assignment. A lack of skills or a lack of good judgment will result in a job that is done poorly. While skills are primarily a byproduct of an educational process, learning how to apply them successfully is a byproduct of experience. However, having experience is not simply a matter of "putting in time" while carrying out the responsibilities of a particular job. Ten years of experience can be gained in one of two ways: First, the same learning experience is repeated each year for ten years. Second, each year of experience is in a new area. In the first case, the individual actually has one year of experience repeated ten times, while the second individual has 10 years of real experience. Aspiring telecommunications managers should acquire the second type of experience.

OVERVIEW

Part 1 provides a summary overview of the basic skill areas that the reader should have prior to proceeding to Parts 2, 3, 4, and 5. Part 1 answers five basic questions:

1. What is telecommunications (technology)?
2. What is management?
3. What do telecommunications managers do?
4. How is managerial success measured?
5. What skills do telecommunications managers need?

Questions 1, 2, and 5 highlight the prerequisite knowledge and skills that prospective telecommunications managers should possess prior to covering the information contained in Parts 2 through 5. As already stated, it is necessary to understand certain basic topics before attempting to learn how to be a telecommunications manager. Some of this prerequisite telecommunications and management knowledge is included as the content provided in academic programs. Typical course subject titles might include professional writing, public speaking, college mathematics, natural sciences, personal computer applications, business organization, management principles, financial accounting, managerial accounting, economics, telecommunications technology, and system analysis. These general skills provide an enabling knowledge base that is a prerequisite to acquiring specialized skills in organization management and technology management.

Unless readers have a good enabling knowledge base, they may find the terminology and concepts used in Parts 2, 3, 4, and 5 to be confusing and abstract in nature. While some management topics are discussed at a detail level in Parts 2 through 5, many problem solving examples presume a prior knowledge of the academic subjects listed previously.

To address the five questions raised earlier, Part 1 contains five chapters:

Chapter 1: Telecommunications Management Overview

Chapter 2: What is Telecommunications?

Chapter 3: What is Telecommunications Management?

Chapter 4: Criteria for Managerial Success

Chapter 5: Telecommunications Manager Skill Requirements

Chapter 1 provides an executive summary of the information that is discussed in Chapters 2, 3, 4, and 5, and is intended to allow someone to quickly assess the type of information contained in Part 1 chapters. If readers find that Part 1 topics are familiar, they are probably ready to proceed to Parts 2 through 5. If this is not the case, it may be advisable to acquire additional skills prior to tackling Parts 2, 3, 4, and 5. This can be done either as part of a degree program or as a personal development program.

1

TELECOMMUNICATIONS MANAGEMENT OVERVIEW

LEARNING OBJECTIVES

1. Understand the impact that regulations have had on the development of telecommunication technology.

2. Understand the impact that the business environment has had on the development of the current telecommunications technology environment.

3. Understand how telecommunications technology has evolved through three technology eras.

4. Understand the difference between organization and technology management requirements.

5. Understand how telecommunications can support business profitability objectives.

6. Understand the criticality of upper management communications and the appropriate structure for this type of communication.

7. Understand the 50%/50% Telecommunications Management Model and its implications for telecommunications managers.

8. Understand three business oriented criteria used to measure managerial success in the telecommunications area and their implications for telecommunications management.

9. Understand what telecommunications managers do and what the term *bona fide manager* means.

10. Understand the Telecommunications Management Skill Triangle and its component parts.

11. Understand the format of the text and how it is organized.

Telecommunications can be defined as the science and technology of communicating at a distance by using the electronic transmission of pulses, such as by **telegraph,** cable, **telephone,** radio, or television. Prior to January 1, 1984, telecommunications in the U.S. was considered by many to be the exclusive domain of the **Bell System,** the regulated entity that dominated the U.S. communications industry for over a hundred years. The Bell System was regulated at the state and federal level by government agencies and the regulatory agencies controlled the availability and cost of **telecommunications** products and services.

Prior to 1984, life was simple for residential and business customers. One call to the local telephone company **(local exchange carrier [LEC])** took care of any equipment, wiring, or service problems. Customers located in remote areas received the same level of service as customers living in heavily populated areas—and everyone paid the same rate regardless of the actual cost for providing the service. All communications related charges showed up on one telephone company bill, and calling one telephone number would resolve the billing problems for equipment, installation, local calling services, or long distance calling services. For business customers, a single call to the telephone company was all that was needed to initiate a project that installed a telephone system that could handle 10,000 employees or installed a complex communications network. A single call also initiated repair activities for all telecommunications services. Before 1984, management of business telecommunications was delegated to the telephone company and the solution for any communications problem was only a phone call away.

However, that was then and this is now. Today, the remnants of the telephone company operate in a restricted mode and—based on regulatory and legal rulings—may face extinction at some future time. This chapter describes the challenges confronting telecommunications managers who have the responsibility for delivering up-to-date telecommunications products and services to businesses and organizations.

THE TELECOMMUNICATIONS TECHNOLOGY ENVIRONMENT

Telecommunications managers must be effective as organization managers in order to achieve personal success in business. However, telecommunications managers must also have the knowledge and skills necessary to manage telecommunications technologies. Telecommunications managers must have a good understanding of the external telecommunications environment where telecommunications products and services will be acquired including technology developers, manufacturers, distributors, regulators, and standards organizations. The external environment controls the availability of telecommunications goods and services. A failure to operate within the constraints of these environmental factors will result in poor decisions being made when selecting telecommunications technologies. Poor selection decisions will generate higher costs and poorer performance (including more down time).

At the semantic level, "tele" means "operating at a distance." The word "telecommunications" can be translated literally as "communicating at a distance." In this context, smoke signals and signal fires are examples of telecommunications. However, the text will use the generally accepted technical text definition of telecommunications: the transmission and reception of information by sending electrical or optical signals over different communications media.

The telecommunications era in the U.S. began when the first public telegram was sent in 1844, using Samuel F. B. Morse's telegraph invention. While public and private telegraph services are still available today, they have been largely superseded by newer technologies. In 1876, Alexander Graham Bell received a patent for an experimental telegraph device and established the Bell Telephone Company. The experimental device was called a telephone, and the Bell Telephone Company operated for a number of years under patent protection laws. The original Bell Telephone Company went through a series of business changes during the late 1800s and was eventually purchased by the American Telephone and Telegraph Company (AT&T) in 1900. AT&T (a.k.a., the Bell System) dominated the telecommunications industry in the U.S. until its breakup in 1984—an event frequently referred to as the AT&T Divestiture or as the Bell System Breakup.

Regulatory Issues

Regulations dominated the early history of the telecommunications industry, both in the U.S. and internationally. Today, the U.S. has deregulated many telecommunications products and services, but regulated products and services still exist outside of the U.S. A telecommunications manager involved with international communications must be familiar with the regulatory constraints that exist in different parts of the world. The constraints imposed by international regulations should be incorporated into the telecommunications planning process.

By 1919, AT&T owned virtually all long distance telephone circuits (**inter-exchange carrier [IXC]**) and controlled 80% of the U.S. local telephone marketplace through its Bell telephone companies. Local telephone companies provided telephone services to residential and commercial customers and the federal government considered long distance and local telephone company operations to be natural monopolies whose benefits could best be managed by regulating telephone service providers. Prior to 1984, U.S. telecommunications services were controlled by various federal and state regulatory agencies. In 1984, the Justice Department implemented a court ruling that resulted in the split up of the Bell System: AT&T Long Lines, Western Electric, Bell Laboratories, and the 22 Bell Operating Companies (local telephone companies). The implementation of the 1984 Justice Department requirements resulted in:

1. immediate deregulation of the communications equipment marketplace

2. opening up the long distance calling market to competition

3. the creation of seven independent Regional Bell Holding Companies (RBHCs) to continue to provide local telephone services

Congress passed the Telecommunications Act of 1996, which continued the trend of deregulating telecommunications services initiated by the 1984 Justice Department decision. The Telecommunications Act of 1996 eliminated the requirement that U.S. long distance carriers had to file domestic tariffs, allowed increased competition in the local telephone market, and eased restrictions that prevented RHBCs from providing long distance calling services.

INTERNATIONAL COMMUNICATIONS. While the U.S. used private companies (AT&T and other independent telephone companies) to provide telephone services to its citizens, other countries used government operated **postal, telephone, and telegraph (PTT) agencies** to provide telephone services. Outside of the U.S., telephone services were seen as a natural extension of the existing postal system, and private firms were allowed to provide neither telephone equipment nor services. The 1984 divestiture triggered a wave of international telecommunications privatization activities—the selling of government owned telephone agencies to private industry companies—which still continue today. However, in this privatized environment, the government normally maintains a majority ownership in the hybrid (private + government ownership) telecommunications companies.

Telecommunications managers responsible for providing international communications services must be aware of the regulations that exist in each of the countries where communications are required and must take the appropriate steps to operate within the local regulatory environment. Because regulations vary on a country-by-country basis, a significant effort may be required to keep track of international regulations.

Business Issues

The U.S. regulatory environment that existed between 1844 and 1984 reflected the prevailing attitude of business organizations toward telecommunications services. Prior to the 1970s, businesses viewed telecommunications as an overhead expense that should be minimized. They had little interest in expanding its use as a business resource. The underlying philosophy for measuring the effectiveness of managing internal telecommunications costs prior to the 1970s was that any cost incurred for telephone services was too high. In this environment, customers were expected to pay for the calls they made to businesses, and a heavy emphasis was placed on minimizing the time and cost of outgoing calls. Many organizations had **accounting** departments set up to scrutinize monthly billings and track calling costs. Employees who made personal calls using business phones were expected to reimburse the company and the accounting function frequently monitored personal call activity closely.

The 1970s presented U.S. businesses with challenges that had never existed previously. For the first time, U.S. corporations were facing serious competition from international companies. During the 1970s, Japanese car makers had succeeded in gaining a significant percentage of the U.S. automobile market. Foreign competition was spreading into electronics, office equipment, and other technology areas that had formerly been the exclusive domain of U.S. businesses. One of the responses of American businesses was to increase their use of new computer and telecommunications technology. The focus of this effort was to manage their operations more effectively and to become more "customer-friendly." During the 1970s, the **upper management** perspective of telecommunications changed from one where telecommunications was viewed as a cost to be minimized to one where telecommunications was seen as a business resource that allowed companies to compete more effectively in the marketplace.

Wide area telecommunications services (WATS) was introduced during the 1980s and became generically referred to as 800 services. 800 services were based on the direct distance dialing (DDD) services commonly referred to as POTS (Plain Old Telephone Services), but introduced a new billing approach that allowed businesses to pay for calls made by their customers—a behavior that would have been considered financial insanity in the 1950s. In the highly competitive, post 1970 environment, businesses found it necessary to provide free customer services in order to retain customers. Businesses were under continual pressure to develop creative strategies so they could survive in the new, customer-driven sales environment. U.S. businesses were competing against high quality, low priced foreign products and services from foreign competitors and thus increased their internal use of computers and communication as a competitive response.

New Pressures For Telecommunications Deregulation

As a result of the changes in the U.S. business environment, businesses could no longer tolerate the slow technology development process that was controlled by regulatory agencies. Businesses needed faster, more complex telecommunications products and services to respond to foreign competition, and it was not a coincidence that the Bell system breakup occurred during the 1980s when American businesses were frantically looking for more technology-based business tools in order to gain a competitive edge. Although the change in the regulated monopoly status of the Bell system in 1984 was caused by a judicial initiative, it can also be viewed as a political response to increase the availability of telecommunications products and services in the U.S. There was a need to have better telecommunications products at lower costs, and these two requirements could not be met by a regulated telecommunications industry. The **1984 Modified Final Judgment** decision was driven by a Justice Department antitrust action (a business issue)—not by Congress—and this antitrust action began the deregulation of U.S. telecommunications products and services. Congress then picked up the deregulation initiative and placed pressure on the **Federal Communications Commission (FCC)**—the government's telecommunications regulatory agency—to continue the deregulation of telecommunications products and services.

Today, the telecommunications product and service environment continues to be driven by commercial pressures. More telecommunications technology has been developed since 1984 than during the 140 years preceding the AT&T divestiture.

Technology Issues

Chronologically, the development of telecommunications technologies can be placed into three technology eras:

1. telegraph communication
2. telephone (voice) communication
3. data (computer) communication

While this listing provides a neatly bundled way of reviewing telecommunications technology developments, the current reality is that telegraph, voice, and data classifications have blurred and are in the process of being supplanted by multimedia communication applications. The new multimedia technologies are expected to provide a holistic (global), any-to-any approach for any form of telecommunications. Of the three classifications listed, computer-based communication has quickly become the dominant technology. It is expected to retain this dominance during the foreseeable future.

First generation (vacuum tube) computer technologies were introduced during the 1950s, and by the mid-1960s, the centralized computer mainframe providers were under heavy pressure by their customers to provide computer communication capabilities. A major breakthrough for computer communication took place during the 1970s, when Internet communication was introduced. The Internet was an outgrowth of a U.S. Department of Defense military network project, **ARPANET,** which was initiated to ensure the availability of military computer information in the event of an enemy attack. However, it was the introduction of web browser applications in the 1990s that transformed the Internet from a technical toy into the commercial success that exists today. The continuing development of sophisticated, easy-to-use search engines has accelerated the growth of electronic-commerce (e-commerce) and the Internet infrastructure has become the standard transaction broker between buyers and sellers.

TECHNOLOGICAL OBSOLESCENCE. In the computer technology arena, the half-life of any new technology is less than two years, as is evident when the functional lifetime of a personal computer (PC) is examined. A PC purchased today will typically have twice the speed and storage capability than one that was produced two years ago, and it will also cost less to purchase. This cost *v.* performance phenomenon also exists in telecommunications—a somewhat distressing problem when a telecommunications manager explains to business management that it makes sense to replace equipment that has not yet been written off. Depreciation is the mechanism used by accounting to recover the cost of equipment purchased by the business enterprise, and a depreciation life of five years is commonly established by the Internal Revenue Services (IRS) guidelines for computer and communications equipment. Writing off equipment before depreciation has been completed is a disruptive process that can adversely affect a business's financial performance.

In the U.S., telecommunications services are provided by regulated and unregulated entities and telecommunications equipment is provided by unregulated entities. Long term, it is highly likely that all U.S. telecommunications services will be offered in a totally deregulated marketplace with only a few regulations left to underwrite the costs for providing limited services to address social issues.

TELECOMMUNICATIONS SUPPLIERS. There are two types of telecommunications suppliers in the U.S.

1. deregulated suppliers
2. regulated suppliers

In the deregulated marketplace, purchasers of telecommunications products are free to choose between different vendor offerings based on price and performance. Regulated suppliers are remnants of the totally regulated environment that existed in the U.S. prior to 1984, and are best described as formerly regulated suppliers that are in the process of being deregulated. Local telephone companies remain regulated entities where the pricing of their products and services continue to be regulated by state Public Utility Commissions (PUCs). The FCC continues to provide loose control over long distance service providers (a.k.a. inter-exchange carriers [IXCs]), and the FCC's current role is primarily one of ensuring a smooth transition into a totally competitive long distance marketplace.

In other parts of the world, product and service availability varies on a country-by-country basis. Some countries have more products and services available than other countries. The U.S. develops and uses more telecommunications technology than any other country—a phenomenon that makes the U.S. marketplace a key target for foreign telecommunications suppliers.

TELECOMMUNICATIONS STANDARDS. Prior to the deregulation and privatization activities triggered by

the 1984 AT&T divestiture, the term *telecommunications* was synonymous with telephone (or voice based) communication, and this area was the exclusive domain of individual country governments or government appointed agencies. In the U.S., private companies (AT&T and others) were regulated, but in the rest of the world governments provided telephone services directly through their PTT agencies.

During the telegraph and telephone phase of telecommunications technology development, telecommunications was a country managed phenomenon and the use of government or government regulated agencies worked quite well. Standards were established at the national level, and each nation had a telecommunications infrastructure based on its own national standards. Some level of coordination took place between national standards organizations when telegraph or telephone communication was desired between countries, or if the cooperating countries were attempting to minimize the cost of independent research efforts.

During the 1960s, **computer** mainframe communication needs emerged as more business organizations wanted to provide remote locations with access to centralized mainframe computers. In this early computer environment, businesses found they were locked into using the proprietary computer communication offerings of the computer vendor from whom they had purchased their mainframe computer system. Communication interoperability between different mainframe computer systems was difficult, if not impossible.

A user driven organization emerged—the **International Standards Organization (ISO)**—for the purpose of developing computer communications standards. The underlying objective of the ISO was to create a set of standards that would be used by all computer communication developers to allow communications interoperability between proprietary products and services. In this any-to-any vision, business customers could purchase telecommunications products and services based on price and performance, and be sure that they would operate in a plug and play mode. Business users would no longer be limited to telecommunications products that were provided by their mainframe computer supplier.

ISO issued the **7-layer Open System Interconnect (OSI) model** during the 1970s, and this model has become the conceptual standard used by all computer communication equipment suppliers and users. The OSI model identified seven communication protocol categories, called layers in the model, and established interface standards between the protocol layers. The OSI model allowed vendors to maintain their proprietary protocols within each layer, as long as they provided a standard interface between layers—an interface that would allow OSI-compatible products to be attached. In theory, equipment produced by OSI-compatible suppliers could be connected to each other and would operate smoothly. Today's relatively transparent communications equipment environment exists because of these initial ISO/OSI activities.

Computer networking standards are a major factor in telecommunications, and they allow end users to have an extraordinary degree of flexibility when selecting equipment and services. However, this flexibility comes at a price, because highly skilled technicians are needed to develop, install, and operate the software and hardware interfaces between different equipment vendors.

WHAT IS TELECOMMUNICATIONS MANAGEMENT?

Telecommunications management is the management of **people, time, and money (PTM)** resources to provide communications products and services for use by business organizations. Telecommunications management skills can be broken into two areas: business management and technology management skills. Business management activities direct and administer the efforts of employees who provide telecommunications products and services. Technology management activities are concerned with selecting, implementing, and operating the appropriate telecommunications technologies that will be used within a business enterprise and between an enterprise and its customers and suppliers.

This text addresses business telecommunications activities and discusses how **business management and technology management** skills are needed to effectively and efficiently provide business telecommunications services.

Business Management

A business is an organization that buys and sells goods, makes products, or provides services to customers. Business managers direct the efforts of their organization [employees] to achieve business goals. Business management theories had their origin during the 18th century, when manufacturing organizations were created in Great Britain at the beginning of the Industrial Revolu-

tion. The Industrial Revolution was triggered by a technical breakthrough—the development of coke from regular coal. Coke properties allowed a high-quality iron to be produced, which allowed the production of the high-quality iron needed to build machines. High-quality iron allowed the construction of large, durable machinery products for converting various forms of energy into mechanical motion. The discovery of coke, coupled with the invention and development of the steam engine, transformed society from a craftsman-oriented production environment to a factory-oriented, mass production environment.

With the consolidation of people resources into a factory environment, the need for people-managers emerged. Although the central focus for factories was to house machines, it was quickly evident that factory employees were essential for the "care and feeding" of these wonderful machines. The machines were immobile and had voracious appetites for fuel and raw materials. Factory employees were originally viewed as machine attendants, whose value was measured by the output of the machines they cared for. Under the previous craftsman-oriented environment, individual workers were only accountable to themselves, or perhaps to a small group of peer workers. In the new factory environment, many workers were needed to support the machine-based environment and employees were paid to perform machine-driven tasks. If workers were idled because the machines were not running, products were not being produced and factory owners would not achieve their profit objectives. From an owner's perspective, underachieving machines were clearly unacceptable. Factory owners found that productivity problems were not with the machines but with the human caretakers of the machines. When factory employees were used effectively, the machinery output was high. Factory owners found that the difference between profit and loss was directly related to how effectively the factory employees were managed.

Factory owners soon found that the job of coordinating the efforts of people, machines, and materials was a difficult one, and that the use of professional managers greatly improved factory performance—and the owner's profits. By the early 1900s, scientific management theories were being formulated by professional factory managers. These theories became the basis for the formal pool of knowledge taught today as principles of business management.

A key contributor to early scientific management theory was **Henri Fayol** (1841–1925), the operating director of a French mining business. He identified and documented four key management activities performed by factory managers:

1. planning
2. organizing
3. leading
4. controlling

His view was that all management activities—regardless of the specific product being produced—required skills in these four areas. Many management theories have been developed since the early 1900s, but Henri Fayol's observations continue to be fundamental in current management theories. His **POLC Model** (plan, organize, lead, and control) will be used as a central management theme throughout this text. The POLC Model is illustrated in Figure 1–1 and will be discussed in greater detail in Chapter 4.

Figure 1–2 provides a goal-centric version of the POLC Model in Figure 1–1, but it emphasizes the need for having *goals* drive the development of a management plan. Conceptually, a plan is developed that meets the goal objectives and identifies the labor and material resources (organize) and managerial component (lead). The managerial (lead) component continually monitors the progress in attaining established goals and makes any necessary changes [control] to bring actual implementation performance in line with the original plan. If the POLC Model is used correctly, the outcomes of the managerial process will achieve the goal objectives identified in the original plan.

This text's primary concern is with getting the telecommunications management job done successfully, and provides only a general overview of management theories—past and present—in Chapter 3 (*What is Telecommunications Management?*). Many excellent books have been written about the different management theories developed since the scientific management era began in the early 1900s. Readers can find more detailed information about management topics by researching those resources. This text will focus on the application of various managerial techniques and processes to effectively utilize telecommunications products and services.

Businesses were initially subdivided into areas of functional specialization, called *departments*, where each department consolidated individuals with similar skills. Departments included accounting, manufacturing, sales, marketing, customer services, computer information services, legal services, personnel (human resources), and administrative services. Departments continue to be a primary building block for many businesses.

The application of general POLC model principles by a specific department manager may vary depending upon the department's responsibilities, but all departments in a business will have the responsibility of meeting the business's enterprise goals. Good management in a manufacturing department context would mean producing a high-quality product at a low cost, while good management in a marketing department context would focus on the selection of the right product to meet customer requirements.

Managing telecommunications requires the skillful application of basic management methods and tools in a business context. The real world measurement of telecommunications functions' effectiveness will be based on how well the telecommunications resource assists in achieving an enterprise's business objectives.

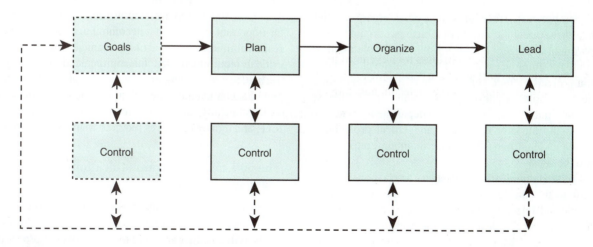

Figure 1–1. The POLC management model.

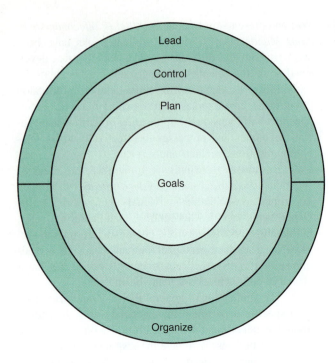

Figure 1–2. A goal-centric POLC model.

OTHER ORGANIZATION MANAGEMENT ACTIVITIES. The term *upper management* refers to the top management level found in a business organization—typically a president and those managers reporting directly to the president. Upper management is accountable directly to the owners—**stockholders** in today's business environment—and has the primary responsibility for meeting stockholders' profitability expectations. Upper management sets strategies and corporate goals, and establishes policies, procedures, and other organizational standards to direct the efforts of a business organization. Department managers are responsible for implementing policies for employees at the department level. Organization policies include employee benefits, **performance reviews,** employee development planning, holidays, vacation, and work hours. The department manager serves as a translator of upper management procedures and policies, and must frequently maintain confidential employee files.

Telecommunications managers are responsible for serving as the managerial interface between upper management and telecommunications employees. They are also responsible for developing the budgetary information that is used by upper management to manage the business and they must have a good fundamental knowledge of business management and accounting so they can translate telecommunications activities into language that will be understood by nontechnical managers.

Technology Management

In the U.S., the first public telegram was sent in 1844. It used telegraphic equipment invented by Samuel F. B. Morse. Telegraph messages were transmitted over a single wire using a series of electric pulses (dots and dashes) where a specific combination of dots and dashes represented an alphanumeric character. The encoding of electrical signals to represent information continues to be the underlying concept used today by all major telecommunications technologies. Light, electricity, and radio frequency media are all used to carry information across long distances. Modern telecommunications relies heavily on computer technology, and the introduction of the World Wide Web (WWW) during the 1990s has made computer-to-computer traffic the fastest growing category of network traffic.

Specific computer technology and applications are short-lived, a concept that is clearly demonstrated by the two-year technical life of PCs. A 3-year old PC is unable to meet many operating system performance requirements expected by new PC operating systems and software applications. While a PC may remain fully functional for many years, its capability and performance will quickly be superseded by cheaper, faster, more reliable alternatives within two years of its introduction. This same obsolescence effect exists for all computer-based telecommunications technologies and is likely to continue for the foreseeable future.

The timely replacement of obsolete technologies is an important element of telecommunications managerial responsibilities, and technology management skills are a critical requirement for telecommunications managers. Technology management includes the ability to develop technology implementation plans that are sound financially and technically, and effectively coordinate the people, time, and money resources required to implement them.

The 50%/50% Telecommunications Management Model

An effective telecommunications manager needs a balance of business and technology management skills. Focusing too heavily in either area will lower the overall probability of managerial success.

If a manager's focus is primarily in the business management area, the implicit assumption is that properly managed telecommunications department employees will automatically select the best telecommunications technology for the organization. In a telecommunications department—as in real life—there are people who are skilled at their craft and those whose skills are poor. If telecommunications managers are unable to assess the technical competence of department members, there is a low likelihood that the manager will be able to select and hire the people who have the skills needed to successfully select, design, and implement telecommunications technologies.

When a manager's focus is primarily in the technology management area, the telecommunications department's primary emphasis will be on the technical purity of the selected technology, i.e., selecting state-of-the-art technologies. If this is the case, there is a strong probability that the selected telecommunications technology infrastructure will be expensive (and perhaps technically unstable) compared to other alternatives that can do a similar job of meeting enterprise business objectives. Two scenarios are possible when a business has a purely-technical telecommunications manager running the department: 1) The telecommunications manager is fired because of poor results or high costs; or 2) The stockholders fire upper-level managers for not selecting good department managers. Success of the business is based on business performance, not on having the latest (and potentially, the most expensive) telecommunications infrastructure.

Managerial success in telecommunications requires a balance of organization management and technology management skills, and it is recommended that a 50%/50% model be followed to achieve long-term success in telecommunications areas. This model recommends that telecommunication managers devote 50% of their managerial time to business management and 50% of their time to technology management.

CRITERIA FOR MANAGERIAL SUCCESS

Regardless of the techniques and tools used to manage telecommunications, there is a need to identify the **managerial success criteria.** In the real world, many different alternatives exist for meeting a given objective. The use of a standard measurement tool for determining managerial success would be very helpful in identifying the best managerial options. If telecommunications managers correctly select the best managerial options, they will be recognized and rewarded with the benefits (salary increases and promotions) associated with doing a good job.

The primary emphasis of this text will be on managing communication within a business. As a result, the criterion for determining telecommunications success will be the same one used for other areas of a business enterprise—that of satisfying upper management expectations. Because upper management expectations may vary from business to business, it is important that telecommunications managers be familiar with their environment. Using the same performance measurement yardstick that is used by upper management will ensure that telecommunications department activities directly support business objectives while also achieving managerial success.

Text examples will be based on using manufacturing examples, i.e., companies that design, develop, and manufacture products. However, the concepts that will be used also apply to retail, service, and other businesses.

A key strategy for ensuring success in any job is *to satisfy the boss*. In a business environment, this means supporting upper management initiatives in their quest to satisfy the stockholders to whom they are accountable. While upper management in different organizations may have differing areas of interest, there are three areas that are of great importance to all senior managers:

1. **business profitability**
2. **customer satisfaction**
3. **planning**

Success cannot be achieved by simply assisting upper management to meet their objectives and by doing good things. Business management must be aware of the good things done by a telecommunications manager, and this awareness is not a normal byproduct of business activities. Therefore, we will delay the discussion of the three success criteria to examine the need for effective communication with upper management.

Communicating With Upper Management

If upper management is unaware of the importance of a telecommunications department in: 1) supporting enterprise profitability objectives, 2) satisfying internal and external telecommunications customers, and 3) developing business-oriented telecommunications plans that support upper management goals, there is a low probability that the department will obtain the budgetary support needed to operate an effective telecommunications organization. The following section discusses the format and style of upper management communications, and provides guidelines for communicating with upper-level managers.

Upper management directly controls the use of a business's financial resources and allocates these resources through a budgetary process. The business's budgetary process is used to provide funding for all departments, including telecommunications. The funds obtained through the budgetary process provide the monies needed to purchase new equipment and services and to cover normal operating expenses. The decision criteria used by upper management for allocating funds to a telecommunications function will be based on the perceived value received for the investment when compared to the business benefits that can be gained by investing in proposals submitted by other departments. Therefore, it is important that upper management sees telecommunications projects and operations as being a good investment—a judgment that will be based on the business benefits derived from telecommunications products and services. A primary role of a telecommunications manager is to effectively communicate the business benefits of telecommunications. Effective communication with upper management is essential for the long-term success of an internal telecommunications department, and the effectiveness of the communication will directly impact the level of funding received by the telecommunications department.

A Description of Business Communications.

Upper managers have a broad range of responsibilities and a limited amount of time to carry them out. The internal telecommunications department is just one of many internal areas vying for upper management attention, and it is important that the communication format used by telecommunications managers is readable, timely, and concise. All business organizations have an operating philosophy regarding the appearance and structure that should be used for internal communication. Therefore, upper management will have preset expectations regarding the format and style of any internal communication they receive. A telecommunications manager should be aware of the organization's format and style philosophies, and should make sure that those elements are incorporated into any documents sent within the business.

The term *format* refers to the overall appearance of a document, and *style* refers to the readability. Good business communication relies on the elimination of technical jargon and the use of financial information to explain the merits of proposals. The language of upper management consists of business English and numbers (accounting). Business communication should be concise, unambiguous, use business English, and contain financial data in an appropriate format.

Technical terms should not be used in memos. The use of a **layered writing style** is strongly recommended. A layered style is one where information is structured to provide summary-level information at the beginning of a section, additional details in the middle, and key elements summarized at the end. If the reader is familiar with the summary information provided at the beginning of a memo, the reader can then bail out because further reading (or listening) is not essential. The use of headings in a layered document format provides a quick reference marker for follow-up questions. More details on the format and style of business communication will be covered in Chapter 4 and examples will be provided in Parts 2 through 5 of the text.

Accounting Information.

Accounting (numbers) is a standard part of the information infrastructure found in all businesses. Upper management uses financial statements to understand the impact of business decisions on the bottom line, and it is essential that telecommunications managers also understand the format of the financial reports (general ledger, budget *v.* actual, capital forecasting, balance sheets, and profit & loss statements) used by business management.

Telecommunications managers should use standard accounting formats when financial information is provided to upper management. Using a familiar accounting format increases the likelihood that a business manager will spend the time to review correspondence and increases the document's readability.

Business Profitability

Management's performance is tied directly to the business's financial performance, and they are accountable to the enterprise's owners for delivering good bottom line results. The accounting department issues reports that keep track of revenues and expenses, and upper management uses these reports to assess both external and internal department performance.

The bottom line measurement of profitability can be expressed as:

$$\text{profitability (or loss)} = \text{revenues} - \text{expenses}$$

Profits result when revenues exceed expenses and losses occur when expenses exceed revenues. Continuing to operate in the red (loss) can only be tolerated for short periods of time, and even not for profit businesses must control their expenses to live within the limits of their revenues (typically, from the donations they receive).

When a telecommunications department supports an enterprise's financial objectives by helping to increase revenues or by decreasing expenses, upper management will view the telecommunications department in a positive light. On the other hand, generating high expenses without showing any evidence of business benefits is a high risk activity for any manager.

Customer Satisfaction

Upper management is extremely customer conscious, and is strongly influenced by positive or negative feedback received from customers. They will also extend this same concern with customer satisfaction to all internal operations and will listen carefully to opinions regarding the quality of services provided by internal departments. When the users of telecommunications services communicate satisfaction or dissatisfaction with the service received, upper managers will listen intently and provide feedback (praise or criticism) to the senior manager responsible for the telecommunications department. Even stronger attention will be given if the enterprise's customers give opinions regarding telecommunications service levels. When internal and external customers view an organization's telecommunications services positively and communicate this perception to upper management, upper management will view the telecommunications function positively.

INTERNAL TELECOMMUNICATIONS CUSTOMERS. In a business organization, a telecommunications department's **internal customers** consist of the various departments and functional units supporting the organization's business operations. When poor telecommunications service levels are received, internal departments will have difficulty communicating with their internal and external customers, and this will be reflected in lower organizational productivity levels. Reduced internal productivity caused by poor communications facilities is guaranteed to get upper management's attention—in a negative way. An internal customer who receives poor service from a telecommunications department will normally be quite vocal to upper management about the poor service they are receiving.

It is important to the long term health and welfare of a telecommunications manager that:

1. The telecommunications department provides high quality services to its internal customers.

2. Internal customers perceive the service to be high-quality.

3. Upper management is aware of the high-quality telecommunications service levels provided to internal customers.

EXTERNAL TELECOMMUNICATIONS CUSTOMERS. In today's communications-intensive business environment, a telecommunications department's customers may also consist of **external customers**—individuals and organizations that are not part of the internal organization. External customers would include the organization's customers, their suppliers, and other peer business organizations. Increasingly, customers are being given access to the internal information resources of their suppliers, and this access utilizes a combination of computer and communications technologies. Customer access may be provided by using Web pages that allow the customer to select the information or service that is of interest to them. An increased emphasis is being placed on e-commerce (electronic-commerce), where e-commerce is the use of computer and communications technologies to provide commercial (business) services that had previously been provided by a human contact only. In the current e-commerce environment, customers may browse through a product database, fill a shopping cart with various products, obtain credit approval for purchasing shopping cart items, and be given follow up order status information via e-mail messages.

A business's suppliers may also be provided with access to the customer's internal databases and be assigned the responsibility of ensuring that the customer's product inventory levels are kept at the levels needed for supporting their sales requirements. An example of this would be when a retail organization provides inventory information to its suppliers, who have the responsibility for avoiding out-of-stock situations at the retail organization's locations. Clearly, this requires excellent communications between customer and supplier. The failure of a telecommunications department to provide reliable, effective communication services could negatively impact organizational profitability.

Planning

Good planning means doing the right things at the right times, and nothing impresses upper management more than a manager who is always prepared. Being prepared is not an accident, but a byproduct of a good planning process. Sound planning practices are needed to establish a just-in-time operating environment that is characteristic of well-run companies. Having an enterprise telecommunications plan that is clear, concise, and identifies the business benefits of telecommunications services provides an excellent vehicle for communicating with upper management. The plan should also accurately anticipate future needs and the investment and operating expenses associated with implementing them.

While many elements of an enterprise telecommunications plan may fall into the strategic planning category, the planning process also includes the tactical planning and operational planning elements needed to translate strategic concepts into operational benefits. Selecting an unproven technology too early in its development cycle increases the likelihood of experiencing operating problems or breakdowns after the technology has been implemented. A high level of operating problems resulting from implementing unstable technologies will be reflected in high operating costs and poor performance when compared to the results that would have been generated if a proven technology with a good track record had been selected.

When a new telecommunications technology has the potential for providing a competitive advantage (an extremely positive planning concept for upper managers), the risk and cost elements should be clearly identified to ensure that the introduction of the technology is justified. The issue of timing is also critical in the planning process when funding requests are made. Telecommunications investments must be identified far enough in advance so that funding can be integrated into the overall business capital investment planning process.

> The telecommunications manager is responsible for doing the right things at the right times, i.e., for ensuring that the timing of project and funding requests makes sense in a business context. The creation and execution of good telecommunications plans is the best way to demonstrate strong planning skills to upper management.

WHAT DO TELECOMMUNICATIONS MANAGERS DO?

Telecommunications managers are a category of managers found in businesses. In general, managers direct and coordinate the activities of others to achieve specific objectives, and they are accountable for the efficient and effective use of a business organization's people resource. Good managers are able to leverage the skills and efforts of employees and subordinate managers to achieve synergistic results, i.e., obtain a final result that is greater than the sum of the capabilities of the individual employees in a workgroup. The managerial role in business organizations is an outgrowth of the Industrial Revolution, which began during the 1700s, and it was only during the early 1900s that professional managers were recognized to be an essential element in a business organization.

This text will focus on the role of the telecommunications manager who works within a business organization, and it will assume that telecommunications managers are **bona fide managers.** *Bona fide managers* are managers who have supervisory and developmental responsibilities for subordinates, as opposed to individuals who have the title of *manager* but do not have any supervisory or developmental responsibility for personnel. Bona fide managers have a responsibility to appraise the performance of their subordinates, develop and train the individuals in their managerial workgroup, administer raises and promotions, and support various employee-oriented initiatives organized by the business enterprise.

From a big picture perspective, telecommunications managers are responsible for effectively utilizing the PTM resources provided to them by a business organization. While there is always a strong emphasis on conserving PTM resources (i.e., being cost-effective), there is an implicit understanding that value to be received for expenditures should be justified by the business benefits that are received. Telecommunications managers are responsible for identifying the business benefits that will be received in exchange for an organization's PTM investment and explaining the investment benefits in terms that can be readily understood by business managers.

At the operating level, telecommunications managers are accountable for a broad range of responsibilities, but the primary responsibility is *to get the job done.* **Job descriptions** are used to provide a general overview of the responsibilities associated with each employee position—managerial or nonmanagerial—but job descriptions are primarily a compensation-justification mechanism. A telecommunications manager's accountabilities, in theory, should be based on a formal performance appraisal process that spells out these accountabilities clearly. In practice, a manager's evaluation also includes many informal, ad hoc appraisal elements.

At the beginning of an appraisal period, managerial goals are established to identify: 1) general managerial, administrative, and functional (telecommunications management) responsibilities, 2) nonmanagerial administrative duties, and 3) specific projects, activities, or tasks to be completed during the appraisal period. In addition to being accountable for completing these duties, managers are rated on how they implement them. The how assessment of managers is normally a subjective evaluation provided by higher-level managers, peer managers, subordinates, and end users of the services provided by the manager's organization. Chapter 3 provides additional information regarding job descriptions and performance appraisal activities.

TELECOMMUNICATIONS MANAGER SKILLS

The preceding sections reviewed a wide range of topics and, hopefully, have convinced the reader that the scope and depth of telecommunications management is very broad and complex. The skills needed to be an effective telecommunications manager fall into two general categories: 1) telecommunications management skills, and 2) **enabling skills.**

Telecommunications management skills are the skills needed to carry out the responsibilities associated with the organization management and technology management roles described previously under the *Telecommunications Management* topic. Enabling skills are those skills that allow business management and technology management topics to be learned and assimilated by an individual. They are the basic knowledge skills an individual must have in order to learn new skills.

Figure 1–3 provides a skill triangle that groups knowledge areas into two main categories—Telecommunications management skills and Enabling skills. The Enabling skill area has been subdivided into Basic education

skills, Higher education skills, and PC skills; and Telecommunications managements skills have been separated into Technology management skills and **Business management skills.**

This text focuses on business and project management topics while assuming that the reader has an understanding of telecommunications technologies and the enabling skills necessary to assimilate the text's organization and **project management** subjects.

Knowledge does not ensure the existence of a skill. Skills are developed by acquiring knowledge and then applying it to different situations. The application phase is commonly called *experience*, a necessary element for the development of skills. Without the experience factor, there is a low likelihood that an individual will be able to apply knowledge effectively to achieve real world results. Therefore, our use of skill in the text implies that an individual has both the knowledge and the necessary experience to effectively apply the knowledge.

Knowledge and experience are time dependent factors, as each requires a period of time (and personal effort) to obtain. This text—or any text—cannot totally bypass the time requirements needed to acquire knowledge and obtain the experience needed to become a professional telecommunications manager. However, personal learning tools can help individuals manage their learning time more effectively and reduce the time needed to acquire experience. Personal learning tools also allow one to learn independently of a

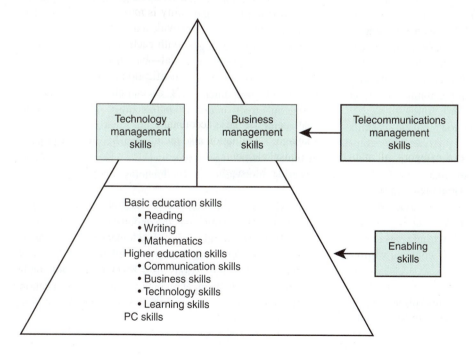

Figure 1–3. The telecommunications management skill triangle.

classroom environment and focus narrowly on specific areas of personal and professional interest.

There is an old adage, "If it sounds too good to be true . . . it probably is." The enabling tools referenced previously are not mysterious incantations. They consist of procedures and practices that are time proven. Unfortunately, personal effort is normally required to acquire enabling skills. The good news is that acquiring learning skills is a one-time effort that is easily updated, and it provides ongoing dividends every time the tools are used. The bad news is that a heavy initial effort may be required if the enabling skills were not developed during an individual's primary education period. If someone's basic education background is strong, many learning and enabling skills will already have been developed. However, if this is not the case, it will be necessary to compensate for past deficiencies by learning basic enabling skills after the primary education process has already been completed.

Enabling Skills

This section will discuss the three enabling skills areas shown in Figure 1–3, which include:

1. Basic education skills
2. Higher education skills
3. PC skills

Basic Education Skills

Basic education skills consist of the three R's–Reading, 'Riting, and 'Rithmetic—that are provided by a sound primary (kindergarten through grade 8) and secondary school (grades 9 through 12) education. Secondary school education skills in oral and written communications, sciences (biology, physics, chemistry), mathematics (algebra, geometry, trigonometry, and calculus), humanities, and other courses provide a foundation for learning higher education skills. If an individual's secondary education skills are weak, it is unlikely that success is possible in telecommunications management or any other technology field until these skill deficiencies are corrected.

The communications and mathematics skills acquired during the basic education process provide the basis for developing effective problem-solving skills. Communications skills in reading and writing areas are essential for long-term survival in a world where new information is continually generated.

READING SKILLS. Good reading skills are important skills in a technology-driven society. Reading skills provide the ability to quickly identify key information elements contained in a written document. This includes being able to understand both the explicit and implicit implications of the written material. A typical scenario for someone in a technical position is to be given a manual and then be told to "fix the problem." Unless one can quickly assimilate written information and identify the key elements needed to solve a problem, there is a low likelihood of succeeding in a technical or managerial position. In addition, good reading skills are needed to learn new skills, and someone without good reading skills is likely to be relegated to a role where someone else is directing their efforts. The individual doing the directing probably has reading comprehension skills necessary to explain written material to others.

If someone finds themselves with weak reading skills after they have completed their high school education, the responsibility for correcting this deficiency falls upon the individual. Compensating for reading weaknesses may require a significant time and study effort by someone, but the alternative—being relegated to doing only what you are told—should be a sufficient motivator for someone to invest the time and effort that is required to correct the weakness.

WRITING SKILLS. While reading skills are strong enablers for supporting self teaching efforts, writing skills provide the vehicle for an individual to communicate their knowledge and capabilities to others. During the self teaching process, the ability to succinctly and accurately restate information demonstrates an understanding of information to others, and writing skills can also be used as a learning tool.

Effective writing is a key skill for directing, motivating, and influencing others in both a managerial and technology context. Good writing skills can be used to improve oral communication skills—another prerequisite for being an effective telecommunications manager. While oral communication skills may be viewed as being secondary to reading for self teaching purposes, it is at least an equal partner to good writing skills when the focus is on directing, motivating, and influencing others.

MATHEMATICS SKILLS. Mathematics—the study of number relationships—is the underlying structure of all technologies. It provides a basis for logical reasoning capabilities. At the elementary education level, the primary focus is on the arithmetic functions of addition, subtraction, multiplication, and division; at secondary and higher education levels, the focus is on algebra, calculus, geometry, and trigonometry.

A good foundation in mathematics is essential for learning technologies and developing the analytical skills required for making sound managerial decisions. While mathematics by itself may be perceived as being an academic subject, its role in the telecommunications management area is similar to one that good physical conditioning plays for an athlete. Just as an athlete would be unable to achieve good performance levels without physical conditioning, a telecommunications manager would not have the necessary mental conditioning to perform managerial functions effectively unless their mathematical conditioning is sound.

Higher Education Skills

Higher education skills refer to those skills gained by earning a college or university degree, such as a Bachelor of Telecommunications Management degree. In the current business environment, there is a low likelihood of advancing into the managerial ranks of medium and large companies without having a college degree. This does not mean that an individual doesn't know their job unless they go to college, but existing hiring and promotion criteria frequently require managerial candidates to have a college-level degree.

While having a degree may provide someone with the credentials to qualify for higher-level managerial or technical positions, the real value of a higher education degree is in acquiring "learning how to learn" skills and then using these skills to teach oneself. College students must learn how to acquire knowledge quickly and efficiently, or they will not survive the rigors of a strong academic program. While the ability to learn is an important asset in a formal education program, it is even more critical in a real-world job environment. If graduates of a program can only learn in a classroom environment, their future success will be limited because more than 90% of all job knowledge must be acquired on-the-job, which requires a self-initiated learning process.

In telecommunications, it is common for entry-level employees to be given six or more technical manuals and then be asked to figure out and solve the problem. On-the-job learning is very difficult for individuals who don't have good communication (reading, writing, and speech), mathematics, and learning skills.

Personal Computing Skills

The introduction of PCs during the 1970s revolutionized the telecommunications networking environment. It also changed the way an individual learns, stores information,

and communicates with others. The introduction of **PC desktop applications**—particularly word processing, spreadsheet, and presentation applications—has added a new dimension to the historical (Three R's) learning environment. Word processing, spreadsheet, and presentation graphics skills are today's basic personal productivity tools. Every aspiring telecommunications manager needs to have strong PC skills to do their job effectively. Today, it is necessary to have strong basic education skills *and* basic PC skills.

Telecommunications managers must have a good understanding of basic computer topics: hardware, the operating system, and the user interface (typically Windows). This technical knowledge is required because PC communication is the major networking technology, and computer technologies are the primary technology infrastructure for today's business networking environment.

WORD PROCESSING. With the introduction of word processing applications in the 1980s, the traditional role of the secretary changed. While upper management executives may still (sometimes) be provided with dedicated secretarial services (telephone answering, typing, file management, and schedule maintenance), most managers are expected to generate their own written documents and to communicate directly with others by using e-mail services.

Typing is no longer a clerical skill to be avoided (the "real managers don't type" syndrome of the past). It is a skill essential to using PC application software effectively. While it may be argued that the use of a Graphical User Interface (GUI) with easy-to-understand icons or the use of voice response applications may negate the need for acquiring the mundane skill of typing, the reality is that a lack of keyboard skills is an impediment to using a PC effectively, communicating via e-mail, or interfacing with any computer applications.

It is strongly recommended that prospective telecommunications managers acquire touch-typing skills early in their educational development. It is a skill that will be valuable for an entire lifetime—both on the job and for personal use. A good knowledge of word processing software allows someone to create written documents with the content being limited only by their imagination. Strong basic education skills and strong word processing skills allow someone to create or modify document content to fit any situation. From a self-learning perspective, word processing skills provide a vehicle for storing and retrieving personal and professional information.

SPREADSHEET SOFTWARE. The introduction of VisiCalc spreadsheet software during the 1970s is considered, by many PC historians, to be the application that drove the initial development of personal computers. Accountants in large corporations found that VisiCalc spreadsheet software could address accounting "what-if" questions quickly and efficiently and avoid the limitations imposed by cumbersome mainframe computer operations. This realization triggered a wave of PC purchases by corporate accounting departments who were able—in some mysterious way—to find the funds needed for PC purchases. Simple "what-if" questions that would slow down mainframe computer processing to unacceptable levels were handled easily by a dedicated PC processor.

Today's PC spreadsheet software is unbelievably powerful. Even the most sophisticated user is probably only using a fraction of the total capability of the software. Spreadsheets can be used for number calculations, sorting, database functions, and producing a broad range of graphs and other graphical formats. Learning 10% of a spreadsheet program's capability should handle 100% of most end-user requirements. Spreadsheet applications also provide a learning tool to speed up the storage and retrieval of numerical information. The number-crunching capability of spreadsheet software is essential for ad-hoc managerial and technical analytical efforts.

PRESENTATION SOFTWARE. Presentation software (Microsoft's PowerPoint) is primarily used for presenting information at meetings (or when teaching subjects in a classroom environment). Although presentation software is not particularly useful for the self teaching process, it provides an excellent vehicle for displaying information clearly and is useful for making presentations to business management.

Business Communication Skills

Communication skills were discussed as a generic skill requirement previously. However, the importance of business communication warrants a separate discussion, because there are significant differences between academic communication skills and **business communication skills.** Effective business communication involves taking basic communication skills and tweaking them into a format and style that is business oriented. Someone who has strong communication skills should have little problem modifying their writing and speaking skills to accommodate business communication requirements.

Business Skills

Business skills for a telecommunications manager means that the managers have a good understanding of the roles, responsibilities, and operating procedures of nontelecommunications departments. This knowledge is essential for customizing generic telecommunications products and services to meet the specific user needs of internal departments.

It is also important for telecommunications managers to understand upper management's operating philosophy. Upper management is concerned with strategic issues that include economic conditions, competition, government regulations, and long-term business trends. Understanding this viewpoint provides two advantages: 1) it allows a telecommunications manager to anticipate upper management concerns and initiatives, and 2) it can prepare the telecommunications manager for learning how to become a member of upper management.

TEXT OVERVIEW

Telecommunications management is a complex, multifaceted topic that requires skills in managerial and technology areas. Anyone attempting to understand telecommunications management without strong foundational skills faces a task similar to the one confronting Alexander the Great (356 BC–323 BC) when he was asked to unravel the Gordian knot. The Gordian knot was an intricately intertwined ball of twine and was accompanied by a prophecy that whoever could untie the Gordian knot would rule all of Asia. Many had tried but none had succeeded until young Alexander attempted to unravel the knot—and was also unable to unravel it. However, this did not discourage Alexander from taking decisive action. He unsheathed his sword and with one stroke cut the Gordian knot into two halves. The prophecy had been fulfilled and Alexander the Great went on to conquer much of Asia.

This text attempts to cut the Gordian knot of telecommunications management by focusing on real world telecommunications management topics and using a building-block process of identifying skills and applying them to case study problems. It assumes that the reader has previously acquired the basic learning and knowledge skills needed for using the text as a sword to cut their telecommunications management Gordian knot.

The text is organized into five parts:

Part 1: Telecommunications Management Basics

Part 2: Telecommunications Planning

Part 3: Project Management

Part 4: Managing Telecommunications Operations

Part 5: Acquisition Management

Part 1: Telecommunications Management Basics

Part 1 provides an overview of the telecommunications management area and reviews topics by addressing five basic questions:

1. What is telecommunications (technology)?
2. What is telecommunications management?
3. What do telecommunications managers do?
4. How is telecommunications managerial success measured?
5. What skills do telecommunications managers need?

Part 1 describes the prerequisite skill set that aspiring telecommunications managers should have prior to addressing the topics presented in Parts 2 through 5. Without these prerequisite skills, telecommunications management topics will appear to be as complex and intricate as the original Gordian knot confronting Alexander the Great in his quest to become ruler of the world. With the prerequisite skills identified in Part 1, readers will be in a position to effectively utilize the sword-knowledge contained in the text, cut their Gordian knot, and continue their quest to rule the telecommunications management world.

Part 2: Telecommunications Planning

The effective selection and use of telecommunications products and services requires a blend of business, technology, and planning skills. Part 2 assumes that the reader has met the basic telecommunications management skill requirements identified in Part 1 and describes the relationship between business and telecommunications strategic planning efforts. It outlines the steps needed to convert strategic plans into practical results, and it also examines advanced organization and technology management topics.

A case study format is used to demonstrate the application of advanced telecommunications management tools and techniques to real world situations.

Part 3: Project Management

Telecommunications managers are typically confronted with a never-ending series of technology and administrative projects as part of their managerial responsibilities.

Part 3 reviews the project management tools and techniques available for a telecommunications manager to handle both types of projects. For large, complex technology projects, Critical Path Method (CPM) concepts are explained and examples of how they can be applied to telecommunications technology projects are provided.

Telecommunications managers will find that non-technology projects (i.e., administrative projects) normally are a larger part of their workload and are also more important for achieving good managerial performance. Tools and techniques for administrative projects are reviewed and examples are provided.

A case study format is used to demonstrate the application of project management tools and techniques to technology and administrative projects.

Part 4: Managing Telecommunications Operations

Telecommunications operation functions have a direct responsibility for providing products and services to a business organization's employees, customers, and suppliers. Part 4 describes the telecommunications operations manager's responsibilities for managing the day-to-day operations of a business telecommunications system and network infrastructure. A strong focus is placed on controlling expenses, because this is a key, ongoing concern of upper management. The "budget v. actual" control process is examined in detail.

A case study format is used to demonstrate the application of the "budget v. actual cost" budgeting and control process.

Part 5: Acquisition Management

Telecommunications products and service are expensive to purchase and expensive to operate. To complicate matters, telecommunications technologies are complex and are in a constant state of change. Part 5 describes the tools and techniques that are available to effectively select and evaluate telecommunications equipment and service alternatives. It includes discussions of the Request For Information (RFI), Request For Quotation (RFQ), and Request For Proposal (RFP) procedures and the application of a Life Cycle Cost Model to the evaluation process. Different quantitative techniques are used to generate acquisition selection decisions.

A case study format is used to demonstrate how different tools and techniques are applied to the acquisition of telecommunications products and services.

SUMMARY

This summary is organized to correspond with the learning objectives found at the beginning of the chapter.

1. U.S. regulatory environment dominated the development and use of telecommunications technology for a hundred years, ending with the Bell System Divestiture on January 1, 1984. The divestiture decision deregulated telecommunications products immediately and initiated the ongoing deregulation of long distance call services. The deregulation trend continues today.

2. The regulatory environment that drove the development and use of telecommunications technology mirrored the existing business climate. When in the 1960s an era of highly competitive, global competition began, telecommunications technologies became a business asset. The regulatory pace of technology development and its pricing was no longer acceptable and created the climate that led to the 1984 divestiture decision.

3. Three major networking periods have existed since the introduction of the telegraph in 1844: 1) telegraph networks, 2) telephone (voice) networks, and 3) computer networks. Since the Bell System Divestiture, there has been an explosion of telecommunication technologies, and the need for computer-to-computer networking is the dominant technology driver. The WWWeb (Internet) is a byproduct of the computer-to-computer networking developments.

4. Telecommunications managers need skills in two managerial areas: 1) business management, and 2) technology management. Business management activities deal with directing and administering the telecommunications responsibilities within the business. They require skills in supervision, budgeting, and effectively using department resources. Technology management responsibilities include the selection, design, implementation, and operation of telecommunications systems and networks to meet internal and external customer needs.

5. The telecommunications department can support business profitability objectives by effectively managing telecommunications expenses and by supporting customer-oriented initiatives to improve customer access to the business enterprise. Increasingly, telecommunications technologies have become an integral part of a product offering by incorporating the technology into the product or by using it for post-sales support functions.

6. Upper management will determine the salary levels of telecommunications managers, and their promotion potential. It is important for telecommunications managers to communicate effectively with upper management.

7. The 50%/50% Telecommunications Management Model states that an effective telecommunications manager must have a skill set that is 50% technology-management based and 50% business-management based (organization + technology). Failure to have a balance of technology and managerial skills makes a manager vulnerable to making poor decisions.

8. The long-term criterion for achieving organizational success in a business enterprise is to support upper management objectives. The three areas that upper management is highly interested in are: 1) meeting organizational profit objectives, 2) satisfying internal and external customer constituencies, and 3) planning ahead to ensure that organizational objectives can be met in the future.

9. The primary responsibility of telecommunications managers is to direct and coordinate the efforts of subordinates and other managerial personnel to provide telecommunications products and services for use in the business. "Bona fide managers" have individuals reporting to them, and bona fide managers have supervisory and development responsibilities for the workers that are part of the manager's telecommunications workgroup. The responsibilities of bona fide managers include evaluating the performance of subordinates, ensuring that workgroup members receive the training needed to do their jobs, administering salaries and promotions, developing workgroup members for advancement to better positions, and administering the personnel policies of the parent organization.

10. The Telecommunications Skill Triangle includes three basic elements: 1) business management skills, 2) technology management skills, and 3) enabling skills. The organization and project management skills fall within the broad category of "telecommunications management skills," while the enabling skills provide the education and knowledge infrastructure needed to effectively and efficiently acquire telecommunication technology and telecommunications management skills.

11. The text is organized into five parts: 1) Telecommunications Management Basics, 2) Telecommunications Planning, 3) Project Management, 4) Managing Telecommunications Operations, and 5) Acquisition Management. A case study format is used to demonstrate the use of the various telecommunications management tools and techniques within a business problem context.

KEY TERMS AND CONCEPTS

The language of telecommunications management is multifaceted and includes words and phrases from managerial, technological, accounting, regulatory, and other business areas. The definitions of these key terms and concepts can be found within the chapter and in the glossary.

1984 Modified Final Judgment
accounting
ARPANET
Bell System
bona fide manager
business communication skills
business management
business management skill
business profitability
computer
customer satisfaction
enabling skills
external customer

Federal Communications Commission (FCC)
50%/50% Telecommunications
    Management Model
Henri Fayol
inter-exchange carrier (IXC)
internal customer
International Standards Organization (ISO)
job description
layered writing style
local exchange carrier (LECs)
management success criteria
PC desktop application
performance review

plan
POLC Model
Postal, Telephone, and Telegraph (PTT)
    agencies
project management skills
PTM
7 Layer OSI Model
stockholder
technology management
telecommunications
telegraph
telephone
upper management

REVIEW

The following questions are open-ended—predefined answers are not included as part of the text. The purpose of these questions is to allow the readers to test themselves on the chapter material.

1. Define *telecommunications*.

2. What do telecommunications managers do?

3. When was the business management profession established?

4. What is a bona fide manager?

5. Why are job descriptions used?

6. What are performance appraisals?

7. What is business management?

8. What is technology management?

9. Describe the POLC Model and its use in the managerial process.

10. Who was Henri Fayol?

11. What is upper management?

12. What responsibilities does a telecommunications manager have?

13. Explain the 50%/50% Telecommunications Management Model.

14. What is the potential downside for managers who do not have a 50%/50% balance of managerial skills?

15. Describe three areas used by upper management to measure managerial effectiveness.

16. Explain the importance of good communication with upper management.

17. Describe the attributes of a good business communication format.

18. What is the value of accounting information to upper management and telecommunications managers?

19. Who are internal and external telecommunications customers?

20. What is the importance of good telecommunications planning in a business enterprise?

21. What are PTTs?

22. What is the ARPANET?

23. What was the purpose for establishing the ISO?

24. What are enabling skills?

25. What are project management skills?

26. What are organization management skills?

MULTIPLE CHOICE

1. The business managerial profession was established in _____.
   a. 800 B.C.
   b. 1000 A.D.
   c. 1776 A.D.
   d. 1900 A.D.
   e. 2000 A.D.

2. The primary responsibility of managers is to _____.
   a. write reports
   b. utilize FUD Model principles
   c. coordinate the efforts of employees
   d. have technical expertise

3. Bona fide managers _____.
   a. select telecommunications equipment
   b. design communications networks
   c. attend meetings
   d. supervise personnel
   e. create strategic plans

4. Bona fide managers _____. (Select all that apply.)
   a. appraise employee performance
   b. have no direct reports
   c. provide training opportunities
   d. administer raises
   e. none of the above

5. PTM consists of _____. (Select all that apply.)
   a. budgets
   b. technology management
   c. time
   d. POLC Model
   e. personnel

6. Technology management refers to learning the technical details of telecommunications technologies.
   a. True
   b. False

7. Business management is concerned with managing the people resource to achieve business objectives.
   a. True
   b. False

8. An important technology management responsibility is to _____.
   a. maintain personnel files for department employees
   b. develop department budgets
   c. coordinate PTM resources
   d. administer corporate personnel policies

9. The functional life of computer-based technologies is typically _____,
   a. 3 months
   b. 24 months
   c. 5 years
   d. set by the accounting department
   e. none of the above

10. The 50%/50% Telecommunications Management Model is a balance of _____ skills. (Select all that apply.)
    a. industrial management
    b. information resource management
    c. organization management
    d. enabling
    e. technology mangement

11. A key managerial success criterion is _____.
    a. cutting costs
    b. having strong public speaking skills
    c. installing the latest technologies
    d. satisfying upper management expectations
    e. obtaining technical certification

12. Effective communication with upper management is not important for technical managers.
    a. True
    b. False

13. Format in a business document refers to _____.
    a. what it says
    b. the use of technical jargon
    c. how it reads
    d. how it looks
    e. data organization

14. The language of upper management consists of _____ and _____. (Select two.)

a. business English

b. alphanumeric characters

c. technical writing

d. numbers

e. executive summaries

15. Internal customers refer to the employees at a customer's location.

a. True

b. False

16. External customers include _____ and _____ (Select two.)

a. suppliers

b. internal employees

c. upper management

d. consumers

e. executive summaries

17. The dominant network technology is _____.

a. telegraph-based

b. telephone-based

c. computer-based

d. voice-based

e. satellite-based

18. Outside of the U.S., _____ were responsible for providing telecommunications services in the predivestiture environment.

a. PTTs

b. STTs

c. private agencies

d. corporations

19. From a managerial perspective, the major importance of the 7-Layer OSI model is that it _____.

a. established technical standards

b. created interoperability standards

c. created telephone standards

d. established communications protocols

e. mandated standards

20. Telecommunications management skills include _____ and _____ skills. (Select two.)

a. industrial management

b. higher education

c. organization management

d. project management

e. PC skills

2

WHAT IS TELECOMMUNICATIONS?

LEARNING OBJECTIVES

1. Understand the underlying concepts of the basic communication and telecommunications models.

2. Understand the role that the regulatory environment has played in the development of telecommunications technologies since the introduction of the telephone and since the terms of the 1982 Bell System Divestiture Agreement.

3. Understand the role that the business environment has played in determining the regulatory environment and in the development of telecommunications technology.

4. Understand the role of ARPANET in the development of TCP/IP and the Internet (the WWW).

5. Understand the role that the telegraph had in the development of telephony technology.

6. Understand telephone equipment and network technology and their contributions to digital computer network technology.

7. Understand the impact that mainframe computers have had on telecommunications networking technology.

8. Understand the impact that PCs have had on the development of LANs and internetworks.

9. Understand the impact that the OSI model has had on equipment and networking interoperability.

Telecommunications can be defined as the science and technology of communicating at a distance by using the electronic transmission of pulses, as by **telegraph,** cable, telephone, radio, or television. This technically oriented definition is neat and concise but does not give any hint of the impact that the regulatory and business environment has had—and continues to have—on the development of telecommunications technology.

This chapter will present telecommunications as a multifaceted, highly complex subject that cannot be neatly wrapped up in a one-sentence definition. A problem that frequently arises when a complex product is used is that specialized skills are required to obtain the benefits of the product—which is the case with telecommunications technology.

Approaching the complexity found in telecommunications is analogous to the old Indian fable about four blind wise men who were given the opportunity to *see* an elephant for the first time by using their sense of touch. The elephant was an extremely large specimen, so all of its dimensions were at the upper end of an elephant's size scale. Because the "sight" of the wise men was based on touch, they were led to the elephant, where they proceeded to use their hands to gain an understanding of how an elephant looked. The first wise man was placed at the front of the elephant. When he felt the trunk, he commented that an elephant was a thick, flexible animal similar in structure to a very large snake. The second wise man had been placed by a leg. He disagreed vehemently with the first observation, stating that the elephant was like a large, immovable building column that had disappeared into the sky. The third wise man, who was placed by the side of the elephant, disagreed with the first two observations and commented that the elephant was like the wall of a building covered with a thick, leathery hide, and the animal extended out horizontally and vertically. The fourth wise man, who had been placed at the back of the elephant, had grasped the elephant's tail. He commented that the other three were clearly mistaken and that the elephant was an animal shaped like a thin, very strong rope. Which wise man was right? They all were. However, unless they combined their different views of the elephant, they would not have an accurate picture of the elephant.

Telecommunications is seen differently, depending on whether its technology, regulatory, business, or end-user perspective is being viewed. The experienced telecommunications manager must see both the sum and the parts of telecommunications to understand it and use it effectively.

TELECOMMUNICATIONS TECHNOLOGY: AN OVERVIEW

Telecommunications technology was introduced in the U.S. during the mid-1840s, when public telegraph networks were installed. These networks consisted of long stretches of wires held above the ground by wooden poles—typically alongside a railroad track. Railroads had the advantage of being able to place the poles and wires on railroad property and avoid the right-of-way issues that could emerge when private property was crossed. When telephone technologies came on the scene during the late 1800s, they also used networks that required the presence of wires between sending and receiving locations. Telephone network right-of-way issues were resolved by designating telephone service providers as a regulated industry and allowing them to place wires on public lands (roads, parks, etc.) while also providing them with the authority of eminent domain—the power to appropriate private property for installing telephone facilities. Telecommunications providers—notably the Bell System—used this charter to create the vision of universal service where the objective was to connect each business and home to the public network. This **universal service** vision is one of the reasons for the ease of access that is taken for granted in today's Web-oriented society. The charter to provide this government-controlled communication environment would remain largely intact until the mid-1980s, when an antitrust decision by the courts forced a restructuring of the regulated telecommunications industry.

During the 1950s, technical "toys" called *computers* appeared—initially, the expensive, complex playthings of scientists and operations research groups. By the 1960s, the improved cost *v.* performance profile of **mainframe computers** attracted the interest of business organizations that wanted to use computer technologies for increasing the efficiency of their business operations. These early mainframe computers were extremely crude by today's **PC** performance standards, and they were very expensive to purchase and operate. However, corporate accounting departments found that primitive mainframe computers could do a wonderful job of "crunching numbers" in an era of manual adding machines. As a result, many early mainframe computers were justified primarily on their ability to provide improved accounting information. Once the computer system was installed to meet accounting needs, its use quickly expanded to address other internal business needs such as product pricing, and maintaining customer databases.

PCs were introduced in the 1970s, and by the mid-1980s they had radically altered the role played by computers in the business environment. The low cost and high power of PCs allowed computers to be distributed throughout an organization at lower costs than by using a centralized mainframe computer. However, the PC environment required the installation of a distributed networking architecture to allow the exchange of information between PCs. As a result, business PC users became the driving force behind the development of computer-based networking technologies that included **local area networks (LANs), wide area networks (WANs),** and internetworking technologies that allowed WANs and LANs to be interconnected.

To examine the telecommunications "elephant," four topics will be reviewed:

- telecommunications regulations
- business needs
- technology development
- **World Wide Web (WWW)**

These topics also provide a chronological description of the telecommunications change drivers from 1844 to the current time. The term *change driver* refers to the events initiating technology development. Although technology breakthroughs (the invention of the telegraph and telephone) were required to originate the telecommunications era, the regulatory climate dominated the telecommunications industry from 1900 into the 1980s and controlled the rate and nature of technology development. During the 1970s, business issues and computer technology emerged to become the primary forces driving the development of new telecommunications technologies. In the last 25 years, the need for computer-based communication networks dominated telecommunications technology development activities.

Currently, the need to expand computer-based WWW applications has become the driving force behind the continued development of telecommunications networking. WWW applications are frequently described as **e-commerce** applications, where *e-commerce* refers to using computer-based applications for commercial activities. These commercial activities include providing product information, taking orders, and providing order status information.

COMMUNICATION BASICS

Telecommunications is an extension of the communication process that takes place when two people exchange information. In a person-to-person communication environment, a sender, a receiver, and a communications medium are required, and the communicating parties will assume either sender or receiver roles during the communication process. The human messaging process would typically consist of verbal, written, or visual communication and the medium would be air in a normal conversation.

The Basic Communication Model

The basic communication model is illustrated in Figure 2–1, which displays a sender, a receiver, and a transmission medium. In the human communication environment, the distance for effective oral communication depends largely upon the lung power of the sender. Long distance communication in early times relied on either written communication or some form of long-range visual communication such as flags, mirrors, or smoke signals.

The quality of the transmission medium and the ability of a sender or receiver to effectively fulfill his or her function affected the outcome of the communication process. If the sender and receiver were not using the same language or if an individual does not speak clearly, communication problems arise. Likewise, the transmission medium may introduce interference that impedes good communication between a sender and a receiver. Interference in an oral communication mode could consist of unclear speech characteristics or a noisy environment. In written communication, the quality of the writing, the writing instrument, and the writing vehicle (paper, stone, etc.) would determine the effectiveness of the communication process.

The Basic Telecommunications Model

If we add "*tele*" (operating at a distance) to "communications," we enter into the world of telecommunications. In an electronics-based telecommunications environment, technology elements introduced major changes in the transmission medium element of the basic communication model. Copper wire (twisted pair cable, coaxial cables, etc.) can be used to carry electrical signals, air can be used to carry radio frequency signals, and fiber optics can be used to provide the transmission medium for light signals. Electronic telecommunications also requires signal conversions at the interface between the sender or receiver and the medium selected for transmitting the information.

Figure 2–2 illustrates a technology-oriented telecommunications model that substitutes different technical elements for the sender, receiver, and transmission medium elements shown in Figure 2–1.

Figure 2–1. The basic communications model.

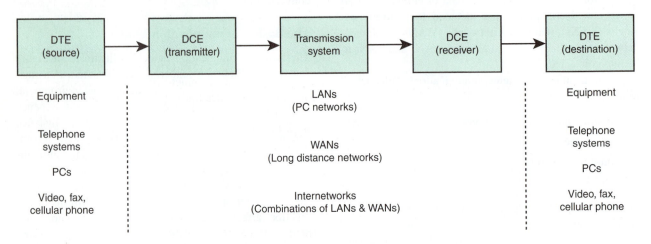

Figure 2–2. The basic telecommunications model.

With telecommunications, interactive communication is no longer limited by the distance that sound can travel across an air medium or on the ability of a person to see distant signaling devices. However, the introduction of a technology-based transmission medium capable of sending and receiving electrical, radio frequency, or light signals comes at a price of increased complexity because sounds, visual images, and text must be converted into electronic signals. The following technical terms are introduced in Figure 2–2 and are examples of technical telecommunications jargon.

Data Terminating Equipment (DTE): A communication device that is the source or destination of signals carried by a network. It is typically a PC, telephone set, or other device that provides an interface between a person and a telecommunications network.

Data Communication Equipment (DCE): A device that establishes, maintains, and terminates a communication session on a network. It may also convert DTE signals into a format compatible for the transmission medium being used (copper, air, or fiber optics). For example, modems are DCEs that are used for analog transmission of data, and a DSU/CSU (Data Service Unit/Channel Service Unit) is used for digital transmission.

Source DTE: Converts human-compatible information into a data format (analog or digital DTE signals) that

may be used directly by the transmission medium or may require an additional signal conversion. PCs, video transmitters, and telephones are examples of DTEs.

Source DCE: Encodes DTE data into a transmission system compatible format for the specific medium (copper, air, or fiber) that is being used to carry the signals. The DCE format may be analog or digital.

Transmission System: Carries signals between source and destination DCEs. Two basic media exist: guided and unguided. Guided media include copper and fiber optics that constrain (i.e., guide) signals within the medium being used. Unguided media consist of an air or a vacuum environment. In unguided media, radio or laser signals are not constrained to a specific path by the air or vacuum medium.

Destination DCE: Decodes a transmitted signal into a DTE-compatible signal.

Destination DTE: Accepts incoming DTE data and converts it to a (human) readable format. PCs, video receivers, and telephones are examples of devices used for this purpose.

Hopefully, this brief description of communications concepts is familiar to readers—unless they are using this portion of the text as an introduction into additional telecommunications topics. In the latter case, it will be necessary to develop a technology background prior to proceeding into Parts 2, 3, 4, and 5.

50%/50% TELECOMMUNICATIONS MANAGEMENT MODEL COMMENTS. Figure 2–2 used the names of basic telecommunications technologies in the diagram—LANs, WANs, and internetworks. Aspiring telecommunications managers should be familiar with the conceptual details for all of the equipment and transmission system technologies shown in Figure 2–2.

Weakness in either business management or technology management areas will translate into overall managerial weakness. Poor business management skills are a liability when managing the people resource within a business organization, while a lack of technology management (not *technical*) skills is a liability when telecommunications investment and operating decisions are needed. A balance of strong organization management and technology management skills allows a manager to make the best use of personnel resources while having the capability to see the technical trees in a technology forest without becoming overwhelmed by the minutiae found in technical details. A 50% organizations management and 50% technology management balance is recommended.

A TELECOMMUNICATIONS CHRONOLOGY

During the last 150 years, many change drivers have influenced the development of telecommunications technology. These change drivers include political regulation, voice technology developments, computer technology developments, postcomputer business needs, and consumerism.

The Beginning (1844–1980)

Public telegraph services, introduced in 1844, set the stage for the subsequent development of all telecommunications products and services. The next technology breakthrough development took place in 1876 when Alexander Graham Bell, a speech teacher in Boston, was given a patent for an experimental telegraph device that could reproduce voice. As a result of Bell's research efforts, voice-based communication technology dominated the long distance networking environment between 1876 and the mid-1980s.

The Middle (1981–Today)

The next major telecommunications technology breakthrough was driven by the introduction of the mainframe computer and the business need to provide access to computing systems. Given the high cost for purchasing and maintaining a mainframe computer system, a single mainframe computer was housed in a central site (a *glass house*) to handle all corporate processing needs. As departments converted from manual systems to computerized systems, more departments required access to the central location. Before long, remote locations also needed access to the central computer. As the cost of computer technologies came down, companies found that they could afford multiple mainframe systems, and computer-to-computer communications needs emerged. Early data networks supporting mainframe computer communications were point-to-point or multipoint networks, which proved to be expensive and unreliable.

PCs became commercially viable during the 1980s, and PC communication requirements radically changed data networking needs. PC-based communication has been the technology driver for data communication networks since the 1980s, and has driven the development of LAN and internetworking technology.

To Be Continued . . . (The Future)

Today, the **Internet** is a PC-oriented application that has become the primary network infrastructure for PC-to-PC communications. For the foreseeable future, Internet applications and the supporting technology will continue to dominate the telecommunications environment.

Telecommunications Change Drivers

Most telecommunications technology developments have been driven by environmental factors. For the 140 years after the introduction of telegraph services, the U.S. regulatory environment determined which telecommunications products and services would be developed and offered to customers. Businesses saw telegraph and telephone services as necessary overhead costs that should be minimized. Customers or suppliers calling a business were expected to pay for the calls, and the primary directive used within a business was to minimize the length of outgoing calls or avoid making them by sending letters. Long distance call usage was monitored, and employees who made personal calls would be contacted so they could reimburse the business.

At the regulatory level, telegraph and telephone services were seen as **natural monopolies**—technology that could best be provided at a reasonable cost by using a single regulated entity, or at least a small number of regulated entities. In the early years, telecommunications services were seen as a logical extension of mail services, and were accorded the same regulatory treatment.

In the U.S., private firms (**AT&T** and other local independent telephone companies) were regulated by federal and state government agencies. In other parts of the world, PTTs were set up as government run institutions, and the country's telecommunications facilities were managed by the same organization that provided mail services.

Telecommunications technology development was controlled by regulating entities, which viewed telecommunications as an electronic form of mail. It was treated as a public utility, where the focus was on universal service, stability, and low cost. The universal service requirement meant that everyone should have access to telecommunications products and services and that the cost should be the same for everyone, regardless of where customers were located. The regulatory mandate was that a farmer who lived fifty miles outside of town, at the end of a dirt road, should receive the same level of service as a large business customer located in a major metropolitan area.

During the 1980s, worldwide competitive pressures accelerated business use of computer-based technology by businesses. This was followed by a wave of aggressive consumerism during the 1990s that was stimulated further by the introduction of WWW services. Web surfers viewed networking as a natural right for gaining access to multiple suppliers to compare products and prices before making a purchasing decision. Today, a network-based consumer culture exists, where many individuals view access to private and public computer databases as a normal way of life.

Although the different telecommunication change drivers are interrelated, it is sometimes difficult to see key elements clearly when they are embedded in a descriptive potpourri. (In other words, it is sometimes difficult to see the forest because of all the trees being in the way.) Change driver topics will be reviewed in the following sequence:

1. regulatory change drivers
2. business change drivers
3. WWW change drivers
4. telecommunications technology

The first three topics drove the need for telecommunications products and services from 1844 to the current time, and the last topic, *telecommunications technology*, is the technology result that was created in response to the change drivers.

REGULATORY CHANGE DRIVERS

The telecommunications regulatory environment varies widely in different parts of the world and telecommunications managers must take this variability into account when attempting to provide remote locations with international networking services. Failure to conform to local regulations or to provide sufficient project lead times to meet local lead time requirements can adversely affect the implementation schedule for international network projects.

The U.S. telecommunications industry was viewed as a public utility that required easy access to individual households. This meant that the regulated enterprise had to be given the right to run communication networks across public and private property. The **FCC** was the federal agency responsible for regulating long distance calling services, and state **Public Utility Commissions (PUCs)** were given the responsibility for regulating local equipment and calling services for locations within their state boundaries. Under this regulatory umbrella, the federal government regulated interstate communications services and the PUCs regulated intrastate communications services.

The U.S. telecommunications industry had a single long distance network provider—AT&T Long Lines— and many local telephone companies. **Bell System** telephone companies accounted for approximately 80% of U.S. telephone revenues at the local level, and the remaining suppliers were independent telephone companies. The FCC monitored and controlled AT&T Long Line rates and services, while the state PUCs monitored and controlled local telephone company rates and services.

The U.S. telecommunications industry regulatory environment can be divided into two major time periods: the pre-1984 era and the post-1984 era.

The Pre-1984 Regulatory Environment

Alexander Graham Bell and a group of financial backers established the Bell Telephone Company in 1877. The **Bell Telephone Company** used the protection afforded by patent law to exclude competitors from the telephone business until 1894—the expiration of the patent protection period. At that time, many independent telephone companies entered the marketplace, and a competitive environment was created in many cities. AT&T was established in 1885 and purchased the Bell Telephone Company in 1900. By the early 1900s, AT&T was referred to as the Bell System, and it controlled approximately 80% of the local telephone market through twenty-two local telephone companies. Approximately 5,000 independent telephone companies serviced the remainder of the U.S. local telephone marketplace.

During the early competitive stage in the telephone industry, state regulatory agencies were established to protect consumers from the negative effects associated with local competition. These agencies—Public Utility Commissions (PUCs)—monitored and regulated the availability and cost of intrastate telephone products and services to the public.

By the early 1930s, Bell System companies dominated telecommunications in the long distance, local telephone, and equipment manufacturing markets. In 1934, the FCC was established as an independent federal government agency that was given the charter to control U.S. long distance telecommunication services. The FCC gave AT&T Long Lines exclusive long distance telephone service rights in the U.S., while local calling services remained the exclusive domain of state PUCs. The U.S. telephone industry consisted of local Bell and non-Bell telephone companies connected to each other through the AT&T Long Lines network. The FCC regulated interstate calling rates, and local state agencies regulated the cost and availability of local equipment and calling services.

REGULATED TELEPHONE SERVICES. Prior to 1984, telephone sets were not sold to customers. They were part of a rental service package that included the telephone set, the communication line to the local telephone company central office (CO), and access to local and long distance calling networks. Telephone customers were charged a basic service rate that covered the cost of the equipment, repair of the equipment and wiring, access to the telephone company's CO, and a package of specific local calling services. Additional charges were levied for other local and long distance calling services.

By regulatory decree, residential and business customers were guaranteed a uniform level of service regardless of their location. Someone living in an isolated rural area would be provided telephone service at the same cost as someone living in a densely populated urban area. The cost for running a single telephone line (with telephone poles) to a remote location was balanced by those customers where the population density allowed the telephone company to make money on telephone services. In addition, long distance calling services were priced at a level that generated high profits. These profits were shared with the local telephone companies who provided the customer with access to the long distance calling network. Long distance profits were placed into the local telephone company's income pool and were used to lower the cost of local telephone services.

Regulated service standards guaranteed high quality services and low basic rate charges to local customers. On the other hand, long distance calling rates were priced at levels that ensured a high profit margin for local telephone companies. The upside of the pre-1984 regulated environment was that local calling services were high quality, universally available, low cost services; the downside was that regulations controlled the rate of technology development. Because a key regulatory mandate was to keep basic rates low, equipment development and installation costs were recovered over long time periods—typically twenty or more years. This meant that the rate of telecommunications innovation was also placed on a twenty-year cycle, and telecommunications equipment was expected to last twenty years before it was replaced. This is a sharp contrast when compared to the technical life of current telecommunications products that normally have a technical life of less than two years.

In the precomputer era (the 1960s), long cost recovery times were not an issue. The ability to recover expenses over a long time period helped finance the Bell System's vision of *universal service*—to provide high quality, low cost telephone service to every household in the U.S. Because the Bell System was the dominant telephone service provider, this vision continued to drive the U.S. telecommunications marketplace until 1984, when the **1984 Bell System Divestiture** requirements effectively scrapped the regulatory view of universal service.

The universal service vision came at a price—high costs to business customers, limited communication technology, and the lack of competition to reduce costs and foster innovation. In the pre-1984 environment, any attempt to attach non-Bell communication devices to AT&T's long distance networks encountered the full wrath of the Bell System. The Bell System rationalized their obsession with protecting the long distance network from foreign attachments by assuring regulators that the entire network would be in jeopardy if non-Bell equipment were connected to the network. The Bell System insisted that only Bell-manufactured equipment would be safe to use on the Bell System networks, therefore ensuring their sales revenues.

ANTITRUST ACTIVITIES. The nation's long distance calling network was owned and operated by the Bell System, and this ownership allowed network access to be monitored very closely to make sure that attached equipment conformed to Bell System specifications. If a device did not conform to Bell System network interface specifications, network access was not permitted.

During the 1960s, the Carter Electronics company of Dallas, Texas, developed the **Carterfone**—a device that would allow radio transmissions from Carter Electronics' customers to be transferred directly into the telephone network. Southwestern Bell, the local telephone company in the area where Carter Electronics operated, ordered the removal of the Carterfone. Carter Electronics took the case to court. To the Bell System's consternation, the courts sided with Carter Electronics, and AT&T was forced to sign an agreement in 1968 that allowed independently manufactured (non-Bell) communications devices to be attached to the AT&T network. The agreement specified that the non-Bell equipment must use a Bell **data access arrangement (DAA)** interface when connecting into the Bell network. During the 1970s, the FCC eliminated this requirement, which allowed non-Bell equipment that met network interface standard specifications to be attached directly to public network facilities.

The Carterfone proceedings initiated a series of events that eventually resulted in the 1984 Bell System Divestiture decision. Prior to the Carterfone decision, the Bell System (AT&T) felt that the Telecommunications Act of 1934 had provided them with a monopoly to provide long distance calling services, and that this charter included the right to restrict access to their network. AT&T's monopoly charter came under attack again in 1974 when the MCI Communications Corporation went to court and directly challenged AT&T's right to maintain a monopoly over long distance calling services. The MCI case was presented as an antitrust suit in which MCI claimed that AT&T was unjustly suppressing competition in the long distance calling market. The federal courts were again being asked to determine whether the 1934 Telecommunications Act provided AT&T with a monopoly charter. As was the case in the Carterfone decision, the courts ruled against AT&T, deciding that telecommunications products and long distance services were not protected by federal regulations. In a **1982 Consent Decree** settling MCI's antitrust suit, the courts issued rulings that resulted in the 1984 breakup of the Bell System. In the Consent Decree, the federal government agreed to drop antitrust proceedings against AT&T in return for AT&T's agreement to begin the process of implementing divestiture requirements on January 1, 1984.

The Post-1984 Regulatory Environment

As part of the 1982 AT&T Consent Decree, AT&T agreed to split the Bell System into three major parts:

1. the AT&T Long Lines division (long distance network)
2. the Western Electric equipment manufacturing division
3. local Bell operating companies

This split is commonly referred to as the AT&T (or Bell System) Divestiture, which took place on January 1, 1984. It provided for the immediate deregulation of telecommunications equipment and set the stage for the eventual deregulation of long distance calling services. Local telephone services would continue to be regulated by state regulatory agencies.

REGIONAL HOLDING COMPANIES. The twenty-two local **Bell operating companies** were grouped into seven **Regional Holding Companies (RHCs)** that would continue to provide local telephone access and services under the direction of state regulatory agencies.

(**Note**: regional holding companies are also referred to as RBOCs (regional Bell operating companies.) However, the seven RHCs (NYNEX, Bell Atlantic, BellSouth, Ameritech, Southwestern Bell, US West, and Pacific Telesis) would also be allowed to set up separate divisions for providing deregulated telecommunications equipment and other unregulated service offerings in the newly formed competitive marketplace. The separation of the RHC's regulated and deregulated organizations would be monitored closely by state regulatory agencies to ensure complete separation of revenues and expenses between the two organizations.

The Consent Decree provided a two-year time period—January 1, 1984 to January 1, 1986—to complete the necessary restructuring of the Bell System.

COMMUNICATIONS EQUIPMENT. In the post-1984 environment, voice and data communications equipment would be provided within a competitive marketplace environment, and AT&T would have to restructure its regulated manufacturing division—Western Electric—to operate in this competitive environment. Western Electric, renamed **AT&T Information Systems (ATTIS),** was also allowed to enter the computer equipment marketplace—an area that had been off limits to Western Electric under the regulated environment.

In the pre-1984 telecommunications environment, all Bell equipment was provided on a rental or lease basis, with the cost specified by tariff regulations. Under the AT&T Divestiture provisions, Bell System rentals and leases would be phased out over a two-year period, and customers using Bell equipment would either have to buy or lease the equipment from ATTIS, or buy or lease new equipment from a non-ATTIS supplier. This ruling applied to all residential and business customers of the Bell System. Because the local telephone companies were no longer part of AT&T, it meant that the equipment provisioning and repair role of the local telephone companies would be eliminated. In addition, the wiring and cabling systems at residential and business customer locations could no longer be serviced by the regulated telephone companies; these customers would have to find new suppliers in the deregulated marketplace.

PBX TELEPHONE SYSTEMS. Most large business customers of the Bell System relied upon **PBX telephone systems** or **Centrex telephone systems** for their voice communications needs. Investment decisions regarding the disposition of existing PBX or Centrex telephone system installations were required, because the equipment market had been deregulated. If they were using Bell System PBX telephone systems, they either had to purchase or lease the existing equipment from ATTIS or replace it with a non-ATTIS alternative.

CENTREX TELEPHONE SYSTEMS. If business customers were using Centrex telephone services, and chose to stay with Centrex, they had to purchase or lease the station sets and other equipment from ATTIS or replace it with non-ATTIS equipment. All **CPE** would have to be purchased or leased from an unregulated equipment supplier. A new contract with the regulated local telephone company was required so they could continue to provide central office-based Centrex services. A separate contract was required with the unregulated provider of the Centrex telephone sets and other CPE.

While a two-year window was provided for the Bell System restructuring, the actual impact was closer to a ten-year period, as business customers coped with the need to establish their own in-house telecommunications organizations. A positive byproduct of communications equipment deregulation has been the increased availability of new technology and a significant reduction in the cost of telecommunications equipment and support services.

LONG DISTANCE SERVICES. The Divestiture Agreement mandated the establishment of a competitive long distance calling marketplace and its **equal access** provision required local telephone companies to provide their customers with access to all long distance network providers. Because AT&T had provided 100% of the long distance services in the U.S., the equal access requirement meant that former Bell telephone companies would now have to provide each local subscriber with the opportunity to select any long distance carrier's services. In addition, local telephone companies had to prove that they were not giving any long distance provider's services preferential treatment—particularly to AT&T. The implications of the equal access requirement had a significant impact on the local telephone company's technical and administrative operations, because its implementation required major investments in new CO hardware and software.

As was the case for the equipment deregulation requirement, it took longer than two years to fully implement the deregulation requirements for long distance calling services. Today, the equal access requirement has been implemented in all local telephone company offices, and all long-distance providers are provided equal access to telephone company customers.

The court's divestiture ruling created independent RHCs to ensure that all corporate ties to AT&T's long distance network would be severed. In the brave new world of divestiture, RHCs and their local telephone companies were set up as competitors of their former AT&T parent company to ensure the equitable implementation of equal access requirements.

The FCC monitored AT&T long distance activities closely during the early divestiture period, and they continue to monitor long distance carriers (although more loosely) today. All long distance service providers fall under the regulatory umbrella of the FCC, but the postdivestiture regulatory environment is very lax compared to the predivestiture environment. Today, the long distance calling market is highly competitive and voice call rates are a fraction of their cost compared to the predivestiture rates. (A $.25/minute rate for long distance was normal in 1982; today, some long distance providers advertise calling rates of under $.05/minute.)

The major benefactor of deregulated long distance services has been the business customer. In the predivestiture period, business users were charged rates that included a subsidy allowance for residential customers' basic service costs. The phasing out of this subsidy continues to be of vital concern to consumer advocate groups and is still an ongoing activity at this time.

Local Telephone Services

The twenty-two former Bell Operating Companies were grouped into the RHC structure referenced previously. RHCs continued to have the responsibility for providing residential and business customers with telephone services within their designated areas. Local telephone companies (former Bell companies and other independent telephone companies) continued to operate under the regulation of state agencies and receive long distance subsidies for providing services to residential customers. However, the overall objective of the 1984 divestiture decision was to totally deregulate all telecommunications products and services, and all currently regulated services are seen as candidates for deregulation. The divestiture agreement included provisions that that allowed long distance customers to bypass local telephone companies and directly access the COs of long distance network providers.

THE TELECOMMUNICATIONS ACT OF 1996. When congress passed the **Telecommunications Act of 1996,** most observers saw it as an extension of the original 1982 antitrust Consent Decree. The 1996 Act did not address telecommunications equipment because the

1982 act had completely deregulated this area. However, it did contain provisions that continued the deregulation trend for long distance calling services and local telephone access services.

The 1996 Telecommunications Act called for the elimination of the FCC tariffs used to regulate the long distance calling market. This meant that domestic long distance carriers would no longer be required to file tariffs with the FCC and obtain FCC approval for rate changes. It is interesting to note that the existing long distance providers appealed this change and, as a result, the elimination of tariffs was delayed until January 31, 2001 instead of being implemented on January 1, 2000.

BYPASSING THE LOCAL TELEPHONE COMPANIES. In the predivestiture era, the local telephone company was the only interface with the long distance network. Under equal access requirements, access to long distance calling services still used telephone company access facilities. However, the divestiture ruling also included provisions that allowed long distance customers to access the COs of their long distance providers. These provisions clearly indicated that the long term objective of the consent decree was also the eventual deregulation of local telephone access services.

The divestiture provision allowing direct access to long distance networks was referred to as a *bypass* because it allowed long distance network customers to bypass the local telephone company's CO facility. Regulated telephone companies expressed great concern about bypass because it meant that they would not receive the long distance subsidies they relied on to offset losses incurred when they provided certain mandated public services.

Since 1984, there has been increased pressure by cable system providers, wireless service operators, interexchange carriers, and other utility companies to totally deregulate local telephone access services. The 1996 Telecommunications Act opened up the lucrative local telephone market to competition while allowing the parent organizations (RHCs) to compete in the long distance network services market. With these new provisions, the local telephone company may eventually become just another access option for local customers as new competitors enter the local access market.

It will take a number of years before the full impact of the 1996 Act can be determined. However, it is clearly another step in the telecommunications deregulation process initiated by the 1984 decision.

DEREGULATION POSTLUDE. The telecommunications deregulation activity scenario is not complete. The general consensus seems to be that when it runs its full course in the U.S., regulated activities will remain in areas where social issues exist but competitive services will determine the cost and product availability for most customers.

The 1984 divestiture has had a major impact on the availability and cost of telecommunications equipment and services in the U.S. and in the rest of the world. Telecommunications has been a major growth industry since 1984, and the current popularity of WWW services will continue to drive the development of telecommunications technologies. More telecommunications products and services were developed in the sixteen years following divestiture than had been developed in the 150 years prior to divestiture. Many industry forecasters believe that this trend will continue for the foreseeable future.

The U.S.'s deregulation of telecommunications has been mirrored throughout the world. The U.S. continues to provide worldwide leadership in the telecommunications field by providing innovations in telecommunication regulations, technology, and products.

BUSINESS CHANGE DRIVERS

While regulatory requirements directly influenced the availability of telecommunications equipment and services in the U.S., these regulatory requirements were established within the context of the existing economic, business, and social environment. As these conditions continue to change, the regulations will change to accommodate their new requirements. The 1984 Bell System Divestiture decision is a clear-cut example of this phenomenon.

The following discussion will examine the U.S. business environment during four time periods, and will describe the impact on the telecommunications regulatory environment. The four time periods include:

1. 1900–1959
2. 1960–1979
3. 1980–1989
4. 1990 and beyond

The first fifty-five years (1844–1899) of telecommunications history, covering telegraph services and the development of Alexander Graham Bell's telephone is not included, but this will not detract from the discussion because the telecommunications industry did not attract strong regulatory interest until the early 1900s.

The Business Environment (1900–1959)

The purchase of the Bell Telephone Company by AT&T in 1900 created the telecommunications industry that dominated the U.S. business environment until the mid-1980s. During the early 1900s, individual states found it necessary to create regulatory agencies (PUCs) to: 1) protect consumers from the inconsistent service levels provided by telephone industry entrepreneurs, and 2) protect smaller telephone companies from the predatory practices of larger telephone service providers. During this time period, AT&T (the Bell System) either eliminated or absorbed many local telephone company competitors. This activity resulted in the federal government enacting the Telecommunications Act of 1934 to define the operating limits of the Bell System and the remaining telephone service providers.

Significant worldwide events took place during the time between 1900 and 1960, including World War I, the Great Depression in the U.S., and World War II. One industry dominated the U.S. business environment during this time period—the automobile industry. The introduction of mass manufacturing concepts by Henry Ford during the early 1900s established an era of entrepreneurship in the U.S. where many business men entered the automobile business to seek their fortunes and further advance the love affair between Americans and their cars.

By 1916, the Ford-dominated U.S. industry was producing a million cars per year—an output level that England would not achieve until the 1950s. During the era before World War II, American automobile companies went through a survival of the fittest era when over a hundred automobile companies either went out of business or were consolidated with other companies. At the start of World War II, the "Big Three" auto makers (General Motors, Ford, and Chrysler) dominated the U.S. automobile industry, and only a handful of independent car manufacturers (Hudson, Packard, American Motors, Willys, and Studebaker) still remained in business.

> The role of the automobile industry during this time period is best illustrated by a statement Charles E. Wilson, Chief Executive Officer of General Motors, made in 1953 to a Senate Committee: " . . . *what is good for our country is good for General Motors, and vice versa.*"

During the pre-World War II period, businesses only used long distance telephone services for necessary communications. They viewed long distance telephone calls as overhead costs that should be closely monitored, controlled, and minimized. Customers calling a business were expected to pay for the cost of their call. (800-services,

which allowed businesses to pick up call charges, would not be available until the 1970s.)

Residential customers had basic telephone services installed (primarily by Bell System telephone companies), which allowed them to make local calls as part of the basic monthly telephone rate. Residential telephone customers viewed long distance calls as an expensive luxury, and they minimized their use of long distance calling facilities.

During the pre-1960 era, the regulatory objective was to provide high-quality, inexpensive basic telephone services for the local telephone company area. This operating philosophy matched both the business and residential view of how telephone services should be utilized. For a very modest fee, telephone services would be installed (including the necessary internal wiring and the equipment), and the cost for these basic services was kept to a minimal level by charging high prices (luxury taxes?) for long distance calls. Also, long distance call profits were used to subsidize local telephone services. Most long distance calls were made by business organizations, and residential customers were able to enjoy high quality local services (including local calls) for a very affordable cost.

The Business Environment (1960–1979)

The automobile industry's dominance of the American industrial environment was challenged in the mid-1960s. By the end of the decade, changes were taking place in the automobile industry that would significantly reduce the economic role of U.S. auto makers.

Historically, U.S. companies had been concerned only with U.S. competitors, and international competition had been token competition, at best. U.S. automobile companies saw the U.S. market as their exclusive territory, and the post-World War II success of the automobile industry was reflected in the unparalleled period of economic prosperity being enjoyed by American consumers. The love affair Americans had with their automobiles was stronger than ever. The hot rods of the fifties had been replaced in the sixties by stock muscle cars produced by American manufacturers. In 1960, 73,868,000 vehicles were registered in the U.S., and 61,569,000 of these were passenger cars. Imports accounted for less than 10% of total domestic sales (Volkswagen was the major import).

However, in 1968, Detroit's auto manufacturers viewed import autos as the domestic automobile industry's biggest worry when foreign auto makers sold an unprecedented 1,009,800 cars.

On the telecommunications front, business ran as usual. The Bell System dominated the U.S. marketplace, and their internal vision of universal service (providing a telephone to every U.S. residence) was very close to being a reality. However, AT&T was now being chastised for being too protective of the public telephone network by not allowing the attachment of Carterfone devices to the public network. In a 1968 settlement, AT&T agreed to allow non-Bell equipment to be attached to its network, provided they met the Bell System technical standards published by the FCC. Business users continued to use telephone services as they had in the past—as an expensive business necessity whose cost should be minimized.

Mainframe computers were introduced during the 1950s. By the 1960s, IBM had assumed a dominant market position in the mainframe computer marketplace—a leadership position they still enjoy today. IBM shipped its first Model 752 computer system in 1955, and this technical "toy" of the fifties matured into computer mainframe products that became a business necessity for American businesses during the 1960s. By the mid-1960s, U.S. corporations viewed computers as necessary for corporate survival in an increasingly competitive business environment.

By the end of the 1970s, many business organizations had multiple mainframe computer installations. From a business perspective, there was a need to interconnect mainframe computer systems and also to connect individual **dumb terminals** in smaller locations back to centralized mainframe systems.

Personal computers—the next wave of technical "toys"—had begun to appear. However, it seemed obvious to IBM at the time that they would never be a significant factor in the business environment. If there was any doubt concerning the continued dominance of mainframe computers, all business leaders had to do was ask IBM.

The Business Environment (1980–1990)

By 1980, the greatest concern of the automobile industry—significant competition from automobile imports—was a reality. Japanese manufacturers accounted for almost 27% of all car sales, and one of the "Big Three" auto makers—Chrysler—had already gone through a major reorganization that was triggered by poor sales. A government bail out loan of $1.5 billion had been given to Chrysler to ensure their continued existence. Even General Motors was experiencing major sales reductions, largely because of foreign competition.

Other manufacturing industries were facing similar problems. Competition was now a worldwide phenomenon, and all domestic manufacturers were under competitive attack from overseas competitors. The "good old days" of facing competition from domestic suppliers only was past. Mergers and acquisitions became a commonplace activity during the 1980s, and corporate size was not a significant ob-

stacle for the new breed of corporation raiders who purchased corporations, dismantled low profitability business segments to pay for the initial purchase, allowed the profitable segments to stay in business, and went on to look for additional acquisitions so the company dismantling cycle could be repeated.

Although mainframe computers were still the primary computing resource, PCs were beginning to make their presence felt. By the end of the 1980s, LAN technologies were becoming commonplace. An "upstart" company called Microsoft was being talked about in business circles, and the vision of a mainframe-centric business environment was under serious attack. The interest in PCs was not limited to businesses. Consumers found that PCs provided personal productivity tools for home use and a wide range of entertainment software was becoming available. Consumers were starting to voice product preferences in many areas, and the "good old days" of brand loyalty were under attack as computer-based technologies allowed small competitors to rapidly reproduce high-quality products at significantly lower prices than name-brand products.

800-SERVICES. The 1970s also saw the introduction of 800-Services (**inbound wide area telecommunications services; or INWATS**) by AT&T. **800-services** were still plain old telephone system (POTS) voice services, but with a twist—the called party would pay for the call. This meant that a company could provide 800-numbers to its customers, making them easy to do business with. When 800-services were implemented, it was obvious to most prudent businessmen that it was akin to insanity to pay for calls that their customers made. After all, customers had always paid for their own telephone calls in the past. Instead, 800-services have become a standard cost of doing business for most corporations, and customers have come to expect suppliers to pay for any calls that are made to them.

LONG DISTANCE CALL COST PRESSURES. In an effort to reduce voice communication costs, many corporations had installed voice networks during the 1970s and early 1980s. For a Bell customer, this meant purchasing high-capacity leased lines, connecting them between their business locations, and using this fixed-cost facility to save money compared to the cost of direct distance dialing (DDD) rates. Bell telephone companies gladly provided this service to large customers, and it gave business customers a way to reduce the high business expense associated with making long distance calls—especially because telecommunications services were now becoming business resources.

MCI had already been authorized to provide long distance telephone services between Chicago and New

York, and the business telephone call had emerged from a role as cost to be minimized to being viewed as a competitive tool for providing business customers with improved accessibility to products and services. Providing 800-services to customers had become a standard way of doing business.

The U.S. telecommunications industry—dominated by the Bell System—was under intense pressure by business customers to reduce the cost of voice and data communication long distance services. Corporations were using telecommunications as a business tool to gain competitive advantage in the battle to maintain or increase sales. Computer-to-computer communications requirements were escalating—not just between computer mainframes but also between PCs and between PC-based LANs.

THE INTERNET.   A Department of Defense (DOD) network project called **ARPANET** (*A*dvanced *R*esearch *P*rojects *A*gency *Net*work) had been converted to **NSFNET** (National Science Foundation Network)—an academic PC network that was the predecessor of the Internet. The technology infrastructure developed for ARPANET is the technology infrastructure that is used to support today's WWW. TCP/IP (Transmission Control Protocol/Internet Protocol) communications protocols were developed as part of ARPANET activities during the 1980s and they are still used as the major underlying internetworking protocols for the WWW and for private internetworks.

COMPUTERS AND COMMUNICATION.   By the end of the 1980s, the business environment had little in common with the business environment that had existed in the 1950s. Competition was fierce, mergers and acquisitions were commonplace, and business strategies were based on using computer and communication technology to gain competitive advantage. Consumers expected manufacturers to meet consumer-imposed expectations—at low costs—or they would go elsewhere to buy a cheaper product. Business management frequently employed the phrase, "strategic use of information technology," and computers and communication were no longer viewed as costs to be minimized but were viewed as business requirements.

THE 1984 DIVESTITURE—A NATURAL OUTCOME.   Considering the business pressures to reduce telecommunications expenses and use the newfound *computer + communications* asset as a business tool, it is not surprising that the 1984 divestiture was a product of the 1980s. High long distance calling costs, the regulatory bottleneck for telecommunications product development, and the inability of the old telecommunications infrastructure to respond to business needs created a judicial climate conducive to deregulating the Bell System-dominated telecommunications industry.

The Current Business Environment (1990 and Beyond)

By 1990, most of the 1984 divestiture mandates had been implemented. Data communication needs continued to escalate sharply as LAN technologies were being developed and installed at a breakneck pace in U.S. businesses. The Internet was an established reality, even though its use was largely limited to academic and technology-oriented users.

On the business front, competition was still fierce, cost pressures were intense, and survival meant either finding a niche market to generate profits or committing to generating new products on a continuous basis. The survival race belonged to the swift—*if they had the right information and were agile; that is, if they had computers and communications resources that allowed them to respond quickly to marketplace conditions.*

THE WORLD WIDE WEB.   Network browsers, brought into the Internet environment during the early 1990s, transformed the Internet from being a technical "toy" used by academics into a combination business and pleasure resource called the World Wide Web (WWW). The terms **e-mail** and *e-commerce* were incorporated into the vocabulary of every businessman and consumer. Individuals became addicted to the WWW and spent countless hours looking for bargains, information, and amusement. Entrepreneurs became overnight millionaires by using WWW facilities to sell products directly to consumers and bypassing the need to establish traditional channels of distribution to the consumer marketplace. Corporations without a home page were likely to suffer the same fate as companies that had continued to base their success on making buggy whips for horses after the automobile had became a reality.

The 1984 divestiture was ancient history, and all telecommunications equipment was being provided in an unregulated environment. Although remnants of regulatory tariffs existed, the cost per minute of long distance calls for both residential and business customers was less than 20% of the cost in 1984. RHCs had separate divisions in both the deregulated side of telecommunications (equipment and long distance calls) and the regulated side of the telecommunications industry (local calls).

The business need for increased computer-to-computer communications continued to drive technology developments. New telecommunications products were computer communications-oriented products, which provided increasingly higher data rates for steadily decreasing costs. Computer-driven multimedia applications were the focus for telecommunications technology development efforts. There were a few remaining regulated telecommunications services in the U.S., but they had a minimal impact on the availability and deployment of telecommunications products and services.

The U.S. deregulation philosophy was evident in the worldwide telecommunications environment, as many countries liberalized (privatized) government-run telecommunications facilities to provide their corporate citizens with access to the worldwide, communications-intensive business environment. The business need for computer and communication services was reflected in a worldwide trend where countries were implementing national policies to accelerate their internal development of worldwide communication networks.

WWW CHANGE DRIVERS

One of the early developments in computer networking was the ARPANET project. ARPANET was a U.S. DOD initiative, undertaken in 1969, to develop a distributed computer network architecture that would have the necessary intelligence to reroute (**bypass**) traffic if communication links between different military mainframe computer systems failed. The military was starting to use computers extensively, and their networks were using point-to-point and multipoint leased line connections to interconnect computer systems. They realized that point-to-point communications links were the weak link in being able to access military information during wartime. Their solution was to underwrite the development of a self-healing network that would allow computer systems to maintain communication by directing the network to automatically reroute computer traffic over undamaged communication links.

The task of creating a distributed computer network was turned over to academic research groups in the form of grants made to universities. The original ARPANET connected the different research groups that were located in participating universities. As the project developed, more and more university groups participated in the ARPANET project and were added on as ARPANET network users. This research-oriented network evolved into the Internet infrastructure that provides the basic infrastructure for today's e-commerce environment—the WWW.

The Internet

In 1990, ARPANET was officially retired and replaced by **NSFNET**—a backbone network infrastructure providing connectivity between university campuses across the U.S. The term *Internet* had originally been associated with

government-funded networks but was being used for any networks using the **TCP/IP** protocols that had been developed for ARPANET. In 1991, three companies, 1) IBM, 2) Merit, and 3) MCI, formed a nonprofit organization to build a new Internet backbone. Today, the Internet, which consists of networks spanning the world, is based on the use of TCP/IP protocols.

Web Browsers

The Internet provided the physical and technical infrastructure that allowed computer information packets to be transferred between different network devices. While the growth of the commercial Internet during the post-ARPANET time period was significant, another strategic product—the **Web browser**—was needed to transform the Internet into the commercial success that today is called the WWW.

The WWW browser was developed within a university environment. A British physicist and computer scientist, Timothy Berners-Lee, began working with hypertext in 1980. His Web browser protocol was an operating application introduced in 1989 at the European Center for Nuclear Energy Research. The first major commercial Web browser, Mosaic, was developed in 1993.

The current WWW is based on a combination of Internet facilities and Web browser servers. Today, the Internet provides the data transmission fabric and Web browsers provide the information access logic essential for the seamless operation of the WWW. As is frequently the case when new technologies are introduced, the Internet was considered by many to be a technical "toy." It evolved from being a plaything or experiment into becoming a worldwide encyclopedia of commercial and private information—an evolution that required the introduction of Web browser technologies. Since the introduction of browsers, the growth of the WWW has been explosive. Business, government, educational, and military organizations without a Web home page are considered to be technology dinosaurs, and Web home pages are now maintained by many private organizations and individuals.

E-Commerce

The term *e-commerce* refers to the commercial activity that takes place across interconnected computers. It is a term that is commonly used when describing the social impact of the WWW. E-commerce can occur between a user and a vendor through an Internet provider or directly between vendor and customer computers by using EDI (Electronic Data Interchange) technologies.

While the Internet (WWW) is a technology-based phenomenon, its impact has clearly affected the social and economic fabric of our society. Privacy and security issues have emerged. It will be a difficult, time-consuming task to sort out the social, economic, and legal implications of satisfying a society where its members have instant access to all forms of information.

TELECOMMUNICATIONS TECHNOLOGY

The technology reviewed in the following section is a direct byproduct of the environments discussed under the *Regulatory Change Drivers* and *Business Change Drivers* sections. Technology developments were direct reflections of the prevailing business and social environment that existed when the products were produced. This statement is clearly supported by the correlation of worldwide business competition in the U.S. with the rate of change in telecommunications technology. Business activities (and technology development) proceeded at a relatively leisurely pace until the 1960s, when worldwide competition and the maturation of computer technology forever changed the economic landscape. Since the 1960s, changes in the business and telecommunications environments have taken place at a dizzying pace. The only constant is continual change.

Telecommunications, as previously stated, is the science and technology of communication at a distance through the electronic transmission of impulses, as by telegraph, cable, telephone, radio, or television. A key phrase in this definition is "at a distance" and the focus of this section will be on *networking technology—the technology infrastructure needed to transport electronic impulses over a distance*. While user-oriented equipment—telephones, cell phones, facsimile, and video cameras—are the most visible telecommunications components, it is the hidden network technology infrastructure that transports voice, video, and data across long distances and represents the real telecommunications phenomenon. During the last fifty years, the network infrastructure has migrated from one based on voice-oriented technologies to one using computer-based digital technologies. Additional digital network technology developments are needed to support WWW and other computer-to-computer networking applications.

Telephony-based (voice) technology was the dominant networking technology in the U.S. and in other nations between 1900 and 1984. Except for a niche market filled by telegraph services, telephone services dominated the telecommunications industry. In 1955, IBM introduced the mainframe business computer but it was not until the mid-1960s that computer communications issues emerged. This 10-year gap existed because the early period of mainframe computer development focused on transforming an unreliable, quirky [computer] technology into a reliable business tool. It was only after computer reliability issues had been resolved that computer communication issues began to attract heavy attention.

By the mid-1960s, most corporations had several mainframe computer systems—a phenomenon that was not possible during the 1950s because of the extremely high cost of purchasing computer hardware coupled with the high cost of developing software to run on the mainframe computer. With the number of mainframe computer installations increasing, coupled with the development of remote terminal technologies, a new need for mainframe-to-mainframe and mainframe-to-terminal data communication emerged. Computer communication needs were initially addressed by using point-to-point leased analog (voice) lines that were conditioned to handle data transmission requirements by adding electrical and electronic components into each individual data link and fine-tuning them to handle computer traffic. Fortunately, all-digital communication facilities were already in place as part of the voice communication backbone network that connected major long distance COs. However, it was necessary to use analog lines (and their conditioning requirements) to access the digital backbone network. This analog segment of the network was the weak link.

The following list categorizes telecommunications technology developments into three networking eras:

1. the telegraph network era: 1844–1875
2. the telephone (voice) network era:1876–1984
3. the computer network era: 1985–present.

The Telegraph Networks Era (1844–1875)

The telegraph era started with the introduction of public telegraph services in 1844. Telegraph services still exist today, although in a limited form compared to other communication technology. While it is now largely relegated to a curio status in museums, it served as the technology base on which current communications technology was built.

Telegraph services were developed as a response to the need for communicating beyond line-of-sight distances. Within a line-of-sight, semaphore signaling was being used in Europe and Native Americans in the U.S. used smoke signals. Semaphore relay stations could be used to extend line-of-sight communication, but the actual line of sight distances were limited by weather and the available light conditions. Horse and coach facilities were used for carrying mail, but this option was also constrained by weather, lighting conditions, and the geographic terrain.

By 1840, a fundamental knowledge existed about the phenomenon called electricity, and wire conductors

Figure 2–3. The telegraph system.

```
A ._         N _.          1 .____
B _...        O ___         2 ..___
C _._.        P .__.        3 ...__
D _..         Q __._        4 ...._
E .          R ._.         5 .....
F .._.        S ...         6 _....
G __.         T _          7 __...
H ....        U .._         8 ___..
I ..          V ..._        9 ____.
J .___        W .__         0 _____
K _._         X _.._
L ._..        Y _.__
M __          Z __..
```

Figure 2–4. International Morse code.

connected to batteries were able to carry electrical current beyond line of sight distances. Early researchers found that opening and closing electrical circuits produced equivalent current fluctuations at both ends of the line and that these current fluctuations could be encoded to transmit information beyond line of sight distances. These encoded signals were the basis for telegraphy—a method of long-distance communication that uses coded electric impulses transmitted through wires.

In the U.S., Samuel Morse had developed electrical instruments for sending and receiving telegraphic transmissions and had also developed an encoding scheme to send alphanumeric characters across the telegraph system (refer to Figures 2–3 and 2–4). Morse's encoding scheme was based on using two electrical current states: a short duration electrical current flow and a long duration current flow, i.e., a dot and a dash. The telegraph receiver generated a short noise burst for the dot and a longer noise burst for the dash. The sending telegraph operator would read the original message, convert the message's words and

numbers into Morse code equivalents, and transmit the resulting dots and dashes across the telegraph wires. At the receiving end, the telegraph operator would listen to the received dots and dashes and convert them back into letters and numbers to recreate the original message.

Telegraph operators continued to be the key elements of long distance telegraph systems until the 1920s, with the introduction of typewriter-based Teletype equipment. Teletype equipment is still in limited use today.

BINARY COMMUNICATION. Morse Code is actually a binary encoding scheme. It uses two states, a dot and a dash, to encode the letters, numbers, and punctuation characters. (In today's binary communication world, dots and dashes could easily be called zeros and ones.)

The Telephone (Voice) Network Era (1876–1984)

Telephony, the technology based on communication between telephones, dominated U.S. networking requirements for over 100 years. In the U.S., the telephony era was begun by Alexander Graham Bell while he was conducting telegraph equipment experiments. Early telecommunications networks were designed to carry voice conversations over long distances. Voice communication still accounts for a significant percentage of today's network traffic. Alexander Graham Bell's early business efforts became the basis for establishing the Bell System, which dominated the telecommunications environment from 1876 to 1984. Therefore, this time period has been selected to represent the Telephone Network Era in the U.S.

THE BEGINNING. In 1874, while working on telegraph experiments, Alexander Graham Bell developed the basic ideas for the telephone. Instead of using the on/off concept of telegraphy to encode information, he varied the current flow in a wire to replicate the sound waves of human speech. Bell used a carbon granule microphone to convert sound signals into electrical signals that were then transmitted across a copper conductor. A receiving earphone equipped with a diaphragm created a replica of the sound waves that had originally created the current flow variations.

> Humans are able to hear frequencies in the range between 50 Hertz and 20,000 Hertz. Early telephony researchers found that it was only necessary to accurately reproduce a relatively small range of this hearing spectrum to have intelligible conversations. As a result of this observation, telephony equipment and network services were designed to accurately reproduce the audible speech spectrum only between 400 Hertz and 4,000 Hertz. This bandwidth range is still the basis for voice telephony equipment design.

In 1875, communication lines consisted of bare copper wires that were strung between telephone poles and supported by insulators to minimize electrical signal losses. Electronic amplifiers had not yet been invented, and the distance a voice signal could travel between the sending and receiving locations was determined by the strength of the initial signal and the transmission quality of the communication line. During rainy periods, transmission capabilities of bare copper wires degraded sharply and it was difficult to have intelligible conversations for distances of more than a mile or two.

ELECTRONIC TELECOMMUNICATIONS. The development of telephony and electronics are interrelated. Telephony needed electronics to provide reliable, long-distance communication and electronics research needed the investments that telephone network providers—primarily the Bell System—were willing to make. Because of electronics, **telephony** evolved from a point-to-point transmission technology requiring a dedicated line between the calling parties to a highly complex technology capable of using a single conductor to carry thousands of individual telephone calls. Electronic switches were installed in telephone COs, allowing multiple conversation pathways to be used for routing calls anywhere in the U.S. This capability meant that long distance calls could be routed over a network consisting of a small number of high capacity lines deployed to a small number of major locations. Once the call had traversed the long distance pathway, lower capacity lines were used to connect local telephone company COs to the long distance node.

Local telephone company COs provided both the entry and exit points for gaining access to the complex, long distance network. They provided connections between local subscribers in the local calling area and gave local subscribers access to long distance network services. Driven by the Bell System's self proclaimed vision of universal service, Bell Labs led the telecommunications product development effort required for providing reliable, cost effective telephony services to residential and business customers.

DIGITIZED VOICE. Coaxial cable, multiconductor cable, and microwave transmission technologies were developed to meet telephony long distance networking requirements. In 1939, the development of **pulse code modulation (PCM)** algorithms provided the means for using digital encoding to convert analog voice conversations into digital signals. Digitized voice signals were then transmitted across the long distance network and converted back to the original analog voice conversation signals at the destination telephone CO, which provided a high quality voice signal at the receiving telephone set. This process involved an analog-to-digital signal conversion at the originating telephone company CO and a digital-to-analog conversion at the destination telephone company CO—a technically complex process but one that provided reliable, high quality long distance calling services. **Digital communication had begun.**

TELEPHONE NETWORKS. By 1984, a high quality, *digital* long distance backbone network spanned the U.S. Microwave transmission was the primary voice transmission networking technology being used. Fiber optics technology was starting to be developed and implemented at an increasing rate, and this light-based technology was destined to become the medium of choice for future high speed, high bandwidth digital communication.

Table 2–1 summarizes the chronological development of telephony transmission media. The voice-based infrastructure that was implemented prior to the development of computer technology still forms the basic platform for most forms of current network transmission: voice, data, and multimedia communication.

TELEPHONE EQUIPMENT. Between 1900 and 1984, communication equipment was primarily voice-based equipment: telephone sets, operator switchboards, PBX telephone systems, key telephone systems, facsimile, teletype terminals, modems, and network interface equipment. Modems converted digital computer signals into an encoded analog signal suitable to be carried by the existing voice-based telephone network. Network interface equipment was used to provide high capacity voice communication between PBX telephone systems or for specialized computer communication needs. In the predivestiture environment, equipment was designed, built, and rented from the local

TABLE 2–1   Transmission Media Development Chronology

When	Medium	Comments
1900s	Open pair wires	Bare copper wire pairs were spaced 8″ to 18″ apart to minimize crosstalk effects, stretched between telephone poles, and suspended from insulators. Open pair facilities provided unamplified conversations and were limited to distances equal to, or less than, the distance from New York City to Chicago. Open pair wires were highly susceptible to crosstalk and attenuation effects. Open pair wires were used for many years to provide telegraph services.
1920s	Twisted pair cables	Twisted pair cables consisted of insulated copper conductor wires twisted into pairs and grouped into one cable. Loading coils and amplifiers were connected to twisted cable pairs to compensate for crosstalk and attenuation effects. Electronic multiplexing techniques allowed twisted pair wires to carry twelve to twenty-four separate conversations on one pair of wires.
1920s	High frequency radio telephone	High frequency telephone radio transmissions were used for transatlantic telephony prior to 1956. Radiotelephone facilities are still used for international telegraph and ship-to-shore telephone communications.
1930s	Coaxial cable	Coaxial cable's external metallic shield minimized the effect of crosstalk and other electromagnetic phenomena that plagued early telephone networks. Multiple coaxial cables and twisted pair cables were combined into larger cables, and amplifiers were placed at 3–4 mile intervals. Multiplexed conversations were transported on .4 to 10 MHz carrier signals. Coaxial cable could carry 10,800 multiplexed analog voice conversations compared to the twelve to twenty-four analog voice channels that could be carried by twisted pair conductors.
1950s	Microwave radio	Microwave links utilized high frequency (1,000 MHz) signals and became the medium of choice for long-haul telephone trunks until the 1980s. Microwave has the capability for concurrently carrying thousands of voice analog channels and hundreds of high bandwidth television signals. Microwave transmission requires a line of sight visibility between the two microwave antennas— a requirement that normally limits the microwave link span to twenty or thirty miles because of the earth's curvature.
1956	Submarine cable	The first submarine cable was installed under the English channel, between England and mainland Europe, in 1858 for telegraph services. It failed after 16 days of use. Although transatlantic telegraph cables had been utilized since the early part of the 1900s, the first transatlantic telephone cable was not installed until 1956.
1960s	Satellite	Satellites provide a "microwave relay" tower in the sky, where the satellites filled the role of microwave antennas. If satellites are placed in a geosynchronous orbit 22,300 miles above the equator, they remain in a fixed location relative to the earth and a geosynchronous satellite can be used as a fixed microwave tower for earth stations that are within the satellite's line of sight. Satellite antennas operate in the four to six GHz and twenty to forty GHz range, and their operation can be adversely affected by atmospheric conditions. Because it requires approximately 1/2 second for round-trip transmissions to and from satellites, its use for voice was limited because most people had difficulty using satellite communication. New data communication protocols were required to allow mainframe computers to handle these delays, because 1/2 second is a lifetime in the computer processor environment. For some applications, the satellite communications delay was unacceptable.
1980s	Fiber optics	Fiber optics (FO) is based on transmitting light signals across hair-thin glass fibers, and has become the current medium of choice for all long distance and high bandwidth applications. FO is unaffected by electromagnetic interference, and amplifiers are spaced at distances of ten to fifteen kilometers (six to nine miles).
1990s	Cellular radio	Cellular radio is based on using low power radio frequency transmitters to serve small geographic areas (cells). The cells are interconnected by means of conventional telephony trunking facilities. Because they use low power transmitters, nonadjacent cells can use the same radio frequencies without creating interference for each other.

telephone company. If the telephone company did not provide the desired equipment, it was simply not available.

The Computer Network Era (1985–Present)

The development of computer technology was driven by the need for data processing—the collection and analysis of data. The Census Bureau, as part of its charter to collect data for the government, initiated the first major data processing application in the U.S. In 1890, the Census Bureau had hired an American engineer and inventor, Herman Hollerith, to build a special purpose data processing system for tabulating and evaluating census data.

HOLLERITH CARDS.

The Hollerith system was based on the use of punched cards about the size of a dollar bill, and utilized a coding structure based on the location of the punched holes in the card. Census takers recorded numerical data by manually punching the appropriate holes in the card. These punched cards were taken to the census office where mechanical card readers read the holes in each card, interpreted the meaning of the punched holes, and provided a listing of the raw data contained in the card. Mechanical adding machines [with human operators] were used to tabulate the census information.

THE INTERNATIONAL BUSINESS MACHINE CORPORATION (IBM).

Herman Hollerith founded the Tabulating Machine Company in 1896, which later merged with several other companies to form the International Business Machine Corporation (IBM). In 1924, the Computer-Tabulating-Recording Company acquired IBM and the new company assumed the IBM name. Until the 1950s, IBM's business focus was on developing and manufacturing time clocks, punched-card tabulating equipment, and typewriters.

COMPUTERS: THE BEGINNING.

During World War II (1939–1945), scientists developed a variety of computers designed for the specific data processing functions needed to support the war effort. At Harvard University, a Mark 1 computer was built using a combination of electrical and mechanical devices (mainly relays) to perform calculations for the U.S. Navy. Between 1943 and 1946, the U.S. armed services underwrote the development of a general-purpose electronic computer named Electronic Numerical Integrator And Calculator (ENIAC). ENIAC was used to calculate the paths of artillery shells and missiles.

The developers of ENIAC—Presper Eckert and John Mauchly—organized the Eckert-Mauchly Computer Corporation in 1948. In 1949, Eckert-Mauchly delivered a computer called *BIN*ary *A*utomatic *C*omputer (BINAC) to the

Northrup Corporation for use as an aircraft-based, onboard missile control system. Eckert-Mauchly followed up its BINAC development effort with the development of another computer—the *UNIV*ersal *A*utomatic *C*omputer (UNIVAC).

The Eckert-Mauchly Computer Company was purchased by Remington Rand in 1950 and was renamed the UNIVAC Division of Remington Rand. The first UNIVAC computer was delivered to the U.S. Census Bureau in 1951 and several additional UNIVAC computers were sold to other government agencies.

In 1950, IBM was the dominant force in the electronic adding machine (EAM) market—a technology based on using Hollerith punched cards. EAM equipment was used by U.S. businesses while ENIAC computers were still viewed as a research device. IBM and Remington Rand exchanged patent rights for EAM and UNIVAC technologies, respectively, during the 1950s.

MAINFRAME COMPUTER SYSTEMS: CORPORATE "GLASS HOUSES."

IBM produced its first mainframe computer in 1951—the IBM 701—and by the early 1960s IBM had established itself as the market leader in the mainframe computer industry. Early mainframe computers were extremely expensive and unreliable, and required 24 hour × 7 day support by trained personnel to achieve some semblance of continuous service. Because of the high cost and their unreliable operation, they were housed in special climate-controlled facilities, and access to them was restricted to authorized personnel. These facilities were commonly called **glass houses,** because corporations owning them frequently placed them behind glass panels so they could be shown off to their customers. This physical separation of mainframe computers from the individuals using computer services resulted in a credibility gap that would not be closed until the introduction of the PC.

COMPANY-SPECIFIC SOFTWARE DEVELOPMENT.

Computer communication in the early mainframe computer environment was simple—*there wasn't any computer communication*. The complexity of incorporating mainframe computers into the business environment absorbed all of the time and talent that was available. Application software was nonexistent and computer programmers were required to write company-specific software applications that could run on their own mainframe computers. During the 1960s, the primary mainframe computer focus for businesses was to convert existing manual systems into computer-based application software.

Computers were a very expensive investment and could only be justified by using them on a 24 × 7 (twenty-four hours per day, seven days per week) basis. Computer processing consisted of running company applications in a continuous stream—an activity referred to as **batch processing.** The computer operations objective was to have the expensive mainframe computer resource continually processing applications in order to justify its existence. Communication in the early years of the mainframe computer meant delivering printed reports to users as quickly as conventional delivery methods (train, truck, and airlines) permitted.

COMPUTER COMMUNICATION. The introduction of the IBM System/360 (S/360) family of computers in 1964 provided a general-purpose computer architecture that included computer networking options. A broad range of S/360 processing capabilities also minimized the need for using individual, special-application computers because the new operating system included many capabilities. The S/360 architecture allowed S/360 mainframes to be interconnected and also let "dumb terminals" be connected to the intelligent mainframe computers.

At this time period, computer communication required the installation of dedicated, conditioned, point-to-point communication lines between host computers and from host computers to dumb workstations. The conditioning process required the attachment of electric and electronic components to the dedicated analog line so that it could handle high speed computer communications. With conditioning, speeds up to 9,600 bps could be achieved.

COMPUTER COMMUNICATION PROTOCOLS: THE OSI MODEL. Computer communication in the early mainframe computer environment required running specialized computer software applications, and the physical, electrical, and logical (software) conventions used for providing communication between computer system devices were called **protocols.** In the 1970s, computer protocols were vendor-specific, proprietary protocols. Computer system customers had to purchase communication hardware and software directly from the computer vendor. Therefore, the purchase commitment made to a computer system vendor also meant that a purchase commitment was also being made to purchase the vendor's communication hardware and software products.

As computers became increasingly important to business operations, business organizations wanted an environment where computer communications was standardized (nonproprietary). Businesses wanted the ability to select equipment from different vendors without encountering the incompatibility issues that existed when communication between different mainframe computers was necessary. The focus for this user-driven standardization

effort was the **ISO.** In 1984, the ISO released the **7-layer OSI Model.** Computer communication equipment that conformed to OSI interface standards would be interoperable with the equipment of other vendors, who also adhered to OSI interface standards. Although OSI protocols never were established as mandated standards, the OSI model concept was incorporated into major vendor products.

These early standardization efforts are the reason why today's networks are able to have interfaces with different types of equipment. Today, LANs and WANs using equipment manufactured by different vendors can be combined into a single internetwork that provides seamless, end-to-end, computer-to-computer communication capabilities between any two workstations attached to the internetwork.

UNFULFILLED EXPECTATIONS. By the mid-1980s, mainframe computers were an integral part of both large and medium-sized businesses. The hardware and software problems encountered in the 1960s were distant memories—the only issues were cost and user control. Although mainframe computers cost much less than earlier models and had much higher processing power capabilities, they still were not a viable option for small companies or for personal use. Mainframe computers required a glass house environment where skilled specialists could maintain them.

Computer programming departments also had large application design backlogs. Even applications that seemed simple to end users took months—even years—to complete. New computer systems processed information hundreds of times faster than the previous generation of computers, but the application programming backlog grew even faster. A major gap now existed between user service expectations and the service levels they received. Data processing centers had backlogs measured in programmer years, and users wanted solutions within hours.

User organizations found mainframe program development services to be unacceptably slow. To make matters worse, the data processing gatekeeper organizations constrained access to critical computer resources except on a precise standardized time schedule. It was time to find a better way for providing end users with computing resources, and the availability of PCs provided the better way.

INTEGRATED CIRCUITS. In the mid-1940s, analog computers were the size of houses and as expensive as battleships without providing the ease of operation or computing power that is expected today in the simplest, least-expensive PC. Mainframe computer development investments had initially been underwritten by government projects. As commercial customers started using them heavily during the 1960s, businesses became the major investors in computer technologies. The invention of integrated circuits in the 1970s was a technology breakthrough that revolutionized the computer industry and allowed PCs to achieve the status they have today. With integrated circuits, the PC could provide the same processing power as a mainframe computer at a fraction of the cost, while sporting a compact desktop size.

PCs: THE BEGINNING.

Three pilot projects undertaken during the 1970s by the Xerox **Palo Alto Research Center (PARC)** would be major catalysts for the commercial development of PCs and LANs:

1. The Alto Personal Computer
2. Alto Graphical User Interface (GUI) software
3. Ethernet LANs

Although the Xerox Corporation never profited directly from these three projects, their research efforts were key developments in PC history. The Alto Personal Computer was a model for the Apple Computer, and Apple's follow up product, the Macintosh computer, incorporated the Alto GUI concepts into its design. Ethernet LANs continue to be the most popular LAN technology in existence today.

However, it remained for IBM to legitimize the use of PCs with the introduction of the IBM PC in 1981. While many industry analysts felt the IBM product was inferior to other PC alternatives (notably Apple Computer products), there is little question that IBM's prestige in the mainframe computer marketplace legitimized the use of PCs by major businesses. Today, the IBM PC architecture is the dominant PC architecture.

PC COMMUNICATIONS: LANs.

Today, the desktop PC provides more power, capability, and ease of use than could ever have been imagined in the 1970s. In addition, the PC has revolutionized computer communications. PCs spawned the development of LANs and the widespread use of LANs created the need for distributed computer communications architectures (versus a centralized mainframe architecture that was based on a centralized mainframe computer architecture).

The IEEE (Institute of Electrical and Electronics Engineers) was set up as the LAN standardization organization by the ISO in February of 1980 and continues to play a major role in the development of LAN standards. By the mid-1980s, LANs were the dominant networking technology used by business organizations to integrate and distribute PC capabilities.

COMPUTER INTERNETWORKING: WANs.

WANs—communication networks spanning long distances—were initially developed to handle voice communication. These same WANs were initially used to handle mainframe computer communication needs. Mainframe computer networks were based on having a single, intelligent host computer provide services to a large number of workstations that did not have computing capability (dumb terminals). Network addressing in the mainframe communication environment meant assigning unique addresses to the devices connected to the mainframe network and using these addresses to exchange information between terminals and mainframes. From a mainframe computer perspective, computer networks were seen as mainframe networks, and WANs were used to extend the range of the mainframe network.

As the number of mainframe computers increased, the number of separate mainframe networks increased. The introduction of the PC network—the LAN—exponentially increased the need for communication between and across networks (internetworking). Packet switching technology already existed and TCP/IP protocols were used for developing computer internetworks. As PC communication increased, the need for faster, higher bandwidth networks increased dramatically and TCP/IP protocols have become the protocols of choice for Internet (WWW) and private internetwork purposes.

SUMMARY

This summary is organized to correspond with the learning objectives found at the beginning of the chapter.

1. The basic (human) communication model consists of a sender, a receiver, and a communication medium, and was limited to hearing and line of sight distance limitations. Telecommunications models replaced the communication medium with a transmission system and provided technology interfaces to the transmission system. These interfaces converted information flows into the appropriate format for humans or telecommunications, as required.

2. The U.S. telecommunications regulatory environment determined the availability and cost of telecommunications services until the 1982 Bell System Divestiture Agreement that deregulated telecommunications equipment and long distance calling services. The

deregulation trend is continuing in areas previously considered the exclusive domain of state regulatory agencies (PUCs).

3. The telecommunications regulatory environment reflects the business and social environment in which it exists. Until the 1960s, businesses considered telecommunications expenses as an overhead cost that should be closely controlled and minimized. During the 1960s, international competition became a way of life. Computer and communication technologies were needed to respond to the competitive pressures. The slow development pace of telecommunications technology and its high cost was an unacceptable business constraint.

4. ARPANET was a U.S. DOD project whose objective was the development of a distributed network architecture that could ensure the ongoing availability of military computers if individual network links were broken. Funding was provided to various universities for the project, and the initial ARPANET interconnected project teams at the different universities. ARPANET evolved into the network infrastructure known as the Internet, which is the technical infrastructure of today's WWW.

5. Samuel Morse's telegraph networks illustrated how technology could be used effectively to span long distances, and telegraph technologies were the basis for the subsequent development of telephones that had the capability of transmitting voice over wires. Morse Code—the telegraph language—was a binary encoding scheme (a two-element code consisting of dots and dashes) that electrically transmitted alphanumeric information.

6. Telephone products and networks were the dominant telecommunications technologies until the mid-1980s, when the emphasis shifted to providing computer communications. Digital transmission facilities were introduced in the late 1930s to provide high quality voice transmission over long distances. These digital facilities are still used today for handling computer communication needs.

7. Mainframe computers were introduced in the 1950s, but were not viewed as a viable business resource until the 1970s, when mainframe technology problems had been solved and integrated circuits were developed. The integrated circuit technology allowed mainframe functionality to be placed in small, inexpensive packages called PCs. Mainframe communication needs drove the development efforts for computer communication technology, including ARPANET.

8. PCs were accepted during the 1980s by American businesses as being a viable business resource, and all subsequent LAN and WAN developments have been driven by PC communication. PCs continue to run faster, become easier to use, contain more storage capability, and cost less than the last year's model. PCs drive computer network developments, and their users have an insatiable appetite for multimedia applications requiring higher-speed, higher-bandwidth LANs, internetworks, and "capital I" Internet services.

9. The ISO developed the 7-layer OSI Model during the 1980s to provide a design standard that telecommunications product designers could use to ensure operating compatibility between different vendor products. Few of the original standards have actually been implemented, but telecommunications vendors continue to use OSI design concepts. It is the underlying reason why a high level of interoperability exists today between proprietary equipment and network products.

KEY TERMS AND CONCEPTS

The language of telecommunications management is multifaceted and includes words and phrases from managerial, technological, accounting, regulatory, and other business areas. The definitions of these key terms and concepts can be found within the chapter and in the glossary.

AT&T	Carterfone	E-mail
ARPANET	Centrex Telephone System	Equal Access
AT&T Information Systems (ATTIS)	Customer Premises Equipment (CPE)	FCC
Batch Processing	Digital Communication	Glass House
Bell Operating Companies	Data Access Arrangement (DAA)	International Standards Organization (ISO)
Bell System	Dumb Terminals	Internet
Bell Telephone Company	800-Service	Inbound Wide Area Telecommunications
Bypass	E-commerce	Services (INWATS)

Local Area Network (LAN)	PC	Telecommunications Act of 1996
Mainframe Computer	Protocol	Telegraph
Natural Monopoly	Public Utility Commission (PUC)	Telephony
1984 Bell System Divestiture	Pulse Code Modulation (PCM)	Universal Service Vision
1982 Consent Decree	Regional Holding Companies (RHCs)	Wide Area Network (WAN)
NSFNET	7-layer OSI Model	Web Browser
Palo Alto Research Center (PARC)	TCP/IP	World Wide Web (WWW)
PBX Telephone System	Telecommunications	

REVIEW

The following questions are open-ended—predefined answers are not included as part of the text. The purpose of these questions is to allow the readers to test themselves on the chapter material.

1. Describe how the Basic Communication Model relates to the world of telecommunications.

2. What is the primary advantage offered by the Telecommunications Model when compared to the Basic Communication Model?

3. Explain the universal service concept as applied to the U.S. telecommunications environment.

4. Describe the events leading up to the deregulation of the U.S. telecommunications industry and why it was probably an inevitable event.

5. Why was the introduction of telecommunications technology innovation comparatively slow during the predivestiture era?

6. What is the importance of the 1968 Carterfone decision for U.S. telecommunications?

7. Why did the Justice Department feel it was necessary to split the Bell System into three major operating entities?

8. What impact did the invention of the computer have on the telecommunications industry?

9. What was the major breakthrough that allowed the Internet to evolve into the information-rich WWW environment that currently exists?

10. What similarities exist between Morse's original telegraph design and the current computer communication environment?

11. When was the first transatlantic cable installed for international telephony?

12. What is the 7-Layer OSI Model?

MULTIPLE CHOICE

1. The Basic Communication Model consists of _____. (Select all that apply.)
   a. LANs
   b. a sender
   c. a communication medium
   d. DTEs
   e. a receiver

2. In the Telecommunications Technology Model, the _____ encodes the transmitted information into a format suitable for the selected transmission medium.
   a. source
   b. destination
   c. equipment
   d. DTE
   e. DCE

3. The medium of choice for light-based transmissions is _____.
   a. coaxial cable
   b. shielded twisted pair
   c. fiber optics cable
   d. satellite relay stations
   e. unshielded twisted pair (UTP)

4. The first telecommunications technology introduced in the U.S. was _____.
   a. fire signals
   b. telephone
   c. computer networks
   d. telegraph
   e. microwave

5. The U.S. government agency given responsibility for regulating long distance calling services is the _____.

   a. ISO

   b. OSI

   c. ICC

   d. PUC

   e. FCC

6. Local telephone company activities were regulated by _____.

   a. ISOs

   b. FCCs

   c. ICCs

   d. OSIs

   e. PUCs

7. The first telephone company in the U.S. was established in _____.

   a. 1812

   b. 1844

   c. 1876

   d. 1900

   e. 1934

8. In the regulated telephone environment, the profits made for _____ services were used to subsidize local telephone company operations.

   a. long distance calling

   b. local calling

   c. equipment rental

   d. data communication

   e. CPE

9. In the regulated telephone environment, equipment development and installation costs were typically recovered _____.

   a. within one year

   b. over a two-year period

   c. over a five-year period

   d. over a ten-year period

   e. over a twenty-year period

10. During the regulated telephone era, _____ company owned and operated U.S. long distance telephone networks.

    a. one

    b. two

    c. five

    d. many

    e. none

11. The Bell System Divestiture took the twenty-two local telephone companies and set up _____ RHCs.

    a. three

    b. five

    c. seven

    d. ten

    e. none

12. The 1982 Consent Decree provided _____ years to complete Divestiture requirements.

    a. one

    b. two

    c. three

    d. five

13. Equal access requirements provided the mechanism to _____.

    a. deregulate local telephone services

    b. provide local calling services

    c. deregulate telecommunications equipment

    d. deregulate long distance calling services

14. The need to file long distance tariffs with the FCC was eliminated by _____.

    a. the 1982 Consent Decree

    b. the Telecommunications Act of 1996

    c. the Telecommunications Act of 1934

    d. the 1984 Modified Final Judgment

15. Long distance digital networks were in use by _____.

    a. 1900

    b. 1934

    c. 1984

    d. 1996

    e. 2000

16. The first transatlantic telephone cable was installed in _____.

    a. 1900

    b. 1925

    c. 1934

    d. 1956

    e. 1984

3

WHAT IS TELECOMMUNICATIONS MANAGEMENT?

1. Understand the organization management skills that a telecommunications manager should have.

2. Understand the technology management skills that a telecommunications manager should have.

3. Understand the 50%/50% Telecommunications Management Model, and understand why it should be used to develop telecommunications manager skills.

4. Understand the underlying concept of managerial accountability and its implications for prospective managerial candidates.

5. Understand the functions performed by different types of telecommunications managers.

6. Understand the criteria to consider when deciding whether to pursue a career in telecommunications management.

7. Understand the concept of situational management.

8. Understand POLC Model elements and their application within a telecommunications management context.

9. Understand the importance of the POLC Model's *Plan* element and its role in managerial activities.

The concept of being a **manager** is relatively new. It originated during the 1700s, when machines were first introduced as an alternative to manual labor. The invention of this machinery in Great Britain heralded the Industrial Revolution and created a factory environment where buildings housed machines and the factory workers were assigned tasks that included their "care and feeding." Factory owners quickly found that simply placing machines and people together did not ensure that the manufacturing process would run smoothly and generate profits. The need for professional factory managers emerged. These professionals coordinated the efforts of workers and machines. As factory operations became larger and more complex, a need for developing managerial specialties also emerged. These managerial specialists headed up functional departments like production, inventory control, purchasing, or sales.

However, it was not until the early 1900s that academic programs acknowledged the new management phenomenon and started to quantify and document the attributes and characteristics needed to be a "professional manager." Since then, a large pool of managerial knowledge has been developed and many theories have been formulated to explain what managers do (or should do). Managerial topics include information about management theories, **accountabilities,** supervision theories, motivation principles, business structure and design, strategic planning, tactical planning, and operational planning.

In Chapter 1, it was stated that telecommunications management required managerial skills in two areas:

1. **business management**

2. **technology management**

The common denominator for both topics is *management.* The POLC Model was also introduced in Chapter 1 as a fundamental process associated with the managerial function. It also will be used as a **management** model in this chapter.

This book is not a text about management theory, but it is one that describes how to apply business management and technology management skills to run an effective business-oriented telecommunications department. This chapter will discuss management from a very basic "what is management" perspective, and Chapters 6 through 22 will describe the application of general management principles to telecommunications management situations.

WHAT IS MANAGEMENT?

The process of becoming a manager typically begins when someone joins a business and is placed within a department that is headed up by a manager. Part of the learning experience necessary for becoming a manager is learning to be a good employee. If someone is incompetent or ignorant as a subordinate, it is highly unlikely that they can become good managers, because they will be unable to explain what they expect from their subordinates. To be a good employee, it is necessary to have answers to the following questions:

- What am I supposed to do?
- How will I know if I am doing a good job?

Good managers should be able to address these two questions quantitatively and with documentation that addresses them directly. **Job descriptions** and job appraisals are the documents used to let employees know what their job responsibilities are and how well they are doing their jobs. The content of these documents is detailed and job specific. Therefore, their discussions will be postponed until Chapter 15, when job descriptions and performance appraisals are discussed within a telecommunications context. Appendix C provides examples of a managerial job description and a managerial performance appraisal. The following section discusses general telecommunications management responsibilities.

Managerial Attributes

In Chapter 2, the fable of four blind wise men describing an elephant was used to highlight the reality that perception is based on individual viewpoints that may vary depending upon both the viewpoint from which observations are made and the senses used for interpreting situations. A similar analogy exists when different people are asked to describe managers by using key words to summarize their opinions. Key words range significantly between positive and negative descriptions, depending upon an individual's personal perspective. The following provides a listing of words that could be used to describe the managerial function:

administration

bureaucracy

control

cost-benefit analyses

decision making

diplomacy

implementation

leadership

manipulation

mastermind

orchestration

organize

oversight

plan

regulation

scheme

tact

very important persons (VIPs)

Some of these words are less than flattering (manipulation and masterminding), but they are words that have been used to describe negative managerial traits. Depending upon one's personal experience when being managed by others, the selected key words may be positive, negative, or neutral.

The range of opinions that can be generated about different managers should not be surprising, because managers are human beings, and human beings have wide ranges of attributes and characteristics. Because managers can have a major influence on the lives of their subordinates and peers, it is important to develop a prototype manager definition that highlights the best managerial characteristics. This text will focus on tools and techniques—*the objective side of management.* However, in the real world, managerial results are strongly influenced by the way that objective tools and techniques are applied to subordinates—*the subjective side of management.* The text assumes that individuals' moral and ethical character was developed prior to becoming a manager, and that the managerial tools and techniques described in the text are used within the appropriate social and interpersonal context.

THE 50%/50% TELECOMMUNICATIONS MANAGEMENT MODEL

According to the 50%/50% Telecommunications Management Model, a telecommunications manager (**50%/50% manager**) should have a 50%/50% balance of skills in business management and technology management.

Business management skills include those skills needed to effectively operate a functional unit (a telecommunications department) within a business enterprise environment. The skills needed to be an effective business manager include planning, supervisory, department administration, organization design, accounting, and human communication skills that a department manager needs to direct employees and coordinate department activities. Technology management skills are those skills needed to effectively select, develop, and implement technology solutions. When the proper balance of business and technology management exists, the technology decisions will support the business objectives of the organization.

Figure 3–1 shows an organization chart for a business that has six departments—marketing, finance, production, distribution services, human resources, and information services—which all report to a president. The telecommunications department is shown as a department within the information services function.

For discussion purposes, we will consider each department that reports to the president as being headed up by a vice president. Each department reporting to one of the six departments consists of autonomous departments headed by a manager. Therefore, the telecommunications manager would report to the vice president of information services, and the vice president of information services would report directly to the president.

In a large organization, the telecommunications department could consist of additional departments reporting to the telecommunications manager, and a manager would head up each department. Figure 3–2 provides an organization chart that shows this type of telecommunications organization.

Business Management

The Telecommunications manager in Figure 3–2 has five direct reports: the planning manager, the development manager, the operations manager, the administrative services manager, and the help desk manager. He or she would have overall responsibility for managing people in the different departments, establishing and administrating department budgets, and carrying out the managerial responsibilities associated with operating a function that provides business communications services. A similar breakdown could be generated for the sales department that is shown under the marketing department in Figure 3–1, where multiple departments also report to the sales manager.

The president, vice presidents, and various managers in Figures 3–1 and 3–2 have a primary responsibility to operate as business managers and a secondary responsibility to manage their departments. While the functions performed by individual departments may vary significantly, the managerial functions performed by the various managers will be quite similar. These similar managerial activities are considered business management activities, and they have the common goal of ensuring that the business organization survives and is profitable. Business management activities include supervisory, personnel, planning, and budget activities that would coordinate resources to achieve business profitability objectives.

The depth and breadth of business management skills needed by different managers would vary according to the individual manager's position. The president would need a different set of business management skills than the help desk manager—but all managerial levels between the

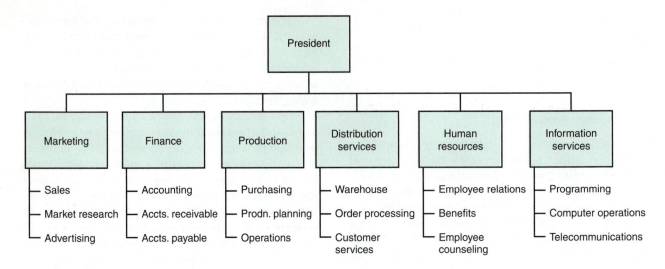

Figure 3–1. Business organization chart.

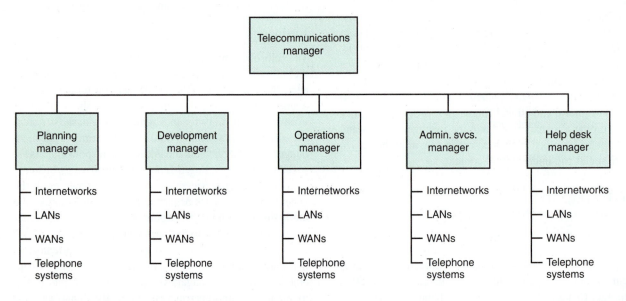

Figure 3–2. Telecommunications department organization chart.

president and the lowest level manager in the organization should have a common understanding of the supervisory, personnel, planning, and budget skills needed for their positions. While business management skills may be used in different functional areas, the management information generated between department managers requires the use of a common language—business English and accounting information—to communicate plans and results. Business English and numbers will be the language used to assess the performance of individual managers, regardless of the manager's departmental responsibilities.

The preceding discussion is not intended to discount the need for a manager to possess strong functional skills. However, it does mean that a manager's functional performance will be assessed based on an organizational measurement yardstick. It is necessary for everyone in a **departmental management** position to have functional skills and business management skills. Managers must be able to explain functional activities in the appropriate organizational context to other business managers, while being able to explain business objectives to the employees they manage directly.

Technology Management

Telecommunications is a technology-based function. Good technology skills are required to design, implement, and operate telecommunications systems and networks. In today's technology environment, telecommunications systems and networks rely on computer-based equipment that runs communication software. The software logic allows normally incompatible devices and equipment to operate as a system or network, and technical specialists with strong hardware and software skills are needed to support this complex environment.

Technology skills can be divided into two basic categories: technical skills and **project** management skills

The term *technical skills* refers to those skills typically associated with the engineering and operational aspects of telecommunications systems and networks—hardware, software, and networking protocol skills. Technical skills are essential skills for understanding how to design, develop, and operate telecommunications systems and networks.

However, technology projects also require another set of skills: *technology management* skills. They are the skills that allow administrative, technical, financial, and business elements to be coordinated so that a project is implemented on time and within budget. They are not engineering-based skills, but are planning and control skills used to convert technology concepts into practical results. It is possible for someone to have outstanding technical skills but not be able to implement large technology projects effectively. Achieving a balance of business and technical management skills is difficult and should not be taken lightly.

TECHNICAL SKILLS. The development of strong technical skills requires a good educational foundation in mathematics and science and is acquired through formal education and on-the-job training. There are many programs that certify individuals in a variety of telecommunications technical skills. These certification programs also provide a means for gaining the different technical skills needed in telecommunications.

A good conceptual understanding of telecommunications technology is essential for effectively managing a telecommunications function. However, this does not mean that a telecommunications manager should be able to perform all the tasks that technicians perform. The effective manager must be able to understand the relevance of technical tasks to the technology infrastructure and—when necessary—become immersed in technical details to ensure technological accuracy of desired results. A telecommunications manager needs this conceptual understanding to ensure that proposed technical projects make sense and that the technical difficulty involved with implementing a project is clearly understood before the project is undertaken.

Technical skills require technical training. This text assumes that the reader has the telecommunications technical skills necessary to understand technology management topics (Parts 2–5). Technical terminology will be used because technical terms are needed to explain technology management concepts. A lack of technology knowledge places a technology manager in the position of relying totally on subordinates for technology decisions and having a tendency to make business management commitments that do not make technical sense. A competent technology manager is able to assess the technical competence of his or her subordinates and also be able to assess the technical viability of technology projects.

TECHNOLOGY MANAGEMENT SKILLS. Technology management skills utilize many of the same tools and techniques as business management skills, but the application is different. The primary activity used to implement telecommunications products and services are project activities. Projects are one time implementation efforts within a technology product's life cycle. Once a project is implemented, the implemented product enters an operational phase where it is maintained until it is scrapped or until a major upgrade extends its functional life.

Business management focuses on managing the people and budget resource of a business while technology management focuses on managing the people, budget, and technology resources associated with implementing a project. The primary difference between the business and technology management requirements is the technology resource management aspect. The same people management and budget management skills are needed for managing large technology projects as for managing a department. Large technology projects may require a higher level of business management skills than is needed to manage a department.

In addition to requiring technology management skills, specialized skills are needed to manage and implement technology projects. Detailed project management requirements will be covered in Part 3, *Project Management*. This chapter provides an overview of technology management requirements.

Business Management *v.* Technology Management

Business management and technology management spans a wide range of topics. Where should you concentrate your primary efforts? Unfortunately, the proper answer is probably not the one you want to hear. The following section will discuss the implications of focusing in one of the two areas—business management or technology management—and use this dialogue as a way of reinforcing the 50%/50% Telecommunications Management Model concept.

WEIGHTED TOWARD BUSINESS MANAGEMENT. If the development and application of management skills focuses on the business management area, at the expense of the technology management area, the likely outcome is a managerial toolset heavily weighted toward organization design, people management, policy administration, communication, supervision, written and oral communication, financial analysis and planning, and business. Someone who has this skill set and few technology skills would have a tendency to focus on the people and numbers aspect of management—areas that are important in a business management context. However, without a strong set of technical skills, the organization manager would have difficulty identifying competent technical personnel, communicating effectively with technical specialists, or understanding the technical implications of selecting one product or service over another. By necessity, these decisions would be delegated to someone else within the business manager's area of responsibility.

If this line of reasoning were carried further, a situation could exist where the business manager provides an excellent interface within the business and does everything right from an organizational perspective. However, the selection of business communication products and services and the selection of telecommunications technical personnel would probably be delegated to someone else. In this case, two scenarios could exist: 1) the person to whom the responsibility is delegated is technically competent, or 2) the selected person is technically incompetent. In the former case, the business manager can interject the organization skills and the telecommunications function will run smoothly because the correct business and technology decisions will be made. However, if the person to whom the technology responsibility has been delegated is incompetent, it is likely that business communication investment decisions will be expensive or unwise, and that operating problems will become a way of life.

The business-focused manager is placed in the role of depending upon someone without having the technology knowledge needed to assess the individual's performance. In the real-world, bad decisions are typically covered up until they have reached such monumental proportions that they can no longer be hidden. When the hidden problem becomes visible, it is frequently too late to easily rectify it.

WEIGHTED TOWARD TECHNOLOGY MANAGEMENT. This scenario involves someone commonly referred to as a *techie*—an individual who focuses on telecommunications technology. In the absence of business management skills, a techie evaluates technology in terms of its technical purity, and has difficulty compromising this purity to provide the somewhat mundane requirements found in most businesses. In the extreme, a techie may be someone who has a deep interest in leading edge technology applications and who may see operating problems as the normal environment needed to develop new technology.

When business management skills are weak, the people management, business communication, financial planning, and policy administration areas will be weak. There is a strong likelihood that even without technical disasters, techies cannot survive without having a strong business manager between them and the internal organization. In the absence of business awareness, the communication products and services selected by a techie may be too sophisticated for everyday use and may not provide the appropriate cost-to-benefit profile expected in a business environment. The lack of business management effectiveness will be translated into the inability of the techie to obtain internal funding because he or she will be unable to communicate business benefits effectively.

The most likely scenario for techies in a high-level telecommunications management position is that they will, at some point in time, have many new opportunities to expand their technical knowledge outside of their current organization. In other words, they will be fired.

THE 50%/50% MODEL REVISITED. With a balance of strong business management and technology management skills, a 50%/50% telecommunications manager would be able to:

1. Develop enterprise telecommunications plans that address business, organization, and technology requirements.
2. Administer policies effectively and fairly.
3. Administer hiring, employee development, **salary administration,** and firing requirements effectively and fairly.
4. Identify the technology and business benefit differences between various telecommunications products and services.
5. Select, design, implement, and operate telecommunications hardware and technology effectively and efficiently.
6. Have the necessary personal technical and managerial competence to select good telecommunications, people.
7. React effectively to changing needs.

MANAGERIAL ACCOUNTABILITY

From a business context, management can be defined as being the skillful handling of resources and being accountable for the results achieved when using those PTM resources. Poor managerial performance can occur because inappropriate or unreasonable objectives had been selected initially, or because the managerial process was executed poorly. Regardless of the reasons for not doing the job, any time the desired results have not been achieved in a business environment, the root cause should be considered a breakdown in the managerial function. Stated another way, if telecommunications managerial responsibilities are accepted, the manager will be held accountable for the results (good or bad) achieved.

Bottom line: telecommunications management is responsible for effectively and efficiently using the PTM resources with which he or she is provided.

TELECOMMUNICATIONS MANAGEMENT POSITIONS

Telecommunications managerial positions vary significantly in terms of the specific responsibilities they entail. Normally, telecommunications managers must demonstrate strong technical skills within a specific technology or administrative area and have an established track record of outstanding technical performance before being seriously considered for filling a managerial position. Telecommunications skills may be acquired from a variety of assignments, because there are many different technical and administrative positions available in the telecommunications field. Different lateral (same job level) assignments early in an aspiring manager's career can provide him or her with a variety of technical and administrative skills that can be used as the underlying knowledge base for future managerial responsibilities.

Creating job titles is frequently a creative writing exercise. Sometimes it is difficult to determine the exact responsibilities associated with a job title. There are six generic telecommunications manager titles that can be used to classify managerial responsibilities and gain an understanding of the types of functions performed by telecommunications department managers:

1. planning manager
2. development manager
3. operations manager
4. administrative services manager
5. help desk manager
6. manager of managers

Figure 3–3 provides an organization chart showing these six generic positions and Table 3–1 provides a summary description of the general job responsibilities associated with each position.

Table 3–1 provided a tidy definition of managerial operating responsibilities and a good reference for understanding functional responsibilities. However, real world telecommunications environments are not that simple. The neatly separated functions in Table 3–1 are more likely to

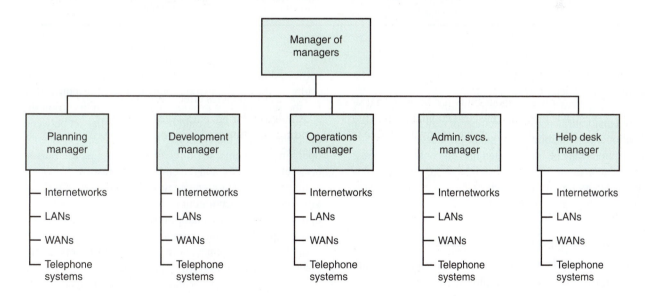

Figure 3–3. A generic telecommunications organization.

TABLE 3–1   Generic Job Descriptions

Managerial position	Description
Planning manager	Responsible for capacity planning, long range technology planning, evaluating new technology, and assisting in the preparation of capital expenditure forecasts.
Development manager	Responsible for the technical design and implementation of new telecommunications technologies and carrying out major modifications to existing systems and networks. Develops the operating procedures that will be used after a major project has been implemented.
Operations manager	Responsible for operating existing telecommunications systems and networks and maintaining them in peak operating condition. Operations personnel perform minor upgrades to existing installations and provide problem resolution services for users of telecommunications services.

Operations hours frequently require 24 × 7 operation (24 hours per day and 7 days per week) coverage. |
| Administrative services manager | Responsible for maintaining system and network inventory databases, authorizing the payment of outside service vendor bills, allocating expenses to users when user chargebacks are used, and handling the administrative requirements of users and other telecommunications departments. These requirements could include establishing accounts for e-mail and telephone system clients and the issuing of electronic and hard copy telephone and e-mail directories. |
| Help desk manager | Responsible for providing a single point of contact (SPOC) to telecommunications clients and providing problem resolution. The help desk is a customer-oriented department that is expected to act as an ombudsman for service users. The help desk assumes ownership for user problems and monitors reported problems until they are satisfactorily resolved from an end user perspective.

The help desk division maintains an incident reporting system (IRS) database that records the nature of a problem and its resolution. The IRS database is used to identify telecommunications service quality levels and equipment performance.

May be a 24 × 7 operation. |
| Manager of managers | The *manager of managers* has managers reporting directly to him or her. The number of direct reports and their functions will depend upon the size of the telecommunications division and the range of services they provide. In a simple business (Figure 3–3), the manager of managers position may be a vice president or director who has department managers reporting to him or her.

In a larger business, multiple levels can exist and different managerial positions may have several managers as direct reports. The operations manager may have the telephone system operations manager and LAN operations manager as direct reports. The operations manager in this case would typically report to a director or vice president. |

be allocated differently and some functions may not exist within a given department structure.

The size of the telecommunications department will have a major influence on the number of managers and their functional responsibilities. In small businesses, Table 3–1 descriptions may be incorporated into one or two positions; in large telecommunications divisions, there may be multiple managers reporting to each of the first-line managers shown on the organization chart.

Different Managerial Responsibilities

In a one person telecommunications department serving an enterprise that has fifty employees, the manager may have the title of telecommunications director and may be given the responsibility for installing, monitoring, and re-solving vendor service problems. In the small shop environment, the vendors would have technical responsibility for the services they provide. The telecommunication director's primary role would be to act as a liaison between the business and the vendor. When employees experience operating problems, the director would act as the liaison between the vendor and the employee to resolve any operating problems. (In a one person telecommunications environment, the telecommunications manager really has no option but to be a facilitator between telecommunications services providers and business employees.)

In a larger organization, a telephone system operations manager may have thirty-five individuals as direct reports (this could include one or more technical manager[s]) and may be responsible for providing telephone services to 1,500 employees. The telephone service provisioning role could include maintaining the telephone equipment, handling all moves and changes of telephone station equipment, correcting all telephone system operating problems, maintaining a corporate directory ("soft" and hard copy), and dealing with executive secretaries in a world headquarters location.

Which manager has more responsibility—the telecommunications director or the telephone system operations manager? Which managerial position requires more managerial, technical, administrative, and political expertise? Based on job title alone, the director position appears to be a higher-level position. Based on the responsibilities handled, the telephone system operations manager position requires more technical, administrative, managerial, and political skills. If the skill levels of the two positions are as stated, the telephone system operations manager should have the inside track over the telecommunications director for a director position in a large corporation.

> **Commentary:** A position's title is not an accurate indication of the position's responsibilities and the skills necessary to perform them. A VP in a small business environment may have less "real" responsibility than an operations manager working for a large business.

The telephone system operations manager is a bona fide manager—an authentic manager. Bona fide managers have individuals reporting directly to them and are expected to direct the efforts of their subordinates, formally assess their performance in written **performance appraisals,** and determine pay raises. A manager without direct reports is not a bona fide manager.

> This text is written for bona fide managers—managers who have supervisory responsibility for subordinates.

WHY BE A TELECOMMUNICATIONS MANAGER?

Being successful at doing a job is normally a good thing—unless you hate the job that you are doing.

There are different entry points for getting into the telecommunications field. Someone starting their first telecommunications job may be given a general overview of their responsibilities, but it is unlikely that they will understand what the job really entails until several months are spent carrying out job responsibilities. During the early stages in a telecommunications career, individuals will have the opportunity to observe the functions performed

by different departments and gain diversified experience through lateral moves within the company. Individuals who have gained first hand experience doing different telecommunications jobs have a better chance of making a smooth transition into a managerial position.

Points To Consider

There is normally an evolutionary process involved with becoming a telecommunications manager, and this process allows someone to grow into a position. However, there are also times when a managerial position opportunity is thrust upon someone before he or she has had time to assess the implications of assuming managerial responsibilities. The following provides a general overview of some managerial responsibilities. If the reader has a negative viewpoint of these responsibilities while entertaining visions of becoming a manager, it would be appropriate to spend more time considering the implications of becoming a manager.

Managers must frequently spend periods of time outside of normal working hours to fulfill managerial responsibilities. Observing effective managers in action and having the opportunity to serve in a subordinate capacity is probably the best way to understand the implications associated with assuming managerial responsibilities. The decision to pursue a career in telecommunications management should include a commitment to acquire the skills and experience needed to be a competent manager. This includes a commitment to carry out the job requirements associated with the position. Position responsibilities will, at times, require a manager to assume responsibility for the actions of others and to deal with interpersonal conflicts.

A wide range of positions is available for aspiring telecommunications managers. These include technical, administrative, and managerial positions that differ significantly in the level of technical skills needed and the level of managerial experience they provide. Lower-level managers have a higher amount of flexibility to move laterally and broaden their knowledge base than higher-level managers, and a good career strategy is to fill a variety of positions during the early stages of one's career. In lower-level positions, a manager's performance appraisal is weighted heavily toward job specific performance, with managerial performance being a secondary factor. At higher management levels, the managerial responsibilities become the most important appraisal factor when job performance is being evaluated.

While the pay and benefits associated with higher-level managerial positions may provide a strong incentive for pursuing a managerial career, aspiring managers should carefully assess their own ability to fulfill the organizational and technical responsibilities of the position. This includes assessing their own maturity when dealing with the personnel issues of hiring, firing, supervision, subordinate development and training, and other situations that have the potential for generating personal stress.

Individuals interested in becoming telecommunications managers should use the early stages of their career to gain technical, administrative, managerial, and business knowledge by working in a variety of positions. The primary focus of top-level positions (vice president of telecommunications) is to facilitate the efforts of others and handle nontechnical managerial responsibilities. Individuals who have a broad understanding of technical and business issues are better equipped to handle a facilitation role than individuals who only have strong technical skills.

Telecommunications manager positions can be rewarding both personally and financially if you like the job you are doing. Become a telecommunications manager if you have an interest and aptitude in technology and are willing to assume a facilitation role with others. Your success as a manager will be based on the results achieved by the people you manage, not by your personal results.

MANAGEMENT THEORY

Today's business management profession, which has existed for a relatively short time, is an outgrowth of the Industrial Revolution that began during the 1700s. During the Industrial Revolution, entrepreneurs acquired machines and established factories to harvest the high-volume production benefits offered by the machines. Factory owners found that it was necessary to hire large numbers of unskilled factory workers to feed and care for these new "beasts of burden." Prior to the introduction of machines that provided an alternative to hand labor processes, individual tradesmen and artisans produced consumer products on a piecemeal basis. Each product they produced was unique—nonstandard. In this craftsman-driven environment, the component parts of any assembled product produced by one craftsman were not normally interchangeable with the component parts of other similar products.

The new factory environment was based on standardization. Component parts of any machine-produced products were designed to be interchangeable with the component parts of other machine-produced products. Machine-driven tasks were kept simple so that workers could be trained quickly and the parts produced by machines were identical and interchangeable. Factory workers fed the machines raw materials, monitored machine operations, made any required adjustments, and moved machine produced goods into storage areas. These high capacity, high speed machines generated products at rates that were mind boggling when compared to the output of individual tradesmen and artisans. However, factory owners quickly discovered that factory workers were not able to efficiently run factory operations unless they were given directions by someone who had a good knowledge of the factory environment. As a result, the need for factory foremen—the first business managers—arose. Initially, the managerial focus was on supervising the labor efforts of factory workers but it quickly broadened in scope to include the other elements associated with supporting a manufacturing operation—purchasing, inventory control, and distribution services.

By 1911, factory managers were being used by factory owners to run factory operations and Frederick Winslow Taylor published a book entitled *Principles of Scientific Management,* which many consider to be the beginning of a formal management profession and a field of academic study. Business managers and academics quickly adopted the management principles contained in Taylor's book, and these principles became the foundation on which modern management theory was built.

The Prescientific Management Era

Organized endeavors involving the skillful handling or use of something such as resources clearly existed long before Frederick Taylor published his book in 1911. The Egyptian pyramids and the Great Wall of China are examples of projects whose scope and size required effective managerial processes to design, develop, and implement. While the documentation of business management principles and methodologies is fairly recent, the application of managerial processes is evident in the legacy buildings and monuments left by the architects and engineers of the past.

Business Management Theory

This text will apply the term *business management* to the pool of managerial knowledge compiled since 1911. Business management theory has been applied to many areas since 1911—including manufacturing, marketing, sales, personnel, computers, and telecommunications. Many management theories have evolved since 1911, and many have faded into oblivion when they were unable to handle the needs of new business requirements. However, a few old management theories have prevailed and have been periodically repackaged and presented as part of new theories that address current managerial needs.

One current management theory views the various management theories developed since 1911 as tools and techniques that should be applied, as required, depending upon the managerial situation that is being addressed. This situational perspective recommends that each managerial activity uses the methods and procedures that best address the activity's needs. Once the specific situational environment is clearly understood, the manager can use different managerial tools and techniques (theories) to resolve the managerial problem. This situational approach recognizes that a given problem may have multiple solutions. The situational management model will be used in the text to solve organization and technology management problems in Parts 2 through 5.

The situational management approach is analogous to stating that the tools of a fine furniture craftsman can be used to make many different wood products. A common set of tools provides the craftsman with the ability to create a wide range of furniture—cabinets, bureaus, beds, or chairs. The same tools are used for each product but are applied in a different way to achieve the desired results. The same situation exists when business management tools are used and the following section will provide a framework for applying managerial tools and techniques.

POLC PROCESS MODEL

In the early 1900s, Henri Fayol, a pioneer of the scientific management era, identified five managerial process elements: 1) planning, 2) organizing, 3) staffing, 4) directing, and 5) controlling. He viewed these processes as being common managerial activities that should be performed by all managers regardless of the operating environment they were managing. Fayol also left a rich legacy of other insights about the managerial process, and these will be described further in Chapter 6, *What is Enterprise Planning*? Management theorists subsequently reclassified the staffing element to be part of the organizing element. As a result, Fayol's theory is now presented as a four-element model: 1) planning, 2) organizing, 3) leading, and 4) controlling. These Fayol managerial elements continue to be used widely.

The author has taken the liberty of using Fayol's management theory to create a goal-centric **POLC Model** that will be used throughout the text as a basic functional framework for carrying out managerial activities. This goal-centric POLC Model is shown in Figure 3–4.

Table 3–2 provides a brief description of the management process elements shown in Figure 3–4.

Note: The author has added the *goals* element to the four process elements listed previously. This action changes the goals (a.k.a., *objectives*) element from an implicit element to an explicit element in Figure 3–4.

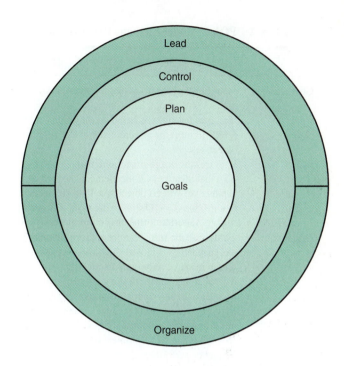

Figure 3–4. A goal-centric POLC model.

Individual goals will vary depending upon the managerial task, but the existence of a goal element is essential prior to starting any managerial assignment. If the four managerial functions were applied without having a measurable objective, the managerial effort would simply be an example illustrating the ultimate bureaucracy—working hard but never successfully completing the activity.

Applying the POLC Model

Figure 3–5 provides a flow chart that illustrates how the POLC Model in Figure 3–4 would be applied to managerial activities. As indicated, the initial step is to define goals and develop a plan that identifies all the necessary elements needed to implement it (organize, lead, and control). The plan is then implemented with the managerial role being one of directing the use of PTM resources while ensuring that controls are applied to achieve goals.

The control element encircling the plan element in Figure 3–4 is applied continuously to each POLC Model element—including the goal element—and uses a plan *v.* actual comparison to measure deviations between the original plan and the results that are achieved. Deviations from the plan are evaluated and the appropriate action is taken to align actual results with the plan standards. If the goals are found to be unreasonable, they should also be evaluated and steps should be taken to make them realistic.

TABLE 3–2   POLC Model Element Description

POLC model element	Description
Goals	Identifies the objectives that the managerial process will accomplish. The success of the managerial activity is based on the ability of the results to meet the requirements of the objectives.
Plan	Requires the development of a management plan that identifies all the elements needed to achieve the desired objectives. Plan elements identify the Goal, Organize, Lead, and Control requirements for completing the project.
Organize	Obtains all the resources (people, equipment, etc.) needed to complete the activity. It is based on the resource requirements identified during the "planning" phase of the activity.
Lead	Identifies the managerial responsibility (who) for coordinating the "Organize" resources and monitoring the various activities to ensure that they are completed on time and within any budget or performance constraints.
Control	The ongoing monitoring and feedback activity used to ensure that process activities are accomplished in accordance with the initial plan (Plan v. Actual).

From an overview perspective, the following activities must be carried out for the successful application of Figure 3–4 concepts:

- define the desired objectives/goals
- develop a plan for achieving the objectives/goals
- execute the plan and control plan v. actual activities
- successfully complete the assignment on time and within budget

A Large Project Example

All projects—large and small—need to be managed. The commitment of resources to the project management activity will largely depend upon the size, complexity, and criticality of the project. All projects can be managed by applying the basics presented in Figure 3–4.

1. **Goals** are established.
2. A **plan** is established to identify project tasks and resources.
3. The resources (**Organize**) are acquired.
4. Managerial **leadership** is assigned.
5. A Managerial plan v. actual **control** is exercised.

The following is a description of the Aswan Dam Project, a project that was completed in Egypt during 1970. At the time it was started, the project was one of the largest and most expensive projects ever undertaken. Many articles were written about the project results in terms of its benefits and liabilities. The intent of this description is to point out that even large, expensive projets can generate unplanned results.

Was the Aswan Dam Project a *successful* project? It probably depends upon the perspective that is taken. From an engineering perspective, the structures were built as designed and they are still in place. Flooding in the lower river is a now distant memory and hydroelectric power is being generated.

However, there have been costs: 1) the elimination of the natural farmland renewal process in the lower Nile, 2) the elimination of ancient tribal cultures, 3) ongoing health and economic concerns for individuals who were displaced from their homes for the project, 4) major silt buildups in the upper river areas, requiring an ongoing dredging operation, 5) concerns with the long term environmental impact of the project, and 6) lower hydroelectric power production than was initially estimated. If all of these issues that now exist were known initially, would the same decisions have been made?

The moral to this story is that the planning element of the managerial process is the single most critical contribution to the long term success of a project. Failure to effectively evaluate benefits and risks in the beginning of a project can lead to unexpected results once the project is implemented.

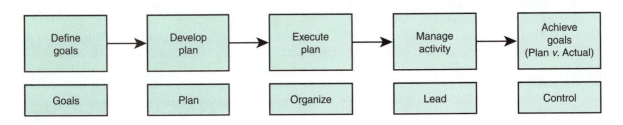

Figure 3–5.   The POLC model application process.

Aswan Dam Project

The Aswan Dam Project was completed in 1970 at a cost of over $1 billion—an astronomical amount of money at that time. It took ten years to complete.

The vast majority of Egypt's population is located along the Nile River, which begins deep in Africa and eventually exits into the Mediterranean Sea. Over the centuries, the Nile's water has provided irrigation to an otherwise parched land. The river was the focal point for Egypt's early civilization.

Project Description

A dam was built across the upper Nile River to provide flood control in the lower Nile and to provide hydroelectric power. The Aswan Dam project was a joint venture between Egypt and the USSR, with the Russians underwriting one third of the cost of the project. Soviet personnel were the primary architects and engineers for the project. The project required building a large reservoir above a dam, which was needed to hold back the annual floods that flowed downstream each year. As a result, major Egyptian landmarks had to be relocated away from the river. Entire villages were forced to leave lands they had occupied for centuries.

The dam's environmental impact has been mixed, at best. While it eliminated the lower-river flooding problems and provides hydroelectric power, it also eliminated the fertile farmland that had been renewed each summer during the Nile's annual flooding cycle. It is now necessary to apply chemical fertilizers to these farmlands and concerns have emerged concerning the impact that fertilizers are having on the environment.

Project Results

The upper river and reservoir area is subject to silt buildups, so ongoing reservoir dredging operations are required. The decreased water flow in the lower river has resulted in a higher salt content seeping from the Mediterranean into the soil and water areas of the Nile delta region. Many of the people displaced from their homelands in upper river areas currently live in conditions of disease and poverty.

Hydroelectric power generation capacity is significantly below initial estimates.

What Happened?

The initial planning did not fully identify the potential environmental impact that the dam project would create. One of the problems was that the effect of dry, hot Sahara winds blowing across the reservoir was not taken into account. The reservoir has never contained more than 50% of its capacity because the water evaporates from the reservoir more quickly than the river can fill it up. The silt buildup problem in the reservoir was also underestimated, as were the positive benefits associated with the silt deposit on the Nile delta lands.

SUMMARY

This summary is organized to correspond with the learning objectives found at the beginning of the chapter.

1. Telecommunications managers are an integral part of a business. The managerial skills needed to operate effectively as a member of the enterprise's management team are referred to as *business management skills.* Business management skills include supervisory, personnel, planning, and budgeting skills. Managers are responsible for directing and coordinating the efforts of employees within their area of responsibility and managerial effectiveness will be measured by the results produced by a manager's organization. While telecommunications managers may have been hired for their telecommunications technology skills, they are expected to be business managers and have the capability to effectively use telecommunications technology to support business needs. Business management skills focus on effectively directing the efforts of department employees to meet business management objectives and being able to operate within the business management context.

2. Telecommunications technology skills consist of technical skills, people management skills, and project management skills. Technical telecommunications skills are engineering-oriented skills that require a strong mathematical and science background. These skills enable someone to be good at designing and developing telecommunications systems and networks. These skills are typically learned through a combination of formal education and on-the-job training with technical certification programs frequently being used to assess technical skill levels. Project management skills are those skills needed to successfully implement telecom-

munications systems and networks on time and within budget constraints. Good technical skills are needed to design, develop, and operate telecommunications systems and networks while good project management skills are needed to implement them successfully. A telecommunications manager should have a good conceptual understanding of telecommunications technologies—but not necessarily have detailed technical skills. Telecommunications managers will coordinate the efforts of others to whom they have assigned project responsibilities. The manager's primary role is to select and use technical PTM resources effectively.

3. Three criteria commonly used by upper management to rate managerial performance are 1) supporting business profitability objectives, 2) satisfying internal and external customers, and 3) effectively planning telecommunications requirements. However, for a telecommunications department to receive credit for its contributions, telecommunications managers must communicate with upper management in an effective format and style.

4. *Managerial accountability* refers to the philosophy that a manager accepts accountability for the function that is being managed. This implies that managers are responsible for the results of employees within their area of responsibility and measure managerial results based on the effective use of the PTM resource provided by the enterprise organization. In a simplistic statement, it can be referred to as the philosophy that "the buck stops here," where the manager accepts responsibility for subordinate employee actions. Unless managers accept accountability for the results of the employees that they manage, there is low probability that they will be successful as business or technology managers.

5. The generic titles used for telecommunications managers are: planning managers, technology development and implementation managers, operations managers, administrative services managers, and help desk managers. In addition, there are manager of managers positions that would include the top manager (vice president). The number of managerial positions and the specific responsibilities assigned to them will vary, but the generic requirements identified will be needed by all telecommunications organizations.

6. A career in telecommunications management requires strong skills in management and technology and a 50%/50% managerial/technology balance is recommended. Managers need strong facilitation skills, a willingness to commit time outside of normal working hours, and a willingness to delegate responsibilities and rely upon the results of others to achieve managerial success. Anyone deciding to become a telecom-

munications manager must be willing to perform the duties associated with managing others.

7. The situational management approach is one of the current management theories. It is based on having a good understanding of the environment within which any managerial action is taken and using any existing managerial theory as a tool or technique to complete the managerial assignment. A heavy emphasis is placed on a manager's ability to accurately assess different situations and select the appropriate actions to successfully complete the assignment. Within the situational management context, the tools and techniques used to resolve the situation may vary and the primary focus is to successfully address the specific situation. Managers with broad skills and experience will typically utilize a wider range of managerial tools and techniques to resolve managerial situations. The selection of the appropriate tools and techniques will rely on managerial judgment—the primary element needed to be an effective manager.

8. The POLC Model is based on the efforts of Henri Fayol, a scientific management theoretician whose works were published during the early 1900s. The POLC Model provides a "thinking methodology" that can be applied within the context of the situational management approach reviewed in the previous learning objective commentary. There are five elements in the goal-centric POLC Model: 1) Goals, 2) Plan, 3) Organize, 4) Lead, and 5) Control. Application of the POLC Model to a management situation utilizes a four-step approach: 1) Define the desired objectives (goals); 2) Develop a plan that identifies the necessary resources (the "organize" element), leadership, and control activities; 3) Execute and control the POLC Model plan; and 4) Successfully complete the assignment by meeting POLC Model objectives within time and money constraints.

9. The POLC Model plan element is the most important element in the model. It requires the initiator of an activity to clearly state the objectives (goals) in a format that can be used to determine the successful outcome of an assignment. The activities and resources needed to execute POLC Model elements (Organize, Lead, and Control) are identified and documented in a Plan format. The "Plan" becomes the measurement standard during a project or activity using the POLC Model, and the control of the activity effort will be based on a continuous Plan v. Actual measurement. Deviations from the plan should be addressed immediately, and the appropriate actions should be taken to bring the activity under control. Within the Plan v. Actual context, the two most important elements are the initial plan and the ongoing control activity that ensures conformance of actual results to the Plan.

KEY TERMS AND CONCEPTS

The language of telecommunications management is multifaceted and includes words and phrases from managerial, technological, accounting, regulatory, and other business areas. The definitions of these key terms and concepts can be found within the chapter and in the text glossary.

Accountabilities
Business Management
Departmental Management
50%/50% Manager
Job Descriptions

Management
Manager
Organization Management
Performance Appraisals
POLC Model

Project
Salary Administration
Technology Management

REVIEW

The following questions are open-ended—predefined answers are not included as part of the text. The purpose of these questions is to allow the readers to test themselves on the chapter material.

1. Describe the 50%/50% Telecommunications Manager Model.

2. What are business management skills?

3. What are technology management skills?

4. What is the difference between technical and technology skills, as they relate to telecommunications?

5. What is project management?

6. Describe the goal-centric POLC Model.

7. Explain the purpose of an employee job description.

8. Explain the purpose of an employee performance appraisal.

9. What is the role of human resources in creating job descriptions?

10. What is the difference between performance requirements and performance appraisal document?

11. What do telecommunications managers do?

MULTIPLE CHOICE

1. The 50/50 Telecommunications Manager Model refers to _____.
   a. 50% technology management/50% technical management
   b. 50% scientific management/50% business management
   c. 50% business management/50% technology management
   d. 50% business management/50% technical management
   e. a set of ambivalent management skills

2. An example of business management is _____.
   a. selecting telephone systems
   b. managing technical projects
   c. delivering a LAN on time and within budget
   d. salary administration activities
   e. life cycle analysis activities

3. A manager's functional performance rating will primarily be based on _____.
   a. the ability to select appropriate technology
   b. business management measurements
   c. project management skills
   d. certification programs

4. A functional management responsibility would be _____.
   a. managing a department
   b. writing a report
   c. completing a mathematical analysis
   d. public speaking

5. Technical skills include _____ skills.
   a. project management
   b. engineering
   c. business management
   d. salary administration
   e. writing

6. The objective of project management skills is to implement projects _____. (Select all that apply.)
   a. by year end
   b. within budget
   c. after the cutover date
   d. at zero cost
   e. on time

7. The current era of "professional business management" actually began in _____.
   a. 84 BC
   b. 1776
   c. 1812
   d. 1911
   e. 2001

8. The POLC Model _____.
   a. was developed using computer modeling techniques
   b. has been replaced by project management processes
   c. listed the performance requirements for managers
   d. is one of the oldest management theories
   e. is one of the newer management theories

9. The element missing from Henri Fayol's original POLC Model is _____.
   a. organize
   b. control
   c. lead
   d. plan
   e. goals

10. The primary purpose of employee job descriptions is _____.
    a. to provide performance feedback
    b. to meet HRS documentation requirements
    c. to identify a position's skill requirements
    d. to establish a project plan

11. Job descriptions contain two types of information: _____ and _____.
    a. to provide performance feedback
    b. the critical responsibilities of the position
    c. legal requirements
    d. the characteristics needed to carry out job responsibilities

12. From a human resources perspective, job descriptions are _____.
    a. a means of determining pay scales
    b. a responsibility of the employee
    c. a responsibility of functional managers
    d. not required

13. Performance appraisals _____.
    a. are handled by human resources personnel
    b. don't require employee participation
    c. list position skill characteristics and attributes
    d. are not required after the first year
    e. are employee specific

14. Performance appraisal accountabilities _____.
    a. describe the employee's position
    b. are lower-level categories
    c. are major appraisal categories
    d. are rating levels
    e. meet expectations

15. The term *boilerplate* _____.
    a. is used to build boilers
    b. refers to the use of standard language in documents
    c. is used to provide employee-specific information
    d. lists position skill characteristics and attributes

16. Managerial performance appraisals _____.
    a. list only organization management accountabilities
    b. list only technology management accountabilities
    c. are the same as nonmanagerial employee appraisals
    d. are more complex than nonmanagerial employee appraisals
    e. are completed by human resources personnel

17. What do managers do? (Select all that apply.)
    a. complete work assignments on time and within budget
    b. set business policies
    c. delegate performance appraisal responsibilities
    d. take accountability for organization results

18. Managerial positions _____.
    a. normally have well-defined responsibilities
    b. normally have open-ended responsibilities
    c. don't require job descriptions
    d. don't require performance appraisals

19. Current business management theories _____.
    a. are used only by upper management
    b. are based on computer modeling programs
    c. view management theories as tools
    d. were used to build Egyptian pyramids

20. The Plan *v.* Actual activity is a(n) _____ element.
    a. organizing
    b. goal-setting
    c. leading
    d. controlling
    e. planning

4

CRITERIA FOR MANAGERIAL SUCCESS

1. Understand what is meant by the term *upper management*.

2. Understand the different viewpoints that upper management can have about the telecommunications department.

3. Understand the criteria used by upper management to measure managerial performance.

4. Understand how the telecommunications department can support upper management interests.

5. Understand the format to use when communicating with management.

6. Understand "mom and pop" management concepts.

7. Understand what personal skills are needed to succeed as a telecommunications manager.

Managerial success can be measured from many perspectives. This chapter will review success from several viewpoints and will recommend a conceptual framework to use for measuring success as a telecommunications manager. The conceptual framework is a universal one that can be applied to any managerial position—technical or nontechnical. Managerial success is relative, it depends upon: 1) liking your job and 2) believing the benefits (pay, benefits, etc.) are commensurate with the job's responsibilities. The content of a technical manager's job is significantly different from a nontechnical manager. The final determination made by someone regarding his or her own level of managerial success will depend upon his or her definition of success and how much he or she likes the job.

The following will discuss several viewpoints for measuring personal and managerial success and will discuss the application of a generic performance **appraisal process** put in place to assess employee performance.

HOW IS SUCCESS MEASURED?

Three definitions of success are:

1. something that turns out well
2. attainment of fame, wealth, or power
3. achievement of something planned or attempted

The first definition of success would probably apply to many situations, but it is too general to use when defining **managerial success.** The second definition is fairly specific and clearly identifies some of the attributes that one may expect if they become successful. However, it has some shortcomings when used to define success for telecommunications managers. Fame is not a description normally used to measure managerial success, and the use of the power attribute would probably have to be modified. Even money (wealth) is a relative term, particularly in today's environment of million-dollar salaries for entertainment, entrepreneurial initiatives, and lawsuits. The last definition assumes a puposeful, directed approach when achieving success. However, this is not always the case since opportunities for achieving success may be seredipitous in nature. When serendipitous opporunities arise, they should be grapsed quickly and firmly.

One novel example of serendipity would be the development of Post-It notes by 3-M. 3-M has an ongoing research and development effort for creating strong bonding agents (chemicals) that are used to glue objects together.

The bonding agent used in 3-M's Post-It notes is one that does not bond strongly. Serendipity occurs naturally but it requires a gift to be able to shift thought patterns so that it is recognized. Someone intent on developing strong bonding agents can easily discard a weak bonding agent as being unusable.

In the same way, opportunities for achieving managerial success may exist but will require an individual to recognize the opportunity.

Personal Viewpoints

Individuals have different personal goals and aspirations and, as a result, each person's perception of *managerial success* may also differ. One person may be satisfied with being a first level manager who handles technical projects and is very happy with the prospect of continuing to do the same job for the foreseeable future. Another person may see lower level managerial positions as simply being stepping stones that lead to higher level managerial positions. Clearly, the definition of success for these two individuals would vary significantly and each definition would be correct when viewed from a personal context.

Compensation is another criterion that is frequently used to measure managerial success. Someone who is making $200,000 per year may be perceived as being significantly more successful than someone who is being paid $50,000 per year—even if the job responsibilities are similar. On the other hand, someone working at a lower paying position may have a better self image and may be happier with carrying out his or her job than someone who has a higher paying position. The impact that compensation has on an individual's view of their own success—assuming that basic needs are met by their salary level—is frequently a matter of personal perception.

Need for a Scoring System

An objective measuring system would be useful when measuring managerial success or failure. All sports have a scoring system that is unique to the sport—baseball uses runs; football uses touchdowns, extra points, field goals, and safeties; soccer uses goals. However, when comparisons are attempted between different sports, the only comparison that provides some level of meaning is: 1) wins and losses or 2) the ranking of a team versus its competitors. When the focus is on measuring individual performance, the measurement of success becomes even more difficult because an all-star may be playing on a mediocre team while an average player may play only a supporting role on a team that wins consistently.

In baseball, the emphasis is on learning how to control runs—a key measurement of baseball success. Pitchers concentrate on learning how to minimize runs while position players concentrate on finding ways to maximize their run generating capabilities by developing hitting skills. Position players also must have fielding skills to minimize the number of runs another team can score. A team that has better pitching and fielding skills, and scores more runs than the opponent, will win the game. Baseball players concentrate on developing physical skills and learning those playing skills that allow them to be effective in their positions. Therefore, the final game score is basically a byproduct of how well team members are doing their job individually and collectively.

The following will propose a **managerial scoring system** for telecommunications managers and will describe the skills required by individual telecommunications managers to achieve winning scores and be successful at their personal telecommunications game.

Accounting: The Business Scoring System

Since the late 1800s, accounting measurements have provided the criteria used to measure **business** success. Accounting uses a standard form of measurement for all accounting activities—*dollars*. A business's assets, liabilities, expenses, salaries, and time are converted to dollars and then placed into the appropriate accounting context to measure the impact they have on organizational profitability. A profitability score is assigned to a business's performance for a given period of time (typically, a fiscal year) by using the following calculation:

$$profit = revenues - expenses$$

A business is considered successful when profits are high (when **current performance** is good). Successful businesses pay higher salaries, make more telecommunications technology investments, and are more fun to work for than unsuccessful businesses. If a telecommunications manager works for a company that is barely surviving (low profits), the role of the telecommunications department will be to act as a **facilitator** for minimizing telecommunications expenditures—a role that is not normally enjoyable. On the other hand, working for a profitable enterprise that views technology as a business resource can be an interesting and fulfilling experience. Working at any job is more enjoyable when working for a successful company, because the rewards (salary and personal benefits) are normally higher and the opportunity to grow professionally and technically is greater. When upper management sees that the telecommunications department is a strong contributor to the success of the company, telecommunications managers and personnel will be rewarded through appropriate compensation and promotion mechanisms.

Upper Management: The Score Keepers

Upper management is responsible for organizing and controlling business affairs. The most common tool used to measure their effectiveness is profitability. If a business does not generate sufficient profits, upper management options are limited. Most large and medium sized U.S. businesses have external **stockholders** who own the corporation. The authority to manage the corporation is delegated by the stockholders to a **board of directors** (refer to Figure 4–1).

The board of directors varies in composition from company to company but generally consists of several officers of the corporation and several outside directors. The **management board** of a corporation, sometimes referred to as the operating officers or upper management, consists of the president, vice presidents, a controller, a treasurer, a secretary, and other positions that report directly to the president.

The board of directors establishes the business policies of the corporation, declares dividends, and appoints management board members. The management board executes the policies established by the board of directors and manages the day to day operations of the firm. In this **corporate structure,** some management board members may be members of the board of directors—a dual membership that provides direct communication between the policy generation group (board of directors) and the implementers of the policies (management board).

In the organization chart (chain of command) shown in Figure 4–2, the management board members include the president, the vice president of human resources, the vice president of finance, the vice president of sales and marketing, the vice president of manufacturing, the vice president of telecommunications, an appointed secretary, and an appointed treasurer. The board of directors would typically consist of outside directors, the president, and selected members of the management board.

The management board would meet on a regular basis to evaluate the firm's operational performance and develop managerial initiatives, as needed, to ensure that the annual goals are being met. Management board actions include approving financial budgets for operating expenses and capital expenditures and approving the managerial appointments to key positions within the organization.

Note: the **planning manager, development manager, operations manager, administrative services manager,** and **help desk manager** all report to the vice

Figure 4–1. Corporate organization structure.

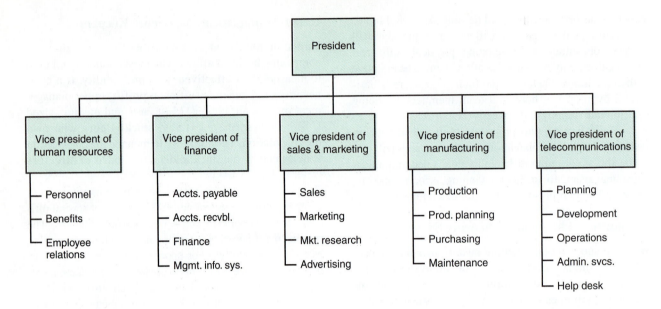

Figure 4–2. A business organization chart.

president of telecommunications. The vice president is a **manager of managers** (a **bona fide manager**). His or her direct reports may or may not be bona fide managers.

WHO IS UPPER MANAGEMENT?   Chapter 1 stated that the primary criterion for achieving long term success in telecommunications was to satisfy upper management expectations. Upper management, in this context, refers to the management board members who are responsible for the day to day operations of the business. Upper management in the Figure 4–2 organization chart would consist of the president and the vice presidents who report to the president.

Although specific upper management objectives may vary from organization to organization, they use similar accounting criteria to measure operating and managerial performance. The charter given to upper management by the stockholders is that upper management should run the day to day business operations and implement the policies established by the board of directors. Board of director policies are designed to meet stockholder goals—to make money so that the stockholders are rewarded for investing in the business. The ultimate performance assessment of both the board of directors and the management board will be based on their ability to produce an operating profit that satisfies stockholder expectations. Creating an operating environment that generates a good level of stock dividends and a strong growth in stock value will satisfy stockholders. If upper management meets or exceeds stockholder expectations, they will be given a great deal of flexibility in how they manage the business. Upper management members

who are successful will also have great latitude in determining employee compensation and capital investment levels.

Employees of a business see members of upper management as their bosses in the same way that members of upper management see stockholders as their bosses. Upper management determines how much money will be made available for employee raises (including managerial raises), capital investments, and providing an attractive work environment. Upper management needs to create a high profit environment if they are to play the role of a generous boss to employees by liberally allocating money for employee raises and asset investments. In a competitive environment, managers who are business oriented and contribute significantly to organizational profitability will be recognized by upper management and will be rewarded accordingly.

> A telecommunications manager's primary objective should be to satisfy the boss (upper management). Individuals who assist upper management in achieving goals will be rewarded and will also help members of upper management satisfy their ultimate bosses—the stockholders.

UPPER MANAGEMENT VIEWS OF TELECOMMUNICATIONS

Upper management is "the boss" for all business departments, including the telecommunications department, and it is always important to know how the boss perceives your efforts. While the specific viewpoints of upper management may vary, there are three general philosophical viewpoints that members of upper management have regarding the value of a telecommunications department. The **three views of telecommunications** include:

1. Telecommunications is a cost to be minimized.
2. Telecommunications is a tool for improving (internal) organizational efficiency.
3. Telecommunications is a strategic asset that can be utilized to achieve success in the marketplace.

A Cost to be Minimized

From a cost-driven perspective, an effective telecommunications manager will be seen as one whose primary focus should be on finding (telecommunications) cost reduction opportunities and taking the necessary action to minimize telecommunications costs. Telecommunications costs would consist of the budgets allocated to the telecommunications department, the cost of internal personnel and operations, and the cost of external telecommunications services.

Cost control is an ongoing reality in all businesses. All managers should be involved with cost control initiatives. A reduction in organization expenses may be required to achieve a given year's profit objectives when sales revenues have not met forecast estimates and a one-time cost reduction effort is required to maintain profitability. Even highly successful businesses will regularly apply the expense reduction strategy to achieve consistent financial performance.

The effective manager must know the places where budget reductions can be achieved without incurring long term damage to the organization. Therefore, a key requirement for a telecommunications manager is to have an excellent accounting knowledge of the operating expense and capital expenditure process that is being used by the business. Telecommunications managers must also understand the short- and long-term implications of reducing telecommunications expenses for various budget line items, and must be able to effectively and objectively communicate these implications to business management. For example, reducing long distance call expenses by 10% may mean that existing customer service activities will be negatively impacted. In this instance, an apparent reduction in telecommunications department costs may result in losing customers because of expense limitations. If telecommunications managers understand cost reduction alternatives in terms of their business impacts, dumb mistakes can be avoided when addressing cost reduction mandates by upper management. Being able to explain the potential downsides of cost cutting actions is extremely important.

A Tool for Improving Internal Efficiency

Upper management may see telecommunications as a means for improving internal efficiencies and may be comfortable with spending money in the telecommunications area to achieve improvements and savings in nontelecommunications areas. For example, the use of 800-services could be used to centralize multiple customer service locations into a single location to generate cost savings, while also providing a better level of service to customers.

The same approach can be applied to other internal departments in order to centralize or decentralize operations and improve the efficiency of internal operations by leveraging people resources. The effective use of communications and computer technology can be used to create a networked organization where any-to-any communications is applied as needed to provide accessibility to critical personnel resources in a cost effective manner.

A Strategic Asset

In this view, upper management sees telecommunications services as a business tool that "makes it easier for customers to do business with us" or "that can be made part of an existing product." Customers and suppliers can be provided with access to internal resources by installing telecommunications-based computer applications or by using **WWW** technologies to develop e-commerce applications. The underlying objective is a strategic one where telecommunications is viewed as a tool for increasing business revenues. Improving customer access to corporate resources and service personnel is one example of supporting revenue objectives.

A direct approach for increasing revenues would be to incorporate telecommunications capabilities into the product. The Automated Teller Machine (ATM) example described later in this chapter used telecommunications technologies as a technology alternative for providing 24 hour per day human teller services. If a company sells and services complex, expensive equipment, the use of computer technology coupled with telecommunications technology could be used to market a product that automatically calls for service when its internal intelligence detects a deteriorating performance pattern or the abrupt termination of operations. Under this scenario, it would be possible for a service representative to request access to the equipment before the customer using the equipment is aware of the problem. The latter example is clearly a significant enhancement to the basic product, which could be offered as a new product service option.

Situational Opportunities

The three business management viewpoints of the telecommunications department—a cost to be minimized, a vehicle for improving internal effectiveness, or a vehicle for improving external (i.e., revenue) performance—may exist separately or concurrently. A telecommunications manager must be able to effectively manage all three environments.

The most attractive viewpoint is the strategic viewpoint, i.e., a revenue-based viewpoint. While cost reduction activities are an ever-present reality that must be carried out effectively, the ability to increase revenues by incorporating telecommunications technology is a more dramatic and eye-catching way to gain upper management's attention. This contrasts with the cost to be minimized viewpoint, where the primary focus is on reducing costs. The fortunate telecommunications manager will be one who operates within an environment that supports all three perspectives. The managerial skills required for balancing the three scenarios are significantly greater than the skills needed for any single philosophy area.

UPPER MANAGEMENT SCORE KEEPING

A "success factor" can be thought of as something that positively influences a successful outcome. In this context, anything that upper management views as desirable characteristics of managers can be referred to as success factors. If present, success factors will result in managers being viewed as good managers. Because promotions and raises reward good managers, telecommunications managers should identify upper management's success factors and use them as guidelines for making managerial decisions.

Upper management has one primary job—providing a return on investment (ROI) that meets the expectations of their bosses (stockholders). Upper-level managers pursue the stockholders' ROI goal by directing the efforts of internal departments (sales, manufacturing, accounting, telecommunications). Upper management members may have strong skills in the department they head but may have a limited understanding of what other internal departments do. In addition, the amount of time upper managers have to manage internal organizations will be drastically limited by their need to interface with many external entities that include customers, peer managers, suppliers, stockholders, professional organizations, and charitable organizations.

Upper management must satisfy their bosses—the stockholders—by meeting profitability goals while imposing major constraints on the amount of time they can dedicate to managing the internal department. This dilemma can be met only by relying heavily on their direct reports (managers) to run individual departments effectively and efficiently. Therefore, upper management relies heavily on the managers to whom they delegate the managerial authority to run departments, and will quickly recognize managers who consistently get the job done.

Upper Management Performance Standards

Because upper-level managers have a limited amount of time to spend in selecting and managing internal managers, what criteria will they utilize for selecting managers and determining good managerial performance? The upper management success criteria for evaluating the performance of internal managers will typically be based on managerial performance in three areas:

1. supporting profitability objectives
2. providing **customer satisfaction**
3. planning ahead

Profitability Performance

In theory, members of upper management can initiate actions based on their own personal preferences. However, their freedom in making unilateral managerial decisions is limited significantly by their accountability to stockholders. Upper managers are accountable to the board of directors, and the board of directors (including the external directors) is directly accountable to the stockholders. The board of directors will evaluate upper management's performance in meeting profitability objectives and, if profitability goals are not met, a change in management board membership will normally result. However, it is more likely that the lower-level managers will be the first to go. Good profitability performance requires having a strong track record in meeting both short- and long-term management goals. Upper managers who consistently generate a high level of profits will be rated as being successful. They achieve this success by focusing on two basic areas:

1. increasing revenues
2. decreasing expenses

Any activities that help to increase profits or decrease expenses will result in higher profits. Higher profits create satisfied stockholders, satisfied stockholders create satisfied upper management, and satisfied upper management is more willing to reward individual performance and make internal investments. Successful organizations will have the financial resources to continue the pursuit of future success.

During the annual budget cycle, the accounting department receives input from all departments in the business regarding their budgetary needs for the future year. Revenue estimates are obtained from the sales departments. This revenue and expense information is combined to create a profitability forecast for the future year. If sales estimates and department's expense estimates are accurate, and the economic environment is a positive one, the organization will meet its profitability forecast. When revenue estimates are not met and/or actual expenses exceed forecast values, the organization may be unable to meet profit objectives. When this profitability shortfall occurs during any given budgetary cycle, revenue and expense projections are scrutinized closely and adjusted to meet the original profit objectives.

Unless the organization has a unique product that allows them to demand a premium price for products or services, profitability shortfalls can be addressed only if customer sales are increased or if internal department expenses are reduced. While sales increases are largely in the domain of the sales-oriented departments, all internal organizations can influence direct and indirect expenses.

Increasing Revenues

Four sales-oriented departments have a direct impact on increasing revenues by influencing the sale of products: 1) the marketing department, 2) the research department, 3) the manufacturing department, and 4) the sales department.

The marketing department must identify the product characteristics that are desirable to its customers and must use this information to direct internal product development activities. These product characteristics will become the input to a research project whose objective is to develop a product that fulfills the needs identified by the marketing department. If both the marketing and research departments do their jobs effectively, a product will be developed in a timely fashion to meet customer needs and will be turned over to the manufacturing department. Manufacturing must produce the product at the right price in sufficient quantities to meet customer demands, and the sales department must convince customers to buy the product. If marketing has identified customer needs accurately, research has developed the product that meets customer needs, and manufacturing produces the product at the right price in sufficient quantities, the burden of meeting revenue forecasts now falls on the sales department.

As an added incentive for sales personnel, many businesses provide sales-based incentives. Under a sales-based incentive plan, the sales representative will receive additional compensation for each product unit they sell. In sales-oriented corporations, it is not unusual for "super sales representatives" to earn more money (salary + commissions) than the vice president of sales.

However, other internal departments can have major impacts on increasing product sales. The following provides an example of a telecommunications-based application that revolutionized the banking industry and had a major positive impact on increasing the revenues (deposits, in this example) of the initial innovators.

INCREASING REVENUES WITH TELECOMMUNICATIONS. During the last twenty-five years, telecommunications technologies have played a key role in providing services that directly impact business revenues. Telecommunications technology has been used to:

1. provide a high speed, responsive interface to a business's customer service department.
2. improve products and services by incorporating communications technology into the products or services.

A desire frequently expressed by upper management as a way to gain customer sales is to become "easy to do business with." From a customer perspective, this means having fast, easy access to a supplier's personnel and information resources. Methods commonly used to improve customer-to-supplier communications include telephone, e-mail, or e-commerce. E-commerce activities include order taking, obtaining order status information, and having access to other sales-related information. The WWW has emerged as the primary means of supporting e-commerce.

Businesses rely upon their internal telecommunications departments to provide the telephone, e-mail, and e-commerce services used by external customers. An internal communications infrastructure is also needed to support ongoing customer service activities. This internal infrastructure usually consists of LANs, WANs, and data internetworking facilities. A customer who finds that it is easy to access customer service facilities and receive a quick response has been provided with a positive experience. Customers receiving good service are more likely to return than those receiving poor service.

Another approach for using telecommunications technology to support sales efforts is to integrate networking capabilities into an existing product or to substitute a computerized service representative for a human sales representative. Use of computerized service representatives that are connected to network facilities can provide customers with 24-hour access to internal services and products.

ATM—TELECOMMUNICATIONS AT WORK. One example of substituting a computerized representative for a human representative is the ATM. When initially introduced by a few banks in the 1980s, ATMs were viewed with skepticism by many banking managers and seen as "technical toys" with little or no business value. These banking managers believed that customers would demand a human interface and would reject the impersonal, technical interface associated with computerized banking services. They felt that a few techies would use ATMs but that bank tellers would still be needed to handle most banking deposits and withdrawals. Instead, ATM usage increased rapidly and created a new type of customer who utilized ATM services during and outside of normal banking hours. In hindsight, ATM created a new customer market of computer-oriented individuals who relied heavily on the use of ATM facilities to meet all of their personal banking needs. ATMs initially provided a competitive advantage to early banking innovators; today they are a competitive necessity that must be offered by all major banks as a standard service. ATMs are examples of how telecommunications technology can be used to enhance an existing process (bank teller deposits and withdrawals) and attract new customers while holding on to existing ones. ATMs generate revenues for banks and provide a cost effective way of offering off-hour access to banking services—and more technical positions needed to support these services.

The creators of the early ATM environment were business visionaries who saw how telecommunications technology could be used to enhance customer service. These innovators were rewarded, because ATMs brought them new customers while providing an off-hour service option for existing customers. The net result was an increase in bank deposits—a way of increasing revenues in the banking industry.

Reducing Expenses

Expenses are incurred by businesses when money is spent to buy or do something. Expenses are incurred by businesses when money is spent to buy or do something and directly affect organizational profitability (profit = revenues − expenses). Expenses can be deducted from any revenues received during the same time period. While many revenue-increasing initiatives may be limited to specific departments (sales or marketing), expense-reduction activities involve all departments in the business. Expense control activities are an ongoing upper management concern but they become a key issue when profitability objectives can't be met because of reduced sales. In this event, expense reductions are frequently used to offset low sales. For every dollar of expense reduction, a dollar will be added back into the profitability shortfall gap.

If a company is profitable, cutting expenses provides a means for increasing profitability levels if a company is marginally profitable, cutting expenses may be necessary for survival. Upper management will automatically initiate expense-reduction actions if sales estimates for the current period indicate that sales levels will be significantly below forecast values. The degree of cost cutting initiated by upper management will vary according to the magnitude of projected revenue losses and the operating philosophy of upper management.

CONTROLLING EXPENSES. Controlling expenses is an ongoing discipline and activity in companies. Internal departments have two types of budgets: 1) operating budgets, and 2) capital expenditure budgets. Operating budgets provide funds for supporting day to day operations and include funding for employee salaries and benefits, subscriptions, equipment rental and maintenance, and office supplies. The capital expenditure budget is for purchasing new assets such as land, buildings, equipment, and other property that must be depreciated in accordance with Internal Revenue Service (IRS) regulations.

Reducing capital expenditure budgets is an easy way to conserve cash during times when sales are low. The impact of reduced sales can be offset by reducing capital expenditure budgets and capital expenditures reductions are relatively painless when capital budgets are reinstated the following fiscal period. If the capital investment is made to support an expected increase in sales, delaying the capital expense until the following fiscal period will not negatively affect current operations. In other instances, the benefits derived from a capital expenditure are not time critical. Deferring the expenditure has no impact on business activities.

Internal department budgets undergo considerable scrutiny when they are originated during an annual planning process. If the original budgets are good estimates of actual revenues and expenses, they will be left intact during the year they are implemented. However, if revenue shortfalls take place, department budgets become a focal point for expense cutting activities such as attempts to maintain profitability by offsetting the impact of reduced revenues by reducing expenses.

Upper management typically initiates two types of operating budget cost cutting activities: 1) discretionary, and 2) mandated. Discretionary initiatives provide a budget reduction target (e.g., 5%) and department managers must reduce their department operating budget by this percentage. Department managers can eliminate or reduce budgeted line items at their discretion. Discretionary budget cuts are relatively painless because the department manager does not normally have to terminate employees to achieve the required expense reduction target.

Employee costs are the largest single expense item in most department budgets. Reducing the number of employees in a department eliminates many employee-related expenses (salaries, wages, benefits, social security, or 401K contribution). Upper management may mandate a reduction in employees (**downsizing**) when severe revenue losses are expected and the expense reductions in nonsalary budget areas are unable to offset the expected shortfall in revenues. Under severe circumstances, sales losses may mean that many employees will not have any work to do and that the company is faced with the prospect of paying idle employees.

Making staffing reductions can create problems in the future if company sales rebound quickly and the business is unable to produce enough product to meet customer demands. However, when difficult times are encountered, skilled production, sales, and customer service personnel may have to be laid off. If former employees are not available for rehire when sales rebound because they have found other jobs or because they have relocated to other parts of the country, the company may encounter production constraints, quality problems, and reduced levels of customer service as they attempt to restore their former operating capabilities. Therefore, the option of reducing personnel through mass layoffs is normally one of the last cost cutting options considered.

REDUCING TELECOMMUNICATIONS EXPENSES.
Telecommunications managers will participate in the cost cutting activities described above. Discretionary initiatives require them to review the department operating budget and apply upper management's cost cutting guidelines to meet expense reduction guidelines. It may also be necessary to defer the implementation of telecommunications technology projects to conserve capital investment funds and make it available for the tough times that are being encountered.

Telecommunications management also has the responsibility for managing all telecommunications related expenses. Internal department employees use the communication services provided by the telecommunications department and this usage translates into company expenses. Any telecommunications cost reduction initiatives requiring a reduction in usage must involve the departments that are using the internal services. **Chargeback systems** identify the end-user costs and allow them to manage their use of the service. If a chargeback system is in place and departments are accountable for their communication costs, the expense-reduction burden is placed on the department. When a chargeback system is not in place, it may be diffi-cult to identify who is using internal telecommunications services and any unilateral attempt by a telecommunications manager to reduce costs can adversely affect individual department operations.

There are some telecommunications expense reduction activities that a telecommunications manager can pursue unilaterally. Internal telecommunications expenses can be reduced without impacting the use of internal services by:

1. purchasing outside services at a lower cost.
2. **leveraging** internal resources to accomplish more with less.
3. eliminating noncritical services.

Reducing the cost for outside services requires a reevaluation of existing service provider products and identifying alternative suppliers capable of providing equivalent or better services at lower costs. Leveraging internal resources means using a smaller number of internal (telecommunications) employees to provide internal services. Elimination of telecommunications services is straightforward when redundant services are involved but requires an impact analysis when services used by internal departments will be eliminated. The operational impact on the end-users losing the service must be understood and considered during any expense reduction process.

LEVERAGING TELECOMMUNICATIONS EXPENSES.
The direct approach of having each department reduce its budget is fairly intuitive and has been discussed. Another approach for achieving overall expense reductions is to increase the expense in one budget but offset the expense increase with major expense reductions (savings) in another budget. An overall expense reduction is achieved by offsetting smaller expense increases in one area with larger savings (expense reductions) generated in other areas. This is referred to as **leveraging expenses.**

Employees have become a high cost expense ever since government mandated benefits and employee taxes were implemented, and these mandated costs are a significant percentage of an employee's base salary. As a result, the expense reduction impact associated with a reduction in workforce is higher than just the employee salary amount. In addition, the elimination of employees not only impacts the current fiscal period but will also benefit future periods. Eliminating a small number of employees can generate significant savings when the cumulative impact on current and future fiscal costs are calculated.

Telecommunications technologies can provide an effective catalyst for reducing the total number of employees required to perform a job when the employees are located in several locations. The basic approach is to consolidate employees into a single location and use telecommunications technologies to provide easy access to the central resource. A single, large central group can be managed more effectively than managing multiple smaller sized groups. A single group can also provide better service levels. Redundant functions (the duplicate facilities needed at multiple sites) can be eliminated without impacting the quality of the services provided from the central location and the cost for installing new telecommunications facilities would be more than offset by the elimination of the redundant employees and equipment required when multiple locations are maintained. In addition, the larger employee base in the central location can frequently justify investments in reengineering improvements that are not economically viable in a smaller organization—while maintaining or improving preconsolidation service levels to enterprise customers.

If the employee downsizing is done as part of a long-term plan, employee reductions can be achieved by not replacing employees that leave as part of normal employee turnover.

DOWNSIZING ISSUES. When department employees are laid off as part of a direct department expense reduction initiative, the action is carried out unilaterally by a department manager and the remaining department members must pick up the work performed by laid-off employees. Some departments may find that the incremental workload inherited from laid-off employees is very high, while other departments will find that the added workload is minimal.

In some departments, the workload may remain constant regardless of any variations in sales. In others, there is a direct correlation between sales activities and department workload. Even sales-oriented departments can face problems when staffing reductions are initiated because of poor sales. If the sales-oriented department has five specialists performing different tasks and one employee is eliminated, the four remaining employees may have to assume a workload that requires different skills than their current workload. The disruptive effect of training and added workload that takes place when downsizing activities are instituted can create a difficult work environment for the remaining employees.

REENGINEERING JOBS WITH TELECOMMUNICATIONS. A logical way to address a situation where fewer employees are available for completing a given set of tasks is to **reengineer** the job—do the job differently. Reengineering may involve applying task specialization techniques to improve operational performance, eliminat-

ing redundant operations, or balancing the workload between several existing locations. Telecommunications technologies can be used as a catalyst to achieve indirect expense reductions. In this case, telecommunications expenses will increase while savings are generated in another department's budget. The following provides two examples of increasing telecommunications expenses to achieve overall expense reductions.

AUTOMATIC CALL DISTRIBUTOR PROJECT EXAMPLE. An **Automatic Call Distributor (ACD)** is a piece of telephone equipment that is used to handle large volumes of incoming telephone calls being answered by a relatively small number of people (agents). An ACD receives an incoming call and routes it to an agent if one is available or places it in a queue if an agent is not available. Queued calls are then routed to the first available agent, based on the order in which they were received. An ACD system provides reports that analyze calls by providing wait time, answering agent, length of the call, and other operating statistics. A call center manager can use ACD report information to identify call coverage requirements during different times of the day and maximize the use of call center agents.

Using an ACD in a high call volume customer service department will result in requiring fewer agents than if the same workload were handled without an ACD system. The ACD will balance the workload more effectively and will provide critical managerial information that can be used to increase operating efficiency with lower staffing levels. The expense associated with operating an ACD system for a call center is normally small compared to the personnel savings it generates.

800-SERVICES PROJECT EXAMPLE. Let's review another example, where a company maintains three customer service locations to handle orders generated by customers in the eastern, middle, and western areas of the U.S. These locations are open from 8 a.m. to 5 p.m. in their respective time zones and each location is staffed with fifteen employees. A workload analysis has shown that the eastern area could operate from 8 a.m. to 7 p.m. and would only require thirty employees to provide the same service levels that the three locations currently provide. The analysis shows that additional nonpersonnel savings can be achieved by closing the two office locations and eliminating the rental and equipment operating costs (personal computers, LANs) needed to support them.

However, a telecommunications investment would be required at the central location. This would consist of installing a large 800-service network to handle customer calls and upgrading the existing LAN and telephone equipment to handle the additional requirements. The telephone system upgrade would include the addition of call processing features (ACD) to improve customer access capabilities and utilize customer service personnel more efficiently. The technical and financial analysis of the eastern area location requirements has shown that a $200,000 telecommunications investment will be needed and that annual operating expenses would increase by $225,000. On the benefit side, the investment would generate net savings of $1,500,000 in customer services department expenses.

The net annual savings of $1,225,000 per year clearly warrants attention and justifies the initial investment. However, it is important for upper management to be aware of the impact that the customer services department savings will have on telecommunications expenses. This issue becomes academic if a telecommunications chargeback system is in place to allocate the telecommunications expense to the customer service department budget. If a chargeback mechanism is used, the department savings will offset the telecommunications expense increase, and the net customer services budget effect will be an expense reduction. However, if a chargeback approach is not used, the telecommunications department budget could have a major increase without any offsetting benefits being seen in the telecommunications department budget.

The use of leveraging a small increase in one department's budget to generate significant savings in another department's budget will frequently generate greater organizational savings than can be realized by having each department focus narrowly on controlling its own expenses.

Improving Customer Satisfaction

Given the time constraints that upper management must operate under, they rely heavily on the opinions of the constituents in their internal and external business environment. Upper management is constantly polling these constituencies to determine their satisfaction with the service levels they are receiving, and this information is used to form opinions about the service provider. This polling is both formal and informal, where the informal approach tends to be on a direct, person-to-person basis. Critical feedback obtained during an informal conversation can quickly trigger an upper management initiative within the internal department.

External customers are a key information source for upper management feedback, and any negative comments from the external constituency will quickly be routed to the appropriate department responsible for addressing it (sales, marketing, customer service, research and development,

engineering, or manufacturing). Suppliers are also part of the external constituency, and key suppliers will have a strong influence on the opinions of upper management. The same applies to regulators, government agencies, and other organizations that can impact the external business environment.

Upper management is also extremely concerned with internal constituencies—the operating departments in the business's infrastructure. Upper management's job is to ensure that cooperation exists between different departments, so that external customer needs can be addressed effectively, and any department that negatively impacts another department's customer-oriented activities will quickly get upper management's attention.

Telecommunications services are essential for carrying out external and internal activities. When an external or internal constituency perceives that they are receiving substandard services from a business's telecommunications department, there is a strong likelihood that an upper-level manager will hear about it during his or her ongoing search for feedback. When this occurs, the top telecommunications manager will be assigned the responsibility for correcting the situation. Failure to comply quickly and effectively can be a career-threatening incident for any managers who are part of the organization's managerial chain of command.

The "casual" upper management customer satisfaction examples described in this section can be viewed as an informal appraisal process, where upper management obtains feedback on different departments and personnel. Doing a good job in a telecommunications context means that upper management receives positive feedback regarding the level of telecommunications support received by external and internal constituents—feedback that will enhance a telecommunications manager's credibility and career opportunities.

> From an upper management perspective, good telecommunications management performance means that the telecommunications department's external and internal customers perceive that they are receiving good service.

Planning Ahead

Upper management has the responsibility for ensuring that stockholder profitability objectives are met. The initiation of activities to offset unexpected revenue losses requires a proactive response by upper management, and the response is typically one of reducing expenses to offset revenue losses. Therefore, expense reduction is always in vogue and internal organizations that achieve ongoing expense reductions without upper management initiatives contribute to profitability in an ongoing manner.

Telecommunications managers who support upper management's concern with maintaining profitability by planning ongoing cost savings initiatives and highlighting these plans during the budgeting cycle will be recognized and rewarded. When telecommunications managers are perceived as being good business managers—not just "techies"—they gain credibility and respect of upper management. Telecommunications services are uniquely able to address both revenue and expense issues, and a competent telecommunications manager should be able to demonstrate the value of the telecommunications department when supporting profitability objectives in both areas.

The appropriate vehicle for demonstrating good business judgment is the financial planning process—the annual planning cycle. During the annual planning cycle, department budgets and capital investment information is developed by all internal departments and forwarded to upper management for budgetary approval. When telecommunications operating budgets and capital investment budgets are presented and clearly indicate the benefits associated with the expense, upper management will be given the opportunity to perform an informal return on investment (ROI) analysis. On the other hand, poorly constructed telecommunications planning documents will only convey the expense information without indicating the benefits associated with them.

A telecommunications manager who consistently provides timely financial information and avoids financial surprises (unexpected requests for emergency funding) by managing their budget will receive good marks from upper management.

> Telecommunications managers who develop a track record for creating telecommunications plans that reduce operating expenses, enhance internal and external communication, and identify ways of using telecommunications to support business objectives will be recognized and rewarded by upper management.

MANAGERIAL COMMUNICATION

Communicating effectively with upper management is a prerequisite for achieving success as a telecommunications manager. Upper management-oriented communications must be clear, easy to read, unambiguous, concise, and timely. Communication that meets these criteria and is appropriate for upper management will also be suitable for other managerial and nonmanagerial personnel. When business communications sent to upper managers is effective, it will also be sent to managers within the upper manager's organizational chain of command.

A Multipurpose Communication Framework

For telecommunications managers, upper management is the boss who controls the allocation of corporate funds. Communicating effectively with upper management is essential for obtaining a fair share of the discretionary funds that are available for (telecommunications) compensation and (telecommunications) project investments. This section will describe an approach for developing written communication, but the written communication framework also applies to any form of upper management communication, including presentations, e-mail messages, and conversations.

A prerequisite for developing an effective written or verbal communication style is to know your audience. The focus for internal business communication should be an upper management audience. The following discussion assumes that *upper management is always the audience for any communication created by the telecommunications manager*. This means that all written and verbal communication created by the telecommunications manager is organized and written for an upper management audience. There are two good reasons for using this approach. First, any form of communication that can be easily understood by upper management will be easily understood by anyone. Second, when written communication is sent to someone in the organization, there is always the potential that it may be forwarded up the chain of command to an upper manager.

The following provides an overview of the three basic elements used in developing written and verbal communications:

- **format**
- **style**
- **content**

These three elements have been ranked in terms of their importance when communicating with an upper management audience. While someone might assume that a message's content should be the first element listed, the reality is that this element is a secondary concern in establishing good communication. If the format and style of the communication are inappropriate for upper managers, they will not be inclined to read the content—regardless of its merit. This is another way of saying that initial impressions of appearance will determine if someone decides to invest the effort for reading a document.

To carry this theme further, consider the following illustration of a project guaranteeing a 20% increase in corporate revenues that is being presented to the management board of a large, conservative corporation. The individual making the presentation in the executive boardroom shows up in sandals, unshaven, and dressed in dirty jeans and a tank top. To complicate matters further, the presenter does not speak English and the only language known by the board members is English. Even if the board could get past the appearance issue (an unlikely event), they would not understand the information being presented.

If project documentation is illegibly handwritten on 500 pages of dirty notebook paper, it will generate the same reaction as noted for our boardroom example. Business management will not read poorly prepared documents.

> For the message to be understood by upper management, the appropriate format and style must be utilized.

FORMAT. Format refers to the way information is packaged, presented, organized, and arranged—how it looks. Appearance is a key requirement when communicating with business management. If the appropriate format is not used, there is a high probability that the communication will be discarded without being read. Upper managers have a limited amount of time available to read documents and the document's appearance will frequently be the basis determining whether it will be read by the manager. Documents that are professional in appearance and conform to organizational format standards are more likely to be selected for reading than documents that are poorly prepared. If the appropriate format is selected, the document's appearance will not be a factor, and the reader can concentrate on the document's message.

A wide range of format options is available when using word processing software. Headings, bulleted lists, tables, and different text fonts can be used to assist the reading process, clarify the information structure, and highlight critical points. A key element in any form of communication with upper management is to clearly identify what is being requested in a next-steps conclusion section. Chapter 5, *Telecommunications Manager Skill Requirements*, will discuss business writing in detail, and will provide examples.

STYLE. Style refers to the way it is written—how it reads. Upper management's time is critical, and they deal with many diverse topics that are frequently outside of their areas of individual expertise. Therefore, written or verbal communication that is concise, unambiguous, and

TABLE 4–1 Translating Technical Terms

Technical term	Translation
PBX	Telephone system
Frame relay network	Data communication network
Universal Resource Locator (URL)	WWW address
Centrex	Telephone system
WAN	Long distance network
LAN	Personal computer network

uses basic business English will be understandable and will gain upper management's interest and attention. Business English means avoiding the use of technical jargon and using numbers in an accounting format. The use of business English will improve the level of communication between a technical department (telecommunications) and a business management department (upper management).

Telecommunications personnel frequently use technical terms and technical jargon in their normal work environment. While this technical shorthand simplifies and speeds up information exchange in a work environment, it is unsuitable for communicating with upper management. Technical shorthand is unintelligible to most of the business world, and it is essential that technical terms and jargon be converted into a generic business format and style when telecommunications proposals are being explained to business management. Some examples of how technical terms can be translated into business English are shown in Table 4–1.

Accounting information is the basic language of business management. Accounting reports convert PTM elements into dollars, where dollars become the basis for making business decisions. Justifying a project based on the technology advantages it provides will result in a request by business management for a manager to go back and do the numbers. This means that the benefits and costs must be given an accounting value so that an accounting assessment can be made of the project's value. Effective telecommunications managers need to understand and utilize local accounting procedures to explain telecommunications proposals.

CONTENT. Content provides the issues, topics, recommendations, or questions being addressed in the document. A business style should be used in presenting the information, and when recommendations are made, they should answer the question, "Why should resources be allocated or approval be given to the subject being addressed?" The answer would be structured in terms of the business benefits (refer to *Upper Management Score Keeping*) to be derived from the proposal that is being submitted for approval.

Managing Expectations

Communication with upper management is a critical element for achieving success as a telecommunications manager. Without the appropriate communication from telecommunications management, upper management's view of the telecommunications department will be based on the flow of information received from third party sources. The accounting department will summarize telecommunications in terms of their operating expense and capital expenditure budgets, the human resources department will provide input regarding telecommunication personnel issues, and the sales and marketing departments will provide input regarding the support provided to their customer service department. In the absence of direct input from the telecommunications department, upper management will find it necessary to use a patchwork quilt of third party opinions to identify the telecommunications department's contribution to the business enterprise.

The head of the telecommunications department (the vice president of telecommunications in Figure 4–2) is responsible for establishing a direct dialog with the management board. Managers reporting to the vice president are responsible for providing the appropriate telecommunications information that will be sent to upper management. This information may consist of telecommunications project proposals, status updates for projects that are in progress, and periodic updates highlighting the efforts of telecommunications in controlling expenses, supporting internal department activities, and improving customer-to-enterprise communication.

Written or oral communication directed to business management should be concise, direct, and unambiguous, and should utilize nontechnical language. While the primary responsibility for forwarding effective communication to the management board resides with the vice president, it is likely that the requirement for effective business communication will be delegated to the VP's direct reports.

When approvals for concepts and projects are desired, the appropriate financial analysis should be included. If significant investment dollars will be requested, the accounting department should be consulted in advance and comments to that effect should be included in the documentation. Involving accounting in the early stages of a project can help gain an ally that can support the financial recommendations reviewed.

APPROPRIATE COMMUNICATIONS. The format, style, and content of the telecommunications information should address management board needs and interests. Presentations and executive-level reports would be in the appropriate format expected by upper managers, and updates to key reports and presentations should be provided on a regular basis, as needed.

ONGOING COMMUNICATIONS. It is also important that the flow of communication to upper management takes place within the appropriate context. If a telecommunications manager initiates a dialog with upper managers during times of crisis only, there is a high probability that business management will expect to receive bad news whenever a communication is received from the manager. On the other hand, if the normal communication flow (a flow, not a flood) is positive, concise, proactive, and concerned with topics of interest to business management, a positive context is established for future communication between the telecommunications manager and business management.

Communication with business management should be an ongoing process that is customized to address the interests of the recipient(s). Credibility gained in this way will provide a positive context. When bad news is being communicated, it will be placed within the context of the total, ongoing communication that exists between the telecommunications manager and business management. Appropriately utilized, this context of credibility will allow greater flexibility to the telecommunications manager across a broad range of topics.

ADAPTING TO CHANGE

> **Adapting**: the process or state of changing to fit new circumstances or the changes that result from new circumstances.

The one constant in the business environment is change, which provides windows of opportunity that open and close quickly. The ability to assess new situations, understand their positive or negative implications, and initiate the appropriate response (action or inaction) will have a great influence on the outcome in addressing new situations. A strong response at the wrong time will court disaster; a strong response at the right time can convert a disastrous situation into a political and practical advantage.

> Success is not an accident. Being able to accurately evaluate a changing environment and select the appropriate reaction, or inaction, will frequently be the difference between success and failure.

The Experience Factor

At first glance, it may seem that experience should be an advantage in being able to manage a changing environment. However, experience may or may not be a positive factor in adapting to change. Someone who is a casual observer during a period of change does not acquire the same experience as someone who has been an active participant during the change process, just as observing several rocket launches does not make the observer a rocket scientist.

The Knowledge Factor

The basic skills needed to manage change include the ability to solve problems, make good decisions, and anticipate potential problems. While formal and informal education may be used to acquire the knowledge base required to develop skills, the application of this knowledge base will be based on individual capabilities. Someone who has developed a systematic framework for problem solving, decision making, and potential problem analysis has a high probability for being able to adapt in a changing environment. When an individual uses a systematic problem-solving framework, the individual will be able to evaluate why certain actions work and others do not. Strong analytical skills coupled with real world experience will provide the skill set needed to adapt and flourish in a changing environment.

> Having a high level of detailed knowledge about a topic without having a good set of analytic and decision tools is analogous to having a high-speed automobile without a steering mechanism.

The "Mom and Pop" Grocery Store Concept

In the days before the advent of big business and nationwide chains, Americans went to small "**mom and pop**" grocery stores to obtain food and miscellaneous items. These small stores were family-run businesses that featured personal service and a limited selection of food and food-related goods. The proprietors (mom and pop) knew all phases of the business and personally handled all transactions with customers and suppliers. These transactions were typically cash transactions, and mom or pop could quickly assess the status of the business by looking in their cash drawer. If there was cash in the cash drawer, the business was solvent; if the cash drawer was empty, they were in trouble. When slow moving items were stocked, cash was tied up and if fast-moving items were not stocked properly, profits were adversely affected.

Mom and pop proprietors were directly accountable for the success or failure of their stores. Success was based on the ability to correctly stock goods based on customer needs. These needs would vary by time of year, time of day, or holidays. Accurate assessment of the selling environment would provide them with a good cash flow, but miscalculating it could quickly drive them out of business.

A good telecommunications manager (or business manager) should have a mom and pop attitude toward the department they are managing. The failure to detect changes in the telecommunications environment and respond appropriately has the potential for driving them out of business—getting fired. Successful assessment of the environment will result in better cash flows (good budgets) and the ability to continue operations (their jobs).

DEVELOP PERSONAL TOOLS

The following provides a few definitions that will be used when discussing the **managerial toolset:**

Craft: a profession or activity that requires skill and training, or experience and specialized knowledge.

Craftsman: somebody who does something with great skill and expertise.

Journeyman: somebody who is a competent and reliable performer without being brilliant or outstanding. Somebody who has completed an apprenticeship and is fully trained and qualified but still works under the direction of a craftsman.

Craftsmen exist in all professions and occupations and are identified as individuals who have skills that place them in the upper echelons of their chosen calling. They have successfully made the transition from apprentice, to journeyman, to craftsman.

Regardless of the occupation, a craftsman relies upon tools to develop products. Without a good set of tools, it is difficult for a craftsman to create a quality product. Therefore, most craftsmen take very good care of their tools. Over time, craftsmen develop new techniques that improve the quality of their products and their desire for improving output will cause them to modify, add, or delete tools. A superior craftsman will have developed specialized tools that are used for specific applications and will know when to use them.

Knowledge and Experience

The key elements that separate a craftsman from a journeyman are knowledge and experience. A craftsman and journeyman can use the same tools but create products that differ greatly in appearance and quality. Perseverance, experience, and a burning desire to enhance their individual skills will allow a select number of craftsmen to emerge from a large pool of journeymen.

Telecommunications management is a profession that requires skills, training, experience, and specialized knowledge. Telecommunications management craftsmen also evolve from beginner, to journeyman, to craftsman. Telecommunications managers must acquire knowledge and develop a good set of skills to become craftsmen in their chosen profession.

The Managerial Toolset

A telecommunications manager's toolset is largely knowledge-based and includes interpersonal communication, mathematics, computing, management, business, and technology skills. Formal education can help in acquiring basic skills but—as was the case for the craftsman—it is the application of basic skills and the self-development of personal skills that separates the craftsman from the journeyman. Most of the knowledge gained by a professional over his or her lifetime is through informal education channels—on-the-job training, personal reading, and personal observation. The drive to become better is a personal characteristic. Perseverance over long periods of time is required to achieve excellence in any field.

Additional details about the managerial toolset are provided in Chapter 5, *Telecommunications Manager Skill Requirements*.

CLOSING COMMENTS

A wide range of topics has been presented and it is appropriate to summarize them in an outline format and provide summary comments:

1. How is success measured?
2. upper management views of telecommunications
3. upper management scorekeeping
4. managerial communication
5. adapting to changes
6. develop personal tools

This chapter's topic, *Criteria For Managerial Success*, has been addressed by discussing these six topics. Different measurements of success were reviewed but the final criterion established for determining managerial success was based on satisfying upper management per-

formance criteria. The conceptual philosophies that an upper manager may have of the telecommunications department was discussed. The three philosophical criteria that members of upper management will use when assessing managerial performance were also addressed. Therefore, items 1–3 addressed the "what" of managerial success and provided managerial goals for a telecommunications manager.

Items 4–6 focused on the "how" aspects of developing the skills needed to successfully achieve the goals established in items 1–3. The how elements are simple ones that are universal in nature:

- communicate effectively
- acquire knowledge and gain experience
- adapt to changing conditions

There are no magic tricks available to achieve managerial success. It means working hard, working long hours, and having a dogmatic insistence on doing the right things at the right time.

The contents of this chapter is analogous to the advice given by a wise man to a young man who had inherited a large farm that was tended by many farmhands. The young man had largely dissipated the monies he had inherited from his father by gambling and drinking, and the farm was no longer generating the profits it had generated in the past. In addition, the young man suddenly found himself on the verge of losing the land because of debts he had incurred. In desperation, he went to the wise man and asked for help resolving his problems. The wise man listened, nodded knowingly, and gave the young man a small sack of magic granules with instructions to place one granule at each corner of the farm at 5 a.m. each morning.

The young man followed the advice of the wise man. During his morning trips he found that the farmhands were not working the land as they were supposed to and he stopped to get them to do their work. He continued his morning rituals, and his farmhands now worked diligently all day under the direction of the young man. Soon the prosperity of the past had been regained and the farm was more profitable than ever. Ten years later—and no longer a young man—the farm owner found that he had used up his magic granules. In a panic, he visited the wise man and requested a new supply.

The wise man smiled and informed him that the magic granules were nothing but ordinary sand. The magic was not in the sack—but in the mind—of the young man. By paying attention to his farm and managing it properly, the farm owner had "magically" transformed his holdings to its former productivity and usefulness. Items 4–6 are this chapter's magic management granules.

SUMMARY

This summary is organized to correspond with the learning objectives found at the beginning of the chapter.

1. *Upper management* refers to the management hierarchy in a business who report directly to the president/chief executive officer of the enterprise. This group of managers is also known as "the management board," and is accountable for daily operations and the achievement of the profitability goals established by the board of directors on behalf of the stockholders.

2. The upper management view of the telecommunications department can be categorized into three areas: 1) a cost to be minimized, 2) a tactical asset that can be used to improve internal operating performance, or 3) a strategic asset that can help to increase sales. The information provided to upper management by telecommunications management will be a major factor in determining which view(s) is/are held.

3. Upper management is accountable for generating profits. The criteria they will use to assess organizational and managerial performance is based on the contribution made by managers to attain these profitability objectives. Managers who make contributions that help increase revenues and manage expenses will be recognized by upper management and will be rewarded accordingly. The contributions upper managers make will be determined based on the satisfaction of the manager's customers and the quality of the planning information. Three areas of interest for upper management are: 1) maintaining organizational profitability, 2) satisfying internal and external customers, and 3) having good plans for directing business activities.

4. The telecommunications department can support upper management's profitability objectives by providing innovative technology solutions for customer communication and by providing an internal communication infrastructure that enables the efficient and effective operation of department-level functions.

5. Communication with upper management should be business-oriented, should avoid the use of technical jargon, and should include accounting information to justify telecommunications investment recommendations. If the appearance and style of the communication is inappropriate for an upper management audience, they may never bother reading the content of the message.

6. The "mom and pop" management concept refers to managing a department as though it were a personal business. The owner (manager) should know all operating details and should be accountable for adapting to changes in the business environment. Success will be measured based on the revenue (budget) received by the department and the services provided to internal customers.

7. A telecommunications manager needs a strong set of interpersonal communications, mathematics, computing, management, business, and technology skills. Formal education provides basic skills, but most managerial skills are self taught and must be applied in real-world applications. Knowledge, experience, and a personal desire for excellence are the key ingredients for becoming an outstanding telecommunications manager.

KEY TERMS AND CONCEPTS

The language of telecommunications management is multifaceted and includes words and phrases from managerial, technological, accounting, regulatory, and other business areas. The definitions of these key terms and concepts can be found within the chapter and in the text glossary.

Administrative Services Manager
Appraisal Process
Automatic Call Distributor (ACD)
Board of Directors
Bona Fide Manager
Business
Chargeback Systems
Corporate Structure
Current Performance
Customer Satisfaction

Development Manager
Downsizing
Facilitator
Help Desk Manager
Leveraging
Leveraging Expenses
Management Board
Manager of Managers
Managerial Scoring System
Managerial Success

Managerial Toolset
Mom and Pop
Operations Manager
Planning Manager
Reengineer
Stockholders
Three Views of Telecommunications
Upper Management
World Wide Web (WWW)

REVIEW

The following questions are open-ended—predefined answers are not included as part of the text. The purpose of these questions is to allow the readers to test themselves on the chapter material.

1. Describe criteria for achieving managerial success.
2. Why should a telecommunications manager understand the employee appraisal process?
3. Describe a generic telecommunications business.
4. What do planning managers do?
5. What do development managers do?
6. What do operations managers do?
7. What do administrative service managers do?
8. What do help desk managers do?
9. What do managers of managers do?
10. Why don't manager titles accurately define what a manager does?
11. What are bona fide managers?
12. What are the positive aspects of becoming a telecommunications manager?
13. What are the potential downsides of becoming a telecommunications manager?
14. Describe the managerial scoring system.
15. Describe the corporate organization structure.
16. What is the role of a corporation's owners/stockholders?
17. What is the role of a board of directors?
18. What is the role of the management board?
19. Who is upper management?
20. Discuss the three upper management managerial success factors.
21. How can a manager help to meet a business's profitability objectives?
22. How can telecommunications be used to support a business's profitability objectives?
23. What is a drawback associated with downsizing to meet profitability objectives?
24. What is the difference between downsizing and reengineering?
25. How can telecommunications expenses be leveraged?
26. How does upper management obtain customer satisfaction information?
27. Why is planning an important managerial skill?
28. Describe the three views upper management may have of the telecommunications department.
29. Describe the general characteristics of good managerial communication.
30. Describe the format, style, and content attributes of business communication.
31. What is technical jargon?
32. Describe the mom and pop operating philosophy.
33. What is the difference between a craftsman and a journeyman?
34. What is a managerial toolset? (Define, then provide an example.)

MULTIPLE CHOICE

1. _____ managers are responsible for maintaining systems and equipment.
   a. Planning
   b. Development
   c. Operations
   d. Administrative services
   e. Help desk

2. _____ managers are responsible for developing strategic technology forecasts.
   a. Planning
   b. Development
   c. Operations
   d. Administrative services
   e. Help desk

3. _____ managers are responsible facilitating the telecommunications problem resolution process.
   a. Planning
   b. Development
   c. Operations
   d. Administrative services
   e. Help desk

4. _____ managers are responsible for the design and implementation of large telecommunications projects.
   a. Planning
   b. Development
   c. Operations
   d. Administrative services
   e. Help desk

5. _____ managers are responsible for providing support services to telecommunications customers and for auditing user billing.
   a. Planning
   b. Development
   c. Operations
   d. Administrative services
   e. Help desk

6. The term 24×7 is frequently applicable to _____.
   a. technical design projects
   b. performance appraisal efforts
   c. employee development programs
   d. a universal calendar
   e. network center operations

7. A manager of managers is frequently found in small telecommunications departments.
   a. true
   b. false

8. Bona fide managers _____. (Select all that apply.)
   a. appraise employee performance
   b. have no direct reports
   c. provide training opportunities
   d. administer raises
   e. none of the above

9. The unit of measure for measuring business success is _____.
   a. speed
   b. response time
   c. time duration
   d. dollars
   e. capacity

10. The business criteria for success is _____.
   a. innovation
   b. sales volume
   c. profitability
   d. number of employees
   e. number of locations

11. The owners of large corporations are _____.
   a. the board of directors
   b. the management board
   c. upper management
   d. the stockholders
   e. the employees

12. The _____ establishes a corporation's business policies and declares dividends.
   a. the board of directors
   b. the management board
   c. upper management
   d. the stockholders
   e. the employees

13. The _____ implements a corporation's business policies and has responsibility for managing day-to-day operations.
   a. the board of directors
   b. the management board
   c. the stockholders
   d. the employees
   e. the telecommunications department

14. Telecommunications management can help upper management meet profitability objectives by _____.
   a. investing in new systems
   b. using the latest technology
   c. installing computer networks
   d. reducing telecommunications expenses

15. The two basic ways of increasing business profitability are by _____ and _____.
    a. increasing expenses
    b. reducing expenses
    c. increasing revenues
    d. decreasing revenues
    e. making capital investments

16. When upper management finds that profitability objectives are not being met it could be due to _____. (Select all that apply.)
    a. low expense forecasts
    b. high expense forecasts
    c. low revenue forecasts
    d. high revenue forecasts
    e. capital forecasts

17. When ATMs were initially introduced, they _____. (Select all that apply.)
    a. increased operating expenses
    b. reduced operating expenses
    c. increased revenues
    d. reduced revenues
    e. reduced capital investments

18. The normal response to reduced profitability by upper management is to _____.
    a. increase expenses
    b. reduce expenses
    c. increase revenues
    d. reduce revenues
    e. increase capital investments

19. The largest budget item in most department budgets is _____ expenses.
    a. capital investment
    b. office equipment
    c. property tax
    d. employee payroll and benefits
    e. outside services

20. When leveraging telecommunications expenses, an increase in telecommunications expenses must be offset by _____.
    a. an increase in telecommunications expenses
    b. a decrease in telecommunications expenses
    c. a decrease in operating revenues
    d. an increase in nontelecommunications expenses
    e. a decrease in nontelecommunications expenses

21. Upper management can view telecommunications in three ways: (Select all that apply.)
    a. an expense to be increased
    b. an expense to be minimized
    c. an internal productivity tool
    d. an external productivity tool
    e. a strategic resource

22. Business communication *format* refers to _____.
    a. what it says
    b. why it is written
    c. how it looks
    d. how it reads
    e. the operating environment

23. Written business communication *style* refers to _____.
    a. what it says
    b. why it is written
    c. how it looks
    d. how it reads
    e. the operating environment

24. Business communication *content* refers to _____.
    a. what it says
    b. why it is written
    c. how it looks
    d. how it reads
    e. the operating environment

25. *Business language* consists of _____. (Select all that apply.)
    a. accounting information
    b. headings
    c. computer generated reports
    d. basic grammar
    e. stockholder reports

26. In a mom and pop operating environment, proprietors relied on _____ to manage their businesses.
    a. accounting reports
    b. cash drawer management
    c. budget *v.* actual reports
    d. profit and loss statements
    e. stockholder reports

5

TELECOMMUNICATIONS MANAGER SKILL REQUIREMENTS

1. Understand the differences between *knowledge* and *skills*.

2. Understand the "catch 22" implications when people without experience apply for positions in telecommunications.

3. Understand the importance of attitude when attempting to achieve success as a telecommunications manager.

4. Understand types of skills included in *enabling skills* and their relationships to project management and business management skills.

5. Understand the types of skills included as *basic academic skills* and understand how they are obtained.

6. Understand the value of higher education skills and know the most important element in that skill set.

7. Understand the nature of business skills and how they are acquired.

8. Understand the types of PC application skills that businesses expect employees to have, and understand their use as personal productivity tools.

9. Understand the key requirements for effective business communication and the importance of format and style when communicating with upper management.

An old proverb states that "knowledge is power," and this wisdom has been restated many times. Franklin D. Roosevelt once (humorously) observed that, "A man who has never gone to school may steal from a freight car, but if he has a university education he may steal the whole railroad." John F. Kennedy made a more realistic observation, "The greater our knowledge increases the more our ignorance unfolds." The Swiss novelist and poet, Hermann Hesse noted, "Knowledge can be communicated but not wisdom."

To be successful as a telecommunications manager, knowledge is required. However, this is simply restating the conventional wisdom regarding the power of knowledge. Realistically, the ability to successfully leverage knowledge will be influenced by two factors: 1) the type of knowledge someone has, and 2) the ability of an individual to apply the knowledge effectively. The former is a matter of formal education or training while the latter is gained through experience. The level of success in acquiring knowledge and being able to apply it effectively will be influenced by an individual's attitude. This chapter will discuss knowledge, skills, and attitudes and how they apply to the telecommunications management department.

TELECOMMUNICATIONS MANAGEMENT AND CATCH-22

In Joseph Heller's satire written about World War II, *Catch-22*, he described a situation where a pilot in a bomber group became aware that his personal behavior is becoming abnormal. The pilot is concerned that he will go over the edge during a bombing flight and that this could result in the death of himself and his bomber crew. He expresses these concerns to the base psychiatrist and requests preventative treatment to avoid having a mental breakdown. However, the base psychiatrist has administrative guidelines he must use for addressing psychiatric problems involving flight crews, and these guidelines result in the classic catch-22 scenario, where following the rules for solving a problem eliminates the possibility of solving the problem.

In Heller's *Catch-22* environment, flights take place every day, and heavy casualties are normal. Only a very small percentage of the pilots flying these bombing runs ever survive to complete the required number of flights that would allow them to be rotated out of the group. It is not unusual for flight members to lose touch with reality during a bombing run, be classified as insane upon their return (if the plane makes it back), and be sent home for mental treatment. The base psychiatrist meets with all flight members on a regular basis for the purpose of finding those who can be classified as being insane so they can be sent home.

The *Catch-22* bomber pilot has flown more than 80% of the required flights, finds that he is unable to concentrate on normal activities, and has developed unreasonable fears about simple, daily matters. He is concerned that he may go insane during a flight and cause the death of his flight crew—an event that is not uncommon in this squadron. Therefore, he meets with the base psychiatrist to get excused from making additional flights until he has received the appropriate treatment.

The psychiatrist is extremely sympathetic but informs the pilot of a military regulation—*Catch-22*—stating that any pilot who is rational enough to want treatment cannot possibly be insane and is therefore fit to fly. Following the *Catch-22* rule only allows treatment for mental illness after the breakdown takes place. Therefore, if the breakdown occurs during a flight, it is necessary for the individual to return—unless the individual who breaks down is the bomber pilot. In this case, a crash is likely and any possibility of followup treatment is eliminated. In the novel, following the *Catch-22* rule did not allow the base psychiatrist to prescribe treatment until an individual has a mental breakdown—that is, the rule did not allow the physician to prevent psychiatric problems.

The Telecommunications Catch-22

How does this relate to telecommunications management? Consider the following scenario for individuals beginning their career in telecommunications. One of the questions all prospective employers ask of an applicant is to list their experience in telecommunications. Applicants without experience are frequently eliminated from further consideration because they don't have the necessary experience, hence the telecommunications **Catch-22.**

> The **telecommunications catch-22**—Human resources personnel have instructions to hire only people with experience. *How can someone without experience gain experience if they won't be hired because they don't have experience?*

Fortunately, there is a way to break the circular reasoning pattern of the telecommunications catch-22 scenario. It involves getting the necessary educational credentials to act as a substitute for the experience factor. A degree that covers telecommunications topics can provide the credentials needed for entry into the telecommunications field, because it is viewed as an acceptable alternative for the human resources gateway screening function. Once entry has been granted to compete for a position, it will then be necessary to convince the decision maker(s) that you are the best candidate in the pool of prospective employees.

KNOWLEDGE *V.* SKILL

Being able to speak an ancient Greek dialect fluently is not likely to help someone to manage a telecommunications department. However, the individual effort required to acquire knowledge about an ancient Greek dialect is significant, and someone having knowledge of the dialect may be valuable in a university environment where the study of ancient Greece is part of a degree program.

In addition, having a knowledge of an ancient Greek language will not make someone a fluent speaker of the language. The ability to speak fluently requires developing a speaking skill, which is applying what has been learned. Learning to speak the ancient Greek dialect fluently will require a combination of knowledge, training, and experience. The likelihood of finding a good speaking environment for practicing ancient Greek is low.

> **skill**: Something that requires training and experience to do well.

To be successful as a telecommunications manager requires a person to have a broad set of skills—not to simply have good knowledge. The ability to translate telecommunications technology into a business asset is the underlying skill that will determine success as a telecommunications manager within a business.

A Skill Framework

This chapter will review different skills that are needed to achieve success in telecommunications management. Many of these skills will require a knowledge base found in an academic subject and applying them to solve real world problems. In a 1974 *Harvard Business Review* article written by Robert L. Katz, entitled "Skills of an Effective Administrator," he discussed the requirements for being a successful business executive. The article identified three skill areas:

- **technical skills**
- **human skills**
- **conceptual skills**

While the article focused on the skill requirements needed to be an outstanding performer in an upper management (executive) position, the three areas identified in the article are applicable to all managerial and technical positions. A brief discussion of the Katz skill framework will be used to provide the readers a perspective for developing their own individual skills.

Note: The Katz article and its application to the telecommunications management area will be discussed in greater detail in Chapter 7, *Managerial Tools and Techniques*.[1]

TECHNICAL SKILLS.   In the Katz article, technical skills are those skills that might be categorized as "subject matter skills"—topics that are normally learned in an educational environment. These skills would include English, writing, speech, mathematics, humanities, or telecommunications technology. Subject matter skills are normally assessed by using some form of testing, which is a common way to determine an individual's subject matter skill. The tests may be written or oral, and students are assigned a grade based on their test results.

It is important to note that the term *technical skill* in the Katz article does not mean a technology skill but a skill in a specific area—typically a subject or a course. Most of the skills discussed in this chapter will be referring to "technical skills"—skills acquired in a course or subject context.

HUMAN SKILLS.   Human skills refer to skills that involve interpersonal communication with people from different social or business levels. Human skills may vary depending upon the audience, and having effective skills when dealing with one type of audience does not ensure that someone will be equally effective when dealing with other audiences. Human skills in the Katz article can be referred to as *influencing skills*—skills that allow an individual to influence others. To be an effective influencer of others typically means that the influencer is viewed to be credible and trustworthy.

Although an individual may have strong technical skills in English, speech, and written composition, it does not mean that the person will have strong influencing skills. Someone who has strong technical skills in communication may have great difficulty communicating with others, while someone who has marginal technical skills may have outstanding skills managing others and working as a team member.

---

[1] Katz, Robert L. 1974. "Skills of an Effective Administrator," *Harvard Business Review 52*(5): 90–102.

CONCEPTUAL SKILLS. As defined in the Katz article, **conceptual skills** refers to the ability of an executive to understand the business as a whole, while also understanding the interrelationships of all the functional departments. From a telecommunications management context, this same view could apply to upper level managers, because an upper-level telecommunications manager would be a business executive.

However, the conceptual skills—the ability to see the total picture while understanding the elements included in the picture—applies to all complex managerial and technical areas. The need for having technical, human, and conceptual skills would apply to all telecommunications managers, but the areas of emphasis would differ, depending upon the area of responsibility and managerial level.

KEYS TO PERSONAL SUCCESS

The bottom line is that the likelihood of being successful in telecommunications management will be based on a combination of attitude and skills. Good **attitude** traits include having a desire to learn new things, being a self-starter, having the ability to adapt to change, viewing problems as opportunities, and being able to constructively motivate others to carry out required tasks and activities.

Formal education provides a knowledge foundation, but success in any field requires the effective application of knowledge—you must develop skills by gaining experience and applying knowledge. Developing telecommunications management skills requires a personal commitment to a lifetime learning process. You must also learn to accommodate the changes that inevitably are a part of life. Without a positive attitude, there is little likelihood that this lifetime commitment to change can be fulfilled.

The advice, "Show up on time and be ready to play," is also appropriate for telecommunications managers. In this instance, "be ready to play" means having the necessary skills (Figure 5–1) to effectively carry out telecommunications management responsibilities, and "be on time" means doing the right things at the right time.

Attitude

In organized sports, a competitive hierarchy exists in which athletes begin competing at lower competitive levels in the sport, then advance to playing at higher skill levels as their own skills improve. Many athletes will find their competitive niche at some intermediate level in the competitive hierarchy and will never rise above that level.

A few will find that their skills place them at the top level of the competitive hierarchy, and these individuals will have the option of becoming a professional player and will be able to make a living by playing the sport.

While skill requirements may vary from sport to sport, all competitive sports typically require some minimal level of physical skills before individuals can begin learning the sport. If someone is unable to run more than fifteen feet without being out of breath, there is no chance that that he or she will play in any competitive sport involving running—regardless of his or her book knowledge about how the sport is played.

In sports, there is an additional factor: attitude. Having a great deal of talent is only part of the formula for achieving team success. Attitude is the other key ingredient. To become team players, players must be coachable—they must be willing to follow instructions from a coach. Typically, coaches require players to follow a rigorous training program to sharpen physical skills while learning how to coordinate his or her efforts with other team members. Players without the right attitude are a liability in team sports and are unlikely to advance in a team sports hierarchy unless they achieve an individual superstar status. Players with outstanding physical skills who won't coordinate their efforts with other team members will be passed over in favor of players who coordinate their efforts with team members and focus on helping the team.

In the telecommunications management game, there are entry level skills that are required before you will be selected to "play"—be promoted to a managerial position. However, as is the case for sports players, enabling skills are only part of the requirement to become a management team player. The other factor is attitude. Attitude in a telecommunications management context means being willing to work with others, support organizational objectives, and do whatever is necessary to achieve organizational success. You must be willing and able to do what it takes to achieve telecommunications objectives presented by your superiors.

Attitude is #1

Telecommunications is a complex field driven by computer technology that is updated every twenty-four months. As a result, telecommunications managers must continually update their technology skills and business management skills. Managerial philosophies have undergone radical changes during the last thirty years in response to major changes in the demographic composition of the workforce and to changes in the business environment. These changes mean that a manager must continually assess the application of business management tools

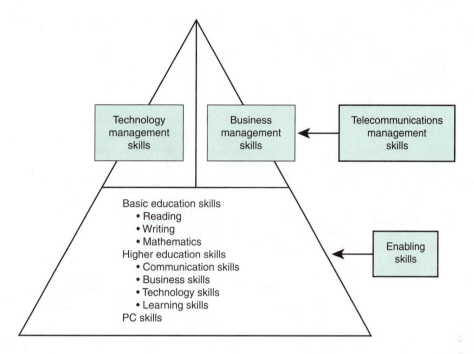

Figure 5–1. Telecommunications manager skill requirements.

to ensure that the appropriate tools and methods are applied to managerial situations.

Having a good attitude means having a positive attitude toward change and having a positive attitude when dealing with others. Telecommunications managers need a positive attitude toward people, technology, and the changes that the future will bring. Without a positive attitude, managers will have negative feelings about themselves, their jobs, and their subordinates. In turn, subordinates who find themselves working in a negative environment will typically assume these characteristics so they can fit in.

Enabling Skills

A telecommunications manager needs managerial skills in business management and technology management. However, these two skill areas are simply part of the skill requirement for aspiring telecommunications managers (or anyone entering a complex profession). Unless someone already has a strong set of **enabling skills** prior to addressing business and technology management skill topics, there is a low likelihood of being able to successfully learn new skills.

Enabling skills are the skills that allow an individual to learn and apply technology and business management skills. Enabling skills include:

• basic education skills (reading, writing, and mathematics)

• higher education skills

• business skills

• business communication skills

• personal computer skills

Figure 5–1 provides a graphical representation of the enabling skills needed to develop technology and business management skills and shows enabling skills as the base that supports the telecommunications management skills. Geometrically, Figure 5–1 is clearly a stable configuration when telecommunications management skills have been placed on top of a broad base of enabling skills.

On the other hand, if someone's enabling skill base was weak, the analogous geometric shape would be as shown in Figure 5–2. Any attempt to rest Figure 5–2 on a surface using the enabling skill base would be an adventure with unpredictable results. The geometric analogy applies to the skill structure shown in Figures 5–1 and 5–2. A broad base of enabling skills is a prerequisite for being able to develop good business and technology management skills.

Basic Academic Skills

Public secondary school (high school) education was rare in the U.S. until 1874, when a Michigan supreme court decision ruled that the city of Kalamazoo was allowed to use local property taxes to support high school educational

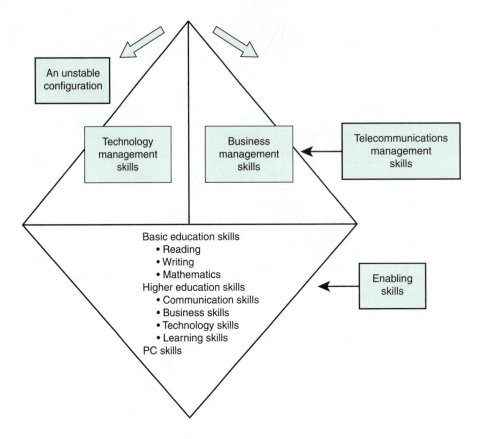

Figure 5–2. Figure 5–1 skills with a weak enabling skill base.

programs. The basic academic skills referenced in this section's heading refers to the "Three Rs"—the reading, 'riting, and 'rithmetic—topics covered in a sound elementary, middle, and secondary school education program.

Telecommunications is a complex, technical subject, and a telecommunications manager must have knowledge that covers a wide range of topics. The ability to effectively learn these topics assumes a prerequisite level of strong verbal and written communication skills. Students attending secondary schools are offered a range of educational opportunities, and a student can graduate with minimal skills or advanced skills. Basic academic skills from the perspective of this text means that a student has mastered the following secondary school subjects:

- English (four years)
- social studies
- humanities
- general science, biology, and chemistry
- elementary algebra, geometry, and trigonometry
- intermediate algebra, introduction to calculus

A student who has done a good job of acquiring skills in these knowledge areas is well equipped to advance to higher education and develop telecommunications management skills. Key skills for understanding any technology are the English skills (grammar, verbal, reading, and writing) and mathematics skills (algebra, geometry, trigonometry, and calculus). Aspiring telecommunications managers who find that their secondary education is weak must address these weaknesses if their objective is to achieve long term success in the telecommunications field.

A practical translation of the academic course listing is that an individual entering the telecommunications field should be able to:

- read, write, and speak effectively
- perform mathematical calculations and operations
- apply scientific method concepts, including deductive and inductive reasoning processes

While technology-oriented students tend to discount the importance of non technical subjects, nothing is further from the truth. Unless someone has the ability to understand written text, to clearly communicate thoughts, or to think logically (this normally requires mathematics-oriented thinking), it is unlikely that someone will be able to learn technology skills, business management skills, or any other complex skill.

READING SKILLS. Technical information is found in publications. It is normal for someone working on a technical project to be given a stack of publications when he or she asks, "How does it work?" Most of an individual's real world technical knowledge is gained through on-the-job training, and the primary tool for on-the-job training is being able to extract information from difficult-to-read, technical descriptions. Even accessing Web-based information requires the ability to comprehend written material. An individual who has good reading comprehension skills has a major competitive advantage over his or her peers who have weaker skills.

A telecommunications manager will receive a never ending stream of correspondence from superiors, peers, employees, and vendors. The ability to read and interpret written correspondence quickly is an essential skill for handling the technical and managerial responsibilities of a telecommunications manager.

WRITING SKILLS. Managers and technical personnel who know what has to be done and can communicate with others clearly have a much higher probability of successfully implementing large, complex projects. In today's e-mail oriented environment, there is an even greater need for writing skills—one must minimize verbiage while clearly and completely communicating important information.

Business communication differs from creative writing, even though creativity is encouraged in business documents. There is a general business writing style that should be followed for business communication. The style will be discussed in a section entitled *Business Communication*. Many businesses have documented standards for their internal written communication requirements, and failure to follow them can relegate a document to the "round file" (a.k.a. waste basket) without being read.

> **Mathematics**: The study of relationships between numbers, shapes, and quantities. Mathematics uses signs, symbols, and proofs and includes the study of arithmetic, algebra, geometry, and calculus.

MATHEMATICS SKILLS. The importance of mathematics in not limited to being able to perform mathematical calculations, it also includes the ability to see relationships between apparently diverse logical elements. Individuals who have strong mathematics skills have an advantage when learning telecommunications technology because technology is based on the use of mathematics. Unless someone has good mathematics skills, his or her technical understanding of telecommunications will be limited. Logical thinking processes are valuable for dealing with people issues and telecommunications issues. The knowledge provided by humanities subjects also are useful.

SUMMARY. The basic education skills—reading, writing, and mathematics—provide a stable infrastructure on which telecommunications management knowledge can be built. Weakness in basic education areas will undermine an individual's efforts to achieve success in a complex field like telecommunications. Someone focusing only on telecommunications topics, without having a good foundation of basic education skills, will find that on-the-job learning can be extremely difficult.

Higher Education Skills

The term *higher education* refers to the academic work completed in a college or university setting. Successful completion of a college program will earn someone a bachelor's degree in a four year program or an associate's degree in a two year program. Degrees are available in both telecommunications management and telecommunications technology areas.

Breaking The Telecommunications Catch-22 Cycle. College degrees break the catch-22 cycle. Human resources departments see a degree in telecommunications as a substitute for experience, and will place job applicants who have degrees in the competition queue for internal telecommunications jobs. From a human resources perspective, a bachelor's degree has significantly higher value than an associate's degree. Aspiring telecommunications managers who have an associate's degree should view the associate's degree as a stepping stone to a bachelor's degree. In today's business environment, a bachelor's degree should be earned as soon as possible because a four year degree is frequently a job requirement for managerial jobs—particularly higher-level positions.

A telecommunications degree in a management or technology program can provide the necessary credentials for aspiring telecommunications managers. While degrees in other topics may be used for entry into telecommunications, the advantage of having a telecommunications-oriented education should be obvious. An approach that could be used by someone with a bachelor of business administration degree would be to get a master of telecommunications degree. This approach could also provide the necessary credentials to break the telecommunications catch-22 cycle.

Someone interested in obtaining a degree in telecommunications can use Web access to various schools that offer degree programs. The program requirements for many schools can be accessed through the school's home page, and a comparison of program topics can easily be made.

LEARNING SKILLS: THE REAL OBJECTIVE.

Someone who receives a bachelor of telecommunications degree also receives another benefit—a performance track record. A telecommunications degree program is a difficult undertaking that requires ability, commitment, and perseverance. Frequently, these personal attributes are more important to prospective employers than the specific telecommunications subjects that an individual has taken as part of the program.

There is a low likelihood that anyone who has a technology-based education will directly utilize more 15% of the degree's course content during his or her careers. This is not because the program is flawed. It is due to the reality that it is impossible to accurately predict the work environment that individuals will encounter during their careers. However, this does not mean that learning unused skills is a waste of time. On the contrary, the ability to learn a wide variety of subjects is the primary value of higher education. The most important skill acquired while earning a degree is to learn how to learn.

Learning skills include the ability to: 1) extract information from books, Internet home pages, and other information sources, 2) comprehend the meaning of the extracted information, and 3) effectively apply this knowledge within a wide range of contexts. There is a very low likelihood that specific answers for any business or technology problem will be found in a text. (If the answer does exist, which text will contain it?) The educational process provides students with an opportunity to develop learning skills. Applying these learning skills will have a greater influence on the long-term performance and success of individuals than the subject matter they covered in their degree programs

In the real world, managers and employees are normally given problems without being given answers or potential answers. Employers expect a good manager to evaluate problem situations, identify alternative solutions, and select a solution that best meets short- and long-term requirements. When technical issues are involved, the answer is frequently embedded in technical manuals that contain a stream of "techno-babble" that is difficult to understand. The same "fuzzy focus" exists when business management problems arise.

Managers who have the ability to evaluate a specific problem situation (technical or managerial) research the background information needed to solve the problem, and successfully implement solutions have the qualities desired by prospective employers. Employers are not looking for managers who can memorize problem-solution pairings and do well on multiple choice tests. Employers are looking for highly motivated individuals who learn quickly, use current information to solve problems, and implement these solutions within budgeted resources and time constraint of a given situation.

The key is to learn quickly. Unless someone has strong learning skills, there is a low likelihood that the problem solving stage can be reached—much less carried out effectively.

Business Skills

The term *business skills* refers to knowledge about the business environment that exists outside of the telecommunications department. It includes knowing the roles and responsibilities of the other departments commonly found in a business—sales, marketing, human resources, accounting, manufacturing, purchasing, customer services, and accounts receivable. Having good business skills also implies that someone has a good knowledge about the external business environment outside of the internal organization—economic conditions, competitors, customers, suppliers, transportation, and international communications.

Basic business skills should be part of telecommunications management degree requirements. A student earning a bachelor of telecommunication degree is expected to understand the context of how telecommunications products and services are used. This requires a knowledge of business structure and a knowledge of the general responsibilities of different business departments. The selection of communication services for internal customers must be matched to their business needs, and these needs are best understood by knowing the different tasks performed by them.

ACCOUNTING SKILLS.

The level of business knowledge required by telecommunications managers will vary according their roles and responsibilities. Regardless of the level of business knowledge required by managers, all managers need a good understanding of accounting. For lower-level positions, knowledge of internal budgeting procedures is extremely important. At higher levels, knowledge of external reports—profit and loss statements or balance sheets—takes on increased importance in addition to understanding budgeting requirements.

Accounting covers a wide range of topics—managerial accounting, standard cost accounting, financial accounting, accounts payable, and accounts receivable. It also includes the technical accounting processes that generate profit and loss statements, balance sheets, budget *v.* actual reports, and capital appropriations.

ACCOUNTING—THE LANGUAGE OF BUSINESS.

Not only is knowledge of accounting topics and processes required for accountants, it is important knowledge for all business managers to have. Telecommunications managers must understand how to use and apply accounting information so they can control costs, purchase assets, and communicate effectively with upper management.

Accounting terminology is the standard language of business. Investment proposals made by different departments must be translated into the appropriate accounting cost *v.* benefit format used by the organization. Upper management uses the cost *v.* benefit format to determine where critical financial resources will be invested. If telecommunications investment proposals are not presented in the correct format, the chance of receiving funding is lowered.

> To communicate effectively with upper management, aspiring telecommunications managers must commit themselves to learning the financial language used by upper management—accounting processes and procedures.

PC Skills

Businesses expect their employees to be PC literate and, more specifically, to know how to use IBM-compatible PCs. IBM-compatible PCs dominate the market, and the majority of existing PC software applications are designed for them. Prospective employees are expected to know how to navigate within a Windows environment and to have a good working knowledge of the PC applications used in a normal business office environment: word processing, spreadsheet, presentation, graphics, Web browser, and e-mail applications.

Upper management is accustomed to receiving information in a highly sophisticated format. At meetings with upper management, multimedia projectors are used to present information that has been formatted with PC soft-

ware applications. Documentation is professional in appearance and contains tables, graphs, and other pictorial information—frequently in full color.

Telecommunications managers have the responsibility for conducting meetings and for providing high-quality documentation. In the pre-PC era, secretarial support services were used to create meeting and document deliverables. Today, PC applications are used to create meeting documents and slides. Managers who know how to generate their own documentation have two major advantages over those who cannot:

1. documentation preparation time is shorter
2. last minute changes are easy to make

The bottom line is, managers who create their own documentation are more productive than those who rely on support personnel, because fewer people are involved in the documentation effort and the communication time required between multiple parties is eliminated.

The PC applications that a telecommunications manager should know fall into three general categories:

- general purpose office applications
- e-mail and Web browser applications
- special purpose applications

The following provides an overview of how PCs evolved to their current status as personal computing tools, and reviews the applications referenced in the list above.

THE PC'S BEGINNING.

At the beginning of the 1980s, PCs were seen as "technical toys" by business management. After all, IBM knew computers and IBM knew the business needs of its customers. If PCs had any merit for use in a business environment, IBM would let them know about it. Until that happened, business managers would continue to rely on IBM mainframe computers to run business software applications and let children and techies play with PCs.

In the early 1980s, some accountants were bringing in PCs to run a PC-based software product called **VisiCalc**—an application introduced by Apple in 1978. VisiCalc could perform all the calculations made by financial systems run on mainframe computers—but at the convenience of the accountant. Mainframe computers shared limited processing resources with many users, but this sharing philosophy had a price. Only a limited number of applications could be run at one time, and they had to be run sequentially to maximize the utilization of the mainframe computer processor. Financial systems had their scheduled times, and it was too expensive to interrupt the

```
Date:      Month 00, 0000

To:        Recipient
From:      Sender
Re:        Subject

[Purpose]
Text of first paragraph [begin flush left with no indentation]. xxxxxxxxxxxxxxxxxxxxxxxxxxxxxxxxxxxxxxxxx
xxxxxxxxxxxxxxxxxxxxxxxxxxxxxxxxxxxxxxxxxxxxxxxxxxxxxxxxxxxxxxx.

[Details—bold heading]
Text of second paragraph. xxxxxxxxxxxxxxxxxxxxxxxxxxxxxxxxxxxxxxxxxxxxxxxxxxxxxxxxxxxxxxxxxxxxxxxx
xxxxxxxxxxxxxxxxxxxxxxxxxxxxxxxxxxxxxxxxxxxxxxxxxxxxxxxxxxxxxxx.

Details Subheading(s)
Text for subtopic of second paragraph. xxxxxxxxxxxxxxxxxxxxxxxxxxxxxxxxxxxxxxxxxxxxxxxxxxxxxxxxxxxxx
xxxxxxxxxxxxxxxxxxxxxxxxxxxxxxxxxxxxxxxxxxxxxxxxxxxxxxxxxx.

[Details—bold heading]
Text of third main paragraph using bulleted list:
• first point
• second point
• third point
(Subordinate points expressed as bulleted lists provide visual relief and guide the reader.)

[Impact—bold heading]
xxxxxxxxxxxxxxxxxxxxxxxxxxxxxxxxxxxxxxxxxxxxxxxxxxxxxxxxxxxxxxxxxxxxxxxxxxxxxxxxxxxxxxxxxxxxxxx
xxxxxxxxxxxxxxxxxxxxxxxxxxxxxxxxxxxxxxxxxxxxxxxxxxxxxxxxxxxxxxx

[Action/Conclusion—bold heading]
Text of conclusion. xxxxxxxxxxxxxxxxxxxxxxxxxxxxxxxxxxxxxxxxxxxxxxxxxxxxxxxxxxxxxxxxxxxxxxxxxxxxxxx
xxxxxxxxxxxxxxxxxxxxxxxxxxxxxxxxxxxxxxxxxxxxxxxxxxxxxxxxxxxxxxx
```

Figure 5–3.   Business memo format guideline.

tion into a format that is easy for a reader to follow and understand. All word processing applications provide a simple table creation option. Tables can be used to present a wide range of information. They can contain detailed expense and capital forecast budget information while also providing summary and grand total information.

Network drawings developed with a graphics package can display a complex network and can be used to highlight detailed elements within the drawing. The use of network graphics for a nontechnical audience should be done carefully because an overuse of network graphics can overwhelm, confuse, or alienate a nontechnical audience.

CONTENT.   Content is determined by the topic. The preceding format and style guidelines can be used to present the content effectively, but the responsibility for selecting appropriate content is a writer's responsibility.

Poor content can be hidden only temporarily within a good format and style. Just as the best ideas may be sidetracked because poor judgment is used when selecting formatting and style elements, the worst ideas can get sold because of excellent packaging. However, a poorly conceived idea will fail, regardless of the packaging (format and style) that was used to gain its approval.

Business Writing Examples

Up to this point, the discussion has been largely theoretical and subject to interpretation. The following provides examples of the use of format and style elements discussed previously:

Figure 5–3: A general format example

Figure 5–4: Figure 5–3 applied to a business memo

Date: August 14, 2004

To: Isaac Newton, Vice President of Finance
From: I.M. Analyst
Subject: Year 2005 Telecommunications Forecast Recommendation

The following provides a preliminary forecast recommendation for ABC Company telecommunications expenses for the fiscal year 2005. The year 2005 expense forecast is $485,004, which represents a 0.2% increase above year 2004 expense estimates.

Background

The ABC Company currently has 217 telephones installed. All ABC Company telecommunications expenses are charged back to the using departments, which are provided with monthly Budget *v.* Actual reports for the following expense categories:

- long distance calling charges
- local calling charges
- station equipment charges
- PBX equipment charges
- OCC (charges for equipment adds, moves, or changes)
- misc (telephone office lines and nonstandard charges)

Year 2005 Forecast

Based on year to date information, it is estimated year 2004 expenses will be $484,149 (Appendix A provides details for these expenses). The year 2005 forecast is based on using the year 2004 annual expenses estimates and modifying them to reflect rate changes and internal usage trends. (Because the staffing forecast provided by the accounting department is flat, it has been assumed that the number of telephone extensions will not change next year.) Expense forecasts have been reviewed with the various department managers.

Detailed forecast information is provided in Appendix B.

2004 Expense Estimate v. 2005 Expense Forecast

A comparison between current year expense estimates and the year 2005 expense forecast is provided in the following table. A 0.2% expense increase has been incorporated into the 2005 forecast.

Department	# Extns	Total ($)	Basic ($)	Eqpt ($)	Local ($)	LngDst ($)	OCC ($)	Misc ($)
2005 annual F/C summary	217	485,004	84,701	79,104	33,360	178,183	25,200	84,456
2004 annual est. summary	217	484,149	80,601	76,800	32,064	186,228	24,000	84,456
Difference ($)	0	855	4,100	2,304	1,296	(8,045)	1,200	0
Difference (%)	0.0%	0.2%	5.1%	3.0%	4.0%	−4.3%	5.0%	0.0%

Although long-distance call volumes are expected to increase by approximately 5%, the overall increase in long distance expenses will actually be reduced by $8,000 compared to 2004. This reduction is due to an 8% rate reduction negotiated with our new long distance provider.

Recommendations/Next Steps

It is recommended that the 2005 telecommunication forecast be accepted and included in the 2005 annual budget. A meeting will be set up for next Tuesday (August 22) to review these recommendations and address any questions you may have.

Figure 5–4. a) Business memo: page 1 of 3. b) Page 2 of 3.

Appendix A
Year 2004 Expense Estimate

Department	# Extns	Total ($)	Basic ($)	Eqpt ($)	Local ($)	LngDst ($)	OCC ($)	Misc ($)
Executive	20	30,017	7,429	7,800	1,464	11,112	2,212	0
Finance	12	33,876	4,457	7,500	1,368	12,324	1,327	6,900
Human resources	14	31,684	5,200	8,400	1,824	14,712	1,548	0
Information services	11	22,667	4,086	4,596	1,728	11,040	1,217	0
Marketing	107	299,689	39,743	38,700	10,764	121,092	11,834	77,556
Order processing	53	66,216	19,686	9,804	14,916	15,948	5,862	0
2004 Actual	**217**	**484,149**	**80,601**	**76,800**	**32,064**	**186,228**	**24,000**	**84,456**

2004 annual basic rate $371.43

Appendix B
Year 2005 Forecast

Department	# Extns	Total ($)	Basic ($)	Eqpt ($)	Local ($)	LngDst ($)	OCC ($)	Misc ($)
Executive	12	27,196	4,684	8,034	1,523	10,632	2,323	0
Finance	20	37,039	7,806	7,725	1,423	11,792	1,393	6,900
Human resources	14	31,716	5,465	8,652	1,898	14,076	1,625	0
Information services	11	22,667	4,294	4,734	1,798	10,563	1,278	0
Marketing	107	298,668	41,765	39,861	11,199	115,861	12,426	77,556
Order processing	53	67,718	20,687	10,098	15,519	15,259	6,155	0
2005 Forecast	**217**	**485,004**	**84,701**	**79,104**	**33,360**	**178,183**	**25,200**	**84,456**

2005 basic rate $390.32

Figure 5–4. c) Business memo: Page 3 of 3.

The general format example's (Figure 5–3) purpose provides a conceptual format, while Figure 5–4 provides a real world application of using the format in Figure 5–3. Additional examples will be provided in the case studies in Parts II, III, IV, and V. Electronic versions are included on the text's CD.

SUMMARY

This summary is organized to correspond with the learning objectives found at the beginning of the chapter.

1. Knowledge is normally acquired through formal education or training, while a skill is the application of knowledge so that a useful result is achieved. The differences between knowledge and skill are similar to the differences between data and information. Knowledge and data, by themselves, are without purpose; skill and information are useful applications of knowledge and data.

2. The telecommunications catch-22 scenario arises when someone who does not have experience applies for a telecommunications position. Because most human resources screening criteria require experience, the applicant will probably be rejected. Obtaining a degree in telecommunications can help break the catch-22 cycle.

3. Attitude includes intangibles such as being a self starter, being adaptable, viewing problems as opportunities, and being able to motivate others in a positive way. A good attitude is essential to personal achievement and working effectively with others.

4. While project management skills and business management skills are the primary skills required by a telecommunications manager, they can't be learned unless a strong foundation of enabling skills exists. Enabling skills include basic education skills, personal productivity skills, learning skills, and various business skills.

5. Basic academic skills are the skills provided by elementary, middle, and secondary education. A good secondary education would provide skills in reading, writing, mathematics, algebra, geometry, intermediate algebra, trigonometry, calculus, physics, chemistry, and biology.

6. The most important skill that higher education (college) can provide is the ability to learn—to independently acquire skills by reading and research. Most telecommunications job skills are gained by reading documents and technical publications. Telecommunications managers are expected to "figure things out" on their own with minimal—if any—guidance.

7. The term *business skills* refers to knowledge about the internal and external business environment outside of the telecommunications area. This includes understanding the roles and responsibilities of different departments found in a business, having strong skills in accounting practices and procedures, and understanding the impact that the external environment has on the success of a business.

8. PC application skills have become essential skills for succeeding in a business organization. These would include skills in Windows, word processing, spreadsheet, and presentation applications. In telecommunications, an understanding of network diagramming and project management software is also essential.

9. Effective communication with upper management must be clear, easy to read, unambiguous, concise, and timely. Failure to provide management with information presented in the appropriate format and style significantly lowers the probability that an upper-level manager will spend the time to read the document.

KEY TERMS AND CONCEPTS

The language of telecommunications management is multifaceted, and includes words and phrases from managerial, technological, accounting, regulatory, and other business areas. The definitions of these key terms and concepts can be found within the chapter and in the text's glossary.

Attitude	Content	Style
Business Writing	Enabling Skills	Technical Skills
Catch-22	Format	Upper Management
Conceptual Skills	Human Skills	VisiCalc

REVIEW

The following questions are open-ended, predefined answers are not included as part of the text. The purpose of these questions is to allow the readers to test themselves on the chapter material.

1. Explain the differences between knowledge and skill.

2. Based on the Katz article, provide definitions of technical skills, human skills, and conceptual skills.

3. What are technology management skills?

4. What are enabling skills?

5. How can education help overcome the telecommunications catch-22?

6. Provide examples of having a good attitude.

7. Why are reading skills important for technology managers?

8. Of what value are writing skills for technology managers?

9. What is the value of learning how to learn?

10. Why is it recommended that business communication be oriented toward upper management?

11. Provide definitions of format, style, and content as they apply to business writing.

12. Why does the text only provide a 20% weight value for the content of a business document?

13. How does the mnemonic AIDA relate to business writing?

14. List and describe the five elements in the "business style outline."

15. Why are PC skills important for a telecommunications manager?

16. Describe business skills and their value to a telecommunications manager.

17. Why are accounting skills important to a telecommunications manager?

MULTIPLE CHOICE

1. An example of an enabling skill is a(n) _____.
   a. project management skill
   b. organization management skill
   c. telecommunications management skill
   d. PC skill

2. Most of an individual's technical knowledge is gained through _____.
   a. formal education
   b. higher education
   c. self learning
   d. training courses

3. The term *Format*, as it applies to business writing, refers to _____.
   a. what it says
   b. how it looks
   c. how it reads
   d. creative writing
   e. why it is sent

4. Business writing _____.
   a. is similar to academic creative writing efforts
   b. is more tolerant of individual writing styles
   c. is less tolerant of individual writing styles
   d. does not require good grammar

5. The five business style outline sections include _____.
   a. tables, graphics, details, impact, and conclusions
   b. purpose, details, impact, and conclusions
   c. conclusion, impact, purpose, details, and appendix
   d. appendix, purpose, details, conclusions, and content

6. Business writing content has a _____ impact on likelihood that a document will be read.
   a. 10%
   b. 20%
   c. 30%
   d. 40%
   g. 50%

7. VisiCalc is a _____ software application.
   a. word processing
   b. presentation
   c. graphics
   d. spreadsheet
   e. project management

8. An example of a business writing format element is _____.
   a. the use of a layered writing style
   b. the technical details
   c. the use of different font styles
   d. providing next steps

9. "Intranet" refers to _____.
   a. the WWW
   b. Internet technology
   c. Web browsers
   d. the use of Internet technology for private networks

10. The standard language of business consists of _____.
    a. business communication
    b. accounting terminology
    c. technical standards
    d. WWW protocols

11. At lower managerial levels, the most important accounting knowledge is about _____.
    a. profit and loss statements
    b. balance sheets
    c. department budgets
    d. annual reports

TELECOMMUNICATIONS PLANNING

Part 1, *Telecommunications Management Basics*, provided an introduction to the subject of telecommunications management. It was prefaced by the suggestion that readers should possess a certain knowledge level prior to moving on to the topics presented in Parts 2 through 5. Basic skill set weaknesses should be addressed prior to continuing with the text, or should be covered concurrently while the text is being used as part of a broader program offering.

Telecommunications management is a multifaceted subject that requires an in-depth knowledge of business management, technology management, and telecommunications technology topics. This in-depth knowledge cannot be gained by reading any single text or by simply completing a formal education. The journey to becoming a skilled craftsman in the telecommunications management area is a lifelong commitment, during which new skills must constantly be developed to enhance or replace older skills.

A strong managerial and technology skill set is based upon the use of fundamental thinking processes with an emphasis on learning those concepts, methodologies, and procedures that can be applied on an as-needed basis to provide solutions to management problems. A good methodology will ask the same questions for all situations but will result in different solutions, depending upon the input provided by the specific situation. The emphasis of this text will be on providing a general managerial methodology while describing the various tools and techniques that can be used within a managerial framework.

The managerial problem solutions that will be discussed in Part 2 will require the application of technical (telecommunications technology) and nontechnical (reading, writing, mathematics, accounting, business organization, PC software skills, etc.) skills that are part of a sound business and technology education program.

PART 2: TELECOMMUNICATIONS PLANNING TOPICS

The topics presented in Part 2 are neither more difficult nor complex, and are not drastically different from those topics identified as prerequisite knowledge in Part 1: professional writing, public speaking, college mathematics, natural sciences, PC applications, business organization, principles of management, financial accounting, managerial accounting, economics, telecommunications technologies, and system analysis. However, Part 2 topics will selectively use elements of these prerequisite topics, and readers may encounter information gaps that disrupt the learning process of applying management techniques if their knowledge base is incomplete.

General Education and Business Knowledge Requirements

Most of the prerequisite subjects are nontelecommunications subjects. Students whose major interest is telecommunications frequently view these subjects as distractions from their primary areas of interest because they do not see their relevance to telecommunications. A key objective of Part 2 is to highlight the importance that nontelecommunications topics have for aspiring telecommunications managers. This importance should become more evident as nontelecommunications knowledge is consistently used as the underlying fabric for solving technology and managerial problems.

Part 2, *Telecommunications Planning*, consists of five chapters:

Chapter 6: *What is Enterprise Planning?*

Chapter 7: *Managerial Tools and Techniques*

Chapter 8: *Organization Management Skills*

Chapter 9: *Technology Management Skills*

Chapter 10: *Telecommunications Planning: A Case Study*

Chapter 6: What is Enterprise Planning?

The underlying theme of the enterprise planning chapter is that business needs should drive the selection and implementation of telecommunications technologies used within a business. A telecommunications manager must be familiar with business planning processes to ensure that an enterprise telecommunications plan supports the organization's business objectives.

Chapter 6 provides a summary of the business planning process, the use of benchmarking in the planning process, and various management theories that have emerged during the last hundred years for managing business enterprises. A composite management theory based on the current views of management process and contingency management theories is discussed, and will be used as the basic managerial decision framework used throughout this text.

Chapter 7: Managerial Tools and Techniques

Chapter 7 addresses the concepts introduced in Chapter 5 and reviews a variety of advanced management skill topics. Just as a skilled wood craftsman would be unable to convert raw wood into beautiful furniture without having the right tools, the skilled telecommunications manager will be unable to successfully manage the telecommunications department without having a strong set of managerial skills. Chapter 7 discusses different managerial tools and techniques that can be used to handle business management and technology management responsibilities.

Chapter 8: Business Management Skills

Chapter 8 topics examine the managerial skills required to manage a telecommunications department within a business context. Issues addressed in this chapter include leadership (*v.* management), budgeting, personnel development, and telecommunications department organization structure options.

Chapter 9: Technology Management Skills

Chapter 9 examines the role that telecommunications managers fulfill during the design, development, and implementation of telecommunications networks and systems. It identifies the range of telecommunications technologies that should be included in an enterprise telecommunications plan. An Excel-based enterprise telecommunications planning model is described and is used as the basis for developing the technical and financial planning elements of an enterprise telecommunications plan.

Chapter 10: Case Study

Chapter 10 provides readers with the opportunity to apply the planning tools discussed in Chapters 6, 7, 8, and 9. A five-year enterprise telecommunications plan is established for a hypothetical company—the PetroProd Corporation—and the telecommunications model reviewed in Chapter 9 is used to establish the telecommunications equipment and financial requirements for a five-year PetroProd telecommunications plan.

6

WHAT IS ENTERPRISE PLANNING?

LEARNING OBJECTIVES

1. Understand high level business planning process elements.

2. Understand the nature and scope of business and telecommunications enterprise planning.

3. Understand the benefits to be gained from an effective enterprise planning process.

4. Understand the relationship of planning to the managerial POLC model process.

5. Understand the annual financial planning cycle and its role in the overall planning process.

6. Understand the purpose and value of vision statements.

7. Understand the relationship of strategic, tactical, and operational plans, and their individual planning horizons.

8. Understand the depth and breadth of management theory knowledge that is available for addressing managerial issues.

9. Understand the basic top-level business planning strategies that may be deployed by upper management.

10. Understand how benchmarking activities can be used to support the planning process.

11. Understand the top-down management planning process concept.

both the tangible and intangible benefits of gaining lead time, improving internal communications, and providing a performance measurement standard.

GAINING LEAD TIME. A good planning process will create a just-in-time management environment, where organizational resources are made available at the right time. A just in time operating environment will generate tangible expense savings by providing the lead time to use internal resources more effectively. Being able to predict and compensate for potential marketplace pitfalls can result in maintaining or increasing revenue streams—another tangible benefit.

BETTER COMMUNICATION. The intangible benefits of a sound enterprise planning process may be greater than the benefits provided by tangible factors. Enterprise planning provides a blueprint for all employees. Managers and employees who understand (and support) enterprise objectives are more likely to perform effectively than employees who are uninformed. In addition, individuals in the external environment (stockholders, financial analysts, customers, and suppliers), who understand and agree with an organization's plans, will become supporters of the organization's short- and long-term planning efforts.

ESTABLISHING MEASUREMENT STANDARDS. From a managerial perspective, a byproduct of the planning process is the establishment of performance standards based on the operational forecasts (budgets) generated during the planning cycle. Managers who generate budget information know that it will become the yardstick by which their operational performance will be measured. **Budget variance** is highlighted by the equation:

$$\text{budget variance} = \text{budgeted expense} - \text{actual expense}.$$

When budget variances exist, it indicates a deviation from planned performance levels. Large deviations require explanation and also provide upper managers with a performance assessment tool. Although negative variances are given more attention than positive variances, all large variances should be evaluated and explained. The importance of controlling variances will be discussed further in Chapter 8, *Business Management Skills*.

Disadvantages of Enterprise Planning

If the enterprise planning process creates disadvantages, they are caused by poor managerial execution—not the planning concept. The root cause for poor enterprise planning is either poor planners, poor planning procedures, or poor management.

HOW DO YOU PLAN?

The following discusses four planning terms that are commonly found in business planning processes: vision statements, strategic plans, tactical plans, and operational plans. The discussion provides definitions of these terms, and any subsequent use of these terms adheres to these definitions.

It has been stated that the most important element of planning is to select the right goals. Therefore, the subject of benchmarking will be discussed before getting into the mechanics involved with developing different types of plans.

Identify The Right Goals

Unless the right goals are clearly identified during the planning process, there is little likelihood that the planning process will be effective. You may be tempted to establish new goals based on the ones that have been used in the past. Benchmarking provides a means for ensuring that the goal development process does not become ineffective because the wrong goals were selected.

Benchmarking refers to the use of a standard as a reference point for measuring something. Competitive benchmarking is a term that was created during the 1970s, when the Xerox Corporation developed benchmarking processes to identify inefficiencies in their domestic manufacturing processes by comparing them to the manufacturing processes of a Japanese affiliate. Competitive benchmarking is used to evaluate internal processes against an external standard, and is an excellent way to objectively assess internal performance.

Although benchmarking can be conducted informally, by using general information that is publicly available, a detailed approach to benchmarking is better. Formal benchmarking activities require the establishment of a relationship with another organization and exchanging information so that both parties can assess their internal performance. Information confidentiality is an issue when two organizations exchange benchmarking information. The relationship between the two parties must be one in which both parties are comfortable.

The benchmarking process can be a time consuming, labor intensive process that requires participants to evaluate their operations in great detail and collect quantifiable measurement information to be shared with other

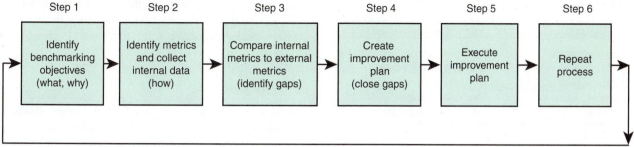

Figure 6–4. A six step benchmarking process.

benchmarking participants. Participants must agree on the measurements that will be used to evaluate internal operations, which requires the establishment of a standard set of metrics (measurements) that are understood and used by both parties. The use of standards provides a way for comparing the operating performance differences between the two organizations. Quantitative metrics provide a quantifiable assessment of operating performance. They allow the relative efficiency of the benchmarked operations to be compared accurately and allow follow up changes to be measured. Figure 6–4 illustrates a six step benchmarking process.

To minimize the clerical effort associated with benchmarking, the following planning criteria should be addressed in the early stages of a benchmarking effort:

- Benchmarking criteria must be clear and unambiguous.
- Benchmarking criteria must be measurable (metrics).
- Data must be easy to collect.
- Data must be reliable and free of contradictions.
- Benchmarking benefits must be worth the benchmarking efforts.

When a performance gap is found between any of the operations being benchmarked, benchmarking metrics provide the means for identifying specific areas where poor performance exists. Experience has shown that the identification of gap areas is the most time consuming phase, and that identification of the required corrective action steps are frequently obvious once gap areas have been accurately identified.

Benchmarking techniques may be used for evaluating the operations of competitors or noncompetitors. Competitive benchmarking is normally accomplished by examining data that is available publicly, because there is a low likelihood that some competitors will be willing to exchange confidential operating information with other competitors. (If competitors exchanged infor-

mation, they would be violating antitrust regulations.) Noncompetitive benchmarking can profit both parties and avoids the antitrust issues involved if competitors exchange information. Noncompetitive benchmarking is particularly useful for examining generic operations that are common to both benchmarking parties. For example, a large mail order firm and a large distributor of medical products could review the metrics of their individual customer service operations and identify ways to improve and benefit the operations of both parties. When key attributes have been defined by an organization, an ongoing benchmarking process is appropriate. This is shown in Figure 6–4 by the feedback link between steps 6 and 1.

Assuming that a planning process has specified the proper goals and objectives, the planning process itself will now be addressed.

Planning Horizons

Plans are developed in advance of the associated implementation activities, unless the implementer is winging it. Each of the four planning stages that will be reviewed—vision statements, strategic plans, tactical plans, and operational plans—has a different planning horizon, that is, they develop planning objectives for different time periods. A planning horizon may range between values of infinity and zero. The infinity **planning horizon** would imply that the planning element is timeless and appropriate during all time frames. For example, a 30% profitability goal could apply to any future period or to the current time. A zero-planning horizon would imply that a plan is being implemented, and the only appropriate actions are those directed at meeting the objectives of the plan being implemented and managing operations within the plan's financial constraints.

The planning horizons associated with the four planning categories are summarized in Table 6–1.

TABLE 6–1 Planning Horizons

Category	Planning Horizon
Vision statement	Statement elements are timeless and always appropriate.
Strategic plan	Beyond three years.
Tactical plan	One to three years.
Operational plan	Zero (implement today).

Plans are normally developed for specific time periods (for a specific year). With the passage of time, the specific plan will evolve through strategic, tactical, and operational planning stages. For example, a 2004 plan may be initially discussed in 1999, five years before it would be implemented. The 2004 plan would then be reviewed during 2000, 2001, 2002, and 2003 prior to becoming the 2004 operational plan. During 1999, 2000, 2001, 2002, and 2003, the same 2004 strategic plan established in 1999 would be, respectively, a strategic, tactical, tactical, tactical, and operational plan. The 2004 plan information would be continuously modified to reflect current thinking. The final 2004 tactical plan generated in 2003 will become the operational plan to be implemented in 2004. This transitional planning process is illustrated in Figure 6–5.

The information contained in short range planning horizons is expected to be very accurate, while long range planning horizon information may frequently be, at best, an educated guess about future events that will affect business activities. As the time period covered by long range plans becomes closer, the plans are refined to reflect current events and are converted into more accurate short range plans. The planning process involves generating a strategic plan for a given year and updating it periodically to refine existing information and add new information.

The actual planning process varies in different businesses, and the following provides a generic description of a planning process. Well run businesses devote considerable time to the planning effort, but there is always a need to ensure that the benefits received from the planning effort are commensurate with the resources expended to develop them.

Annual Planning Cycle

Planning is a businesswide activity that includes business-level and department-level planning requirements. The vehicle used by many companies to develop enterprise plans is a financial **annual planning cycle,** where the annual planning cycle is initiated and managed by a department (such as the finance department). While a primary focus for annual planning efforts is to develop the tactical plan that will become next year's operational plan, other concurrent tactical and strategic planning needs are also addressed during the annual planning cycle.

Tactical plans (plans that will be implemented 1 to 3 years in the future) quantify strategic planning elements by establishing budgets and assigning costs to the necessary implementation efforts. These budgets may be capital expense or operating expense budgets, depending upon whether fixed assets are being purchased or existing operations are being maintained. Tactical budgets translate business and technology strategic planning elements into dollars, and these budgets will be used to identify the staffing, facility, and expense requirements for implementing plan objectives.

From a telecommunications manager's perspective, most of the planning time will probably be spent on next year's budget—the budget that will become the financial operating plan for the following year. Failure to accurately identify the budget requirements for next year can adversely affect a manager's performance. Table 6–2 provides an annual planning calendar as seen from a department manager's perspective. It identifies those annual planning activities that focus on the preparation of the next year's budget, and is based on a fiscal calendar that begins on January 1.

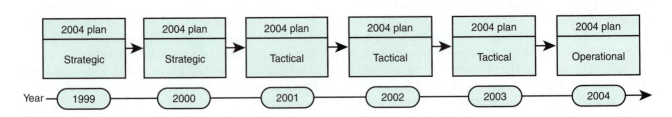

Figure 6–5. Strategic, tactical, and operational planning stages.

CHAPTER 6

TABLE 6–2   Generic Annual Planning Cycle Calendar for Next Year's Budgets

Date	Description
July 1	Detailed budget worksheets and year to date actual expense reports are issued to each department manager. These worksheets will typically have between twenty and forty expense line items that must be filled in by the department manager.
	During this process, department managers will review the budgets with their managers and will obtain their managers' approval prior to submitting the worksheets to finance.
September 1	Completed budget estimates will be returned to the finance department. The finance department will review them and will determine how overhead costs (property taxes, building depreciation, human resources) will be allocated to the departments using them. The overhead items are referred to as noncontrollable costs on the department budgets and the remaining costs are labeled as controllable costs. Department managers will be given direct accountability for staying within their controllable budget estimates.
	Any questions regarding specific department budgets will be reviewed with the responsible department manager.
October 15	The finance department will consolidate all the department budgets and submit the consolidated package to the enterprise's management board. Finance will conduct meetings with the management board both individually and collectively to explain the budgets and answer any questions that arise. Individual department managers may also be asked to provide supporting documentation explaining their budget request.
	The management board will convene to collectively approve the final budgets.
November 15	A copy of the approved budgets will be distributed to the various department managers. These budget estimates will be used in the following year to calculate budget variances (variance = budget $ − actual $).

BUSINESS PLANNING *v.* ANNUAL PLANNING

From a practical perspective, the annual planning cycle just described is also the business planning cycle. While the annual plan's primary focus is on the next year's operating budget items (both revenue and expense budget line items), other strategic and tactical planning efforts also take place. These business planning efforts are the primary responsibility of upper management, although many of the planning mechanics may be delegated to the accounting department.

The following discussion will address planning horizons for the four planning elements commonly found in business planning: vision statements, strategic plans, tactical plans, and operational plans.

Vision Statement

The planning horizon of a **vision statement** is unlimited because the vision statement is a guiding theme that is applicable in any time period. For a business, it would be the guiding business theme of the business, and would be supported by other high-level planning instruments. These could include mission statements or definitions of customers, markets, products, or services. They could also include a statement of organizational values or beliefs that upper management will use as an underlying philosophy when running the business and when dealing with organization stakeholders—customers, suppliers, employees, communities, and owners (typically stockholders).

Vision statement elements are heavily oriented toward enterprise level business objectives, and upper management has the primary responsibility for developing them. From a departmental perspective (the telecommunications department), similar instruments may be used to identify how the department is supporting the business's vision statement. A telecommunications vision statement might indicate that the (organization name) telecommunication department's objective is "to derive business value from the innovative use of communications technology in order to support customers and suppliers." Business management should approve any vision statement issued by an internal department prior to its release.

A well run business will have a detailed set of guiding principles that provide long-term guidelines for its management and employees. Departments within the business (accounting, human resources, manufacturing, telecommunications) may also provide similar operating principles for their department, and these principles would be linked back to the business's principles. The specific documentation of vision principles may utilize different formats and names: they may be called vision statements, mission statements, or business value statements.

The area of principles and vision statements is characterized by vagueness and a lack of definition that may be unsettling for technically oriented individuals. When telecommunications principles or vision statements are developed, they should be consistent with the vision statement used in their business.

Strategic Planning

The **strategic planning** horizon is three years or longer, and estimates of strategic business activities become extremely fuzzy for longer planning horizons. Many uncontrollable factors—economic conditions, competition, and customer demands—are the driving forces that determine the success or failure of business ventures. In strategic planning, a heavy reliance is typically placed on jury of opinion forecasting and other qualitative forecasting methods, because there is normally very little hard data available for strategic topics.

Strategic business plans become the driver for generating strategic plans at the department level, where the strategic goals of the business plans will be converted into operating plan objectives. However, the telecommunications department may also be asked to generate strategic telecommunications information without having strategic business plans as input. Chapter 9, *Technology Management Skills*, will review techniques for generating telecommunications plans when detailed business plan information is not available.

Tactical Planning

A **tactical planning** horizon ranges between one and three years. Tactical plans provide a transition between strategic plans and the operational plans that will be implemented in a real world operating mode. Tactical plans identify the resources (PTM) needed to convert strategic elements into operating results. As a result, a heavy tactical planning focus is on providing detailed financial plans that identify the resources needed to implement strategic concepts. During a three-year tactical planning phase, implementation details for strategic goals must be developed and converted into a financial cost *v.* benefit format. Yearly budget estimates are developed and documented, and the budgets are then modified as they continue through the annual planning stages illustrated in Figure 6–5.

Budgetary accuracy and completeness becomes more critical as the implementation year draws closer. A tactical budget developed two years prior to implementation should be more accurate than one developed three years prior to implementation because there will be newer information available. The highest tactical plan accuracy is needed for the plan that is developed during the year just prior to implementation. This final tactical plan will become the performance measurement standard used to measure managerial performance. As a result, the budgeting effort for plans that will be implemented the following year is typically a very intense activity. The manager responsible for preparing the budget is held accountable for implementing the plan within its budget provisions—implementing operating objectives on time and within budget.

REAL WORLD ACCOUNTABILITIES. Strategic plans focus more heavily on business activities and are used to provide "guesstimates" for future revenues and expenses. The revenue forecasting activity is normally limited to a few departments (typically sales-oriented organizations), while all departments must provide expense forecasts. Departmental expense forecasts would include estimates for staffing (a head count), salaries, and direct department expenses. These detailed expense forecasts are used to finalize profit projections for the future year and to make expense adjustments, as required, to ensure that profitability objectives are met.

The accounting format for department planning is a budget document containing line items used to identify budget categories (salaries, overtime, subscriptions, office equipment repair), and approved line item expense forecasts become the basis for the operational budgets used by department managers. For example, a 2006 operating plan would be developed in the year 2005, and its expense line items would be approved during the fourth quarter of 2005. When January of 2006 arrived, the department reports would show budget values for each expense line item, based on the forecast values established during the previous year (2005). As actual expenses are incurred during 2006, the report would provide a comparison between actual expenses and the forecasts developed for the year 2006 budget.

Operational Planning

The **operational planning** window has a zero-duration horizon. The forecasts developed during the last tactical planning period provided funding for the operational activities that must be carried out *now*. The manager's task is to meet budget objectives on time and within the budget's financial constraints. Managers who implement an operational budget normally have little flexibility when obtaining additional funding. If requests for additional funding are made for an operational budget, managers will have to explain why these new needs were not identified during the normal budgeting process.

MANAGEMENT THEORY AND PLANNING

Managerial skills are key elements of any planning tool set. Many theories have evolved regarding the best way to manage businesses, and planning approaches can vary depending upon the managerial philosophy supported by upper management. Some students of management theory see the various theories as tools—not as systems that must be implemented. When the different theories are viewed as tool sets, it is appropriate to select those tools individually and employ them on a situational basis.

The following provides a review of topics that are covered in typical principles of management courses. The intent is not supersede the need for management theory courses, but to highlight the use of individual managerial theories as managerial tools whose selection is based on the specific needs of a given situation. Emphasis will be placed on the management theories that are currently in vogue, while allowing the reader to gain an appreciation for the scope and breadth of the management theory knowledge base. Some management theories have fallen out of vogue because they were unable to effectively address the new needs of an ever changing managerial environment. In other cases, newer theories were viewed as being more effective than older theories.

Table 6–3 groups managerial theories into a pretheory category and five management theory categories.

Examination of Table 6–3 reveals some interesting facts: 1) management theory only began to be formalized in 1911, and 2) many management theory categories were developed concurrently. The six items in Table 6–3 are discussed in the following sections and a summary (Composite View of Management Theory) has been added to summarize how management theory is used in this text.

Preclassical Theory Contributions (pre-1911)

The building of the Egyptian pyramids and the Great Wall of China are examples of mammoth projects that required extensive managerial skills. Clearly, these wondrous works could not have been built over the span of many years without managing the efforts of thousands—possibly tens of thousands—of laborers. Good managerial skills were needed to translate the vision of these projects into a physical reality, although some of the worker motivation techniques used would be unacceptable today.

Another frequently cited example of preclassical theory management is the Roman Catholic Church. The Catholic Church is based in Rome, Italy, and has coordinated the religious efforts of individual Catholic Churches worldwide for over 1,500 years. It utilizes a centralized management style to maintain religious control. The number of years that it has been used is impressive by any managerial measurement, because modern management theory is less than 100 years old.

The industrial revolution was the primary driving force for the management era in which we currently live. The industrial revolution began in Great Britain during the 18th century and was the culmination of a trend during which Europeans had been inventing and using machines as replacements for human labor. Great Britain introduced new machinery-based production methods in several key industries during the mid-1700s, and developed mass production techniques that required the consolidation of workers into a single location to "feed and care for" machines. This new factory environment created the need for management skills because factory owners soon found out that the efforts of machines and workers must be coordinated. A brief period of worker idleness was magnified hundreds and even thousands of times, depending upon the number of employees at the factory. Issues that were minor in a small workshop environment became critical in a factory environment that housed hundreds of workers. In addition, the capability of manufacturing large quantities of product also meant that improved channels of distribution had to be developed to dispose of large quantities of mass-produced product.

New skills were needed in this industrial setting to ensure that factory driven businesses could operate effectively to generate profits for the factory owners. This skill set included:

forecasting market demands

obtaining raw materials

assigning tasks to factory personnel

directing daily activities

coordinating different tasks

TABLE 6–3   Management Theory Categories

Time Period	Theory
Pre-1911	Preclassical theory contributions
1911–1960	Classical management theorists
1911–1960	General administrative theorists
1911–1960	Human resources theorists
1911–present	Quantitative theorists
1960–present	Integrative theorists

maintaining factory equipment

establishing and maintaining performance standards

finding buyers for products

selling products

In 1776, Adam Smith (a British philosopher and economist), published a book titled *The Wealth of Nations*, and described the division of labor concept that was being used in British factories. While it was not until 1911 that the era of formal management theory began, the industrial revolution of the 1700s was clearly the key change driver of the classical management theory phase that set the stage for 20th century management theorists.

Classical Management Theorists (1911–1960)

1911 is commonly used as the starting point for modern management theories and is the year that Frederick Taylor published a book titled *Principles of Scientific Management*. The basic theme of scientific management theorists was that there was a best way to do a factory job. Frederick Taylor is credited with being the originator of the scientific management movement. The scientific management era heralded the beginning of the modern management era, and individuals in the classical management category were supporters of the management principles set forth by Taylor. Key classical management theorists in this period also included Frank and Lillian Gilbreth and Henry L. Gantt.

Frederick Taylor was a scientist who believed that factory managers were responsible for maximizing the work output of factory workers. He identified four scientific management principles that managers should use to increase worker output:

1. Replace existing experience-based work elements with work elements developed through the use of scientific methods.

2. Scientifically select, train, teach, and develop factory workers.

3. Managers should deal with workers in a cooperative mode to ensure conformance to scientific management standards.

4. Various factory tasks should be allocated appropriately between managers and workers. Factory managers should have a proactive role in directing the efforts of workers. This was an extension of the division of labor concept identified by Adam Smith.

Most readers are unlikely to find Taylor's four principles revolutionary. However, at the time they were intro-duced, they were radical departures from accepted practices. Factory managers were owners of the facilities and did not participate in the day to day manufacturing operations. This was left to worker supervisors who had been promoted to their current positions through a system of trial and error experience. Factory owners selected supervisors based largely on their ability to control workers through fear and intimidation techniques. New workers were not given instructions on how to do their jobs. They were held responsible for figuring out how to do their jobs by watching others perform the same tasks.

Taylor's principles identified a new role for managers and set them up as a separate entity from ownership—professional managers who have the responsibilities of determining the best way to perform a factory task and directing the work efforts of others to maximize work output. Using Taylor's approach, the manager's responsibilities would supersede many responsibilities that factory owners had viewed as being an owner's prerogative. A factory owner who used scientific management principles would not use tyrannical supervisors who relied on fear and intimidation, but would instead delegate the operational responsibility of the factory to trained professional managers. Scientific management principles heralded the start of the professional management era.

Frank and Lillian Gilbreth, a husband and wife team, focused on finding the best way to perform a factory function by using time and motion principles that identified the most time efficient way to carry out manual operations. They would carefully document the existing way of running the equipment, eliminate redundant or wasteful motions, and install procedures that specified precisely how machine operators should perform their tasks. These same techniques were applied to process and production line operations.

Henry L. Gantt introduced the concept of incentive pay for achieving high work performance while using scientific method work standards. Incentive systems were developed. The incentive systems provided high pay for workers who exceeded scientific method standards established by management. Very high pay levels could be achieved if workers exceeded the standard. Gantt also was responsible for introducing the graphical representation that bears his name, the Gantt chart (Figure 6–6). The **Gantt chart** was used to show the relationship between planned work and a time line. The vertical axis (y-axis) was used to list various planned work elements and the horizontal axis (x-axis) was used to show time information—typically dates. The work

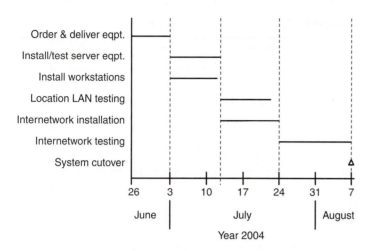

Figure 6–6. An example of a Gantt chart.

elements were shown as bars or lines. The beginning of the bar represented the start of the work element and the end of the bar indicated the completion schedule of the work element.

The U.S. was a leader in the development of scientific management techniques. This knowledge provided the U.S. with a competitive edge in manufacturing processes—a competitive edge that it enjoyed for much of the 20th century. The manufacturing dominance of the U.S. up to and including World War II was due to the development of efficient mass production techniques and the development of managerial skills and methods.

General Administrative Theorists (1911 – 1960)

While the classical theorists were efficiency oriented and focused on improving work methods, the general administrative theorists focused on developing general theories of management by examining the management process itself. Two leading theorists in the general administrative school of thought were Henri Fayol and Max Weber.

Henri Fayol (1841–1925) was an operations manager—the director of a French coal mine. He approached management theory from an organizational perspective and identified fourteen principles that should be followed by managers (refer to Table 6–4).

When Henri Fayol introduced his fourteen principles of management, the ideas were as revolutionary as the scientific management principles developed by Frederick Taylor. Fayol also advocated the use of trained, professional managers to run factory operations. However, while Taylor's professional manager focused primarily on work tasks and the techniques for making them more efficient, Fayol addressed management organization issues. These included the relationships that should exist between managers and the organization and between managers and workers (Table 6–4). Inspection of Fayol's principles would show that the topics are as relevant today as they were when they were first published in the early 1900s.

POLC: PLAN, ORGANIZE, LEAD, AND CONTROL. Henri Fayol also formulated theories regarding the process that managers should follow to carry out their responsibilities. The processes he identified are the basis for the POLC Management Process Model (plan, organize, lead, and control) discussed previously, and they remain a key element in contemporary managerial theory.

Max Weber, another general administrative theorist, also focused on the organization aspect of management and formulated the concept of an ideal bureaucracy based on the division of labor, authority hierarchies, formal rules and regulations, impersonality, managerial careers, and the formal selection of workers and managers. As was the case with all classical and general administrative theorists, the concepts that Weber presented were revolutionary compared to the manager-owner structure that was in place when these theories were first published.

Human Resources Theorists (1911–1960)

Concurrent with the development of classical and general administrative theories, human resources theorists provided another approach to managing employees. Human resources theorists focused on the organization's employees—factory workers—and the underlying philosophy of their theories was that the managerial key to achieving higher productivity was through employee motivation. A wide range of approaches was offered. All of them were directed at the employees. These efforts

TABLE 6–4   Henri Fayol's Fourteen Principles of Management

Principle	Description
1. Division of work	Specialization increases output by making employees more efficient. (The same viewpoint expressed by Adam Smith's division of labor proposals.)
2. Authority	Managers must be able to give orders. Authority gives them this right. Whenever authority is exercised, responsibility is assumed.
3. Discipline	Employees must obey and respect the rules that govern the organization. Good discipline is the result of effective leadership.
4. Unity of command	Every employee should receive orders from only one superior.
5. Unit of direction	One manager with one plan should direct each group of organizational activities that have the same objective.
6. Subordination of individual interests	The interests of any single employee or group of employees are secondary to the interest of the organization as a whole.
7. Remuneration	Workers must be paid a fair wage.
8. Centralization	The degree of centralization (of decision making) should be based on optimizing any given situation.
9. Scalar chain	The line of authority from upper management to the lowest level represents the scalar chain, and communications should follow this chain of command. Cross-communications can be allowed if agreed to by all parties and superiors are kept informed.
10. Order	People and materials should be at the right place at the right time.
11. Equity	Managers should be fair and kind to their subordinates.
12. Stability of personnel tenure	High employee turnover is inefficient. Management is responsible for minimizing turnover and ensuring that qualified replacements fill vacancies.
13. Initiative	Employees will exert higher levels of effort if they are allowed to originate and carry out plans.
14. *Esprit de corps*	Promoting team spirit will build harmony and unity within the organization.

resulted in the establishment of new professional fields—industrial psychology, human relations, and behavioral science management.

Early pioneers who provided input to the field of human resources management theory included Robert Owen, Hugo Munsterberg, Mary Parker Follet, Chester Barnard, Abraham Maslow, and Douglas McGregor. The underlying theme presented in Robert Owen's works was that it was profitable to show concern for employees because happy and satisfied employees are more productive employees. Hugo Munsterberg developed the study of industrial psychology—the study of human behavior and attitudes in the workplace.

Abraham Maslow introduced a **hierarchy of needs** theory that could be used to identify the appropriate motivation methods to use with employees in a workplace environment. These needs are summarized in Table 6–5. Maslow identified five needs basic to all individuals, where the highest level need was the need for self-actualization and the lowest level need was to satisfy physiological needs. Maslow believed that individuals must satisfy lower-level needs before they can become concerned with fulfilling higher-level needs. This meant that

it would be ineffective to use higher need benefits to motivate someone who still had unfulfilled lower-level needs.

Mary Parker Follet proposed that organizations should be based on group ethics—not on individualism—and her works identified ways to achieve this objective. One of Douglas McGregor's contributions was the Theory X and Theory Y approach to managing employees. He stated that employees could be placed in one of two groupings and that different approaches were required in each case. Theory X employees were naturally lazy, disliked work, and shunned responsibility. They could best be managed with a system of rewards, threats, and punishments. Theory Y employees wanted to work, wanted to take on additional responsibility, had an innate desire to work, and could best be managed by satisfying their higher-order needs (refer to Table 6–5).

Chester Barnard, president of the New Jersey Bell telephone company, had viewpoints that bridged the classical and human resources theory categories. His managerial model was based on applying scientific management principles *and* having the manager communicate effectively with employees in order to achieve high levels of performance.

TABLE 6–5 Abraham Masolow's Hierarchy of Needs, 1954

Level	Need	Description
1	Self-actualization	Growth, self fulfilling, achieving personal potential
2	Esteem	Internal: Self respect, autonomy, achievement External: Status, recognition, attention
3	Social	Need for affection, belongingness, acceptance
4	Safety	Need for security, protection from physical and emotional harm
5	Physiological	Food, drink, shelter, and sexual needs

Quantitative Theorists (1911–present)

Quantitative theorists focus on managerial decision-making techniques that use statistics, creating organizational mathematical models, and conducting computer simulations for organizational analysis. This approach has also been called either *operations research* or *management science theory*, and it continues to be used in the area of computerized managerial planning and control. The widespread availability of sophisticated computer hardware and software added a major dimension to the quantitative research approach.

Integrative Theorists (1960–present)

By 1960, a significant pool of knowledge existed for the four management theory categories already described, and contributions were continuing to be made to each area. Simplistically, it could be stated that: 1) classical theorists provided a first line supervisor's view of managerial needs based on maintaining efficient operations 2) general administrative theorists believed that managers should address management issues based on a holistic view of the entire organization; 3) human resources theorists felt a manager's primary role was to interact with, direct, and motivate employees; and 4) quantitative theorists advocated the use of quantitative modeling for making managerial decisions.

Integrative theorists believed that no single approach (classical, general administrative, human resources, or quantitative) was able to answer the managerial issues confronting managers. Integrative theorists wanted to synthe-size the individual approaches developed previously and provide a universal management theory. Three different integration methodologies emerged: 1) process methodology, 2) systems methodology, and 3) contingency methodology. The effort for developing a unifying framework to consolidate the various management theories began in the early 1960s and is viewed by some as being a maturation stage for managerial theory development.

PROCESS METHOD. In 1961, Professor Harold Koontz published an article describing different management theory approaches and concluded that: 1) the human resources and quantitative approaches were not management theories but were tools that could be used by managers, and 2) a process approach could encompass and synthesize the various management theory viewpoints that existed. The process approach advocated by Koontz was Fayol's process model (plan, organize, lead, and control). His proposals generated a great deal of controversy but the Fayol Process Model evolved as a key element that allowed different management theories to be integrated.

SYSTEMS METHOD. The Systems approach also emerged during the early 1960s. This approach viewed the various management theories as a set of interrelated and interdependent elements. Systems theorists identified two basic systems: 1) closed systems and 2) open systems. Closed systems did not interact with the external environment. An example of a closed system would be the scientific management approach advocated by Frederick Taylor. Scientific management methods focused only on internal elements—people, machines, and organization—and were not concerned with external environment effects. An open system interacts with the external environment and recognizes the impact that factors outside the enterprise can have on internal activities.

CONTINGENCY METHODOLOGY. The contingency (situational) approach states that each managerial situation is unique and therefore requires a customized solution. The contingency approach is intuitively logical because organizations that have different attributes (size, organizational objectives, tasks being performed) will have different managerial requirements.

Composite View of Management Theory

The following summarizes the managerial approach used in this text. In keeping with modern management theory,

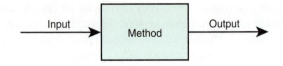

Figure 6–7. Composite management model.

it represents a blend of the process and contingency (situational) methodologies described in the integrative theory section. The text approach for addressing business management or technology management issues will be to emphasize the use of time proven theories and methodologies as managerial tools that can be applied to a variety of situations. This concept is illustrated in Figure 6–7. Based upon the specific managerial situation, an appropriate methodology would be selected and used. The parameters of the specific situation become the input for the methodology process, and the output will be a set of managerial decisions customized for the situation. Using this model, the same methodology (managerial tool) may generate different solutions (output) for different input scenarios.

The text's composite model reflects an integrative theorist's thinking regarding management theory and provides the flexibility for adapting to different situations. The appropriate management theory (methodology) would be selected based on the specific situation. It should be noted that using the composite model allows different approaches to be used for the same problem—recognizing the fact that there is frequently more than one way to solve a problem. The responsibility for selecting and successfully using a given methodology lies with the manager, and the manager is accountable for making the selected approach work.

Current Trends and Issues

The six management theory sections provided a conceptual overview of the different theory areas and the seventh topic described a way to use all of these approaches to solve managerial problems. Because this is not a management theory text, minimal coverage has been given to specific theory areas. Each management theory area has a large pool of documentation, and a full-time effort would be needed to fully assess and understand each theory.

Just as the factory working environment triggered the creation of different management theories during the last 100 years, today's working environment can be expected to result in new theories that augment or replace existing ones. The issues and buzzwords being used in today's workplace that are likely to be incorporated into new managerial approaches include workforce diversity, business ethics, changing ground rules, total quality management, reengineering, empowerment and teams, the bimodal workforce, downsizing, and contingent workers. The current focus is on reorganizing and restructuring existing management theories. Only time will reveal if any revolutionary approaches will emerge.

The seventh section, *Composite View of Management Theory*, described how the various management theories and methodologies will be used as tools for different managerial situations. It is based on the thinking of integrative management theorists.

ENTERPRISE-LEVEL BUSINESS PLANNING

The philosophy of top management in a business will strongly influence the strategies used by internal departments. A proposal to aggressively invest in leading-edge telecommunications technology in a conservatively oriented enterprise is not likely to gain upper management support. Therefore, it is important for telecommunications managers to understand the basic strategies being used by upper management when setting their enterprise goals. Aligning the telecommunications department strategy with the business strategy is likely to gain support from upper management and enhance the career of a telecommunications manager. The following describes four general strategic directions available to upper management:

1. a stability strategy
2. a growth strategy
3. a retrenchment strategy
4. a combination strategy

In all business planning strategies, a top-down planning approach is used and this same approach is relevant to business and departmental planning. The following discusses the **top-down planning** concept prior to reviewing the four general strategies.

Top-Down Planning

Top-down management planning establishes general objectives and then develops the detailed plans needed to support them. Most business plans utilize a top-down approach. The alternative is a **bottom-up approach,** where the details or specifics are established and general strategies are then developed based on consolidating and analyzing lower-level details.

In a typical business management hierarchy, each level of management provides subordinates with general requirements and relies upon subordinate managers to develop and control the specific implementation of the general requirements. In reality, the communications process associated with top-down planning is a two-way street. Upper management provides broad objectives that are passed down a hierarchical organization structure. The upward responses to these requests utilize a bottom-up planning process. The bottom-up process is important because it provides the mechanism for allowing lower levels to communicate with upper levels regarding the practicality of the top-down directives they have been given and to provide feedback regarding the level of difficulty involved with achieving them.

Top-down planning is also used in technical design. For example, in network planning the top-down design approach would start by identifying customer needs and then proceeding through logical and physical design phases that are based on meeting these needs. If a bottom-up approach were used, the output of the design phases may or may not meet the customer needs, because detailed technical planning begins with technical details. This text will utilize the top-down approach for both telecommunications department and technology planning.

Stability Strategy

The stability strategy is employed when an organization is satisfied with its position in the market and its current profitability performance. Upper management wants to retain its current position and will deploy strategies that support that objective. This could include product development and pricing strategies that create barriers to competitors or, if the enterprise's market share is based on being a low-cost product provider, the implementation of strategies that continue to reduce expenses. On the other hand, if product innovation is used to maintain market position, department-level strategies that provide product differentiation will be initiated by upper management.

A stability strategy is not a strategy of cutting back (this strategy will be covered under the retrenchment strategy discussion), because maintaining current performance levels in a volatile business environment requires proactive managerial action. In some respects, it is analogous to maintaining the position of a boat in a river that has strong, fluctuating currents where many large rocks jutt above the water's surface. If the boat relied only on the use of an anchor to maintain its position, the results would be disastrous if the rope broke or if the anchor was unable to firmly grasp the river bed. A better strategy would be to use a motor and the skill of an experienced pilot to maintain the boat's position in treacherous waters. In the business world, proactive upper management would be both the pilot and the motor.

When a business stability strategy is being deployed, telecommunications department strategies that improve communications with customers, reduce internal operating expenses, or provide product differentiation for the enterprise's product line are appropriate. Upper management would view these activities in a positive way.

Growth Strategy

A growth strategy is based on following a "bigger is better" philosophy. Growth can be achieved in one of two ways: 1) by increasing market share in existing markets or 2) by entering new markets. Market share can be increased by enhancing existing products or by developing new products for a specific market. New markets may be entered with existing products or by acquiring companies that have existing market shares in the target marketplace. In a growth environment, new product development is very important. It could be accomplished by either developing products internally or acquiring them externally.

As was the case for the enterprise stability strategy, telecommunications department strategies that improve communication with customers, reduce internal operating expenses, or provide product differentiation of the business's product line are department-level strategies that would be viewed positively by upper management.

Retrenchment Strategy

A retrenchment strategy is one of contracting operations. It is normally used when market share is permanently lost because of severe competition or because of poor economic conditions. Regardless of the cause, it is a strategy employed by upper management when profitability objectives cannot be met by maintaining the enterprise's current operating status. Reductions in staffing levels, closing locations, and reducing the diversity of operations are typical strategies employed by upper management when implementing a retrenchment strategy. The retrenchment strategy may be used as a stopgap measure for maintaining short term profitability objectives, or it may be used as a long range strategy if upper management is convinced that the conditions that led to the retrenchment strategy are permanent.

The telecommunications department's responses to retrenchment are far more limited than strategies for stability or growth. Cost reduction is the primary concern of upper management, and the only appropriate telecommunications response is one that would help reduce (or contain) costs. These plans could involve the direct reduction of telecommunications expenses or by leveraging a small investment in telecommunications technologies in order to generate large savings in other parts of the organization.

Combination Strategy

The combination strategy may contain elements of all three strategies discussed previously. It is an amorphous strategy that is difficult to categorize. As a result, it is equally difficult to formulate any single telecommunications department strategy that would be viewed positively by upper management.

BUSINESS-LEVEL TELECOMMUNICATIONS PLANNING

A comprehensive business plan identifies key business objectives, describes how these objectives will be achieved, and explains the expected business benefits. Business plans may be used to establish a new business or provide a master plan for operating an existing business. Business plans are normally an upper management responsibility, and the business plan is a master plan established to ensure the ongoing success of a new venture or of an established business.

A business plan contains the basic information needed to manage the businesses and evaluate the merits of new business opportunities. It includes specifics regarding the firm's products and services, markets, customers, and competition. The business plan would normally include a business mission statement, a marketing plan, an operating plan, and a financial plan. It would also identify specific goals and objectives that must be achieved to ensure the long-term viability of the firm.

The term *enterprise* refers to a commercial business or firm that is organized specifically to achieve growth and profit. This text will use the term *enterprise planning* when the planning objectives are for the entire business. By its nature, telecommunications planning typically involves enterprise planning because its basic objective is to provide communication links between the employees, customers, suppliers, and external entities who have a relationship with the business. The range and scope of the business's telecommunications effort will depend upon the firm's specific business plan objectives and the size of the firm.

Telecommunications enterprise planning is primarily network oriented, and it focuses on providing internetworking capabilities. Internetworks provide linkages between different networks (WANs and LANs) and business internetworks contain a variety of equipment, systems, and subsystems.

> Telecommunications enterprise planning methodologies are appropriate for business unit or location planning. In those cases, the full sets of enterprise planning methodologies are not required, and it is a matter of selecting those that are appropriate for the planning situation.

The concept of enterprise planning is not the exclusive domain of for-profit businesses—it can be applied to nonprofit businesses or government agencies. The enterprise business plan deliverable is a document that identifies the business activities that must be undertaken to ensure the long-term viability of the business. In addition, departmental (telecommunications) enterprise plans would contain those telecommunications technology infrastructure elements required to support the enterprise business plan. A telecommunications enterprise plan should be linked directly to the enterprise plan objectives and should identify the telecommunications resources needed to implement business plan objectives. Although the telecommunications enterprise plan will address technology elements, this information should be translated into the language of upper management—business English and dollars—and should answer the recurring managerial questions—What, Why, How, Where, and When?

Telecommunications Benchmarking

Benchmarking can be very useful to telecommunications managers. The establishment of informal benchmarking relationships between noncompetitive organizations is common. Membership in user groups, professional societies, or technology database services can provide a telecommunications manager with valuable information based on the experience of others. Under the right circumstances, detailed metrics can be exchanged between two firms.

The use of benchmarking standards provides an objective metric for measuring internal performance and avoids the pitfall of becoming complacent if the current operating performance looks good compared to last year's internal operations. It may not look as good when compared to an external standard.

SUMMARY

This summary is organized to correspond with the learning objectives found at the beginning of the chapter.

1. High-level business planning process elements consist of business-level planning, business unit planning, and departmental planning elements. The enterprise planning process provides the broad, general goals of the organization, while the business unit plans identify the specific objectives needed to ensure business unit profitability. Departmental planning is used by internal organizations to develop plans that support the attainment of business unit goals.

2. Telecommunications enterprise planning refers to the development and implementation of a technology infrastructure that provides rapid, easy to use communications between an enterprise's employees, customers, suppliers, and external entities. The telecommunications plan elements should be linked to the enterprise's business plan and should support the efforts for achieving business objectives.

3. An effective enterprise planning process provides a business with the lead time needed to effectively meet changing business conditions. It also provides a conceptual business blueprint that can be used by employees and individuals outside the enterprise to understand basic enterprise goals and the management process necessary for attaining them. A third benefit is that it provides a measurement standard (budget) that can be used to assess organizational performance.

4. Planning is one element of the POLC Model (plan, organize, lead, and control). The successful implementation of any plan requires the effective use of the POLC Model managerial process. Focusing too heavily on the planning element of the POLC Model may create an environment where plan objectives are rarely achieved.

5. The annual financial planning cycle is used by businesses to establish a budget that will be used in the following year. During the annual planning cycle, capital and operating expenditure budget needs are documented for use in the following year. The annual planning cycle is frequently used to update all strategic and tactical plans for all the business's various planning horizons.

6. Vision statements provide consistent, long-term goals that are general in nature and appropriate as guiding principles. A good vision statement contains business objectives that can provide direction within any planning time frame and are seldomly changed.

7. Strategic, tactical, and operational planning are three stages of an overall planning scheme. Strategic plans may be thought of as forecasts or "guessimate" of goals that will not be implemented for three or more years. The tactical planning time frame is one to three years before its goals will be implemented, and is characterized by a heavy emphasis on financial planning—the preparation of budgets. Operational planning operates within the financial constraints and time constraints imposed by the previous year's tactical plan. Operational planning is limited to activities focused on meeting the tactical plan objectives.

8. Upper management can use one of three basic business strategies: 1) a stability strategy, 2) a growth strategy, or 3) a retrenchment strategy as a basic operating principle. A stability strategy is used to maintain a business's current business position, while a growth strategy is based on increasing size through growth. A retrenchment strategy is a containment strategy based on cutting back staffing and other expenses to survive periods of lower revenues. Upper management can deploy any combination of these three strategies.

9. Benchmarking compares internal operations to equivalent external operations for determining the effectiveness of the internal department. It relies on the use of metrics to identify performance gaps between the benchmarked elements. When performance gaps are found, the business that has the poorest performance can focus on improving its operations to meet or exceed the benchmark performance standards.

10. Management theory has been formalized since 1911, when Frederick Taylor published *Principles of Scientific Management*. Many different managerial theories have been developed since 1911, and the current integrative management theory views them as being different managerial tools that can be applied, as required, to a wide range of managerial situations.

11. A top-down management process is a planning process where broad, general objectives are identified, then the detail-level elements needed to achieve the general objectives are developed. Top-down planning provides an operating framework that lower-level implementation activities can use as goals for planning activities.

KEY TERMS AND CONCEPTS

The language of telecommunications management is multifaceted and includes words and phrases from managerial, technological, accounting, regulatory, and other business areas. The definitions of these key terms and concepts can be found within the chapter and in the glossary.

Annual Planning Cycle	Enterprise Planning	POLC Model
Benchmarking	Function Plan	Strategic Planning
Bottom-Up Approach	Gantt Chart	Tactical Planning
Budget Variance	Hierarchy of Needs	Top-Down Planning
Business Unit Plan	Operational Planning	Vision Statement
Enterprise	Planning Horizon	

REVIEW QUESTIONS

The following questions are open-ended—predefined answers are not included as part of the text. The purpose of these questions is to allow the readers to test themselves on the chapter material.

1. Complete the phrase, "Strategic planning is useless . . . . "

2. Explain the working concepts behind the POLC Model.

3. What are vision statements?

4. What is the relationship between business planning and telecommunications planning?

5. What is top-down planning?

6. What is bottom-up planning?

7. What are the respective planning horizons for vision statements, strategic planning, tactical planning, and operational planning?

8. What is the value of enterprise planning?

9. List and explain the three risk factors that may exist in telecommunications projects.

10. How does departmental planning differ from enterprise-level planning?

11. What are the four enterprise-level business strategies that the top management in a business can follow?

12. Identify a calendar schedule for a typical annual planning cycle and the associated budgeting process.

13. What is the primary value of benchmarking?

14. Describe the six step benchmarking process.

15. What are the main differences between current management theories and earlier (pre-1960) theories?

MULTIPLE CHOICE

Answers to the multiple choice questions are provided in the text's Instructor's Manual.

1. The initial step when applying POLC Model principles is to _____.

   a. correct deviations from the plan
   b. establish a plan
   c. assign resources
   d. identify objectives
   e. look for leadership

2. The planning horizon for strategic planning is _____.

   a. three or more years
   b. one to three years
   c. one year
   d. zero
   e. open-ended

3. The planning horizon for tactical planning is _____.

   a. three or more years

   b. one to three years

   c. one year

   d. zero

   e. open-ended

4. The planning horizon for vision statements is _____.

   a. three or more years

   b. one to three years

   c. one year

   d. zero

   e. open-ended

5. If a plan is developed for the year 2007, and it is now 2004, it is a/an _____ plan.

   a. operational

   b. visionary

   c. strategic

   d. tactical

   e. none of the above

6. If a plan is developed for the year 2008, and it is now 2004, it is a/an _____ plan.

   a. operational

   b. visionary

   c. strategic

   d. tactical

   e. none of the above

7. Budgetary accuracy is most critical for a/an _____ plan.

   a. operational

   b. visionary

   c. strategic

   d. tactical

   e. none of the above

8. A key objective of the tactical planning process is to _____.

   a. reduce risk

   b. develop financial plans

   c. identify future events

   d. provide guiding principles

   e. complete projects on time

9. An intangible benefit of sound enterprise planning processes is to _____.

   a. provide budgets

   b. identify budget variances

   c. plan ahead

   d. communicate with employees

10. A business unit plan _____.

   a. answers basic questions about business-level issues

   b. identifies plans in terms of customers and products

   c. is prepared by stockholders

   d. has a planning horizon of zero

11. Department planning _____ enterprise planning.

   a. precedes

   b. runs concurrently with

   c. follows

   d. avoids the need for

12. An upper management "stability strategy" is used when _____.

   a. expenses must be minimized

   b. business conditions are poor

   c. business conditions are good

   d. growth is desired

   e. the current state of business is good

13. When a top-down planning approach is used, _____.

   a. operational plans are not required

   b. plan details are initially identified

   c. strategic planning is not required

   d. plan details are identified in later planning stages

   e. operational plans are not required

14. Competitive benchmarking _____.

   a. negates the needs for developing metrics

   b. is rarely done

   c. uses external standards to measure performance

   d. uses internal standards to measure performance

15. In benchmarking, performance gaps _____.

   a. are not used

   b. provide performance information

   c. should be avoided

   d. involve confidentiality issues

7

MANAGERIAL TOOLS AND TECHNIQUES

LEARNING OBJECTIVES

1. Understand the skill framework concept and its relevance to achieving managerial success.

2. Understand the importance of attitude in attaining managerial success.

3. Understand the importance of managerial style and its appropriate application.

4. Understand microdecision concepts and how they relate to the managerial POLC Model.

5. Understand the importance of benchmarking and its relevance to the microdecision process.

6. Understand macrodecision concepts and how they relate to the managerial POLC Model.

7. Understand the value of using macrodecision concepts within a life cycle analysis format.

8. Understand the importance for a telecommunications manager to have a good understanding of accounting procedures.

9. Understand the two basic budgeting approaches that may be used in the budget preparation process.

10. Understand the value of forecasting and its limitations.

11. Understand the relationship of project network diagrams to the project management process.

Many tools and techniques have been developed for use when addressing and resolving managerial issues. They are available to telecommunications managers – *if they know about them and are willing to expend the effort to learn to apply them effectively*. While some tools are explicitly identified as being managerial tools, many tools are simply the application of common logical and mathematical techniques that are combined to solve managerial problems. Real managerial tools frequently rely on the creativity of the individual manager to evaluate problems and construct a solution based on combining several common techniques. There is a low likelihood that managers will find the problems they encounter to be in a neat question and answer format with multiple choice options. Defining the parameters of a problem is the initial step in solving a problem, and accurately defining a problem is the single largest step in resolving it.

Some managerial tools can be used intuitively but others require skill levels in (apparently) unrelated topics (accounting, mathematics, PC applications, etc.) and require the problem solver to define the problem, select a reasonable solution methodology, and create a real world management solution. This chapter will review some of the available tools and techniques, and will provide examples of how they can be applied to common managerial situations. In those cases where the topic is (or should be) a major course topic in a telecommunications program, a limited amount of time will be spent describing it, based on the assumption that it will be covered in those courses.

PERSONAL SKILLS

Chapter 5, *Telecommunications Manager Skill Requirements*, summarized some of the basic skills needed to be an effective telecommunications manager. A strong emphasis was placed on the value of **enabling skills** — those skills that allow someone to learn and develop skills outside of a formal training or degree program. Figure 7–1 describes the enabling and telecommunications management skills that a telecommunications manager should possess.

A good set of enabling skills provides the tools needed to learn on the job and provides the adaptability and flexibility to react to new situations. Without strong basic education skills, it is extremely difficult to acquire a good set of higher education, PC, business management, or technology management skills. Figure 7–2 provides a modified form of the Figure 7–1 triangle—there are additional details.

While the skill triangles display knowledge areas needed for telecommunications managers, it is appropriate to discuss the role of experience. Experience is the factor that, coupled with knowledge, provides someone with skill. It is recognition of the fact that knowledge, which is not applied to real world situations, may have academic interest but has limited interest for most individuals. How-

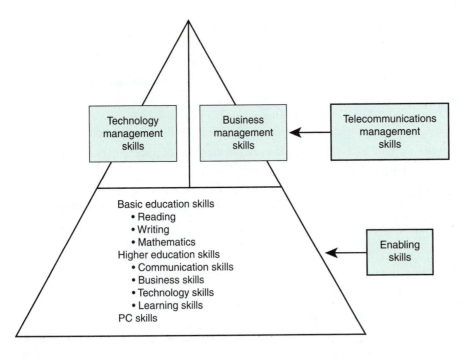

Figure 7–1. Telecommunications manager skill requirements.

ever, experience must be the right type of experience if it is used to hone skills. There are two ways of gaining ten years of experience in a specific skill area:

1. one year of the same experience repeated ten times
2. ten years of diversified experience in the area

Clearly, the initial example of experience is actually only one year of experience unless the skill area is unusually complex. From a personal development perspective, individuals in the early stages of their careers should concentrate on acquiring the second type of experience. It is valuable to acquire diversified experience, which is normally more available during the early stages of a manager's career.

Gaining diversified experience will frequently require a conscious effort by an individual to leave a comfortable, stable position and start over in a new position—a move that includes a risk of failure. Professional growth is based on acquiring new skills and then continuously using the new skills to acquire another set of skills throughout one's career. The easiest way to assess one's own personal skill set is to undertake new experiences that will highlight the strengths and weaknesses of the skill set. This assessment should be used to identify areas where skill improvements are needed. It can be made by undertaking a personal development or formal education program to start the process. A skill can be acquired only by applying knowledge.

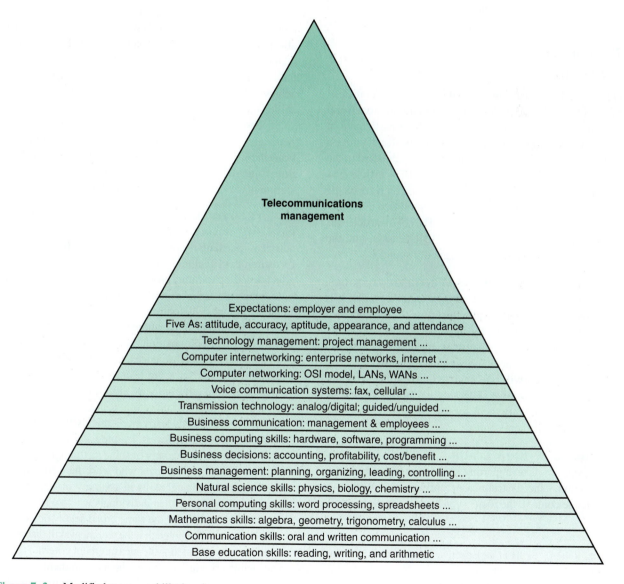

Telecommunications management

Expectations: employer and employee
Five As: attitude, accuracy, aptitude, appearance, and attendance
Technology management: project management ...
Computer internetworking: enterprise networks, internet ...
Computer networking: OSI model, LANs, WANs ...
Voice communication systems: fax, cellular ...
Transmission technology: analog/digital; guided/unguided ...
Business communication: management & employees ...
Business computing skills: hardware, software, programming ...
Business decisions: accounting, profitability, cost/benefit ...
Business management: planning, organizing, leading, controlling ...
Natural science skills: physics, biology, chemistry ...
Personal computing skills: word processing, spreadsheets ...
Mathematics skills: algebra, geometry, trigonometry, calculus ...
Communication skills: oral and written communication ...
Base education skills: reading, writing, and arithmetic

Figure 7–2. Modified manager skill triangle.

Katz Article: A Skill Framework

In 1955, Robert Katz wrote an article for the *Harvard Business Review*, titled "Skills of an Effective Administrator."[1] It identified the attributes that an ideal executive needed to cope effectively with organizational problems. It was written as a response to the conventional (1955) wisdom regarding the criteria used for selecting individuals for the fast track, which leads to senior executive positions. The conventional wisdom was that potential executives should be selected based on their innate traits and characteristics. Katz believed that the subjective approach of measuring a person's innate traits and characteristics was not the best selection methodology and he proposed that there were three basic, developable skills that would provide better selection criteria:

1. **technical skills**
2. **human skills**
3. **conceptual skills**

He believed that focusing on what a person can do instead of what he or she is would be a much better approach and should be used for selecting individuals to participate in executive development training programs. Katz wrote a follow-up article in 1974, which was also published in the *Harvard Business Review* (HBR). The 1974 article was based on twenty years of experience gained by Katz on the topic. As a result of the experience, he modified a number of the ideas in his original article. The 1974 article has earned the status of becoming an HBR Classic, and the views of the article are still conceptually sound.[2]

TELECOMMUNICATIONS MANAGEMENT SKILLS. While the Katz articles focused on executive skills, it is proposed that the effective administrator skills referenced in these articles are equally applicable as management skills because business executives are basically a subset of business management (upper management). The following discussion will reference the three traits—technical, human, and creative skills—found in the 1974 Katz article and will modify them for use within a telecommunications management context.

SKILL V. KNOWLEDGE. The focus of educational programs is on imparting knowledge to the student—information, facts, truths, or principles. Within a knowledge context, the focus is on testing a student's ability to retain (memorize) information and demonstrate the ability to intellectually apply it within an academic environment. A problem, which confronts students when they earn a degree and leave the academic world to enter the real world, is that they are given real world assignments. The assignments are frequently open ended problems with fuzzy, disorderly requirements. Someone who has a strong academic knowledge base can easily be overwhelmed by the lack of clarity in real world problems and will find it difficult to identify the parameters of the problem so that a good solution can be implemented.

The ability to apply knowledge in a real world environment is normally a combination of on the job training and experience gained when solving real world problems. When someone can apply knowledge to solve problems consistently, they are said to be skilled in that area. A knowledgeable person may have a high level of knowledge but may be unable to achieve good results, while a lesser skilled individual with a strong level of practical know-how will be able to achieve good results. Within this context, management needs skilled managers—not simply well educated managers.

The following sections will review technical, human, and creative skill attributes within a telecommunications management context. It will also discuss the relative importance of these skill areas based on the managerial assignments and the managerial levels held by individuals.

TECHNICAL SKILL. In the Katz article, *technical skill* refers to gaining proficiency in a specific activity—particularly one involving methods, procedures, or techniques. Technical skills are normally taught in an educational or training program format and are the skills with which we are most familiar. The term *technical,* used in the technical skill context, does not refer to technology skills but to subject skills where technical skill areas would include English composition, speech, algebra, principles of management, social sciences, and telecommunications. These are the skills we are accustomed to learning in a formal education environment. Skill levels in subjects are assessed by taking written or oral tests.

Some individuals learn more quickly than others, but individuals who have lower learning skills can acquire strong skill levels in a variety of subjects through hard work and perseverance. Individuals who work hard to acquire a broad range of technical skills in a variety of subjects will have a better skill base than individuals who are more intelligent but did not acquire the same broad set of subject matter skills. It should be noted that the technical skill discussion is academically oriented—the measurement criteria is based on academic criteria. Therefore, the measurement and identification of technical skills is only a partial measurement of practical skills and does not guarantee that an individual with

---

[1] Katz, Robert. "Skills of an Effective Administrator." *Harvard Business Review* 33 no.1 (1955).

[2] Katz, Robert. "Skills of an Effective Administrator." *Harvard Business Review* 52 no.5 (1974):90–102.

strong technical skills will be effective when achieving real world managerial results. To determine an individual's real world effectiveness ability to apply technical skills, it will be necessary to evaluate an individual's results within the context of real world assigned activities.

HUMAN SKILLS. Human skills are those skills needed to work effectively within a leadership or group activity environment. From a managerial perspective, this could involve: 1) leadership ability as the manager of an organization or 2) influencing skills when participating with other groups, peers, or subordinates. In either instance, the human skills that individuals have will be strongly affected by their personal philosophies and the ability to react quickly to new situations. In a supervisory role, human skills are needed to build an atmosphere of trust and security with subordinates for the purpose of creating an effective, cooperative organization. In a subordinate or peer role, human skills are needed to create a harmonious, effective working relationship with others.

Some of the technical skill subjects that are assets in the human skills area are verbal and written communications, technical skills, and supervisory skills. However, someone who has outstanding technical skills in subjects may have great difficulty interacting with others. For example, a first line supervisor who is foreign born and who retains a heavy accent may be a much better leader of people than a native-born individuals who has strong speech skills. The final factors that influence others are the credibility, sincerity, and other human attributes the speaker evokes in the listener. While leadership qualities are not byproducts of the technical skill learning process, acquiring technical skills can help strengthen innate leadership qualities by allowing someone to interact more effectively in a range of situations.

The ability to influence others includes being able to change the opinions and beliefs of others and being able to convince others about the course of action being proposed. To complicate matters, the ability to influence others also depends upon the background of the individual who is being influenced. A speaking or writing style that may be effective when influencing one group may be ineffective when dealing with other groups. The ability to influence (lead, motivate, direct, etc.) is best measured by evaluating the results, not by taking a series of tests that evaluate an individual's technical communication skills.

A good measurement of an individual's human skills would be to evaluate the end results of activities involving others to determine: 1) if the desired task or activity objectives were achieved satisfactorily and 2) if the individual's human interaction elements were positive or negative factors in completing task or activity objectives.

The measurement of human skills is much cloudier than the measurement of technical skills. Human skills measurement factors would include an assessment of the ability of an individual to effectively influence, direct, supervise, manage, cooperate, and coordinate with others. This would involve a degree of subjectivity on the part of the rater, and this subjectivity can affect rating scores when different raters provide different assessments of the same situation. The context of the rating—supervision of personnel, interaction with peers, following orders of upper management, etc.—must also be understood because good performance in one area does not ensure good performance in other areas. For most telecommunications managers, their human skills performance rating will be heavily influenced by two factors: 1) their boss, and 2) the organizational environment. Satisfying the boss will typically result in good human skills ratings—assuming the boss has good human skills. Different organizations may have different viewpoints on desirable interpersonal skills, and a manager must conform to these viewpoints if he or she is to receive good human skills ratings within the organization context.

Katz believed that influencing [human] skills were best learned through practice and experience. As was the case for technical skills, hard work and perseverance can be used to compensate for individuals who have lower levels of innate influencing skills.

CONCEPTUAL SKILLS Influencing (human) skills are more difficult to describe and more difficult to measure than technical skills. Conceptual skills are the fuzziest of the three skill areas. It is extremely difficult to evaluate conceptual performance. Phrases that are frequently used to describe conceptual skills include: *creative skills*, *abstract thinking skills*, *cerebral skills*, and *innovative skills*. Katz referred to conceptual skills as those skills that allowed the executive to see a business as a whole, while also recognizing how the various organization departments relate to each other. In his 1955 article, he stated that an individual could develop conceptual skills by holding various departmental positions in a business as part of an overall management training process. However, in his 1974 article, he concluded that unless the individual had innate conceptual skills there was a low likelihood that job rotation would develop them.

Conceptual skills can also be viewed as the unifying, coordinating skills that provide an individual with the ability to step outside the frame of reference being investigated and arrive at a solution that is outside the sphere of existing solutions—an original solution. Another phrase that could used to describe creativity is *thinking outside the box*. The existence of good technical skills can be an asset to someone who has strong conceptual skills, but Katz considered the two skill areas to be mutually exclusive. An individual may have strong technical skills but may have weak conceptual skills. The reverse is also possible. In addition, individuals may have strong conceptual skills in one area and be weak in other areas. It is not uncommon to find individual creativity limited to specific areas.

The following provides an example of how conceptual skills could relate to technology skills. Let's assume that there is a hypothetical class of 100 students who are enrolled in a course to learn how to fix PCs. None of the students has prior experience in repairing PCs, and they have been selected to attend the course based on the use of standard test scores that assessed their intelligence, mathematical aptitude and knowledge, and mechanical ability. The students selected in our hypothetical class have achieved scores that are very close in all testing areas—they are all believed to have the same capabilities for learning how to become a top notch PC repair person.

Real world experience has shown that, at the end of the training course, there will be one student (possibly two) who will intuitively be able to identify the solution for virtually any PC problem when given the basic symptoms of the problem. The proposed solution may not have been covered during any class work, but the problem solver would feel that it was an obvious way to solve the problem. It is also possible that the individual who exhibits this conceptual ability may not be able to describe exactly how the solution was determined.

Another scenario could take place when a research product is being evaluated to determine its potential for being a good seller in the competitive marketplace. In the marketing department of large corporations, there is likely to be one individual who is able to consistently and accurately predict the likelihood of product success. This individual will have access to the same information as others in the department, but other department members will be unable to provide forecast accuracy approaching the accuracy of our creative forecaster.

Instances similar to these two examples recur consistently in life, where one individual seems to have an uncanny ability to identify the outcome of complex situations. Despite many attempts to teach creativity, it still requires the existence of innate skills that can be nurtured and expanded. Katz's conclusion in his second article was that individuals who do not have the innate conceptual skill are unlikely to develop creative skills through education or training.

RELATIVE IMPORTANCE. The level and relationship of technical, human, and conceptual skills required for any given telecommunications management position will vary depending upon the specific position and the level of the position.

If a telecommunications manager holds a technical position that makes him or her responsible for designing internetworks that consist of routers that use different network protocols, he or she will require a different set of technical skills than a manager who provides administrative services to the users of a telephone system. The human skill needs will also vary because the two managers will have different organization and interorganization communication requirements. In general, the technical and human skills required for different telecommunications management positions will be based on the job requirements of the position.

The conceptual requirements will also vary according to the area of responsibility, because conceptual skills in one area are not normally transferable to other areas. A technical manager who has a strong, intuitive understanding of networking technology could be at a loss when confronted with decisions about the structure and appearance of a business's telephone directory—an essential skill for an administrative services manager.

POSITION REQUIREMENTS. Generally speaking, higher-level telecommunications managers require a lower level of telecommunications technology skills (Katz's technical skills) than lower-level managers—assuming that higher-level managers have technically competent lower-level managers reporting to them. As was the case in the previous section, the specific technical (subject) skills required in a given managerial position will vary depending upon the job responsibilities assigned to the position. A manager of managers will have less need for technology skills than lower-level managers who are directly responsible for a technical department.

Human skills needs will also vary by level. A higher-level manager will require a stronger set of intergroup communication skills than a lower-level manager whose primary focus is on running a department made up of highly technical individuals. Following this same reasoning, a lower-level manager will usually have a larger number of direct reports than an upper-level manager who only manages other managers. Therefore, a lower-level manager needs stronger human skills for interfacing with individuals in a departmental context.

Higher-level telecommunications managers will need strong conceptual skills in business organization, technology concepts, and decision-making areas and their long-term success will be based on their ability to see the (technology) forest and the (technology) trees concurrently.

COMMENTARY. The Katz article reference was presented to provide readers with a conceptual framework for understanding the relationships between different skills. It is not intended to be a solution for understanding or developing personal skills. It is intended to provide readers with a reference framework that they can apply to their own skill development efforts.

Attitude—The Catalyst For Success

> **catalyst:** Somebody or something that makes a change happen or initiates an action without actually generating the change.
>
> **attitude:** A general feeling about something or someone.

At the macrolevel, **attitude** refers to a person's opinion of humanity, the world, and life. At the microlevel it can refer to the likes or dislikes associated with food, entertainment, or other people. Someone who has a positive attitude will see a problem as an opportunity to solve it and will correct the problematic situation, while someone with a negative attitude will see the same problem as someone else's fault and will try to find the guilty culprit so that the appropriate punishment can be administered. In general, people enjoy working with individuals who have positive attitudes and are uncomfortable or find it depressing to work with people who have negative attitudes.

Managers achieve results by directing, leading, coaching, and motivating others. A negative attitude interferes with interpersonal communication, while a positive attitude fosters a better exchange of ideas. In the previous section, the effectiveness of human skills was based on the ability to influence (lead, motivate, change opinion, and coordinate) others. Individuals will voluntarily be influenced when the influencer generates a feeling of credibility and trust within the person being influenced. Credibility and trust are earned by an individual's appearance, words, and actions. An individual who consistently finds fault with peer workers and "tells it like it is" to anyone who will listen is unlikely to gain the confidence and respect of peer workers.

At some point during their careers, managers will have to deal with difficult situations or with difficult people. These difficult people may be a boss, upper management, subordinates, or peers. The way that managers deal with both difficult or easy to work with individuals will determine their effectiveness in the organization. Managers who have difficulty communicating with others will be resented by subordinates, avoided by peers, and viewed with concern by superiors.

Inspirational quotes that relate to attitude:

- You are not interesting if you are not interested.
- Answering dumb questions is easier than correcting dumb mistakes.
- Never let your face shout what you would never let your lips utter.
- Nothing motivates a person more than seeing his or her boss put in an honest day's work.
- Fight the issue, not the person. Keep all conflicts impersonal.

MANAGEMENT STYLE. Leadership is one of the qualities associated with managers. The approach to leadership can range between two extremes: total employee-oriented leadership or total production-oriented leadership. Leaders who are employee oriented emphasize the role of interpersonal relationships when dealing with others, while leaders who are production oriented emphasize the technical or result-oriented aspects of a job. On the surface, it might seem that the employee-oriented approach has clear cut advantages over the production-oriented approach. Some well publicized management studies have shown that employee-oriented managers head groups that have high productivity and high job satisfaction levels, while production-oriented managers headed groups with lower productivity and lower job satisfaction levels.

As with many stereotypes, the general characterizations of employee-oriented and production-oriented leaders may be inaccurate. Let's consider a hypothetical situation in a manufacturing environment where the production-oriented manager ensures that equipment is operating properly, raw materials are always available on time, working conditions are safe, and the pay scale rewards high output. In this production-oriented environment, rules and regulations are consistently applied equitably to all employees. In this same hypothetical manufacturing environment, an employee-oriented manager is continually communicating with subordinates but pays little attention to the equipment, with the result that equipment outages are longer than those of the production-oriented manager. In addition, while the employee-oriented leader is spending time communicating with others, raw material deliveries do not always arrive on time. The net result is that employees in the employee-oriented manager's group incur more downtime, have lower productivity, and are paid less than the production-oriented group. As a result, the employees who work for the production-oriented manager are well paid and have excellent working conditions, while the employees who work for the employee-oriented manager make less money and have more spare time (downtime), but are able to freely discuss their concerns with their manager. Which environment is a better work environment?

The objective of this example is to illustrate that the use of generalities or stereotyping can be dangerous. In the previous chapter, different management theories formulated during the last ninety years were discussed. Theories that were developed more recently tend to use a situational, contingency theory, and process-oriented approach. Use of a situational approach means that the details of the environment must be known before general management theories are applied to solve a problem. In our hypothetical example, the conditions for the employee-oriented scenario required understanding the situation prior to assuming that the employee-oriented approach was best.

SELECTING A MANAGEMENT STYLE. Managers will adopt the leadership style with which they are the most comfortable. The **management style** they use early in their careers will be greatly influenced by personal attitudes and the guidance given by their bosses or other mentors. With maturity and experience, individuals will be exposed to many different leadership styles and will have the opportunity to observe their own and others' strengths and weaknesses. Unless their work environment is highly stable (an unlikely scenario), they will find that different styles work best under different situations and that the specific work environment may determine which leadership style is most effective. This is another way of saying that a situational leadership style may be the most effective leadership style.

Commentary On Selecting A Management Style:
"Read, listen, discuss, observe, think."

John Patterson, NCR Chairman

The ability to manage effectively will depend upon a manager's individual skills and attitudes and the skills and attitudes of the people being managed. The ability to effectively evaluate different managerial situations, initiate the appropriate actions, and achieve positive results will be the final yardstick for measuring managerial effectiveness. This is similar to the observations made in the Katz article, where the assessment of someone's human (influencing) skills is based on results, not on a technical testing process.

MICROPLANNING AND MACROPLANNING CONCEPTS

The *Integrative Theory* section in Chapter 6 discussed process and situational management theories. Under the in-

tegrative management theory approach, existing management theories would be viewed as tools that can be applied to a range of managerial problems on an as needed basis. Fayol's **POLC Model** (plan, organize, lead, and control) would be used in the integrative approach, and any appropriate methodology could be applied in the different model phases. The POLC Model is shown in Figure 7–3.

The goals provide the focus for the plan, organize, lead, and control elements, where those steps would continually be monitored and adjusted, as required, to ensure that the goals are achieved. It may appear that the management process model can be used as both a **microplanning** and a **macroplanning** model. However, a brief analysis will show that POLC Model is best suited for the microplanning process when it is applied as a multipurpose tool. Macroplanning models must be modified for the environment in which they operate, while a microplanning model can be used in any planning process.

The following will discuss microdecision and macrodecision requirements. As is frequently the case in the real world, the techniques that are discussed are a few of the many approaches that are available. The tool selection decision relies on the judgment of the individual.

Microdecision Concepts: A Thinking Method

The term *microdecision* refers to the basic thinking processes that take place when a problem or situation is encountered.

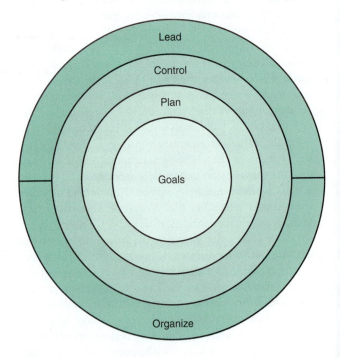

Figure 7–3. The POLC Model.

The POLC Model is a basic, flexible thinking process that can be applied to handle a wide range of managerial problems. The *P* in POLC identifies the planning phase, where managerial objectives are defined—objectives that become the criteria for determining the success or failure of the management solution. The specific situation being addressed with the POLC Model may be technical or nontechnical, but is one that requires managerial action to resolve. Let's assume that the manager of an order processing department calls the telecommunications manager responsible for LAN operations in a medium-sized company. The order processing manager informs the LAN operations manager that customer orders cannot be processed because the LAN is not working properly. What does the telecommunications manager do to solve this problem?

The correct answer to the previous question requires a balance of diplomacy and corrective action. Diplomacy requires the manager to acknowledge that the order processing manager has a problem and that the LAN operations department will respond quickly to fix the problem—despite the fact that the LAN operations manager does not yet know whether a LAN problem exists or not. The reality is that the LAN operations manager will be unable to initiate any meaningful corrective actions until the root cause of the problem has been identified. If any action is taken without fully understanding the nature of the problem, there is a strong likelihood that these actions may be ineffective. The following discussion will review three general thinking methodologies that are needed to initiate corrective action:

1. problem analysis
2. decision making
3. potential problem analysis

The framework used for this discussion will be based on company training received by the author of this text during the 1960s. The text used for the training course was *The Rational Manager* by Charles H. Kepner and Benjamin B. Tregoe. This book is no longer in print, but the topics are as relevant today as they were forty-five years ago.

PROBLEM ANALYSIS. A problem refers to questions or situations that require a solution. Problems may be characterized in many ways —complex, simple, technical, nontechnical, administrative, or personnel. If problem solving methods were developed for every type of problem that exists, the selection of the correct solution specific methodology would be come a difficult and time consuming effort. What is needed is a general method that provides a thinking framework that is applicable to a wide range of problems.

Students of engineering and other science-based programs are introduced to the scientific method early in their educations. The scientific method is used to develop solutions to problems. The method involves defining the problem, collecting appropriate data through observation and experimentation, and then testing different hypothetical answers to select the one that best fits the problem. Scientific method thinking concepts are the basis for virtually all problem-solving methodologies, including the ones that will be discussed in this section of the text.

A (NOT THE) PROBLEM ANALYSIS APPROACH. The primary objective of the problem analysis phase is to determine if the problem is real and, if it is real, to assess its scope and severity. For a problem to exist, there must be an acceptable standard of performance used to identify good performance. Therefore, the first step when analyzing a problem (or situation) is to identify the expected standard of performance and compare the current level of performance to it. For example, if a production line normally produces 100 widgets per hour, acceptable performance would be a production of 100 or more widgets per hour. If the maintenance foreman responsible for maintaining the widget production line is told that the line is not operating properly, the first question that should be asked is "At what speed is it running?" If the response is 100 widgets per hour, the foreman's response might be, "The line is running at normal speed, what other problems exist?" The return response might be, "Oh, the line is operating allright but the light above the labeling machine is burned out." Therefore, the problem to be addressed is replacing a light bulb—one that does not require mechanical maintenance of the widget-manufacturing equipment. Dispatching a mechanic to fix the widget line would have been inappropriate and a waste of the mechanic's time. Instead, someone from building services could be dispatched, and the problem could addressed directly. Figure 7–4 provides a flowchart that summarizes the **problem analysis process.**

The problem analysis process in Figure 7–4 is a generic process. However, it should be clear that applying it effectively assumes that the individual who uses the process has an appropriate level of knowledge about problem parameters. The model process raises many questions during its application. Unless these questions are answered properly, the results of the model are likely to be flawed. If the problem solver does not have personal knowledge of the problem or situation, there is a low likelihood of finding a successful solution unless there is access to someone who has knowledge about the problem.

Telecommunications managers frequently find that they are asked to solve problems in areas where they do not have detail-level knowledge or in areas where they have limited skills. When a knowledge gap exists, the first

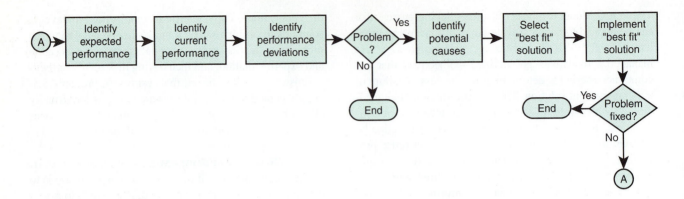

Figure 7–4. A problem analysis process.

step is to obtain the required knowledge by identifying and utilizing appropriate information resources. These resources would include department members, written documentation, other internal resources, and external resources. Telecommunications managers manage many individuals who have a detailed knowledge of telecommunications technology, *but those individuals may have limited problem solving skills*. If the telecommunications manager has strong problem solving skills, these skills can be used in a synergetic mode with someone else's technical knowledge to determine the correct solution. When this marriage of problem solver + problem knowledge occurs, the manager becomes a facilitator—a catalyst that provides a focus for effectively using someone else's technical knowledge.

The problem-analysis process illustrated in Figure 7–4 is conceptually simple, but its effective application is more difficult. As with many knowledge areas, applying problem solving process knowledge is normally learned through experience. Because this is not a course in problem solving, the problem solving discussion ends now. The problem solving approach presented in this section will be used for all the case studies provided in this text.

BENCHMARKING: A PROBLEM ANALYSIS TOOL.
During the discussion on problem solving, it was stated that the initial step in the problem solving process was to determine if a problem actually exists. This step requires knowledge of the expected standard of performance, so that actual operating performance can be compared to the expected standard. The idea of comparing actual performance to a standard is the underlying concept behind **benchmarking.** Benchmarking is an analytical approach that gained attention during the late 1970s, when the Xerox Corporation used a competitive benchmarking process to identify inefficiencies in their U.S. manufacturing operations.

During the 1970s, Xerox found that they were selling copiers at a significantly higher price than equivalent Japanese copiers being sold in the U.S. marketplace. A concern voiced by some U.S. legislators was that Japanese manufacturers might be engaged in "product dumping"— the illegal practice of selling exported goods below the cost of making them. If this were the case in the U.S. copier market, it would become a matter for Congress to resolve with the Japanese government.

Xerox initiated a benchmarking project with one of its Japanese affiliates to evaluate its manufacturing operations and determine if internal U.S. manufacturing costs were competitive compared to those in Japan. The Xerox Corporation established a database of the appropriate metrics for their copier manufacturing operation, then compared the database to the manufacturing costs of their Japanese affiliate. They found that the U.S. manufacturing costs were significantly higher than the affiliate's manufacturing costs, and concluded that this was due to differences in the manufacturing processes. The U.S. manufacturing facility was found to be inefficient when compared to the Japanese affiliate's operations. Therefore, it was most likely inefficient compared to the manufacturing processes of other Japanese copier manufacturers.

The root cause of the problem was not product dumping by Japanese competitors. The problem was that Xerox manufacturing facilities were being operated inefficiently compared to their Japanese competitors. Once the root cause had been identified, Xerox focused on improving its manufacturing processes. As a result of these efforts, Xerox manufacturing costs were reduced, and the company was able to compete effectively with Japanese copier pricing.

The benchmarking process involves applying problem-analysis method to see if performance problems exist compared to an external standard. When a significant

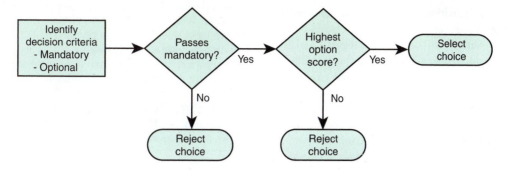

Figure 7–5. A decision making process flowchart.

performance gap is found, it becomes a matter of identifying the changes required to modify the activity or process and improve its performance. From a management perspective, the use of benchmarking provides a means of ensuring that internal operations are being run efficiently and effectively as compared to external benchmarking standards. If the selected external benchmarking standard being used is a valid standard, any internal comparison to this standard ensures that the selected operation is being measured objectively. Benchmarking may be applied to business level or department-level operations.

DECISION MAKING.   Managers must make decisions, frequently without knowing the details of the decision or problem solving activities that generated the need for the decision. Therefore, it is important for managers to use a decision making method that is able to operate effectively with the information that is available. Part of the decision making process is to ask questions of the individuals who are requesting the decision. It should be noted that the degree to which a manager may question superiors is more limited than the level of questioning that a peer or subordinate employee will tolerate.

A good **decision making process** should compare alternative solutions to the problem for which a decision must be made and should also provide a reliable process for selecting the best alternative. A telecommunications manager may be approached by others (subordinates, peers, or senior managers) and may be asked to determine which of several alternatives is best for a given situation. On the surface, this situation may appear to be a "no win" situation for the manager, while in reality, it is an opportunity to demonstrate a key managerial **attribute**—a sound, logical, decision making skill. Good managers make good decisions, while poor managers make poor decisions.

The following examines a decision making method that, when properly applied, will generate good decisions.

Figure 7–5 provides a decision process flowchart that will be used as the basis for the decision making discussion in this section. While the text will primarily use it for evaluating acquisition alternatives, the methodology is appropriate for use with any decision activity:

Two decision making elements, shown on the chart, that will be further examined are:

1. mandatory requirements

2. optional requirements

For every decision process, there must be criteria for making the right decision, otherwise it would be impossible to ever make any decisions. Various decision criteria will have different levels of importance for the decision process. A good decision process must provide a way of allowing for different levels of importance and ensuring that the high-importance factors weigh most heavily in the decision making process. In some cases, the level of importance may be so high that the criterion becomes a mandatory decision factor.

MANDATORY AND OPTIONAL CRITERIA.   Two types of decision criteria will be established for our decision making model—those that are mandatory and those that are not mandatory, but are important. Mandatory criteria will be called **mandatory requirements.** This designation means that the decision criteria must be met—or the decision cannot be made. If multiple mandatory requirements exist for a decision alternative, failure of the alternative to meet any mandatory requirement would disqualify it from further consideration.

Nonmandatory but important criteria will be called *optional requirements* to reflect the qualitative nature of their characteristics. The relative desirability of different optional requirements will be measured through the use of a scoring system. A table should be used to list the various optional requirements provided by different decision alternatives and the desirability of individual optional requirements will be rated against other individual optional requirements.

A simple example will illustrate the use of mandatory and optional requirements for generating a decision between different decision alternatives. In the example, a family wants to purchase a car that will meet the needs of the family. There are six family members—two parents and four children—and one of the mandatory requirements would be that the new car must be able to seat six comfortably. Therefore, any opportunity to purchase a two-seater sports car at a wonderfully low price would be summarily dismissed, and only cars capable of comfortably transporting six people would warrant further consideration.

The decision makers (probably the parents) may feel that gas mileage and reliability history are very important but car color and exterior trim options are unimportant. They might also feel that criteria of medium importance would include the type of seat upholstery and the luggage carrying capacity of the car. It should be apparent that continuing to list criteria in this format would result in many entries that are hard to compare individually or collectively. A table will be used to organize what could become a long list. This list will also indicate: 1) the importance or desirability of the option to the family, and 2) the rating assigned to the option for each decision alternative.

Table 7–1 provides a preliminary Optional Requirements Evaluation Table that lists the various option requirements selected by our hypothetical family. It shows four columns—Optional Requirement, Weight, Rating, and Score.

The Optional Requirement column lists the various optionals that the family considers important (not mandatory) elements for the decision process. The Weight column indicates the relative importance of the listed criteria, where a *10* is the highest possible weight and a *1* is the lowest weight that will be used in the table.

Note: Weights are relative ratings. The attributes that are most desirable would be rated with a *10* and other attributes would have lower weights. The same weighting values can be assigned to multiple attributes if the different attributes are considered to be of equal importance. Table 7–1 shows that the Reliability history was considered the most important attribute and was assigned a 10. The least important attribute was Color, which was assigned a 3.

The Rating column would list the rating values assigned to an option for a given choice. The ratings would be made on a comparative (not absolute) basis. This means that the car choice that best meets a given optional requirement would be assigned a 10 and all other ratings for that option would be assigned a comparative rating. If two car choices provided an optional requirement that was considered equivalent, the same rating would be given to both car choices.

Table 7–1 should be prepared prior to beginning the evaluation of various car models, so that it can be used during the preliminary screening phase when comparing the choices.

Only cars that met the mandatory requirement of being able to seat six comfortably would reach the evaluation process shown in Table 7–1. A separate rating would be carried out for each car choice, which would probably require establishing multiple tables. Table 7–2 provides a completed option evaluation table for one of the cars that passed the mandatory requirement of being able to seat six passengers comfortably.

An individual score was calculated for each attribute by multiplying the weight with the rating. The total score for any car alternative would be the sum of its individual optional requirement scores.

TABLE 7–1   Optional Requirement Evaluation Table

Optional Requirement	Weight	Rating	Score
Reliability history	10		
Gas mileage	9		
Luggage capacity	7		
Upholstery material	6		
Exterior trim	4		
Color	3		
Total score			

TABLE 7–2   Completed Option Evaluation Table

Optional Requirement	Weight	Rating	Score
Reliability history	10	10	100
Gas mileage	9	8	72
Luggage capacity	7	9	63
Upholstery material	6	8	48
Exterior trim	4	5	20
Color	3	7	21
Total Score			**323**

Individual score = weight × rating total score = sum of individual scores

Table 7–2 shows that a total score of 323 was assigned to one of the car choices. If the correct criteria were identified, weighted, and rated, the total score should provide a relative measure of satisfaction for this car choice compared to other choices. The car choice that had the highest score would have the best fit for the evaluator's optional requirement criteria. However, it is important to remember that the table results will only be as accurate as the rater's application of weights and ratings and the inclusion of all options that are important for the selection decision. Otherwise, the results will be inaccurate. If the total rating scores differ by only a small percentage (less than 5%), there is really no significant difference between the choices, and evaluator judgment is required (sometimes referred to as common sense). In the event of very close scores between top contenders, either choice could be selected, with a high degree of confidence that it would meet family needs.

The use of mandatory requirements ensures that essential criteria are included in the decision process, while the use of the option scoring technique provides a means of converting subjective criteria into a measurement metric. Tables provide an excellent way to organize a great amount of information into an easy to read format and provide others with an easy to understand tool.

POTENTIAL PROBLEM ANALYSIS. At this point, two microdecision areas have been reviewed: 1) a problem solving method and 2) a decision making process. For both areas, it is possible to compensate for a lack of evaluator knowledge by asking the right questions of someone who has the necessary knowledge. This flexibility allows a manager who has strong problem resolution and decision making skills to work with someone who does not have those skills.

The problem analysis and decision making methods are examples of thinking within the box—they are focused on the end result of obtaining a solution within the constraints of the specific situation. **Potential problem analysis** (PPA) asks a broader question, "What will happen if I use this problem solution?" or "What will happen if I use the decision I have selected?" PPA involves looking at both the problem solving and decision making processes in a broader context, other than simply finding an answer. PPA examines solutions that are beyond of the scope the problem solving and decision making environments that generated them.

Returning to our car selection problem, suppose a car has been selected. It meets the mandatory criterion of seating six passengers comfortably, and it also scores highest when rating the optional requirement categories. Looking for potential problems may reveal that the closest

dealership is forty miles away, and that the complexity of servicing and repairing the selected car requires the owner to have the car serviced at a dealership. The evaluator now has another issue to address prior to making a decision.

> **Note:** This potential problem analysis example is analogous to establishing a plan in the POLC Model and realizing at a later time that it may be necessary to redefine the plan so that the desired goals can be met.

THINKING METHOD SUMMARY. Thinking method skills can help someone solve problems outside of his or her knowledge boundaries by asking the right questions of someone else who is familiar with the situation. A good question asker who has minimal knowledge of a subject can solve complex problems by applying sound problem solving and decision making methods.

Successful managers are assigned many responsibilities, and good managers may be asked to manage departments about which they have limited knowledge. The key to being an effective manager, when confronted by problems in areas where personal expertise is low, is to ask the right questions of individuals who are familiar with details of the situation. The manager would structure the received information into a problem solving or decision making format to develop solutions. The ability to solve problems, make decisions, and identify potential problems are key skills for any aspiring manager, and they become increasingly important as they advance to higher managerial levels and personally handle fewer details.

This introduction to thinking methods is intended to stimulate interest in acquiring and effectively using thinking skills. The concepts that have been presented will be used throughout this text.

Macrodecision Concepts: A Decision Framework

The POLC Model works very well as a basic method for carrying out simple activities, but it has shortcomings when activities are part of a large work effort, such as the development and implementation of telecommunications projects. In large projects, many activities must be coordinated. It is often necessary to create an overall project framework to ensure the most efficient and effective implementation of project activities. It is necessary to supplement the microdecision POLC process with a broader framework to address organizational and technology issues.

Figure 7–6 illustrates a macrodecision process flowchart that places telecommunications systems and networks into a product life cycle framework. This

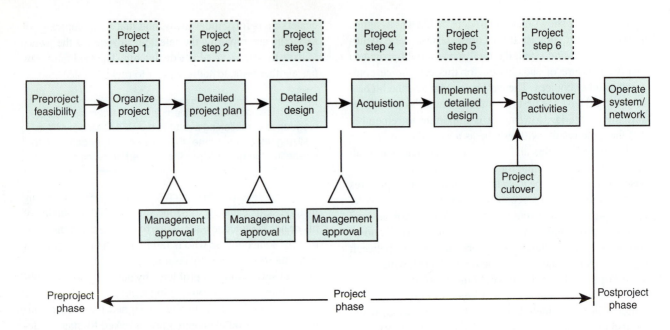

Figure 7–6. A macrodecision framework.

framework consists of three major life cycle phases—preproject, project, and postproject phases. These three phases can also be thought of as conceptual, development, and operational phases. When telecommunications resources (products, systems, and networks) are being developed, it is necessary to ensure that their implementation viability is maintained during the development phase. This is done by providing project exit points that allow a project to be scrapped if: 1) the initial justification for the project no longer exists or 2) more current information (higher implementation costs, project delays, etc.) changes the economic viability of the project. Project exit points provide the opportunity to bail out of a bad project and avoid or at least minimize the losses associated with it.

The decision framework in Figure 7–6 can be used for technical or nontechnical projects by modifying it for the appropriate context. Conceptually, the macrodecision framework breaks a project or activity into phases, evaluates the ongoing viability of the effort in increasing detail as the project or activity is executed, and determines if the project or activity remains viable during the course of the project. A project that looks very attractive initially may become less attractive as additional information is obtained.

The larger or more complex the project is, the greater the need to use a macrodecision structure. While the POLC Model would continue to be applied within each framework phase, each phase would also be evaluated from an enterprise perspective that requires a decision. If

the project remains viable up to the last approval point shown in Figure 7–6, the project will be implemented; otherwise, it will be terminated and the unused resources can be allocated to other investment opportunities.

Figure 7–7 places the Figure 7–6 macrodecision framework elements into a flowchart format.

LIFE CYCLE ANALYSIS. When telecommunications projects are undertaken, the work effort typically results in the creation of a fixed asset that is expected to function over some time period. Therefore, the development effort—the part of the project preceding the implementation of the project—is an effort that is intended to provide benefits over a finite time period. The total costs incurred for selecting, implementing, and operating the asset over its lifetime are *life cycle costs*. Figure 7–8 has taken Figure 7–6 and relabeled it as a product life cycle model. This figure will be used to review the **life cycle analysis** (LCA) concept, and this model will be used throughout the remainder of the text.

Costs are incurred during the development, implementation, and operational phases of a technical product's life cycle. In Figure 7–8, a network is being developed and placed into operation. Most of the network project costs for the Organize project, Detailed project plan, and Detailed design phases will consist of the paperwork costs involved in developing a design and selecting vendor equipment for the network. As indicated in Figure 7–8, the Acquisition,

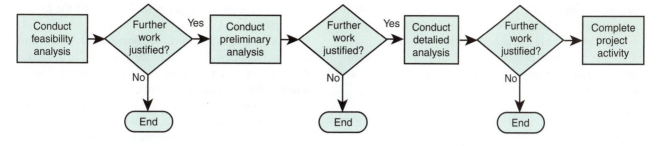

Figure 7–7. The Macrodecision process.

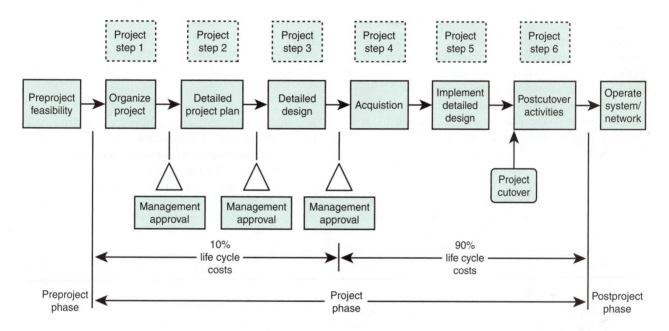

Figure 7–8. Product life cycle model.

Implement detailed design, Postcutover activities, and Operate system/network phases account for 90% of total Life cycle costs, while the Organize project, Detailed project plan, and Detailed design phases account for approximately 10% of total Life cycle costs. This should not be surprising, because the Acquisition phase is when equipment and services are purchased, which is normally the largest single cost incurred during the product life cycle.

> **Note**: Annual maintenance costs typically amount to 10% of the initial equipment purchase cost.

Figure 7–8 used a value of approximately 3% of the total LCA budget for each development phase. While the actual percent of LCA budget may vary from project to project, the Acquisition, Implementation, Postcutover, and Operational phases will normally range between 80% and 90% of total LCA costs (LCA$).

As additional details are gained during a project development period, a project that was initially judged as being financially attractive may be found to have unexpected new costs or be less desirable because the initial decision criteria are no longer valid. Providing upper management with a periodic review of projects during a project life cycle helps them identify poor decisions early in the development cycle and take action to minimize losses. These monies can then become available for implementing other projects that were bypassed in favor of the project that should be discontinued.

CLOSING COMMENTS. The life cycle framework in Figure 7–8 provides a mechanism for ensuring the ongoing viability of a project during its implementation phase, and provides periodic opportunities to terminate poor projects. The use of periodic checkpoints also ensures that enterprise level decision makers are provided with assurances that their (perhaps limited) investment dollars are being spent wisely.

THE ACCOUNTING TOOL

Since 1894, when the first laws governing the activities of Certified Public Accountants (CPAs) were created, businesses have used financial criteria to measure internal and external business activities. Money (dollars in the U.S.) is the standard unit used for measuring business performance in the marketplace, evaluating investment alternatives, and measuring internal operating performance.

Technology investments are translated into a cost *v.* benefit format to facilitate their understanding by nontechnical business managers and to provide business managers with the information they need to make sound investment decisions. Employee staffing represents an investment of dollars. Productivity measurements are frequently used to determine the effectiveness of an organization in managing its people resource. People-time is assigned a monetary rate ($/hour) for different departments, and the time value of money is also assigned a cost value by using interest rates to translate investments spanning different time periods. In a lifetime financial analysis, expenses incurred in different time periods are converted to standard dollars (typically current-year dollars), appropriate interest rates are used, and an allowance is provided for inflation's effects. These parameters are part of the accounting framework used by most businesses.

> **Bottom line:** Accounting terminology and principles are embedded in current management techniques. A good working knowledge of general and business accounting procedures is a mandatory skill for telecommunications managers.

The timing of revenues and expenses determines the cash flow status of a business. Operating expenses and capital investment activities must be timed to ensure that an organization's short-term and long-term profitability objectives can be met. If expenses exceed revenues in any fiscal period, it will be necessary to have cash available to meet the profit shortfall until operational profits can sustain day to day operations. Timing of activities is an ongoing concern to upper management, and cash flow

financial planning is a key responsibility of the finance department.

All business activities—maintaining staffing, buildings, and equipment—require the expenditure of money. Activities in all business areas must be converted to the standard business measurement unit—*dollars*. When the financial benefits outweigh the financial costs, a project is considered viable. However, because organization funds are limited (unless a government agency is involved), telecommunications department spending proposals must compete with all of the other internally generated spending proposals. These proposals must be in the format used by the business to evaluate investment alternatives. Failure of a telecommunications manager to conform to internal proposal format guidelines will reduce the probability of receiving funding for telecommunications activities.

Budgeting

Budgets are the financial mechanism for identifying future plans. They are generated by establishing forecasts for a future period's assets and liabilities and converting these forecasts into dollars. Last year's budget becomes this year's operating plan, and the operating plan contains detailed information for employee compensation, equipment costs, equipment maintenance costs, subscriptions, employee overtime, etc. Budgets also provide forecasts of future revenues. This combination of revenue and expense budgeting become an internal tool for measuring managerial performance. Two budgeting approaches are used by businesses:

1. **incremental budgeting**
2. **zero based budgeting (ZBB)**

INCREMENTAL BUDGETING. The underlying philosophy of incremental budgeting is that the current year's actual revenues and expenses become the operating base on which the next year's budget will be built. The implications are that current year revenues and expenses have already been justified, and the services they covered will continue to be provided. If they are eliminated, a budget adjustment will be made. The normal incremental approach is to compare the current year actual expense history against the current year budget, identify the best estimate for total current year actual expenses, and use this actual expense estimate as the base for establishing next year's forecast (budget). The difference between the current year actual expense forecast and next year's expense forecast should include adjustments for rate changes, volume changes, and the implementation of new initiatives.

A downside of the incremental budgeting process is that it is difficult to identify inefficiencies and waste that have become embedded in budget line items. The advantage is that it allows managers to focus on changes without going through the pain of an in-depth analysis of each budget line item.

ZERO BASED BUDGETING. In the ZBB process, every line item in a budget must be explained in terms of its benefits when a new budget is being prepared. The ZBB preparation process requires managers to justify all budget requests in detail and assumes that annual expenses start from a zero base and any budget line items are justified in every annual budget. In ZBB, the budget preparer is required to follow four steps:

1. Separate each department activity into a decision package.
2. Rank these decision packages in terms of their importance.
3. Allocate the proposed budget into the various decision packages.
4. Submit the decision packages for approval.

Creating a decision package (step 1) requires the budget preparer to initially identify the key products and services provided by the department and then generate a listing that separates them into logical groupings. These logical groupings become the basis for individual decision packages that are part of the ZBB process.

In step 2, product/service groupings (the decision package) are ranked in importance by using an enterprise-based ranking process, where the most important products and services are placed at the top of the ranking list. In step 3, the budget preparer would then allocate line item expense forecasts (salaries, office supplies, and equipment) to individual decision packages. The end result would be a series of minibudgets established for each decision package, where the total budget being submitted is the sum of the individual minibudgets.

The detailed decision package/minibudget information is then submitted for approval. The budget preparer would be told which decision packages had been accepted and which had been rejected.

Carried to the extreme, ZBB can be a tedious, painful process. Managed effectively, it provides a process for ensuring that the value of a department's products and services are validated on a regular basis. The use of ZBB should also include an ongoing assessment that ensures that the pain of ZBB is justified.

ZBB is an excellent approach for comparing outsourcing options to internal operations. Separating internal activities into decision packages and then comparing out-

sourcing proposals to these decision packages will identify exactly what is covered by an outsourcing proposal and what is not. Used in this way, ZBB can prevent a company from signing an outsourcing contract and then discovering that essential products or services were erroneously omitted from the outsourcing contract.

Financial Reports

A business's accounting department generates many reports used by upper management for assessing the business's financial condition. These reports include income statements, retained earnings statements, balance sheets, and cash flow statements that provide a financial report on the overall status of profitability, assets, and liabilities. At the operational level, department budget reports and capital forecasting reports are used to measure internal performance and provide a financial plan for major internal investments. Department managers have the responsibility for forecasting department needs, then they assume the accountability for ensuring that their forecasts are met when budgets becomes current operating plans.

Department forecasts are consolidated within departmental areas (purchasing, manufacturing, accounting, telecommunications, etc.) and the manager of the department is responsible for developing department expense and capital expenditure forecasts. Department forecasts are consolidated into division forecasts, and the consolidated forecasts are formally submitted to the business's management board for final approval. Final approval by the management board means that the forecast becomes the operating budget for the next year, and internal managers will be evaluated on their ability to manage their budgets.

The financial department acts as the facilitator for this financial planning process—a process frequently referred to as the **annual planning cycle.** The annual planning cycle is scheduled and carried out each fiscal year, and the approved final revenue and expense forecasts become the basis for the future year's profitability forecasts. Approved forecasts are then sent back to the departments that generate them. Department managers are provided with budgets in a format where each revenue or expense line item forecast category is listed, and a plan *v.* actual comparison will be provided as actual expenses are incurred during next year's operations.

Revenue forecasting is an activity normally limited to upper management and the business's sales department. However, all departments are involved in forecasting expenses (including capital expenditure forecasting). Expense forecasting is a time consuming activity that is of great importance to management personnel. Expense forecasts (budgets) become the performance standard by which department managers are measured. In the year the budget is implemented, each expense line item forecast is listed alongside the actual expense incurred. Differences between the forecast and the actual expense are referred to as variances. Large variances require explanations.

Budget *v.* Actual: The Variance Report

The budget *v* .actual (**BVA**) equation is a simple one:

$$\text{Variance} = \text{forecast (budget)} - \text{actual}$$

Each expense line item listed on a BVA report shows both a forecast value (generated during the previous year's annual planning cycle) and the actual expense incurred during the forecast period. Example 7–1 shows the basic format that is used for BVA reporting. To simplify this discussion, only a few expense line items have been shown.

The normal frequency for BVA reporting is monthly, and each monthly department report should contain a listing of forecast expense line items (the budget) and the expense actually incurred (actual) during the current time period. Variances are calculated for each line item, so that the manager can quickly identify large variances. Example 7–1 uses parentheses to highlight negative calculations instead of using the minus (–) sign. Parentheses are frequently used for negative variance quantities because they are easier to see than minus signs.

Variances are easily seen in a BVA format. The review process is simplified by using an **exception management** approach, where the primary focus is on line items that have significant variances. In Example 7–1, the total department budget shows an overall negative variance of $3,543.68 (a negative 4% variance). While this may appear reasonable on the surface, it can be seen that a negative variance of $1,000.00 was incurred in the Overtime salaries category—a major (20%) negative variance. The Overtime salary clearly warrants investigation to determine the reason for the variance and to see if corrective action is required to bring this account under control.

Variance reporting is a key tool for both department and business management. Telecommunications managers will be evaluated on their ability to forecast accurately and meet their budget estimates.

MANAGING BY EXCEPTION. When addressing variances generated in a BVA reporting environment, the volume of information presented on the reports can easily overwhelm a novice telecommunications manager. Each expense line item contains budget, actual, and variance values. Category subtotals and grand total information are also provided in BVA reports. The key to retaining one's sanity when confronted with large amounts of data is to identify the critical data elements and resolve them in a priority sequence. Using this approach, the variances on a BVA can be scanned, the larger ones should be highlighted, and any follow up efforts would focus on the highlighted items. Therefore, the first step when managing variances is to categorize variances according to sign (positive or negative), magnitude, and expense category. Some expense categories warrant higher attention than others.

The process described in the preceding paragraph is an example of exception management, where specific elements are separated from a large group of elements. While the exception example was used to find a way of evaluating variances, the concept can be applied universally for any area within a telecommunications manager's control. Managers must be able to determine what is critical and what is not critical, including instances where criticality assessments may change over time because of priority changes. The ability to work on the right things at the right times separates good managers from mediocre managers.

Example 7–1 BVA Reporting

Expense Description	Budget	Actual	Variance ($)	Diff (%)
Salaries, regular time	$50,000.00	$49,500.00	$500.00	1%
Salaries, overtime	$10,000.00	$11,000.00	($1,000.00)	(20%)
Subscriptions	$350.00	$350.00	$0.00	0%
Petty cash	$150.00	$132.50	$17.50	12%
Etc.				
Department totals	**$85,000.00**	**$88,543.68**	**($3,543.68)**	**(4%)**

Everyone has a limited amount of time to spend doing a job. Applying limited time resources to the most important issues is the best way to increase managerial performance.

Other Financial Analysis Tools

There are many activity-specific financial tools and techniques used to manage a business department. Managers should be aware of the ones used in their business, and should be able to use them appropriately and accurately. Typically, these tools are used for investment analysis—evaluating a project's benefit to the business. Investment analysis tools provide a standard way of identifying the value of investment alternatives for the business by using a standardized cost/benefit format. If capital investment proposals are prepared accurately, and if they include all the proper evaluation elements, upper management will be able to select the best choice for the allocation of limited corporate funds.

OTHER PLANNING TOOLS

Over the years, different tools have been developed and used by managers. These include sophisticated tools like linear programming, queuing theory, probability theory, and model simulation techniques. While many techniques are not operationally viable without the use of computer technology to handle the associated processing requirements, simplifying assumptions can frequently be made to use them in a practical way. However, while mathematically complex methods may be important for certain applications, they will not be used in this text.

Three tools are reviewed in the following sections: 1) forecasting, 2) Gantt charts, and 3) project network diagrams. The forecasting and project network diagram discussion are technically detailed topics, while the Gantt chart discussion reviews an old tool that still is useful for simplifying large, complex projects. Project network diagrams will be discussed in greater detail in Part 3, *Project Management*. and forecasting techniques will be covered in Part 4, *Operations Management*.

Forecasting Tools

Forecasting, the ability to predict accurately what is likely to happen in the future—provides obvious advantages for individuals or organizations that possess accurate forecast information. Good forecasting information can be used to introduce new products at the best time, retrench activities for temporary economic downturns, and avoid making investments in the wrong areas.

Forecasting has had a long, inconsistent history. One of the celebrated forecasters in the past, the oracle of the Greek god Apollo, resided in the Greek town of Delphi. The oracle was located on the slope of Mount Parnassus and was operated by Apollo's priestesses. When the Persians approached the oracle and wanted to know the outcome [forecast] of a war they planned to wage with Greece, they were informed that a great nation will be destroyed. Armed with this valuable bit of information, they attacked the Greeks. As predicted at Delphi, the Persians were defeated. The point of this fable is that *all forecasts should be viewed with skepticism.* There is always a degree of uncertainty in the forecasting process, regardless of how celestial the forecasting source claims to be.

Used appropriately, with an understanding of its strengths and limitations, forecasting is a powerful business and managerial tool. Accurate forecasting is a detailed, complex activity requiring strong mathematical skills and common sense. In this text, discussions and illustrations of managerial forecasting will be based on using a practical approach instead of relying on complex mathematical calculations.

Most forecasting techniques used in business are mathematically based and assume the existence of accurate historical information. They also assume that projections of historical trends will provide accurate indicators of future performance in the same area (sales, expenses, staffing). The use of historical data trends to predict future values is based on utilizing quantitative forecasting methods. There are also forecasting methods for estimating events in the absence of historical trend information, and these techniques rely on probability and jury of opinion forecasting techniques. These are qualitative forecasting methods, which are scientific forms of guessing.

Using estimates based on past history is commonly used when forecasting telecommunications expenses. In the absence of specific historical data, educated estimates (jury of opinion) can provide reasonably accurate results—if the estimator has good judgment. Simplifying assumptions about historical data can significantly reduce the work effort needed to provide reasonable forecasts.

Gantt Charts

Henry L. Gantt, one of the contributors to the scientific management movement during the early 1900s, developed the **Gantt chart** to provide a way to summarize multiple managerial activities that take place during different time periods. The Gantt chart, still in use today, provides a fairly intuitive way of portraying the different elements of a

Figure 7–9. An example of a Gantt chart.

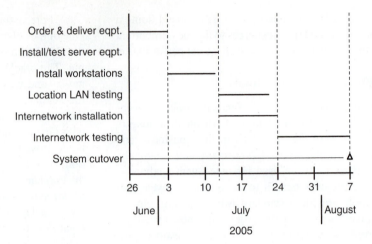

technical or nontechnical project that spans different time periods.

Projects are broken down into activities and tasks, and activities consist of multiple tasks. The Gantt chart portrays the time relationship between various project activities by showing each activity's start time, end time, and duration, as shown in Figure 7–9. The vertical axis (*y* axis) is used for listing the different work elements (activities), and the horizontal axis (*x* axis) is used to show time-related information (dates). The work elements are shown as bars or lines. The beginning of the bar/line is the start of the work element and the end of the bar/line indicates the completion of the work element.

Gantt charts are used for conveying project information to others in a simple, easily read format. When correctly labeled, the information that Gantt charts contain is fairly intuitive and easily understood. Gantt charts provide a good way to highlight major project activities and explain project schedules to nontechnical personnel.

Project Network Diagrams

Individual project activities have sequence and time relationships to each other. Some activities must be completed before others can start, some activities must start or end at the same time, and some activities must start or end at other specific times. The Gantt chart provides a simple, two dimensional (activity/time) view of a project, but problems may become apparent as the number of project activities increases. Large, complex projects may have thousands of activities associated with them. The sheer volume of activity information makes them difficult to manage and impossible to display in a meaningful manner on a Gantt chart.

Prior to the 1960s, the major project management tools were paper and personnel. Mountains of paperwork supported intricate Gantt charts and required many labor hours to develop. During the 1960s, the **Critical Path Method** (CPM) of project management was developed to handle large projects. It is a network-based approach for managing projects, in which key project activities become nodes in the diagram. Connections between nodes indicate activity relationships. Individual activities (nodes) may consist of many tasks and subtasks, and the use of **project network diagrams** is an effective way of showing these relationships.

The size of a project network diagram is limited only by the ability to perform tedious mathematical CPM calculations. Therefore, it is not an accident that CPM, with its network-based logic, was created during the 1960s—when computer technology first became available for business use. Today, PC software provides CPM-based applications that can handle projects of virtually any size and complexity.

Figure 7–10 provides a simple example of a project network diagram for a telephone system project. The project network contains twelve nodes, and each node represents a project activity. When the CPM calculations are performed manually, the number of nodes is kept to a minimum. However, the same telephone system project, using PC-based project management software, would contain 100 or more nodes (activities). The software is able to quickly and accurately determine the implications of different project options.

Having an understanding of CPM concepts is valuable. The CPM approach to shortening projects and effectively using critical resources applies to all managerial areas—not just for technology projects. Telecommunications managers should understand CPM concepts and should be capable of using manual calculations to manage simple projects. While there is a low likelihood that managers will be asked to perform manual CPM calculations in the real world, the conceptual understanding of CPM can be applied to many managerial activities.

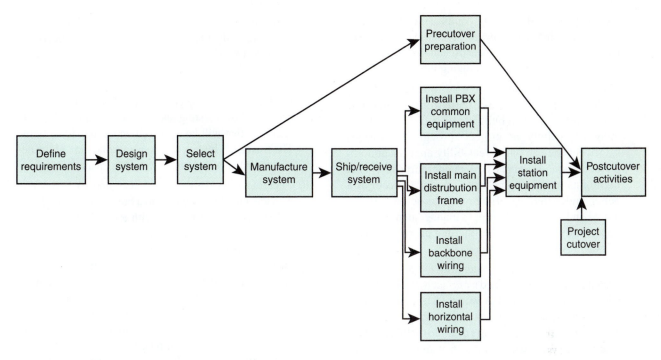

Figure 7–10. A telephone system project network diagram.

SUMMARY

This summary is organized to correspond with the learning objectives found at the beginning of the chapter.

1. In a 1974 *Harvard Business Review* article, Robert Katz described a three-part skill framework consisting of technical skills, human (influencing) skills, and conceptual skills. This framework was intended to highlight those skills needed to be an effective administrator (manager). Technical skills are those skills acquired during a formal education process (English, accounting, mathematics, speech, etc.), while influencing skill are normally acquired by experience and can be measured by the results achieved when motivating, leading, and influencing others. Creativity (conceptual) skills are the integration element that allows an individual to "step outside the box" and develop original solutions to problems.

2. A good attitude is a necessary catalyst for achieving managerial success. When operating at the interpersonal level, a good attitude includes those qualities that generate feelings of trust, confidence, and credibility in other people—necessary qualities for an effective leader. A positive attitude encourages teamwork and is a necessary attribute when dealing with difficult individuals.

3. Leadership is a key attribute associated with managers, and "managerial style" is one of the parameters

used to describe a leader's qualities. A wide range of leadership styles have been recognized and documented in managerial theory resources, and the leadership style is frequently linked to the attitude of the individual manager. Different leadership styles are more effective in different situations. A practical approach is to have the ability to use different leadership styles, depending upon the situation.

4. Microdecision concepts include problem solving, decision making, and potential problem analysis skills. These skills are used as part of the thinking process when solutions are required for different situations or activities. In this text, microdecision skills are applied within the POLC Model framework—a framework that is a key element in current integrative management theory thinking. Good decision making skills allow individuals to solve problems outside their area of specialization by obtaining the details from others and formatting them into an appropriate problem or decision analysis context.

5. Benchmarking consists of using an external standard, normally a best-of-the-best activity or process, and comparing it to internal activities and functions. The use of an external benchmarking standard minimizes

the potential for developing complacency because of self-serving, internal analyses. A microdecision problem solving process can easily incorporate benchmarking within its problem solving methodology.

6. Macrodecision concepts are used to ensure that microdecision processes make sense from an enterprise level. They provide a built-in mechanism for evaluating an activity or project through the various stages between an initial feasibility analysis and implementation. It serves two major purposes: 1) it highlights justification changes that may occur as a better understanding of a project or activity is obtained and 2) it provides upper management with the opportunity to validate the ongoing progress of projects and activities.

7. A life cycle analysis (LCA) identifies the costs incurred during the lifetime of a fixed asset, such as a network or telephone system. An LCA would identify all the lifetime costs including feasibility analysis, design, implementation, and operating costs over the useful life of the asset. An LCA, used in conjunction within a macrodecision framework, provides a "truer" picture of an asset's cost than only looking at the initial purchase cost.

8. Telecommunications managers require a good understanding of general accounting procedures and those procedures that are used within the business they are part of. Accounting is the language of business, and telecommunications managers must be able to accurately translate technical benefits into a financial format that can be understood by upper management. Failure to follow internal accounting justification procedures can adversely affect the likelihood of receiving funding approval for critical telecommunications projects.

9. The two basic budgeting approaches used in a business environment are incremental budgeting and zero based budgeting (ZBB). Incremental budgeting assumes that the activities that are covered by a budget will continue to be carried out unless specific action is initiated to re-move the activity. As a result, the primary focus of incremental budgeting is to identify new requirements and adjust last year's budget to fund the new requirements. Under ZBB, all managers start with a zero budget, and all managers must justify every activity that will be performed for the budget period. ZBB requires managers to prioritize both existing and new activities into decision packages that will be approved on an individual basis. The final ZBB budget will be a consolidation of the decision packages that are approved by management.

10. Accurate forecasting of revenues and expenses can provide a major advantage to a business. It would provide an accurate forcaster with a competitive advantage by allowing him or her to plan for both good times and bad times. Quantitative forecasting is based on using historical information, and it assumes that past trends will be continued. If unexpected events take place, they will not be detected by quantitative forecasting techniques until they have developed a history of their own. Forecasts are tools that are only as good as the relationship between the future and the past. Forecasting results should be viewed with pragmatism and a sense of skepticism to minimize the potential for blindly accepting mathematical calculations that don't reflect real world conditions. Forecasting remains an important tool for managing businesses.

11. Project network diagrams provide an excellent way to show the relationships among the various needed to complete a project. When durations can be assigned to activities, a mathematical calculation can be applied to determine how long a project will take. CPM calculations were developed for this purpose, but it was only when mainframe computers were introduced in the early 1940s that it became practical to use project network diagrams for large, complex projects. Today, PC project management software applications are based on using project network diagrams to manage and control all types of projects.

KEY TERMS AND CONCEPTS

The language of telecommunications management is multifaceted and includes words and phrases from managerial, technological, accounting, regulatory, and other business areas. The definitions of these key terms and concepts can be found within the chapter and in the glossary.

Annual Planning Cycle	Conceptual Skills (Katz)	Gantt Chart
Attitude	Critical Path Method (CPM)	Human Skills (Katz)
Attribute	Decision Making Process	Incremental Budgeting
Benchmarking	Enabling Skills	Life Cycle Analysis (LCA)
BVA	Exception Management	Macroplanning

Management Style
Mandatory Requirement
Microplanning
POLC Model

Potential Problem Analysis (PPA)
Problem Analysis Process
Project Network Diagram
Technical Skills (Katz)

Variance
Zero Based Budgeting (ZBB)

REVIEW

The following questions are open-ended—predefined answers are not included as part of the text. The purpose of these questions is to allow the readers to test themselves on the chapter material.

1. Describe the role of enabling skills when obtaining business and project management skills.

2. Describe Robert Katz's technical, human, and conceptual skill categories.

3. Describe the relative importance of Robert Katz's technical, human, and conceptual skills for different managerial levels.

4. What is the difference between knowledge and skill—if there is any difference?

5. What role does personal attitude play for a telecommunications manager?

6. Describe the extremes of managerial styles.

7. Explain the difference between microplanning and macroplanning.

8. Describe a generic problem analysis process.

9. Describe a generic decision-making process.

10. What is *potential problem analysis*?

11. Describe the role of benchmarking in the problem analysis process.

12. Describe the difference between mandatory requirements and attribute requirements.

13. Describe the mechanics for scoring multiple attributes during a decision-making process.

14. Explain the macrodecision framework used for projects.

15. What does life cycle analysis mean?

16. Why should telecommunications managers have strong accounting skills?

17. Explain the difference between incremental budgeting and ZBB.

18. How are variances calculated, and how would a manager evaluate them?

19. Explain *managing by exception*.

20. What is the value of forecasting expenses and revenues?

21. How are project network diagrams used?

MULTIPLE CHOICE

1. Enabling skills include _____. (select all that apply)
   a. project management skills
   b. PC skills
   c. organization management skills
   d. reading

2. In the Katz article, *technical skills* refers to _____.
   a. innate traits and characteristics
   b. telecommunications skills
   c. organization management skills
   d. skills measured through testing

3. From the Katz article, higher-level managers require _____ technical skill levels than lower-level managers.
   a. more   c. the same
   b. fewer   d. no

4. The first step in a problem analysis process is to _____.
   a. define the problem
   b. assign attribute weights
   c. identify the constraints of other problems
   d. implement the "best fit" solution

5. The primary objective of competitive benchmarking is to _____.
   a. share performance information with competitors
   b. implement concurrent solutions
   c. objectively assess internal performance
   d. avoid the use of detailed metrics
   e. combine dissimilar metrics

6. In the decision-making process, attributes are used to _____.
   a. identify mandatory requirements
   b. define the problem
   c. provide detailed metrics
   d. quantify subjective decision criteria
   e. identify dissimilar products

7. In the decision-making process, attribute scoring is used only if _____.
   a. the decision will be important
   b. mandatory requirements have been met
   c. mandatory requirements have not been met
   d. the rater has technical skills
   e. the rater has business management skills

8. PPA is used _____.
   a. before problems are solved
   b. during work hours
   c. after problem solutions are generated
   d. when mandatory requirement scores are high

9. A key ability for solving problems is _____.
   a. to have strong technical skills
   b. to be able to ask the right questions
   c. to provide answers to questions
   d. to have strong managerial skills

10. In the seven-step macrodecision framework, 90% of a fixed asset's cost is incurred _____.
   a. before the asset is acquired
   b. before the prefeasibility phase
   c. after the system operation phase
   d. after the asset is acquired
   e. during the design steps

11. Annual maintenance costs for equipment typically are about _____ of the initial purchase cost.
   a. 1%
   b. 5%
   c. 10%
   d. 15%
   e. 25%

12. The use of management checkpoints in the macrodecision model helps to _____.
   a. define the problem
   b. provide a project cutover point

c. hold meetings
d. evaluate life cycle costs
e. reaffirm a project's viability

13. A variance is defined as _____.
   a. $2 \times$ budget
   b. budget $-$ actual
   c. actual $-$ budget
   d. an attribute
   e. equivalent to a forecast

14. The standard measurement unit in business is _____.
   a. money (U.S.$)
   b. attributes
   c. forecast factors
   d. mandatory requirements
   e. decimal units

15. In an annual cycle, the next year's budget is _____.
   a. rejected
   b. next year's operational plan
   c. this year's operational plan
   d. strategic in nature
   e. this year's strategic plan

16. In the _____ budgeting process, next year's budget must be justified in detail.
   a. budget $v.$ actual
   b. incremental
   c. life cycle analysis
   d. ZBB
   e. forecasting

17. If a budget value is 50 and the actual expense if 60, the variance is _____.
   a. $+10$
   b. -10
   c. 0
   d. inconclusive
   e. 110

18. Gantt charts _____.
   a. generate a project network diagram
   b. show activities and times
   c. are no longer used
   d. require external benchmark

8

BUSINESS MANAGEMENT SKILLS

1. Understand the nature and scope of business management responsibilities.

2. Understand the managerial responsibilities associated with being a telecommunications manager.

3. Understand the differences between managers and leaders and understand the need for a manager to also be a leader.

4. Understand the need for structure in a business environment.

5. Understand the basic design principles used when developing an organization structure.

6. Understand the advantages and disadvantages of centralized and decentralized management approaches.

7. Understand the purpose of the vertical and horizontal dimensions of a business organization chart.

8. Understand span of control from both classical and current management theory contexts.

9. Understand the advantages and disadvantages of the functional organization structure.

10. Understand the advantages and disadvantages of the divisional organization structure.

11. Understand the advantages and disadvantages of the matrix organization structure.

12. Understand the advantages and disadvantages of the team organization structure.

13. Understand the functions found in a generic telecommunications organization structure.

14. Understand the basic rationale used when selecting a specific organization design structure for a telecommunications department.

15. Understand the role of telecommunications project teams and the role that a telecommunications manager plays.

Organizational functions are roles or activities assigned to people working within a business—accounting, purchasing, sales, marketing, human resources, or telecommunications. From a business organization perspective, personnel performing these functions are grouped into departments and a managerial reporting hierarchy is established within the department and between departments. The reporting relationship established by upper management for these departments will determine the roles and responsibilities of individual department managers.

Telecommunications managers are assigned the responsibility of managing telecommunications departments and for providing telecommunications services internally (employees and departments) and externally (customers, suppliers, and other organizations) to allow business activities to be carried out. All department managers must have knowledge of the business management skills that: 1) allow them to run their assigned functions within the context of the overall business and 2) to manage employees within the guidelines established by personnel policies.

This chapter will review key skill areas that telecommunications managers should use for managing their departments.

WHAT IS BUSINESS MANAGEMENT?

During the initial stages of the industrial revolution in the 1700s, factory owners quickly found out that factories did not run themselves and that the consolidation of the resources needed to create a factory—machines, labor, and raw materials—was a double edged sword. A factory was a machine-driven business and factory owners found it necessary to coordinate different manufacturing processes to allow the machines to run at full capacity. Workers maintained the machines, fed them raw material, and the machines produced products at speeds hundreds of times faster than the most efficient craftsman. However, if any element of the labor, raw material, and machine process was not available, the entire production line stopped.

Factory owners found it necessary to create business managers (factory foremen) who were given the responsibility of keeping the machines running and keeping the factory workers busy. Initially, foremen were the biggest and strongest workers and they utilized fear and intimidation tactics to supervise workers. However, by the late 1800s, the best results were being achieved by factory managers who worked smarter and improved worker output through job design improvements and training. As factory operations became more complex, different skills were needed to coordinate equipment, workers, raw materials, and finished goods in a manufacturing operation. A **three stage business process model** for these manufacturing-oriented steps is shown in Figure 8–1.

Early business managers found that the most effective way to maximize production output in this new, complex environment was to create areas of specialization within the factory environment. Factory foreman divided labor requirements into areas of specialization and created assembly lines that limited the roles of workers to carrying out simple, repetitive tasks. One worker's output became the input for the following worker, and the last worker in an assembly line handed a completed product to the warehouse worker for storage as a finished good. The **division of labor** into simple work elements allowed workers to be trained quickly and produce output at a high (if tedious) work rate.

The same division of labor philosophy used to produce product was also applied to nonmanufacturing work operations. Factory operations were set up as individual specialized departments—purchasing, manufacturing, sales, inventory control, accounting, etc. Just as it had been necessary to create factory foreman positions to improve the efficiency of workers and machines, different types of business managers were needed to coordinate internal department functions and ensure that the owners' profit objectives were met. The functional form of organization was a natural evolution of the scientific management philosophies that dominated the early era of professional management.

Business Management Responsibilities

Professional management principles were formalized when scientific management principles were first published in the early 1900s. Factory managers created management documentation based on their experience overseeing the resources of business operations. By this time, many business owners relied on professional managers to run the business and generate profits and—unlike the early owners—were not involved with the day to day operations of the business.

Figure 8–1. A three stage business process model.

In addition, the maturation of manufacturing-based operations resulted in a management organization that required managers who had different skill sets. Department managers were needed, and the efforts of these departments had to be coordinated. The overall effectiveness of the business became dependent upon the skills of its department managers.

> **Business management skills** are those managerial skills that allow individual managers to work effectively as team members in a business, where the primary objective is to satisfy the operating and profit objectives of business owners.

Business management skills are best described by examining the **POLC Model** skills discussed in Chapter 7, *Managerial Tools and Techniques*, while at the pragmatic level they include any enabling skills needed to carry out the POLC process. Management enabling skills will include supervisory, budgeting, and any functional skills needed to get the job done and fulfill expectations.

The specific managerial activities assigned to a telecommunications manager will depend upon the management position that is held (first level manager, middle manager, or upper management), department staffing size, department budget size, the business culture, and other job specific responsibilities.

Managers *v.* Leaders

Leaders are individuals who are able to influence others—to change beliefs, motivate, and have others willingly perform activities they would not otherwise undertake. There are informal and formal leaders. Informal leaders influence others through personal credibility or charisma, while formal leaders influence others because of the position they hold.

The formal power that a **manager** has is defined by the managerial position that is held. The power that the person has is assigned by the business. Managerial authority is clearly defined and will vary by functional area and by managerial level. Managers who are also informal leaders will have performance advantages over managers who only rely on their position to influence others.

Leadership based on the ability to influence others does not contain an element that may be part of the position leadership role—fear. Use of fear through threats, intimidation, or direct physical action is not considered leadership in the context of this text. The use of fear as a leadership "skill" could be labeled as a dictatorship or absolutism. It is not an appropriate management model.

In the managerial POLC Model, the "L" stands for "lead," and its application is consistent with the definition given above—although other early management definitions of leadership may have included fear. This text will assume that managers possess the nucleus of positive, non-threatening, leadership elements and the desire to develop them further. It will also be assumed that managers are leaders—an assumption that may not always be consistent with real world experience.

BONA FIDE MANAGERS. The title of "manager" is assigned by businesses for a wide range of responsibilities. Some managers may not have any subordinates, while in other cases a manager may have many subordinates. Clearly, the managerial responsibilities assigned to these two positions will vary widely.

Managers who have people management responsibilities are referred to as **bona fide managers** (literally, authentic managers) to identify managers who have supervisory responsibilities. When the term "manager" is used in the text, it refers to a bona fide manager. The discussion of managerial responsibilities is in the context of bona fide managers. However, managers who do not have supervisory responsibilities can also apply many of topics that are provided in the text.

MANAGEMENT RESPONSIBILITIES

Managers can be assigned a wide range of responsibilities. Their job descriptions frequently include the catchall phrase, ". . . and perform all other duties as assigned by the manager." Bona fide managerial responsibilities include supervisory, personnel, planning, budgetary, technology implementation, telecommunications operating, and other responsibilities. Each of these categories will be discussed within the context of a telecommunications management position, and Chapters 8, 9, and 10 will focus on telecommunications-specific activities.

Supervisory Responsibilities

Supervisory responsibilities for a bona fide telecommunications manager involve directing other employees (direct reports), who could be technical or administrative employees, or could be other managers if the manager is a middle-level or senior-level manager. Managers are responsible for developing the technical and administrative skills of their direct reports and indirectly responsible for other employees within the organization they manage. Managers are also responsible for developing the managerial skills of those direct reports who have the potential for assuming managerial positions in the future. A key objective of a good manager should be to develop the managerial skills of potential managers, so that they become capable replacements for the manager. There is a twofold benefit to training your potential replacement: 1) it demonstrates strong managerial skills, and 2) it can free you up for promotional opportunities. When managers have not developed potential replacements, they may be categorized as being irreplaceable and may have limited access to promotional opportunities.

Supervisory skills include delegation skills—the assignment of authority and accountability responsibilities to others, by allowing them to demonstrate their ability to carry out assignments. The delegation of responsibilities provides a manager with a way of assessing the potential of employees as prospective managers, technical specialists, or administrators.

Managers need to keep subordinates informed about organizational activities. The best way to do this is to hold regular staff meetings—typically on a weekly basis. The manner in which a manager conducts staff meetings will be a reflection of the manager's skills, and will be a role model for direct reports. Well-managed meetings have an agenda, cover all relevant topics, start on time, and end on time. Department managers will also be asked to attend meetings called by their manager. Managerial staff meetings provide the information linkage between lower and upper management and ensures that critical business information is communicated quickly and accurately throughout the business. An important managerial responsibility is to make sure subordinates are aware of ongoing events and activities.

Personnel Responsibilities

Bona fide managers have employees reporting to them. A middle- or senior-level manager can have many employees working within his or her area of responsibility. A manager of managers has responsibility for direct reports and the employees who report to their direct reports. A key responsibility for managers is salary administration—determining starting salaries and the raises that will be given to department employees. The amount of dollars available for salaries and salary increases will be established at the enterprise level, and the dollars for implementing them will be distributed to departments. Salary administration is normally a performance-driven activity, and managers are responsible for conducting periodic (typically annual) performance appraisals for all employees in their area of responsibility. When telecommunications managers have other managers reporting to them,

they must facilitate the overall performance appraisal process. This includes ensuring that the salary administration process is administered fairly and equitably to all employees within their managerial domain.

Telecommunications managers are responsible for obtaining and allocating monies for employee training. Because of the ever changing technical environment, telecommunications training budgets can be large compared to other department training budgets. A telecommunications manager must ensure that the training dollars are used effectively. In-house training is available in larger organizations and is used to address nontechnical subject areas, but external training resources are needed for most telecommunications-specific skills.

Facilitating conflict resolution between department members or between members of different departments is also a management responsibility. The demeanor and process used by a manager when resolving conflicts will have a major impact on the opinions held by department members regarding the business, because managers represent the company.

Meetings should be held periodically with department employees. Department meetings allow managers to communicate business and department-specific information directly to department members, and they also provide the opportunity for direct employee feedback—a mechanism that is highly effective in an organization that holds regular meetings. If meeting intervals are infrequent or are held only when there is bad news to communicate, employees will view department meetings negatively.

Depending upon the company policies and procedures, a telecommunications manager may also perform a record-keeping role for employee files. This would include updating training history, updating performance appraisal information, filing special award information, and recording any disciplinary actions taken against employees. Employee files may be stored in a central human resources area, in the telecommunications department, or in both areas. Employee records kept in the telecommunications department must be kept in a secure environment, and the appropriate measures must be taken to ensure the confidentiality of the information while still providing employees with access to their files.

Planning Responsibilities

Planning responsibilities (the "P" of the POLC Model) are some of the most important roles that a telecommunications manager has. Unless department goals are established, performance cannot be measured effectively, and it will be difficult to explain to upper management how operating expense and capital investment dollars are being utilized. Telecommunications management planning responsibilities include business management and technology management planning activities. Business planning efforts are directed toward the telecommunications department, while technology management planning efforts are directed toward the implementation and maintenance of telecommunications facilities and services.

BUSINESS PLANNING.   Business planning for the telecommunications department is a personnel-oriented activity, and the magnitude of the planning effort is dependent upon the number of department employees. Managers are responsible for establishing individual employee development plans to identify an employee's current skills, new training needs, and potential for new assignments. Depending upon the technology plan and the impact of outsourcing activities, it may be necessary to recommend staff additions or staff reductions as part of the department planning activity.

As the size of the telecommunications staff changes, organizational structure plans must be developed. Growing organizations will be providing new services, and it may be necessary to restructure functions into more manageable operating units. Business restructuring involves dividing department employees into logical resource groupings based on the tasks and accountabilities that will be assigned to them. Organization design and structure will be discussed in detail in the *Organization Design and Structure* section of this chapter.

Planning may be required to address enterprise level initiatives, such as participation in an enterprise-driven total quality management program or self assessment activity.

TECHNOLOGY PLANNING.   The telecommunications department is assigned the responsibility for providing telecommunications services that support business operations. These responsibilities may involve: 1) installing and operating equipment to provide the services, or 2) purchasing services from external telecommunications service providers. Good planning and execution skills are needed to ensure the efficient and effective use of telecommunications technologies. Technology planning details for will be covered in Chapter 9, *Technology Management Skills*.

Budget Responsibilities

Dollars are the standard measurement unit used for business activities, and budgets provide the measurement yardstick that is used by upper management to assess internal performance. A key managerial responsibility is to participate in the development of financial operating expense and capital expenditure forecasts (budgets) for strategic, tactical, and operational planning purposes. These forecasts become the basis for predicting profitability when a strategic plan (normally a 3 to 5 year planning horizon) evolves into a tactical plan (1 to 3 year planning horizon) and finally becomes an operational plan (current year plan). The operational budget that is established during the tactical planning cycle becomes the standard for measuring managerial financial performance where:

managerial performance (variance$) = budget$ − actual$

Upper management views positive variances kindly (unless their size indicates inept forecasting), while large negative variances are the equivalent of getting a failing grade in school. Ideally, the goal is to achieve a zero variance for all line items while successfully completing all the activities planned in the budget. Within this context, a zero variance would normally indicate good performance if the plan has been successfully carried out. Nonzero variances (both negative and positive) will require explanations if their values are large.

Under certain situations, large negative expense variances could be viewed positively. For example, if a large negative variance occurs in the order processing department's telephone budget, and is due to a large increase in customer order activity, the negative variance will be viewed in a positive light. In general, department managers should: 1) review their monthly budget vs. actual (BVA) reports as soon as they are received, 2) highlight budget variances, and 3) identify the reasons for them so they are prepared to answer questions raised by others (normally, their boss).

The accounting department facilitates the budgeting process and also issues guidelines for documenting operating expense and capital expenditure forecasts. The budgeting process is part of an annual planning cycle, which updates strategic, tactical, and operational plans while creating budgets (forecasts) for revenues and expenses. Telecommunications managers are responsible for meeting annual planning deadlines and participating in the associated budgeting activities. Because many internal departments use telecommunications services, the telecommunications department may develop, or assist in developing, the telecommunications budgets for other departments. Revisions of current year forecasts may be required during a budget year to address unexpected revenue increases or decreases.

Details on preparing operating expense forecasts and capital expenditure forecasts will be covered in Part 4, *Operations Management*, and Part 5, *Acquisition Management*.

Technology Implementation Responsibilities

The development and implementation of telecommunications technology is a major responsibility of the telecommunications department. Telecommunications technology may be implemented by using internal staff or by using outside services. When outside services are used to implement or operate telecommunications products or services, it is referred to as **outsourcing** the activity. The use of internal personnel is sometimes referred to as **insourcing.**

Project management skills are essential skills for successfully implementing telecommunications technology. Telecommunications managers play a variety of project management roles. In smaller organizations or in technically organized departments, the telecommunications manager may be the project manager for telecommunications projects. In larger organizations, the telecommunications manager may act as an overseer, delegating most project management activities to others. Regardless of whether projects are outsourced or insourced, the telecommunications manager is ultimately responsible for completing the project on time and within budget.

Telecommunications Operating Responsibilities

Once telecommunications projects have been implemented and the system or network is in place, it must be operated so that services are available for use by enterprise employees, customers, and suppliers. The facilities must be operated and maintained effectively to ensure that they perform as designed, and this operations management function may be done internally or may be performed by an external service provider.

Telecommunications systems and services include telephone systems, LANs, WANs, internetworks, and WWW functions. In some organizations, enterprise telecommunications systems and services may also be made available to customers and suppliers. When this is the case, the telecommunications department has greater responsibility for ensuring the ongoing availability of telecommunications equipment and services. Network performance-monitoring activities will become even more critical for large networks, and a higher investment in customer-support services will be required.

Enterprise telecommunications systems and services may use private network facilities—network facilities designed and implemented by the business—or public network facilities, or a combination of both. Private or public network facilities may be managed in-house (insourcing) or by using outsourcing services.

In telecommunications, WAN services have historically been supplied by common carriers. The use of outsourcing is common for many other telecommunications services. The use of outsourcing has become commonplace for many functions that formerly used internal personnel—data processing, telecommunications, accounting, human resources, transportation, etc. More outsourcing options exist today than did in the past, and upper management may have a strong bias toward outsourcing business functions.

Telecommunications managers should continually evaluate outsourcing options by comparing the costs and service levels of outsourcers to the products and services provided by internal operations. The bias toward or against outsourcing telecommunications services may depend upon the importance of telecommunications services in daily operations. If a telecommunications service is integrated with an enterprise product, any decision to outsource the telecommunications service may have product confidentiality or product development implications. These implications should be considered prior to making an outsourcing decision.

Other Responsibilities

Depending upon the enterprise environment, and the level of the managerial position held, telecommunications managers may find themselves accountable for other responsibilities. These can include a responsibility to maintain enterprise memberships in professional organizations and telecommunications-oriented user groups, and encouraging department members to participate in professional organization activities. A telecommunications manager may participate in enterprise-related activities such as ad hoc task forces that are established to address enterprise-level concerns.

These activities typically fall under the catchall managerial job description phrase referenced previously – " . . . and perform all other duties as assigned by your manager."

Handling Managerial Responsibilities

Responsibilities assigned to managers can cover a wide range of managerial, administrative, personnel, financial, and technical activities, and there is zero likelihood that any formal education program will provide the skills necessary for handling all areas. Telecommunications man-

TABLE 8–2 Business Functions *v.* Organiz
Functions

Business Function	Line Function	St...
Buy labor, material, and services	Purchasing	Le...
	Distribution services	Ac...
	Research	
	Engineering	
	Human resources	
	Information services	
Produce goods and services	Production	Le...
	Distribution services	Ac...
	Research	
	Engineering	
	Human resources	
	Information services	
Sell goods and services	Marketing	Le...
	Distribution services	Ac...
	Research	
	Engineering	
	Human resources	
	Information services	

ment members may have a wider range of skills,
organization grows, increased specialization is ty
troduced. This will result in the existence of larg
ments that consist of highly specialized emplo
example, in a small company, the accounting de
may take care of accounts payable, accounts re
cost accounting, and financial reporting. In large
nies, these functions are assigned to individual dep
In very large firms, there may be multiple departn
provide similar functions but service different
groups. Departments may be combined into divi:
divisions may be combined into corporations, in
meet the basic business needs of the business.

TASKS AND ACCOUNTABILITIES. Job

tions should exist for the employees who work w
department. These job descriptions would specify
and accountabilities (responsibilities) associated
position. Job descriptions should exist for all
managerial, supervisory, technical, and administ
assigned to employees. Job descriptions become
for employee appraisals, which are used to info
ployees of their job performance. Performance a
results then become the basis for identifying the
needs, future assignments, advancement potential,
raises of employees. Job descriptions are establish

agers will find that they must learn new skills on their own
and use real world experience and sound judgment to effectively apply skills for a specific situation. The commitment to telecommunications management excellence is a
never-ending journey throughout a career and managers
will find it necessary to periodically assess and reengineer
their existing skills.

ORGANIZATION DESIGN AND STRUCTURE

The industrial revolution of the 1700s created a working
environment that consolidated workers into a single (factory) location, and it was imperative to keep factory workers busy. Workers were machine-driven, and allowing
workers to be idle had two negative consequences for factory owners: 1) idle workers meant that machines were not
running and product was not being made, or 2) idle workers who were not making money would look elsewhere for
employment, creating a labor shortage.

Early management theorists focused strongly on the
efficiencies to be derived through the application of division of labor concepts presented by Adam Smith in his
book, *Wealth of Nations*. Division of labor techniques provided production efficiencies at the worker level by simplifying tasks and creating single task specialists. While
individual worker tasks were kept simple, the coordination
structure needed to ensure that tasks were done in the correct sequence became more complex and required the addition of managerial functions. Organization structure and
design was used to create the organization chart needed to
effectively and efficiently manage different internal business functions. The design process consisted of identifying
the various tasks needed to carry out the business activities
and providing an organization structure that coordinated
the efforts of its people. A good organization design
ensures that overall enterprise goals and strategies are
incorporated into the organization structure, and that
function-level goals are consistent with enterprise-level
business goals.

There are a number of standard functions found in
most businesses—accounting, human resources, purchasing, data processing, and telecommunications, etc. These
basic departments may be arranged in a variety of ways on
an enterprise organization chart and, while the basic functions they perform remain relatively constant, upper management may periodically reorganize their relationship to
each other. Some corporations intentionally change their
organization structure on a regular basis to create an inter-

nal climate of constant change, while other businesses
view organizational changes as a superficial exercise, so
their organizational structure is seldom changed. While
disagreements may exist regarding the optimal structure
for a given business, there are guidelines available to
avoid some obvious poor choices when a business structure is established.

Business Design Considerations

The objective of establishing an organization infrastructure is to create a business framework that utilizes an enterprise's people resource efficiently and effectively.
When business units were small—a single proprietorship
or a craftsmen guild—there was a minimal impact when
the proper raw materials or tools were not available. The
impact caused by the absence of raw materials and tools in
a factory environment is hundreds or thousands of times
worse than that in a single proprietorship environment. If
a factory employs 100 employees on an assembly line, a
raw material or tool shortage would result in idle employees being paid for doing nothing or—if they are not paid
unless they produce product—unpaid workers would seek
alternative employment. In either instance, it created an
undesirable situation that threatened the long term viability of a business. The need to keep manufacturing operations running smoothly and continuously led to the
development of managerial positions and an associated organization infrastructure.

Henry Ford perfected mass production techniques
during the early 1900s and used them to build automobiles that the average American family could afford to
buy. As a result of Ford's mass production expertise, the
Ford Motor Company dominated the early U.S. industrial
environment. However, during the 1930s, General Motors (GM) developed a decentralized organizational
structure whose superior performance allowed GM to
supplant Ford's position as the dominant automobile pro-
ducer in the U.S. GM continued this dominance of the
U.S. automobile industry until the next wave of change in
the 1960s, when Japanese manufacturers introduced inexpensive, high-quality automobiles and forced a reengineering of existing management philosophies. It is
interesting to note that the organizational structure of
Japanese automobile manufacturers in the 1960s was significantly different from that of their U.S. counterparts. It
is unlikely that this dissimilarity was simply a coincidence. Today, the U.S. and Japanese automobile manufacturing organization structures are more similar than
they are different.

During the last forty years, companies ha
solidated, merged, and reengineered at a dizzy
attempt to address the challenges and issues 1
the global competition environment establish
1960s. Today, there are a relatively small nun
automobile manufacturers that have surviv
have done so by adopting the best industrial p
organization structures) of their competitors.
sic organizational design procedures still rem

- cluster jobs into organization units
- assign tasks and accountabilities to the orga
- install a coordination process between orga

ORGANIZATION UNITS.

Businesse
wide range of goods and services for their cu
these businesses vary significantly in size ar
presence. Regardless of their size or business,
of their organization charts will show that r
nies are similar in organization structure. Ta
vides a listing of common department (organi
titles, and groups them by function (a.k.a.,
some enterprises, the departments may be pla
ent divisions—production planning may be
manufacturing division.

All business enterprises perform three
tions to meet profitability objectives:

1. purchase labor, material, and services
2. produce goods and services
3. sell goods and services

Other organization classifications used
the nature of organizational units are "line"
Line organization units have primary respo
carrying out the business objectives of the
and are typically sales- and production-orient
Staff organization units support the line org
carrying out their business responsibilities. Ta
solidates Table 8–1 functions and assigns thei
propriate line or staff category.

While major differences exist between
dustries, the basic organization functions
same: finance, human resources, sales, marke
and development, customer services, order pro
puter information systems, and telecommun
Technology-based functions are relatively ne
information systems and telecommunication
organization functions have been in place f
management theory concepts have existed. E

CENTRALIZATION V. DECENTRALIZATION.

Centralization and **decentralization** refer to the degree that decision-making is concentrated in upper management. Prior to the introduction of computers and computer communication, the centralization and decentralization description was directly related to the geographic distribution of locations. Decentralization of managerial authority meant that operating units were also dispersed geographically, and central management influence was minimal. Today's computer and communication technology environment provides the means for upper management decisions to be encoded in the applications that are used throughout a business. Using computer-based technology, multiple geographically dispersed operating units can be managed easily by using centralized management controls.

Enterprises that employ a centralized philosophy normally operate in a management mode where key decisions are made at higher management levels and then passed down through the organization. The vehicle for transferring these decisions could be by chain of command communication or by embedding decisions in enterprise supported computer applications.

Decentralization of decision making means that many decisions are made in lower organization levels, but a few key areas are reserved for upper management control. Inherent in the process of delegating authority to geographically dispersed locations was an implicit belief that local management best understood their customers and would be more effective when dealing with them.

Traditionally (classical management theory), organization charts utilized a pyramid structure, with a concentration of power and authority at the top of the pyramid. The pyramid shape is generated automatically if each managerial position uses six as the span of control for individual managers. Under the contemporary view, the situational approach is more commonly used, and the amount of centralization or decentralization found in the organization will be based on using the combination that is believed to be best suited for meeting objectives. There is now a trend toward delegating authority to lower levels. This concept of empowerment may supersede the formal managerial lines shown on the organization chart. Empowerment is also a key concept in the formation of work teams and is a way of delegating authority to lower organization levels (team members).

IMPACT OF COMPUTERS AND COMMUNICATIONS.

With the availability of computers and communication technology, the implicit assumptions regarding the appropriateness of centralizing or decentralizing managerial authority are less of an issue. Telecommunication networks can connect geographically dispersed customers to centralized customer service facilities by providing toll-free services. The rapid access to customer information at these centralized locations creates the impression that the customer service department is located nearby, and computerized customer service applications track a customer's purchasing history and preferences. When a customer service representative answers a customer's call, the customer will not know whether the enterprise employee is ten miles away or 1,000 miles away. Application databases provide the same information to all customer service representatives, and the customer should receive the same level of service—regardless of which service agent is responding to an inquiry about pricing, order status, or product availability.

It is no longer true that a small, decentralized organization can best respond to its customers and can react more quickly. However, if the organization does not use computers and communication technology effectively, the traditional concerns with poor, centralized customer service may be true. The effective use of computer and communication technology allows a business to assume any shape it wishes. Large, highly centralized organizations can appear to be small, nimble business units that are highly responsive to customer requests. However, small, decentralized organizations can appear to be larger organizations that have vast resources at their disposal. This blurring of the lines between centralized and decentralized organizations is most easily understood by considering the effect of e-commerce. With e-commerce, customers use a WWW interface to connect to vendors and place their orders. From a customer perspective, it is impossible to differentiate between large corporations and newly formed companies based on the appearance of their home page (the website's opening page).

Span Of Control

Span of control refers to the number of subordinates that a manager can effectively control, and is a topic that received a great deal of attention from scientific management theoreticians during the early 1900s. The classical management span of control limited the number of direct report to six, while contemporary management span of control standards are more liberal—typically a maximum of ten to twelve employees. The contemporary view is consistent with the situational approach to management theory advocated by integrative theorists. Contemporary theories argue that there can be no single span of control that is best for all organizations because employee and environmental factors differ in each case. If employees are well trained, there is little need for direct supervision. If all the tasks performed by employees were similar and simple, a larger span of control may also be appropriate.

When all the subordinates are in close physical proximity, a larger span of control can be used. A smaller span of control may be appropriate for a physically dispersed organization, however. Supervisory positions can be used to limit the number of employees reporting directly to a manager—a manager who manages 100 employees could have six supervisors who provide a direct supervisory interface to employees while keeping the managerial span of control within the design standards of the enterprise.

If span of control is used in organization design, it will have an impact on the number of levels (vertical dimension) in the organization chart and the breadth (horizontal dimension) of the organization chart. The scope and breadth of an organization will determine the number of management positions required and will also determine how many departments will be created. Table 8–3 illustrates the mathematical application of different spans of control to identify the potential effect on hierarchical organization charts. It assumes a starting point of one individual at the top of the organization chart (the President), providing each management position with the same span of control.

Table 8–3 indicates that if the span of control is six (i.e., each manager has six direct reports), an enterprise that has five management levels will require 1,555 managers (1 + 6 + 36 + 216 + 1,296). Similar calculations can be performed for different spans of control and different numbers of levels.

Smaller spans of control are used when tighter managerial control is desired because lower level managers are inexperienced or because decision making is centralized in the chain of command (a management philosophy issue). When managers are experienced, or if decision making is

delegated to lower managerial levels, a larger span of control is used. Decentralized organizations have distributed decision making authority, have shorter chains of command, and utilize fewer managers. Centralized organizations impose a tighter control on decision making, have longer chains of command, and may utilize managers in the hierarchy structure.

The span of control concept also applies to the number of nonmanagement employees assigned to managers. Worker span of control issues are primarily related to first-level managers, because the workload for upper-level managers is more likely to be based on managerial span of control while lower level management workloads are based on managing nonmanagement employees.

The span of control approach can be used to identify the number of workers that first-level managers can support. Table 8–4 assumes that there are 1,296 first level managers in an organization that has five managerial levels (refer to Table 8–3). Different worker span of control values have been calculated for Table 8–4.

The Total column shows the total number of managers and workers for a given span of control. Workers who perform simple, repetitive, machine-driven tasks will require less managerial control than unskilled workers who perform more complex tasks. In this simple scenario, a larger span of control could be used, while a smaller span of control could be used for the complex environment. If the workers are highly skilled, they will require minimal managerial control, whether the tasks they perform are simple or complex.

Applying these principles would allow a single supervisor to manage fifty employees who operate machines in a machine-driven production environment, while an engineering manager might only manage six employees when a new computer chip is being developed. Larger spans of control are more efficient in terms of cost (lower management costs per employee) while smaller spans of control are more effective when controlling operations. The selection of an appropriate span of control is based on balancing business requirements.

TABLE 8–3 Managerial Span of Control by Organization Level

Level	SOC = 4	SOC = 6	SOC = 10
1	1	1	1
2	4	6	10
3	16	36	100
4	64	216	1,000
5	256	1,296	10,000
6	1,024	7,776	
7	4,096		

Note: SOC = Span Of Control

TABLE 8–4 Worker Span of Control

SOC	Managers	Workers [1]	Total
4	1,296	5,184	6,480
6	1,296	7,776	9,072
10	1,296	12,960	14,256

Note: SOC = Span Of Control

[1] Employees without managerial responsibilities.

SPAN OF CONTROL IMPLICATIONS. The information provided in Tables 8–3 and 8–4 shows that when more managerial control is desired, more managers are required. Managerial decisions regarding manager and worker span of control standards will have a direct impact on the number of managers found within an organization. Regardless of the span of control selected, effective management requires management personnel to have a good set of managerial tools and to be able to apply them appropriately.

While span of control principles can be applied mechanically, managerial judgment is the best criteria for many situations. Situational management requires an ongoing appraisal of the managerial outcomes being achieved and modification of different managerial variables (including span of control) to meet organizational objectives effectively. There is a low likelihood that applying any single managerial philosophy will automatically ensure success for a given situation.

Business Structure Dimensions

Organization charts have two dimensions: a vertical dimension and a horizontal dimension. Managerial positions shown on the same horizontal line have the same level—they are considered peer managerial levels even though they may be in different departments. The vertical dimension indicates the level of managerial positions—the top position is the top-level manager (upper management) who typically has the title of *President* or *Chief Executive Officer*. Reading an organization chart from the top to the bottom will indicate managerial levels from the President (the highest position

level) to the lowest managerial level in the organization. Figure 8–4 provides an organization chart showing these relationships.

In an organization chart, the management title box typically contains three information elements:

department name

manager name

manager title

Figure 8–5 illustrates the title box format for James Martin, Manager of the LAN operations department.

Organization charts may be presented in different ways. Three commonly used format structures are shown in Figure 8–6, and the information contained in each of the three examples is identical. The center example does save space, when compared to the other two examples, and that format will be used in this text.

Department boxes are placed at the appropriate horizontal position to indicate the correct managerial level, and the vertical connecting lines will identify the departments (and managers) in the same department. Organization charts contain a great deal of information. In large organizations, it is sometimes difficult to identify the relationships among functions.

VERTICAL DIMENSION DESCRIPTION. In the classical view of management theory, each employee reported to a single manager. This concept was formalized in Henri Fayol's principles of management (Chapter 6, *What is Enterprise Planning?*) and was initially used to ensure that employees were treated fairly and were not placed in the position of having to choose between requests made by

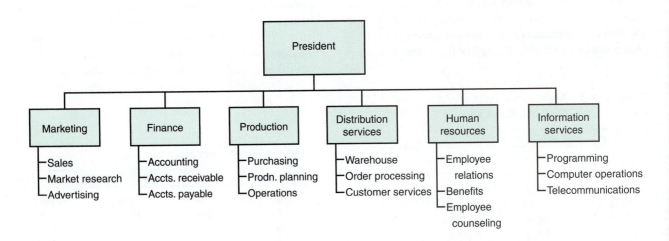

Figure 8–4. Organization chart example (departmental structure).

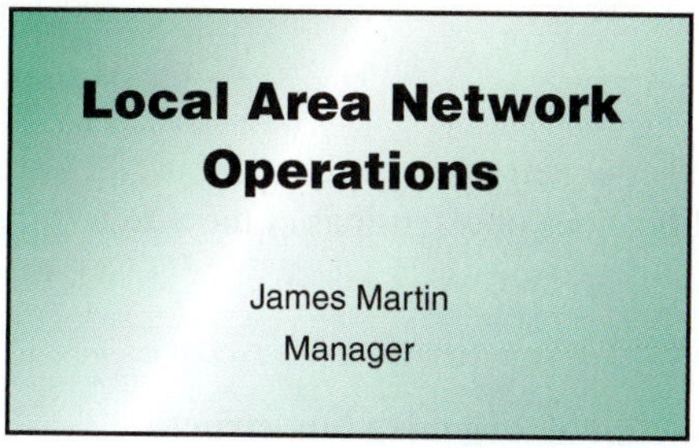

**Local Area Network
Operations**

James Martin

Manager

Figure 8–5. Organization chart title box example.

different managers (the unity of command principle). The organizational chain of command travels from a given organization chart element, up through the organization chart, to the top manager (President or Chief Executive Officer) of the enterprise.

In the contemporary view of management theory, the concept of having a single boss is not a prerequisite for developing an organization. (This view will be expanded further during discussions about matrix organization and work team organization structures.) In addition, contemporary management theory takes issue with the assumption that subordinates accept managerial authority automatically. It argues that authority comes from the willingness of employees to accept it—a discussion involving the issue of power *v.* authority. To simplify matters, this text will assume that employees carry out instructions given by their manager.

HORIZONTAL DIMENSION DESCRIPTION. While the vertical dimension of an organization addresses the integration and coordination of activities taking place be-

tween business units, the horizontal dimension addresses the issue of the best way to perform the functions assigned to different departments. The horizontal level is primarily concerned with department level activities and determining the best way to subdivide functional tasks within a department or division.

Under the classical approach, the focus was on efficiency. Manufacturing assembly line production methods were developed by applying division of labor concepts to break down manufacturing processes into a series of interrelated tasks. This same concept is still used in fast food operations, where a series of standard tasks is established to result in the creation of a final product.

A point is reached when employing division of labor concepts affects employee motivation. Contemporary views encourage the enlargement of tasks and the use of other techniques to reduce employee boredom, absenteeism, job stress, and high turnover found in many assembly line jobs. In fast food environments, tasks that require different skill levels are developed. Jobs can then be assigned to employees based on their individual skills and capabilities. Skilled tasks pay more than unskilled tasks, and the existence of many different jobs provides a progression path for advancement and better pay. In this case, an old concept (division of labor) has been modified to meet contemporary requirements. Contemporary modifications typically include a stronger customer orientation and the use of teams consisting of people who have different skills.

DEPARTMENTALIZATION. Departmentalization is used to group employees into separate organization units within a department. The department's specific location in the organizational hierarchy should indicate the role that

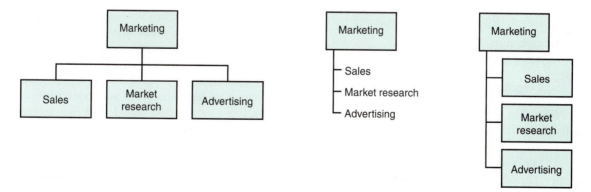

Figure 8–6. Equivalent formats for organization chart information.

its efforts have in supporting the attainment of enterprise objectives.

Classical theorists divided factory jobs into specialized tasks and placed these specialists in departments directed by a manager. The departments would be placed in different parts of the organization, based on the internal criteria regarding the approach to support customers. Contemporary organization designs continue to use many of the department-oriented approaches of the classical theorists. Contemporary trends focus more strongly on having department functions provide a customer-oriented interface than in the past, when customer support was provided by specialized departments. In addition, there has been an increased use of cross-functional teams. Cross-functional teams group individuals who have different skill sets and conceptually create a miniprocess organization that is able to handle complex processes and produce products within a small organization setting.

ORGANIZATIONAL STRUCTURE OPTIONS

Organizational structure refers to the relationship that exists between various departments and, to a lesser extent, the relationship between different departments. The decision factors that influence how a business is structured should include: 1) identifying the departments needed to run the business, 2) the type of business the enterprise is in, and 3) the managerial philosophy of upper management. These factors are shown in Figure 8–7.

The detailed design of the organization—location and quantity of boxes (departments) on an organization chart—is based on upper management's philosophies regarding topics that were discussed in the organization design section. These include:

- degree of complexity, formalization, and centralization
- vertical organization dimensions
- horizontal organization dimensions

Four types of organizational structures will be discussed:

- functional
- divisional
- matrix
- team

While other organization structures exist, they are primarily modifications or extensions of these four.

Functional Organization Structure

The **functional organization structure** is the oldest form of organization structure. It is an organization format designed initially for manufacturing organizations, where assembly line procedures were based on consolidating related tasks to achieve the advantages of specialization. As business enterprises evolved from small mom and pop businesses into complex, multidivision enterprises, the basic functions needed to efficiently operate a business became larger and more complex. Early scientific management theorists focused on making all business functions efficient by eliminating redundancy, simplifying activities into basic tasks, and providing formal guidelines for the management of business functions. The functional structure was a natural outgrowth of scientific management theory and Figure 8–4 provided an example of a functional organization structure. (The organization chart in Figure 8–4 has been replicated in Figure 8–8 to avoid the need for paging back to the earlier chart.)

Individuals who carry out similar functions are managed as a single department entity, and departments that carry out similar functions are managed as independent entities. In Figure 8–8, sales, market research, and advertising are grouped under a marketing manager, who is typically a vice president and reports to the president. In addition, the finance, production, distribution services, and human resources department heads also report to the president. As the organization grows in size, the separate functions shown under vice presidents will be set up as individual departments headed by a manager. In a large organization, the marketing vice president's department would consist of a vice president and an executive assistant only. The marketing department employees would actually be members of the individual functional departments that report to the marketing vice president. A manager who reports directly to the marketing vice president would head each marketing department: sales, market research, and advertising.

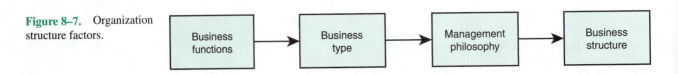

Figure 8–7. Organization structure factors.

Business functions → Business type → Management philosophy → Business structure

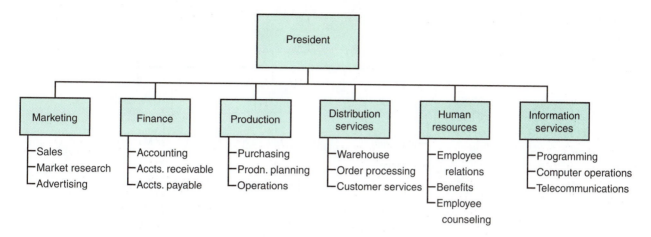

Figure 8–8. Organization chart example (functional structure).

ADVANTAGES. The advantages of the functional structure are that it 1) achieves economies of scale as the functional organization's size increases, 2) minimizes the duplication of personnel and equipment, 3) increases the quality of technical expertise, and 4) creates a good environment for the development of functional skills.

DISADVANTAGES. As the functional organization's size increases, personnel frequently adopt a function-oriented perspective of their roles within the business enterprise. This perspective can adversely affect overall enterprise performance. As the functional departments become larger, slow response and poor intraorganizational communications can also result.

Divisional Organization Structure

The **divisional structure** provided a way to respond to the potential weaknesses of the functional organization structure while retaining its advantages. It consists of limiting the size of the individual functions by subdividing the business into smaller divisions (a decentralization technique) and providing a full set of functions for the various divisions. The divisional concept can be used to create independent management organizations based on product, customer, or geographic location. Figure 8–9 shows a divisional organization structure. Note that each of the departments shown in Figure 8–8 has been duplicated within each division.

ADVANTAGES. The divisional organization structure retains many of the advantages of a functional structure while focusing on results (products, customers, or geographic locations). By constraining the organization

to the size necessary for meeting limited objectives, many of the functional organization disadvantages are minimized to allow division members to focus on meeting specific goals.

DISADVANTAGES. Inherent in the divisional structure is the existence of resource and equipment duplication, and overall enterprise functional redundancy. From a scientific management perspective, the multiple functional organizations could be consolidated to provide the same level of service with fewer personnel and equipment resources. (In today's advanced computer and communication environment, a large centralized resource could appear to be as small and nimble as a division organization.)

Matrix Organization Structure

The **matrix organization structure** was another attempt to circumvent the disadvantages associated with a functional structure. It evolved out of the aerospace industry's needs for concurrently supporting many large project efforts within the enterprise. The divisional approach, with its inherent redundancy and duplication of personnel and equipment, was considered unsuitable. The aerospace industry wanted to have the advantages of maintaining a large pool of highly skilled technical workers, and wanted the skilled labor pool to handle multiple projects efficiently.

The matrix organization format continues to be popular in project-oriented enterprises. From an enterprise perspective, it leverages critical skills by being able to fully utilize individual employees on multiple projects. This approach increases the utilization of individuals by allocating their time to multiple assignments. It allows the

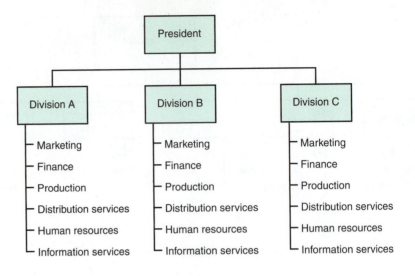

Figure 8–9. Divisional organization structure.

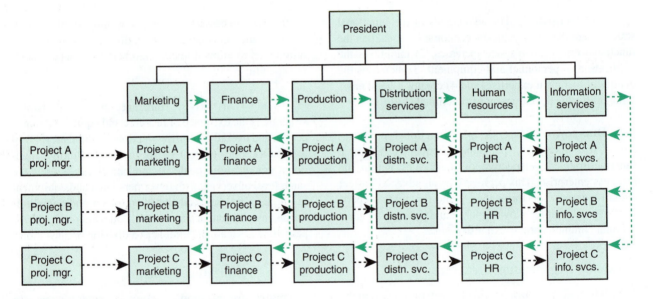

Figure 8–10. A matrix organization structure.

hiring of expensive, highly skilled specialists, because their expense can be spread across multiple projects. Individual projects may require only part time, highly skilled support and would be unable to justify hiring expensive employees for part time jobs. However, when expensive worker resources can be kept busy on a full time basis, their costs can be fully justified.

Figure 8–10 illustrates the matrix organization structure. It is a modified functional organization where ad hoc project teams are established by assigning them from the enterprise organization's departments. Project managers request project staffing from the functionally organized departments. Those department employees normally work on several projects concurrently while reporting to their functional department manager.

Individual project managers are able to afford the use of specialists, because the project is required to pay only for the time that the specialist spends working on the project. Once a project is completed, personnel return to their functional assignments and become candidates for new projects. Because matrix personnel are full time employees of the enterprise, they are immediately available for new projects or other temporary assignments—assuming their individual work loads allow this.

ADVANTAGES. The matrix organization provides an excellent environment for utilizing and developing technical specialists, because the services of scarce, expensive specialists can be shared across multiple projects. In effect, the matrix organization uses the same philosophy as the divisional structure by substituting project goals for the customer, product, or geographic location goals of division organizations.

In the matrix structure, enterprise personnel are fully utilized, and the matrix approach has the same advantages as both the functional and divisional organization structures. Teams can be created, changed, and dissolved without difficulty.

DISADVANTAGES. The primary disadvantage of the matrix approach is from the employee viewpoint. Employees have a dual chain of command—the functional department manager and the project manager(s). Employees must balance the needs of two or more bosses and must personally mediate any conflicts that arise when multiple assignments are due at the same time.

The matrix philosophy is a contentious one by nature, because project managers must negotiate with functional managers for personnel resources. The project manager has a single focus—their project—and the functional manager must balance the availability of department staffing between projects and the day to day responsibilities of the department. An ongoing tug of war takes place between project managers and between project managers and the functional department managers as the project managers attempt to get the best specialists assigned to their projects.

The functional organization structure handles projects in the same way as the matrix structure. The difference is that the sponsoring organization normally provides the specialists and looks for facilitation assistance from other organizations. In the functional structure, there is no employee conflict because functional management has responsibility for both the project and the people assigned to it.

Team Organization Structure

Team management utilizes concepts similar to those discussed under both the functional and matrix organization discussions. A key difference is that the individuals assigned to work teams are primarily accountable to the work team—not to functional managers or to a temporary project manager.

The **team organization structure** may be viewed as an evolution of the matrix structure. In the matrix approach, project members were in the position of constantly juggling their priorities to meet the requirements of many bosses, and satisfying one boss's needs could negatively impact another boss's needs. In a team environment, team members have one objective—that of meeting the team's objective. Team members are assigned as full time members to their team. Figure 8–11 illustrates the team organization structure.

Figure 8–11 is similar to Figure 8–10 (a matrix structure), except that the functional organization linkages have been removed. Each team (Team A, B, or C) is autonomous. Members assigned to the team are accountable only to their team. As a result, team members must monitor, appraise, and control other team members—a responsibility that was normally assumed by functional department managers in the functional and matrix organization structures.

Teams are self-managed entities, and team members are accountable for results and have wide latitude in defining how they will achieve the results. Two common types of teams are cross-functional teams and work teams.

CROSS-FUNCTIONAL TEAMS. Cross-functional teams are made up of individuals who have skills in different specialized areas. The composition of the team is based on the function or task they are performing, and individual members are accountable for integrating their specialized skills with the skills of other team members to complete team activities. Team members measure their success based on meeting team objectives. Individual success is secondary to the overall achievement of team goals. Cross-functional teams were initially developed to bypass development delays inherent in many functionally designed organizations. In functionally designed organizations, there is always a conflict between working on project objectives *v.* working on function objectives. This conflict can affect personnel selection (keep the best employees to address function work) and the allocation of time to projects.

Cross-functional teams typically report directly to a senior manager and are usually used for mission-critical projects. Car manufacturers have used cross-functional teams to shorten the development time for creating new car designs.

WORK TEAMS. Work teams are sometimes referred to as self-directed teams. They consist of six to eighteen individuals responsible for generating a well defined unit of finished work. This concept represents an alternative to the division of labor approach that dominated scientific management theory in the U.S. between 1900

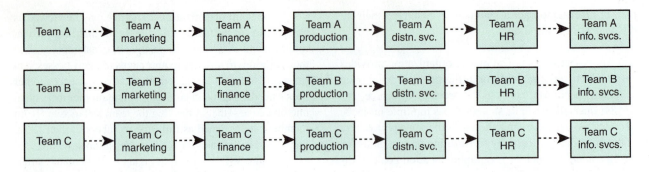

Figure 8–11. A team organization structure.

and 1950. Each member of the team is selected based on his or her ability to provide a specific set of skills (similar to cross-functional teams), and team members are responsible for solving problems, scheduling and assigning work, and addressing personnel issues such as absenteeism and poor work performance—issues that may arise in the team environment.

ADVANTAGES. In a team structure, work goals and team goals are the same, and success in achieving work goals means that team goals are being met. Even though team members may have different functional skills and different viewpoints about how they should be utilized, the likelihood for compromise between team members is higher because the team objectives clearly supersede the functional interests of team members. Because the teams are autonomous and self-managing, minimal supervision is required.

DISADVANTAGES. The potential for the success of a team is closely tied to the selection of team members and the training provided to team members. In a traditional organization, the functional manager responsibilities include:

- establishing and controlling operating budgets
- hiring and terminating department employees
- performing annual employee performance appraisals
- recommending employee salary increases and promotions
- establishing employee development plans
- establishing and monitoring employee vacation schedules
- establishing department tactical and strategic plans
- facilitating interdepartment communication
- providing intradepartment communication

These responsibilities do not disappear in a team organization—the team becomes accountable for providing them. Without the appropriate training or experience, these tasks can be very difficult for team members to carry out.

TEAM ORGANIZATION COMMENTS. The team structure organization is the newest of the structures reviewed in this section, and its use has met with mixed success. Like any organization design option, it should be evaluated carefully. When implemented, it should be evaluated periodically after its implementation to assess its effectiveness and, if necessary, modify it. Organization needs change with time and the team structure is one of several organization options that are available.

TELECOMMUNICATIONS ORGANIZATION

The telecommunications department is expected to operate within the context of a business enterprise as one of the many departments set up to achieve enterprise objectives. It may exist as a stand-alone department or it may be incorporated into another technology department, such as the computer information services department. The following sections discuss telecommunications as an individual department within the business enterprise. If the telecommunications department exists within another functional organization, the stand-alone discussion will still apply. The only difference is that it will be shown on the organization chart as a subset of the organization it is part of.

Enterprise Organization

Figure 8–12 provides an organization chart for the business enterprise that will form the context for the telecommuni-

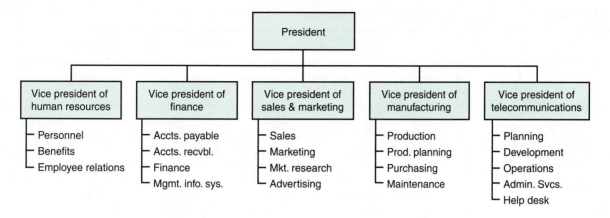

Figure 8–12. Business enterprise organization.

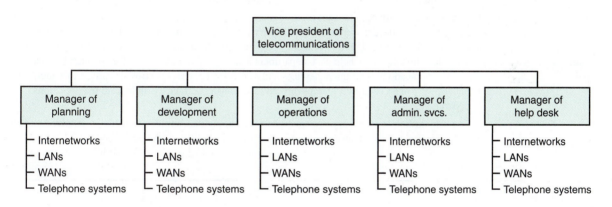

Figure 8–13. Telecommunications organization chart.

cations business design discussion. Figure 8–12 utilizes the functional organization design format discussed previously.

Figure 8–12 contains five major functional organizations: human resources, finance, sales & marketing, manufacturing, and telecommunications. Vice presidents head each functional area and report directly to the President of the enterprise. The President and five Vice presidents make up the enterprise's Management board—the upper management group that is accountable for profitability and performance. The Management board establishes the rules and policies used to manage enterprise departments.

Each Vice president (VP) has several direct report departments. The department names are shown in Figure 8–12. Although not indicated, a manager heads up each department with individual department staffing ranging between 10 and 100 employees. Total staffing for our hypothetical enterprise organization consists of 230 employees.

Telecommunications Organization Options

Figure 8–13 expands the telecommunications organization shown in Figure 8–12. The listing shown below each of the five telecommunications managers is not intended to provide organizational information but to highlight the telecommunications services supported by each department. For discussion purposes, we have shown the major telecommunications technologies supported by telecommunications departments: LANs, WANs, internetworks, and telephone systems. Table 8–5 summarizes the activities performed by each department.

The telecommunications organization functions in Figure 8–13 are typical of a technology-oriented function. The figure was developed by using a functional organization structure design.

All department managers have responsibilities for: 1) preparing operating expense forecasts, 2) conducting

TABLE 8–5 Telecommunications Department Functions

Department	Functions Performed
Telecommunications planning	The telecommunications planning department is responsible for capacity planning, preparing a five-year strategic plan, evaluating new telecommunications technologies, and helping to develop capital expenditure forecasts.
Telecommunications development	The telecommunications development department is responsible for implementing large projects and facilitating project management responsibilities. This includes the design and development of the operating procedures that will be turned over to the operations department. This department has responsibility for developing capital expenditure forecasts.
Telecommunications operations	The telecommunications operations department prepares operating expense forecasts, provides technical support for solving equipment and network problems, and has primary responsibility for the proper performance of telecommunications systems and networks. They will install minor additions and changes to equipment and network facilities but will defer larger projects to the development department.
Telecommunications administrative services	The telecommunications administrative services department maintains the system and network equipment inventory databases, pays the bills for outside services, and issues monthly reports to users of telecommunications services. All telecommunications departments use the databases.
	Administrative services manages the chargeback function, through which all service expenses are charged back to the departments using the services. They also maintain the enterprise directories for telephone, LAN, e-mail, and WWW services, and provide an online directory for enterprise users.
Telecommunications help desk	The telecommunications help desk department is a single point of contact for all enterprise users of telecommunications department services and networks. They receive trouble calls, create incident tickets, resolve procedural problems directly, and transfer technical problems to the operations department.
	The help desk retains primary responsibility for ensuring that service problems are resolved quickly and completely. They maintain incident reporting databases and act as an ombudsman for user problems. They furnish problem reports to the administrative services, operations, development, and planning departments.

employee performance appraisals, 3) preparing employee development plans, and 4) ensuring the quality of services provided in their area of responsibility. The VP of telecommunications holds weekly staff meetings with the five telecommunications managers.

Enterprise functions can be organized in several ways: functionally, by customer, by location, or by product. The selection of a particular organization approach is a situational decision based upon the organization environment that exists at the enterprise level. Small telecommunications organizations (less than ten employees) tend to be organized functionally (Figure 8–13) and usually combine multiple department functions into one department.

The use of different telecommunications organization structures will depend upon the department's future growth, because a major increase in the number of telecommunications employees may require a new organization structure. Table 8–6 shows how the functional organization chart could be mapped into different organization formats.

TABLE 8–6 Different Telecommunications Organization Options

Telecommunications Function	Telecommunications Customer	Telecommunications Product	Location
Planning	X	X	X
Development	X	X	X
Operations	X	X	X
Admin. services	X	X	X
Help desk	X	X	X

Table 8–6 is interpreted as follows: A telecommunications organization with a structure similar to Figure 8–13 can be set up for each customer group or for each physical location (effectively a division structure format). A telecommunications product-oriented organization is shown in Figure 8–14. This structure would have telecommunications services consolidated under one functional organization with each product department

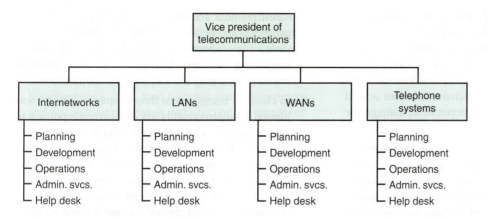

Figure 8–14. A telecommunications product-oriented organization.

providing its own planning, development, operations, administrative services, and help desk staffing. The number of departments and the staffing for each will be based on the scope and complexity of services needed for the specific situation.

Project Teams

The transient, one-time nature of projects—for both technical and nontechnical projects—does not normally justify the hiring of full time employees unless the enterprise is heavily involved in consulting or other activities that require ongoing projects. A telecommunications department normally implements systems and network facilities as a temporary assignment. Project-oriented activities end when the project is implemented.

Telecommunications managers may use outside consultants or vendor personnel, or they may assign projects to their own employees. When projects are implemented using internal personnel, the project assignments are viewed as temporary assignments and project personnel are "on loan" from functional departments. The understanding is that the project personnel will be returned to their original responsibilities (or will be candidates for promotion to new positions). Project assignments may be part time or full time activities for the individuals assigned to them.

Project personnel continue to have a primary responsibility to the manager of the "lending" department.

SUMMARY

This summary is organized to correspond with the learning objectives found at the beginning of the chapter.

1. Department management responsibilities refer to those managerial responsibilities associated with running a department within a business. It is assumed that department managers are bona fide managers—managers who have supervisory responsibilities for managerial and/or nonmanagerial personnel. Department management environments include accounting, human resources, manufacturing, or telecommunications, etc. Department management methods rely heavily on applying the POLC Model processes to department management activities.

2. In his or her role as a telecommunications manager, an individual has a broad set of accountabilities, includ-ing supervisory, administrative, personnel, planning, budgeting, and technology responsibilities. A managerial role is an open-ended assignment and telecommunications managers must be ready to "perform all other duties as assigned by their superior."

3. Managers hold positions of power assigned by business organizations. The person who occupies the position is empowered to use this power when carrying out his or her responsibilities. Leaders are individuals who are able to influence others so they willingly perform activities they would not normally perform. Ideally, managers should also be leaders.

4. The need for organization structure and design was triggered by the consolidation of workers into factory locations and the need to utilize worker resources

REVIEW

The following questions are open-ended—predefined answers are not included as part of the text. The purpose of these questions is to allow the readers to test themselves on the chapter material.

1. Describe the three stage business process model.
2. What are organization management skills?
3. Explain the role of leadership for managers.
4. What responsibilities does a bona fide manager have?
5. Describe division of labor concepts and why they were not used prior to the industrial revolution.
6. What are the three basic steps used in organizational design?
7. What is the difference between line and staff organizations?
8. What are employee job descriptions used for?
9. What is the purpose of employee performance appraisals?
10. Describe the differences between hierarchical and flat organization structures.
11. Why are centralization and decentralization organization structures less of an issue today?
12. Discuss span of control and the factors that influence it.
13. Describe what a chain of command is and what determines its length.
14. Describe the functional organization structure, its advantages, and its disadvantages.
15. Describe the divisional organization structure, its advantages, and its disadvantages.
16. Describe the matrix organization structure, its advantages, and its disadvantages.
17. Describe the team organization structure, its advantages, and its disadvantages.
18. What is the difference between cross-functional teams and work teams?
19. Describe the functions performed by various telecommunications departments: planning, development, operations, administrative services, and help desk.

MULTIPLE CHOICE

1. The field of professional management started in _____.
   a. 907 B.C.
   b. 1489 A.D.
   c. 1911 A.D
   d. 1965 A.D.
   e. 2045 A.D.
2. Organization management skills include _____. (Select all that apply.)
   a. budgeting skills
   b. project management skills
   c. technology skills
   d. supervisory skills
   e. PC skills
3. Bona fide managers _____.
   a. report to upper management
   b. have higher education degrees
   c. design organization charts
   d. supervise personnel
4. Employee performance appraisals are used to _____.
   a. define a position's responsibilities
   b. issue certificates
   c. determine raises
   d. conduct meetings
5. Technology planning responsibilities include _____.
   a. organization chart design
   b. project planning
   c. conducting performance appraisals
   d. maintaining employee files
6. The primary purpose of budgeting is to _____.
   a. measure performance
   b. keep track of actual expenditures
   c. define functional responsibilities
   d. generate profit and loss statements

7. If a department's budget is $100,000, and it spent $110,000, the variance would be _____.

   a. $100,000

   b. $110,000

   c. 0

   d. + $10,000

   e. − $10,000

8. Outsourcing involves the use of _____ personnel.

   a. telecommunications

   b. internal

   c. financial

   d. external

   e. affiliate

9. The _____ organizational design structure was the first structure used for factory environments.

   a. matrix

   b. team

   c. functional

   d. divisional

   e. flat

10. The basic unit used most commonly in organization design is _____.

   a. the team

   b. the department

   c. the president

   d. the manager

   e. the worker

11. Job descriptions are used to _____.

   a. evaluate employees

   b. obtain medical benefits

   c. coordinate organizational units

   d. establish performance expectations

12. The chain of command _____.

   a. identifies the reporting hierarchy of a manager

   b. is long in flat organizations

   c. is dependent upon the organization breadth dimension

   d. determines the number of direct reports

13. Managerial communication lines are shortest in a _____ organization structure.

   a. functional

   b. flat

   c. matrix

   d. hierarchical

   e. divisional

14. Project teams have more direct control over their activities in a _____ organization.

   a. functional

   b. divisional

   c. matrix

   d. hierarchical

15. Organizational formalization is most likely to occur in _____ organizations.

   a. functional

   b. matrix

   c. growing

   d. mature

   e. team

16. Span of control refers to _____.

   a. the depth of an organization

   b. the number of direct reports a manager has

   c. the vertical dimension of an organization structure

   d. the number of managerial levels in an organization

   e. use of cross-functional teams

17. Span of control has _____ staffing implications in large organizations.

   a. no

   b. small

   c. large

   d. none of the above

18. The vertical dimension of an organization addresses _____.

   a. how to perform department functions

   b. how to create team structures

   c. peer department relationships

   d. how organization activities are coordinated

19. The horizontal dimension of an organization addresses _____.

   a. how to perform department functions

   b. how to create team structures

   c. peer department relationships

   d. how organization activities are coordinated

20. The horizontal dimension of an organization addresses _____.

    a. how to perform department functions
    b. how to create team structures
    c. peer department relationships
    d. how organization activities are coordinated

21. The duplication of personnel and functions is minimized in the _____ organization structure.

    a. matrix
    b. functional
    c. team
    d. divisional

22. The _____ organization structure is best suited for focusing narrowly on specific objectives.

    a. matrix
    b. functional
    c. team
    d. divisional

23. In a team organization structure, traditional managerial responsibilities are performed by _____.

    a. upper management
    b. customers
    c. suppliers
    d. team members
    e. department managers

9

TECHNOLOGY MANAGEMENT SKILLS

LEARNING OBJECTIVES

1. Understand what *telecommunications technology management* means.

2. Understand what the term *telecommunications architecture* means.

3. Understand the elements that should be included in a business's telecommunications plan.

4. Understand how to estimate basic requirements for business telecommunications planning purposes.

5. Understand the advantages of the ANSI/TIA/EIA-568-A standard and describe why telecommunications managers should be familiar with it.

6. Understand cable model estimating procedures and how to apply them.

7. Understand the purpose of estimating factors and know how to use them.

8. Understand the elements used to develop a business's telecommunications financial plan.

9. Understand how to utilize the telecommunications planning model.

Chapter 8 discussed the business management responsibilities of a telecommunications manager. Those responsibilities focused on integrating the telecommunications department into the enterprise organization and managing it to operate effectively within a business context to provide technical services to customers (external and internal). Basic business management skill requirements are similar for all department managers, and each department manager is charged with ensuring the effectiveness of his or her department while supporting overall enterprise objectives.

Technology management skills are also generic—basic technology management skills can be applied to different situations and in different technical areas. Implementing technologies within the telecommunications department requires the coordination of PTM resources to create or modify telecommunications systems and networks. Projects are the primary instrument used to create or modify telecommunications systems and networks, and *project management skills* are a critical technology management skill for successfully implementing technical projects. Project management skills can be used for all projects—technical or nontechnical (administrative) projects. A key requirement for managing telecommunications technology is to have a good understanding of telecommunications technology to ensure that technology project proposals are realistic and do-able. This technical requirement is beyond the scope of this text, and it will be assumed that the reader has acquired a technical knowledge base prior to reading this chapter.

Good technology management skills cannot compensate for a poor technical design. However, poor technology management skills can take a technically sound design and create a project that costs more to implement than was budgeted, is not implemented on time, and does not operate properly. A **telecommunications technology planning model** will be used develop a multiyear business telecommunications plan, and the discussion of the model assumes the reader has a good conceptual understanding of telecommunications technology and terms.

WHAT IS TECHNOLOGY MANAGEMENT?

Technology management can be viewed as the study, development, and application of devices, machines, and techniques for productive processes. In a telecommunications context, technology would include communication equipment and systems, **LANs, WANs, internetworks,** and WWW facilities. A telecommunications department is

part of a business, and has the responsibility for selecting and installing the appropriate telecommunications technology to support business activities. While the technology management discussions will minimize the use of technical terms, it is not possible to discuss telecommunications projects without introducing some level of technical jargon.

Technical skills are needed to execute many aspects of the technology implementation activity. However, many technology implementation skills are managerial skills based on applying the same concepts described in Chapter 7, *Managerial Tools and Techniques,* and Chapter 8, *Business Management Skills.* A key technology management skill is project management, the managerial and organizational skills required to successfully implement technology and nontechnology projects. Project management skills are such an important part of the technology management process that Part 3, *Project Management* will be devoted to the project management topic. This chapter will focus on describing technology planning concepts for the purpose of answering two questions:

1. What is an appropriate format to use for documenting the **business enterprise telecommunications plans?**
2. How can strategic and tactical (one to five year planning horizon) telecommunications plans be developed in the absence of specific business requirements?

Telecommunications managers frequently find themselves in the uncomfortable position of having to meet implementation deadlines that did not include input from the telecommunications department. As a result, planning can become a reactive process that does not allow sufficient lead time to design and order complex systems and networks. Managers who find themselves in this uncomfortable position can spend unproductive time complaining about the need to meet unreasonable deadlines, but the bottom line is that meeting unreasonable deadlines frequently goes with the job of being a telecommunications manager. It is far more productive to: 1) respond quickly to requests for information, and 2) initiate activities that encourage business planners to incorporate telecommunications requirements into the business planning process at an earlier phase.

Note: One of the reasons that technical managers are not invited to participate in early planning efforts is because many technical managers are uncomfortable talking in nontechnical terms and about general planning elements. Most business planners are interested in business concepts and are not interested in listening to technical solutions when conceptual planning elements are being discussed. The best way for a technical manager to become involved with business planning is to effectively communicate the business impact of technology planning without the use of technical jargon.

Technology Management Overview

From a macroplanning perspective, technology management consists of:

1. *selecting* telecommunications technologies
2. *designing* telecommunications systems and networks
3. *implementing* telecommunications systems and networks
4. *operating* telecommunications systems and networks

The selection, design, and implementation elements are carried out within a project management context when projects are established to create operational systems and networks. When individuals are assigned to projects, preliminary planning has frequently resulted in the creation of a project budget and a set of project objectives. If budgets have already been established before the project team is formed, the primary focus of project management team members will be to implement the project on time and within budget while implementing project objectives.

How are the appropriate resources allocated to a project before the project implementation phase is initiated? The preproject phase, which allocates funds during the budgeting process, requires a technology planning effort to identify project goals and allocate sufficient money and time to complete the project. The focus of this chapter is identifying project budget requirements before the actual project is started and Part 3, *Project Management,* will discuss the procedures used to develop project plans for implementing technology projects.

Telecommunications Project Funding

The need for telecommunications projects is identified during the strategic planning process, when business goals are identified and the telecommunications department is given the assignment of supporting business planning efforts. Once a strategic business goal has been identified and approved by business management, a request for supporting details is made to different departments. When telecommunications products and services are involved, a telecommunications manager will be asked to: 1) identify the technical requirements and 2) establish capital expense estimates that cover the cost of implementing technology requirements.

At this level of planning, a minimum amount of detail is available and the manager is expected to provide a reasonable budget estimate for implementing telecommunications requirements. Unless the project is very large, the manager will be assigned the primary responsibility for establishing preliminary budget values. Once preliminary estimates have been developed, the budget becomes part of the tactical planning process that translates strategic requirements into a final financial budget format in preparation for the project implementation effort. The financial format for purchasing **fixed assets** (telecommunications equipment, networks, and systems are fixed assets) is a capital forecasting process that conforms to the financial department's format. The **capital expenditure** forecast coverts the project implementation requirements into the budgetary format used to allocate enterprise investment expenses. Capital budgets will include all the costs needed to implement the system or network, and this planning phase should also provide estimates of the project's operating costs during its operating lifetime.

> The expression "capital dollars" is the accounting term used to identify budgets that have been established to purchase fixed assets. Equipment, buildings, land, and furniture are examples of fixed assets.

Life Cycle Costs

As discussed in Chapter 7, telecommunications products (fixed assets) have an operating life. When they reach the end of their useful life, the product is retired (scrapped). Refer to Figure 7.8 for a diagram of a project life cycle. From an accounting perspective, the costs associated with purchasing and operating fixed assets are recovered over the assets' lifetime and are referred to as *life cycle costs.* Some fixed assets, such as land and buildings, have lifetimes of twenty or more years, but most of telecommunications equipment used to build systems and networks have an operating life of just five years. The IRS establishes the tax life of fixed assets (in years) and companies are given annual tax credits called depreciation allowances during the asset's IRS life to recover asset acquisition costs. Depreciation tax credits allow companies to recover the cost of the initial purchase over the operating life of the asset. Telecommunications managers should understand depreciation concepts.

The total cost of owning a fixed asset during its operating life consists of the initial purchase price plus the annual operating expenses incurred during its lifetime. This total cost is referred to as the asset's life cycle cost, and the accounting format used to identify these costs is the **LCA.** LCA identifies the true cost of owning a fixed asset by identifying all the design, implementation, and operational costs associated with the **telecommunications system** or network during its lifetime. Documentation submitted to upper management for the purpose of obtaining project funding should include a financial analysis that conforms to the internal accounting department's guidelines—a format that may include a request for life cycle costs.

Capital expenditure documentation frequently requires a cost *v.* benefit analysis so that upper management will have a means for comparing, evaluating, and ranking capital expenditure requests made by different departments. All businesses have funding limitations, and the capital forcasts submitted by different departments will be reviewed and ranked. The criteria used to rank different projects are established by the finance department. Managers submitting capital expense requests must complete forms that identify the project's value to the business. During the ranking process, a final cut-off point will be established, and only capital requests whose benefits meet or exceed the cut-off point will receive funding.

Capital expenditure forecasts are normally identified several years before they will be implemented, and will be updated during the organization's annual planning cycle. During the last annual cycle prior to implementation, capital forecasts become budget values for the project and will be used to measure the financial performance of the project management team.

TECHNOLOGY PLANNING ELEMENTS

Telecommunications has evolved into a network-centric technology. During the early stages of telecommunications technology development, the focus was on disparate pieces of equipment or large systems (telephone systems) made up of many equipment components. Today, upper management expects telecommunications systems and networks to be a single, homogeneous network infrastructure that provides any-to-any communications between all business locations for voice, data, and multimedia information needs. The following telecommunications technology planning elements should be incorporated into any business telecommunications planning model:

technology architecture

premises cabling systems

telephone systems

LANs

WANs

internetworks (LAN/WAN communications)

Technology Architecture

The term *technology architecture* refers to the underlying technology framework that determine the design, structure, and interaction of technology elements in systems, networks, or equipment. In a networking environment, the architecture defines the underlying standards that form the basis for selecting the hardware, software, and communication protocols used to create a seamless, transparent network-based communication infrastructure. Telecommunications technology elements include LANs, WANs, internetworks, and telephone systems. The technology architecture defines the method of device control used in a network—distributed or centralized—and specifies device access methods used in a LAN environment, such as Ethernet or Token Ring.

A prerequisite for developing a viable business enterprise telecommunications plan is the existence of a technology architecture plan. Using equipment that conforms to technology architecture standards ensures the interoperability of communication elements and technical scalability as new devices and technologies are added in the future. The topic of selecting technology architectures is well beyond the scope of a managerial text and requires a high level of technical expertise. The architecture selection responsibility should be delegated to technical specialists who have the necessary technology skills.

A technology-based approach should be used to select the technology equipment and services, and these technology elements will be converted into a cost format for financial planning purposes.

Premises Cabling Systems

Communication equipment and systems are distributed throughout businesses on desktops, in wiring closets, and in equipment rooms. The network and system devices are normally interconnected with a physical cabling infrastructure, although wireless technology is currently receiving a great deal of attention. The text's selection of the term, **premises cabling system,** broadly refers to the location connectivity system—whether guided or unguided media is utilized.

A copper or fiber optic cabling medium is frequently used to provide location device connectivity, and the entire location cabling infrastructure is commonly referred to as a premises cabling system. The premises cabling system is a key architectural element for any technology design process and initial investments for installing a premises cabling system can be high. If poor judgment is used during the initial selection and installation of a premises cabling system, the cabling infrastructure will generate ongoing operating problems and high operating costs.

A good premises cabling infrastructure should be able to handle all types of telecommunications equipment and networks. Fortunately, a significant effort has already been applied to designing a premises cabling infrastructure and a premises wiring system standard has been developed by telecommunications and electronic industry organizations. Following this existing standard will avoid initial installation problems and ensure that the initial installation can be expanded to handle new requirements. The **Electronic Industry Association/Telecommunication Industries Association (EIA/TIA) standard** is called the "Commercial Building Telecommunications Wiring 568A/569" standard. It provides detailed specifications for the selection, installation, and maintenance of cabling facilities to handle voice, data, and multimedia communication requirements.

Today, the EIA/TIA standard has been adopted as a national (U.S.) standard and has been designated as the ANSI/TIA/EIA 568-A Standard. From a telecommunications management perspective, any premises cabling installation should conform to ANSI/TIA/EIA standards.

Telephone Systems

Telephone systems have provided voice communication capabilities to business enterprises for many years; telephone technology is stable and reliable. Telephone system vendors provide a wide range of interface specifications to allow the interconnection of their systems with different WAN and LAN environments. WAN and LAN interface requirements should be identified during the design phase and should be specified to the telephone system supplier.

Telephone systems come in two basic versions: 1) a premises-based telephone system, and 2) a telephone central office (CO) based telephone system. These are normally referred to as PBX or Centrex systems, respectively. Centrex services are available from large telephone company COs only, while PBX systems can be used in any customer location. The text uses the PBX option for case study examples because it is used more universally than Centrex alternatives.

LANs

LANs provide a desktop interface for PCs and have become a critical business technology infrastructure element. LAN equipment decisions should be made within the enterprise technology architecture framework refer-

enced previously. Equipment and software selection decisions are frequently based on selecting equipment offered by dominant vendors because it is easier to gain business management support for brand name product investments (Microsoft or IBM, for instance) than for second-tier suppliers. Some of the LAN issues that must be resolved at the technical level include the selection of:

- Ethernet *v.* Token Ring access method
- Novell *v.* Microsoft network operating systems (NOSs)
- IBM PC compatible *v.* Macintosh workstations
- Microsoft PC operating system *v.* other vendors' operating systems
- Microsoft Office desktop software *v.* other vendors' spreadsheet, word processing, and presentation software

Without becoming embroiled in a discussion of technical purity, today's business and political environment favors the following selections. The astute telecommunications manager needs a sound business reasoning process to deviate from them. Failure to adhere to these popular standards is likely to generate a series of questions from business managers who base their technical knowledge on the advertising of the major telecommunications vendors.

- Ethernet LANs
- Microsoft network operating systems
- IBM PC compatible workstations
- Microsoft PC operating systems
- Microsoft Office desktop software

WANs

WANs provide the communication interconnection infrastructure between enterprise locations and use regulated common carrier services. In the 1970s, high-speed data communications over WAN facilities used dedicated (leased) lines. These facilities were expensive and only provided point-to-point or complex multipoint configurations. During the 1990s, viable data communication switched services emerged. When available at the location level, data switched services is the preferred way of meeting data communication WAN needs.

WAN carriers have always provided switched communication services to handle voice communications needs. The emergence of data communication switched services allows the application of a cost per minute approach to both voice and data communication traffic. The telecommunications planning model will assume the use of switched services for both voice and data WAN communication needs and voice and data WAN costs will be developed based on using on a rate × minutes used ($/min × minutes) cost algorithm.

Internetworks (LAN/WAN Communication)

Internetworks consist of multiple LANs and WANs interconnected to create the impression of a single, homogeneous network. Repeaters, bridges, routers, and gateways are the devices used to create networks and internetworks, and the planning model will include estimating factors for selecting networking and internetwork equipment.

A TELECOMMUNICATIONS PLANNING MODEL

Telecommunications spans a wide range of technologies, including telephone systems, LANs, WANs, and internetworks. Each of these technology application areas is implemented by using a complex blend of hardware, software, communication links, services, and people skills.

As a result of this inherent complexity, it is not unusual to find telecommunications planning focused on individual technology areas, with little attention paid to using common infrastructure elements to handle multiple technologies. For example, if a PBX system is installed to handle only voice communication, the telephone system cabling could not be used for data transmission purposes. However, if ANSI/TIA/EIA 568-A standards (568 standards) are utilized, the wiring system will handle both telephone system and LAN communication requirements. Using 568 standards avoids the need for installing and maintaining two separate wiring systems, and the additional cost for using 568 standards to initially install the telephone system wiring would be more than offset by the savings derived when desktop PCs can be installed without installing additional premises wiring.

An enterprise telecommunications plan should address all the needs of all telecommunications technology areas discussed in the previous sections and should leverage the opportunity to share infrastructure elements as a common resource. The enterprise plan should translate required technology investments into a format that can be understood by nontechnical personnel, because business decision makers in a corporate environment are not normally technologists. Requests for telecommunications project funding will be weighed against other corporate investment needs, and it is important that upper management understands the business benefits of the proposal. Unless a business justification format that uses business English and financial numbers is utilized, there is a low likelihood that management will understand the need for investing critical funds into a telecommunications infrastructure.

Another related area beyond the scope of this discussion is the need to link any technology plan to the corporate business planning process. Telecommunications investment costs must be presented in terms of their impact on business expenses and revenue. Clearly, an investment will be viewed differently if: 1) it generates savings that return the initial investment within a year or 2) will result in a 10% (or higher) increase in sales because of benefits provided to enterprise customers.

To summarize, a sound enterprise telecommunications planning process should:

1. address all telecommunications technology areas
2. translate investment requirements into business English and numbers
3. identify the financial benefits of the telecommunications investment

The following technology planning procedures will address the first two items. The last item—*business benefits*—is situation specific and should be based on real world requirements.

Telecommunications Model Concept

Table 9–1 lists the telecommunications technology elements that will be used in the enterprise telecommunications plan to generate a financial proposal that can be shared with upper management.

Estimating factors will be used to convert staffing and location-dimension information into equipment and cabling quantity estimates, respectively, in Table 9–1. While the estimating factors used in this text are "guesstimated" planning factors, telecommunications managers in a real world environment would be responsible for developing planning factors that are appropriate for the operating environment for which costs are being estimated. Individuals who have good technical design skills should be able to generate good estimating factors.

Structured Method Approach

It is conceptually easy but tedious and time consuming to develop a telecommunications plan when detailed information is already available. However, there is frequently little or no detailed information available, and it becomes necessary to estimate telecommunications costs without

TABLE 9–1   Business Telecommunications Model Elements

Element Description	Telephone System	LAN	WAN	Cabling
Estimating factors	X	X	X	X
Staffing (number of users)	X	X	X	X

Floor plan
  Equipment type/location*
  Wiring closets (MDFs,
  IDFs, etc.)*
	X	X	X	X

Hardware
  Quantities
  Standards*
  Unit costs
	X	X	X	X

Software
  Quantities
  Standards*
  Unit costs
	X	X	X	X

Cabling
  Cable type*
  Cable lengths
  Termination locations*
	X	X	X	X

Cost analysis
  Life cycle analysis
  Inflation factor
  Capital investment costs
  Operating costs
  Total costs
	X	X	X	X

System description*	X	X	X	X
Location addresses*			X	

* Important in real world planning but not required for preliminary estimates.

real world information. The following technology planning discussion assumes that minimal information is available to the telecommunications manager and preliminary cost estimates have been requested.

A sound technology planning process (model) should be based on a structured planning process that remains constant whether facts or assumptions are used as input. Then the planning model can be used to develop plans based on actual requirements or one based on assumed requirements. When the same planning model is used to estimate actual or estimated costs, the difference between the calculated results will depend upon the accuracy of the assumed values. With experience, this difference can be minimized and allows the planning model to be an accurate planning tool. When reasonable assumptions are used with a sound structured planning methodology, good estimating results can be obtained.

Figure 9–1 illustrates the use of a planning model that can use either real or estimated input. The output of the telecommunications planning model in Figure 9–1 will have the same format and appearance regardless of the input source. The output examples provided in the text are considered representative examples of what telecommunications planning documents should look like, whether real world or estimated values are used as input.

> *Disclaimer: If facts (detailed requirements and design information) are known, use them.* The text's use of estimates as input for the telecommunications planning model is intended to demonstrate how a telecommunications plan can be developed when the facts are not available. However, it is always preferable (and more accurate) to use real world information.

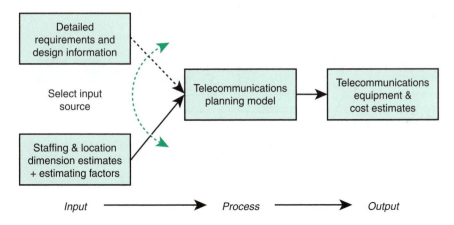

Figure 9–1. Telecommunications planning model.

Planning Process Overview

The telecommunications planning model utilizes a three step planning process for developing an enterprise telecommunications plan:

1. Identify the basic requirements driving the need for telecommunications services and then calculate equipment and service requirements.
2. Develop detailed worksheet costs for each telecommunications investment category.
3. Summarize the equipment and service investment requirements into a financial LCA plan format.

This three step process is shown in Figure 9–2.

The first step, *Identify/estimate basic requirements,* will determine the technology requirements for meeting business requirements, while the second step, *Calculate worksheet costs,* will convert the product and service estimates into costs by using appropriate cost and rate esti-

mates. The last step, *Develop Life Cycle Costs,* converts the cost information into an accounting format that summarizes the total cost implications of the telecommunications plan into a standard accounting format. This last step converts future depreciation costs and operating costs into equivalent current year costs.

Excel spreadsheets are used to calculate values for the planning model steps in Figure 9–2. The first step can be broken down further, as shown in Figure 9–3.

Figure 9–3 shows that basic requirement estimates are initially driven by Staffing (actual or estimated) and Estimating factors (planning values). The Step 1 output from the Basic requirements step (WAN, desktop equipment, and premises cabling requirements) is entered into worksheets where their costs and the costs of shared resource requirements are calculated. After the worksheet costs (Step 2) have been calculated, the cost information is consolidated into a financial Life Cycle Analysis/Net Present Value (LCA/NPV) plan format (Step 3) that conforms to the financial department's budgeting format.

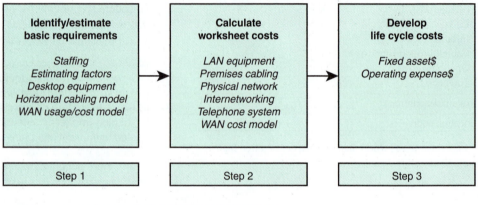

Figure 9–2. A Three step enterprise telecommunications planning model.

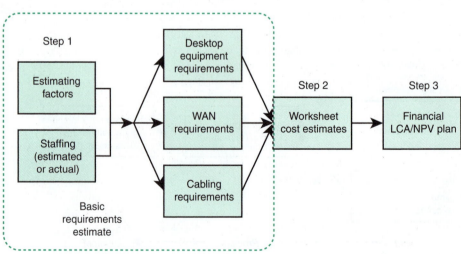

Figure 9–3. Expanded step 1 (basic requirements estimate).

CHAPTER 9

Step 1: Estimate Basic Requirements

Telecommunications is a network-centric technology where the number of devices used in a network environment is directly related to the number of individuals attached to the network. Desktop devices (telephones, PCs, and other input/output devices) provide a direct user interface and network servers to respond to user requests to provide these services. In a business location, a premises cabling system typically provides the connectivity infrastructure for different desktop devices and server resources. The 568 standard will be the conceptual basis for the cabling building infrastructure used in the planning model.

System and network users who require access to external resources will use WANs as the connectivity infrastructure and the planning model will be based on using a measured service ($/min) WAN infrastructure. Excel worksheets have been developed to generate requirements for desktop equipment, WAN services, and premises cabling. Staffing and estimating factor information provide the information used as input to develop Excel worksheets (Figure 9–3). Staffing, estimating factors, desktop equipment, WAN services, and premises cabling assumptions will be reviewed in the following sections.

STAFFING. The first step in developing a telecommunications plan is to identify the staffing levels on which product and service quantities will be based. Staffing information should be provided at the department level because departments normally consist of individuals who perform similar jobs and, therefore, who have similar communication needs. Staffing levels and estimating factors will be used to develop desktop equipment, horizontal cabling, and WAN requirement estimates.

ESTIMATING FACTORS. Estimating factors are used to convert staffing levels into desktop equipment, WAN service needs, and premises cabling requirements. The desktop equipment requirements will subsequently be used to estimate the different network shared resources required to provide system and network services to desktop equipment.

The concept of estimating factors is frequently used when a relationship exists between one variable and another, such as the relationship between square feet of ceiling and gallons of paint. If a paint container states that a gallon will cover 500 square feet, and the ceiling area to be painted is 500 square feet, one gallon of paint will be required. In this example, the paint coverage (500 square feet per gallon) is the planning value and the area to be covered (square feet) is equivalent to using staffing to identify desktop equipment needs.

Estimating factors are used in the telecommunications planning model to estimate a wide variety of telecommunications products. Normally, a detailed design effort is needed to identify real world equipment requirements. However, examination of real world design procedures will show that a calculation structure exists where different variables are entered to design calculations to create a system or network that has specific capacity and functionality attributes. The model's estimating factors have been selected as an approximation of the real world design process for the purpose of providing a planning template that can be modified, as needed, as better information becomes available. The primary objective of the planning model is to identify the various components that should be addressed in a telecommunications plan, and a secondary emphasis is placed on using the technically correct design process.

Note: The absence of hard information during strategic and tactical planning efforts does not normally provide the accurate input required for detailed design calculations.

Table 9–2 lists the estimating factors that will be used in the telecommunications planning model to develop an ABC Company telecommunications plan for a CSE (customer services & engineering) location.

> In a real world environment, telecommunications managers would have to develop the estimating factors that are appropriate for the specific enterprise technology environment for which estimates are being developed. The validity of estimating factors will be based on the skill of the estimator and the degree to which estimates apply to the planning environment.

DESKTOP EQUIPMENT. Business organizations provide desktop equipment (telephones and workstations) for their employees and the selection of features would be based on job requirements. From a macroplanning perspective, telephone and workstation needs can be grouped into categories and these categories can be matched with end user job requirement needs. In practice, there is a high likelihood that a relatively small number of equipment categories will be needed to meet the needs of most network/system users. A small percentage (under 5%) of an enterprise's employees may require unique equipment. These special requirements are best addressed on an individual basis when the implementation budget is being developed.

The following will discuss the use of standard categories for addressing employee commuting needs, and is intended to demonstrate the rationale of providing a few standard options instead of relying on an individual selection process. The primary decision criteria used in the commuting

TABLE 9–2   ABC Company Project Estimating Factor Table

Worksheet Name	Estimating Values
Desktop equipment estimates:	*Calculate workstation and telephone set quantities.*
Staffing assumptions:	Each line item is a department and is headed by a manager, e.g., president, vice
Managers	president, or dept. manager (default). For the CSE location, there are four supervisors in the customer departments who are considered managers for desktop equipment allocation purposes.
Executive assistants	Each manager has an executive assistant.
Equipment calculation rules:	
Super workstations	Engineering research & production departments
	Widget production = 3; widget development = 8
Manager workstations	1 per manager (defined previously)
General purpose workstations	All employees not assigned a super or manager workstation
Desktop printers	Pres, VP, and all executive assistants
Call director telephone sets	1 per 15 dept. members*
Manager telephone sets	1 per manager (defined previously)
ACD telephone sets	Order processing: 66; customer service: 13
General purpose telephone sets	All employees not assigned a call director, manager set, or ACD Set.
Cabling model	Use horizontal cabling model. Assume 225 sq. ft. per employee and ceiling = 15 ft.
	Calculate per floor and building cabling needs.
	Backbone cabling assumes a 1-floor building
WAN usage estimates:	*Determine empl/loc, monthly$ and annual$ values.*
	Usage & rate estimating values shown on worksheet.
Empl/loc value:	Establish links to appropriate desktop TelSet quantities.
Customer services: INWATS (800)	Number of ACD TelSets
Customer services: OUTWATS	Number of ACD TelSets
Other OUTWATS & local calls	All except ACD TelSets
Direct Outward Dialing(DOD)	All TelSets
Frame relay (data) locations	To 10 Locations
LAN equipment:	*Determine quantities and cost$ values.*
Workstations	Establish links to appropriate desktop workstation quantities.
Shared printers	1 Printer/12 users* who don't have a desktop printer
Servers	1 per 15 workstations*
Network Interface Cards (NICs)	1 per workstation, shared printer, or server
Network management system	1 at HQ; none at other locations
Microsoft office software	1 copy per user workstation
Workstation user training	$100 per workstation
Installation labor	1 allowance per NIC device
LAN annual maintenance:	
Hardware:	
Workstations, printers, servers, network management Systems	Hardware$ x 10%
Workstation moves, adds, changes (MAC)	(# workstations x 15%)* x $250 per MAC
Premises cabling system:	*Determine quantities and cost$ values.*
Service entrance components	1 per building
Equipment room components	1 per building
Backbone facilities	1 per building with wiring closet(s)
Wiring closets	1 per floor @ HQ and CSE

TABLE 9–2   ABC Company Project Estimating Factor Table (continued)

Worksheet Name	*Estimating Values*
Horizontal cabling	*Link to cabling model worksheet (HorizCable).*
Backbone/riser fiber cabling	*Link to cabling model worksheet (BBCable).*
Work area hardware (plugs, jacks, etc.)	1 per NIC device
Service entrance cable	Assume distance from road to building (feet): 200 assumed
Horiz. cabling installation hours	1.5 hours/NIC device
LAN physical networking:	*Determine quantities and cost$ values.*
Server racks (equipment room)	1 per 6 servers*
Hub ports	1 per NIC device
Hub chassis	Assume 1 per 60 hub ports*
Hub chassis racks	1 per 3 hub chassis*
Hub network management system	1
Hub switches	1 per 50 NICs (round down)
Bridges	1 per 20 NIC devices (round down)
FDDI hardware	1 @ CSE location
Hub cabling labor	1.5 hours/NIC
Physical networking annual maintenance:	
Hardware:	
Hub ports, network management system, hub switches, bridges, FDDI hardware	Hardware$ × 10%
Internet equipment:	*Determine quantities and cost$ values.*
Local routers	1 per 40 NIC devices*
Remote routers	1 per location
Installation labor	7 hours per router
Technician training	None (HQ location only)
Internetworking annual maintenance:	
Hardware:	
Routers	Hardware$ × 10%
Telephone system:	*Determine quantities and cost$ values.*
Use a key system when total lines are less than or equal to 100 lines;	
A PBX above 100 lines	
PBX tel. system, including tel. sets	$1000/employee
Key tel system, including tel. sets	$700/employee
(Key/PBX)telephone system	Quantity: 1 per location. Unit$ = Tel system cost **without** TelSets
Telephone sets (TelSets)	*Link to appropriate desktop TelSet quantity.*
Telephone user training	$100 per TelSet user
PBX annual maintenance:	
Hardware:	
PBX system + TelSets	Hardware$ x 10%
TelSet moves and changes	(#TelSets x 15%)* x $300/MAC
Wide area network	*Determine quantities and cost$values.*
WAN Frame relay adapter card	1 per remote router (card module in remote router)
Voice comm. trunks	1 trunk per 20 employees*
Data comm. trunks	1 T1 trunk
Annual usage estimates	*Link to appropriate WAN Est quantity.*
Frame Relay (data)	*Link to appropriate WAN Est quantity.*

(continued)

cable runs where each wiring closet will be connected to the MDF with a separate backbone cable. Figure 9–7 provides an illustration of the floor plan grid used for cable length calcuations.

Because the example is for a one-story building, only a single backbone cable run is required. The backbone cable run length between the equipment room and the wiring closet will be:

$$backbone\ cable\ run\ length = H + 6W + 5.5L + H$$
$$= 2H + 6W + 5.5L$$

The H, W, and L values were already calculated (see *Calculating Cable Run Lengths*) to be 15 feet, 15 feet, and 15 feet, respectively. We can then convert the $H/W/L$ formula into feet:

$$backbone\ cable\ run\ length = (2 \times 15) + (6 \times 15) + $$
$$(5.5 \times 15)$$
$$= 202.5\ ft$$

Placed into a table format, this result would be shown as:

Description	Qty.	# H	H	# W	W	# L	L	Length
1st floor backbone	1	2	15	6	15	5.5	15	203

The quantity of '1' indicates a single cable run. When multiple floors exist, the wiring closets for each floor in the telecommunications model are aligned in the center of their floors. Backbone cable runs made to other floors will have a length equal to the first floor run plus the number of additional floors times H. Applying this calculation method to a hypothetical 3rd floor backbone cable run for a $12W \times 11L$ grid layout would add $2H\,[(3-1) \times H]$ and result in the following backbone cable length:

$$3rd\ floor\ backbone\ cable\ length = [2H + 6W + 5.5L] + 2H$$
$$= 4H + 6W + 5.5L$$
$$= 232.5\ ft$$

or, in a table format:

Description	Qty.	# H	H	# W	W	# L	L	Length
3rd floor backbone	1	4	15	6	15	5.5	15	233

HORIZONTAL CABLING CALCULATION.

Figure 9–8 provides another version of the Figure 9–7 layout and highlights the information used for calculating horizontal wiring requirements. Horizontal cable runs will begin at the floor of each cell and end at the floor of the wiring closet, with the length calculated in terms of H, W, and L. However, 132 cable lengths of first-floor horizontal cable runs will be required instead of the single cable backbone cable run.

The cable length from cell #1 to the wiring closet will have the same length as the first-floor backbone cable.

$$cell\ \#1\ length = H + 6W + 5.5L + H$$
$$= 2H + 6W + 5.5L$$

Following the same process for the remaining Figure 9–8 cells generates the results summarized in the following table and shows that the total horizontal cabling requirement for the six cells is 990 feet.

Description	Qty.	# H	H	# W	W	# L	L	Length
Cell #1	1	2	15	6	15	5.5	15	202.5
Cell #2	1	2	15	5	15	5.5	15	187.5
Cell #3	1	2	15	4	15	5.5	15	172.5
Cell #4	1	2	15	3	15	5.5	15	157.5
Cell #5	1	2	15	2	15	5.5	15	142.5
Cell #6	1	2	15	1	15	5.5	15	127.5
Group total	**1**	**12**	**15**	**21**	**15**	**33**	**15**	**990.0**

While this may be an interesting approach, it would be tedious to calculate each cell manually and then total them. Fortunately, symmetry and the use of spreadsheets greatly simplify the process. From a symmetry perspective, inspection of Figure 9–8 shows that the right half of Row 11 would generate the same formula values as the left half. The following table multiplies each Row 11 left-half cell cable length and shows that Row 11 requires 1,980 feet of horizontal cable.

Description	Qty	# H	H	# W	W	# L	L	Length
Cell #1	2	2	15	6	15	5.5	15	405
Cell #2	2	2	15	5	15	5.5	15	375
Cell #3	2	2	15	4	15	5.5	15	345
Cell #4	2	2	15	3	15	5.5	15	315
Cell #5	2	2	15	2	15	5.5	15	285
Cell #6	2	2	15	1	15	5.5	15	255
Row 11 total								**1,980**
Row 11: L/R side	1	12	15	21	15	33	15	990
Row 11: twice L/R side	2	12	15	21	15	33	15	**1,980**

However, there is an easier way to summarize Row 11 requirements—simply add up the $\#N$, $\#W$, and $\#L$ values for the left-hand group to get a group total value (Row 11: L/R Side). Twice the group value (Row 11: Twice L/R Side) will also generate the same answer as doubling each cell value. The algebraic formula for this approach—and

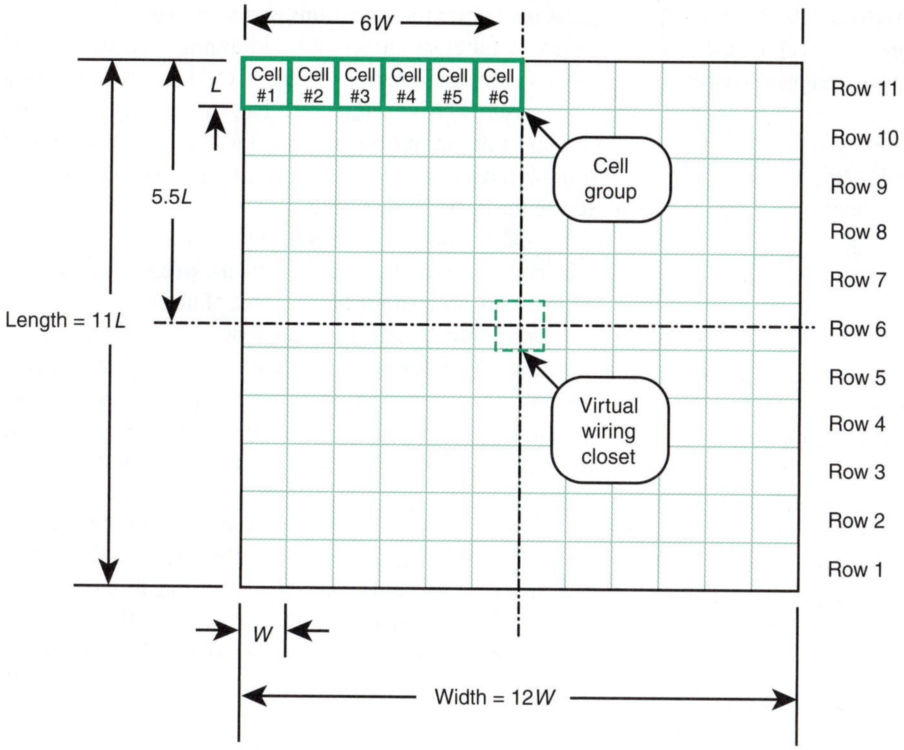

Figure 9–8. Grid plan layout example ($12W \times 11L$ grid).

the one that is used in the spreadsheet length formula calculation of rows 1 and 11 is:

$$\text{length} = 4 \times [(12 \times 15) + (21 \times 15) + (33 \times 15)] = 3,960$$

The following table uses the group total approach to calculate the horizontal cabling requirements for Rows 1 through 11 and shows that 17,280 feet of horizontal cabling is needed for 132 first floor cells. Because Row 6 does not have a mirror image row, its quantity value is 2.

Description	Qty.	#H	H	#W	W	#L	L	Length
Rows 1 and 11	4	12	15	21	15	33	15	3,960
Rows 2 and 10	4	12	15	21	15	27	15	3,600
Rows 3 and 9	4	12	15	21	15	21	15	3,240
Rows 4 and 8	4	12	15	21	15	15	15	2,880
Rows 5 and 7	4	12	15	21	15	9	15	2,520
Rows 6	2	12	15	21	15	3	15	1,080
Floor total								**17,280**

Using this approach, it is necessary to calculate the cable length in terms of $H/W/L$ only for the left side of a row and either multiply it by four or two, depending upon whether an even or odd number of rows results when symmetry is applied.

MULTIFLOOR CABLING REQUIREMENTS. To estimate the cable requirements for a multifloor environment, divide the building staffing by the number of floors and use the same calculation method demonstrated previously. The horizontal cabling requirements will be the number of floors times the horizontal cabling requirements for one floor. Backbone cabling requirements would be calculated for each floor, as discussed previously.

WIDE AREA NETWORK MODEL. One way to estimate WAN costs is to assume the use of measured services for voice and data communication and express these rates in cost$/minute. If the average calling minutes per user can be identified (or estimated) for different WAN services, the cost for using the service will be the number of minutes × the rate (i.e., minutes × $/minute).

As was the case for the desktop equipment, staffing drives the WAN cost estimating process. Table 9–2 assumes that there are three categories of WAN telephone users: customer service department users, noncustomer service department users, and all company personnel (customer service + noncustomer service). Table 9–2 identifies which categories should be used on the WAN estimation worksheet.

Step 2: Calculate Worksheet Costs

Once the staffing, estimating factor, desktop equipment, cabling, and WAN requirements calculations are completed, they become the input for Figure 9–3's Step 2 (worksheet cost estimates). Six Microsoft Excel worksheets are used to calculate telecommunications element costs:

1. LAN equipment cost worksheet
2. structured cabling system cost worksheet
3. LAN physical network cost worksheet
4. internetwork equipment cost worksheet
5. telephone system cost worksheet
6. WAN cost worksheet

The basic calculation performed on the spreadsheets is quantity × unit\$ = cost\$. Quantity values are based on using staffing, estimating factors, desktop equipment model, horizontal cabling model, and WAN model information. The worksheet table format is shown below.

Worksheet Format

Description	Quantity	Unit$	Cost$
		Total	

Step 3: Financial Life Cycle Plan

The objective for developing a telecommunications plan is to identify budget needs and request the necessary funding. Future capital investment needs and the operating expenses associated with these investments should be included with the funding request. A telecommunications plan must include all financial requirements so business management can evaluate its benefits compared to the investment plans submitted by other departments.

A number of financial analysis techniques are used to assess capital investment options, and the techniques vary in complexity and scope. Some of the more commonly used method include LCA, net present value (NPV), return on investment (ROI), and investment payback. The text will use an LCA/NPV financial model to evaluate telecommunications investment options.

LIFE CYCLE ANALYSIS (LCA). LCA refers to a financial analysis process that estimates all the costs required for purchasing and operating a fixed asset during its useful life. The IRS defines an asset's tax life (the depreciation period). However, the useful functional life of a system or of equipment is sometimes longer than its tax life, and the length of an LCA analysis should be based on the expected functional life of the asset.

During the operating life of a fixed asset, hardware maintenance and repair costs, software maintenance fees, personnel costs for operations and administration, and environmental costs (heat, air conditioning, electricity, and floor space) are incurred. Because the functional life of a fixed asset is greater than one year, these costs will be incurred in different time periods and the current values of those future costs will differ depending upon how far in the future the costs are incurred.

LCA financial analysis procedures convert future year costs to current year costs, and the **present value** (PV) approach is utilized for this purpose. Future year costs are converted into current year costs by using PV factors—a conversion tool for determining the current dollar value of revenues and expenses incurred in future time periods. When alternatives are compared, the net present value (NPV) cost for each alternative will be compared.

INFLATION FACTOR. Another important factor used for calculating future costs is the **inflation factor.** Inflation results in goods and services costing more in the future than they cost today. The effect of inflation on an asset's **operating costs** means that operating costs in the future can be higher than today for the same maintenance.

TAX EFFECT. From a tax accounting perspective, different alternatives may generate different tax credits that impact the actual cost seen by a corporation. The complexity of determining the impact of corporate tax rates and other tax credits is significant, and is best left to financial specialists. Most economic studies (financial plans) require examining alternatives that have the same types of deductible costs and that produce similar taxable income. However, in some cases, alternatives may generate different deductible costs and taxable income. A telecommunications plan should accurately identify capital expenditures and operating expenses in the life cycle periods incurring them and rely on the finance department for identifying the tax implications of the plan. The different values shown in the text's LCA/NPV analyses will be pretax values, and any **tax effect** issues will be delegated to the accounting department.

LCA/NPV STANDARD FINANCIAL MODEL. A standard financial model will be used to summarize the capital investment and operating expense implications of telecommunications plans into an LCA/NPV format. It will be based on evaluating pretax costs over the life of the investment (LCA) and include the use of PV and inflation factors. The standard financial model shown in Table 9–5 was developed by:

1. establishing the LCA study length
2. identifying current year product costs (capital and operating)

TABLE 9–5   Standard Economic Model Description

Calculation Category	Description
Common cost data	The **common cost data table** lists the different financial factors that will be used in LCA/NPV calculations, and they would be provided by the accounting department. These would be the standard financial factors used for evaluating different enterprise investment alternatives. inflation rate% inflation factor cost of money (interest rate) asset service life (years) asset salvage (% of initial cost) The cost of money is based on the enterprise organization's rate of return requirements. The inflation factor used to determine future year operating costs is calculated as follows: inflation factor = 1 + inflation rate%. For example, if the inflation rate were 5%, the inflation factor = 1 + 5% = 105% or 1.05.
Fixed asset description	The **fixed asset table** would summarize the individual cost elements associated with the fixed asset purchase description. In a detailed LCA/NPV analysis, it would consist of the various expense elements that will be included in depreciation allowance calculations. In the strategic planning format, it is based on the estimated asset costs provided on the cost worksheets. The total installed cost is the fixed asset value that would be included in the depreciation allowance and would follow IRS depreciation procedures. All Fixed Asset Expenses are shown as negative values because the purchase of the asset generates an immediate cash outflow. Parentheses will be used instead of negative signs to highlight negative values on the LCA/NPV analysis worksheets.
Annual costs	The **annual cost table** lists the maintenance and operating costs associated with operating the fixed assets shown in the fixed asset table. For fixed assets, it would be the maintenance cost for maintaining the asset during the first year of its life cycle. When telecommunications services are purchased instead of using installed equipment, the annual cost would be the estimated cost for purchasing the service. When the LCA/NPV is used for evaluating equipment purchase options, the annual cost would primarily consist of maintenance cost values. In a strategic planning format, the LCA/NPV would include estimates of equipment maintenance costs and telecommunications service costs. The depreciation and salvage annual costs are calculated as follows: salvage value = total installed cost × salvage value% depreciation = (total installed cost – salvage value)/service life The salvage value% and service life factors are gotten from the **common cost data table.** Depreciation and Salvage values are shown as positive values because depreciation and salvage accounting activities generate a positive cash flow during the product life cycle. All other common cost data table elements are expenses and are shown as negative values.
Annual operating costs	The **annual operating cost table** calculates the annual operating costs for the **annual cost table** elements for the selected study length time period. The annual operating cost table includes allowances for inflation and provides a PV calculation to convert future year costs into current year cost values so that a reasonable comparison can be made between future operating costs. Table 9–7 will be used to select the appropriate PV factors for converting future year costs into current year costs. For the strategic financial planning process, Year 0 operating costs will use the pretax annual cost table values. Future year annual operating costs will be calculated using the Inflation factor from the common cost data table: year 0 costs = annual cost table cost future year costs = previous year cost × inflation factor*

TABLE 9–5 Standard Economic Model Description (continued)

Calculation Category	Description
	The **annual operating cost** is the sum of the column costs (remember there are positive and negative signs). These annual costs are converted to current year costs (**PV operating costs**) by multiplying them by the PV factor for the specific year. (The cost of money interest rate from the common cost data table determines which interest rate is used.)
	PV operating costs are used for comparing alternative investments or for strategic planning purposes.
Management summary	The **management summary table** consolidates the information shown in the fixed asset table and annual operating cost table:
	initial cost = total installed cost (fixed asset table)
	total PV operating cost = annual PV operating cost (annual operating cost table)
	This table summarizes both the investment (fixed asset) and operating costs for a specified time period—typically the life of the asset when a product evaluation is being carried out.

*Inflation Factors apply to all operating costs **except depreciation, salvage value, or fixed contract**. These costs are fixed by the IRS (depreciation and salvage value) or by a contractual agreement and are not affected by inflation.

3. calculating future year costs while allowing for inflation

4. using the company's cost of money interest rate for PV calculations

5. calculating LCA costs based for items 1–4

6. interpreting the results

7. making a selection from choices given (optional)

The optional Step 7 would be used when the economic model is used to evaluate the financial implications of two or more choices. Part 5 will use Step 7 as part of the evaluation process for selecting telecommunications equipment. This chapter will use the standard financial model to develop financial plan estimates for strategic planning purposes.

The best way to understand the LCA financial evaluation process is to review one that has been completed. Example 9–1 shows a completed LCA financial plan based on using the standard financial model and is actually the financial evaluation part of the ABC Company case study at the end of this chapter.

Table 9–5 provides the procedures for calculating the different cost elements shown in Example 9–1, while Table 9–6 shows the present value table used for selecting PV factors to convert future year costs into current year costs. Different investment rates and different future time periods would generate different PV values. In our LCA/NPV analysis, the interest rate is based on the value of money to the enterprise organization and is specified by the accounting department (Refer to Table 9–5).

Table 9–6 is a standard PV table. The first year on the table is Year 1, and it refers to the first future year for which a present value calculation is made. In the LCA/NPV format (Example 9–1), this is the second year that is shown, because the first column is for the current year value. For this reason, current year cost calculations are shown as Year 0 on the LCA/NPV format and the first future year is shown as Year 1, the second future year as Year 2, etc. However, when discussing current year costs with nonaccounting personnel, it is more appropriate to use Year 1 to specify the current year.

When the standard economic model is used to evaluate two investment alternatives, the format used in Example 9–1 would be modified to include two analyses and provide a cost comparison between them. The same approach could be used for any number of investment choice, and this use of the LCA/NPV format will be shown in Part 5, *Acquisition Management,* of the text for making decisions between equipment acquisition options. In the real world, an organization's finance department would provide the standard economic model guidelines used for evaluating telecommunications investments.

CASE STUDY: THE ABC COMPANY

This case study will demonstrate the application of the planning procedures described previously in this chapter. It will use the three step planning process (Figure 9–1)

TABLE 9–6 Present Value of $1.00

Years								*PV (a.k.a. DCF) Factor*								
	1%	3%	4%	5%	6%	7%	8%	9%	10%	11%	12%	13%	14%	15%	18%	20%
1	0.9901	0.9709	0.9615	0.9524	0.9434	0.9346	0.9259	0.9174	0.9091	0.9009	0.8929	0.8850	0.8772	0.8696	0.8475	0.8333
2	0.9803	0.9426	0.9246	0.9070	0.8900	0.8734	0.8573	0.8417	0.8264	0.8116	0.7972	0.7831	0.7695	0.7561	0.7182	0.6944
3	0.9706	0.9151	0.8890	0.8638	0.8396	0.8163	0.7938	0.7722	0.7513	0.7312	0.7118	0.6931	0.6750	0.6575	0.6086	0.5787
4	0.9610	0.8885	0.8548	0.8227	0.7921	0.7629	0.7350	0.7084	0.6830	0.6587	0.6355	0.6133	0.5921	0.5718	0.5158	0.4823
5	0.9515	0.8626	0.8219	0.7835	0.7473	0.7130	0.6806	0.6499	0.6209	0.5935	0.5674	0.5428	0.5194	0.4972	0.4371	0.4019
6	0.9420	0.8375	0.7903	0.7462	0.7050	0.6663	0.6302	0.5963	0.5645	0.5346	0.5066	0.4803	0.4556	0.4323	0.3704	0.3349
7	0.9327	0.8131	0.7599	0.7107	0.6651	0.6227	0.5835	0.5470	0.5132	0.4817	0.4523	0.4251	0.3996	0.3759	0.3139	0.2791
8	0.9235	0.7894	0.7307	0.6768	0.6274	0.5820	0.5403	0.5019	0.4665	0.4339	0.4039	0.3762	0.3506	0.3269	0.2660	0.2326
9	0.9143	0.7664	0.7026	0.6446	0.5919	0.5439	0.5002	0.4604	0.4241	0.3909	0.3606	0.3329	0.3075	0.2843	0.2255	0.1938
10	0.9053	0.7441	0.6756	0.6139	0.5584	0.5083	0.4632	0.4224	0.3855	0.3522	0.3220	0.2946	0.2697	0.2472	0.1911	0.1615

This table shows the present value (PV) of $1 received at a future time (FV). To use the table, select the interest rate from the top row and read down the column to the appropriate number of years. The PV factor is the intersection of the Year row and Interest rate column, that is, the NPV of $1 received 10 years in the future discounted at 10% = $0.3855, i.e. FV = $1, NPV = $0.3855

Excel Function: NPV (interest, value1, value2,. . . .)
where Value1 = FV of Year 1, Value2 = Future Value of Year 2, etc.
e.g., NPV of $1 in Year 7 @ 7% = NPV(.07,0,0,0,0,0,0,1) = 0.6227
e.g., @ i = 12%, FV1 = 235; FV2 = 250, FV3 = 679: NPV(.12,235,250,679) = $892

Fixed Asset Description	Purchase
Product costs	
LAN hardware/software	($592,750)
Premises cabling system	($35,319)
Physical network	($31,850)
Internetwork	($8,250)
Telephone system	($143,000)
WAN	($1,000)
Total installed cost	**($812,169)**

Annual Costs	
LAN maintenance	($52,350)
Phys. net. maintenance	($1,670)
Internetwork maintenance	($650)
Tel. system maintenance	($19,000)
WAN maintenance	($31,300)
WAN—voice comm.	($1,058,904)
WAN—data comm.	($37,800)
Total deprectn. (straight line)	$146,190
Total salvage value	$81,217

Common Cost Data	Item
Inflation%	4%
Annual inflation factor	104%
Cost of money	11%
Service life (years)	5
Salvage value	10%

Annual operating costs

Description	Year 0	Year 1	Year 2	Year 3	Year 4	Total
Consolidated comm. costs						
LAN system maintenance	($52,350)	($54,444)	($56,622)	($58,887)	($61,242)	($283,544)
LAN phys. net maintenance	($1,670)	($1,737)	($1,806)	($1,879)	($1,954)	($9,045)
Internetwork maintenance	($650)	($676)	($703)	($731)	($760)	($3,521)
Tel. system maintenance	($19,000)	($19,760)	($20,550)	($21,372)	($22,227)	($102,910)
WAN maintenance	($31,300)	($32,552)	($33,854)	($35,208)	($36,617)	($169,531)
WAN—voice comm	($1,058,904)	($1,101,260)	($1,145,311)	($1,191,123)	($1,238,768)	($5,735,366)
WAN—data comm	($37,800)	($39,312)	($40,884)	($42,520)	($44,221)	($204,737)
Total depreciation	$146,190	$146,190	$146,190	$146,190	$146,190	$730,952
Total salvage	$0	$0	$0	$0	$81,217	$81,217
Annual operating costs	**($1,055,484)**	**($1,103,551)**	**($1,153,540)**	**($1,205,529)**	**($1,178,381)**	**($5,696,485)**
PV factors	**1.0000**	**0.9009**	**0.8116**	**0.7312**		**0.6587**
PV operating costs	**($1,055,484)**	**($994,190)**	**($936,239)**	**($881,473)**	**($776,236)**	**($4,643,622)**

Management Summary

Description	Year 0	Year 1	Year 2	Year 3	Year 4	Total
CSE building costs						
Initial costs	($812,169)					($812,169)
Total PV operating costs	($1,055,484)	($994,190)	($936,239)	($881,473)	($776,236)	($4,643,622)
Totals	**($1,867,653)**	**($994,190)**	**($936,239)**	**($881,473)**	**($776,236)**	**($5,455,791)**

Example 9–1. Telecommunications financial plan: 5-year economic evaluation of headquarters communications plan uses "standard economic model" format & assumptions.

with the final deliverable being a 5-year Telecommunications Financial Plan (Example 9–1). The case study is for a project that will relocate the ABC Company's customer service and engineering departments to a new location. This project is in the early planning stages and decisions have not been made regarding the new building's design or location.

ABC Company Project Information

The ABC Company's management board is discussing the option of relocating their customer services and engineering department into a leased, one-story building within the next six months. The new location would be used for the next five years to alleviate overcrowding at their headquarters, and would provide time to design and implement a new headquarters complex. The five year staffing level projection for the customer services and engineering departments are 100 and 30 respectively.

From a preliminary planning perspective, it will be assumed that new telecommunications equipment and services will be purchased. If existing products and services can be reused, it will simply be a matter of modifying the preliminary numbers to reflect the change. The telecommunications analyst assigned to the project has summarized the forecasting requirements into the general telecommunications plan description shown as follows:

Telecommunications plan description	
Objective:	Develop a preliminary five year business telecommunications forecast for a new customer services & engineering (CSE) location based on the assumption that all new facilities and services will be installed. This forecast will provide estimates for a basic business communication infrastructure including WAN, LAN, internetwork, telephone system, and premises wiring requirements.
Input:	Department staffing levels exist and will be provided. No other information is available.
Output:	The primary deliverable for the preliminary forecast will be a budgetary estimate of capital investment and five year operating expense requirements for the telecommunications infrastructure.

Table 9–7 summarizes the staffing levels for the new CSE location, which will house 130 employees and must be provided with a suitable business communications infrastructure.

It will be assumed that this staffing information is the only hard information that has been made available to the telecommunications analyst. The telecommunications planning model will be used to develop preliminary estimates in a Microsoft Excel file, and information from the various worksheets will be shown in the text.

> The calculations shown in the text are Microsoft Excel-based calculations and selected portions of the Excel worksheets have been "cut and pasted" into the text to make it easier for the reader to see the entire process. However, for Excel-oriented individuals, the electronic version is available in the text's CD. The CD version shows the Excel expressions used for calculations and linking.

Estimating Basic Needs

To identify telecommunications investment and operating expense costs for a five year period, the following information must be known or estimated.

1. staffing levels
2. desktop equipment
3. WAN usage and cost estimates
4. horizontal cabling requirements

Staffing Levels

Staffing levels (Table 9–7) will drive the desktop equipment, WAN usage, and cabling estimates. Staffing information has been summarized into the Excel worksheet format shown in Example 9–2, which provides allowances for entering desktop equipment requirements—requirements that will be developed by using Table 9–2.

Desktop Equipment

The approach for estimating desktop equipment requirements will be to standardize the workstation and telephone set (TelSet) options required at the new facility. Based on a review of customer services and engineering requirements, three workstation and four telephone set options will be used to meet customer services and engineering personnel

TABLE 9–7   CSE Location Staffing

Division	Department	Staff
Customer Services	VP-customer svc & executive assistant	2
	Order processing	80
	Customer services	18
	Dept. totals	**100**
Engineering	VP-Engineering & executive assistant	2
	Widget production	8
	Widget development	10
	Widget field support	10
	Dept totals	30
	Totals	**130**

Division	Department	Staff	Workstation Type				TelSet type				
			1	*2*	*3*	*Tot*	*1*	*2*	*3*	*4*	*Tot*
Customer services	VP customer svc. & exec. assistant	2									
	Order processing	80									
	Customer services	18									
	Dept. totals	100									
Engineering	VP engineering & exec. assistant	2									
	Widget production	8									
	Widget development	10									
	Widget field support	10									
	Dept. totals	30									
	Totals	130									

Example 9–2.   ABC company staffing/desktop equipment worksheet.

Category	Description	Workstation Type			TelSet Type			
		1	*2*	*3*	*1*	*2*	*3*	*4*
Workstation	Super workstation	X						
	Manager workstation		X					
	General purpose workstation			X				
TelSet	Call director TelSet				X			
	Manager TelSet					X		
	Automatic call distributor TelSet						X	
	General purpose TelSet							X

Example 9–3.   Workstation and telephone equipment types.

needs. Example 9–3 lists the workstation and telephone set options needed for staff listed in Example 9–2. .

The descriptions shown in Example 9–3 were discussed previously in the desktop equipment estimates section. Example 9–4 provides a completed staffing/equipment worksheet. The workstations and telephone sets selected for each job category were based on using the estimating factor information contained in Table 9–2.

Example 9–4 assigned three and eight super workstations to the production and development departments, as

Division	Department	Staff	Workstation Type				TelSet Type					Dsk Prtr
			1	2	3	Tot	1	2	3	4	Tot	
Customer services	VP customer svc. & exec. assistant	2	0	0	1	2	1	1	0	0	2	2
	Order processing	80	0	1	79	80	6	4	66	4	80	1
	Customer services	18	0	1	17	18	2	1	13	2	18	1
	Dept. totals	100	0	3	97	100	9	6	79	6	100	4
Engineering	VP engineering & exec. assistant	2	0	1	1	2	1	1	0	0	2	2
	Widget production	8	3	1	4	8	1	1	0	6	8	1
	Widget development	10	8	1	1	10	1	1	0	8	10	1
	Widget field support	10	0	1	9	10	1	1	0	8	10	1
	Dept. totals	30	11	4	15	30	4	4	0	22	30	5
	Totals	**130**	**11**	**7**	**112**	**130**	**13**	**10**	**79**	**28**	**130**	**9**

Example 9–4. Completed ABC company staffing/desktop equipment worksheet.

indicated in Table 9–2. Manager workstations were assigned to VPs and department managers, and other department members were assigned general purpose workstations.

The same approach was used to assign telephone sets: call director, manager, and Automatic Call Director (ACD) telephone sets (Table 9–2). Department members not assigned call director, manager, or ACD telephone sets were provided with general purpose telephone sets.

Location Cabling Estimate

With a staffing level of 130 and a one-story building, the number of employees per floor = 130. In a multifloor structure, divide the number of employees by the number of floors in the building. The 225 square feet per employee estimating factor from Table 9–2 will be applied.

The grid pattern selection and cable length calculations were already completed in the premises cabling discussion of a previous section. The same solution (Figure 9–8) will be used here (Figure 9–9) and only the summary calculation results are shown in Tables 9–8 and 9–9.

> Refer to the cabling model discussion if there are any questions regarding the cable length calculation results shown in Tables 9–12 and 9–13.

WAN Estimate

In the planning model, employees were placed in standard WAN usage categories based on the type of telephone set they used. ACD set users fell into one category and all other

telephone sets fell into another category. Only ACD users will have access to INWATS, and ACD users will have a different OWATS and local call usage rate than the other employees. The estimating factors used in Example 9–5 are listed in Table 9–2. The Min/Day, Day/Mnth, $/Min factors were provided as part of the worksheet. (The Day/Mnth estimates the average number of working days per month [(250/12 = 20.8 = 21)]. These values are estimating factors and should be provided by the telecommunications manager.

The calculation for determining Example 9–5 Monthly$ and Annual$ are:

$$\text{Monthly\$} = \text{Empl/Loc} \times \text{Min/Day} \times \text{Day/Mnth} \times \text{\$/Min}$$
$$\text{Annual\$} = 12 \times \text{Monthly\$}$$

Worksheet Cost Calculations

Table 9–2 will be applied to the cost worksheets. Description and unit cost (Unit$) values are provided on the worksheet, and worksheet quantities are based on the use of previously calculated values (Example 9–5) or calculated values from another worksheet. The cost worksheets are:

Example 9–6: LAN workstation/server equipment worksheet

Example 9–7: Structured cabling system worksheet

Example 9–8: Physical network worksheet

Example 9–9: Internetwork worksheet

Example 9–10: Telephone system worksheet

Example 9–11: WAN worksheet

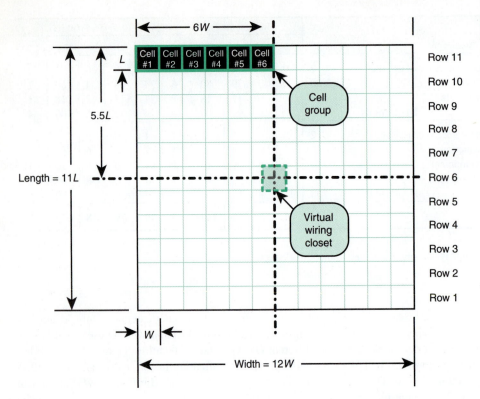

Figure 9–9. Floor plan of horizontal cabling model (12W × 11L grid).

TABLE 9–8   Horizontal Cable Length Calculation Results for 12W × 11L Grid Layout

Description	Qty.	# H	H	# W	W	# L	L	Length
Rows 1 and 11	4	12	15	21	15	33	15	3,960
Rows 2 and 10	4	12	15	21	15	27	15	3,600
Rows 3 and 9	4	12	15	21	15	21	15	3,240
Rows 4 and 8	4	12	15	21	15	15	15	2,880
Rows 5 and 7	4	12	15	21	15	9	15	2,520
Rows 6	2	12	15	21	15	3	15	1,080
Floor total								**17,280**

TABLE 9–9   Backbone Cable Length Calculation Results for 12W × 11L Grid Layout

Description	Qty.	# H	H	# W	W	# L	L	Length
1st floor backbone	1	2	15	6	15	5.5	15	203

ABC Company Telecommunications Financial Plan

The calculations needed to develop the LCA/NPV analysis shown in the Example 9–1 project were discussed previously and summarized in Table 9–5. In the Example 9–1 analysis, the bottom line estimate for the LCA/NPV plan would be $5,455,791 with $812,169 of this amount required for the initial fixed asset investment and $4,643,622 for five years of (PV) operating costs:

If Example 9–1 is examined, the information presented in the Table 9–10 is the same shown in the summary cost section of Example 9–1. The table version eliminated the negative signs (used parentheses instead) and placed the years in a year 1 through year 5 format.

Service	Empl/Loc	Min/Day	Day/Mnth	$/Min	Monthly$	Annual$
OWATS	51	45	21	$0.10	$4,820	$57,834
DOD (10% overflow)	130	4	21	$0.20	$2,184	$26,208
Outgoing LD					**$7,004**	**$84,042**
Customer services						
INWATS (800)	79	240	21	$0.15	$59,724	$716,688
OWATS	79	120	21	$0.10	$19,908	$238,896
					Subtotal	**$955,584**
Local calls	51	30	21	$0.05	$1,607	$19,278
Frame relay (data)*	10	30	21	$0.50	$3,150	$37,800
OWATS summary						
OWATS	51	45	21	$0.10	$4,820	$57,834
OWATS	79	120	21	$0.10	$19,908	$238,896
					Total	**$296,730**
Estimate summary						
Voice comm.						**$1,058,904**
Data comm.						**$37,800**
					Total comm.	**$1,096,704**

Assumes ten locations communicating daily with headquarters location.

Example 9–5. WAN employee usage/cost estimates.

Description	Quantity	Unit$	Cost$
SuperStations	11	$10,000.00	$110,000
Manager workstations	7	$2,500.00	$17,500
General purpose workstations	112	$2,000.00	$224,000
Shared printers	11	$2,500.00	$27,500
Desktop printers	9	$500.00	$4,500
Ethernet NICs	150	$150.00	$22,500
Microsoft Office software	130	$500.00	$65,000
LAN servers w/software	9	$10,000.00	$90,000
Network management system	0	$10,000.00	$0
Installation labor	150	$125.00	$18,750
Training	130	$100.00	$13,000
Annual LAN maintenance		$47,350	
Annual LAN moves & changes		$5,000	
Annual total		**$52,350**	
		Total	**$592,750**

Example 9–6. Workstation/server equipment worksheet.

This change was made to translate a technical financial assessment into a more user-friendly version that can be understood easily by individuals who don't have accounting backgrounds.

Once the financial plan is completed, it is necessary to translate the information into a business report (oral or written) that summarizes the technical and financial implications of the telecommunications plan. It is likely that a presentation would also have to be made to the management board. The presentation should describe the scope of the plan and the basis for formulating estimates. The worksheet quantities from Examples 9.2

Description	Quantity	Unit$	Cost$
Service entrance components	1	$1,000.00	$1,000
Equipment room components	1	$2,500.00	$2,500
Backbone facilities	1	$1,000.00	$1,000
Wiring closets	1	$3,000.00	$3,000
Horizontal cabling (feet)	15,960	$0.15	$2,394
Backbone fiber (ft) w/installation	193	$10.00	$1,925
Work area components	150	$15.00	$2,250
Service entrance cable (feet)	200	$50.00	$10,000
Horiz. cabling labor (installation hours)	225	$50.00	$11,250
		Total	**$35,319**

Example 9–7. Structured cabling system worksheet.

Description	Quantity	Unit$	Cost$
Server racks	2	$300.00	$600
Hub ports: 100BaseT	150	$50.00	$7,500
Hub chassis	3	$1,000.00	$3,000
Hub chassis racks	1	$300.00	$300
Hub network management system	1	$5,000.00	$5,000
Hub switches	2	$400.00	$800
Bridges	7	$200.00	$1,400
FDDI hardware	1	$2,000.00	$2,000
Hub cabling labor (installation)	225	$50.00	$11,250
Annual maintenance		**$1,670**	
		Total	**$31,850**

Example 9–8. Physical network worksheet.

Description	Quantity	Unit$	Cost$
Local routers	4	$1,000.00	$4,000
Remote routers	1	$2,500.00	$2,500
Internetworking labor	35	$50.00	$1,750
Internetworking training	0	$1,000.00	$0
Annual internetworking maintenance		**$650**	
		Total	**$8,250**

Example 9–9. Internetwork worksheet.

through 9.7 would provide the fixed asset and annual operating cost input for the Example 9–1 financial plan. The common cost data would be obtained from the accounting department.

Case Study Recap

The ABC Company case study provided an example of applying the methods and procedures described in Chapters 6, 7, 8, and 9 to a situation where a cost estimate was

Description	Quantity	Unit$	Cost$
130-line PBX system w/VM, ACD	1	$94,300.00	$94,300
Call director TelSets	13	$300.00	$3,900
Manager TelSets	10	$250.00	$2,500
ACD TelSets	79	$300.00	$23,700
Basic TelSets	28	$200.00	$5,600
User telephone system training	130	$100.00	$13,000
Annual PBX maintenance		$13,000	
Annual PBX moves & changes		$6,000	
Annual total		**$19,000**	
Total			**$143,000**

Example 9–10. Telephone system worksheet.

Description		Quantity	Unit$	Cost$
WAN frame relay adapter card		1	$1,000.00	$1,000
	Qty	Unit$	Cost$	
Recurring voice comm.Trunk*	7	3600	$25,200	
Recurring data comm. trunk (T1)*	1	6000	$6,000	
Annual costs		**Annual trunk Oper$**	**$31,200**	
F/R eqpt. annual maint.			$100	
Trunk recurring cost			$31,200	
Total annual maintenance cost			**$31,300**	
Annual usage estimates				
OWATS			$296,730	
DOD			$26,208	
800 services			$716,688	
Local calls			$19,278	
Total voice communications			**$1,058,904**	
Frame relay (data communications)			**$37,800**	
			Total asset$	**$1,000**

Example 9–11. WAN worksheet.

TABLE 9–10 ABC Company Project Cost Estimate in Current Year Dollars: Five Year Plan

Description	Year 1	Year 2	Year 3	Year 4	Year 5	Total
Communications costs						
Initial costs	$812,169					$812,169
Total PV operating cost	$1,055,484	$994,190	$936,239	$881,473	$776,236	$4,643,622
Totals	**$1,867,653**	**$994,190**	**$936,239**	**$881,473**	**$776,236**	**$5,455,791**

required for a strategic thinking session. In the case study, upper management was interested in the financial implications of setting up a temporary (five years) location to house their headquarter's customer services and engineering departments in a one-story building. The information provided to the telecommunications analyst assigned to the project was existing staffing levels and that a one-story building would be used. In a strategic session, the focus is on "what if" thinking and responses to these questions should be fast and conceptually accurate. The ABC Company management board is requesting information from many departments—not just the telecommunications department—and all the information will be consolidated by the finance department to determine the total implications. If the board wishes to proceed based on the initial estimates, the various organizations that provided input would be asked to provide additional details. On the other hand, if the board concludes that the CSE consolidation is inappropriate, the telecommunications department has fulfilled its role quickly, using a reasonable analytical approach.

The most important element of the plan is its format. The estimation models, worksheets, and financial plan clearly document the plan proposal and allow others to see the equipment and service elements it contains. An information database has been established that can be modified, as required, to address any questions raised regarding its scope and content.

SUMMARY

This summary is organized to correspond with the learning objectives found at the beginning of the chapter.

1. *Telecommunications technology management* refers to those activities involved with selecting, designing, implementing, and operating telecommunications equipment, systems, networks, and services. Many technology skills are of a managerial nature and utilize basic management skills. Others are more technical and require a good knowledge of the specific technology or access to specialists who have this knowledge.

2. In today's network-centric environment, telecommunications architecture is a network-oriented architecture that defines the hardware, software, access methods, and protocols used by network devices and devices attached to the network. The architecture decision should be made early in the telecommunications management process, because it becomes the basic blueprint that will be used to select and install hardware and software elements. The architecture determines the operating characteristics of LANs, WANs, and internetworks, and the selection of a specific architecture may limit the selection of devices that can be attached to the network.

3. An enterprise telecommunications plan should include desktop equipment (telephone sets and PCs), LAN equipment, premises cabling, physical networking equipment, internetworking equipment, telephone systems, and WAN services. These technical elements must be translated into business benefits and financial costs so that business management can understand their meaning. The plan should always contain the technical details needed to communicate with telecommunications personnel.

4. In the enterprise telecommunications planning process, staffing level is the primary driver that determines the plan's basic requirements. High staffing levels will require more telecommunications equipment than lower staffing levels. The quantity of desktop equipment (telephone sets and PCs) required is directly related to staffing and the shared facility equipment quantities will be based on the number of desktop devices they support. The equipment estimates are then converted into dollars so that a financial plan can be established for budget planning purposes.

5. The ANSI/TIA/EIA-568-A Standard is a set of premises wiring standards. They provide a complete set of wiring connection and wiring standards for customer premises locations. The benefit of conforming to the 568 Standards is that they provide a wiring architecture that ensures that premises wiring investments are long-term investments that can be modified to meet new future needs while maintaining the existing investments.

6. The cable planning model reviewed in the chapter provides a means for estimating horizontal cabling needs. Horizontal cabling requirements are a major cabling infrastructure investment and are difficult to estimate without detailed floor plans showing wiring closets and desktop equipment locations. The cabling model provides a conservative (high) estimate that is suitable for strategic planning purposes. If floor plans showing wiring closets and desktop equipment locations are available, they should be used to generate a more accurate horizontal cabling estimate.

7. To estimate equipment needs for enterprise telecommunications planning purposes, estimating factors are used to convert staffing information into equipment requirements. The equipment estimates provide a basis for developing telecommunications budget estimates and are key elements when hard facts are not available. Estimating factor values are based on experience and an understanding of the technology environment being planned. If hard information about equipment requirements is available, it should be used to create more accurate forecasts.

8. The elements used to develop an enterprise telecommunications financial plan include desktop equipment (telephone sets and PCs), LAN equipment, premises cabling, physical networking equipment, internetworking equipment, telephone systems, and WAN services. These elements are converted into capital expenditure forecast and operating budget information so that telecommunications requirements can be included in the business's financial planning process. An LCA approach is used to convert future period expenditure to a current dollar base and provide a more accurate picture of life cycle expenses. The telecommunications financial plan should use enterprise accounting standards in its format.

9. The telecommunications planning model is a three step process based on using worksheet calculations to identify telecommunications investment (capital expenditures) and operating budget needs. It is an estimating technique and is not intended to be a substitute for the detailed design and planning needed to develop operational budgets, but is suitable for long-range planning purposes. Model estimating factors used for strategic planning should provide a conservative estimate for expenses. The calculation results should be on the high side, because it is easier to explain lowering cost estimates to upper management than to explain why the estimated costs must be increased.

KEY TERMS AND CONCEPTS

The language of telecommunications management is multifaceted and includes words and phrases from managerial, technological, accounting, regulatory, and other business areas. The definitions of these key terms and concepts can be found within the chapter and in the glossary.

Annual Cost
Annual Operating Cost
Business Enterprise Telecommunications-
    Plan
Cable Length Estimation Model
Capital Expenditure
Common Cost Data
EIA/TIA Standard

Estimating Factors
Fixed Asset
Inflation Factor
Internetwork
LCA
LAN
Operating Costs
Premises Cabling System

Present Value (PV)
Tax Effect
Technology Architecture
Technology Management
Telecommunications Technology Planning
    Model
Telecommunications System
WAN

REVIEW

The following questions are open-ended—predefined answers are not included as part of the text. The purpose of these questions is to allow the readers to test themselves on the chapter material.

1. Define the term *telecommunications technology management.*

2. What are capital expenditures?

3. What is network architecture?

4. What are premises wiring systems?

5. What is the ANSI/TIA/EIA-568-A Standard?

6. What elements should be included in an enterprise telecommunications plan?

7. Provide an overview description of this chapter's telecommunications planning model.

8. What are the primary drivers for developing telecommunications technology estimates?

9. Provide a backbone and horizontal cabling estimate (in feet) for a three-story building that houses 1,000 employees.

10. What is a virtual wiring closet?

11. What are the benefits of developing an LCA of different acquisition alternatives?

12. Outline the seven steps used to develop the standard economic model used in this chapter.

MULTIPLE CHOICE

1. Capital expense dollars are used to _____.
   a. budget operating expenses
   b. purchase current assets
   c. purchase fixed assets
   d. pay dividends

2. The analysis used to determine all the costs associated with owning networks or systems is called a _____.

   a. life cycle analysis
   b. product development analysis
   c. POLC model analysis
   d. perpetual cycle analysis

3. A central office-based telephone system is called a _____.

   a. PBX system
   b. Centrex system
   c. CBX system
   d. Modular telephone system

4. The primary requirement driving the telecommunications planning model is _____.

   a. fixed assets
   b. current assets
   c. staffing
   d. operating costs
   e. estimating factors

5. How many different types of telephone set options were provided in the telecommunications model?

   a. 1
   b. 2
   c. 3
   d. 4
   e. 5

6. What percentage of moves and changes are allowed for in the telecommunications model?

   a. 10%
   b. 5%
   c. 25%
   d. 15%
   e. 20%

7. How many standard areas are covered in the ANIS/TIA/EIA-568-A premises cabling standard?

   a. 2
   b. 4
   c. 5
   d. 6
   e. 8

8. In the cabling model grid, each cell represents _____.

   a. L
   b. W
   c. H
   d. an employee
   e. a virtual wiring closet

9. When costs are developed using estimates, the estimated costs should be _____ than the actual costs of implementing the plan.

   a. lower than
   b. equal to
   c. higher than
   d. in future year dollars, rather than

10. Backbone cabling connects between _____.

    a. the work areas and wiring closets
    b. communications devices and the premises cabling
    c. outside services and the equipment room
    d. the equipment room and wiring closets

11. The purpose of the present value calculation is to _____.

    a. identify heat and air conditioning expenses
    b. identify asset costs
    c. calculate operating costs
    d. convert current year expenses into future year dollars
    e. convert future year expenses into current year dollars

12. For LCA/NPV calculations, depreciation is a _____ value.

    a. positive
    b. neutral
    c. negative
    d. indeterminate

13. The LCA/NPV inflation factor is used to _____.

    a. convert current year expenses into future year dollars
    b. convert future year expenses into current year dollars
    c. convert current year costs into future year costs
    d. convert future year costs into present value costs

14. For LCA/NPV calculations, the purchase cost for fixed assets is a _____ value.

    a. positive
    b. neutral
    c. negative
    d. indeterminate

15. In LCA/NPV calculations, the inflation factor is *not* applied to _____. (Select all that apply.)

a. maintenance expenses

b. leasing expenses

c. depreciation expenses

d. rental expenses

16. Depreciation service years (fixed asset life) is established by the _____.

a. telecommunications department

b. IRS

c. accounting department

d. corporate policies

e. ICC

PRACTICE

The following provides manual versions of three types of telecommunications model calculation worksheets: 1) desktop equipment, 2) cost worksheets, and 3) a financial LCA/NPV worksheet. They are provided to allow readers to self-test their understanding of telecommunications model calculations presented in the text and should be completed, with a calculator, prior to completing the case study problem that follows.

1. This problem provides a manual version of the desktop equipment worksheet used to develop workstation, telephone set, and desktop printer quantities for the telecommunications planning model. The only input requirements are: 1) staffing levels and 2) a set of Estimating Factors. Both have been provided.

Complete the calculations for the Desktop Equipment worksheet. A solution is included so that you can verify your answers.

Practice Desktop Worksheet Problem: Estimating Values

Worksheet Name	Estimating Values
Desktop equipment estimates	*Calculate workstation, telephone set, and desktop printer quantities.*
Staffing assumptions	
Managers	Each line item is a department and is headed by a manager (president, vice president, or dept. manager [default])
Executive assistants	Each manager has an executive assistant.
	Other locations: executive assistants by title only
Equipment calculation rules	
SuperStations	Development/advertising: 1
	Production planning: 1
	Programming services: 2
Manager workstations	1 per manager (defined previously)
General purpose workstations	All employees not assigned a SuperStation or manager workstation
Desktop printers	HQ: pres., VP, and all manager executive assistants
	Other locations: executive assistants titles only
Call director telephone sets	1 per VP secretary, 1 per 15 dept. members*
	Other locations: 1 per executive assistant (title)
Manager telephone set	1 per manager (defined previously)
	Other locations: 1 per manager (title)
ACD telephone sets	Order processing: 17
	Customer service: 6
General purpose telephone set	All employees not assigned a call director, manager, or ACD set

*Round calculations up, unless otherwise specified.

Disclaimer: These estimating values have been arbitrarily selected to provide students with a common basis for PetroProd Project calculations. In the "real-world," a great deal of requirements definition, design, and equipment selection effort is needed to identify the actual quantities for the following desktop equipment worksheets:

Desktop Equipment Worksheet:

Branch	Department	Staff	Workstation Type				TelSet Type					Dsk Prtr
			1	2	3	Tot	1	2	3	4	Tot	
Executive												
	President/exec. assistant	**2**										
Finance	VP finance/exec. assistant	2										
	Finance department	7										
	Cost accounting/acct. receivable	10										
	Dept. totals											
Human resources	VP personnel/exec. assistant	2										
	Personnel	6										
	Benefits/employee relations	4										
	Dept. totals											
Marketing	VP marketing/exec. assistant	2										
	Development/advertising	8										
	Sales	8										
	Dept. totals											
Customer services	VP customer svc./exec. assistant	2										
	Order processing	20										
	Customer services	8										
	Dept. totals											
Manufacturing	VP-Manufacturing / exec. assistant	2										
	Purchasing	5										
	Production planning	6										
	Plant operations	15										
	Dept. totals											
Information services	VP-MIS/exec. assistant	2										
	Programming services	6										
	Telecom/LAN operations	5										
	Dept. totals											
	Totals	**122**										

Desktop Equipment Categories

Category	Description	1	2	3	1	2	3
Workstation	Super workstation	X					
	Manager workstation		X				
	General purpose workstation			X			
Telephone set	Call director				X		
	Manager					X	
	Automatic call distributor						X
	General purpose						

Practice Desktop Problem Solution:

Branch	Department	Staff	Workstation Type				TelSet Type					Dsk Prtr
			1	2	3	Tot	1	2	3	4	Tot	
Executive												
	President/exec. assistant	2	0	1	1	2	1	1	0	0	2	2
Finance	VP finance/exec. assistant	2	0	1	1	2	1	1	0	0	2	2
	Finance department	7	0	1	6	7	1	1	0	5	7	1
	Cost accounting/acct. receivable	10	0	1	9	10	1	1	0	8	10	1
	Dept. totals	**19**	**0**	**3**	**16**	**19**	**3**	**3**	**0**	**13**	**19**	**4**
Human resources	VP Personnel/exec. assistant	2	0	1	1	2	1	1	0	0	2	2
	Personnel	6	0	1	5	6	1	1	0	4	6	1
	Benefits/employee relations	4	0	1	3	4	1	1	0	2	4	1
	Dept. totals	**12**	**0**	**3**	**9**	**12**	**3**	**3**	**0**	**6**	**12**	**4**
Marketing	VP marketing/exec. assistant	2	0	1	1	2	1	1	0	0	2	2
	Development/advertising	8	1	1	6	8	1	1	0	6	8	1
	Sales	8	0	1	7	8	1	1	0	6	8	1
	Dept. totals	**18**	**1**	**3**	**14**	**18**	**3**	**3**	**0**	**12**	**18**	**4**
Customer services	VP customer svc/exec. assistant	2	0	1	1	2	1	1	0	0	2	2
	Order processing	20	0	1	19	20	2	1	17	0	20	1
	Customer services	8	0	1	7	8	1	1	6	0	8	1
	Dept. totals	**30**	**0**	**3**	**27**	**30**	**4**	**3**	**23**	**0**	**30**	**4**
Manufacturing	VP Manufacturing/exec. assistant	2	0	1	1	2	1	1	0	0	2	2
	Purchasing	5	0	1	4	5	1	1	0	3	5	1
	Production planning	6	1	1	4	6	1	1	0	4	6	1
	Plant operations	15	0	1	14	15	2	1	0	12	15	1
	Dept. totals	**28**	**1**	**4**	**23**	**28**	**5**	**4**	**0**	**19**	**28**	**5**
Information services	VP MIS/exec. assistant	2	0	1	1	2	1	1	0	0	2	2
	Programming services	6	2	1	3	6	1	1	0	4	6	1
	Telecom/LAN operations	5	0	1	4	5	1	1	0	3	5	1
	Dept. totals	**13**	**2**	**3**	**8**	**13**	**3**	**3**	**0**	**7**	**13**	**4**
	Totals	**122**	**4**	**20**	**98**	**122**	**22**	**20**	**23**	**57**	**122**	**27**

Desktop Equipment Categories

Category	Description	1	2	3	1	2	3	4
Workstation	Super workstation	X						
	Manager workstation		X					
	General purpose workstation			X				
Telephone set	Call director				X			
	Manager					X		
	Automatic call distributor						X	
	General purpose							X

2. This problem provides a manual version of the LAN equipment worksheets used in the telecommunications planning model, which is a good example of cost worksheets. Desktop Equipment and the Estimating Factors are used to develop the worksheet quantities and the operating expense values, and the quantities are multiplied by the table's cost/quantity values to calculate equipment costs.

Complete the calculations for the desktop equipment worksheet. A solution is included so that you can verify your answers.

Practice LAN Equipment Worksheet Problem: Estimating Values

Worksheet Name	Estimating Values
LAN worksheet	*Determine quantities and Cost$ values.*
Workstations	*Establish links to appropriate desktop workstation quantities.*
Shared printers	1 printer per 14 users* who don't have a desktop printer
Servers	1 per 20 users
NICs	1 per workstation, shared printer, or server
Network management system	1
Microsoft Office software	1 per user workstation
Workstation user training	1 per user workstation
Installation labor	1 allowance per NIC device
LAN annual maintenance	
Hardware: workstations, printers, servers, network management system	Hardware$ × 10%
Workstation moves, adds, changes (MAC)	(# workstations × 15%)* × $300 per MAC

*Round calculations up, unless otherwise specified.

Disclaimer: These estimating values have been arbitrarily selected to provide students with a common basis for PetroProd Project calculations. In the real world, a great deal of requirements definition, design, and equipment selection effort is needed to identify the actual quantities for the following:

LAN Equipment Worksheet Problem

Desktop Equipment: Workstations Desktop Printers						
Workstations	Staffing	SuprStations	MgrStations	GPStations	TotStations	Printers
Company totals	315	18	21	276	315	26

LAN Equipment Worksheet	Determine Quantities and Cost$ Values
Workstations	*See desktop equipment table.*
Shared printers	1 Printer/14 users* who don't have having a desktop printer
Servers	1 per 20 workstations*
NICs	1 per workstation, shared printer, or server
Network management system	1
Microsoft Office software	1 per user workstation
Workstation user training	1 per workstation
Installation labor	1 allowance per NIC device
LAN annual maintenance	
Hardware: workstations, printers, servers, network management system	Hardware$ × 10%
Workstation MAC	(# workstations x 15%)* × $300 per MAC

* Round calculations up.

Description	Quantity	Unit$	Cost$
SuperStations		$10,000.00	
Manager workstations		$2,500.00	
General purpose workstations		$2,000.00	
Desktop printers		$500.00	
Shared printers		$2,500.00	
Ethernet NICs		$150.00	
Microsoft Office software		$500.00	
LAN servers w/software		$10,000.00	
Network management system		$10,000.00	
Installation labor		$125.00	
Training		$100.00	
Annual equipment maintenance			
Annual moves & changes maintenance			
Total annual maintenance			
		Total	

Round calculations to nearest dollar.

LAN Equipment Worksheet Problem Solution

Desktop Equipment: Workstations Desktop Printers

Workstations	Staffing	SuprStations	MgrStations	GPStations	TotStations	Printers
Company totals	315	18	21	276	315	26

LAN Equipment Worksheet	Determine Quantities and Cost$ Values
Workstations	See workstation table.
Shared printers	1 Printer/14 users* who don't have a desktop printer
Servers	1 per 20 workstations*
NICs	1 per workstation, shared printer, or server
Network management system	1
Microsoft Office software	1 per user workstation
Workstation user training	1 per workstation
Installation labor	1 allowance per NIC device

LAN annual maintenance:

Hardware: workstations, printers, servers, network management system	Hardware$ × 10%
Workstation MAC	(# workstations × 15%)* × $300 per MAC

* Round calculations up.

Description	Quantity	Unit$	Cost$
SuperStations	18	$10,000.00	$180,000
Manager workstations	21	$2,500.00	$52,500
General purpose workstations	276	$2,000.00	$552,000
Desktop printers	26	$500.00	$13,000
Shared printers	21	$2,500.00	$52,500
Ethernet NICs	352	$150.00	$52,800
Microsoft Office software	315	$500.00	$157,500
LAN servers w/software	16	$10,000.00	$160,000
Network management system	1	$10,000.00	$10,000
Installation labor	352	$125.00	$44,000
Training	315	$100.00	$31,500
Annual equipment maintenance		$102,000	
Annual moves & changes maintenance		$14,400	
Total annual maintenance		**$116,400**	
		Total	**$1,305,800**

Round calculations to nearest dollar.

3. This problem provides a manual version of the financial LCA/NPV worksheet used in the telecommunications planning model. Normally, the input for the worksheet is gathered from the various cost worksheets and the common cost data table with information gathered from the enterprise's financial department. An abbreviated present value table is included. (A complete table is provided in Appendix D.)

Complete the calculations for the fixed asset, annual costs, operating costs, and summary costs tables, making sure to use the appropriate signs ($+$ or $-$) for depreciation- and expense-oriented data, respectively.

Financial LCA/NPV Practice Problem Present Values: Present Value of $1

PV Factors DCF Factors

Years	3%	4%	5%	6%	8%	10%	12%	14%	20%
1	0.9709	0.9615	0.9524	0.9434	0.9259	0.9091	0.8929	0.8772	0.8333
2	0.9426	0.9246	0.9070	0.8900	0.8573	0.8264	0.7972	0.7695	0.6944
3	0.9151	0.8890	0.8638	0.8396	0.7938	0.7513	0.7118	0.6750	0.5787
4	0.8885	0.8548	0.8227	0.7921	0.7350	0.6830	0.6355	0.5921	0.4823
5	0.8626	0.8219	0.7835	0.7473	0.6806	0.6209	0.5674	0.5194	0.4019
6	0.8375	0.7903	0.7462	0.7050	0.6302	0.5645	0.5066	0.4556	0.3349
7	0.8131	0.7599	0.7107	0.6651	0.5835	0.5132	0.4523	0.3996	0.2791
8	0.7894	0.7307	0.6768	0.6274	0.5403	0.4665	0.4039	0.3506	0.2326
9	0.7664	0.7026	0.6446	0.5919	0.5002	0.4241	0.3606	0.3075	0.1938
10	0.7441	0.6756	0.6139	0.5584	0.4632	0.3855	0.3220	0.2697	0.1615

This table shows the PV of $1 received at a future time (FV). To use the table, select the interest rate from the top row and read down the column to the appropriate number of years. The PV Factor is the intersection of the Year row and interest rate column, e.g. the NPV of $1 received 10 years in the future discounted at 10% = $0.3855, i.e. FV = $1, NPV = $0.3855

Excel Function: NPV(interest, value1, value2, . . .)

where Value 1 = FV of Year 1, Value 2 = Future Value of Year 2, etc., e.g., NPV of $1 in Year 7 @ 7%; = NPV(.07,0,0,0,0,0,0,1) = $0.6227), e.g., @ i = 12%, FV1 = 235; FV2 = 250, FV3 = 679: NPV(.12,235,250,679) = $892.42

Financial LCA/NPV Practice Problem: 5 Year Economic Evaluation

Pretax Analysis; Includes Inflation Allowance
Uses Standard Economic Model Format & Assumptions

Fixed Asset Description	Purchase
Product costs	
LAN equipment	$76,000
Premises cabling	$25,000
Physical network	$25,000
Internetwork	$21,000
Telephone system	$51,000
WAN	$1,300
Total installed cost	

Annual Costs	
LAN maintenance	$12,000
Phys. net. maintenance	$2,800
Internetwork maintenance	$1,300
Tel. system maintenance	$5,200
WAN maintenance	$1,000
WAN svcs.—voice comm.	$82,000
WAN svcs.—data comm.	$29,000
Total deprctn. (straight line)	
Total salvage value	

Common Cost Data	Item
Inflation%	4%
Annual inflation factor	
Cost of money	6%
Service life (years)	5
Salvage value	10%

Description	Year 0	Year 1	Year 2	Year 3	Year 4	Total
Operating costs:						
LAN maintenance						
Phys. net. maintenance						
Internetwork maintenance						
Tel. system maintenance						
WAN annual maintenance						
WAN services—voice comm						
WAN services—data comm						
Total depreciation						
Total salvage						
Annual operating costs						
PV factors						
PV operating costs						

Summary Costs

Description	Year 0	Year 1	Year 2	Year 3	Year 4	Total
Consolidated comm. costs						
Initial costs						
Total PV operating cost						
Totals						

Round calculations to nearest dollar.

The telecommunications manager was asked to discuss three areas at the board meeting:

- telecommunications standards
- a shared networking environment
- telecommunications budgetary estimates

The Telecommunications Manager's Plan

The telecommunications manager had been at PetroProd for three weeks, and had conducted a preliminary survey of PetroProd's communication environment. The manager had found that a potpourri of communication equipment and services had been implemented at different PetroProd locations, and that there were no telecommunications standards currently being used.

As a first step, the telecommunications manager decided to prepare a personal planning document to identify the activities that had to be completed for the March 12 management board meeting. The project plan below shows the personal project plan developed by the telecom manager after the March 5 meeting. Its purpose was to identify activities that must be completed and outline how the activities will be carried out (*plan* in the POLC Model).

While the project plan may appear to be a document specifically prepared for inclusion in a text, it is also one that can easily be generated in approximately thirty minutes by anyone who is competent in the use of word processing software and has the necessary managerial skills. Word processing software is the best tool to use when establishing a personal plan. The planning approach is simple—list the time available for completing the assignment and identify the tasks that must be completed during that time period. Because managers must coordinate the efforts of others when meeting organization deadlines, a word

The Telecommunications Manager's Personal Project Plan

PetroProd Consolidation Project Feasibility Analysis	
Date	*Task Description*
3–5–04 (Friday)	Assignment given by VP-MIS to the telecommunications department for developing a PetroProd telecommunications plan recommendation to be presented at a March 12, 2004, management board meeting. The plan should include recommendations for: • PetroProd telecommunications standards • developing a shared network environment • budget estimates for the recommendations
Weekend (Saturday + Sunday)	Create PC-based telecommunications planning model for developing consolidated system and network requirements (equipment and budgets). Most of the specific input used to drive the model (staffing, location size, and estimating factors) will be finalized on Monday (3–8–04).
3–8–04 (Monday)	1. Meet with human resources to obtain consolidated location staffing levels for the new PetroProd organization. 2. Meet with engineering to obtain PetroProd location floor plans. 3. Meet with telecom department personnel to finalize estimating factors and assign tasks.
3–9–04 (Tuesday)	1. Complete initial run of telecommunications planning model (dept. members). 2. Review with telecom department members. 3. Modify input as required. 4. Create PowerPoint presentation (manager). 5. Write cover letter for management board meeting (manager).
3–10–04 (Wednesday)	1. Complete telecommunications planning model. 2. Review/finalize planning model results with telecom department. 3. Complete PowerPoint presentation. 4. Complete cover letter for management board meeting. 5. Review management board presentation with telecom department members.
3–11–04 (Thursday)	1. Review management board presentation with VP-MIS. 2. Modify presentation, as required.
3–12–04 (Friday)	1. Make telecom plan presentation to management board. 2. Obtain feedback for follow-up activities.

processing document is an excellent way of communicating schedule deadlines and the nature of the required deliverables. The telecom manager's project plan is a professional looking document that can be shared with telecommunications department personnel, the VP-MIS, or anyone else without being concerned about its appearance. The table format provides a professional statement of the assignment requirements that a handwritten or oral format cannot match in clarity or professionalism.

The manager did not attempt to discuss the reasonability of the assignment in the project plan. While there is always the option of telling the VP-MIS that the assignment is unreasonable and cannot be completed in five working days, such a comment is likely to be a career threatening move—one that will limit the manager's future within the PetroProd organization. On the other hand, carrying out the assignment and satisfying the VP's request will demonstrate great resourcefulness and creativity while probably enhancing the manager's future potential in the new PetroProd/LubProd environment.

> The primary purpose of the telecom manager's personal project plan is to identify the key activities and the schedule deadlines that must be met to complete the assignment on time. Once that information is laid out, he or she can then worry about *how* the work will be done.

By completing the project plan quickly, the telecom manager is able to schedule the necessary meetings and coordinate the telecommunications department resources. Because the manager had strong PC skills and knew how to develop a telecommunications planning model, it was undertaken as a personal project during the weekend—not an uncommon occurrence for managers. If the manager did not have these skills, it would be necessary to find someone in the telecommunications department who had these skills, and he or she would have to develop the model. If internal personnel skills were not available, an outside consultant might be needed. This is really not a viable option for the short time period provided in the case study.

The following will focus on the results of carrying out the project plan and will utilize the telecommunications planning procedures discussed in the previous chapter.

ASSIGNMENT DELIVERABLES.

The telecommunications manager identified the three following deliverables that must be completed to fulfill the VP-MIS's assignment:

1. telecommunications model calculations
2. management board [PowerPoint] presentation
3. cover letter for management board presentation

This information must be reviewed with the VP-MIS prior to the meeting, to ensure that the telecom manager has full support for the information that will be presented. Deliverable and schedule information was listed in the manager's project plan.

TELECOMMUNICATIONS MODEL COMMENTARY.

Without strong PC skills in word processing, spreadsheet, and presentation graphics applications, the manager has little likelihood of successfully creating the required deliverables in the time frame that was provided. Fortunately, this was not the case, and the telecom manager was able to coordinate most requirements personally—a major advantage when confronted with very short lead times for completing assignments.

Unless estimation methods are used, it will not be possible to complete the assignment within the time provided in the case study problem. However, it is also necessary to maintain the proper perspective regarding the equipment and costs generated when using a telecommunications planning model—*they are only estimates and should be presented as such*. Determining the actual equipment requirements will require a design effort and a better understanding of equipment pricing —a topic that will be addressed in Part 5, *Acquisition Management*.

PLANNING FRAMEWORK.

The manager is concerned that management board members will give the telecommunications model estimate more credibility than it warrants, so he or she should use a product life cycle model (Figure 10–2) to discuss the entire process that must be followed when implementing the final project.

The telecommunications model information provided in response to the management board request will be positioned as being a preproject activity in Figure 10–2, a strategic planning activity. Within this context, the purpose of model planning information is to provide a preliminary estimate of the financial resources needed to develop and implement the six project steps shown in Figure 10–2. To develop a realistic budget for completing Figure 10–2 project phase activities, it will be necessary to obtain current information about:

1. installed telecommunications equipment and services
2. staffing forecasts
3. building location site and floor plan layouts

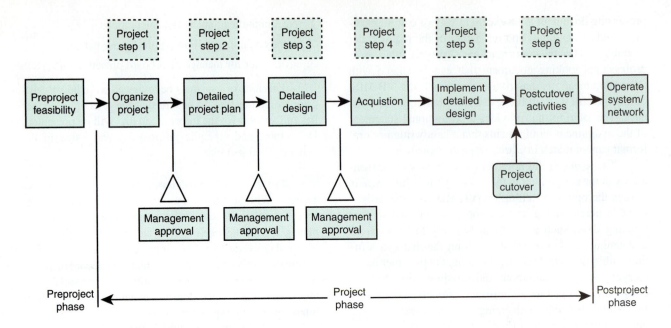

Figure 10–2. Telecommunications product life cycle model.

4. the business operation needs of various departments

5. the availability and cost of different equipment and service options

6. implementation schedule requirements

The planning model output used for the management board meeting does not include information about these six items. While the model will identify the types of equipment and services needed to address the board's request for information, its accuracy depends on the accuracy of the information used to generate the model output. The information referenced in the list cannot be assembled in time for the management board meeting, but is required to develop an accurate telecommunications plan.

As a result, the information that will be provided to the management board should be presented as a "ball park estimate" that is complete in identifying general requirements but requires additional information to generate an accurate budget value.

TELECOMMUNICATIONS MODEL INPUT

The Chapter 9 telecommunications planning model will be used to estimate equipment needs and the associated costs. This information will be placed into a five year LCA format

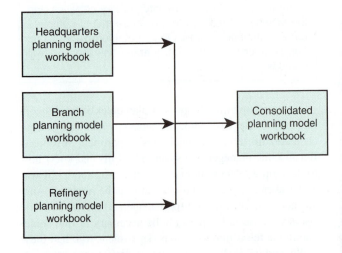

Figure 10–3. Telecommunications model spreadsheet structure.

for providing financial details in the format desired by the finance department. Because there are twelve locations, the enterprise plan will require the use of three models to determine the requirements for each location type (headquarters, refinery, or fuel depots). The information calculated by the individual models will be consolidated into a final enterprise planning model. This approach is shown in Figure 10–3.

TABLE 10–1   PetroProd/LubProd Locations

Description	Location
Headquarters	Trenton, NJ
Refinery	Linden, NJ
Fuel depots	Camden, NJ
	Phillipsburg, NJ
	Trenton, NJ
	Albany, NY
	Elmira, NY
	Syracuse, NY
	Allentown, PA
	Harrisburg, PA
	Philadelphia, PA
	Wilmington, DE

An LCA/NPV financial plan format will be used to summarize the capital expenditures (fixed asset costs) and operating expenses required over a five year period. On March 9 (see the Personal Project Plan, page 228), the telecom manager obtained the necessary staffing and location size input for the telecommunications model and also finalized the model's estimating factor information during a meeting with telecommunications department personnel. The consolidated PetroProd/LubProd locations and their respective staffing levels are summarized in Tables 10–1, 10–2a, 10–2b, and 10–2c.

Building Dimensions

The location building dimension information is summarized in Table 10–3.

The refinery building dimensions are 300 ft × 150 ft, and an 85 ft × 80 ft office area exists in one corner of the refinery. For safety reasons, it will be necessary to install six telephones in the refinery's production area for production and research personnel when they are near the equipment. It will be assumed that 300 ft cables will be run to each production area telephone.

PROJECT PLANNING CALCULATIONS

The planning model calculations will be provided in this section. The tables used to show the results are from spreadsheet software worksheets. An electronic version of the actual Microsoft Excel model is provided on the text CD, so that readers can view spreadsheet cells to see the link and formula elements.

Multilocation Workbook

Because all PetroProd fuel depots are identical in staffing and size, a single workbook can be used to identify fuel depot needs. The single location worksheets will be linked to a set of total fuel depot worksheets, whose values are linked to the single location worksheets multiplied by ten—the number of fuel depot locations. The multilocation worksheet will be used for identifying the costs required in the consolidation worksheet (Figure 10–3.)

Estimating Factors

The creation of estimating factors requires an extensive set of technical and managerial skills, and the decisions they incorporate are only evident to someone who has the appropriate technical and mangerial skills. Example 10–1 contains the estimating factors that will be used in this case study. The telecommunications manager and telecommunications department personnel developed this estimating factor table, which identifies the processes used to develop worksheet calculations.

> While the Case Study in Chapter 9 uses formulas to indicate the relationship between different pieces of equipment, the process in the real world will typically be a much more direct process, requiring technical specialists to use their skills to provide "guesstimates" for equipment requirements.

The planning deliverables used for the PetroProd enterprise plan will require setting up eight Microsoft Excel worksheets to calculate requirements for:

1. desktop equipment
2. backbone and horizontal cabling
3. WAN services
4. LAN equipment
5. Premises wiring
6. LAN physical network equipment
7. Internetworking equipment
8. Telephone system equipment

As shown in Figure 10–3, a workbook is created for the headquarters, fuel depot and refinery locations. A fourth workbook consolidates the information calculated in the first three workbooks. Each workbook contains eight worksheets, except for the fuel depot

Example 10–7b. Fuel depot LAN physical network cost estimate: LAN physical networking devices.

Description	Quantity	Unit$	Cost$
Server racks	1	$300.00	$300
Hub ports	20	$50.00	$1,000
Hub chassis	1	$1,000.00	$1,000
Hub chassis racks	1	$300.00	$300
Hub network management system	0	$5,000.00	$0
Hub switches	0	$400.00	$0
Bridges	0	$200.00	$0
FDDI hardware	0	$5,000.00	$0
Physical network labor	30	$50.00	$1,500
Annual maintenance		**$1,000**	
		Total	**$41,000**

Example 10–7c. Refinery LAN physical network cost estimate: LAN physical networking devices.

Description	Quantity	Unit$	Cost$
Server racks	1	$300.00	$300
Hub ports	35	$50.00	$1,750
Hub chassis	1	$1,000.00	$1,000
Hub chassis racks	1	$300.00	$300
Hub network management system	0	$5,000.00	$0
Hub switches	0	$400.00	$0
Bridges	1	$200.00	$200
FDDI hardware	0	$5,000.00	$0
Physical network labor	53	$50.00	$2,650
Annual maintenance		**$195**	
		Total	**$6,200**

Example 10–8a. Headquarters internetwork equipment cost estimate.

Description	Quantity	Unit$	Cost$
Local routers	5	$1,500.00	$7,500
Remote routers	1	$2,500.00	$2,500
Internetworking labor	42	$50.00	$2,100
Internetworking training	2	$1,000.00	$2,000
Annual internetwork maintenance		**$1,000**	
		Total	**$14,100**

Example 10–8b. Fuel depot internetwork equipment cost estimate.

Description	Quantity	Unit$	Cost$
Local router	0	$1,500.00	$0
Remote router	10	$2,500.00	$25,000
Internetworking labor	70	$50.00	$3,500
Internetworking training	0	$1,000.00	$0
Annual internetwork maintenance		**$2,500**	
		Total	**$28,500**

Description	Quantity	Unit$	Cost$
Local routers	0	$1,500.00	$0
Remote routers	1	$2,500.00	$2,500
Labor	7	$50.00	$350
Internetworking training	0	$1,000.00	$0
Annual internetwork maintenance		**$250**	
		Total	**$2,850**

Example 10–8c. Refinery internetwork equipment cost estimate.

Description	Quantity	Unit$	Cost$
175-line PBX system w/VM, ACD	1	$131,950.00	$131,950
Call director TelSets	34	$300.00	$10,200
Manager TelSets	33	$250.00	$8,250
ACD TelSets	30	$300.00	$9,000
Basic TelSets	78	$200.00	$15,600
User telephone system training	175	$100.00	$17,500
Annual PBX maintenance		**$17,500**	
Annual PBX moves & changes		**$8,100**	
Annual total		**$25,600**	
		Total	**$192,500**

Example 10–9a. Headquarters telephone system cost estimate.

Description	Quantity	Unit$	Cost$
16-line key system w/VM	10	$7,800.00	$78,000
Call director TelSets	10	$300.00	$3,000
Manager TelSets	20	$250.00	$5,000
ACD TelSets	0	$300.00	$0
Basic TelSets	130	$200.00	$26,000
User telephone system training	160	$100.00	$16,000
Annual KeySys maintenance		**$11,200**	
Annual KeySys moves & changes		**$9,000**	
Annual total		**$20,200**	
		Total	**$128,000**

Example 10–9b. Fuel depot telephone system cost estimate (ten locations).

Telephone System Equipment

The telephone system equipment requirements for the various locations (headquarters, fuel depots, and refinery) are shown in Examples 10–9a, 10–9b, and 10–9c. A PBX telephone system will be installed at the headquarters location, and key systems will be installed at the refinery and ten branch locations.

WAN Equipment and Service

The WAN equipment and service (CO trunks, OWATS, INWATS, local calls, DOD, and Frame Relay) requirements for the various locations (headquarters, fuel depots, and refinery) are summarized in Examples 10–10a, 10–10b, and 10–10c. Because calling services is a major category, the operating costs for WANs are much higher than the fixed asset costs (Frame Relay adapter card).

Investment Requirements

- LANs
  - Workstations
  - Servers
  - Software
    - ◊ Business applications
    - ◊ Network operating systems
- Telephone systems
- Premises wiring
- Data internetworking
- WAN access

Figure 10–4l. Management board presentation (slide 12 of 16).

Investment Overview
Preliminary Estimates

- Equipment
  - Initial investment
    - ◊ $2,424,403
  - Five year PV operating costs
    - ◊ $4,330,098
      - Depreciation
      - Maintenance
      - WAN networking: data
      - WAN: voice

> **Corporate finance procedures were followed**

Figure 10–4m. Management board presentation (slide 13 of 16).

Date: March 14, 2004

To: VP of MIS
From: I.M. Telecom ma
Subject: Enterprise telec

The following provides pr
infrastructure as part of tl
telecommunications stan
information needed to de

Planning approach
The preliminary telecomn
of 365 employees that wil
utilized preliminary planni

PetroProd telecommunica
period and its focus is on
the new consolidated Petr
consultant be retained to

Planning elements
A telecommunications fina
details are attached. Appe
quantities used in the ana

    A. Staffing and desl
    B. Horizontal cablin
    C. WAN model estir
    D. LAN equipment
    E. Premises wiring
    F. LAN physical net
    G. Internetworking e
    H. Telephone syster
    I. WAN facilities an
    J. Five year life cycl
The proposed PetroProd te

Financial analysis
The financial analysis usec
preliminary results have be
analysis includes an estim
operating this equipment. (

If all new equipment were
equipment would cost appr

Five year summary costs

Description
Consolidated costs
Initial costs
Total PV operating costs
Totals

PV: Present value dollars.

Figure 10–5. Example of a pr

Investment Details
Preliminary Estimates

- **Initial investment**
  - Total: $2,424,403 (100%)
    - ◊ HQ: $1,098,098 (45%)
    - ◊ Fuel depots: $1,098,300 (45%)
    - ◊ Refinery: $226,005 (10%)
- **Five-year PV operating costs**
  - Total: $4,330,098 (100%)
    - ◊ HQ: $2,807,713 (65%)
    - ◊ Fuel depots: $1,307,580 (30%)
    - ◊ Refinery: $214,806 (5%)
- **Details in handout**

Figure 10–4n. Management board presentation (slide 14 of 16).

1. Get
   - Bud
   - Obt
2. Con
   at co
3. Doc
   - Sul

Figure 10–4o. Manager

4. Dev
   mar
   - Pri
   - Pro
5. Sub
   mar
   - Pro
6. Afte
   - Ea
     life

Figure 10–4p. Manage

a teaching format—it will assume that readers are unfamiliar with the topic. Therefore, the primary prerequisite for undertaking Part 3 topics is that the reader has good fundamental skills in mathematics, written communication, and PC software applications including word processing, spreadsheet, networking graphics, and presentation software. A secondary prerequisite is that the reader has technology skills, because the technical project discussions require the use of technical terminology.

Part 3 consists of four chapters:

Chapter 11: What is Project Management?

Chapter 12: Critical Path Method Concepts

Chapter 13: Project Organization

Chapter 14: Project Management: A Case Study

Chapter 11: What is Project Management?

Projects are a series of activities that must be completed in a specific sequence to successfully achieve a final outcome. Key project attributes include: 1) a starting time, 2) an ending time, 3) an operating budget, and 4) a limited set of project resources. Projects come in all sizes and shapes and may have administrative or technical objectives as their final outcome. A telecommunications manager's workload will typically consist of many small, administrative projects interspersed with a few larger, technical projects.

This chapter provides an overview of the generic project management process and uses the telecommunications project life cycle model discussed previously in Chapter 7, *Managerial Tools and Techniques,* as a common framework for projects. The managerial tools and techniques discussed in Part 2 are applied to the life cycle model framework and are used to provide a generic approach for project management activities.

Chapter 12: Critical Path Method Concepts

Telecommunications technology projects can be very large and can require the coordination of many diverse activities to successfully achieve project objectives. The Critical Path Method (CPM) was developed during the 1950s, when computer technologies were initially introduced to the business environment. CPM has become the basic methodology used to manage large projects. CPM views individual project activities as nodes in a project network diagram, and CPM software provides the analytical tools needed to document project requirements, develop and control schedules, and assign project resources. Many PC-based software CPM applications are now avail-

able for use in managing and controlling projects. During a project, CPM calculations are used to identify schedule deviations and evaluate the implications for implementing the various options that can be used to get back on the original schedule.

The underlying concepts of CPM have not been changed significantly since its inception, and these concepts are relatively simple. Unfortunately, CPM project management concepts are concealed when computerized software applications are used. Chapter 12 uses a manual approach to describe CPM—an approach that will allow the reader to understand the underlying philosophy of CPM and its applicability in a common-sense mode. A case study is used in the chapter to illustrate the use of manual CPM.

Chapter 13: Project Organization

The first two chapters in Part 3 describe the procedures and methods used to manage administrative and technical projects. Part of the project management activity is the need to develop the organization structure that runs the project and coordinates various project activities. The project organization may consist of one person for administrative projects (typically the telecommunications manager) or may consist of a project manager and many team members when large projects are undertaken.

Chapter 13 reviews the role of the telecommunications manager in establishing the appropriate organization structure to carry out administrative and technical projects while continuing to maintain overall control of project activities. For large projects, the telecommunications manager becomes a facilitator who has the responsibility for making sure the project is successfully implemented. For smaller projects, the telecommunications manager may be both an overseer and the person directly responsible for carrying out project tasks.

Chapter 14: Case Study

The Chapter 14 case study provides readers with the opportunity to apply the administrative and technical (CPM) project management procedures described in Chapters 12 and 13. The case study requires the application of manual CPM procedures to identify the project's critical path and adjust activity durations so that the target implementation date can be met.

Appendix B provides an overview of Microsoft Project (MS-Project), a popular project management software product, and provides a software solution for the Chapter 14 case study. The MS-Project software solution is provided on the CD that accompanies the text.

11

WHAT IS PROJECT MANAGEMENT?

1. Understand the definition of a project in a project management context.

2. Understand the types of projects that a telecommunications manager will have responsibility for.

3. Understand the four project management attributes and their meanings.

4. Understand what tools and techniques are used for carrying out project management processes.

5. Understand the need for telecommunications managers to have strong project management skills.

6. Understand project risk elements and how they can be addressed to minimize their effects.

7. Understand the relationship of the POLC Model to project management activities.

8. Understand the telecommunications asset life cycle model and its project elements.

9. Understand the business planning process and its relationship to the project life cycle model.

10. Understand the project management process, the six project steps, its application to technology projects, and the process for ensuring that projects remain viable during their development phase.

11. Understand how to manage administrative projects.

WHAT IS A PROJECT?

Projects may be small or large. The building of the Great Wall of China and the construction of the Egyptian pyramids clearly fall into the large project category. Small projects might involve the installation of a mailbox or the building of an elementary school project demonstrating how volcanoes function. Most projects fall somewhere between these large and small project examples.

For telecommunications managers, projects are a way of life. Good project management skills are needed for handling both managerial and technical projects. There are two types of managerial projects: 1) personal projects, and 2) delegated projects. Personal projects are those that a manager must handle because of confidentiality, security, or time constraints. For example, if the human resources department needs to obtain information regarding an employee's availability for promotional opportunities, the manager would handle this request directly. Delegated projects are those projects that require a manager to coordinate the effort of other managers, such as preparing budgets during an annual planning process. The senior telecommunications manager should direct and coordinate the budget preparation efforts of subordinate managers to ensure that the budgets are prepared on time and contain the required information.

Technical projects require the acquisition of equipment components, and interconnecting them to construct a telecommunications system, network, or internetwork. A telecommunications manager may exercise direct or indirect control over technical projects. When direct control is involved, the manager becomes the project manager, who is responsible for coordinating all the resources and activities needed to successfully implement the project. In an indirect control mode, the manager delegates project responsibilities to a project manager who will have direct control of all project-related activities. The project manager will be directly accountable to the telecommunications manager. However, although the project manager has been assigned direct control, the telecommunications manager still retains the ultimate responsibility for ensuring that the project is completed on time and within budget.

Some Definitions of Project

While the preceding discussion gave examples of different types of projects, it is more useful to have a more specific definition to use when discussing projects. The following provides four definitions:

1. project: a unit of work that requires a large amount of planning, time, and effort to complete.

2. project: a group of activities whose completion will meet a specific goal or objective. Projects are established when there are many tasks to be coordinated and when the project outcome is so critical that the administrative overhead associated with project management is justifiable. Projects come in all sizes—large, medium, and small—and the complexities associated with managing vary greatly.

3. project: a sequence of interrelated activities that have a common goal that must be completed by a specific time, within an assigned budget, and according to specifications.

4. project: a set of nonroutine tasks, performed in a certain sequence, that lead to a final outcome. Projects include specified start and finish dates and utilize a set of limited resources that may be shared with other projects.

Which definition of a project is correct? They all are. Examination of the different definitions will show that they are similar conceptually. For the purposes of this text, definition number 4 is probably the best.

Project Attributes

Four attributes are used to describe a project:

1. project description
2. sequential activities
3. schedule
   - start
   - finish
4. budget

PROJECT DESCRIPTION. A project description states the purpose of the project and provides a nontechnical overview of project objectives and the project's implementation environment. The project description is the most important attribute of a project, because its objectives will be used to measure the success or failure of a project. The project description should describe a project completely and should contain the following elements:

1. the reasons (objectives) for initiating the project
2. the justification (tangible and intangible) for the project
3. constraints imposed on the project
4. objective measurement criteria for project goals

Failure to identify and quantify these four elements before major resources have been committed to a project has the potential for creating a no-win situation, in which the project will never be completed. If it is completed, it will not meet the expectations of those who originated the project. A project that is extremely attractive when discussed in abstract terms can become a money pit that absorbs all the resources allocated to it while never providing real world benefits. All projects should be monitored on an ongoing basis to ensure that:

- the original objectives are still desirable objectives
- the justification parameters have not changed
- new constraints don't change the project's desirability

When a project covers a multiyear period, there is always a possibility that the project's originator (the primary stakeholder) may be assigned new responsibilities or may leave the company. The new project primary stakeholder is likely to bring in a different perspective regarding the project's value and the potential exists that the original benefits used to justify the project may not be seen in the same light by the new manager. There is nothing more traumatic for technical personnel assigned to a project than being told that, "We don't really need those features now. Here is a list of twenty-eight features we really need. How long will it take you to change the (system or network) project to provide them?"

In addition, the accuracy of information changes over time. When a project is initiated, an estimate of **PTM** resources is developed and the project's benefits are compared to this estimate. If either the benefits or the resource requirements change, a reassessment of the project's merit is appropriate and should be reviewed with upper management. A telecommunications manager should continually assess projects to ensure that changing conditions do not negate the original value of the project.

SEQUENTIAL ACTIVITIES. Projects consist of multiple activities that must be performed in a specific sequence to complete the project effectively and efficiently. When the wrong activity sequence is followed, higher costs and lost time can result.

Completing a project is similar to creating a meal. Each food item (salad, sauce, meat, vegetable, etc.) has a separate recipe that must be followed to create the food item. The food items are then combined for each meal course (appetizer, salad, entree, dessert, etc.) and these different courses are then presented in a specific sequence. Project activity ingredients consist of tasks that must be combined in a specified sequence to complete the activity, and the various project activities must also be combined in a specific sequence to optimize the use of PTM resources.

Failure to combine cooking ingredients in the proper sequence can spoil a meal course, and failure to properly carry out the tasks within an activity or carrying out activities in the wrong sequence can achieve negative results. The project may not meet original time and budget constraints, or—in a worst case scenario—it may not work at all. Just as the skill of the cook heavily influences the meal outcome, the skill of the project manager and the technical specialists will determine the quality of the project's outcome.

PROJECT SCHEDULES. Projects have a start time and an end time. If this is not the case, it is not a project, it is an ongoing process. To meet a project's completion target (ending time), individual project activities that make up the project must each have starting and ending times that are coordinated within the overall project completion time requirements.

PROJECT BUDGET. Technology projects always have budgets that provide the means to obtain the required project resources, while **administrative projects** typically do not have budget resources assigned. Most administrative projects are assigned to existing personnel, and the cost for the project resources are embedded within an operating budget.

When a budget is provided, the project must be completed within the budget's financial constraints. The basic requirement for completing any project can be stated simply as, "complete the project on time and within budget," where failure to meet either constraint has the potential for being career-threatening.

Project Types

Telecommunications managers have the responsibility for completing two basic types of projects:

- administrative (nontechnology) projects
- technology projects

Administrative projects come in all sizes and shapes. Most of them are handled personally by the telecommunications manager without the use of any other resources, although the manager may delegate supporting assignments to department personnel. Telecommunications (technology) projects result in the installation of new communication systems or networks, and these projects will range in size. Small projects may be handled by a single technical specialist or require the creation of a project management team whose members have the necessary skills to manage and implement highly complex projects.

While the underlying principles used in administrative and technology projects are similar, technology projects tend to require a more formalized project approach than administrative projects. Large technology projects frequently use computerized project management applications based on **Critical Path Method (CPM)** or **Program Evaluation and Review Technique (PERT)** mathematical models.

WHAT IS PROJECT MANAGEMENT?

Project management is the art of managing a project to ensure that it meets the objectives used to justify its creation. Depending upon the size of the organization and the size of the project, telecommunications managers may be expected either to manage a project directly or delegate the project management responsibilities to a dedicated project manager.

Telecommunications managers typically have many more administrative projects to complete than they do technical projects. Examples of recurring administrative projects are budget preparation, salary administration, employee performance appraisals, and budget reviews. A telecommunications manager is responsible for coordinating the efforts associated with these projects, and may be required to handle some activities directly because of organizational or personnel confidentiality requirements. The ability to handle small- and medium-sized administrative projects quickly and effectively is a managerial skill that pays ongoing dividends. Those ongoing dividends would include the time benefits gained through increased personal productivity and the positive feedback obtained from peer and upper managers who appreciate the quick response time.

Project Management Tools and Techniques

Projects have been around for a long time. Therefore, project management techniques have also been used for a long time. However, during the last forty years, a new tool—the computer—emerged and revolutionized project management activities. The primary impact of computers has been on large, technical projects that require the coordination of many complex activities over long time periods. However, there are many more small projects than there are large, complex ones. Manual methods are still used for the majority of projects, particularly administrative projects.

THE POLC MODEL... AGAIN. Project management is not a technical process, *it is a managerial process*. In management theory, the POLC Model

(plan/organize/lead/control) is used to provide a process framework for carrying out managerial responsibilities. The POLC Model (Figure 11–1) is a generic problem-solving approach that can also be applied to project management activities.

Executing POLC Model elements provides a managerial process that contains all the elements needed to successfully carry out both managerial and project-oriented responsibilities. In a project context, the *goals* provide the focus for the four POLC elements (plan, organize, lead, control). The POLC *plan* element identifies the *what, why, how,* and *when* of the project and provides a measurement standard against which ongoing activities can be compared (the *control* element). Activities are then evaluated to measure progress toward achieving project goals. The POLC *organize* element is the formal project phase that obtains the PTM resource identified in the plan, and the *lead* element assigns managerial responsibilities for directing project activities. When a project plan is being executed by using the POLC process, the actual results are compared to the project plan to ensure that the project objectives (goals) are successfully achieved. If the actual results do not match planned results, a control mechanism (a leadership responsibility) is applied and the project process is modified to get the project back on track. The

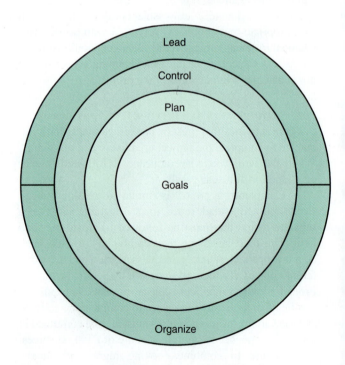

Figure 11–1. Goal-centric POLC Model (management process model).

original project plan may have to be modified. The proper application of POLC Model principles will result in a project that is completed on time and within budget. The POLC Model can be applied to any manual or computerized project management method.

MANUAL PROJECT MANAGEMENT METHODS.

In the precomputer era, manual project management methods were the only means for managing projects. Managing large, complex projects required many manual calculations and created a paperwork-intensive process that required a major administrative resource investment. In the precomputer era, tables and **Gantt charts** were the primary tools used for managing projects and presenting project information.

Henry L. Gantt, a pioneer in the development of scientific management methods during the early 1900s, developed the Gantt chart. Gantt charts graphically display project activities and show the relationship of these activities against a time scale. Figure 11–2 provides an example of a Gantt chart.

Various colors and line weights can be used in a Gantt chart to clarify different project activities and provide a plan v. actual summary. However, as the size of the project increases, the requirement for more Gantt charts increases sharply and large volumes of paperwork are needed to display project information. The selection of a Gantt chart timescale is also critical because a large time span (such as a year) will result in a compressed, hard-to-read document. Using too short a time span does not allow someone to see the entire project picture.

Tables were found to be the best way to manage large volumes of project information, and the combination of Gantt charts and tables were the primary project management process elements in the precomputer era. In the

precomputer era, the need for multiple copies of tables was satisfied by typing carbon-paper copies or by creating a typed stencil that allowed multiple mimeograph copies to be printed.

Table 11–1 provides an alternative format to the Gantt chart—a word processing or spreadsheet table—to display the same information shown in Figure 11–2. Most people will find the table format easier to understand and interpret than the Gantt chart.

A comparison of the Figure 11–2 and Table 11–1 information should quickly highlight the advantages of using tables to provide the detailed information shown on the Gantt chart. The Table 11–1 information was embedded into the Gantt chart, but required a translation step to develop the information that is shown directly in the table. If a large timescale were used on the Gantt chart, it would be very difficult to determine the exact dates that are clearly displayed in Table 11–1.

Table 11–1 contains a large amount of information but requires a very small amount of paper space. However, as project details increase, the table approach also encounters problems because more tables will be required and the contents of these multiple tables must be linked in some way. Managing large, complex projects in the precomputer era required many support workers who operated mechanical calculators to obtain the needed project information. Mechanical calculators could not handle multiplication and division calculations effectively, and calculations that are done instantaneously with today's handheld electronic, computer-based calculators required a long, error prone, manual calculation process. Mechanical calculators were the only game in town until the late 1960s, and a combination of mechanical and manual calculations were used during the precomputer era to develop project information.

Figure 11–2. A Gantt chart example.

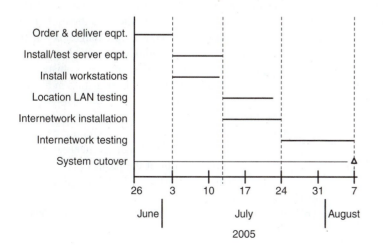

TABLE 11–1   Information from Figure 11.2 in a Table Format

Activity Descriptions	Duration (Days)	Start Date	Stop Date
Order & deliver equipment	5	6–27–05	6–30–05
Install & test server equipment	7	7–5–05	7–12–05
Install workstations	6	7–5–05	7–11–05
Location LAN testing	7	7–14–05	7–22–05
Internetwork installation	8	7–14–05	7–23–05
Internetwork testing	10	7–21–05	8–6–05
System cutover	0	8–8–05	8–8–05

In this precomputer environment, project management was not an occupation for anyone who had an aversion to paperwork. In addition, the accuracy of the project information was only as good as the accuracy of the person who made the calculations on mechanical calculators or developed manual calculation results.

MANUAL METHODS USING PC APPLICATIONS.

The introduction of PC desktop applications during the 1980s made word processing and spreadsheet applications commonplace. In addition, creating documents became fairly simple as laser and ink jet printers provided a wide range of printing capabilities.

Word processing and spreadsheet programs easily produced tables or Gantt charts, and PC printers provided a wide range of printing capabilities for displaying text, tables, or graphics. A telecommunications manager who had good PC skills could handle most administrative projects with little difficulty, and these same skills were used to handle smaller technology projects.

COMPUTERIZED PROJECT MANAGEMENT METHODS.

Business computing equipment became viable during the early 1960s, when IBM introduced its line of business computers. While these early computers were extremely primitive and underpowered compared to today's PCs, they represented a major calculation and paperwork breakthrough when compared to existing alternatives. During the 1960s, DuPont researchers developed a calculation-intensive project planning model, CPM, to manage large engineering projects. At about the same time, another project planning tool, PERT, was being developed to manage the U.S. Navy's Polaris project. Both applications required the processing capability provided by new computers. Neither effort could have been undertaken during the precomputer era.

Today, CPM and PERT project planning tools are available as PC application software products. Of course,

today's $1,000 PC would have been a bargain at $110 million when compared to the processing capability that was available in the early 1960s.

Comparing the processing and storage capacity of today's $1,000 PC to a 1960s mainframe computer is equivalent to measuring the difference in speed between a one-day old turtle (a 1960s computer) and a modern jet fighter (the PC). PC-based project management software quickly provides calculated results that would have taken a 1960s computer many weeks to complete. PC-based project management applications are very sophisticated and can easily handle most of the projects that a telecommunications manager will encounter. Both CPM and PERT are network-based project management systems, and because CPM is conceptually simpler than PERT, it is the calculation engine of choice for many project planning efforts.

Network-based project planning software represents different project activities as network nodes in a project network diagram, where the connections between the nodes specify each activity's relationship to other activities. As is the case in a communication network, there are multiple paths from the start of the project network diagram to its end. A **project network diagram** example is shown in Figure 11–3. Project network diagrams clearly show the relationships among activities and their relationships within the overall project. Multiple diagrams can be used for different levels of detail. Existing PC-based project management software provides a highly sophisticated CPM database that portrays project information in a variety of easy to understand formats.

The Figure 11–3 example is actually much simpler than the project network diagram that would normally be generated with PC-based project management software. With PC software, the creator of the project network diagram is not concerned with the number of nodes or the complexity of the project network diagram, because the software application handles all necessary calculations at computer speeds.

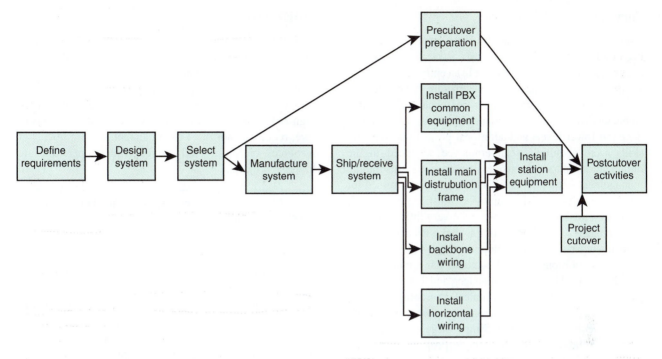

Figure 11–3. Telephone system project network diagram.

WHY LEARN PROJECT MANAGEMENT?

Figure 11–3 will be used in Chapter 12 to demonstrate the use of manual CPM calculations as a project management tool.

A prime responsibility of telecommunications managers is to get assignments done on time and within budget. These assignments may either be administrative or telecommunications technology projects. Unless telecommunications managers have good project management skills, they will find it difficult to effectively carry out their job responsibilities. Good project management skills include the skills needed to modify a potentially "never ending" project into smaller, manageable segments. If good judgment is used when breaking up a large project into several smaller projects, project benefits can be realized earlier because benefits from some of the smaller projects will be derived earlier than benefits from large, "big bang" projects. Big bang projects are projects for which all the project work must be completed before significant benefits are provided. Big bang projects are typically multiyear projects that require very large financial investments. The issue of project size and length will be addressed in greater detail in the *Managing Project Risk* section.

Good project management skills do not require an individual to have a detailed knowledge of project management software unless they are managing a large project. However, a telecommunications manager should have a strong conceptual understanding of both manual and computerized project planning methods used to solve everyday, real world situations. Good project management skills provide a way of thinking that intuitively examines situations or projects, breaks them into components or tasks, and organizes them into a logical flow. This logical thought process can be used by a manager to handle personal (administrative) projects or can be used to facilitate activities with others to whom they have delegated project responsibilities. A person who has strong project management skills typically has good organizing skills because the same enabling skills are needed in both areas.

Project management skills are another tool for managing a telecommunications function and can be used to:

- reduce project expenses
- shorten project schedules without incurring additional costs
- require fewer resources than using an unstructured approach

Survival

During the last fifteen years, business organizations have been under pressure to reduce costs and staffing levels. In the past, someone who started out in an entry-level position would enter a stable management structure that existed between lower level positions and upper management. In this stable environment, project management skills were introduced at lower levels and additional project management skills were acquired as an employee advanced in the organization. In today's business environment, this middle management structure is either sharply compressed or nonexistent. As a result, employees must acquire project management skills on their own, with very little help from their managers. The bottom line is that a telecommunications manager who has developed strong project management skills in premanagerial positions has a much higher likelihood of: 1) becoming a manager, and 2) surviving the project pressures found in a technical environment.

Managerial judgment is required when project management techniques are used. Simple project management methods should be used for simple projects. The more complex techniques (CPM software applications) should be reserved for large, complex projects. Both simple (manual) and complex (computer-based) approaches to project management are discussed in this text, but the primary emphasis is on the manual methods because these are best for teaching basic project management concepts. The text's emphasis on manual methods has two objectives: 1) to provide the reader with an understanding of underlying project management concepts, and 2) to provide a real world tool for handling simple projects.

MANAGING PROJECT RISK

Project risk refers to the possibility that things will go wrong when something is being done. Projects—particularly large, complex projects—have high risks built into them because of the nature of the project. The following will review three risk factors that may be encountered when projects are undertaken, and will also describe ways for minimizing these project risks. The risk discussion is more applicable to telecommunications technology projects than to administrative projects, and applying the concepts introduced in this discussion requires managerial judgment.

There are three risk factors that should be evaluated when undertaking a project:

1. project size
2. project experience
3. project structure

Project Size

Project size refers to the cost, duration, labor (administrative and technical) needs, or the business impact of a project. Projects that are expensive, require long time periods from start-to-finish, require a large quantity of labor resources, or affect the operation of many departments are high risk projects. Conversely, projects that are inexpensive, require a short time to implement, require few labor resources, or don't directly affect business operations are low risk projects.

> Small projects have a low risk factor and large projects have a high risk factor.

MINIMIZING PROJECT SIZE RISK. The risk associated with large projects can be addressed directly: reduce the effective size of the project by breaking it up into smaller subprojects and implement the subprojects in phases or as individual projects. This fragmentation approach replaces the large, risky project with smaller manageable projects that are easier to implement and manage.

Breaking up major parts of the project into smaller elements and distributing the implementation activities over a longer time period can reduce risk by minimizing the potential for overloading limited resources. Splitting a project into multiple, separate projects normally requires an extensive redesign process that can add another layer of complexity to the project. As is always the case in the real world, any simplifying solution has the potential for creating more problems than it solves. If the concept of breaking up a project is carried to an extreme, the result may be a project that will never be fully implemented.

LONG TIME DURATION PROJECTS. Time is a critical **project attribute** in the business world because the benefits to be derived from a project are typically based on a window of opportunity, within which the project must be completed or it will not generate the benefits to justify it. Therefore, a project's duration is a key area of focus when reviewing large projects.

A project that requires several years to implement has the potential for being obsolete prior to, or immediately after, implementation. During a long, multiyear project, key project team members may pursue better career opportunities before the project is completed. The loss of key technical specialists from a project will have a negative impact on cost because of the retraining costs involved with bringing new employees up to speed. However, the problem becomes even more acute if it is not possible to find a suitable replacement for the lost specialist. To minimize the potential for losing personnel and to ensure that a project's justification does not change, most business projects (or subprojects) should be designed to be completed within one year.

Empirical experience suggests that 90% of a project's benefits require 10% of the total project cost, and that the remaining 10% of the benefits absorb 90% of the total project cost. When a multiyear project is planned, it should be broken into two or more subprojects that incorporate overall project benefits into each subproject on a ranked basis. Using this approach, the first project segment would provide the greatest benefit per project dollar, and following project segments would provide lower benefit levels. The primary criterion to create a subproject would be that it can be successfully completed in one year, or less.

A project that requires two years to implement can be split into two projects, each requiring one year to implement. If the new design incorporates many of the project's benefits into the first project phase, several scenarios are possible. When most of the project's benefits are built into the first subproject, many project benefits will become available in half the time of the original project schedule. When project downsizing is handled skillfully, it may even be possible to obtain more than 50% of the benefit in the first year. As a result, the use of subprojects could allow project benefits to be utilized earlier—a major advantage if the project has a limited window of opportunity.

Splitting a project into two parts also creates another decision option. After completing phase one of a two-part project, a more informed decision can be made regarding the value of implementing the second phase. If many key benefits were incorporated into the first phase of the project, the benefits to be gained from implementing the second phase may not warrant the additional effort needed to implement them. If this is the case, the overall project cost savings gained from downsizing the project could be significant.

LARGE PROJECT SUMMARY. When a project is expensive and requires a large commitment of resources to implement, staging its cost over a longer time period can be very attractive from a financial perspective. If a benefit *v*. cost approach is taken, large projects can be restructured so that greater benefits are realized close to the beginning of the implementation effort. When this is done, low benefit project elements may be deferred or eliminated if their incremental benefits cannot justify them as stand-alone projects.

Short, segmented projects (less than 1 year in duration) may be also be used to distribute total project expense and labor needs over a longer time period. This approach can conserve critical cash resources, allow the use of a smaller labor force, and minimize the implementation impact on the business. A phased implementation is particularly effective if new technology is being introduced because it effectively provides a pilot operation environment where the results are implemented on a smaller, more manageable scale before the total project is rolled out.

The downside of breaking a project into smaller segments is that it may require a higher administration effort, a higher project budget, and a longer time period to implement. The upside is that initial results will probably be seen earlier and the cost, labor, or business impact is distributed over a longer time. Distributing the project timeline and resources over longer periods of time may result in negating the need for secondary implementation efforts.

Project Experience

Project experience refers to the experience that project management team members and project technical specialists have when implementing the project. Different types of projects require different skill sets and it is necessary to accurately define the skill requirements for a given project. If project team members have successfully implemented many similar projects, there is a high likelihood that they will implement the current project successfully and will encounter relatively few problems. On the other hand, if project team members are inexperienced, there is a higher probability that they will encounter problems while implementing the project.

> Project teams made up of team members who have strong project-specific skills have a low risk factor, while inexperienced project teams have a higher risk factor.

OBTAINING PROJECT EXPERIENCE. As was the case when addressing the risks associated with large project size, the lack of project experience can be addressed directly by adding experience to the project team. This is done by: 1) training team members, 2) placing experienced members on the team, or 3) by hiring outside consultants to assist with the project. All three alternatives would enhance the skill of the project team and provide inexperienced team members with the opportunity to learn project skills from experienced team members.

When project experience is gained by members of a telecommunications department, the experience becomes available to other members in the telecommunications department.

Project Structure

Structured projects are projects for which standardized procedures can be used to implement the project. The project nodes (activities) of a project network diagram must consist of well-documented activities, and the relationships among individual nodes must be well understood by project personnel.

Going back to our earlier cooking example, an experienced cook can follow a good recipe and can achieve excellent results when the recipe provides accurate ingredient and process instructions. On the other hand, when information is missing from the recipe, there is little likelihood that the results will fulfill the expectations of someone attempting to duplicate a good eating experience. Using the same logic, when a builder uses a standard set of plans to build homes, it is very likely that consistent, successful results will be generated.

Unstructured projects include project activities with requirements that will not be understood until a previous step has been completed and evaluated. A research and development project is an example of an unstructured project. Each step in a research project must be evaluated after it has been completed to determine what the focus should be for the next phase of the project. This is one of the reasons why only a small percentage of research and development (R&D) projects ever result in a successful product. Most R&D projects fail because the poor results they achieve are not known until after the R&D effort has been expended. If they were known in advance, they would not be R&D projects. Telecommunications departments that are responsible for implementing business communication systems and networks for their enterprise should avoid telecommunications R&D projects.

> Structured projects have a low risk factor and unstructured projects have a high risk factor.

MANAGING UNSTRUCTURED PROJECTS. If a project contains activities for which different successor activities will be designed, based on the information received from a predecessor activity, it is virtually impossible to accurately predict the project's cost or duration.

While a worst case scenario could be developed to identify potential problems, few business managers will tolerate the high costs associated with undertaking worst case alternatives. The best recourse a manager can use when an unstructured project must be implemented to meet business needs is to clearly explain the risk element associated with implementing the project and incorporating management go/no go **decision points** after each critical activity. Figure 11–4 displays this concept.

When surprises are encountered during a project because of new information, the use of managerial checkpoints provides the opportunity to reevaluate the original investment decisions. If the project's justification is changed by the new information, terminating the project can minimize enterprise losses. On the other hand, if the project still makes sense, management can approve the project effort and provide additional funding requirements, as needed.

Another approach to addressing R&D projects is to use project management techniques based on PERT. PERT incorporates estimating elements designed for an unstructured project environment by providing statistical estimates (educated guesses) for activity durations. However, if the duration estimates are too high because of the project's lack of structure, business management may be unwilling to make the investment.

UNSTRUCTURED PROJECT SUMMARY. There is little that can be done to structure an unstructured project. If this could be done, it would not be an unstructured project. However, if the potential rewards are great enough

Figure 11–4. Project plan using decision points.

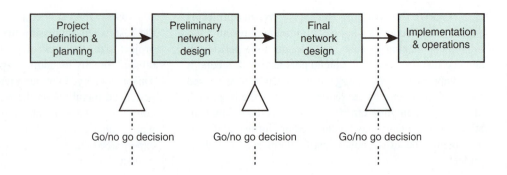

to justify the risk of an unstructured project, go/no go decision points should be built into the project at key project points (Figure 11–4). This approach highlights the risk factor initially and provides the opportunity to bail out if the odds shift too strongly against the probability of success.

Project Risk Summary

The three project risk elements—size, experience, and structure—should be evaluated at each decision point during a project's life cycle. When project funding is established during the budgeting process, the project risk factors should be evaluated and formal statements regarding the level of risk the project is based on should be well documented. These statements should include assessments for each risk element, and these elements can then be reevaluated at various decision points in the project.

The risk information assessment discussed in this section would be incorporated into the project description discussed earlier. This initial assessment would be reaffirmed or modified during subsequent project decision point evaluations.

PRODUCT LIFE CYCLE MODEL

In the previous project description discussion, it was stated that projects must have a beginning and an end, or they are not projects. A generic **project life cycle model** can be used to identify various product stages: 1) the preproject conceptual stage, 2) the project implementation phase, and 3) the product's operational phase during the postproject stage. In telecommunications, the product of a project is typically a system or network. If the descriptions in the model are kept general in nature, they can be applied to all types of telecommunications products *and* the projects needed to develop and implement them. Figure 11–5 provides a preliminary telecommunications product life cycle model. Figure 11–5 was introduced in Chapter 7, *Managerial Tools and Techniques,* during the discussion of macrodecision making to illustrate the need for a decision process that provides decision exit points for telecommunication projects.

The model in Figure 11–5 must be administered with common sense. Complex projects may justify a heavy allocation of project management resources during the product's life cycle, but simple projects should have lower concerns about the project phases shown in Figure 11–5. From a project perspective, the product life cycle can be divided into three major phases as shown in Figure 11–5: a preproject phase, a project phase, and a postproject phase. Formal project management processes address the project phase. However, during the postproject phase, when an implemented project's product is operational, there is a strong likelihood that ongoing projects will be needed to enhance the product's performance or capacity as needs change.

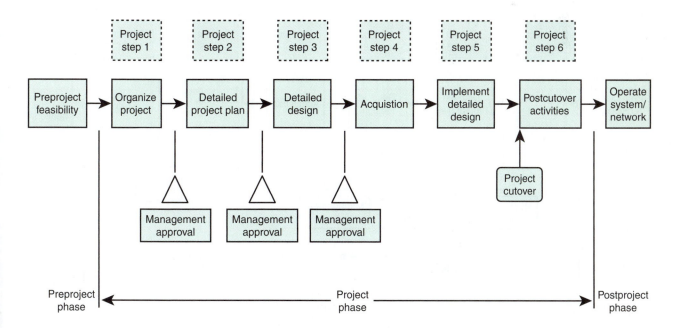

Figure 11–5. Telecommunications product life cycle model.

Project Phase

A technical project's life cycle (Figure 11–5) includes six major project management steps:

1. organize project
2. develop a detailed project plan
3. develop a detailed design
4. acquire project components
5. implement the detailed design
6. complete postcutover activities

While this project life cycle can be used for non-technical (administrative) projects, the smaller size and scope of most administrative projects does not warrant using all the project elements shown in the six-stage project life cycle. Using the six step model for simple projects would be analogous to requiring a formal, typed statement from elementary school students when they want to get permission to go to the bathroom. . . it just doesn't make sense.

The six project steps shown in Figure 11–5 will be discussed individually in the *Project Management Process* section of this chapter.

Management Approval Checkpoints

When a significant expenditure of funds is involved, it is essential that upper management be given periodic up-dates regarding the current and projected status of a project. The management approval checkpoint concept was discussed previously (Figure 11–4) and was incorporated into Figure 11–5 at appropriate project steps.

Management approval checkpoints provide an opportunity to reaffirm the viability of expensive capital projects. These checkpoints also provide telecommunications management with an opportunity to set the expectations of upper management regarding project results. If project performance is substandard, corrections can be addressed at checkpoints; and if new conditions affect the original decision, a reassessment of the original decision may be appropriate.

> Any decision to discontinue a major project in the latter stages of its life cycle will normally require a comprehensive explanation to upper management by the individual who recommended the project's termination. A project's termination due to environmental changes is easily understood; however, termination because it was poorly conceived will require a detailed explanation.

Telecommunication Product Life Cycle Costs

All technical projects go through the project processes shown in Figure 11–5. Figure 11–6 has added cost information to Figure 11–5. This diagram is the final version of the telecommunications product life cycle model.

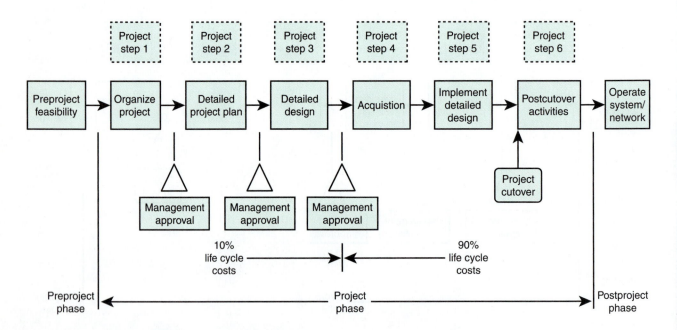

Figure 11–6. Telecommunications product life cycle model.

The telecommunications product life cycle model in Figure 11–6 will be used in the remainder of the text as the standard means of describing the implementation and operating activities associated with telecommunications products (networks, systems, and equipment).

The primary difference between administrative projects and technical projects are size, complexity, implementation schedule, and operating life. Administrative projects are relatively small and normally must be completed in shorter time periods than technical projects. For example, a telephone system will typically be assigned a fixed asset life of five years, although future upgrades and maintenance expenditures may extend its useful life an additional five years. While all fixed assets will eventually be retired when they are scrapped or sold, their project life cycle is significantly longer than administrative project durations.

The total telecommunications fixed asset (product) **life cycle cost** associated with any telecommunications asset (network, system, or equipment) includes the costs of: 1) acquiring the asset and 2) operating the asset over its operating lifetime. These operating costs would include normal maintenance or any upgrades needed to ensure its ongoing operational viability. An asset that cost $1 million to purchase may easily incur a total life cycle cost of more that $10 million during a seven year lifetime.

Total life cycle costs are the best measurement of how much an asset will cost a business. Consider the investment alternative comparison shown in the following table for telephone systems A and B.

Description	Purchase Cost	Five Year Operating Cost	Total Cost
Telephone system A	$1 million	$6 million	$7 million
Telephone system B	$1.2 million	$4.8 million	$6 million
Difference	+ .2 million	($1.2 million)	($1 million)

Difference = B cost – A cost; parentheses indicate a negative value.

While system B costs $200,000 more to purchase than system A, it will save $1.2 million in operating costs over a five year life (a total savings of $1 million). If the purchase price were the only criterion used to select the system, system A would have been selected to save $200,000. However, if the total life cycle cost approach were used, it would clearly show that selection of system B would save $1 million over the five year lifetime of both telephone systems. As a telecommunications manager, which system would you select, system A or system B?

As a rule of thumb, the majority of a telecommunications asset's total life cycle cost will be incurred after the detailed design (project step 3) management checkpoint (Figure 11–6). This checkpoint gives the final management approval to purchase project components and to implement them. Prior to this checkpoint, most of the project expenses have been for the labor required to design and develop a detailed implementation plan.

> It is normal for 90% of a telecommunication asset's total life cycle cost to be incurred after the final management approval checkpoint shown in Figure 11.6.

PROJECT MANAGEMENT PROCESS

Projects come in all sizes and can be technical or nontechnical in scope. The tools and techniques used to manage large, complex projects would be considered "overkill" if they were applied to small, simple projects. Therefore, a certain level of common sense (managerial judgment) is needed during the course of any project. There are many tools and techniques available for managing projects, and the appropriate ones should be selected for the specific project situation. Small, simple projects can use simple tools; large, complex projects may require the use of complex tools.

The following discussion will review the preproject feasibility phase and the individual project steps shown in Figure 11–6. This descriptive information is intended for large, technical projects. An administrative project example immediately follows the technical project discussion, and describes procedures that would make sense to use for smaller, nontechnical projects.

Project Management Process

The telecommunications project management activity is part of the overall **business planning process** shown in Figure 11–7. In the business planning process, concepts evolve into budgeted activities (tactical plans) and the budgeted activities are implemented (operational plans). Projects are the implementation results associated with taking a budget, fine tuning it during its tactical phase, and implementing it during its operational phase. Project management PTM resources are obtained from operational budgets and implemented during the current operating period.

In Figure 11–7, a project that began as a concept in 1999 is implemented as a telecommunications project in 2004. The project resources were provided in an operational

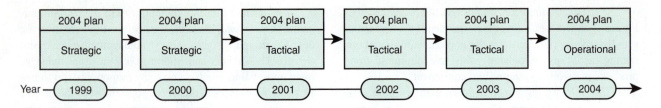

Figure 11–7. Business planning process.

budget that was initially developed as a tactical plan during the 2002 annual planning cycle.

For example, in 1999, business management identified the need to build a new manufacturing plant in 2004 based on forecast growth trends in product sales. This strategic business need then becomes the driver for generating a 2004 telephone system project that will provide telephone services to the manufacturing plant employees. As the 2004 telecommunications project plan reviews get closer to 2004, its budgetary requirements are refined to create a final tactical budget in 2003. The 2003 plan's 2004 budget becomes the operating budget that will be used to implement the telephone system project and the Figure 11–6 telecommunications project life cycle model will be used to carry out the actual implementation requirements during the year 2004.

PREPROJECT FEASIBILITY.   During a strategic planning process (Figure 11–7), major business objectives are defined and preliminary planning efforts identify the supporting projects needed to attain desired business objectives. Strategic plans are based on using a three to five year planning horizon and, at some point, the strategic future year plan becomes the operational plan's current year plan. Changes are made to the annual plan as it evolves from a future status to a current status.

The preproject phase includes the **strategic planning** phase and the **tactical planning** phase of the business planning model. During the tactical planning phase, estimates are made of the PTM resources needed to successfully implement the project and a project budget is established. If the project requires implementing a telecommunications system or network, an associated budget, called a capital appropriation budget, is also established to cover the costs for purchasing the necessary fixed assets that will be installed as part of the project effort.

The final capital appropriation budget and implementation budget will be finalized during the year prior to implementing the project. These final budgets will become the "yardstick" that is used to measure the success of the telecommunications organization while completing the project on time and within budget during the year 2004.

ORGANIZE PROJECT (PROJECT STEP 1).   The preproject budgets become the input for project step 1, and the primary focus for step 1 is to evaluate the strategic and tactical planning information that justified the project. The step 1 evaluation will result in one of three possibilities: 1) a reaffirmation of the project's viability, 2) a modification of the initial project plans, or 3) serious questions about the project's viability arise.

For technical projects of any significant size, the telecommunications manager will appoint a project leader, who will have primary responsibility for managing the project details. When a project manager has been dedicated to a project, the telecommunications manager will oversee the project and provide an information conduit between the project manager and business management. For large projects, the appointment of a project manager is done well in advance of the time period in which that project is scheduled to be implemented.

The deliverables for completing project step 1 requirements would include:

- preliminary project documentation
- preliminary project network plan
- risk assessment observations
- project team organization recommendations
- project financial plan
- recommendations to management

For most projects, the initial identification of objectives, resource requirements, and funding was carried out within the context of the normal annual budgeting processing cycle.

> For large complex projects that require large amounts of funding, project step 1 may be completed prior to finalizing the budget used for measuring project accountability. This approach would provide a more detailed plan than relying on normal tactical planning activities.

When a project manager is assigned to a new project, step 1 provides an opportunity for the project to be assessed from a different perspective than the perspective used to establish the original tactical budgets. The results of the step 1 assessment would be the focus for the management checkpoint review meeting scheduled at the end of project step 1. Normally, the step 1 checkpoint recommendation would simply provide a reaffirmation of the project's viability and include an update of the project's progress. If any new information uncovered during step 1 modifies the project's viability, the step 1 management checkpoint provides an opportunity to update management and inform them of the new information's impact on the project.

Project step 1 is an extremely critical point for the project manager because the preproject budget and objectives will become the performance measurement yardstick unless they are modified at this time. Management approval of step 1 will result in the creation of the project team and will initiate the detailed planning effort needed to complete step 2 **deliverables.**

DETAILED PROJECT PLAN (PROJECT STEP 2).

The first action taken during step 2 is to formally establish the project management organization identified during step 1. Project team members would carry out the work effort requirements for step 2 and would use the step 1 plan deliverables as a starting point. A key step 2 effort will be to establish a detailed project network diagram that identifies project activities, tasks, and resources, and creates the time schedules that will be used for implementing the project. The step 2 project network diagram will become the project management plan that, for large projects, will typically require the use of CPM software. If PC software is used, it becomes the primary managerial tool to control the project management phase of the project. The plan developed in step 2 becomes the baseline plan that will be used as a standard during project implementation efforts—the baseline plan becomes the plan element in the POLC Model and is used to control plan *v.* actual activities.

The deliverables for project step 2 would include:

- detailed project documentation
- detailed project network plan
- updated risk assessment observations
- final project financial plan
- recommendations to management

Step 2 assigned the first significant staffing resource to the project and the new project team will be spending a concentrated effort to ensure that step 2 deliverables are accurate and complete. Step 2 deliverables will be re-

viewed with upper management prior to advancing to step 3.

The step 2 management checkpoint provides a second opportunity for the telecommunications manager to reaffirm the project's viability and update upper management on the project's progress. The step 2 project plan now becomes the final project plan (baseline plan) for controlling the project until its implementation.

Management would be given a positive recommendation to proceed unless the detailed planning effort used in step 2 has uncovered information that changes the project's viability. If this occurs, the telecommunications manager is faced with the uncomfortable task of being a messenger who is conveying bad news. He or she must present the information in such a way that the messenger of the information is not punished unjustly.

DETAILED DESIGN (PROJECT STEP 3).

Project step 2 deliverables become the blueprint for step 3. For a technical project, step 3 is the preimplementation stage, during which all project costs are identified in detail and contractually "locked in" with selected equipment and service vendors.

In step 3, the detailed system or network design requirements would be completed, **requests for proposal (RFPs)** or their equivalent would be developed for selecting specific vendor products, and all the necessary details required to implement the project would be identified and documented. The term *detailed design* indicates that step 3 deliverables contain all elements needed to implement the project—including contracts that provide price protection until final management approval is provided at the step 3 management approval checkpoint meeting. The step 3 checkpoint meeting provides upper management with a last chance to terminate a bad project without incurring the major expenses associated with 1) the purchase of the asset and 2) its life cycle operating costs. At this stage in the project, only approximately 10% of the total asset lifetime costs have been incurred (Figure 11–6). While large projects may have incurred significant costs by this time, they are relatively small compared to the 90% life cycle costs that will be incurred after the fixed assets are purchased (project step 4).

The deliverables for Project Step 3 would include:

- summary evaluation of (acquisition) alternatives
- acquisition recommendations
- recommended supplier(s)
- five year financial plan
- implementation schedule
- final recommendations

A final review would be made of the project's objectives, the various vendor options that were evaluated, the acquisition recommendations, the reasons for selecting the recommended vendor products, the life cycle cost implications of step 3 recommendations, and the detailed design's implementation schedule. Approval of step 3 recommendations would initiate step 4, the project phase during which signed contracts are sent to the selected vendors and implementation activities are initiated.

> Management approval of step 3 recommendations will begin the spending of capital budget funds and indicates the organization's commitment to the ongoing operating costs that will be associated with the acquisition of the asset. The step 3 management approval checkpoint provides conceptual approval for incurring 100% of the fixed asset life cycle costs.

ACQUISITION (PROJECT STEP 4). The actual acquisition (a.k.a., purchase, procurement, or lease) of the project components will not be undertaken until final upper management approval is given in step 3 (Figure 11–6). It is at this time that a commitment is given to spend the "big bucks" needed to complete the project and, realistically, a point of no return has been reached. Any subsequent attempts to terminate the project will have major political and cost liabilities.

The preacquisition work completed during step 3 will now be implemented. The step 3 effort included identifying required project components, evaluating vendor alternatives, and selecting the specific vendor products that will be used in the project. Normally, contracts would have been written to lock in prices, and the contract commitment period would provide sufficient time for the telecommunications manager to get the necessary internal management and legal approvals.

IMPLEMENT DETAILED DESIGN (PROJECT STEP 5). Project step 5 is viewed by many observers as the most difficult step in the project. However, if the four previous project steps were executed properly, step 5 should run smoothly with few, if any, surprises.

Step 3 locked in vendor price and performance commitments, and also established a detailed plan for completing the step 5 implementation phase. Step 5 activities will focus on ensuring that the technical specialists hired to implement the detailed design plans meet project requirements. Any step 5 plan deviations should require only minor adjustments of assigning ad hoc resources to maintain the project's schedule commitment. If the step 3 plan-

ning process was done properly, the step 5 implementation activity should be uneventful.

Step 5 deliverables are simple and direct. They include:

- a fully operational system, network, or device
- operation management documentation

POSTCUTOVER ACTIVITIES (PROJECT STEP 6). Cutover is a point in time when the user of the project deliverables is provided access to a fully operational system or network. From a project management perspective, it signifies the end of the technical project but includes the obligation to close out the project and smoothly transfer operational responsibility to an operations department. Typical activities include resolving implementation problems, obtaining user approval for the satisfactory performance of the system or network, formally transferring operational responsibility to the operations management department, completing project documentation, and tying up any loose ends.

> **cutover:** the synchronized transfer of users to new facilities and equipment, with the objective of ensuring the continuity of business activities and minimizing disruptions to internal users. Cutover is a point in time, not a time period.

The deliverables for step 6 include:

- operations documentation
- client/user acceptance and approval
- closing out the appropriation budget
- postcutover audit
- complete project documentation
- final project report

Step 6 is a critical project phase because it involves a significant amount of administrative paperwork—a task that is tedious but essential for ensuring successful operation during an asset's operating life. Once the project team is disbanded, there is a low likelihood that project documentation requirements or other tedious project tasks will ever be completed. Good project documentation includes addressing all of the elements listed under the step 6 deliverables. These deliverables will be used by operations management personnel to answer any installation or performance questions and for planning any major upgrades in the future.

A final report should be written in a format that is suitable for distribution to upper management. It should include a nontechnical summary of project objectives and the functional, technical, and financial elements of the project. An updated cost $v.$ benefit analysis would be appropriate.

OPERATE SYSTEM/NETWORK. While the operations phase is not a project phase, it is the most important phase in the life cycle of the implemented technology. Implementation activities are relatively brief time durations within the life cycle of a system or network. The useful life of the system or network does not start until it has been turned over to operations management and is providing the benefits for which it was developed.

A high priority should be given to developing effective operating procedures to ensure that equipment will perform as designed and will operate reliably during its operational lifetime. A final responsibility of the project team is to ensure that operating procedures are complete and documented, and that operations management personnel understand all maintenance requirements. The project team has the responsibility for establishing initial maintenance contracts with outside service providers and this task should be done jointly with the operations management organization.

Summary

While the model in Figure 11–6 may appear complex, it is a relatively simple process compared to the technical complexity of designing and implementing large telecommunications projects. The use of the model should be tailored to match the project. Large, complex projects require a highly detailed and controlled project management process, but smaller, simpler projects can be executed with the use of a simplified project management approach.

ADMINISTRATIVE PROJECT EXAMPLE

The previous sections reviewed the telecommunications product life cycle model (Figure 11–6) from a technical project perspective and discussed how the model activities would be implemented for a technical project. In the real world, telecommunications managers will have direct accountability for a large number of administrative projects and for a relatively small number of technical projects. Because of the size and complexity of technical projects, it is normally easier for upper management to understand

that dedicated project management resources must be assigned to control a project. However, ongoing day to day administrative projects typically consume most of a telecommunications manager's time, and additional resources are seldom provided to carry out these administrative projects.

While some telecommunications managers may be technical managers, many telecommunications managers will be generalists who are expected to handle a wide variety of tasks, and they will find that they have little time to dedicate to any individual project—technical or administrative. Higher-level telecommunications managers will frequently act as a facilitator for multiple technical and nontechnical projects but will have little direct involvement with them. The primary responsibility of a senior telecommunications manager will be to get the job done, which requires good motivating, coaching, training, delegation, facilitation, supervision, and management skills. The detailed technical skills for implementing telecommunications projects will be provided by the staff within the senior manager's organization.

The skills needed to handle multifaceted managerial roles—personal skills, learning skills, personal productivity skills, business communication skills, technology management skills, and department management skills—are not obtained casually. They require a combination of three elements: 1) formal and informal education, 2) on the job training, and 3) experience. Each assignment given to prospective or bona fide telecommunications managers provides an opportunity for them to learn new skills. Individuals seeking to become telecommunications manager craftsmen must also exercise personal initiative in developing the skills that will qualify them to become an outstanding professional manager.

Administrative projects are normally assigned to a telecommunications manager without detailed instructions (unlike an academic environment), and the manager is expected to identify: 1) the full scope of what is being requested and 2) the best way to complete the assignment.

If the manager focuses on the way to complete the assignment without understanding the explicit and implicit objectives of the assignment, it is unlikely that the project will be completed to the satisfaction of the requestor. It is more likely that a manager's time will be spent spinning wheels and searching desperately for someone who knows how to do the assigned project. Upper managers seldom give assignments that neatly and completely list all the required deliverables for a manager. It is more likely that the manager will receive vague, general guidelines and be expected to identify the detailed objectives that must be completed. If the manager does not identify project objectives accurately at the start of the assignment, a simple project can become a complex and time consuming activity.

The best way to approach a project is from a top down perspective by using the POLC Model. From a top down perspective, all projects are similar. It is the details that change as the top level elements are dissected and a viable implementation plan is developed. The following administrative project example describes an approach that can be used for administrative projects and is also appropriate when a telecommunications manager acts as an overseer for technical projects.

Administrative Project Description

A case study approach will be used to demonstrate a conceptual approach for handling the project management requirements associated with administrative projects.

CASE STUDY DESCRIPTION. A manager has just been hired to run the telecommunications department of a medium-sized company. He or she has four managers as direct reports—an operations manager, an administrative services manager, a development manager, and a help desk manager. In addition, two administrative assistants report directly to the telecommunications manager. One assistant is dedicated to handling the support services of the various telecommunications departments and the other

administrative assistant is primarily dedicated to supporting the telecommunications manager's individual needs. Each department manager has six direct reports. This telecommunications organization is shown in Figure 11–8.

The telecommunications manager has just left a Friday afternoon meeting held with the vice president of finance, where he or she was told that the human resources department needs all telecommunications department performance appraisal forms completed and submitted to them in three weeks. Because this is the first week on the job, the manager is not sure what this actually means.

> This is a typical business scenario. No additional information was provided and the boss's expectation is that the manager will figure out what has to be done. Attempts by the manager to obtain detailed information from the VP regarding the assignment requirements may be seen as a managerial weakness by the VP.

After the meeting, the manager talked with the telecommunications department administrative assistants and found out that current year performance goals had been established for each employee twelve months ago. It is now time to: 1) update employee appraisal forms by adding the employee accomplishments to them and 2) establish a new set of employee performance goal forms for next

Figure 11–8.
Telecommunications organization.

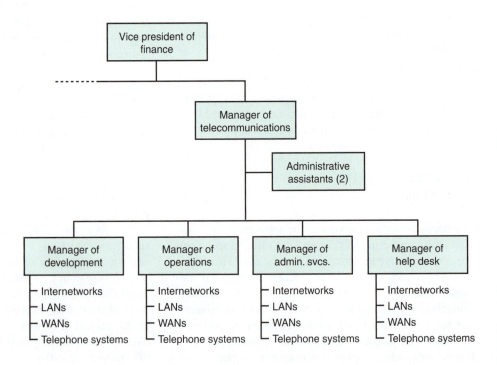

year's performance appraisal cycle. The following summarizes the information received by the telecommunications manager during discussions with the administrative assistants.

APPRAISAL PROCESS INFORMATION. The preparation of current year performance evaluation and future year performance goals involves both the employee and his or her manager. Employees are asked to provide current year performance information and prepare their initial drafts for creating future year performance goals. Word processing templates are used for this process, and managers coordinate the process with their direct reports. Once the managers and their subordinates have agreed on the appraisal document content: 1) approved copies of current year appraisal forms and future year performance goals are given to employees and 2) copies are maintained in telecommunications and human resources department files.

To understand the details of the appraisal process, the telecommunications manager signs out ten appraisal forms for department employees and and will review them over the weekend.

> The manager now has all the information needed to begin the employee performance appraisal project planning process.

The following illustrates an approach for completing this assignment. It will be based on the direct application of POLC Model elements by separating out POLC elements (goal, plan, organize, lead, and control) and identifying the steps taken to develop information for each category.

The personal planning document initially established by the telecommunications manager is shown in Table 11–2. It illustrates the application of the POLC

TABLE 11–2   Telecommunications Manager's Initial Plan

Telecom Employee Performance Project	
Workday	*Task Description*
0 (Saturday & Sunday)	Over the weekend, review the appraisal forms that exist for the different telecom managers, administrative assistants, and selected department personnel to become familiar with the appraisal process. Identify issues and questions about the appraisal forms. Write a memo to telecom department members announcing the appraisal process update cycle and the time frame established for the process. Request employees to add results to current forms and create forms for next year's appraisal process.
1 (Monday)	Issue the appraisal announcement memo. Meet with the human resources manager to review appraisal requirements. Meet with the telecom staff to initiate personnel appraisal process and identify any issues. Schedule initial appraisal review meetings with direct reports starting with workday 6.
2	
3	
4	
5	
18	
19	Deadline for receiving telecom appraisal forms from managers.
20	Review completed employee appraisal forms. Resolve any questions with managers.
21	**Submit telecom appraisals to HR department.**

Model process for establishing a plan that will be controlled during its execution.

Telecommunications Manager's Plan

The planning format used a 21 day calendar for the initial project plan and listed the tasks needed to complete the assignment. Because the project was assigned on a Friday afternoon, the telecommunications manager used the weekend for planning the project.

The primary requirement for this personal project plan was to develop an action plan quickly and notify the individuals affected by the appraisal process. There are only twenty-one workdays available to update old appraisal forms and create new ones for the twenty-six employees in the telecommunications organization. Although the manager was hired only recently and is unfamiliar with the appraisal process, knowledge of the appraisal form's contents was not required to organize the administrative aspects of the project. By doing some homework over the weekend, the telecommunications manager gained first-hand experience with the appraisal process and developed a game plan that could be started on workday 1 of the project (Monday).

> Note that the plan focuses on meeting commitments as assigned by the boss and also meeting the human resources schedule. With a minimal amount of input from the two administrative assistants, a preliminary plan was created and the key project elements were identified.

The use of PC application skills (word processing tables) simplifies the planning effort and helps the manager establish a fill-in-the-blanks document (Table 11–2) where information can be added, deleted, or modified. The manager would continue to add more information to Table 11–1 while working on the project, and would use the completed table as the game plan for next year's appraisal process.

To make the manager's plan a generic one, workdays were used instead of calendar dates on the initial plan (Table 11–2). However, when the plan is actually distributed to others, calendar dates would be provided instead of the workday information.

POLC GOALS. A key requirement when using the POLC Model is to identify the goals in quantitative terms. This was done on workday 21 of the personal plan, which stated that the performance appraisals were to be submitted to the HR department. The goals are very clear, and success or failure can be measured easily. Because this

objective will be covered in the memo that will be issued by the telecommunications manager on workday 1, all telecommunications employees are provided with deadlines for completing their job appraisals.

POLC PLAN. There is a need to establish a planning structure that identifies the project objectives and the individual tasks that will be required to complete the project. These elements should be placed into a format that clearly identifies the required activities and provides a schedule that can be used by others. Because the VP of finance gave a 3 week period for the assignment, this time frame became the planning period for the project.

Table 11–2 shows the word processing table that was initially created by the manager after meeting with the two administrative assistants. It covers a twenty-one workday period and includes the different tasks and milestones that will be used to manage the project and ensure its satisfactory completion.

POLC ORGANIZE. The organize phase of the project was initiated on workday 1 of the project by executing the workday 1 plan shown in Table 11–2. The resources needed to complete the project were the telecommunications department employees and their managers. They were assigned their tasks on workday 1 in the manager's memo (table 11–2) to give them the maximum possible time for completing their tasks. Contacting human resources and meeting with the telecom managers on workday 1, after reviewing appraisal examples during the weekend, quickly educated the telecommunications manager about the appraisal system and also provided an opportunity to identify any issues that might exist.

POLC LEAD. Issuing the memo to telecommunications department employees, holding the meeting with the human resources managers, and meeting with staff members is a leadership role. Given clear, unambiguous instructions in a timely manner, most employees will work very hard to carry them out in the time provided to them. On the other hand, incomplete instructions that are received late are almost certain to create (justifiable) resentment when employees are asked to complete the undefined tasks in an unreasonably short time period.

Holding the meetings with managers and scheduling appraisal meetings with direct reports also provides the new manager with an opportunity to gain additional first-hand information about the existing appraisal process and obtain feedback regarding the instructions that were provided in the manager's memo.

POLC Control. Control for most administrative projects is relatively simple because the time spans are normally short and there are only a few resources that require coordination. Simple, interpersonal communication is frequently the easiest and best approach to use for administrative projects. E-mail and other written communication formats can also be used, as required.

The control element for this case study example would primarily be one of following up on the published schedule developed by the telecommunications manager and issued to department managers and employees. Communication would typically require ongoing, low-key questions like, "How are you coming with your appraisals?" or "Any problems in meeting the workday 21 deadline?"

Observations. Administrative projects are a way of life for telecommunications managers. Most administrative projects have short time spans and can frequently be done by a manager without using additional resources. Projects that are larger and broader in scope may require the delegation of responsibilities to direct reports and other department employees. The control requirements of personally initiated projects should be low, and those involving others will require an ongoing follow up with individuals who have been given various assignments.

Whether the project is small or large, a plan containing tasks and milestones should exist. The plan may be a mental plan, a handwritten plan, or a plan listed in a word processing table.

> The word processing approach is by far the best planning option to use with administrative projects. It provides a hard copy document that can be given to others and is legible (a problem with many handwritten notes) and easy to update. Hard copy documentation is also less prone to misinterpretation (compared to verbal instructions) and is intuitively assigned more importance than verbal statements.

Telecommunications managers who develop good skills handling nontechnical projects will gain two benefits: 1) they will save a great deal of time and 2) they will be viewed in a positive light by their boss, their peers, and members of upper management who are normally the creators of these nontechnical projects. On the other hand, failure to effectively manage nontechnical projects will typically result in negative appraisal comments on a telecommunications manager's performance appraisal form.

In summary, technical projects are frequently more fun to take part in than nontechnical projects, but nontechnical projects are more important to business management commitments. To paraphrase an Abraham Lincoln saying, "(Management) must love (administrative projects) because they make so many of them."

SUMMARY

This summary is organized to correspond with the learning objectives found at the beginning of the chapter.

1. There are many definitions of projects, but the one that applies best in a project management context is that "a project consists of a set of nonroutine tasks that must be performed in a specific sequence to accomplish specified objectives." Projects have a start time and a completion time that must be met, and they utilize a limited set of resources. A project must meet project objectives, must be completed on time, and must operate with the limits of PTM resources.

2. Telecommunications managers have responsibility for two types of projects: 1) technology projects and 2) nontechnology projects. Technology projects acquire: 1) telecommunications equipment and configure them to create telecommunications systems and networks, or 2) telecommunications services. Nontechnology projects are normally administrative in nature and are directed toward fulfilling business management responsibilities, such as employee performance appraisal reviews, budget planning, or budget management (forecast *v.* actual) activities, etc. A telecommunications manager may have direct responsibility for managing technology projects directly or may be responsible for overseeing the activities of a dedicated project manager. Nontechnology projects may be carried out by the telecommunications manager directly or may require him or her to coordinate and delegate the resources of other department personnel.

3. The four attributes used to define a project are: 1) project description, 2) project activities, 3) project schedule, and 4) project budget. The project description

The langu
tifaceted a
technolog

Administra
Business P
Critical Pat
Decision P
Deliverable
Gantt Chart
Life Cycle
Program an
    Techniqu

REVIEW

The follow
swers are r
these quest
the chapter

1. Define
2. What a
3. What a
4. Descri
    activiti
5. Descrit
6. Descrit
    activiti

MULTIPl

1. It is imp
    a. rema
    b. are b
    c. inclu
    d. cove
2. A projec
    outside
    a. proje
    b. proje
    c. proje
    d. proje
    e. proje

pr
ob
su
act
dir
ple
sch
co
the

4. Bo
are
sp
ual
de
he
an
for
ba
for
mi

5. Te
dle
no
the
tiv
lik
ma
wi

6. Pr
an
m
lar
ma
m
ex
tec
me
ce
are
re
the
cu
to

7. Th
ble
be
thi
pr
tha

5. Network diagrams have advantages over Gantt charts because network diagrams _____.

a. show the relationship between project activities

b. have a beginning and an end

c. are not subject to budgetary constraints

d. clearly show project objectives

6. 90% of the telecommunications product life cycle costs are incurred after _____.

a. the detailed project plan phase

b. the organize phase

c. the implement detailed design phase

d. the detailed design phase

e. the postcutover activities phase

7. Life cycle costs include _____. (Select all that apply.)

a. operating costs

b. advertising costs

c. budgetary values

d. fixed asset costs

e. strategic planning costs

8. There are _____ management approval checkpoints in the telecommunications product life cycle model.

a. 1

b. 2

c. 3

d. 4

e. 5

9. The primary purpose of having management approval checkpoints in the telecommunications product life cycle model is to _____.

a. develop project network diagrams

b. obtain additional funding

c. add project staffing

d. validate a project's viability

10. The budgets for telecommunications projects are created during the _____ planning phase.

a. project management

b. strategic

c. operational

d. tactical

e. life cycle analysis

11. The justification for telecommunications projects are created during the _____ planning phase.

a. project management

b. strategic

c. operational

d. tactical

e. life cycle analysis

12. In the year 1999, the 2004 plan is a _____ plan.

a. project management

b. strategic

c. operational

d. tactical

e. life cycle analysis

13. The best forecast of project expenses can be made after the _____ phase is completed.

a. organize project

b. detailed project plan

c. detailed design

d. operate system/network

14. The best planning medium for most administrative projects is _____.

a. CPM project management software

b. PERT project management software

c. technology project management

d. Gantt charts

e. word processing tables

12

CRITICAL PATH METHOD CONCEPTS

1. Understand the advantages offered by project network diagrams compared to earlier project planning approaches.

2. Understand the difference between CPM and PERT project planning techniques.

3. Understand project network diagram labeling conventions and their meanings.

4. Understand critical path concepts and the manner in which they can be used in project planning activities.

5. Understand the four step approach for identifying a project network's critical path and translating the information into a usable format.

6. Understand how to identify the critical path in a project network diagram.

7. Understand the meaning of *float time* and how it can be utilized when planning a project.

8. Understand the differences between top-down and bottom-up planning approaches and their applications.

9. Understand the elements that make up manual CPM project deliverables.

10. Understand the work breakdown structure (WBS) concept and the format used to develop a WBS worksheet.

11. Understand how to determine a project schedule once the critical path has been identified and how to adjust the schedule if the calculated project completion does not equal the target completion date.

In the early 1900s, Henry L. Gantt developed the **Gantt chart** to show the relationship between project activities and the times when they were being executed. The Gantt chart remained a cornerstone of project management activities until computer technologies were introduced in the 1950s, when the underlying logic for developing computer-based project management software began to evolve. A problem associated with the Gantt chart was that it did not clearly show the dependencies and relationships that existed among activities in large projects. As project sizes increased, the usefulness of Gantt charts quickly diminished, as did the usefulness of the other manual tools that predated computerized project management software developments.

ORIGIN OF CPM

Computers initially appeared in the U.S. business environment during the 1950s, and many organizations maintained a management services department whose mission was to find out how this new technology could be used effectively. During the mid-1950s, project management was one of the areas of focus for management services personnel trying to harness the potential of computers. Computerized **CPM** and **PERT** software applications were products generated by management services organizations in the E. I. DuPont Company and the U.S. Navy Special Projects Office, respectively. Both applications were based on using a network-based approach to describe project activities. Network nodes represented project activities (events) and the connections between nodes identified the dependencies and relationships among different project activities. **Project network diagrams** overcame the limitations of Gantt charts and other existing methods of manually displaying project management information. The processing power of computers allowed project management calculations to be made quickly and cost effectively, and eliminated the human calculation bottleneck of existing manual project management methods.

An E. I. DuPont Company management services team consisting of Morgan R. Walker and James E. Kelly set out during the 1950s to develop a computer application that would assist with planning, scheduling, and controlling large engineering projects—a major activity in the DuPont Company. Their joint efforts resulted in the development of the Kelly-Walker network technique, a name that was changed to *Critical Path Method (CPM)* in later publications of their work. In 1958, CPM was used by DuPont to manage the construction of a $10 million chemical plant and implement several smaller maintenance projects. The use of CPM was credited for generating savings

in excess of $1 million for these 1958 projects, and the basic simplicity of the original Kelly-Walker model calculations are still retained in current CPM software versions. No fundamental changes have been made to the original CPM model calculation engine that was developed at Dupont during the 1950s.

At the same time that DuPont was developing CPM, the U.S. Navy was undertaking a major project whose objective was to develop the Polaris Missile System. Three organizations—the U.S. Navy's Special Projects Office; Lockheed; and Booz, Allen, and Hamilton—shared the joint responsibility of managing Polaris project activities. The Polaris project was the largest project undertaken by a government agency and required coordinating the efforts of more than 3,000 subcontractors and government agencies. As a result, the project management work effort implications were monumental and overwhelming if conventional manual methods (Gantt charts, tables, etc.) were employed. In February, 1958, the Special Project Office's management services team introduced a new computerized project management tool—Program Evaluation and Review Technique (PERT)—for use as the Polaris Project's project management system. Like CPM, it was based on showing the project's activities as nodes in a project network diagram. In October, 1958, PERT became the official project management tool for the Polaris project and was credited with reducing the original project schedule by more than eighteen months and providing large cost-savings.

Both CPM and PERT are network-based tools. The primary differences between them are the calculations they use to develop project time schedules. CPM was developed for engineering construction projects, while PERT was developed for managing research and development projects. These projects differ drastically, and the difference is reflected in their calculation methods. In the case of DuPont, engineering schedule **activity durations** could be estimated with a high degree of accuracy, while the Polaris Project involved an extensive R&D effort that could not provide accurate estimates of the time needed to complete individual activities. R&D activities normally have open-ended schedules because the activities are being undertaken for the first time and they do not have a historical database to use for predicting duration requirements. DuPont's engineering-based CPM calculations assumed that the activity times provided are accurate, but Polaris's PERT calculations developed a most-likely completion schedule by using probability-based statistical calculations. Both CPM and PERT are project network diagramming techniques that optimize the use of project resources. The selection of either CPM or PERT as a project management tool will depend upon the project management requirements.

CPM PROJECT NETWORK DIAGRAM

CPM is the network-based project management method that is most likely to be used for telecommunications projects. Like the engineering projects for which CPM was designed, the time durations of telecommunications project activities can usually be estimated with a reasonable degree of accuracy. The basic simplicity of CPM also makes it a good candidate to use with manual calculations because the CPM calculation process involves simple add, subtract, multiply, and divide functions that can be done easily on an electronic calculator or by using spreadsheet software. However, to use PERT effectively, the software user should have a basic understanding of statistics and be able to exercise good judgment in selecting the appropriate statistical approach for different types of activities. This text will use a manual CPM approach to explain CPM concepts and show the type of information obtained when using CPM software.

PC-based CPM project management software masks the underlying concepts of CPM. The software asks questions and uses the information entered through keyboards or other data entry methods to calculate results. The problem with using CPM software without having a knowledge of underlying CPM concepts is that it is difficult for a data entry clerk (the project administrator) to know whether the CPM output makes sense. If erroneous information is entered, the CPM application will generate schedule information regardless of its merit. Even if the software detects the error, the application user will have to evaluate the error output and identify the appropriate corrective action. Someone who has a basic understanding of CPM concepts is less likely to make data entry errors and is more likely to be able to correct problems. This chapter will focus on presenting CPM concepts so that the reader does not fall victim to the data entry clerk syndrome and is aware of the underlying CPM logic in project management.

Although it is possible to simplify many telecommunications projects to allow the use of manual methods, it is far more likely that telecommunications projects will be implemented by using PC-based CPM software. Having an understanding of manual CPM methods provides the manager with another conceptual thinking tool that can be used in project or nonproject situations.

A project network diagram must be created before CPM calculations can be made. The network nodes in the project network diagram represent project activities. The connections that exist between the nodes indicate the relationships among different project activities. Figure 12–1 provides a simple example of a project network diagram. A large project network could contain hundreds or thousands of nodes and could be managed effectively only by using PC-based software.

Network Diagram Conventions

Activity durations (the amount of time required to complete an activity) are the basic elements used to identify the project network's **Critical Path (CP)** and create a CPM project schedule. The CP is the path through a project network, from start to finish, that determines how long a project will take to complete. The CP is the longest path from start to finish, and identifies those activities that must be modified if the overall project duration is to be shortened.

Figure 12–1 illustrates several conventions that will be used during the CPM discussion. Rectangles are used to identify project activities and the arrows (connector) between the rectangles indicate the relationships among activities. Figure 12–2 provides a picture of an activity rectangle.

Each activity is provided with an identifier (a name or number) so that it can be uniquely identified. The activity box also contains information specifying the length of time (duration) needed to complete the activity. **ES, EF, LS,** and **LF** are abbreviations for *early start, early finish, late start,* and *late finish,* respectively, and the objectives of CPM calculations are to determine their values. The ES, EF,

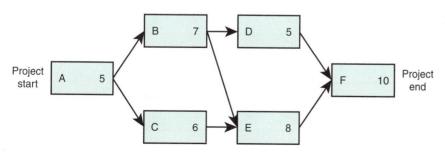

Figure 12–1. Project network diagram example.

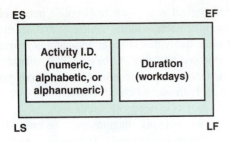

Figure 12–2. Activity node naming convention.

LS, and LF values are then used to identify a project's CP activities—a process described in the following sections.

In Figure 12–1, letters A through F identify different activities, and the numbers within each box indicate the time duration required to complete the activity. Activity A is the beginning activity in the project network diagram and activity F is the ending activity. Activity A will require five units of time. The duration time unit (minutes, workdays, or weeks, etc.) is specified when the project is set up. Activity F will require ten time units to complete. The number in each of the other activity rectangles identifies the duration times.

The arrows connecting the boxes indicate the relationships among activities. When an arrow connects two activities, the arrow-end activity is designated as a **successor activity,** while the "tail end" activity is designated as a **predecessor activity.** Except for the starting and ending activities, each project network diagram activity will have successor and predecessor roles. For example, activity E is the successor activity for activities B and C and is also a predecessor activity for activity F. It is important to understand the successor/predecessor terminology, because this terminology will be used in the following discussion to describe the CPM activity calculations needed to calculate project schedules.

The arrows also indicate when any specific project activity can be started. Work on a project activity can only

be started if all of its predecessor activities have been completed. Referring to the arrow connectors in Figure 12–1, activity A must be completed before activities B or C can be started, and activity F can't be started until both activities D and E have been completed.

> Activity identifiers, activity durations, and the status of successor and predecessor activities are the basic information elements used to perform CPM calculations.

Activity Information

The network convention information in Figure 12–2 identifies the basic data needed to carry out CPM calculations. CPM calculations will identify the ES, EF, LS, and LF values for each activity, and these values will be shown in their respective ES, EF, LS, and LF positions indicated in Figure 12–3. If the Figure 12–2 naming convention is applied to the Figure 12–1 project network diagram, the network diagram format looks like the one shown in Figure 12–3.

CRITICAL PATH CONCEPTS

A key objective in the critical path process is to identify the project network's CP. Multiple paths exist between the start and end points of a network diagram, and the process of identifying them by using manual calculations—even with CPM—can be a tedious, time-consuming task. Fortunately, computers are very fast, very patient, and very accurate. CPM calculations that would take hours for an individual to calculate manually are completed in seconds. In simple project networks (the type of project networks shown in this text), manual CPM calculations can be used. The use of manual calculations provides the advantage of demonstrating the basic simplicity of the CPM approach and highlighting the underlying CPM concepts that make CPM a useful project management tool.

Figure 12–3. Project network diagram showing ES, EF, LS, and LF.

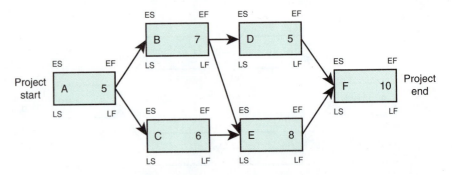

CPM utilizes a mathematical method to examine all path options and identify the CP (the longest path—the network path from start to finish whose activities add up to the largest total duration). The overall duration of a project is determined by adding up all the activity durations along the critical path. Because all other paths through the network diagram are shorter paths than the CP, shortening their duration will not impact the project's duration.

CPM calculates two project network schedules for each activity—an early schedule and a late schedule—and determines the time differences between these schedules. The calculated difference between early and late schedules is called slack time or **float time,** which is the amount of time an individual activity can be delayed without delaying the overall completion time of the project. Critical path activities will have zero float/zero slack, and any delay in completing a critical path activity will delay the completion of the overall project.

An advantage of CPM is that it provides a standard format for evaluating the impact of proposed project changes. Project completion times may be shortened or lengthened by changing the duration of activities. The length of time required for completing an activity is dependent upon the resources with which it has been provided (such as using two people to complete an activity instead of using just one). A project's time duration is also affected by the activity sequence structure. Changing the sequence of project activities to create concurrent work activities can be used to shorten project duration.

Many enhancements have been added to CPM project management software to assist in the process of identifying options for changing project durations and for producing project management information in different formats.

Graduation Project Example

Figure 12–4 illustrates the application of project networking concepts to a student's graduation project: completing twenty activities (courses) during five semesters to obtain an associate's degree. The length of each activity is one semester, and the activity I.D. is the course's alphanumeric identifier. Because there are five semesters, no path through the graduation project network will contain more than five activities/nodes. In our simple world, it will be assumed that the student has already passed the entry exam and must now pass all of the courses shown in Figure 12–4.

Applying the information that has been reviewed to this point, it should be easy to identify the successor and predecessor activities in Figure 12–4. For example, the fifth semester course, T240, has two predecessor activities: C118 and T220. Therefore, T240 cannot be started until both predecessor courses have been completed. The second semester course, E120, has three successor courses: S275, S230, and H210. Until E120 is completed, none of the successor courses can be taken.

In Figure 12–4, the critical path is the longest path that can be taken through the project network. A cursory examination of Figure 12–4 shows that any start to finish path will have a maximum of five courses (activities)—the minimum time required to obtain an associates degree if all the Figure 12–4 courses are completed.

The following lists four critical paths:

1. C108-T128-T235-T220-T240

2. C108-T128-T230-T210-T245

3. M145-T128-T235-T220-T240

4. M145-T128-T230-T210-T245

Interpreting the implication of these critical paths is straightforward. If students fail to successfully complete any of the courses in any critical path sequence, it will require (at least) six semesters to be a candidate for graduation, because retaking any course in the critical path extends the time requirements by one semester. Therefore, our student should identify all three CPs and make sure that all of the courses in the critical path are taken and passed during the semester they are scheduled. Otherwise, the student will require at least six semesters to complete the program.

> Activities along a project network's CP must be completed on schedule or the project's duration will increase by the amount of delay caused by not completing the critical path activity on time.

The CP approach identified those network elements where delays cannot be tolerated. What about those network paths where delays *can* be tolerated? Let's examine path B110. Course B110 is not a prerequisite for any other course and it has a slack time of four semesters. This means that it could be taken in any semester, if allowed by the school scheduling guidelines, and still be completed in time for graduation. If the student can only take three courses during the first semester because of a personal schedule conflict, B110 is the one to take at a later time. If only two courses can be taken, C108 and M145 must be taken to retain the potential for graduating in five semesters. (There are only three nodes in any E108 path, which

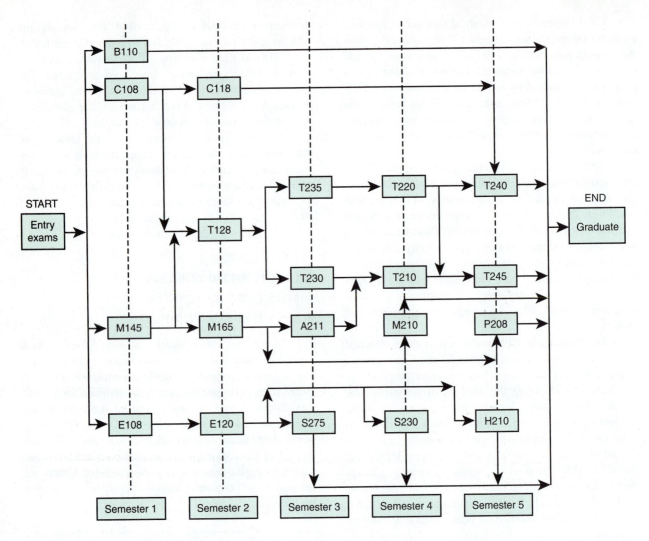

Figure 12–4. Student graduation project example.

would allow doubling up courses if permission is granted by the academic organization.)

If our student does not have attendance policy constraints, the Figure 12–4 project network can be followed and, assuming good academic performance, the student will graduate in five semesters. When scheduling constraints that require a student to take fewer courses because outside time commitments arise, the application of CPM concepts will provide options for taking the correct CP courses and delaying courses that are on paths that have float time. If critical path thinking is applied and executed, the student can still be eligible for graduating in five semesters despite skipping noncritical courses early in the graduation "project."

Project network paths that have float time allow for rescheduling the activities in the path without incurring delays in the overall project.

LESSONS LEARNED. Several observations can be made regarding the graduation project network in Figure 12–4:

1. It becomes difficult to draw, follow, and interpret project network diagrams as the number of activities increases.

2. For small project networks, the CP(s) can be found by inspection.

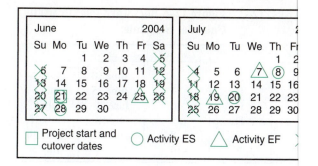

Project start and cutover dates — Activity ES ⃝ — Activity EF △

Next, the ES and EF dates for individual CP activities are determined by counting their durations on the Figure 12–6 calendar. For example, the first CP activity (A) will start on June 21 and will be completed five days later on June 2[...]

Because the CP activities are completed on the same date (August 2), calculated initially by using the thirty C[...] working days, the individual activity date computation[...] were correct. If the project and activity computations di[...] fered, an error exists in either one of the computations an[...] the error must be identified and corrected.

At this time, the ES and EF dates for the CP activi[...] ties have been identified so that the actual project compl[...] tion date of August 2 is known. However, this completio[...] date does not match the required project completion da[...] of July 30, the last workday prior to the project cutover. [...] CP activity duration must be shortened by one day to com[...] plete the project on July 30. The adjustment process wi[...] be discussed in the backward pass schedule section.

FORWARD PASS NON-CP ACTIVITY DATE[...]
Once the CP calendar schedule is established, the non-C[...] activity calendar schedule can be computed. Because th[...] CP activity schedule cannot be changed, a non-CP activit[...] must conform to the CP activity schedule. When a non-C[...] activity has the same predecessor as a CP activity, the no[...]

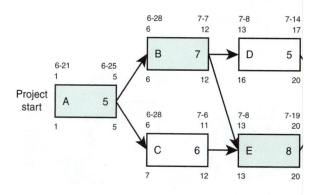

3. The CP identifies project constraints that must be met if the project is to be completed on time.

4. Slack/float paths provide flexibility for rescheduling events/nodes in their path while still allowing overall objectives to be met.

CRITICAL PATH CALCULATIONS

For simple project networks, the CP may be determined by inspection: It is the path through the network diagram that will take the longest time to complete. The following provides a three-step mathematical technique for identifying critical path activities in a project network diagram by applying basic calculations in a predefined process:

1. Determine the early schedule for project network activities (**forward pass** calculation).
2. Determine the late schedule for project network activities (**backward pass** calculation).
3. Identify critical path activities and activity floats.
4. Identify the activity calendar date schedule associated with the critical path.

A fourth step, which translates CPM theory into a real world management tool, has been shown. Project durations have little meaning to managers, but dates clearly identify project management requirements. In our manual CPM procedures, a calendar will be used to determine the activity calendar dates associated with the CP.

Step 1: Calculate The Early Schedule (Forward Pass)

The forward pass calculations begin with the ES of the first project activity node.

ES. The ES is the earliest time when all predecessor activities for an activity will be completed and the activity can begin. The ES time for the first activity is arbitrarily set to one (1) to provide a starting point.
For the other activities,

$$\text{activity ES} = \text{EF}_{predecessor} + 1$$

Note: The ES of an activity that has multiple predecessors is based on selecting the predecessor that has the largest EF.

EF.

$$\text{activity EF} = \text{ES} + (\text{activity duration} - 1)$$

Note: When the first EF has been set to 1 (such as day 1), the last network EF will specify the total number of workdays required to complete the project.

Step 2: Calculate the Late Schedule (Backward Pass)

The backward pass starts with the last activity's LF.

LF. Start at the last activity. The LF time of the last activity is set to the EF time calculated during the forward pass calculation for that activity.

$$\text{activity LF} = \text{LS}_{successor} - 1$$

Note: The LF time of activities that have multiple successors is based on using the successor with the smallest LS.

LS. The LS is the latest time at which an activity can be started without causing a delay in the completion of the project.

$$\text{activity LS} = \text{LF} - (\text{activity duration} - 1)$$

Forward pass and backward pass procedures are used to determine ES, EF, LS, and LF values for each activity. ES, EF, LS, and LF values can be shown directly on the network diagram or listed in a separate table. The following network diagram (Figure 12–5) shows the EF, ES, LS, and LF calculation results when the correct forward and backward pass calculations are made. The CP nodes are highlighted.

Step 3: Identify Critical Path Activities and Activity Floats

The calculated difference between EF and LF or ES and LS is called slack time or float time (float time = LF–EF or float time = LS–ES). It is the amount of time an individual activity can be delayed from the ES time without delaying the overall project completion schedule. CP activities will have zero float/zero slack and any delay in completing a CP activity will delay the overall project completion. The zero float/zero slack activities in Figure 12–5 have been highlighted.

> Because the same duration value is used to calculate individual activity ES, EF, LS, and LF values, the activity float/slack can be calculated by using either LF–EF, or LS –ES.

For critical path activities, there will be zero float, and each critical path activity must be completed by the LF time (also the EF time) or the overall project completion

Figure 12–5. Project network example showing calculation results.

Project start

	1	
	A	
	1	

TABLE 12–1 Figure 12–5 Project Network Calculation Summary

CP	Activity	Duration	ES	EF	LS	LF
X	A	5	1	5	1	5
X	B	7	6	12	6	12
	C	6	6	11	7	12
	D	5	13	17	16	20
X	E	8	13	20	13	20
X	F	10	21	30	21	30
CP Total		**30**				

time will be increased. For noncritical path activitie
float will be a positive number. As long as the noncr
path activity is completed within the time period bet
an activity's EF and LF, the overall project will be
pleted on schedule.

The activity durations, ES, EF, LS, LF, and flo
Figure 12–5 are listed in Table 12–1. LS and LF ca
tions can also be performed directly in an Excel table
out the use of a network diagram. This approach is us
PC-based project management software.

The float column in Table 12–1 shows the resu
the LF–EF (or LS–ES) calculation. Activities A, B,
F have zero float, and the path formed by these acti
will be the CP. Bold type has been used to identify t
activities.

Step 4: Establishing An Acceptable Schedule

The workday calculations described previously m
converted into a calendar schedule by identifying th
cific dates associated with project activities. Allow
must be made for any holidays and weekends be
work is done only on regular workdays. Adding extr
to offset the number of nonworking days provid
lowances for nonworking time. Although work c
done outside the regular working schedule, an ov
penalty is involved, which makes work outside of n

TABLE 12–2 Figure 12–5 Forward Pass Project Calendar Schedule

CP	Activity	Duration	ES	EF
X	A	5	**June 21**	**June 25**
X	B	7	**Jun 28**	**July 7**
	C	6	June 28	July 6
	D	5	July 8	July 14
X	E	8	**July 8**	**July 19**
X	F	10	**July 20**	**August 2**
CP Total		**30**		

BACKWARD PASS NON-CP ACTIVITY DATES.
The CP activities will determine the LF dates that are used to calculate non-CP backward pass schedules. The LF for non-CP activities that have the same successor activity as CP activities will use the CP activity's LF date. If the non-CP activity's LF date is known, the LS date is calculated by counting off the non-CP activity's duration workdays.

Both the CP and non-CP dates are shown in Figure 12–9.

However, another potential conflict arises in the backward pass schedule because the ES for the first activity is calculated to be June 18 (Friday) and the project was

TABLE 12–3 Figure 12–5 Backward Pass Project Calendar Schedule

CP	Activity	Duration	ES	EF
X	A	5	**June 18**	**June 24**
X	B	7	**June 25**	**July 6**
	C	6	June 29	July 6
	D	5	July 12	July 16
X	E	8	**July 7**	**July 16**
X	F	10	**July 19**	**July 30**
CP Total		**30**		

scheduled to start on June 21 (Monday). If the project can be started a day earlier, the backward pass date schedule can be used for the entire project. However, if the project's start date (June 21) and end date (August 2) are firm dates, a schedule adjustment is required. Figure 12–10 and Table 12–4 combine the forward and backward pass schedules so that they can be compared more easily.

Note: Because the last activity's LF date is different from the EF date, the resultant forward and backward pass schedules are not related. The fact that ES date = LS date and EF date = LF date for activity C does not indicate that activity C is a CP activity.

Figure 12–8. Backward pass calendar.

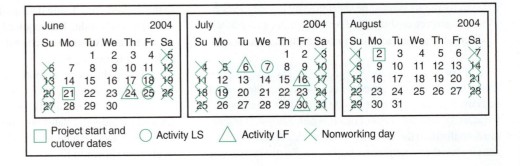

Figure 12–9. Backward pass schedule for Figure 12–5 diagram.

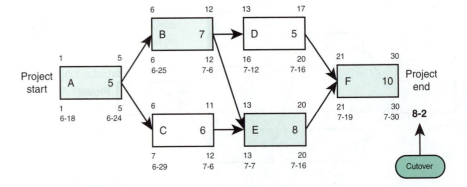

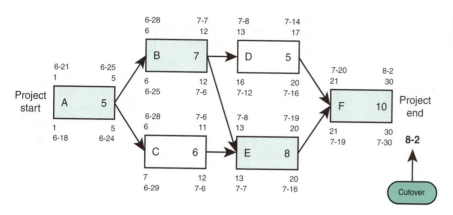

Figure 12–10. Combined forward pass and backward pass schedules.

TABLE 12–4 Figure 12–5 Combined Project Calendar Schedule

CP	Activity	Duration	ES	EF	LS	LF
X	A	5	June 21	June 25	June 18	June 24
X	B	7	June 28	July 7	June 25	July 6
	C	6	June 28	July 6	June 29	July 6
	D	5	July 8	July 14	July 12	July 16
X	E	8	July 8	July 19	July 7	July 16
X	F	10	July 20	August 2	July 19	July 30
CP Total		**30**				

TABLE 12–5 Figure 12–5 Final Project Calendar Schedule

CP	Activity	Duration	Start	End
X	A	5	June 21	June 25
X	B	7	June 28	July 7
	C	6	June 28	July 6
	D	5	July 8	July 14
X	E	7	July 8	July 16
X	F	10	July 19	July 30
CP Total		**29**		

Table 12–4 is a **technical schedule** that displays both a forward pass and a backward pass schedule. The term *technical* is used because the Table 12–4 schedule would make little sense to someone who is unfamiliar with the CPM process. Normally people expect single start and ending dates for activity schedules, not two sets of dates. Therefore, our next requirement is to establish a single set of activity starting and ending dates by selecting either the forward or backward pass dates for each activity, or some combination of the two.

Examination of Table 12–4 shows that the late schedule (backward pass) finishes on time but starts too early and the early schedule starts on time but finishes too late. If the assignment project start and ending dates are considered required dates, it will be necessary to use the first activity's ES date and the last activity's LS date. The duration of one of the intermediate CP activities must be shortened by one workday to meet these dates and the selection of the activity to be shortened is a judgment decision because there are several correct solutions. In this example, activity E will be shortened by one day by authorizing the use of overtime.

Activity E will start on 7/8 (the activity's ES date) and end on 7/16 (the activity's LF date). After an ES/LF schedule change has been used to shorten a CP activity, successor CP activities will use their late schedule (LS and LF). Our final schedule is shown in Figure 12–10 and Table 12–5 and is the one that would be used as a project schedule.

Using the Figure 12–11 schedule will allow the project to end on July 30th—the last workday before the required cutover date of August 2nd. This schedule begins on time (June 21) and completes the project work on July 30 so that the project **deliverable** is available for use on August 2—the project's cutover date.

ACCEPTABLE SCHEDULE SUMMARY. Establishing an acceptable final schedule when using manual procedures is an iterative process that requires good judgment. In the real world, this involves balancing out the cost of overtime for different schedule options and understanding the impact of schedule variations on subsequent activities. The following case study will be used to demonstrate the use of manual calculations and the application of

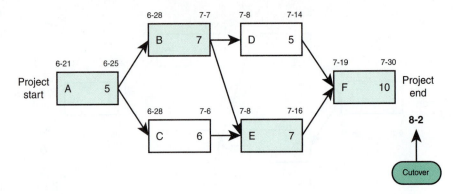

Figure 12–11. Final management project schedule.

reasonable judgment to develop an acceptable project implementation schedule.

In Figure 12–5, the activity F duration was shortened by one workday to seven workdays by authorizing the use of overtime. If activity A, B, or E were shortened by one workday, the same results would have been achieved but would have required a recalculation of other activity schedules.

> The use of a manual CPM example highlights the CPM process used to calculate CPs and determine the associated calendar schedule. PC-based CPM software utilizes similar methods, but much more quickly. In addition, there are many resource allocation options available in project management software that would be far too difficult to do manually.

CPM PROJECT PLANNING

To illustrate the application of manual CPM techniques to a real world project, a PBX implementation project problem has been created where it will be necessary to change the initial schedule to meet project implementation schedule requirements.

Real World Project Planning

In the project network, project nodes represented project activities. In this text, the term *activities* refers to summary-level planning elements that consist of multiple smaller work elements called **tasks.** For example, an activity called "clean the car" would require executing a series of tasks that results in a clean car. CPM could be applied to these tasks, and the CP time to complete the tasks would become the activity's duration. Carrying the concept down another level, some of these tasks may require executing a group of subtasks.

A reasonable question would be, "To what level of detail is CPM applied in project management?" The correct answer is, "It depends." The originator of the project determines the amount of detail contained in activities, tasks, and subtasks. When PC-based CPM applications are used, a lower level of detail can be used without having concerns about the work effort consequences, because the software application does the work and does it quickly and accurately. When manual CPM calculations are used, it makes sense to use a small number of activities (nodes) and keep the project network design simple. When working on similar types of projects that have predictable resource requirements, it is possible to operate at the activity level without becoming involved with the detailed tasks that make up the activity. However, when project experience is limited, external expertise or a detailed planning process should be used to identify activities and the sequence in which they must be carried out so that a detailed plan can be developed.

Top-Down *v.* Bottom-Up Planning

Top-down planning identifies major components and shows them as activity nodes in a project network diagram. The activities are then broken down into tasks and subtasks so that task and subtask CP times can be calculated to establish the time durations of the activity. In **bottom-up planning,** the tasks and subtasks are identified first and grouped into higher-level planning activities.

The top-down approach is more common in business planning and will be used in this text. Bottom-up planning does not have an overall planning framework until the details have been sorted out and grouped into major activities. Top-down planning starts with a structure framework and adds detail to the framework structure.

Work Breakdown Structure (WBS)

Because project activities consist of many tasks, mini-CPMs are frequently performed within each activity to determine the activity's duration. This mini-CPM duration value is used as the basis for forward pass and backward

TABLE 12–6 WBS Worksheet Example

Activity	Task Description	ACP
Define requirements	Conduct user reviews Analyze traffic **Totals**	12
Design system	Obtain jack locations from facilities Determine user features Determine trunks needed Prepare specification documentation **Totals**	7

ACP: activity critical path duration

pass calculations. Activity and task information must be organized, whether a PC application or manual calculation approach is used. A **work breakdown structure (WBS)** is commonly used for this purpose. A WBS is a hierarchical display of project activities and their associated tasks. It is normally a byproduct of project team planning activities and can be used either for a top-down or bottom-up planning process. Table 12–6 illustrates a WBS list of activities and their supporting tasks.

Milestones are a special activity/task designation used in the CPM process, and are assigned a duration time of zero. Their purpose is to allow critical events to be incorporated into the project network diagram and be part of the documentation information without affecting the project schedule. Milestones can be used to identify external tasks that are completed by an outside party or they can be used to highlight checkpoints at critical project stages. The Table 12–6 activity, *Obtain jack locations from facilities,* is an example of an external milestone activity and would be assigned a task duration of zero.

PARALLEL TASK CRITICAL PATH.   When tasks are performed concurrently (in parallel), the critical path is the task that has the longest duration. For example, consider a project in which ten painters are each painting similar rooms, and each painter will leave the job site after painting the room they have been assigned. The time du-ration to complete all ten rooms will be the time required for the slowest painter to complete his or her room. This parallel task approach can be used to estimate mini-CPM calculations if the slowest task time can be identified. When good judgment is used to establish a parallel task model, the activity time duration estimates will be reasonable values.

> In this text, the reader will be provided with the activity's duration to avoid getting mired in the details of mini-CPM calculations. In a normal work environment, PC software would automatically take care of calculating mini-CPM requirements.

A Manual CPM Process

CPM is a complex, multifaceted project planning tool that can overwhelm first time users easily. The key to managing a complex topic is to break it into smaller, more manageable segments. A five step process (refer to Figure 12–12) will be used for the text's manual CPM calculations:

1. Develop a project network diagram that shows all major activities and their relationships to each other.

2. Develop a work breakdown structure worksheet that identifies the duration (workdays) of various project network activity nodes.

3. Use the project network diagram to determine the project's CP by completing workday calculations (ES, EF, LS, and LF).

4. Use a calendar to calculate a project technical calendar schedule.

5. Establish a final project calendar schedule that meets the original project schedule requirements.

It is necessary to 1) understand project requirements before starting the CPM calculation process and 2) to identify required deliverables in advance. The term *deliverables* refers to the documentation requirements

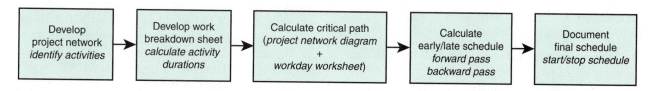

Figure 12–12.   CPM five step calculation process.

associated with the project management activity. These deliverables will become the control mechanism used to manage the project and communicate project information to project stakeholders.

MANUAL CPM PROJECT DELIVERABLES.

The project deliverables that will be created as part of the manual CPM process are:

1. project objectives and constraints description
2. project network diagram
3. work breakdown structure
4. workday calculations
5. project technical calendar schedule
6. project final calendar schedule

Note: The project final calendar schedule will be a nontechnical schedule based on interpreting the project's technical calendar information (deliverable 5).

Some deliverables are byproducts of the CPM process, but others will simply document information that is being used during the CPM planning process. A PBX project example will be used to illustrate the five-step CPM planning process (Figure 12–12) and provide the information needed to illustrate the content of the six project deliverables.

PBX TELEPHONE SYSTEM PROJECT EXAMPLE

The PBX telephone system's initial project schedule will not meet the project's cutover date schedule requirements and it will be necessary to establish a new schedule to meet project schedule requirements. The following calculates the final project schedule by: 1) completing the six project deliverables identified previously, 2) describing the process of creating them, and 3) providing completed examples. The primary objective in going through this tedious, detailed manual process is to highlight the underlying concepts and logic of the CPM approach that would be hidden when project management software is used.

Deliverable 1: Project Objectives and Constraints Description

The project objectives and constraints description defines the scope of the project and establishes a reference standard for measuring project progress during the project and at its completion. A project objectives and constraints description should contain the following (see Example 12–1):

1. project description overview
2. project start date
3. project cutover date (the day that full operations must begin)
4. workday schedules
5. holidays (nonworkdays)

The project information description information would be obtained from a variety of business planning sources. From a CPM perspective, the key elements that should be included in the project description are the project start date (1–2–04) and the cutover date (6–1–04). These dates will become the primary schedule constraints for developing a final schedule. By inspection, it can be seen that the only holidays that impact the work schedule will be New Years Day (1–1–04) and Memorial Day (5–31–04).

Deliverable 2: Project Network Diagram

A top-down approach will be used for the project. The project diagram in Example 12–2 was developed at the beginning of the project. If the project utilized a PC-based CPM application, the project network diagram would be much more complex and would contain many more nodes and many more diagonal links. Example 12–2 was kept simple to minimize the complexity of CPM calculations while still highlighting the key project management elements required in a PBX telephone system implementation project.

The information needed to develop the project network diagram in Example 12–2 would be obtained from technical specialists who are familiar with implementing PBX telephone systems or from files that contain documentation of previously completed projects. While the size and specific tasks within project activity nodes may differ from project to project, the major activities and their relationships will be similar for all PBX telephone system projects.

Deliverable 3: Work Breakdown Structure

Individual project activities (project network nodes) consist of multiple tasks that must be carried out in a specific sequence. A mini-CPM would normally be performed for each activity's tasks to determine the duration of the activity. The activity duration would then be used to calculate the project's CP. Example 12–3 provides the WBS worksheet that will be used for this project.

<table>
<tr><td colspan="2">**Project Description**
Installation of a 1,000 line PBX/voice messaging system in a new corporate headquarters building scheduled for occupancy on June 1, 2004.</td></tr>
<tr><td></td><td></td></tr>
<tr><td>**Current date:**</td><td>October 20, 2003</td></tr>
<tr><td>**Project start date:**</td><td>January 2, 2004</td></tr>
<tr><td>**Cutover date:**</td><td>June 1, 2004</td></tr>
<tr><td></td><td></td></tr>
<tr><td>**Workdays:**</td><td>Monday through Friday, 8 am to 5 pm</td></tr>
<tr><td></td><td></td></tr>
<tr><td>**Holidays:**</td><td>New Year's day, Memorial day, Labor day, Thanksgiving, Christmas day, and Independence day</td></tr>
<tr><td></td><td></td></tr>
</table>

Example 12–1. PBX project description (deliverable #1).

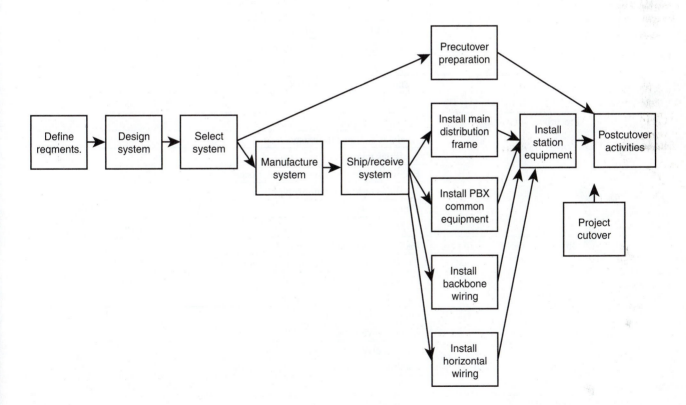

Example 12–2. PBX project network diagram (deliverable #2).

Activity/Phase	Task Description	ACP
Define requirements	Conduct user reviews	
	Analyze traffic	
	Totals	**14**
Design system	Obtain jack locations from facilities	
	Determine user features	
	Determine trunks needed	
	Prepare specification documentation	
	Totals	**14**
Select PBX System	Develop PBX system rating matrix	
	Identify RFP bidders	
	Prepare PBX system RFP	
	Telecom: hold bidder's conference	
	Develop RFP responses	
	Answer ad hoc bidder questions	
	Evaluate RFPs	
	Clarify bidder information	
	Select PBX system	
	Notify selected vendor(s)	
	Notify other vendors of selection decision	
	Prepare PBX system contract	
	Prepare PBX system purchase order	
	Conduct bidder postdecision briefings	
	Totals	**23**
Build system	Manufacture/assemble PBX system	
	Totals	**30**
Precutover preparation	Prepare user guides	
	Analysis stations: train users	
	Facilities task: pass fire inspection	
	Facilities task: obtain certificate of occupancy	
	Facilities task: move in people	
	Cutover system	
	Totals	**40**
Order/ship/ receive equipment	Facilities task: build equipment room	
	Facilities task: install electric in equipment room	
	Facilities task: install halon system	
	Facilities task: test halon system	
	Order TelCo facilities	
	Ship/receive PBX, MDF, IDF, etc.	
	Ship/receive stations, jacks, cable	
	Facilities task: install riser shaft conduit	
	Totals	**10**
Install MDF	Install MDF	
	Connect TelCo netwk. interfc. to MDF	

Example 12–3. PBX project WBS (deliverable 3).

Activity/Phase	Task Description	ACP
	Punch down TelCo cable to MDF	
	Test TelCo trunks	
	Totals	**5**
Install PBX common equipment	Install UPS	
	Install PBX cabinets	
	Install PBX power connection	
	Install PBX to MDF cable	
	Connect PBX trunk circuits to MDF	
	Connect PBX station circuits to MDF	
	Vendor tests PBX hardware	
	Vendor loads generic PBX software	
	Establish software database: ARS, ACD, etc.	
	Acceptance test final	
	Facilities task: seal equipment room	
	Totals	**11**
Install backbone wiring	Facilities task: install electric in telephone closets	
	Install IDFs	
	Install riser cables	
	Punch down risers to MDF	
	Punch down risers to IDFs	
	Test MDF to IDF risers	
	Totals	**6**
Install horizontal wiring	Facilities task: frame drywall offices	
	Facilities task: install ceiling grid	
	Facilities task: install under carpet power	
	Facilities task: install power poles	
	Facilities task: install electric in walls	
	Facilities task: core drill 3rd floor	
	Facilities task: core drill first floor	
	Install first floor cable runs to IDF	
	Install second floor cable runs to IDF	
	Install third floor cable runs to IDF	
	Punch down first floor cables to IDF	
	Punch down second floor cables to IDF	
	Punch down third floor cables to IDF	
	Facilities task: install drywall offices	
	Facilities task: install drywall, electrical boxes	
	Facilities task: install electric in power poles	
	Install cable wire to first floor jacks	
	Install cable wire to second floor jacks	
	Install cable wire to third floor jacks	
	Test IDF to jack cable runs	
	Facilities task: seal core drills	
	Totals	**12**

Example 12–3. PBX project WBS deliverable 3 (continued).

Activity/Phase	Task Description	ACP
Install station equipment	Facilities task: install ceiling tiles	
	Facilities task: install carpets	
	Facilities task: install cubicles and furniture	
	Install stations	
	Test stations	
	Totals	**5**
Postcutover activities	Provide ad hoc user training	
	Provide on site support services	
	Audit and accept PBX system	
	Obtain end user approvals for system operation	
	Complete operations documentation	
	Complete project documentation	
	Close out project	
	Totals	**22**
	Total project days	**192**
	Precutover project days	**170**

ACP: activity critical path duration in workdays.

Example 12–3. PBX project WBS deliverable 3 (continued).

The mini-CPM process will be avoided by assuming that a good knowledge already exists of the time required to complete activities. A single, summary activity duration has been shown for each activity listed in Example 12–3. A listing of activity tasks for each activity has been given to provide the reader with an appreciation for the complexity that actually exists within project network diagram activity nodes. When project management software is utilized, the activity task information (duration and relationship to other activity tasks) would be used to develop a mini-CPM network and calculate the activity's duration. Project management software would use these calculated activity durations to determine the project's CP.

Examination of the WBS (Example 12–3) shows that 192 workdays are needed to complete the PBX project, including the postcutover activities that are required after the cutover date (6–1–04). If the postactivity duration (22 workdays) is subtracted from the total, precutover activity duration is established (170 workdays).

However, if a 2004 calendar is used to identify the number of workdays that are available between 1–2–04 (project start date) and 6–1–04 (project cutover date), it will be seen that there are only 106 workdays available. Deliverable 3 (workday calculations) will address this issue and reveal the *magic of CPM* that allows 170 project workdays to be completed in 106 workdays.

> The WBS would be prepared using input obtained from experienced technical specialists who are familiar with PBX installation requirements. The role of the project leader would be to format the information into the WBS worksheet format required by the PC-based CPM application.

Deliverable 4: Project Workday Calculations

Project workday calculations provide the information needed to identify the CP, and are carried out by inserting activity duration information (deliverable 3) onto the project network diagram (deliverable 2). Once this is done, the forward pass and backward pass calculations are completed to identify each activity's ES, EF, LS, and LF values. These values are then used to identify CP activities and develop a project duration estimate.

CPM CALCULATIONS. When CPM calculations are done manually, the easiest way to perform them is to enter the WBS duration information directly onto

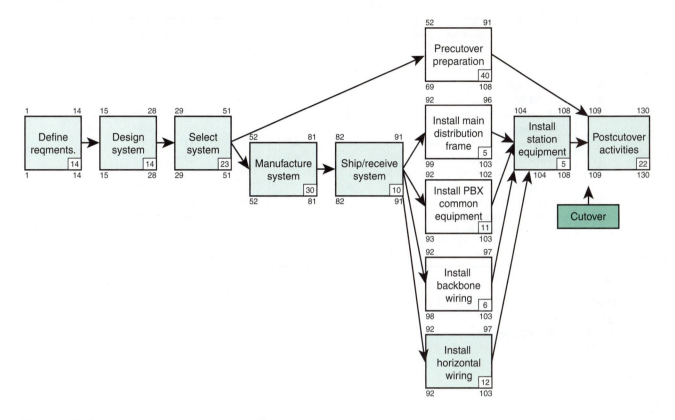

Example 12–4. PBX project network showing CPM calculation results.

the project network diagram and calculate ES, EF, LS, and LF on the project network drawing by using the forward pass and backward pass procedures described previously. Critical path nodes will be those nodes where LF – EF = ∅ (or LS – ES = ∅). Example 12–4 provides a completed diagram showing the various ES, EF, LS, and LF calculated values, and highlights the CP activities/nodes.

While this step would normally be done manually on a project network diagram, it has been provided in a finished format to allow readers to validate their CPM calculation skills by applying the forward and backward pass calculation procedures that were reviewed previously. The Example 12–5 table summarizes the Example 12–4 workday calculations. Critical path information has been identified on the table by placing an 'X' in the CP column and by bolding the activity line.

Earlier in the WBS deliverable 3 section, it was stated that 192 and 170 project workdays were needed to complete the total project and precutover activities, re-

spectively. Example 12–5 shows that the use of CPM can complete the total project in 130 workdays and the precutover activities in 108 workdays (130 days – 22 days). When the precutover duration requirements (108 days) are compared to the 106 workdays available, it can be seen that the install equipment activity will be completed 1 workday after the cutover date. The install equipment activity must be completed two days earlier, on Friday, June 28, to allow the cutover to take place on Tuesday, June 1.

The use of CPM allowed 170 workdays to be accomplished in 108 days. If the project network in Example 12–4 is examined, it can be seen that this time compression occurs because some activities can be carried out concurrently. For example, the four installation activities (MDF, common equipment, backbone wiring, and horizontal wiring) are all done during the horizontal wiring activity's duration of twelve workdays. This means that thirty-three days of project workdays were accomplished during a twelve workday period—a calendar time savings of twenty-one days.

			System Cutover: June 1, 2004					
CP	Activity	Duration	ES	EF	LS	LF	Float
X	**Define requirements**	**14**	**1**	**14**	**1**	**14**	**0**
X	**Design system**	**14**	**15**	**28**	**15**	**28**	**0**
X	**Select system**	**23**	**29**	**51**	**29**	**51**	**0**
X	**Manufacture system**	**30**	**52**	**81**	**52**	**81**	**0**
	Precutover preparation	40	52	91	69	108	17
X	**Ship/receive PBX & stations**	**10**	**82**	**91**	**82**	**91**	**0**
	Install main distribution frame	5	92	96	99	103	7
	Install PBX common equipment	11	92	102	93	103	1
	Install backbone wiring	6	92	97	98	103	6
X	**Install horizontal wiring**	**12**	**92**	**103**	**92**	**103**	**0**
X	**Install station equipment**	**5**	**104**	**108**	**104**	**108**	**0**
X	**Postcutover activities**	**22**	**109**	**130**	**109**	**130**	**0**
	Activity CP total	**130**					

CP: critical path activities; critical path activity: EF = LF + ES = LS

Float: measured in workdays; float = LF – EF, or LS – ES

Example 12–5. PBX project workday worksheet.

Deliverable 5: Project Technical Calendar Schedule

Example 12–6a provides a 2004 calendar that will be used to determine the different activity dates computed for deliverable 6. Two supplementary calendar worksheets are used to provide the activity date information: 1) the forward pass schedule calendar in Example 12–6b, and 2) the backward pass schedule calendar in Example 12–6c.

FORWARD PASS CALENDAR SCHEDULE.
Example 12–6b provides a copy of the completed forward pass calendar schedule. The project start and cutover dates are highlighted with squares, circles are used to identify activity start (ES), and triangles are used to identify end (EF) dates. A preliminary forward pass activity completion date was computed by counting off ninety-nine workdays (the CP precutover project duration workdays) starting on the first activity workday, 1–2–04. The forward pass project completion date (EF) for the last project precutover activity is 6–2–04.

Next, the individual activity ES and EF dates were calculated by counting off the respective CP activity durations. These dates are highlighted with circles in Example 12–6b. The final precutover node EF date was 6–2–04, a result that matched the preliminary activity completion date calculation. Therefore, the 6–02–04 completion date schedule calculation has been verified.

> The postcutover activities shown on Example 12–4 are carried out after the project is implemented—they should start on the cutover date (6–1–04). As shown in Example 12–6b the postcutover activities were completed on 7–2–04 (the EF of the postcutover activities project node). Although this node is shown as a CP node, it does not affect the cutover schedule.

BACKWARD PASS CALENDAR SCHEDULE.
The forward pass precutover activities were completed on 6–2–04, which is one workday after the project must be ready for use on 6–1–04 (the cutover date). The last workday prior to the target cutover date is 5–28–04 (Friday), which will be used as the desired project completion date. The rationale for using this date will be reviewed after Example 12–7 has been discussed.

Example 12–6c shows the backward pass LS and LF activity dates. The LS dates are highlighted with circles while the LF dates are highlighted with triangles.

> As was the case for the forward pass calendar process, the postcutover activities shown in Example 12–4 are carried out after the project is implemented—they should start on the cutover date (6–1–04). As shown in Example 12–6c, the postcutover activities are completed on 6–30–04 (the LF of the postcutover activity's project node).

Example 12–6a. 2004 calendar.

January						2004
Su	Mo	Tu	We	Th	Fr	Sa
				1	2	3
4	5	6	7	8	9	10
11	12	13	14	15	16	17
18	19	20	21	22	23	24
25	26	27	28	29	30	31

July						2004
Su	Mo	Tu	We	Th	Fr	Sa
				1	2	3
4	5	6	7	8	9	10
11	12	13	14	15	16	17
18	19	20	21	22	23	24
25	26	27	28	29	30	31

February						2004
Su	Mo	Tu	We	Th	Fr	Sa
1	2	3	4	5	6	7
8	9	10	11	12	13	14
15	16	17	18	19	20	21
22	23	24	25	26	27	28
29						

August						2004
Su	Mo	Tu	We	Th	Fr	Sa
1	2	3	4	5	6	7
8	9	10	11	12	13	14
15	16	17	18	19	20	21
22	23	24	25	26	27	28
29	30	31				

March						2004
Su	Mo	Tu	We	Th	Fr	Sa
	1	2	3	4	5	6
7	8	9	10	11	12	13
14	15	16	17	18	19	20
21	22	23	24	25	26	27
28	29	30	31			

September						2004
Su	Mo	Tu	We	Th	Fr	Sa
			1	2	3	4
5	6	7	8	9	10	11
12	13	14	15	16	17	18
19	20	21	22	23	24	25
26	27	28	29	30		

April						2004
Su	Mo	Tu	We	Th	Fr	Sa
				1	2	3
4	5	6	7	8	9	10
11	12	13	14	15	16	17
18	19	20	21	22	23	24
25	26	27	28	29	30	

October						2004
Su	Mo	Tu	We	Th	Fr	Sa
					1	2
3	4	5	6	7	8	9
10	11	12	13	14	15	16
17	18	19	20	21	22	23
24	25	26	27	28	29	30
31						

May						2004
Su	Mo	Tu	We	Th	Fr	Sa
						1
2	3	4	5	6	7	8
9	10	11	12	13	14	15
16	17	18	19	20	21	22
23	24	25	26	27	28	29
30	31					

November						2004
Su	Mo	Tu	We	Th	Fr	Sa
	1	2	3	4	5	6
7	8	9	10	11	12	13
14	15	16	17	18	19	20
21	22	23	24	25	26	27
28	29	30				

June						2004
Su	Mo	Tu	We	Th	Fr	Sa
		1	2	3	4	5
6	7	8	9	10	11	12
13	14	15	16	17	18	19
20	21	22	23	24	25	26
27	28	29	30			

December						2004
Su	Mo	Tu	We	Th	Fr	Sa
			1	2	3	4
5	6	7	8	9	10	11
12	13	14	15	16	17	18
19	20	21	22	23	24	25
26	27	28	29	30	31	

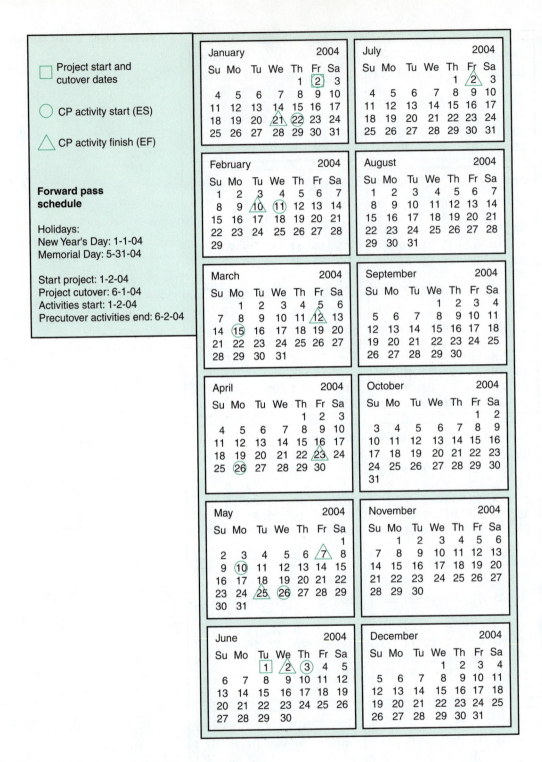

□ Project start and cutover dates

◯ CP activity start (ES)

△ CP activity finish (EF)

Forward pass schedule

Holidays:
New Year's Day: 1-1-04
Memorial Day: 5-31-04

Start project: 1-2-04
Project cutover: 6-1-04
Activities start: 1-2-04
Precutover activities end: 6-2-04

January	2004
Su Mo Tu We Th Fr Sa
1 ② 3
4   5   6   7   8   9   10
11 12 13 14 15 16 17
18 19 20 21 22 23 24
25 26 27 28 29 30 31

| February | 2004 |
| Su Mo Tu We Th Fr Sa |
| 1   2   3   4   5   6   7 |
| 8   9   10 11 12 13 14 |
| 15 16 17 18 19 20 21 |
| 22 23 24 25 26 27 28 |
| 29 |

| March | 2004 |
| Su Mo Tu We Th Fr Sa |
| 1   2   3   4   5   6 |
| 7   8   9   10 11 12 13 |
| 14 15 16 17 18 19 20 |
| 21 22 23 24 25 26 27 |
| 28 29 30 31 |

| April | 2004 |
| Su Mo Tu We Th Fr Sa |
| 1   2   3 |
| 4   5   6   7   8   9   10 |
| 11 12 13 14 15 16 17 |
| 18 19 20 21 22 23 24 |
| 25 26 27 28 29 30 |

| May | 2004 |
| Su Mo Tu We Th Fr Sa |
| 1 |
| 2   3   4   5   6   7   8 |
| 9   10 11 12 13 14 15 |
| 16 17 18 19 20 21 22 |
| 23 24 25 26 27 28 29 |
| 30 31 |

| June | 2004 |
| Su Mo Tu We Th Fr Sa |
| 1   2   3   4   5 |
| 6   7   8   9   10 11 12 |
| 13 14 15 16 17 18 19 |
| 20 21 22 23 24 25 26 |
| 27 28 29 30 |

| July | 2004 |
| Su Mo Tu We Th Fr Sa |
| 1 ② 3 |
| 4   5   6   7   8   9   10 |
| 11 12 13 14 15 16 17 |
| 18 19 20 21 22 23 24 |
| 25 26 27 28 29 30 31 |

| August | 2004 |
| Su Mo Tu We Th Fr Sa |
| 1   2   3   4   5   6   7 |
| 8   9   10 11 12 13 14 |
| 15 16 17 18 19 20 21 |
| 22 23 24 25 26 27 28 |
| 29 30 31 |

| September | 2004 |
| Su Mo Tu We Th Fr Sa |
| 1   2   3   4 |
| 5   6   7   8   9   10 11 |
| 12 13 14 15 16 17 18 |
| 19 20 21 22 23 24 25 |
| 26 27 28 29 30 |

| October | 2004 |
| Su Mo Tu We Th Fr Sa |
| 1   2 |
| 3   4   5   6   7   8   9 |
| 10 11 12 13 14 15 16 |
| 17 18 19 20 21 22 23 |
| 24 25 26 27 28 29 30 |
| 31 |

| November | 2004 |
| Su Mo Tu We Th Fr Sa |
| 1   2   3   4   5   6 |
| 7   8   9   10 11 12 13 |
| 14 15 16 17 18 19 20 |
| 21 22 23 24 25 26 27 |
| 28 29 30 |

| December | 2004 |
| Su Mo Tu We Th Fr Sa |
| 1   2   3   4 |
| 5   6   7   8   9   10 11 |
| 12 13 14 15 16 17 18 |
| 19 20 21 22 23 24 25 |
| 26 27 28 29 30 31 |

Example 12–6b. Forward pass schedule calendar worksheet.

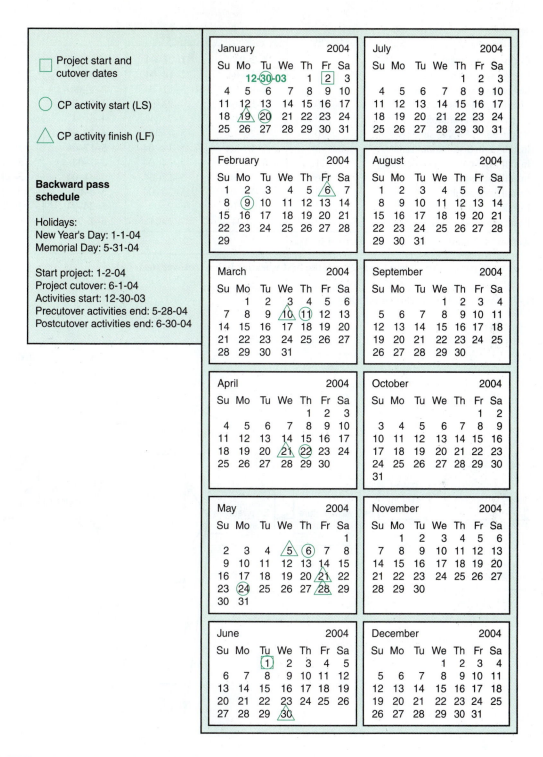

□ Project start and cutover dates

◯ CP activity start (LS)

△ CP activity finish (LF)

Backward pass schedule

Holidays:
New Year's Day: 1-1-04
Memorial Day: 5-31-04

Start project: 1-2-04
Project cutover: 6-1-04
Activities start: 12-30-03
Precutover activities end: 5-28-04
Postcutover activities end: 6-30-04

| January | 2004 |
| July | 2004 |

Example 12–6c. Backward pass schedule calendar worksheet.

CP	Activity	Duration	ES	EF	LS	LF
X	Define requirements	14	**1–2–04**	**1–21–04**	12–30–03	1–19–04
X	Design system	14	**1–22–04**	**2–10–04**	1–20–04	2–6–04
X	Select system	23	**2–11–04**	3–12–04	2–9–04	**3–10–04**
X	Manufacture system	30	3–15–04	4–23–04	**3–11–04**	**4–21–04**
	Precutover preparation	40	3–15–04	5–7–04	**4–5–04**	**5–28–04**
X	Ship/receive PBX & stations	10	4–26–04	5–7–04	**4–22–04**	**5–5–04**
	Install main distribution frame	5	5–10–04	5–14–04	**5–17–04**	**5–21–04**
	Install PBX common equipment	11	5–10–04	5–24–04	**5–7–04**	**5–21–04**
	Install backbone wiring	6	5–10–04	5–17–04	**5–14–04**	**5–21–04**
X	Install horizontal wiring	12	5–10–04	5–25–04	**5–6–04**	**5–21–04**
X	Install station equipment	5	5–26–04	6–2–04	**5–24–04**	**5–28–04**
X	Postcutover activities	22	6–3–04	7–2–04	**6–1–04**	**6–30–04**
	Activity CP total	**130**				

Backward pass work completion date set to 5–28–04, the first workday before cutover (6–1–04).

Example 12–7. Project technical calendar schedule worksheet.

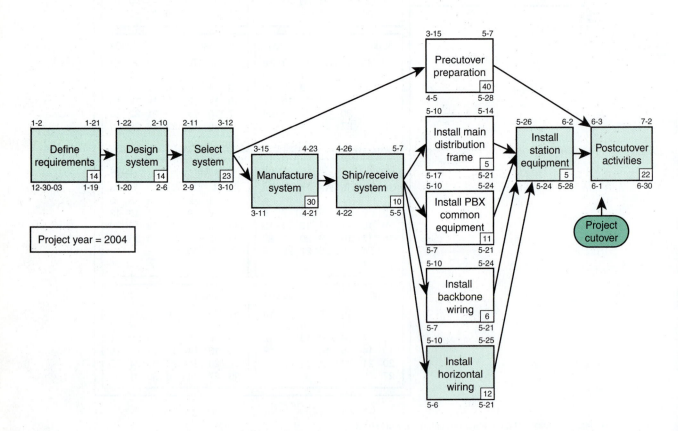

Example 12–8. Technical schedule project network diagram.

Activity	Start	Finish
Define requirements	1–2–04	1–21–04
Design system	1–22–04	2–10–04
Select system	2–11–04	3–10–04
Manufacture system	3–11–04	4–21–04
Precutover preparation	3–11–04	5–28–04
Ship/receive PBX & stations	4–22–04	5–5–04
Install main distribution frame	5–17–04	5–21–04
Install PBX common equipment	5–7–04	5–21–04
Install backbone wiring	5–14–04	5–21–04
Install horizontal wiring	5–6–04	5–21–04
Install station equipment	5–24–04	5–28–04
Postcutover activities	6–1–04	6–30–04

Project cutover date: 6–1–04

Example 12–9. Final project schedule.

The forward and backward pass technical calendar schedules have been consolidated into Example 12–7 and into Example 12–8, a project network diagram.

When the forward and backward technical calendar schedule is reviewed, it can be seen that the forward precutover schedule starts on the first project day (1–2–04) but ends late (6–2–04), while the backward precutover schedule ends on the last workday (5–28–04) before cutover but provides a project start date of 12–30–03.

In the real world, project start dates and cutover dates, are normally fixed dates and a project schedule must meet requirements. In our example, there are 106 normal workdays available to complete 108 workdays of work. To shorten the precutover path length, it will be necessary to select a CP activity and either work overtime or add additional resources to complete it two days earlier than the initial (forward pass) schedule. Therefore, a decision must be made regarding which CP activity will be shortened by two days.

Deliverable 6: Final Project Schedule

Example 12–8 summarizes all the information needed to select and shorten a CP activity for the PBX project. Note that each CP activity has a float of two workdays, which is the number of workdays that the initial schedule is late. This result is a direct outcome of setting the desired LF of the last precutover activity to the last workday before the cutover date. If any CP activity is selected, and work is started on its ES date and completed on its LF date, all suc-

cessor activities can use their late schedules (LS and LF) to complete the precutover activities on the last workday before the cutover date.

As is frequently the case with real world problems, there are several correct solutions, so the decision maker must exercise judgment. In the real world, the decision maker must have a good understanding of both technical and project management requirements when making the final decision. The following provides one solution but is not the only solution that would result in a good project schedule.

The Select System CP activity will be shortened, which will be done by authorizing the use of overtime to finish it by its LF date of March 10. The Select System activity requires a fairly large number of workdays to complete (23) and is an activity that is under the direct control of the project manager. It will be started on its ES date (February 11) and will be completed on March 10. All activities taking place after this activity will use their backward schedule dates and all activities completed before the select system activity will use their forward schedule dates. Example 12–7 uses bolding to indicate this selected schedule; the final schedule is shown in Examples 12–9 and 12–10.

Work schedules used in business discussions should have a single starting and ending date, and the final schedule in Example 12–9 meets this requirement. The final schedule is shown in the technical schedule table (Example 12–7) by bolding the final schedule dates. Good judgment, primarily gained through experience, is the key factor in modifying a schedule to meet project requirements. The PBX example illustrates the mechanics of modifying a schedule, but any schedule modification will only be as good as the judgment used in making the changes.

WHAT IF ... ?

The PBX example provided a fairly straightforward example of using CPM to establish and implement a schedule, matching the project's start date and cutover date requirements. For discussion purposes, it will be assumed that completing a project on time means that it is completed on the last workday prior to the cutover date. In general, there are three potential outcomes when a CPM analysis is made of a project and an initial schedule is calculated:

1. The project will be completed after the last workday.
2. The project will be completed on the last workday.
3. The project will be completed prior to the last workday.

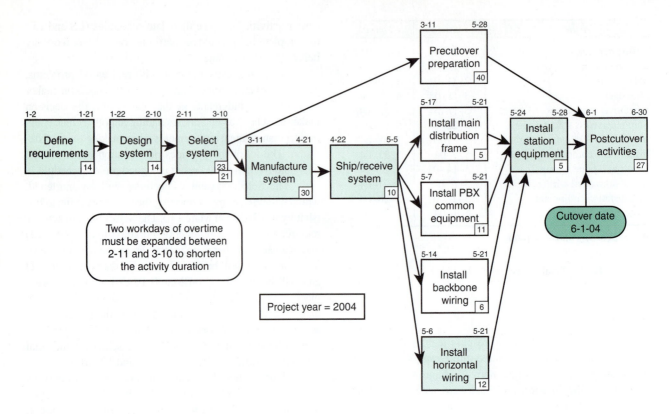

Example 12–10. Final project schedule.

The PBX example was an example of the first outcome, which was resolved by selecting a CP activity, applying additional labor resources to shorten the activity's duration, and completing the project on the last workday before cutover. If the initial forward pass calculation had resulted in a schedule that completed the precutover activities on the last workday before the cutover date, no further action would have been required and the forward and backward calendar schedules would be identical. This case can be viewed as a perfect planning solution on the first try.

However, what happens when the initial forward pass shows that the project will finish early? Finishing early may sound very attractive, but there are some potential downsides. If the installed equipment is left unattended after the installation work has been completed, the potential for vandalism, theft, or inadvertent damage exists and security arrangements must be made. In addition, if the work is completed early, some of the system installers may be reassigned. Therefore, they would not be available during the system's cutover

phase. On the other hand, when the work crew is scheduled to work up to the cutover date, it is relatively easy to continue their assignment through the first few days of cutover to handle any unexpected technical problems.

It is usually desirable to have all projects finish on the last workday before cutover. This project outcome will be referred to as finishing on time. In the PBX example, we modified the schedule of a late project so that it would finish on time. If the project ended early instead of finishing late, we could have inserted additional float into the Ship/Receive activity (refer to Example 12–10). Selection of this activity has the advantage of not affecting the work schedule of other labor-oriented activities.

Multiple schedules can be developed to address late or early project schedules and, in many instances, there are several correct solutions. Which is the best schedule? The answer is primarily a matter of opinion because good results can frequently be obtained by using different schedules.

Another Scheduling Tool

A calendar approach was used to establish a schedule for the project. This approach involved using a calendar and knowledge of the CP activities. Another approach is to use Microsoft Excel's WORKDAY and NETWORKDAY functions to identify ES, EF, LS, and LF dates. This approach is discussed in Appendix A, and an Excel scheduling solution for the PBX example has been provided on the CD provided with the text.

WRAPPING UP THE PROJECT

The information contained in Figures 12–13, 12–14, 12–15, 12–16a, 12–16b, 12–16c, 12–17, and 12–18, as well as in Tables 12–7, 12–8, 12–9, and 12–10 would be used for any presentations, reports, or communications regarding the PBX project plan. Technical personnel may want to see the raw data used to create the schedules, and business management would be primarily interested in the overview information.

SUMMARY

This summary is organized to correspond with the learning objectives found at the beginning of the chapter.

1. Earlier approaches to project planning relied heavily upon the use of Gantt charts and tables to show project activities. This approach did not show the relationships among all project activities and created large volumes of paper as project sizes increased. The project network diagram approach identifies the relationships among various project activities. When coupled with today's PC-based project planning software, it can quickly show macroviews and microviews of the entire project plan or subelements of it. The project network also provides a means to quickly calculate project schedules and vary project activities to change existing project schedules for meeting new requirements.

2. Both CPM and PERT project planning methods are network-based approaches to project planning. CPM is a deterministic approach that assumes that duration times can be accurately estimated based on past experience. PERT utilizes a statistical probabilistic approach to determining activity durations. The CPM approach is best suited to engineering projects where an experience factor exists, while the PERT approach is best suited for a research environment where the options for any given activity will not be known until the previous activity has been completed. Telecommunications projects would normally use the CPM approach.

3. Rectangles are used to identify nodes in a project network diagram and the nodes are connected with arrows. Within each rectangle, a unique activity ID is displayed, along with the duration period needed to complete the activity. Above the rectangle/node, ES and EF dates are displayed, while LS and LF values are displayed below the rectangle/node. The arrows that connect nodes indicate the relationship between the nodes, the arrowhead touches the successor activity for the node touching the tail of the connection arrow. Successor activities cannot be started until all their predecessor activities have been completed.

4. In a project network diagram, there are multiple paths leading from the start node to the end node. The path with the longest duration time (the sum of the activity durations in the path) is called the critical path. To shorten a project, the duration times of critical path activities must be shortened. This can be done by adding more resources to complete the activity. Shortening the time duration of noncritical activities does not affect the time for completing the project.

5. The four step approach for identifying a project network diagram's critical path consists of: 1) calculate forward pass ES and EF values, 2) calculate backward pass LS and LF values, 3) identify critical path activities (zero float), and 4) translate the activity duration times into a project schedule. The last step is required to effectively utilize the information generated from the project network diagram.

6. The critical path of a project network diagram is based on comparing the forward and backward calculation values (ES, EF, LS, and LF) to determine its float (slack). Float = LS – ES or float = LF – EF, where both calculations have the same result. If an activity has zero float, it is a critical path activity and must be completed on time or the project schedule will change.

7. Activities can have zero float or positive float based on the float calculation. If an activity has zero float, it must be completed on time or the project's overall schedule will be affected. If an activity has float (a positive number), work on the activity can be delayed by the amount of float without affecting the overall project schedule.

From a project planning perspective, this allows resources in noncritical activities (positive float) to be used elsewhere until the float has been used up.

8. Top-down planning is based on identifying the major elements of a plan and developing the supporting elements based on meeting the requirements identified in the major elements. Business planning typically uses a top-down approach, in which business objectives are defined broadly and strategies that allow the top-level objectives to be met are developed. Bottom-up planning is based on examining detailed plans, consolidating them into logical groupings, and developing a top level strategy based on the logical groupings. Top-down planning is more commonly used in project planning, but bottom-up thinking is a critical element in determining the viability of top-down plans.

9. Manual CPM deliverables consist of: 1) a project objectives and constraints description, 2) a project network diagram, 3) a work breakdown structure (WBS) worksheet, 4) a project workday worksheet, 5) a calendar, 6) a project schedule worksheet, and 7) a final project schedule. The final project schedule is the primary deliverable used to provide information to business management.

10. The WBS worksheet provides a way of organizing information to the tasks that are part of an activity. All the activity tasks must be completed for an activity to be completed, and it may be appropriate to use the CPM approach to calculate an activity's duration. The activity duration will be used to identify the critical activity nodes in a project network diagram. The tasks and activities shown on a WBS worksheet require a detailed knowledge of the project requirements—a knowledge base that is normally provided by technical specialists in technology projects.

11. Once the critical path has been identified, the critical path node durations are used to identify their individual starting (ES) and ending times (EF) in a forward pass through the calendar. If nonworking days are involved (e.g., holidays and weekends), these days are not counted during the schedule identification process. The calculated completion date is compared to the project's requirements. If the dates are identical, the forward pass schedule becomes the backward pass schedule, and no further work is required. If the calculated and target completion dates differ, the critical path activity durations must be shortened or lengthened to complete the project on the target completion date.

KEY TERMS AND CONCEPTS

The language of telecommunications management is multifaceted and includes words and phrases from managerial, technological, accounting, regulatory, and other business areas. The definitions of these key terms and concepts can be found within the chapter and in the glossary.

Activity Duration	Float Time (Slack Time)	Project Network Diagram
Backward Pass	Forward Pass	Successor Activity
Bottom-Up Planning	Gantt Chart	Tasks
CPM (Critical Path Method)	LF (Late Finish)	Technical Schedule
Critical Path (CP)	LS (Late Start)	Top-Down Planning
Deliverable	Milestone	Work Breakdown Structure (WBS)
EF (Early Finish)	PERT (Program Evaluation and Review	
ES (Early Start)	Technique)	
Final Schedule	Predecessor Activity	

REVIEW

The following questions are open-ended—predefined answers are not included as part of the text. The purpose of these questions is to allow the readers to test themselves on the chapter material.

1. Compare the use of Gantt charts and project network diagrams for project management purposes.

2. Explain the basic difference between CPM and PERT project management tools.

3. Why were network-based project management tools not commonly used prior to the 1950s?

4. How are the CP nodes identified in a project network diagram?

5. Verify the existence of four CP paths through Figure 12–4 (student graduation project example) by calculating EF, ES, LS, LF, and activity float values.

6. What is meant by cutover?

7. Why won't reducing the float of a non-CP activity to zero have any effect on the completion time of a project?

8. Explain the difference between the top-down and bottom-up planning approaches.

9. What is meant by a *mini-CPM*?

10. Outline the five-step manual CPM process.

11. Explain how a project that requires 200 workdays of time to complete can be completed in less than 200 calendar workdays.

12. What is the difference between a technical schedule and a final schedule?

MULTIPLE CHOICE

1. Projects include the following: (Select all that apply.)
   a. specific starting and ending times
   b. final outcome
   c. limited resources
   d. interrelated activities
   e. None of the above.

2. CPM stands for _____.
   a. constant primary motivation
   b. critical project methods
   c. critical path method
   d. clear, perfect, manual
   e. *program* *evaluation* and *review* *technique*

3. In CPM, an activity that has float will not affect the project schedule if _____.
   a. it is started earlier than its ES time
   b. it has a long duration
   c. it is completed before its LF time
   d. it is started later than its LF time
   e. it sinks

4. During forward pass calculations, an activity that has multiple predecessors _____.
   a. uses the largest ES predecessor value
   b. uses the smallest EF predecessor value
   c. uses the largest LF predecessor value
   d. uses the smallest LF predecessor value
   e. None of the above.

5. During backward pass calculations, an activity that has multiple successors _____.
   a. uses the largest ES successor value
   b. uses the smallest EF successor value
   c. uses the largest LF successor value

d. uses the smallest LF successor value
   e. None of the above.

6. Between two nodes in a CPM network diagram, the head of the arrow touches a predecessor node.
   a. true
   b. false

7. Float is calculated by _____.
   a. subtracting EF from ES
   b. subtracting ES from EF
   c. subtracting ES from LS
   d. subtracting LS from LF
   e. None of the above.

8. It is important to eliminate the float in all project network diagram nodes.
   a. true
   b. false

9. *Zero float* means the same thing as *zero slack*.
   a. true
   b. false

10. When a project network node has float, it is a critical path node.
    a. true
    b. false

11. When a project network node has zero float, it is not used in any more calculations.
    a. true
    b. false

12. A project network node can only have a single successor node.
    a. true
    b. false

13. When the critical path has been identified, the project can be shortened by _____.
    a. shortening the duration of a nonzero float node
    b. increasing the duration of a nonzero float node
    c. shortening the duration of a zero float node
    d. increasing the duration of a zero float node
    e. None of the above.

14. Top-down planning _____.
    a. brings long-range plans to reality by budgeting
    b. initially takes place at the macrolevel, then addresses macro details
    c. initially takes place at the macrolevel, then addresses micro details
    d. initially takes place at the microlevel, then addresses micro details
    e. initially takes place at the microlevel, then addresses the macrolevel

15. The critical path in a project network diagram is the path with the longest total time duration.
    a. true
    b. false

16. The critical path duration is the minimum amount of time required to complete the project.
    a. true
    b. false

17. An activity's EF is _____.
    a. the earliest time that it can be completed
    b. the latest time it can be completed
    c. the latest time it can be started
    d. the earliest time that it can be started
    e. None of the above.

18. An activity's ES is _____.
    a. the latest time that it can be completed
    b. the latest time that it can be started
    c. the earliest time that it can be started
    d. None of the above.

19. An activity's LS is _____ and still complete the project on time.
    a. the earliest time that it can be completed
    b. the latest time that it can be completed

c. the latest time that it can be started
d. the earliest time that it can be started
e. None of the above

20. An activity's LF is _____ and still complete the project on time.
    a. the earliest time that it can be completed
    b. the latest time that it can be completed
    c. the latest time that it can be started
    d. the earliest time that it can be started
    e. None of the above

21. Cutover is _____.
    a. when the cabling is cut into the proper lengths
    b. forest land with trees cut down
    c. the start of each activity node
    d. the day the project must be ready for full operational use by the end users
    e. None of the above.

22. An activity's ES is 46 and its duration is 23. Its EF is _____.
    a. 45
    b. 47
    c. 67
    d. 68
    e. 69

23. What is the EF of an activity that has a duration of 38 and has three predecessor activities that have EFs of 29, 30, and 42?
    a. 67
    b. 68
    c. 78
    d. 79
    e. 80

24. What is the EF of an activity that has a duration of 23 and has two predecessor activities that have EFs of 33 and 34?
    a. 57
    b. 58
    c. 59
    d. 24
    e. None of the above.

25. What is the LS of an activity that has a duration of 15 and has two successor activities that have LSs of 56 and 57?

    a. 68

    b. 69

    c. 70

    d. 71

    e. None of the above.

26. What is the LS of an activity that has a duration of 15 and has two successor activities that have LSs of 56 and 57?

    a. 39

    b. 40

    c. 41

    d. 72

    e. None of the above.

27. When using a calendar to calculate a preliminary completion date, the holidays and weekends are subtracted from the total calculated workday duration.

    a. true

    b. false

28. When using a calendar to calculate a preliminary completion date, the holidays and weekends are added to the total calculated workday duration.

    a. true

    b. false

PRACTICE

The following provides two CPM problems that are similar to the ones covered in the chapter's tutorial and case study sections. Problem 1 requires the calculation of forward and backward pass workday values (ES, EF, LS, and LF) and problem 2 converts problem 1's workday values into a project schedule.

    Both problems should be completed before proceeding to the Case Study problem that follows.

1. This is a CPM workday calculation problem that is similar to the ones covered within the chapter and in the Case Study.

• Using project network diagram Figure 12–13 on page 323, calculate forward and backward pass project days showing ES, EF, LS, and LF values on the activity nodes. Next, identify CP activities by placing an X in CP nodes.

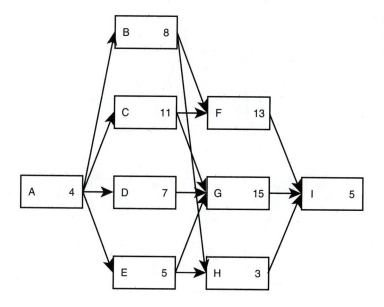

Figure 12–13. CPM workday practice problem.

- Complete Table 12–7 (page 324) and calculate the float for each activity.

A solution is included (Figure 12–14 and Table 12–8) so you can verify your answers.

2. The workday calculations completed for problem 1 must be converted into a calendar schedule by identifying the specific dates associated with project activity workday values (ES, EF, LS, and LF). Allowances must be made for any holidays and weekends because normal work is only done on regular workdays. Allowances can be made by adding days to offset the lost work time.

The project will start on May 17, 2004, and must be ready to use on July 6, 2004, the first workday following the 4th of July weekend. July 4 falls on a Sunday, and it is assumed that the holiday observation takes place on July 5. The workday input is from problem 1 and a 2004 calendar is provided (Figure 12–15 on page 325).

- Develop a technical schedule for the project. Identify the dates for problem 1 forward pass workdays (ES and EF). Next, identify the dates for problem 1 backward pass workdays (LS and LF). Remember to start with the desired project completion date.

TABLE 12–7 CPM Summary

Activity	Duration	ES	EF	LS	LF	Float
A	4					
B	8					
C	11					
D	7					
E	5					
F	13					
G	15					
H	3					
I	5					
CP total						

TABLE 12–8 CPM Summary

Activity	Duration	ES	EF	LS	LF	Float
A	4	1	4	1	4	0
B	8	5	12	10	17	5
C	11	5	15	5	15	0
D	7	5	11	9	15	4
E	5	5	9	11	15	6
F	13	16	28	18	30	2
G	15	16	30	16	30	0
H	3	13	15	28	30	15
I	4	31	35	31	35	0
CP total	34					

Figure 12–14. CPM workday practice problem solution.

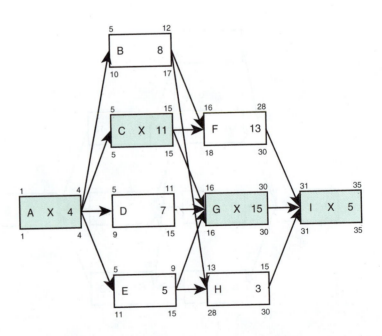

CHAPTER 12

Figure 12–15.   2004 Calendar.

January						2004
Su	Mo	Tu	We	Th	Fr	Sa
				1	2	3
4	5	6	7	8	9	10
11	12	13	14	15	16	17
18	19	20	21	22	23	24
25	26	27	28	29	30	31

July						2004
Su	Mo	Tu	We	Th	Fr	Sa
				1	2	3
4	5	6	7	8	9	10
11	12	13	14	15	16	17
18	19	20	21	22	23	24
25	26	27	28	29	30	31

February						2004
Su	Mo	Tu	We	Th	Fr	Sa
1	2	3	4	5	6	7
8	9	10	11	12	13	14
15	16	17	18	19	20	21
22	23	24	25	26	27	28
29						

August						2004
Su	Mo	Tu	We	Th	Fr	Sa
1	2	3	4	5	6	7
8	9	10	11	12	13	14
15	16	17	18	19	20	21
22	23	24	25	26	27	28
29	30	31				

March						2004
Su	Mo	Tu	We	Th	Fr	Sa
	1	2	3	4	5	6
7	8	9	10	11	12	13
14	15	16	17	18	19	20
21	22	23	24	25	26	27
28	29	30	31			

September						2004
Su	Mo	Tu	We	Th	Fr	Sa
			1	2	3	4
5	6	7	8	9	10	11
12	13	14	15	16	17	18
19	20	21	22	23	24	25
26	27	28	29	30		

April						2004
Su	Mo	Tu	We	Th	Fr	Sa
				1	2	3
4	5	6	7	8	9	10
11	12	13	14	15	16	17
18	19	20	21	22	23	24
25	26	27	28	29	30	

October						2004
Su	Mo	Tu	We	Th	Fr	Sa
					1	2
3	4	5	6	7	8	9
10	11	12	13	14	15	16
17	18	19	20	21	22	23
24	25	26	27	28	29	30
31						

May						2004
Su	Mo	Tu	We	Th	Fr	Sa
						1
2	3	4	5	6	7	8
9	10	11	12	13	14	15
16	17	18	19	20	21	22
23	24	25	26	27	28	29
30	31					

November						2004
Su	Mo	Tu	We	Th	Fr	Sa
	1	2	3	4	5	6
7	8	9	10	11	12	13
14	15	16	17	18	19	20
21	22	23	24	25	26	27
28	29	30				

June						2004
Su	Mo	Tu	We	Th	Fr	Sa
		1	2	3	4	5
6	7	8	9	10	11	12
13	14	15	16	17	18	19
20	21	22	23	24	25	26
27	28	29	30			

December						2004
Su	Mo	Tu	We	Th	Fr	Sa
			1	2	3	4
5	6	7	8	9	10	11
12	13	14	15	16	17	18
19	20	21	22	23	24	25
26	27	28	29	30	31	

- Consolidate the calendar information onto the technical schedule table that has been provided (Table 12–9, page 326).
- Select a suitable final schedule that meets project requirements and complete the final schedule table (Table 12–10, page 326).

Solutions are included so that you can verify your answers. A technical schedule project network diagram is also provided to assist in determining non-CP dates. See Figures 12–16, 12–17 and 12–18 (pages 327–329) and Table 12–11 on page 329. The final schedule solution is further explained, and the final diagram (Figure 12–19) and table (Table 12–12) are shown on page 330.

FINAL SCHEDULE SOLUTION

The forward pass of the technical schedule showed that the project would be completed on July 6, the cutover date. Therefore, the project could not be implemented until the following day, July 7. However, the project must finish one day earlier to meet the cutover date requirement. The backward pass provided a schedule that finished on time but had to start on May 17, one workday before the project start date. Several options exist, and the one shown in the final schedule is one in which overtime was applied to activity I to shorten its duration by one day—from five workdays to four workdays. This allowed activity I to finish on July 2, the last workday before the project cutover date. If other delays are encountered, the weekend is available for additional overtime. If an earlier activity had been selected, it would have been necessary to follow the same procedures as in the chapter's PBX example.

Table 12–12 is the one that would be used to explain the project's schedule to business management (minus the bold highlighting). The final schedule network diagram is shown in Figure 12–26.

CASE STUDY

The following provides an abbreviated description of an 800-station LAN implementation project and follows the same procedures discussed in this chapter. The full description of the LAN project plus an Excel template is available on the CD. The LAN project is scheduled to start on January 2, 2004, and cutover on July 6, 2004. Holidays (nonworking days) are Memorial Day (5–31–04) and Independence Day, which will be observed as a nonworking day on 7–5–04 because July 4 falls on a Sunday.

1. Using project network diagram Figure 12–20 and workday Table 12–13,
   - calculate forward and backward pass project days showing ES, EF, LS, and LF values on the network diagram's activity nodes and
   - identify CP activities by placing an X in CP nodes (The solution—Figure 12–21 and Table 12–14—shades the activities and uses a bold X.)
2. Complete the workday table and calculate the float for each activity.
3. Using the 2004 Calendar (Figure 12–22),
   - determine the forward pass and backward pass project schedules for the CP activities and noncritical path activities and show these dates on the project network diagram,

TABLE 12–9 Technical Schedule

Cutover: July 6, 2004 (Tuesday)						
CP	Activity	Duration	ES	EF	LS	LF
A	4					
B	8					
C	11					
D	7					
E	5					
F	13					
G	15					
H	3					
I	4					
Activity CP total						

TABLE 12–10 Final (Management) Schedule

Cutover: July 6, 2004 (Tuesday)		
Activity	Start	Finish
A		
B		
C		
D		
E		
F		
G		
H		
I		

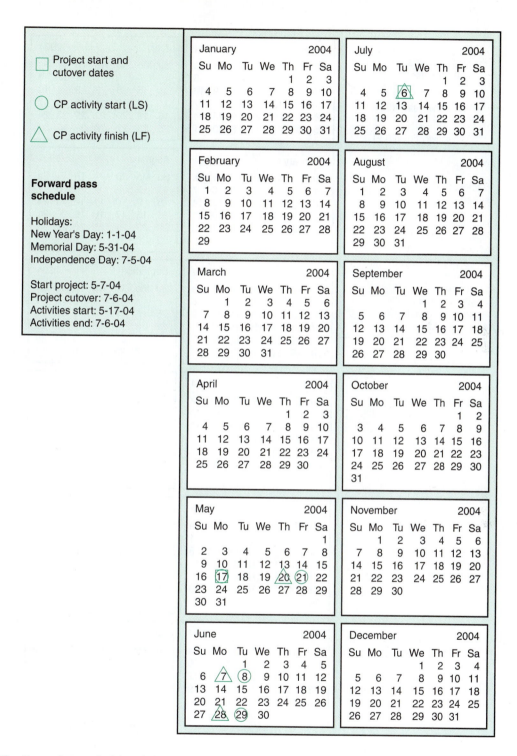

Figure 12–16. Forward pass schedule solution.

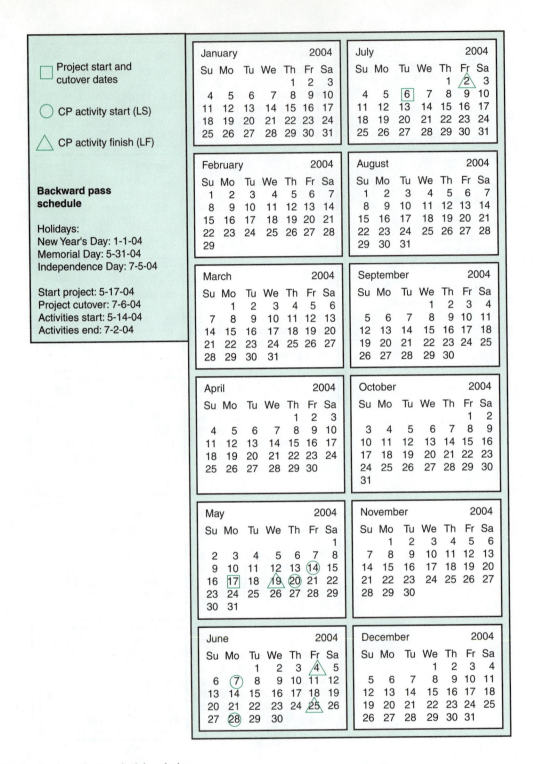

Figure 12–17. Backward pass schedule solution.

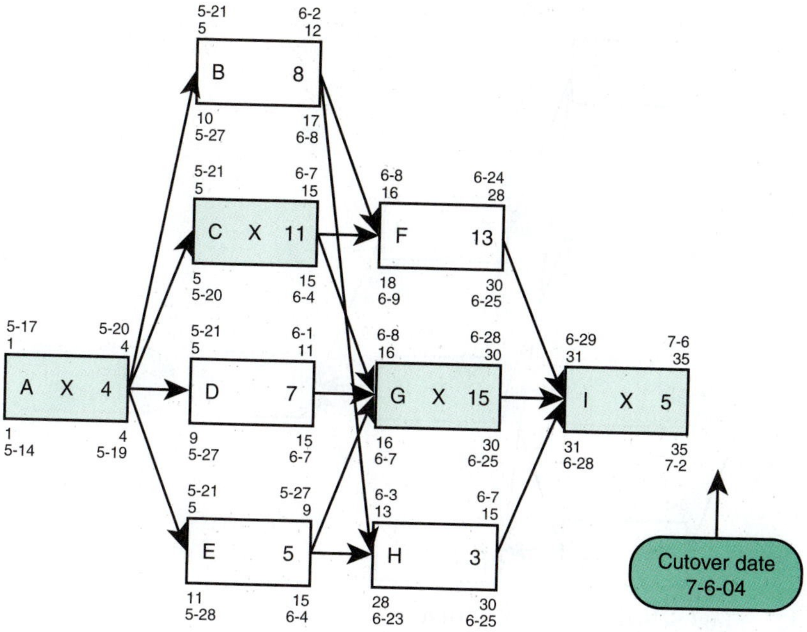

Figure 12–18. Technical schedule network solution.

TABLE 12–11 Technical Schedule Table Solution

			Cutover: July 6, 2004 (Tuesday)			
CP	Activity	Duration	ES	EF	LS	LF
X	**A**	**4**	**5–17–04**	**5–20–04**	**5–14–04**	**5–19–04**
	B	8	5–21–04	6–2–04	5–27–04	6–8–04
X	**C**	**11**	**5–21–04**	**6–7–04**	**5–20–04**	**6–4–04**
	D	7	5–21–04	6–1–04	5–29–03	6–4–04
	E	5	5–21–04	5–27–04	5–28–04	6–4–04
	F	13	6–8–04	6–24–04	6–9–04	6–25–04
X	**G**	**15**	**6–8–04**	**6–28–04**	**6–7–04**	**6–25–04**
	H	3	6–3–04	6–7–04	6–23–04	6–25–04
X	**I**	**4**	**6–29–04**	**7–6–04**	**6–28–04**	**7–2–04**
Activity CP total		**34**				

Bold dates show final schedule recommendation.

Figure 12–19. Final schedule network solution.

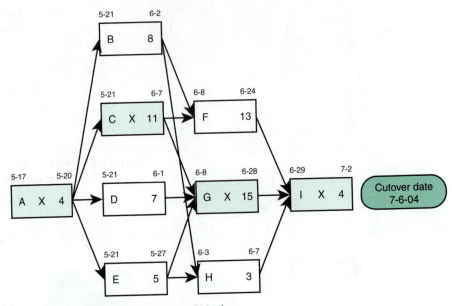

TABLE 12–12   Final Schedule Table Solution

Cutover: July 6, 2004 (Tuesday)		
Activity	*Start*	*Finish*
A	**5–17–04**	**5–20–04**
B	5–21–04	6–2–04
C	**5–21–04**	**6–7–04**
D	5–21–04	6–1–04
E	5–21–04	5–27–04
F	6–8–04	6–24–04
G	**6–8–04**	**6–28–04**
H	6–3–04	6–7–04
I	**6–29–04**	**7–2–04**

Bold activities indicate CP activities.

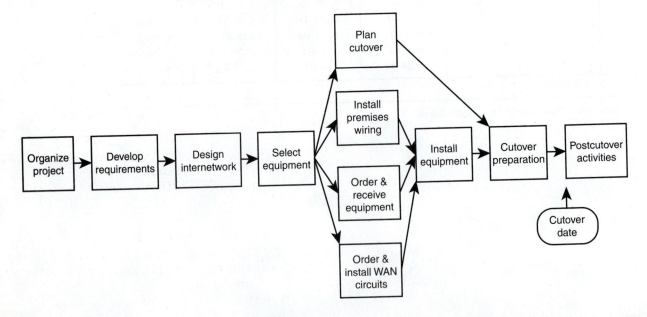

Figure 12–20. Project network diagram.

TABLE 12–13   Workday Table

| | | | Cutover: July 6, 2004 (Tuesday) | | | | | |
CP	Activity	Duration	ES	EF	LS	LF	Float
	Organize project	13					
	Develop requirements	16					
	Design internetwork	22					
	Select equipment	25					
	Cutover planning	15					
	Install premises wiring	26					
	Order & receive equipment	18					
	Order & install WAN circuits	12					
	Install equipment	24					
	Cutover preparation	6					
	Postcutover activities	21					
Activity CP total							

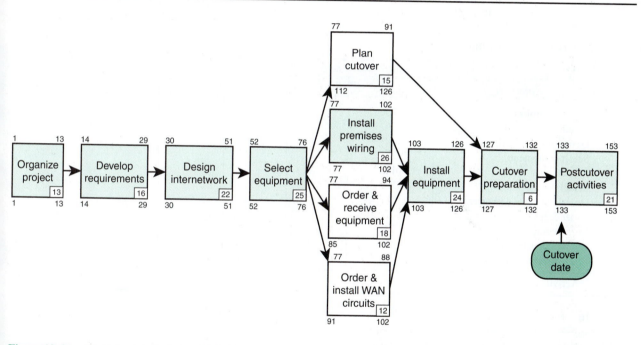

Figure 12–21.   Project network diagram solution.

- complete the technical schedule table (Table 12–15), and
- select an acceptable schedule and complete the final schedule table (Table 12–16). Forward and backward pass schedule solutions are shown in Figures 12–23 and 12–24, respectively. The technical schedule table solution is shown in Table 12–17, and a network diagram is shown in Figure 12–25. The final schedule is further explained, and the final schedule table solution (Table 12–18) and

network diagram solution (Figure 12–26) are shown on page 337.

FINAL SCHEDULE COMMENTS

The technical schedule provides two options: 1) a forward pass schedule that starts on time but finishes two days late (7–7–04), and 2) a backward pass schedule that finishes on time but starts two days early (12–30–03). The desired

TABLE 12–14   Workday Table Solution

			Cutover: July 6, 2004 (Tuesday)				
CP	Activity	Duration	ES	EF	LS	LF	Float
X	**Organize project**	**13**	**1**	**13**	**1**	**13**	**0**
X	**Develop requirements**	**16**	**14**	**29**	**14**	**29**	**0**
X	**Design internetwork**	**22**	**30**	**51**	**30**	**51**	**0**
X	**Select equipment**	**25**	**52**	**76**	**52**	**76**	**0**
	Cutover planning	15	77	91	112	126	35
X	**Install premises wiring**	**26**	**77**	**102**	**77**	**102**	**0**
	Order & receive equipment	18	77	94	85	102	8
	Order & install WAN circuits	12	77	88	91	102	14
X	**Install equipment**	**24**	**103**	**126**	**103**	**126**	**0**
X	**Cutover preparation**	**6**	**127**	**132**	**127**	**132**	**0**
X	**Postcutover activities**	**21**	**133**	**153**	**133**	**153**	**0**

Activity CP total	153	
Precutover activity total	132	

TABLE 12–15   Technical Schedule

			Cutover: July 6, 2004 (Tuesday)			
CP	Activity	Duration	ES	EF	LS	LF
	Organize project	13				
	Develop requirements	16				
	Design internetwork	22				
	Select equipment	25				
	Plan cutover	15				
	Install premises wiring	26				
	Order & receive equipment	18				
	Order & install WAN circuits	12				
	Install equipment	24				
	Cutover preparation	6				
	Postcutover activities	21				

Activity CP total

TABLE 12–16   Final Schedule

	Cutover: July 6, 2004 (Tuesday)	
Activity	Start	Finish
Organize project		
Develop requirements		
Design internetwork		
Select equipment		
Plan cutover		
Install premises wiring		
Order & receive equipment		
Order & install WAN circuits		
Install equipment		
Precutover preparation		
Postcutover activities		

schedule starts on 1–2–04 and completes project work on 7–2–04 to allow the cutover date of 7–6–04 to be met.

The recommended approach is to start with the early (forward pass) schedule and switch over to the late (backward pass) schedule before the end of the project. The schedule shift must take place in a CP activity, which means that the selected activity will use its ES date and LF date. By adding resources (overtime or additional personnel) the project can be finished early (the LF date) to complete the project on time.

Several solutions are possible, but any solution must involve a CP activity. The following solution shortens the *design internetwork* activity by two days (from twenty-two duration days to twenty duration days), which allows the activity to finish on 3–10–04 (its LF

Figure 12–22. 2004 calendar.

January						2004
Su	Mo	Tu	We	Th	Fr	Sa
				1	2	3
4	5	6	7	8	9	10
11	12	13	14	15	16	17
18	19	20	21	22	23	24
25	26	27	28	29	30	31

July						2004
Su	Mo	Tu	We	Th	Fr	Sa
				1	2	3
4	5	6	7	8	9	10
11	12	13	14	15	16	17
18	19	20	21	22	23	24
25	26	27	28	29	30	31

February						2004
Su	Mo	Tu	We	Th	Fr	Sa
1	2	3	4	5	6	7
8	9	10	11	12	13	14
15	16	17	18	19	20	21
22	23	24	25	26	27	28
29						

August						2004
Su	Mo	Tu	We	Th	Fr	Sa
1	2	3	4	5	6	7
8	9	10	11	12	13	14
15	16	17	18	19	20	21
22	23	24	25	26	27	28
29	30	31				

March						2004
Su	Mo	Tu	We	Th	Fr	Sa
	1	2	3	4	5	6
7	8	9	10	11	12	13
14	15	16	17	18	19	20
21	22	23	24	25	26	27
28	29	30	31			

September						2004
Su	Mo	Tu	We	Th	Fr	Sa
			1	2	3	4
5	6	7	8	9	10	11
12	13	14	15	16	17	18
19	20	21	22	23	24	25
26	27	28	29	30		

April						2004
Su	Mo	Tu	We	Th	Fr	Sa
				1	2	3
4	5	6	7	8	9	10
11	12	13	14	15	16	17
18	19	20	21	22	23	24
25	26	27	28	29	30	

October						2004
Su	Mo	Tu	We	Th	Fr	Sa
					1	2
3	4	5	6	7	8	9
10	11	12	13	14	15	16
17	18	19	20	21	22	23
24	25	26	27	28	29	30
31						

May						2004
Su	Mo	Tu	We	Th	Fr	Sa
						1
2	3	4	5	6	7	8
9	10	11	12	13	14	15
16	17	18	19	20	21	22
23	24	25	26	27	28	29
30	31					

November						2004
Su	Mo	Tu	We	Th	Fr	Sa
	1	2	3	4	5	6
7	8	9	10	11	12	13
14	15	16	17	18	19	20
21	22	23	24	25	26	27
28	29	30				

June						2004
Su	Mo	Tu	We	Th	Fr	Sa
		1	2	3	4	5
6	7	8	9	10	11	12
13	14	15	16	17	18	19
20	21	22	23	24	25	26
27	28	29	30			

December						2004
Su	Mo	Tu	We	Th	Fr	Sa
			1	2	3	4
5	6	7	8	9	10	11
12	13	14	15	16	17	18
19	20	21	22	23	24	25
26	27	28	29	30	31	

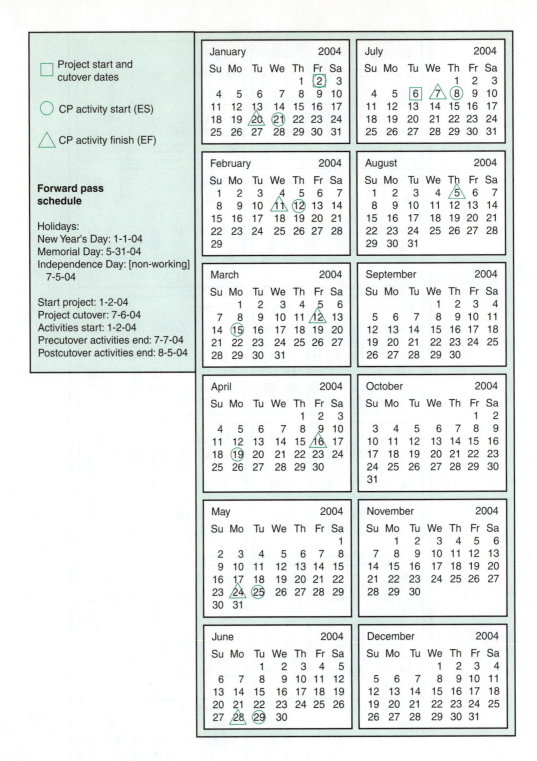

Figure 12–23. Forward pass schedule calendar solution.

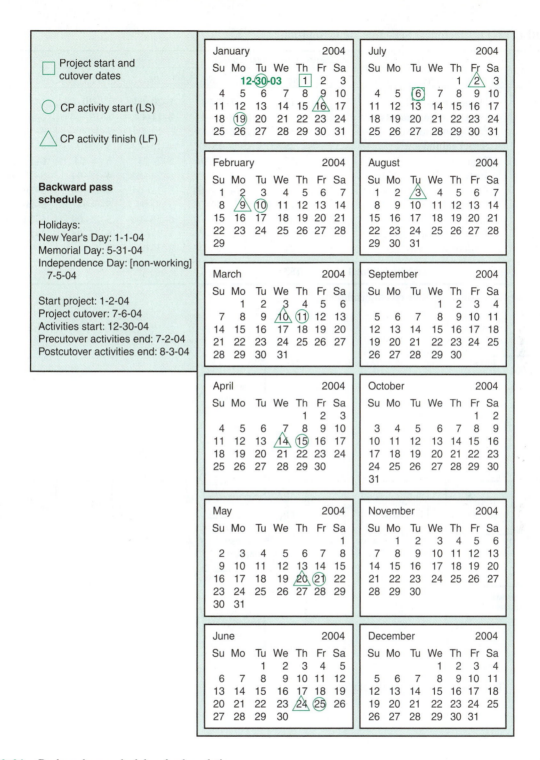

Figure 12–24. Backward pass schedule calendar solution.

TABLE 12–17   Technical Schedule Table Solution

CP	Activity	Duration	ES	EF	LS	LF
	Cutover: July 6, 2004 (Tuesday)					
X	**Organize project**	**13**	**1–2–04**	**1–20–04**	12–30–03	1–16–04
X	**Develop requirements**	**16**	**1–21–04**	**2–11–04**	1–19–04	2–9–04
X	**Design internetwork**	**22**	**2–12–04**	3–12–04	2–10–04	**3–10–04**
X	**Select equipment**	**25**	3–15–04	4–16–04	3–11–04	4–14–04
	Plan cutover	15	**4–19–04**	5–7–04	6–4–04	**6–24–04**
X	**Install premises wiring**	**26**	4–19–04	5–24–04	**4–15–04**	**5–20–04**
	Order & receive equipment	18	4–19–04	5–12–04	**4–27–04**	**5–20–04**
	Order & install WAN circuits	12	4–19–04	5–4–04	**5–5–04**	**5–20–04**
X	**Install equipment**	**24**	5–25–04	6–28–04	**5–21–04**	**6–24–04**
X	**Precutover preparation**	**6**	6–29–04	7–7–04	**6–25–04**	**7–2–04**
X	**Postcutover activities**	**21**	7–8–04	8–5–04	**7–6–04**	**8–3–04**
	Activity CP total	**153**				

Bold dates show final schedule recommendation.

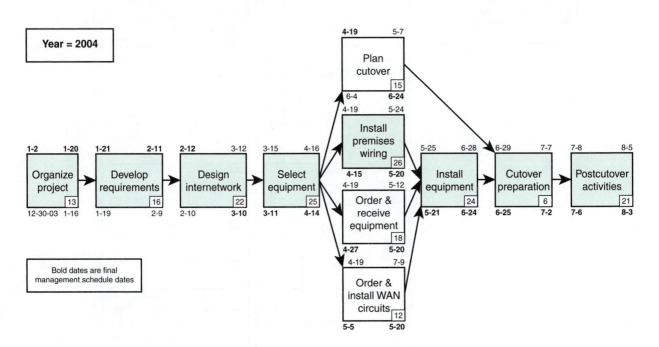

Figure 12–25. Technical schedule network solution.

date). All the activities following the *design internetwork* activity will use their late (backward pass) schedule dates.

The *plan cutover* activity schedule has also been modified based on examining the technical schedule. The selected start date will be 4–19–04 and its end date will be 6–24–04, the activity's LF date. This action adds additional float within the *plan cutover* activity but does not change the amount of time (fifteen workdays) needed to complete the activity.

TABLE 12–18   Final Schedule Table Solution

Cutover: July 6, 2004 (Tuesday)		
Activity	Start	Finish
Organize project	1–2–04	1–20–04
Develop requirements	1–21–04	2–11–04
Design internetwork	2–12–04	3–10–04
Select equipment	3–11–04	4–14–04
Plan cutover	4–19–04	6–24–04
Install premises wiring	4–15–04	5–20–04
Order & receive equipment	4–27–04	5–20–04
Order & install WAN circuits	5–5–04	5–20–04
Install equipment	5–21–04	6–24–04
Precutover preparation	6–25–04	7–2–04
Postcutover activities	7–6–04	8–3–04

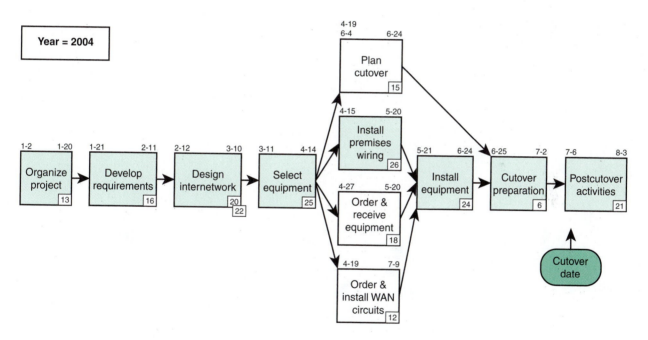

Figure 12–26.   Final schedule network solution.

Note: The selected schedule is one of several "correct" schedules that could be used. The best schedule in a real world scenario will be the one that allows the best coordination of work resources while minimizing costs. A good understanding of real world activities is required to select the best schedule from the many academically correct solutions that are available. The final solutions are shown in Figure 12–26 and Table 12–18.

13

PROJECT ORGANIZATION

1. Understand the purpose of project organization.

2. Understand the project manager's role in project management and the job responsibilities associated with the position.

3. Understand the implicit authority elements that a project manager can use to carry out project objectives.

4. Understand the negative aspects of project management if the process is carried to an extreme.

5. Understand the different organization structures commonly used to develop a project organization in a business environment.

6. Understand the four basic roles that are normally executed by project teams during the project management process.

7. Understand how to apply the project life cycle model to develop a game plan for organizing different project organization requirements.

8. Understand how to use the WBS worksheet as an aid for determining staffing level requirements for a project team.

WHY IS PROJECT ORGANIZATION NEEDED?

Unlike an inflatable life raft, which automatically assumes the correct shape and is ready for use once it is blown up, technology and administrative projects must be designed, developed, and assembled. The project construction and assembly effort requires a broad range of skills ranging from simple administrative skills to highly specialized technical skills. These skills come in a variety of "people packages," where any single individual typically has a limited set of skills. Therefore, when many skills are needed on a large, complex project, there will be many people who possess a wide range of personalities and capabilities assigned to the project. The success of the project will not be based on the technical skills of any single individual but upon the ability to effectively direct and coordinate the skills of many individuals. The clarity of direction and the effective coordination of people resources will be the primary responsibility of the project team that is established to develop and implement the project.

Some common definitions of well designed organization are:

1. a group of people who share a common interest or purpose
2. individual human elements that are coordinated into a common operating structure
3. relationships that are established between organization elements
4. a synergistic framework that helps to use PTM resources more effectively and efficiently

In a project organization, someone (typically a **project manager**) must identify goals, develop a plan, obtain the necessary resources, direct the efforts of individuals, and control project activities to ensure that project goals are met on time and within budget. The potential for project success will be influenced more by the ability of the project manager than by the abilities of the technical specialists assigned to the project. Poor project management performance will negate the efforts of a strong technical staff, and strong project management will frequently be able to compensate for a weak technical staff. Key characteristics of any competent organization include elements of the definitions provided earlier: shared purpose, coordination, relationships, and efficiency. Good organizational performance produces synergistic results—the results achieved by a well managed group will greatly exceed the sum total of the skills possessed by individual members of the group. This concept is highlighted in an ancient Arabian proverb: An army of sheep led by a lion defeats an army of lions led by a sheep.

Deliver Project Objectives

Project manager responsibilities can be stated simply:

1. Convert strategic project goals into quantifiable deliverables.
2. Implement the deliverables on time and within budget.

The following will address the project organization issue by examining a generic project team organization structure, describing the elements contained in the organization structure, and providing a case study example that applies the principles and concepts of project organization.

Project Organization Elements

Telecommunications project organizations consist of two basic components:

1. technical and functional specialists needed to produce project deliverables
2. the project management team that coordinates the efforts of technical specialists and ensures the effective use of the specialists.

THE PROJECT MANAGER. The project manager is the individual assigned the responsibility for completing a project successfully. For project managers, *project success* means successfully completing the six project steps shown in Figure 13–1 and turning over a fully operational system or network to an operations management organization (postproject phase).

Successful completion means that the end product for which the project was created meets all product specifications and is completed on time and within budget. While the technical design of a telecommunications project is the primary responsibility of technical specialists assigned to the project, the project manager is responsible for making sure that technical specialists do their jobs properly.

WHAT IS PROJECT ORGANIZATION?

Project organization is the process of selecting team members, molding them into an organization that has a shared purpose, coordinating project PTM resources effectively and efficiently, and successfully achieving project goals.

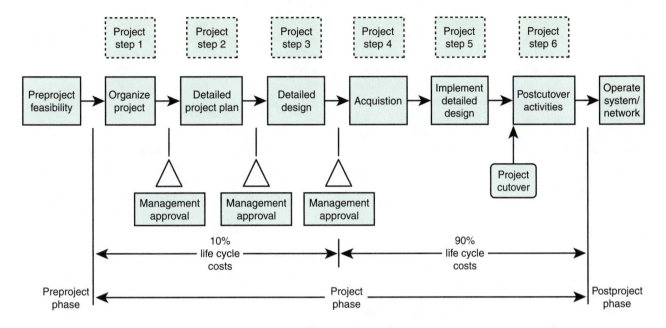

Figure 13–1. Telecommunications **project life cycle model.**

Project Organization Elements

Chapter 6 discussed **organization design and structure** as being one of the skills needed to create and operate a successful business. Unless an organization's human resources are used effectively, it is unlikely that the business can compete effectively with other businesses that have better organization structures and are running them effectively and efficiently.

Project teams are temporary businesses set up to achieve project objectives successfully in the same way that businesses establish business organizations to successfully achieve business objectives. If the same care is taken in establishing a project team organization as should be taken when establishing a business organization, the likelihood for project success is greater. Effective use of organization design principles will result in a project team that does an excellent job of implementing projects.

Good organization design identifies the basic objectives of the organization, determines which specialized skills are needed to successfully achieve business objectives, and establishes an organization structure that defines the roles and responsibilities of its members. Historically, business organization design was based on a department-oriented structure, and an organization chart identified the organizational

relationships between different departments and their managers. The head of the business (president or chief executive officer) was given the responsibility for overseeing all department activities and coordinating their efforts to meet business objectives.

Project organization utilizes many of the same methods used for business organization design, and applies them to achieve project objectives. In the same way that departments were established to support the business, the project requirements will be used to identify the organization structure needed for a project. When a telecommunications manager creates a project organization (team), the design will be driven by the project's objectives and the organizational philosophy of the business that the telecommunications manager works for. The telecommunications manager has the ultimate responsibility for developing a project organization design that provides the necessary project skills to administer and implement the project. This responsibility includes selecting, assigning, and managing project management personnel.

Project Teams

As indicated in Figure 13–1, projects only exist for a brief time span in a telecommunications product's life cycle. Therefore, the organization structure used for projects is transient in nature. A project organization is established at the start of a project, carries out project responsibilities during the project's life, and is disbanded at the end of a project. In some organizations, such as a matrix organization, a structure may exist where individuals are on continuous assignments to various project teams while individual project teams are continually created and disbanded.

The following section discusses some of the unique needs involved with creating temporary teams and discusses the different options that can be used to organize project teams.

Establishing a Project Team

A telecommunications management context will be used to describe project team roles, responsibilities, and authority. The project manager's responsibilities will be used as the focal point for these discussions. However, the ultimate responsibility for a project resides with the telecommunications manager who has selected the project manager role or, for smaller projects, may also be the project manager. Project managers require many of the skills that a **bona fide manager** needs. The effectiveness of a project or bona fide manager will be based on his or her ability to direct the efforts of others. The other members of the project management team may be members of other internal organizations, or individuals from external organizations.

The telecommunications manager responsible for establishing the project organization must identify the appropriate project organization structure and utilize sound organization design methods to ensure the most efficient use of project management personnel. For small projects, this may involve giving one individual the responsibility for developing the telecommunications product and handling any project management reporting requirements. In this case, the individual will fill the role of a project manager and be accountable to the telecommunication manager for both technical and project management details. The telecommunications manager would be closely linked with the project. This close linkage would be used for directing the project manager and for providing direct and indirect support to the project management and technical efforts.

For large projects, the responsibility for coordinating all project details would be delegated to a project manager if the telecommunications manager uses a functional design approach, or, it could be delegated to the team members who make up the project team if a self directed team is established.

Regardless of the organization structure used for the project team, the team's functional manager—typically the telecommunications manager—continues to be accountable to upper management for the project manager's performance in the same way that supervising managers are accountable for the performance of the managers they supervise.

Project Team Organization

When organizing a project team, the same organization options used to develop a business organization can be utilized—functional, divisional, matrix, and team organization structures. It is highly likely that the project team will reflect the organization structure of the business in which it exists.

It is unlikely that project management staffing levels will be of sufficient size for many telecommunications projects to warrant a complex organization structure. In a small project organization, the emphasis is on the individuals who make up the core project management organization, not on the organizational design aspects, because project members will be asked to fill many roles. This may include performing project work while also carrying out project management responsibilities. With the pressures found in most projects and the need to coordinate the efforts of others, a positive attitude is one of the greatest assets that a project team member can possess.

In a typical business environment, the telecommunications manager will develop a project organization that is temporary in nature and relies heavily upon the use of internal personnel. Outside skills may be brought in—at a cost—to supplement the internal skill pool if internal skills are not available. The responsibilities assigned to project members will be based on the skills and experience they possess, and the organization design's focus will be to develop a project team that has all the technology and project management skills needed to successfully implement the project. Individuals who have been borrowed from different internal organizations will expect to return to their original job, and their participation on the project team may be as full time or part time team members for the duration of the project.

The following will discuss the design options that can be used to develop a project team.

FUNCTIONAL TEAMS V. SELF DIRECTED TEAMS. Functional teams are headed by a project manager who has similar authority over project team members as a functional manager has over department employees. This differs from **self directed teams,** for which a designated supervisory project manager is not used, and all team members are expected to share the project manager responsibilities. Self directed teams are a relatively new phenomenon. The experience factor for using them is low compared to the functional team structure.

Functional Teams: Functional teams are frequently staffed with personnel who have been selected from the organization's telecommunications department. The project manager is expected to fulfill a role that is similar to that of a functional manager. Issues such as authority, decision making, leadership, and interdepartmental communication are clear because the project manager has been assigned the responsibility for executing them within the same context as a functional department manager who manages a project.

The project manager is given the managerial responsibility for getting the job done, including the identification of the people, time, and money resources needed to complete the project. The project manager is also expected to initiate any action needed to obtain project resources. Also, he or she is accountable for the project results. These responsibilities include directing the activities of project members, ensuring that project activities are carried out, and evaluating the performance of project team members.

Self Directed Project Teams: Self directed project teams operate without a designated project manager and team members assume a shared accountability for managing the project and meeting project objectives. Self directed teams are expected to carry out all of the same managerial tasks performed by a departmental manager, including completing employee performance appraisals. Self directed teams have become popular for a variety of reasons, and time will be required to assess their effectiveness in handling project activities.

The initial effort for establishing an effective self directed team is significantly higher than the effort associated with functional teams, unless the self directed team members have previously been given training and the opportunity to participate in a self directed team environment. Inexperienced self directed team members can have difficulty with the concepts of evaluating the performance of others and carrying out the responsibilities normally handled by supervisory personnel. Self directed team decisions are based on having a consensus among team members, and achieving consensus in a diverse group can be difficult. Successful self directed teams have addressed the need for strong team skills during the team organization phase by 1) selecting team members carefully, 2) providing the appropriate team training, and 3) allowing time for team individuals to become team members.

SWAT Project Teams: SWAT (special weapons and tactics) has been borrowed from police tactics and applied to project management. **SWAT project teams** are small groups of people whose responsibility is to start projects, establish the project management infrastructure needed to execute the project, then turn the project management infrastructure over to a project team that will complete the project activities needed for implementing the project.

This approach leverages the skills of project management specialists by using their expertise to establish the project plan, resolving tough start up questions up front, then turning over a stable project to a project implementation team. The project implementation team members are provided with a project that has well defined goals, objectives, and operating procedures. The SWAT resource would be available as an information resource to answer questions raised by the implementation team during the implementation period.

The initial organize project phase (step 1) is a difficult step when the concepts driving the project's creation are translated into quantifiable project objectives. In addition, this phase requires a high level of expertise and skill because it is necessary to evaluate the project budget; establish a project network diagram format; and address the budgetary, managerial, and technology issues associated with setting up a project. The use of a SWAT team provides a means of using highly trained personnel for this difficult phase and leveraging scarce skills by using SWAT personnel in the most difficult stage of project management.

In large telecommunications organizations, SWAT project teams can be a temporary assignment given to key personnel who then return to their functional departments. A SWAT team can also be organized by hiring an outside consulting firm that has good project management credentials or using a consultant team to complete SWAT team activities. In both cases, it is advisable to have a project manager who will be assigned responsibilities for completing the project implementation to be assigned as a member of the SWAT team. When SWAT functions are completed, the project manager would seamlessly migrate into the implementation role.

> This text will assume the use of a functional project team organization design during project management discussions.

The Project Team Building Process

As noted earlier, project teams are temporary in natures and it is possible that some team members may not know the other individuals assigned to the team. In an established business environment, new employees are brought into an existing organization infrastructure, where the roles and responsibilities of organization members are well defined. A new employee would be able to identify

TABLE 13–1   Team Building Process for Self Directed Teams

Team Creation Stage	Description
Forming	The initial organization stage when team members are selected, objectives are identified, and shared responsibilities are negotiated.
Storming	Personal conflicts emerge when individual members find that other team members do not share their views about member roles and responsibilities.
Norming	Team members modify individual expectations and develop a team-oriented measure of the roles of team members—including their roles within the team environment. A normalized team philosophy emerges to supersede individually oriented viewpoints. At the end of this phase, the team becomes the project manager.
Performing	Completion of the first three phases results in a team that has common goals and a common approach for accomplishing the work needed to successfully implement these goals.

the roles of others and the role he or she has been hired for, and would concentrate on learning how to fit in as a member of an existing organization.

When a project team is initially established, project team members may find themselves in the same situation as the new employee described in the preceding paragraph. If all of the members of a self-directed project team have not worked together previously, the identification of roles and responsibilities will be one of the key issues that must be addressed prior to addressing project-specific issues. Their individual ability in this area will be dependent upon the education, training, and experience they had before being assigned to the team.

The team-building process for developing team members from individuals assigned to a team typically evolves through the four stages described in the Table 13–1.

While the same four phases exist for functional teams, the functional manager has been given the authority for resolving them—an authority that can be effective or ineffective, depending upon the skills of the manager.

Project Team Members

When designing an organization, you must keep in mind the structure needed to carry out organizational responsibilities and providing the flexibility to address unexpected situations. Creating a good organizational design requires an understanding of the functions performed by departments (functional units) and existing business or functional objectives.

A project team is responsible for implementing the project on time and within budget. If the project is large, individual project functions may be assigned to one or more individuals, while a single individual may handle multiple responsibilities on smaller projects. Project team members working on telecommunications projects may have technology implementation or project management responsibilities—or both. When a project is large enough to warrant dedicating individuals to project management and project implementation activities, project management personnel would not directly perform project work. They would coordinate and direct the efforts of the technical specialists who have the primary responsibility for completing the tasks associated with a technical project.

The key member of a project team is the project manager. He or she is given the responsibility for performing project management activities, assumes a supervisory role, and monitors the individual and group performance of team members.

For highly technical projects, some team members may be technical specialists who have the necessary project management skills to coordinate the activities of the technical specialists responsible for implementing project tasks. While these technical team members are primarily concerned about operating within the project management framework, they also have responsibility for ensuring that technical specialists assigned to the project complete their assignments competently and that their work meets generally accepted technical standards.

For large projects, a separate technical management group may exist as part of the project management team. This group may be given the primary responsibility for directing the efforts of the technical specialists who are assigned project work. The technical specialists doing project work may be members of the internal organization, may be hired as temporary workers to complete specific tasks, or may be members of the supplier organization that has been awarded the contract to install a system or network.

Summary

As noted in the chapter's introduction, projects come in all sizes and shapes. The organizational design applied to a project management team will depend upon the specific requirements of the project. For small projects, the project manager fills all the roles and is an organization of one. For very large projects the project management team may exceed the size of many departments commonly found in a large business.

The selection of the appropriate structure and staffing is a managerial decision—one that should make sense within the project's context. The manager will decide when the final project outcomes will be used to measure the success or failure of the project team. A functional project team design will be used in this text. The following reviews the different functions—project management and technology implementation—that must be provided by telecommunications project teams.

PROJECT TEAM FUNCTIONS

The **project team function** is to implement the project on time and within budget. Depending upon the telecommunications project objectives, typically the installation of a system or network facility, different technology skills will be required. However, regardless of the diversity of technical skills needed for the project, the one constant is the need to provide effective project management to ensure that project objectives are met.

Figure 13–2 provides a conceptual organization template for discussing the functions that a project team must provide. While projects may vary in size and scope, the generic functional project team structure shows those functions required to complete any project. The difference between small and large projects is the staffing level.

Table 13–2 outlines the responsibilities assigned to the people who perform the different functions shown in the organization chart in Figure 13–2.

In a small project, the project manager may not have a support staff and therefore would handle both technical support and project management needs. In a very large telecommunications project, the groups shown in Figure 13–2 may consist of ten or more members. The purpose of the support staff is to coordinate and document project management activities under the guidance of the project manager.

A functional organization structure has been used in Figure 13–2. Different team structures will be discussed, and the actual organization structure of the project team may differ from that shown in Figure 13–2 (while still performing the same tasks). The project team is directed by the project manager, who has the overall responsibility for ensuring that project deliverables are implemented on time and within budget.

The Project Manager

The following discusses some the detailed tasks included in a project manager's job responsibilities—tasks that may be assigned to other project team members if the project's scope and size warrants it. On the other hand, if the project manager is the primary project management resource, then the project manager must personally complete them. A project manager's specific job responsibilities will vary depending upon the size of the project, the business enterprise environment, and the type of project.

Assigned responsibilities may include:

- developing project plans that define activities, tasks, and results in an appropriate WBS, project network diagram, or budgetary format.

- creating a project management team through a process of identifying, selecting, and recruiting qualified individuals for the various positions. This responsibility includes monitoring the performance of individual team members and taking the appropriate action if expected performance levels are not met.

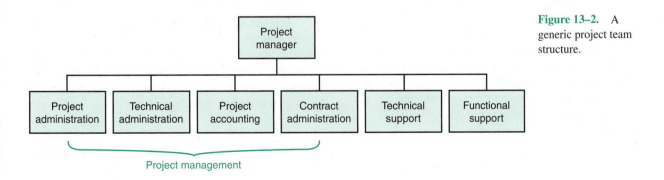

Figure 13–2. A generic project team structure.

TABLE 13–2   Project Team Function Overview (from Figure 13–2)

Project Function	Description
Project manager	The individual assigned primary responsibility for coordinating all the steps shown in Figure 13–1. The project manager may be dedicated full time to the project activity or may be assigned on a part time basis while continuing to handle other responsibilities.
Project management	Performs the various project management functions required to manage and control the project.
Project administration	Develops and documents the project management activities required to define and control the project. Includes the development of a WBS, a project network diagram, resource allocation reporting, project schedules, and ongoing project status reporting. The planning and control function would identify deviations between the project plan and actual project performance.
Technical administration	Coordinates, monitors, and assesses the performance of technical support personnel assigned to the project. Individuals assigned to this area would have strong technical skills in the technology area being implemented.
Project accounting	The project accounting function—under the direction of the project manager—is to develop and maintain the project budgets by using a budget *v.* actual format as money is spent. This phase is a project team responsibility even though the finance department controls capital appropriation budgets as part of its function. The project budget will be examined at a much more detailed level than the financial department budget.
Contract administration	Monitors and controls any contractual arrangements used during project implementation activities. Coordinates the internal approval of RFPs and vendor contracts by the (internal) legal department and ensures that the contractual content of project documents are followed by project participants.
Support staff	
Technical support	Provides the technical specialists for the project. In the case of the Chapter 12 PBX telephone system, technical specialists would survey telephone users, identify equipment and CO service needs, develop telephone system RFPs, order communications services, technically evaluate vendor alternatives, and coordinate the implementation of the telephone system with the selected vendor.
	Technical specialists would also define and create the operations management documentation required to transfer the telephone system into the operating environment supported by the telecommunications operations department. If different technical skills were needed, they would have been coordinated by technical support.
Functional support	Depending upon the nature of the project, input and support may be required from nontelecommunications functions. This interface would coordinate the activities of nontelecommunications representatives. For example, it may be necessary to hire outside expertise to develop the technical documentation that will be used by the network control center to administrate and operate installed network facilities.

- providing ongoing communication during the project life cycle with the various project stakeholders, including functional managers, outside contractors, consultants, internal users, and upper management.

- monitoring project activities to ensure that project plan objectives are being met. If deviations are found between planned activities and actual implementation, the project manager is responsible for initiating the appropriate action to realign project activities with project performance objectives.

- Resolving issues and crises that emerge during the project. These may include interpersonal conflicts, technical and functional problems, escalating problems

that cannot be resolved by the project team, and facilitating the reallocation of project resources.

In effect, the project manager is being asked to carry out the standard managerial responsibilities of the **POLC Model** (Figure 13–3) within the context of the project environment. The goals in the POLC Model become the project goals. The plan, organize, lead, and control processes focus on the desired project results.

IMPLICIT AUTHORITY.   The authority of project managers is normally less than a department manager's authority. An effective project manager must monitor ongoing project activities and implement project decisions

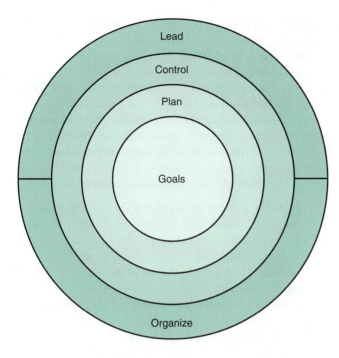

Figure 13–3. Goalcentric POLC model.

while having little direct authority. This requires good judgment, the existence of strong interpersonal and business communication skills, and good working relationships with individuals outside of the project team.

Project managers normally have little direct (explicit) authority when carrying out project responsibilities. However, a project manager may have a significant level of implicit authority. If this implicit authority is wielded effectively, it can generate the same results as those achieved with explicit authority. When the sponsor for a project is a member of upper management, such as an executive committee member, the requests made by the project manager will be viewed within the context of the sponsor's authority limits. If a project manager uses the implicit authority provided by a project's sponsor wisely, there will seldom be a need to exercise explicit authority to resolve issues.

Another source of implicit authority is based on the personal credibility of the project manager. Project managers are members of the business organization, and all organization members have a level of personal credibility based upon their knowledge, skills, contacts within the organization, their position outside of the project environment, and other personal alliances. Project leaders who have personal credibility within a business organization will carry this credibility to the project manager position.

It may be necessary to call upon their direct sponsor (the telecommunications manager) when real managerial authority is needed to eliminate project bottlenecks. The experience gained as a project manager is excellent training for aspiring telecommunications managers.

Project Administration

Project administration activities support the project manager's efforts in planning, monitoring, controlling, and reporting project performance. In a simple environment, the tasks may simply involve documenting the recommendations of others. In a more complex project environment, it may require defining, developing, and documenting project management activities and tasks. These efforts would include:

- managing the project management system (manual or PC-based) by maintaining and updating the WBS, project network diagram, activity schedule, and activity resource information. This includes generating the appropriate reports for controlling project activities by providing plan *v.* actual reporting for activities, vendors, costs, and schedules.

- working with functional managers (technical specialists) to define WBS elements and obtain the actual performance data that will be used to monitor project activities and ensure that project plan objectives are met (implementing the project on time and within budgetary constraints).

- providing administrative control over project work orders, progress reports, budget and schedule revisions, and activity approval documents. This may require getting approval from the project manager (for large projects) or working with a multimember change control board when very large, complex projects are undertaken.

Project Technical Administration

The **project technical administration** role that must be coordinated by the project management team when a system or network is being developed and implemented includes:

- identifying end user requirements and converting them to performance and design specification criteria that can be used to select, develop, and design system and network facilities. Project design must conform to enterprise telecommunications technology standards.

- monitoring the design process to ensure that specification criteria have been incorporated into the design. This includes taking the necessary steps to ensure that the project equipment that has been selected is compatible with the existing equipment.

- providing a quality assurance presence by overseeing the design and implementation process and ensuring that technical specialists meet specification criteria. This responsibility includes a field management role, in which technical activities are reviewed by technical administration personnel to ensure that they are performed satisfactorily.
- monitoring and evaluating the equipment testing process and providing the final technical approval for technical specialist activities.
- ensuring that the appropriate technical documentation is created for both project file and operational management purposes. This includes making sure user manuals and technical operating procedures are provided as part of the project implementation.

Project Accounting

The key project management responsibilities assigned to every project management team are to live within the constraints of: 1) time and 2) money. **Project accounting** activities manage project budgetary performance. The project management accounting team provides a function similar to the role provided by an accounting department in a business organization. Project accounting responsibilities would include:

- reviewing invoices and bills for equipment, labor, and services to ensure that the goods and services have been received. This would include obtaining the necessary approvals within the project team hierarchy and authorizing the payment of approved bills by the accounts payable department.
- providing the necessary input for any enterprise financial system that tracks capital expenditures and operating expenses. In most businesses, this would be a monthly budget *v.* actual (BVA) reporting system.
- preparing periodic financial reports that identify plan *v.* actual expense performance. These reports would be issued to project stakeholders (upper management, functional management providing project resources, project management members, and project service providers).

Project Contract Administration

For large projects, the use of contractual agreements is a way of life. It is necessary to closely monitor contractual products and services to ensure that they are acceptable and they meet project specifications. When formal contracts are used to obtain the services of outside firms, it is necessary to have an internal contact for authorizing work activities and change orders, and to ensure that contract terms are followed by both the contractor and the client. As was the case for the other project management responsibilities, the project manager or project management team is responsible for coordinating the resources needed to provide **project contract administration,** but this includes performing some tasks directly.

Contract administration responsibilities include:

- preparing RFPs to be issued to prospective bidders, obtaining internal legal approval for the RFP, defining and negotiating contract terms with the selected bidder, and obtaining internal legal approval for the final contract. The preparation of RFPs would be coordinated with the project management team's technical administration personnel. The content of RFPs would be a primary responsibility of the technical administration personnel, while the administration of the RFP's terms and conditions would be a contract administration responsibility.
- ensuring that contract terms are fulfilled by the bidder, negotiating and approving vendor change orders, and coordinating with the project administration personnel to ensure that contract work conforms to project schedule requirements. This responsibility includes a field management role, in which vendor activities are reviewed periodically by the contract administration personnel.
- maintaining all appropriate contract documentation, including RFPs, project correspondence, contracts, contract amendments, change orders, bills, and other contract-oriented documentation.
- coordinating contract completion milestones with technical administration, project administration, and project accounting personnel.

Project-Specific Requirements

The skill and support levels required for the Table 13–2 team functions will vary from project to project. The table is intended to provide a checklist for functions that should be provided by a project team, whether it is a one person team or a multiperson team. The depth and scope of how the functions are applied will depend upon the project's requirements.

To build a project organization, it is necessary to understand both the project specific and general project management requirements. Project specific requirements differ from project to project. For telecommunications projects, project specific requirements impose the need to have technically qualified individuals available during the design and implementation phases of the project. For administrative projects (i.e., nontechnical projects), the term *project-specific* takes on a different meaning, because many administrative projects are ad hoc projects in which initial requirements consist of vague, instinctive reactions to the organizational environment. The project specific requirements for technical and administrative projects are quite different but the general project management requirements for technical and administrative projects are quite similar.

Closing Comments

The technical administration, project administration, and project accounting functions are always required for telecommunications projects, but contract administration is only required when contracts are required for the project. Deciding who will carry out these responsibilities will depend upon the staff assigned to the project. For a small project for which the project manager is the only member of the project team, the project manager will provide these roles. When two or more individuals are assigned to a project on a full time basis, the project roles would be distributed among the team members based upon their backgrounds and qualifications. In very large projects, multiple individuals may be assigned to any individual role discussed in this section.

PROJECT MANAGER SELECTION CRITERIA

Large, complex, technical projects are more likely to encounter problems than small, simple projects. A $100,000 project that has a cost overrun of 10% must find an additional $10,000 to complete the project, while a $20 billion project that has a cost overrun of 10% must find an additional $2 billion. Project management skills that are considered excellent in a small project environment may be inadequate for large projects.

Project managers should be selected based upon their potential for successfully completing a project. Small projects can be used to develop project management skills, but experienced, skilled project managers should be assigned to large, business critical projects. Projects provide excellent training for prospective functional managers. Successfully carrying out project management responsibilities is one way of demonstrating that someone has strong managerial potential.

The selection of a project management team will be a balance between the administrative overhead created by assigning a management function for the projects and the benefits derived from project management activities. If project management activities do not provide a measurable value-added benefit, the project management team is either incompetent or unnecessary.

Project Manager Assignments

A project manager is normally appointed at the start of the project phase shown in Figure 13–1, although it may take place during the preproject phase if the project is sufficiently large or important. In the latter case, the project manager will assist in the definition of project parameters and becomes directly accountable for meeting project objectives before the project begins.

When the project manager's first exposure to the project is at the organize project phase (project step 1 in Figure 13–1), the project manager will typically be provided with a general description of the project (goals and performance measurement criteria) and will also be given a predetermined set of PTM resources for achieving project objectives. The information given to the project manager would have been developed during various strategic and tactical planning phases that led up to the creation of the project budget used in the operational phase (Figure 13–4).

Project budgets are operational budgets that were developed as a final tactical budget during the year preceding a project's scheduled startup. While technology considerations drive the preparation of the final tactical budget, the budget development process will normally be

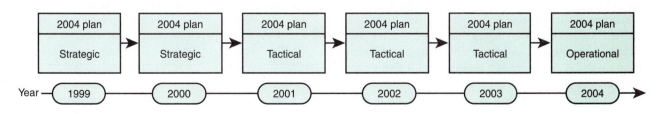

Figure 13–4. Planning process stages.

far less detailed than the planning efforts for steps 1 through 3 shown on the project life cycle diagram (Figure 13–1). As a result, a project manager's first task should be to find out if the resources provided in the project budget are adequate to successfully implement the project. A project manager evaluating a new assignment should normally ask three basic questions:

1. Does the budget information provide sufficient details so that project goals and the criteria for successfully meeting them are clear and measurable?

2. Are the budget resources (people, time, and money) adequate for successfully implementing the project?

3. Has enough project time been allocated for successfully designing and implementing the project infrastructure?

Assuming that the answer to the above questions, after a careful evaluation by the project manager, is "yes," the next question that would arise is: How do I (the project manager) come up with a good project plan?

A project example will be used to address the issues raised by these four questions. Hopefully, it will provide an insight to the project organization process.

Administrative Overhead

Bureaucracy is an administrative system that divides work into specific categories to be carried out by specialists. Based on this definition, project management is a form of bureaucracy, even though its limited (project) life minimizes the potential for project management to assume the negative aspects of a bureaucracy, where complex rules and regulations are applied rigidly and incessantly. President Ronald Reagan is said to have made the following observation regarding government bureaucracies: "A government agency is the nearest thing to eternal life that we'll ever see on this earth." Large, lengthy projects can assume many characteristics of a government agency, and it is the responsibility of the telecommunications manager to ensure that the project team does not become a self-serving, bureaucratic organization.

The telecommunications manager is responsible for the selection of the project manager needed to manage a telecommunications project. Simple projects require a minimal amount of project management and complex projects require a significant investment in project management overhead. While project management activities are necessary for the effective implementation of projects, the cost for project management personnel and their associated support services must be paid from the project budget. A good project manager will minimize the overhead as-

pects of project management and ensure that project management resources are used efficiently and effectively. A poor project manager will absorb an unreasonable amount of the project's budget without providing tangible benefits to the project effort.

Complex Requirements

Complexity is a relative term. A situation that is complex for one individual may be relatively simple for another. The difference between the two viewpoints is normally due to differences in education and experience. The project management process deals with many different project elements and combines them to produce the desired project results. Telecommunications technology introduces a level of technical complexity that makes sense only to individuals who have the necessary technology knowledge. To successfully implement telecommunications projects, a project manager must have good skills in both the project management and telecommunications technology areas associated with the specific project.

Earlier in the text, the 50%/50% Telecommunications Management Model was introduced. It stated that telecommunications managers need a strong set of skills in both business and technology management areas. Unless a balance exists between the two areas, telecommunications managers can find themselves in situations where the lack of knowledge could result in poor business or poor technology decisions. This same requirement applies to project managers. Project managers need to have strong project management skills and a good understanding of the telecommunications technology they are being asked to implement. While the project manager may not require the same skill levels as the technical specialists working on the project, they should be sufficient to understand and logically group the technology project elements required for implementing the project. Actually, project managers need the same conceptual understanding of telecommunications as a telecommunications manager.

> The **ninety-ninety rule of projects:** The first 90 percent of the project's benefits takes 10 percent of the time and the remaining 10 percent of the project's benefits takes the other 90 percent of the time.

If the telecommunications manager has done a good job of structuring the preproject budgetary phase of the project, a great deal of pressure is removed from a project manager and the project manager's focus can be on implementing the project. If the project was poorly conceived or under-funded, the project manager must restructure the project prior to developing the deliverables associated with step 1 in Figure 13–1.

Telecommunications technology projects that are implemented in a business should not be research projects. The telecommunications department should be implementing stable business telecommunications technologies that have a proven performance track record. From a technology planning perspective, there is a limited number of telecommunications project categories implemented within a business enterprise—telephone systems, LANs, WANs, internetworks, and WWW facilities. A common set of project management skills can be used to implement different telecommunications technologies. However, a different set of technology skills is required for different types of projects and a project manager must have the appropriate level of technology skills for the specific project assignment.

At the completion of the organize project phase (step 1 in Figure 13–1), the managerial, budgetary, and technical structure of the project should be understood and preliminary documentation that will become the basis for step 2 should be established. This preliminary documentation will typically consist of spreadsheets for the budgets, a CPM project network diagram, and detailed word processing notes that highlight the key parameters and issues. If this is not the case, the project manager has not met step 1 requirements and the telecommunications manager has not effectively supervised the project manager.

The majority of telecommunications projects have straightforward project management requirements, and a file of records from completed projects should be available to a project manager. By using the experience of others who have implemented similar projects, a project manager can minimize the risk of encountering project problems. If documentation is not available, it will be necessary to add expertise to the project by training or obtaining external consulting services. When outside skills are required, a good manager will make sure that internal personnel work with the outside skill resource (personnel) and have the opportunity to learn these skills so that they become part of the internal organization's skill pool.

The following case study will discuss project management responsibilities from the viewpoint of a telecommunications manager who must develop a project organization to handle a PBX telephone system implementation project.

PROJECT ORGANIZATION CASE STUDY

In the previous chapter, CPM was described and a PBX telephone system example was used to show how a manual CPM approach could be applied. CPM has emerged as the project management control method of choice to use when large, complex technical projects are being implemented. This chapter examines the people side of project management—organizing the project—that has the overall responsibility for coordinating project activities and implementing the project on time, within budget, and meeting project specification requirements.

PBX Telephone System Project

The following will organize the PBX telephone system project discussed in Chapter 12. The project management details have already been discussed and documented so the reader can focus on the project organization aspects without having concerns about the technical implementation requirements, because these are already known. The CPM solution is contained in Chapter 12's *PBX Telephone System Project Example* section and includes WBS information, a project network diagram, workday calculations, the identification of the critical path, and the development of an associated project schedule.

> Before a project can be organized, a good conceptual understanding of the project details are needed. This means that a manager who is organizing a project must develop a project plan model prior to organizing the project. In our case, this was done in Chapter 12. If a solution did not exist, the manager would have to develop a strawman solution (create an estimate of the project details).

The following will examine the organization requirements associated with initiating and implementing the Chapter 12 PBX telephone system and will use the Chapter 12 deliverables for organizing the project. Therefore, it is essential that the reader has completed Chapter 12 prior to proceeding with the project organization discussion and is familiar with the details of the technical (CPM) solution. A key Chapter 12 topic is the WBS worksheet information, because it provides a step by step map of the technical project requirements. The following discussion will follow the procedures described in Chapters 11 and 12 and will also reuse some of the illustrations found in those chapters.

TABLE 13–3   Project Description Information

Project Description Installation of a 1,000 Line PBX/Voice Messaging System in a New Corporate Headquarters Building Scheduled for Occupancy on June 1, 2004.

Current date:	October 20, 2003
Project start date:	January 2, 2004
Cutover date:	June 1, 2004
Workdays:	Monday through Friday, 8 am to 5 pm
Holidays:	New Years Day, Memorial Day, Labor Day, Thanksgiving, Christmas Day, Independence Day

The starting point for organizing a project is the beginning. Table 13–3 shows the project description information used for the Chapter 12 telephone system project.

The time frames provided in the description statement should be used as input to the project organization process. It will be assumed that it is October 20, 2003. The telecommunications development manager is ready to start the project organization effort and has been provided Table 13–3 target dates and the 2004 capital appropriation budget.

The Business Environment

The environment in which the project takes place will have a strong influence on how the project is organized, because the internal organization is normally the source for project staffing (the project manager and the project team members). Therefore, the telecommunications manager should have good knowledge about its structure and people re-

source capability. In Chapter 8 (Business Management Skills), the functional, divisional, matrix, and team organization structures were reviewed. We will assume that a traditional departmental organization structure is the operating environment for this chapter's project management problem. Figure 13–5 shows the enterprise functional organization chart for the project. The telecommunications department is one of five functions that report to the president.

Figure 13–6 provides a more detailed view of the telecommunications department. There are seventy-five employees in the telecommunications organization who provide telephone system, LAN, WAN, and internetworking services to the enterprise. The vice president of telecommunications assigned the manager of development the responsibility of implementing the telephone system project. The development manager established the project budgets and had worked on telephone system implementation projects in the past. The development department has the responsibility for installing telecommunications technology and has experience with implementing various telecommunications technology projects.

Table 13–3 described the project objectives that will be organized in this chapter. The project requires the installation of a 1,000 line PBX telephone system in a new corporate headquarters building. The cutover date is June 1, 2004.

From a project planning perspective, it will be necessary to organize the six step project process shown in the telecommunications project life cycle model (Figure 13–1) to meet the project requirements. The project team member staffing for the PBX project will be temporarily borrowed from the telecommunications organization in

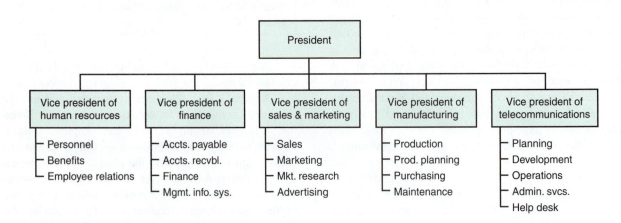

Figure 13–5.   Enterprise functional organization chart.

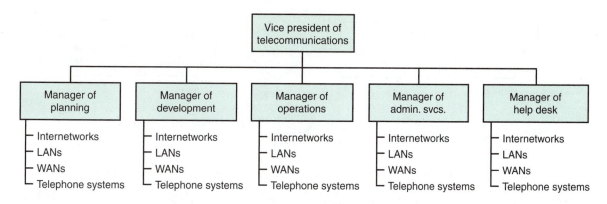

Figure 13–6. Telecommunications organization chart.

Figure 13–6 for the duration of the project. This may include full time and part time project personnel.

The project manager was selected by the telecommunications development manager and, with the approval of the telecommunications vice president, was appointed to head the project. The following section will discuss the project team staffing requirements. Once the required skills have been identified, members from various telecommunications departments will be assigned to the project on a full time or part time basis, depending upon project needs.

Macro-Level Planning

For the following discussion, please refer to the discussion of the telecommunications project life cycle in Chapter 11 and Figure 13–1 on page 341.

While the development manager's planning framework is the entire project phase, the initial focus would be on project step 1, the project organization step. The step 1 deliverables described in Chapter 12 include:

preliminary project documentation

preliminary project network plan

risk assessment observations

project financial plan

recommendations to management

At this point in the project life cycle, funds were allocated during the preproject feasibility phase, and the actual project work is ready to begin. Step 1 is a critical point in the project because it generates the framework for the entire project and provides the opportunity to reevaluate the initial feasibility decision. In a small telecommunications organization, the telecommunications manager may assume the role of project manager. For this example, someone other than the development manager will be appointed to the project manager position. In addition to selecting a project manager, the development manager must be able to explain to prospective project managers the responsibilities associated with the assignment. The development manager needs a project organization plan to provide a framework for developing the project management team.

The Project Organization Plan

Fortunately, the development manager has experience in project management. If this were not the case, the manager would have to initiate a personal self education effort or pay for the use of outside consulting resources. A self education process could involve using documentation sources such as texts, other training material, or may involve talking with someone (who is experienced in project management) about similar types of projects.

> The beginning phase of any project requires stepping back from the details and establishing a game plan. The manager will use the POLC Model to design a preliminary plan that identifies the detailed results that must be implemented to develop a complete project plan.

Before developing the project organization, the telecommunications manager must identify the activities needed to complete step 1 and set the stage for completing steps 2 through 5. While Figure 13–1 identifies the major project elements, it does not indicate the process for selecting project team members. The development manager reformatted the Figure 13–1 information into a

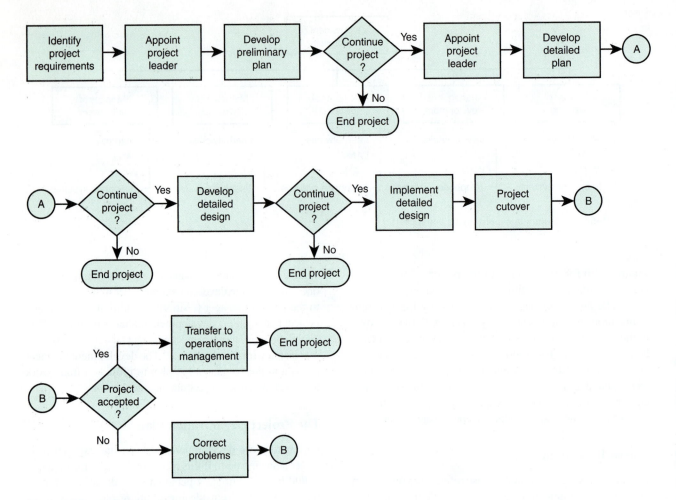

Figure 13–7. Project management flowchart.

flowchart that highlighted the project management staffing requirements and showed the different management approval milestones needed to ensure the ongoing viability of the project. This flowchart is shown in Figure 13–7.

The development manager will use this flowchart as the basis for documenting a game plan that provides a summary overview of the entire project. The flowchart and associated project documentation will serve two purposes: 1) they can be used to explain the project requirements to potential project managers and 2) they provide a plan that can be used by the development manager to monitor project manager activities.

Note: The preparation of the flowchart and associated documentation is a relatively trivial effort for individuals who have good skills in Microsoft's Word and Excel, and Visio software.

A comparison of the Figure 13–7 flowchart with the Figure 13–1 telecommunications project life cycle model will show that the basic elements are similar. In the flowchart, the development manager will initiate step 1 by appointing a project manager, having the project manager develop a preliminary project plan, reviewing the preliminary plan with upper management, and gaining management approval to proceed to step 2.

THE DEVELOPMENT MANAGER'S PLAN. The development manager's approach to organizing the project is to document key activities and identify their target dates. Table 13–4 shows the development manager's preliminary plan, which highlights the beginning and end of each project step. Figures 13–8 and 13–9 provide the calendars for 2003 and 2004, which the development manager used to complete the Table 13–4 plan.

TABLE 13-4 The Telecommunications Manager's Preliminary Project Plan

Date	Task Description
10–20–03 (Monday)	1. Document initial administrative plan for PBX system project. 2. Create project documentation folder (project description, target dates, budget, etc.) for project manager candidates. 3. Document project manager position responsibilities for project steps 1–5. 4. Identify and list potential candidates for project manager position. 5. Schedule initial interviews with project manager candidates and provide candidates with project and position documentation. Schedule follow-up meetings within five workdays of initial meeting.
10–21–03 (Tuesday)	1. Administrative plan completion target date. 2. Project documentation completion target date.
10–22–03 (Wednesday)	1. Compete initial project manager interviews.
10–27–03 (Monday)	1. Complete final project manager interviews.
10–28–03 (Tuesday)	1. Select project manager. 2. Review project manager selection recommendation with upper management and get approval.
10–30–03 (Thursday)	**1. Start project step 1.** 2. Announce project manager appointment.

11–10–03 (Monday)	1. Review/approve project manager recommendations:
	  • preliminary project documentation
	  • preliminary project network plan
	  • risk assessment observations
	  • project team recommendations
	  • project communications plan (meetings, memos, etc.)
	  • project financial plan

11–13–03 (Thursday)	1. Review project manager recommendations with upper management. 2. Get approval for recommendations. **3. Project step 1 completed.**
11–17–03 (Monday)	**1. Start Project Step 2.** 2. Announce project team member appointments. 3. Review project manager plans for completing step 2 requirements.

12–15–03 (Monday)	1. Review/approve project team recommendations:
	  • detailed project documentation
	  • detailed project network plan
	  • updated risk assessment observations
	  • final project financial plan

12–18–03 (Thursday)	1. Review project team recommendations with upper management. 2. Get approval for recommendations. **3. Project step 2 completed.**
1–2–04 (Friday)	**Start project step 3.**

3–22–04 (Monday)	1. Review/approve project team recommendations:
	  • summary evaluation of PBX alternatives
	  • PBX vendor recommendation
	  • five year financial plan
	  • implementation schedule

TABLE 13–4   The Telecommunications Manager's Preliminary Project Plan (continued)

Date	Task Description
3–23–04 (Tuesday)	1. Review project team recommendations with upper management. 2. Get approval for recommendations. **3. Project step 3 completed.** **4. Project step 4 started.**
3–26–04 (Friday)	**Project step 4 acquisition activities completed.**
6–1–04 (Tuesday)	**PBX system cutover: step 5 precutover activities completed.**
6–30–04 (Wednesday)	**Project step 6 completed.** 1. Formal transfer of project to operations management.

The key dates shown on Table 13–4 are: 1) the project's start, 2) the project's end, and 3) the cutover date. These dates were obtained from the project description statement and are critical dates if the project is to be implemented on time. The other dates in Table 13–4 are development manager estimates of when other project phases must be started and completed to meet the project completion date. While there is flexibility to change some dates, the cutover date has no flexibility unless upper management initiates the change.

The primary focus of the initial plan is to identify key project elements and provide an operational framework for the project manager and project team members. When project members know what is expected of them, they can provide feedback to change the plan. The best way to let people know what is expected of them is to provide them with a document they can review and react to. If the only communication is verbal, it is difficult to accurately reconstruct discussions unless they have been recorded.

> At first glance, Table 13–4 may appear to be an academic document that has been carefully structured to allow its introduction into a textbook. This is not the case. One of the skills a professional manager should possess is the capability to effortlessly generate a table by using word processing software. It is easier, and quicker, to generate Table 13–3 using a word processing application than it is to write it out on paper. The word processing version is legible, easy to read, and easy to modify.

COMMENTARY. The development manager's plan has been developed in a format that can be shared with the VP of telecommunications, prospective project managers, team members, upper management, and anyone interested in understanding the scope of the project. The development manager does not view the initial plan as a doctrine that requires blind obedience, but as a guideline that will be modified as needed. The attitude of the development manager, when reacting to proposed changes in this base plan, should be to view it as a baseline reference for ensuring that key plan elements remain intact. Team members will view the need to modify the document in a positive light if their interface with the development manager is a rational one. If the development manager dogmatically defends the preliminary plan, it will reduce the credibility of both the development manager and the organization plan.

At this stage in the planning scenario, the development manager must address two key staffing issues:

1. What are the criteria for selecting an effective project manager?

2. What type of representation should be included on the project team?

These two questions will be answered for the PBX project example by drawing on information reviewed in a previous section (Project Team Functions). The following will describes converting this information into a staffing plan for the PBX project example.

Project Staffing

The first area that needs to be addressed when developing the project organization for our example is to determine the staffing levels needed to manage the project and complete the telecommunications tasks. The PBX project is a relatively small project, and the development manager has

January 2003

Su	Mo	Tu	We	Th	Fr	Sa
			1	2	3	4
5	6	7	8	9	10	11
12	13	14	15	16	17	18
19	20	21	22	23	24	25
26	27	28	29	30	31	

July 2003

Su	Mo	Tu	We	Th	Fr	Sa
		1	2	3	4	5
6	7	8	9	10	11	12
13	14	15	16	17	18	19
20	21	22	23	24	25	26
27	28	29	30	31		

February 2003

Su	Mo	Tu	We	Th	Fr	Sa
						1
2	3	4	5	6	7	8
9	10	11	12	13	14	15
16	17	18	19	20	21	22
23	24	25	26	27	28	

August 2003

Su	Mo	Tu	We	Th	Fr	Sa
					1	2
3	4	5	6	7	8	9
10	11	12	13	14	15	16
17	18	19	20	21	22	23
24	25	26	27	28	29	30

March 2003

Su	Mo	Tu	We	Th	Fr	Sa
						1
2	3	4	5	6	7	8
9	10	11	12	13	14	15
16	17	18	19	20	21	22
23	24	25	26	27	28	29
30	31					

September 2003

Su	Mo	Tu	We	Th	Fr	Sa
	1	2	3	4	5	6
7	8	9	10	11	12	13
14	15	16	17	18	19	20
21	22	23	24	25	26	27
28	29	30				

April 2003

Su	Mo	Tu	We	Th	Fr	Sa
		1	2	3	4	5
6	7	8	9	10	11	12
13	14	15	16	17	18	19
20	21	22	23	24	25	26
27	28	29	30			

October 2003

Su	Mo	Tu	We	Th	Fr	Sa
			1	2	3	4
5	6	7	8	9	10	11
12	13	14	15	16	17	18
19	20	21	22	23	24	25
26	27	28	29	30	31	

May 2003

Su	Mo	Tu	We	Th	Fr	Sa
				1	2	3
4	5	6	7	8	9	10
11	12	13	14	15	16	17
18	19	20	21	22	23	24
25	26	27	28	29	30	31

November 2003

Su	Mo	Tu	We	Th	Fr	Sa
						1
2	3	4	5	6	7	8
9	10	11	12	13	14	15
16	17	18	19	20	21	22
23	24	25	26	27	28	29
30						

June 2003

Su	Mo	Tu	We	Th	Fr	Sa
1	2	3	4	5	6	7
8	9	10	11	12	13	14
15	16	17	18	19	20	21
22	23	24	25	26	27	28
29	30					

December 2003

Su	Mo	Tu	We	Th	Fr	Sa
	1	2	3	4	5	6
7	8	9	10	11	12	13
14	15	16	17	18	19	20
21	22	23	24	25	26	27
28	29	30	31			

Figure 13–8. 2003 calendar.

January 2004

Su	Mo	Tu	We	Th	Fr	Sa
				1	2	3
4	5	6	7	8	9	10
11	12	13	14	15	16	17
18	19	20	21	22	23	24
25	26	27	28	29	30	31

July 2004

Su	Mo	Tu	We	Th	Fr	Sa
				1	2	3
4	5	6	7	8	9	10
11	12	13	14	15	16	17
18	19	20	21	22	23	24
25	26	27	28	29	30	31

February 2004

Su	Mo	Tu	We	Th	Fr	Sa
1	2	3	4	5	6	7
8	9	10	11	12	13	14
15	16	17	18	19	20	21
22	23	24	25	26	27	28
29						

August 2004

Su	Mo	Tu	We	Th	Fr	Sa
1	2	3	4	5	6	7
8	9	10	11	12	13	14
15	16	17	18	19	20	21
22	23	24	25	26	27	28
29	30	31				

March 2004

Su	Mo	Tu	We	Th	Fr	Sa
	1	2	3	4	5	6
7	8	9	10	11	12	13
14	15	16	17	18	19	20
21	22	23	24	25	26	27
28	29	30	31			

September 2004

Su	Mo	Tu	We	Th	Fr	Sa
			1	2	3	4
5	6	7	8	9	10	11
12	13	14	15	16	17	18
19	20	21	22	23	24	25
26	27	28	29	30		

April 2004

Su	Mo	Tu	We	Th	Fr	Sa
				1	2	3
4	5	6	7	8	9	10
11	12	13	14	15	16	17
18	19	20	21	22	23	24
25	26	27	28	29	30	

October 2004

Su	Mo	Tu	We	Th	Fr	Sa
					1	2
3	4	5	6	7	8	9
10	11	12	13	14	15	16
17	18	19	20	21	22	23
24	25	26	27	28	29	30
31						

May 2004

Su	Mo	Tu	We	Th	Fr	Sa
						1
2	3	4	5	6	7	8
9	10	11	12	13	14	15
16	17	18	19	20	21	22
23	24	25	26	27	28	29
30	31					

November 2004

Su	Mo	Tu	We	Th	Fr	Sa
	1	2	3	4	5	6
7	8	9	10	11	12	13
14	15	16	17	18	19	20
21	22	23	24	25	26	27
28	29	30				

June 2004

Su	Mo	Tu	We	Th	Fr	Sa
		1	2	3	4	5
6	7	8	9	10	11	12
13	14	15	16	17	18	19
20	21	22	23	24	25	26
27	28	29	30			

December 2004

Su	Mo	Tu	We	Th	Fr	Sa
			1	2	3	4
5	6	7	8	9	10	11
12	13	14	15	16	17	18
19	20	21	22	23	24	25
26	27	28	29	30	31	

Figure 13–9. 2004 calendar.

decided that the project management function will be the responsibility of the project manager. In addition, the development manager will estimate the requirements for technical specialists (those individuals responsible for completing activity tasks).

The WBS worksheet from Chapter 12 already exists and can be used for this purpose. The WBS listed the requirements associated with each activity, including the subtasks that must be completed to meet activity objectives. It will be used as a guide for identifying project staffing requirements, which will include the project manager and the technical specialist(s) needed to complete the tasks. The project objective is to select and install a PBX telephone system, and the telecommunications department will provide the staffing for the project management needs and the technical resource for defining the technical specifications, issuing an RFP, selecting a system, and coordinating the installation of the system with the selected vendor.

The Chapter 12 WBS was used as the base document for developing the staffing estimate shown in Table 13–5.

Staffing Analysis

The project requires the installation of a 1,000 line PBX/voice messaging system in a new corporate headquarters building scheduled to become operational on June 1, 2004. The

TABLE 13–5 Chapter 12 WBS Elements

Activity	Task Description	Staffing
Define requirements	Conduct user reviews Analyze traffic	1.0PM 1.0TM1
Design system	Obtain jack locations from facilities Determine user features Determine trunks needed Prepare specification documentation	1.0PM 1.0TM1
Select PBX system	Develop PBX system rating matrix Identify RFP bidders Prepare PBX system RFP Telecom: hold bidder's conference Develop RFP responses Answer ad hoc bidder questions Evaluate RFPs Clarify bidder information Select PBX system Notify selected vendor(s) Notify other vendors of selection decision Prepare PBX system contract Prepare PBX system purchase order Conduct bidder postdecision briefings	1.0PM 1.0TM1 .5TM2
Build system	Manufacture/assemble PBX system	.3PM
Precutover preparation	Prepare user guides Analyze stations: train users Facilities task: pass fire inspection Facilities task: obtain certificate of occupancy Facilities task: move in people Cutover system	
Order/ship/receive equipment	Facilities task: build equipment room (ER) Facilities task: install ER electric Facilities task: install halon system Facilities task: test halon system Order TelCo facilities Ship/receive PBX, MDF, IDF Ship/receive stations, jacks, cable Facilities task: install riser conduit	.5PM
Install MDF	Install MDF Connect TelCo network interface to MDF Punch down TelCo cable to MDF Test TelCo trunks	

TABLE 13–5   Chapter 12 WBS Elements (continued)

Activity	Task Description	Staffing
Install PBX common equipment	Install UPS Install PBX cabinets Install PBX power connection Install PBX to MDF cable Connect PBX trunk circuits to MDF Connect PBX station circuits to MDF Vendor tests PBX hardware Vendor loads generic PBX software Establish software database: ARS, ACD, etc. Acceptance test – final Facilities task: seal equipment room	
Install backbone wiring	Facilities task: install telephone closet electricity Install IDFs Install riser cables Punch down risers to MDF Punch down risers to IDFs Test MDF to IDF risers	
Install horizontal wiring	Facilities task: frame drywall offices Facilities task: install ceiling grid Facilities task: install under carpet power Facilities task: install power poles Facilities task: install electric in walls Facilities task: core drill third floor Facilities task: core drill first floor Install first floor cable runs to IDF Install second floor cable runs to IDF Install third floor cable runs to IDF Punch down first floor cables to IDF Punch down second floor cables to IDF Punch down third floor cables to IDF Facilities task: install drywall offices Facilities task: install drywall, electrical boxes Facilities task: install electric in power poles Install cable wire to first floor jacks Install cable wire to second floor jacks Install cable wire to third floor jacks Test IDF to jack cable runs Facilities task: seal core drills	.5PM .3TM1
Install station equipment	Facilities task: install ceiling tiles Facilities task: install carpets Facilities task: install cubicles and furniture Install stations Test stations	.5PM .3TM1
Postcutover activities	Provide ad hoc user training Provide on site support services Audit and accept PBX system Obtain end user approvals for system operation Complete operations documentation Complete project documentation Close out project	1.0PM 1.0TM1

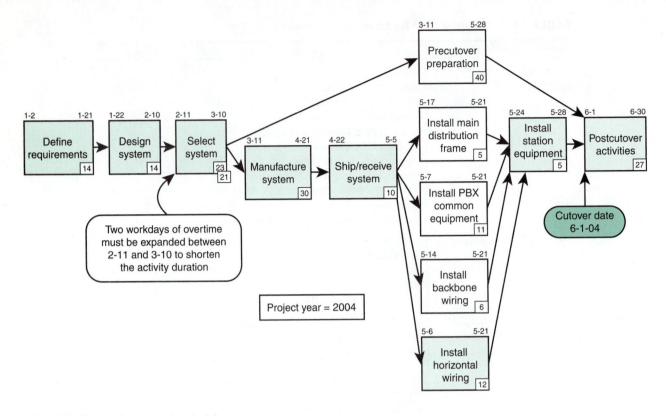

Figure 13–10. Project example schedule.

importance of such a project to the business enterprise should be clear to the reader, and it was the basis for an earlier statement that the development manager would assign a dedicated project manager to the PBX project. However, depending upon the project work requirements, the project manager assignment could be a full time or part time position. In view of the project's criticality, it is also important to ensure that a backup capability is provided in the event that the assigned project manager is unable to complete the project because of sickness, an accident, a job transfer, or leaving the company. Therefore, the development manager will plan for two positions and will use Table 13–5 as a worksheet for planning staffing requirements. The far right column will show the full time equivalent for each position (PM = project managers and TM1 = team member) by using a decimal notation to indicate the amount of each position to apply to a given activity (.5PM means that it estimated that 50% of the project manager's time will be dedicated to an activity). If required, a second team member (TM2) resource will be added.

Note that staffing has been shown for the CP activities only. This is because noncritical activities are completed during the same time periods as the critical path activities. This is seen more easily on the PBX project's final schedule, which is shown in Figure 13–10.

Figure 13–10 shows that: 1) the four installation activities are completed concurrently during the time period between May 6th and May 21st (the CP installation activity length), and 2) the precutover activity is completed during the time period between March 11th and May 28th – a time period that is concurrent with CP activity times.

The actual staffing needs are summarized in Figure 13–11. Both the project manager and team member 1 are dedicated 100% to the project during heavy workload times and are dedicated on a part time (or zero) basis during other time periods. For simplicity's sake, team member 2 was not shown in the figure. Figure 13–11 is basically a Gantt chart. The starting times for different CP activities are shown as the time line (x axis).

ASSIGNMENTS. The subject of assignments is largely academic because of the small project staffing level. There are really only two project team members: the project manager and team member 1 (the project's full time project team resource). The project manager will be accountable for all of the project team functions listed in

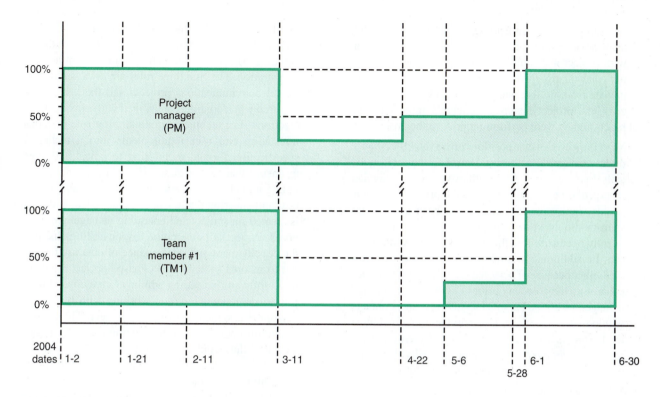

Figure 13–11. Year 2004 project team staffing requirements.

table 13–1 and will delegate some of these functions to team members 1 and 2. In this case, both the project manager and the team members provide project management and technical specialist resources, which is a common occurrence for small projects. Both the project manager and team members must have the technical skills needed to complete the tasks shown on the WBS to fulfill this dual role. The selected vendor will provide the major installation resource under the supervision of the project team.

The development manager completed the planning for the project by developing and documenting a game plan (Figure 13–11 and Table 13–4) and identifying the staffing levels needed for the project in Table 13–5 (a project manager and one full time team member). With this information, the development manager can begin the project organization effort and move the project forward through the project steps shown in Figure 13–1.

SUMMARY

This summary is organized to correspond with the learning objectives found at the beginning of the chapter.

1. *Project organization* refers to the selection of team members to carry out project management responsibilities. Project team members are responsible for utilizing project PTM resources effectively and efficiently to achieve project objectives. Their primary purpose is to complete the project on time and within budget while meeting the goals established for the project.

2. A project manager has the primary responsibility for completing a project successfully and must have many of the managerial attributes needed to be an effective functional manager. Projects come in all sizes. The project manager for a small project may be a telecommunications manager who performs the project manager functions on a part time basis. For larger projects, the project manager will be dedicated to the project and will have supervisory responsibility for other project team members. A project manager's responsibilities may include the development of project plans,

recruiting and recommending individuals for project team positions, maintaining ongoing communication with project stakeholders, monitoring project activities, and taking corrective measures when activities deviate from project plan elements. Once the project ends, the project manager frequently returns to the function they were performing prior to the project.

3. Most project manager positions are given little, if any, direct managerial authority. However, they will typically have two sources of authority they can exercise to expedite project activities. If the project's sponsor wields significant authority in the business and the sponsorship is known, a project manager can frequently operate within the power domain of the sponsor. In addition, an individual can have personal credibility because of personal knowledge or his or her position in the company prior to assuming the project manager position. Personal credibility and contacts within the company can also provide implicit authority. By properly exercising authority elements, project managers can exert influence on the individuals and organizations they deal with during project activities.

4. While good project management practices are essential for successfully meeting project goals, project management is an overhead cost that does not contribute directly to the design and implementation activities. As an overhead cost, it is a matter of balancing the value received by the project versus the cost of executing project management activities. Within this context, large, complex, mission-critical projects can justify project management overhead needs more easily than smaller, simpler projects. Telecommunications managers and project managers should constantly assess the value of project management processes to ensure that they are in balance with the project benefits that are realized.

5. The two most common organization structures used to implement projects in a business enterprise environment are functional organizations and team organizations. Functional project teams assign managerial and supervisory responsibilities to the project manager and to others if the team is large. In a business, team members frequently remain accountable to the functional department that is "lending" them to the project. In a team environment, managerial and supervisory responsibilities are assigned to all team members, and they are expected to function as self directed teams. A specialized project management team structure is the SWAT team. The team members are highly skilled at setting up project structures and turning the project structure over to team members who have lower skill levels.

6. The four basic roles that a project team may assume include 1) technical administration, 2) project administration, 3) project accounting, and 4) contract administration. The first three roles are always required for telecommunications projects and the last role is required when contracts are signed with outside organizations. The technical administration role includes translating end user requirements into a technical specification format, monitoring technical activities to ensure that technical specifications are met, providing a quality assurance check on technical activities, and ensuring that the appropriate documentation is created for project and operating management purposes. Project administration responsibilities include the development and maintenance of data used as input to manual systems or PC-based project management software, providing administrative control over project documentation, and working with functional personnel assigned tasks on the project. The project accounting personnel audit ongoing expenses to ensure that they conform to project budget categories and act as a financial liaison between the business's accounting department and the project. Contract administration is required when contracts are generated as part of the project process, and ensures that the appropriate internal legal reviews are provided. Contract administration also has the responsibility for making certain that the contractor and the project organization meet legal terms and conditions of contracts.

7. The project life cycle model provides a blueprint for the project management process by identifying different stages and milestones that should be incorporated into the project organization process. The telecommunications manager in charge of the project would develop a high-level plan used to identify various project organization elements. The plan would identify staffing requirements, major project steps, and the management approval milestones (used to ensure the ongoing viability of the project) in a schedule format that matches project schedule requirements.

8. A WBS provides a detailed breakdown of the various tasks that must be completed for various project activities. A good WBS provides an insight into the project team skills required on the project and the project management staffing needed to provide oversight management of project activities. Large, complex projects contain many WBS tasks and will require higher staffing levels and higher skill levels than simple projects. The WBS can be used as a basic worksheet to determine project team staffing needs.

KEY TERMS AND CONCEPTS

The language of telecommunications management is multifaceted and includes words and phrases from managerial, technological, accounting, regulatory, and other business areas. The definitions of these key terms and concepts can be found within the chapter and in the glossary.

Bona Fide Manager
Functional Team
Ninety-Ninety Rule of Projects
Organization Design and Structure
POLC Model

Project Accounting
Project Administration
Project Contract Administration
Project Life Cycle Model
Project Manager

Project Team Function
Project Technical Administration
Self Directed Team
SWAT Project Team

REVIEW

The following questions are open-ended—predefined answers are not included as part of the text. The purpose of these questions is to allow the readers to test themselves on the chapter material.

1. Explain the role of a telecommunications manager when the manager has delegated project management responsibilities to a project manager.

2. List and explain the telecommunications product life cycle model's six project steps.

3. Describe the responsibilities that may be assigned to a project manager.

4. What is meant by the term "implicit authority" within a project context?

5. Why is project management referred to as administrative overhead?

6. Describe the ninety/ninety rule of projects and its implications for managing projects.

7. Describe the differences between functional and self directed teams.

8. Explain the advantages with using a SWAT team approach for project management.

9. List and describe the four team building stages.

10. What responsibilities are included under the technical administration category?

11. What responsibilities are included under the project administration category?

12. What responsibilities are included under the project accounting category?

13. What responsibilities are included under the contract administration category?

14. Describe how to utilize a WBS table to estimate project staffing requirements.

MULTIPLE CHOICE

1. When a project is completed in a business that has a functional organization structure, project team members are most likely to _____.

   a. be terminated
   b. be reassigned to another project
   c. return to their functional department
   d. become part of a labor pool
   e. None of the above.

2. Completing a project successfully means _____. (Select all that apply.)

   a. completing performance evaluations
   b. completing the project on time
   c. using a cross functional team
   d. meeting project objectives
   e. creating a project network diagram

3. _____ of telecommunications project life cycle costs are incurred prior to the product acquisition stage.

   a. 10%
   b. 20%
   c. 40%
   d. 90%
   e. 100%

4. There are _____ project steps in the telecommunications project life cycle model.

   a. 2

   b. 4

   c. 5

   d. 6

   e. 8

5. A project manager's responsibilities include _____.

   a. maintaining personnel files

   b. developing a department budget

   c. creating a capital appropriation forecast

   d. monitoring project activities

6. The two skill components referenced in the 50%/50% Telecommunications Management Model are _____. (Select all that apply.)

   a. organization management

   b. technical administration

   c. contract management

   d. project management

   e. technology management

7. The ninety/ninety rule of projects states that _____. (Select all that apply.)

   a. the first 10% of a project takes 90% of the project time

   b. the last 10% of a project takes 90% of the project time

   c. the last 90% of a project takes 10% of the project time

   d. the first 90% of a project takes 10% of the time.

   e. 90% of a project takes 90% of the time

8. In a self directed team, managerial responsibilities are handled by _____.

   a. the functional manager

   b. team members

   c. a functional team

   d. the team leader

9. In a functional team, managerial responsibilities are handled by _____.

   a. the functional manager

   b. team members

   c. a functional team

   d. the team leader

10. The establishment of a team philosophy takes place during the _____ stage of the four step team creation process.

    a. forming

    b. storming

    c. norming

    d. performing

    e. managing

11. A _____ team is used to leverage project management skills when setting up a project.

    a. cross functional

    b. SWAT

    c. functional

    d. self directed

    e. football

12. The project accounting personnel _____.

    a. maintain the project management system

    b. define WBS elements

    c. issue reports to project stakeholders

    d. monitor the design process

13. The project's technical administration personnel _____.

    a. maintain the project management system

    b. define WBS elements

    c. issue reports to project stakeholders

    d. monitor the design process

14. A project's budget is normally established _____.

    a. during the strategic planning process

    b. during the tactical planning process

    c. during the operational planning process

    d. during the organize project phase of a project

    e. upon completion of the project

15. The ultimate responsibility for completing a telecommunications project successfully belongs to _____.

    a. the cross functional team

    b. the SWAT team

    c. the project manager

    d. the telecommunications manager

    e. the functional team

14

PROJECT MANAGEMENT: A CASE STUDY

LEARNING OBJECTIVES

There is one basic learning objective for this chapter: to understand and apply the information reviewed in Chapters 11, 12, and 13 to a hypothetical real world problem and develop a project schedule that has the necessary information for monitoring and controlling project activities. A case study format is used where the telecommunications project has been set within a business environment.

Readers are provided with an opportunity to assess their project management skills. To do this, they should evaluate the basic information provided at the beginning of the chapter, prepare a preliminary project schedule, and develop an administrative game plan from the perspective of a telecommunications manager who has been given the responsibility for establishing the project team that will implement the project. This will require developing a preliminary CPM plan with the same deliverables established in Chapter 12 and used to define project organization requirements in Chapter 13. Results can be checked against the example details that are provided.

In the real world, there are many right answers. The solution provided in this chapter is only one of several correct solutions.

INTRODUCTION

In Chapters 12 and 13, the project planning elements for implementing a PBX telephone system were discussed. Chapter 12 described the process of developing a project network diagram, determining its critical path, evaluating the initial project schedule, and modifying the project schedule to meet the project schedule requirements. Chapter 13 examined the project organization (the people side of project management) and established a project team to implement the Chapter 12 PBX telephone system. The task information from the Chapter 12 WBS worksheets was used to develop staffing estimates for the PBX system project.

In this chapter, the HealthProd Corporation will be moving into a new headquarters facility on September 2, 2003. HealthProd's telecommunications department will be implementing the internetworking infrastructure (LANs, WANs, and internetwork equipment) needed for supporting headquarters employees. A 1,200 station LAN will be installed. One of the telecommunications managers has been assigned to develop a preliminary project schedule and create a project team that will implement the project. The telecommunications manager will also develop an administrative game plan. This plan will include project team organization details and a preliminary project schedule. The schedule will be developed by using manual CPM calculations, and calculation results will be shown.

HEALTHPROD CASE STUDY DESCRIPTION

The HealthProd Corporation is a leading manufacturer and distributor of health care products. Its success in the competitive marketplace has given administrators the problem of managing fast-paced growth. Currently, there are six separate headquarters locations that house a total of 1,200 corporate employees who provide various corporate administrative services to HealthProd locations and employees. One of the ongoing complaints from corporate department heads is that the LAN environment varies from location to location; therefore, interlocation communication is a major problem.

The HealthProd Environment

HealthProd has three manufacturing plants, eight large distribution centers, and four sales division offices in the U.S. Currently, six leased locations house the existing corporate departments, and the upper management of Health-Prod's manufacturing and distribution organizations is located in the geographically dispersed manufacturing and distribution centers. The plan is to consolidate corporate personnel from the six separate locations into a single headquarters location. In addition, the customer services and order processing departments that are located in the eight distribution centers will also be consolidated to provide a centralized customer services and order processing department in the new headquarters location. These changes are seen as a way of standardizing the customer interface and improving support services, while using 800-services to provide an interface for customers.

Once the six corporate locations have been consolidated and the other reorganization changes are completed, the new corporate organization will be as shown in Figure 14–1.

The departments listed below the vice presidents in the Figure 14–1 organization chart are each headed by a director who, depending upon the department, may have multiple managers reporting to him or her.

The management board has been painfully aware of the difficulties caused by the physical separation of corporate departments, so they allocated the necessary funding to establish a new headquarters building capable of consolidating the staff from the separate locations. Planning efforts for the new headquarters have been underway for over three years, and a modular building design has been selected to handle future staffing increases. The property where the new headquarters will be located should be large enough to accommodate HealthProd's needs for at least a fifteen year period.

The new headquarters facility has been under construction for the last year, and September 2, 2003 is the target date for beginning full headquarters operations in the new facility.

Information Services Organization

The headquarters information services department provides computer and communications services to all Health-Prod locations. A small computer and communications staff is maintained in the various manufacturing and distribution center locations, but the corporate function has primary responsibility for handling the information technology needs of the entire corporation. The director of telecommunications heads up the telecommunications department, and the organization chart is shown in Figure 14–2.

There are ninety-five employees in the telecommunications department, which consists of five smaller departments: planning, development, operations, administrative services, and help desk. They provide 24 × 7 network services to all locations and will be providing online

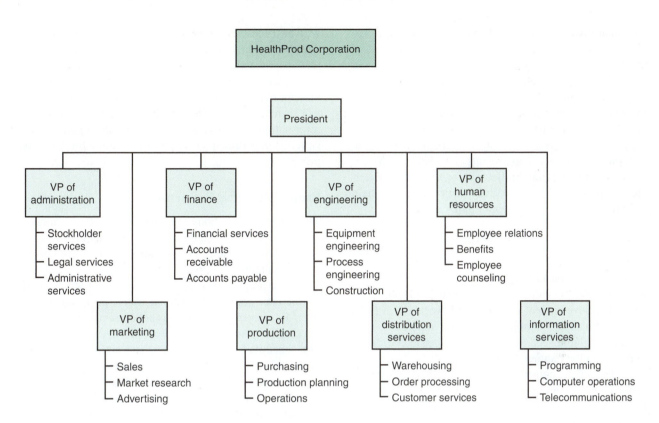

Figure 14–1. HealthProd corporate headquarter organization.

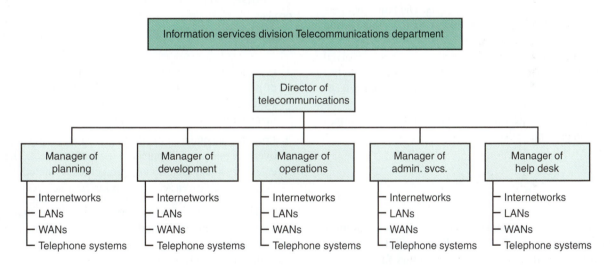

Figure 14–2. HealthProd telecommunications organization.

Web-based access to HealthProd customers in the new headquarters location.

In the telecommunications department, the development manager has the primary responsibility for implementing new telecommunications products and services for all locations and then transferring the operating responsibility to the operations manager. The help desk manager maintains an incident reporting system (IRS) for all telephone system and network operating problems reported by HealthProd network users. The administrative services manager is responsible for providing corporate directory services, generating end of month cost allocation reports for telephone system and network users, and authorizing the payment of bills for all telecommunications expenses. The development manager has the managerial responsibility for implementing the headquarters LAN project and will select the needed project team staffing from within the telecommunications department. This approach has been used for previous projects to broaden the experience of junior and senior technical specialists and help train them for managerial opportunities.

The Telecommunications Project

It is now January 2, 2003, and the development manager has begun work on an administrative game plan for implementing the 1,200 station LAN at the new headquarters facility. The development manager's role will be that of an overseer because the project's size and importance warrants setting up a separate project manager to coordinate implementation requirements.

The VP of engineering has requested that all organizations implementing products or services at the new headquarters provide project schedules for these activities. The corporate construction department will provide an overall coordination role to ensure that the construction facilities are available for these projects. The requested project schedules are to be submitted to the construction department by January 24, 2003.

While the development manager has been involved with the headquarters LAN planning effort during the last two years, the planning focus has been on developing technical and financial information. The request from the VP of engineering requires more detailed schedule information than currently exists.

CREATING A PROJECT ADMINISTRATION PLAN

The development manager will create a project administration plan for the 1,200 station LAN project, which will be implemented in the new headquarters facility. This plan should provide: 1) a preliminary project schedule for the corporate construction department and 2) a project plan for the LAN implementation. The latter step will require selecting project team personnel to staff the LAN project. As a result of HealthProd's rapid growth, many telecommunications department members are new to HealthProd and the development manager feels that it

will be necessary to provide more detailed startup instructions than would normally be required. These project details will be documented in the administrative game plan so that it can be used for discussions with the director of telecommunications and with prospective project team members. The administrative plan's schedule information will be used to provide the corporate construction department with a project schedule for the LAN project.

Project Planning Framework

The telecommunications department uses a telecommunications project life cycle model as the basis for planning and documenting telecommunications services and products (see Figure 13–1, page 341).

The project steps shown in Figure 13–1 will be used as reference points in the administrative project plan.

Because a project team is not currently in place, the development manager must provide a LAN implementation schedule for the corporate construction department. While this may appear to be a major effort, the reality is that the key date is the cutover date (September 2, 2003), which has already been established for all headquarters projects. The primary scheduling effort requires the use of this cutover date to establish reasonable estimates for the different activities needed to implement the LAN project.

The administrative game plan will be used for two purposes:

1. Provide a project framework for directing the efforts of project team members. This project framework would provide guidelines for selecting the project manager and project team members.

2. Provide a calendar of events to use when giving an overseer managerial control of the LAN project. The calendar should identify key project dates, including project postcutover activities and milestone events.

The first item is straightforward. However, the second item is more complicated. The development manager will be establishing a schedule from a minimal amount of information. Therefore, some of the preliminary activity dates may require adjustment when better information becomes available. However, this should not be a problem, because the only inflexible date is the cutover date (September 2, 2003). As long as the corporate construction schedule covers the major areas, any schedule deviations can be handled without problems if sufficient lead time is provided to corporate construction.

Project Administration Planning

Establishing a detailed plan at the beginning of the LAN project planning efforts will provide a framework for the LAN project and allow the development manager to share project plan information with the director of telecommunications and prospective project team members. The manager has found that most individuals are more participative in a planning process when they have a point of reference, and the development of the administrative plan will provide a focal point for LAN project discussions.

The project schedule will drive the administrative plan, and it will be necessary to develop preliminary project schedule estimates before a project team has actually been selected. Therefore, the preliminary schedule is not considered a final schedule but is one that can be modified as required. Administrative project plans should accurately reflect technical project activity requirements. The only way that this can be done is to develop technical project estimates before the detailed technical planning phase is undertaken.

> Preparation of a good, detailed administrative plan for a large technology project can be a tedious, time consuming activity. Failure to spend the necessary time up front will result in a situation where the manager is "winging it" and reacting to issues as they arise. Developing a game plan in advance allows a manager to assume a leadership role and control project activities.
>
> Good managers develop good plans and implement them successfully.

The Project Administrative Plan

The development manager begins the planning process by using a word processing table function and typing in key project dates (Table 14–1). Descriptive information is then added.

Note: The rough draft doesn't look rough because a word processing table function was used. The use of word processing software automatically creates a product that is suitable in appearance for any discussion (formal or informal).

Key milestone activities noted in Table 14–1 include:

- construction department schedule delivery
- communication with the director of telecommunications
- review and approval process meetings with upper management

- meetings to review various project team deliverables
- start/end dates for project steps
- project cutover date
- project completion date

The level of detail contained in the administrative plan is largely based on an individual manager's style. Table 14–1 provides a detailed plan based on examining both macro and micro level elements of the headquarters LAN project. The up-front work effort dedicated to the administrative plan will allow the development manager to delegate detailed activities within a well defined and well documented framework. If the dates on the administrative plan are compared to those in the following preliminary LAN schedule (Table 14–6), you can see that dates between the two overlap. This is because the project life cycle steps do not match the real world project network activities that are used to implement the project—and they are not expected to. The administrative plan schedule provides a "reasonable" schedule estimate and, as the project team creates the final documentation, the actual schedule will be created.

IS THIS "OVERKILL?" It requires a significant work effort to create the detailed plan shown in Table 14–1, and it is easy to discount such an effort as being "overkill." As previously outlined in this chapter, the headquarters LAN project will require hundreds of labor hours to complete and will be a million dollar investment. If the development manager spends several weeks on the administrative effort shown in Table 14–1, it is a small cost compared to the expense of the total project.

There are two major benefits associated with spending time to develop a good plan:

1. When good plans are shared with your manager and other business managers, you may gain personal credibility. The greatest compliment that any manager can be given is in the statement: "This proposal warrants serious consideration because (insert your name) always does his (or her) homework." Good planners are individuals who have done their homework, and managers who do their homework will acquire credibility from their dealings with others.

2. Effective managers utilize people resources effectively. Having a good plan and sharing it with others provides a focal point for further discussion. If the plan is sound, others will use it to increase their own effectiveness and efficiency. If the plan contains problems, it provides a focal point for resolving

TABLE 14–1 Development Manager's Preliminary Administrative Game Plan

Date	Task Description
1–2–03 (Thursday)	Begin work on administrative game plan. Key deliverables will include: 1. Document a preliminary project plan for headquarters LAN Project. 2. Creation of project documentation folder (project description, target dates, budget, etc.) to review with project team candidates. 3. Document project manager position responsibilities for project steps 1–5. 4. Identify and list potential candidates for project manager position. 5. Schedule initial interviews with project manager candidates and provide candidates with project and position description. Schedule follow-up meetings with finalists within five workdays of the initial meeting.
1–17–03 (Friday)	1. Complete initial project documentation for reviews with project manager candidates. This would include a preliminary WBS worksheet and the establishment of a project network diagram that will be used to establish preliminary project schedules. 2. Complete initial administrative game plan. (This table is the completed administrative game plan.) 3. Complete preliminary listing of project manager candidates. This includes having discussions with the candidates' managers prior to selecting candidates. 4. Review administrative game plan and preliminary project plan with director of telecommunications.
1–20–03 (Monday)	Notify project manager candidates and set up initial interview meetings.
1–22–03 (Wednesday)	1. Complete preliminary LAN project schedule. 2. Send letter to director of telecommunications with project schedule for construction department.
1–24–03 (Friday)	1. Meet with director of telecommunications. 2. Delivery of preliminary LAN project schedule to construction department.
2–4–03 (Tuesday)	Complete final interviews for project manager position.
2–6–03 (Thursday)	Complete preliminary selection of the project manager and obtain his/her manager's agreement.
2–7–03 (Friday)	1. Get the approval of director of telecommunications for selected project manager. 2. Notify selected project manager.
2–10–03 (Monday)	1. Formal announcement of project manager appointment. **2. Start project step 1.** 3. Develop LAN project schedule.
2–17–03 (Monday)	1. Review/approve project manager/step 1 recommendations: • preliminary project documentation • preliminary project network plan • risk assessment observations • project team recommendations • project communication plan (meetings, memos, etc.) • project financial plan
2–19–03 (Wednesday)	Review project step 1 recommendations with director of telecommunications. After getting director approval, organize upper management meeting to make recommendations and get approval to proceed with upper management meeting.
2–21–03 (Friday)	1. Review and approval process meeting completed with upper management. **2. Project step 1 completed.** 3. Announce project team member appointments.
2–24–03 (Monday)	**1. Start project step 2.** 2. Review project manager plans for completing step 2 requirements. 3. Kick off meeting with team members (project management + technical specialists).

TABLE 14–1   Development Manager's Preliminary Administrative Game Plan (continued)

Date	Task Description
4–14–03 (Monday)	Review/approve project team step 2 recommendations: • detailed project documentation • detailed project network plan • updated risk assessment observations • final project financial plan
4–16–03 (Wednesday)	Review project team step 2 recommendations with director of telecommunications and obtain approval to proceed with upper management review meeting.
4–18–03 (Friday)	1. Review and approval process meeting completed with upper management. 2. **Project step 2 completed.**
4–21–03 (Monday)	**Start project step 3.**
6–16–03 (Monday)	Review/approve project team step 3 recommendations: • summary evaluation of LAN alternatives • LAN vendor recommendation • seven year financial plan • implementation schedule
6–18–03 (Wednesday)	Review project team step 3 recommendations with director of telecommunications and obtain approval to proceed with upper management review meeting.
6–20–03 (Friday)	1. Last review and approval process meeting completed with upper management. 2. **Project step 3 completed.**
6–2–03 (Monday)	1. **Start project step 4.** 2. **Start project step 5.**
7–18–03 (Friday)	**Project step 4 completed.**
9–2–03 (Tuesday)	**HQ LAN cutover date** 1. **Project step 5 completed.** 2. **Start project step 6.**
9–29–03 (Monday)	**Project step 6 completed.** Review project team step 6 status with director of telecommunications and obtain approval to formally close project.
10–1–03 **(Wednesday)**	1. **Formal transfer of project to operations management.** 2. **Project completed.** 3. **Hold final project review meeting with upper management.**

problems during the planning stage (not after it has already been implemented).

Note: A word of warning is appropriate. The level of planning used for any effort should be proportionate to the value that will be received from the results of the planning. Large, expensive, mission-critical projects warrant high planning levels; small, mundane projects do not warrant a heavy investment in planning. However, the same level of managerial accountability exists for both project types. From a common sense perspective, it will require less effort to obtain good results for simpler projects.

Preliminary Project Schedule Estimate

While it is possible to provide a gross project time duration estimate for the project, it would not provide adequate schedule information for the construction department. The

TABLE 14–2 Project Description

Installation of a 1,200-Workstation LAN + Internetwork at the New HealthProd Headquarters Building Scheduled for Occupancy on September 2, 2003.	
Current date:	January 2, 2003
Project start date:	February 24, 2003
Cutover date:	September 2, 2003
Workdays:	Monday through Friday, 8 am to 5 pm
	Weekend overtime available
Holidays:	New Years Day, Memorial Day, Labor Day, Independence Day, Thanksgiving Day, Christmas Day

development manager has worked on LAN projects in the past and has maintained reference files for these activities. Table 14–2 and Figure 14–3 provide the preliminary project description and project network diagram documentation that the manager has established for the headquarters LAN project.

The preliminary WBS table established by the manager for this project network is shown in Table 14–3.

Table 14–3 shows that 195 project workdays will be needed to complete the project. The manager's notes didn't identify the resources needed to support this schedule—that will be determined as part of step 2 activities. The

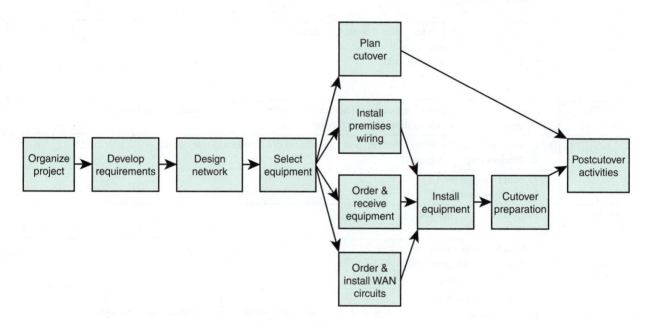

Figure 14–3. Headquarters LAN project preliminary project network diagram.

TABLE 14–3 Headquarters LAN Project WBS

Activity/Phase	Task Description	Days
Organize the project	Set project objectives.	**15**
	Organize project team.	
	Hold kickoff meeting.	
	Set cutover dates.	
	Schedule project team meetings.	
	Project team organization complete.	
	Identify constraints.	
	Develop task list.	
	Develop project network diagram.	
	Develop detailed cutover schedule.	
	Project schedule complete.	

TABLE 14–3   Headquarters LAN Project WBS (continued)

Activity/Phase	Task Description	Days
Develop requirements	Identify applications that will run over the network.	**15**
	Identify need for mainframe connectivity.	
	Identify workstation locations.	
	Identify workstation requirements.	
	Identify printing requirements.	
	Identify LAN remote access requirements.	
	Requirements completed.	
Design network	Select LAN architecture.	**30**
	Select network operating system.	
	Select workstation operating system.	
	Select backbone architecture.	
	Select backbone protocol (Ethernet, FDDI, etc.).	
	Select network transmission medium.	
	Calculate bandwidth requirements.	
	Estimate network load.	
	Identify network management requirements.	
	Determine UPS requirements.	
	Determine hub configuration.	
	Determine switching requirements.	
	Design hub hierarchy.	
	Provide space for hubs.	
	Determine NMS workstation requirements.	
	Determine network security requirements.	
	Determine internetworking requirements.	
	Design IP addressing system.	
	Design subnet architecture.	
	Design domain name and IP addressing structure.	
	Establish computer names.	
	Develop a security plan for the file server.	
	Select type of public network facilities.	
	Identify file server requirements.	
	Design the directory structure.	
	Determine specialized server requirements.	
	Identify outside support requirements.	
	Establish workstation software standards.	
	Determine station wiring requirements.	
	Specifications completed.	
Select equipment	Prepare RFPs.	**25**
	Issue RFPs.	
	Identify product selection criteria.	
	Receive LAN proposals.	
	RFP responses received.	
	Review LAN proposals.	
	Select vendor.	
	Equipment selected.	
Plan cutover	Develop network cutover plan.	**12**
	Develop network testing plan.	
	Develop backup strategy.	
	Develop training plans.	

TABLE 14–3 Headquarters LAN Project WBS (continued)

Activity/Phase	Task Description	Days
	Cutover planning complete.	
Order & receive equipment	Order network hardware.	18
	Order network operating system.	
	Order server.	
	Equipment ordered.	
	Deliver network hardware.	
	Deliver network operating system.	
	Deliver server.	
	Equipment on site.	
Order & install WAN circuits	Order public network (WAN) circuits.	10
	Install WAN circuits.	
	WAN circuits installed.	
Install premises wiring	Install backbone cabling.	20
	Install horizontal and station wiring.	
	Wiring installed.	
Install equipment	Install network hardware.	25
	Install internetworking equipment.	
	Install hubs and switches.	
	Install server.	
	Install network operating system.	
	Install directory structure.	
	Transfer files to file server.	
	Set up users on servers.	
	Install security on servers.	
	Configure network printers.	
	Install network management system.	
	Configure network management system.	
	Create user environment.	
	Install network printers.	
	Install workstations.	
	Test network operations.	
	Installation complete.	
Cutover preparation	Train users.	5
	Set up help desk.	
	Cut over network.	
	Complete cutover preparation.	
Postcutover activities	Provide ad hoc user training.	20
	Provide cutover support services.	
	Audit and accept PBX system.	
	Obtain end user operational approvals.	
	Complete operations documentation.	
	Complete project documentation.	
	Close out project.	
	Total workdays	195

estimates used are based on the development manager's experience with similar projects.

The activity durations shown in the WBS table provided the information needed to make the manual critical path calculations that are shown in Figure 14–4. The critical path activities have been shaded, and the various ES, EF, LS, and LF values for each activity are shown on the project network diagram. Figure 14–4 information was transferred to Table 14–4, where the float (slack) calculations were identified for each activity.

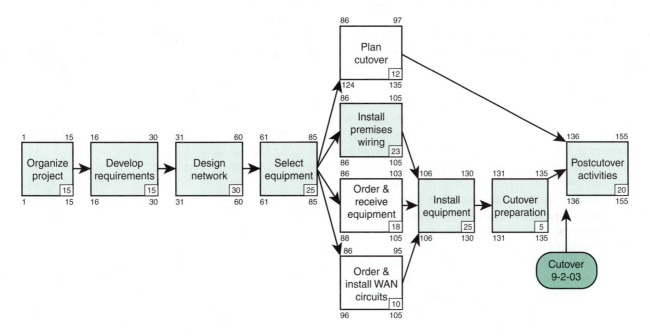

Figure 14–4. Headquarters LAN project preliminary project network diagram.

TABLE 14–4 Headquarters LAN Critical Path Calculations

	System Cutover: September 2, 2003 (Tuesday)						
CP	Activity	Duration	ES	EF	LS	LF	Float
X	**Organize project**	**15**	**1**	**15**	**1**	**15**	**0**
X	**Develop requirements**	**15**	**16**	**30**	**16**	**30**	**0**
X	**Design network**	**30**	**31**	**60**	**31**	**60**	**0**
X	**Select equipment**	**25**	**61**	**85**	**61**	**85**	**0**
	Plan cutover	12	86	97	124	135	38
X	**Install premises wiring**	**20**	**86**	**105**	**86**	**105**	**0**
	Order & receive equipment	18	86	103	88	105	2
	Order & install WAN circuits	10	86	95	96	105	10
X	**Install equipment**	**25**	**106**	**130**	**106**	**130**	**0**
X	**Cutover preparation**	**5**	**131**	**135**	**131**	**135**	**0**
X	**Postcutover activities**	**20**	**136**	**155**	**136**	**155**	**0**
	Activity CP total	**155**					

Note: CP activities are shown in bold.

The use of CPM has compressed the 195 project workdays initially provided on the WBS (Table 14–3) into the 155 workday schedule shown in Table 14–4. The next step will be to identify the project schedule implication of this workday estimate. This will be developed based on using the Table 14–4 information to identify activity forward and backward pass schedules on a calendar.

Figure 14–5a provides the 2003 calendar used to develop the forward pass and backward pass schedule shown in Figures 14–5b and 14–5c.

SCHEDULING PROBLEM. When reviewing the forward pass schedule (Figures 14–5b), it is evident that the preliminary project estimate completes the project on September 3. This means that the LAN facilities would not be available for use until the following day (September 4), two days after the cutover date of September 2. This is clearly an unacceptable situation. The development manager created a backward pass schedule (Figure 14–5c) based on completing the project work on the last workday before the cutover date (August 29).

To simplify the information in Figures 14–5b and 14–5c, it has been summarized in Table 14–5 and in Figure 14–6. (The dates derived in Figures 14–5a and 14–5c could also have been calculated by using Excel functions. The Excel calculations are provided on the electronic solution CD that accompanies the text).

After reviewing Table 14–5 and Figure 14–6, the development manager felt that the simplest solution was to use overtime on the install equipment activity to shorten its duration by two days and allow the project to cutover on September 2, the mandatory cutover date. Extracting the appropriate early and late schedule dates from Table 14–5, the final schedule (Table 14–6) was created.

Note: The technical schedule (Table 14–5) presumes knowledge of CPM because it lists ES, EF, LS, and LF dates—terminology that is not clear to someone who is not familiar with CPM. The Table 14–6 schedule can be understood by anyone, and is the schedule format of choice for business management purposes.

The final schedule information in Table 14–6 was placed on the project network diagram to provide a graphical view of the schedule. This is shown in Figure 14–7.

At this time, the development manager has developed a project schedule that meets project cutover (September 2, 2003) requirements and can be used to fulfill the construction department's schedule needs. In addition, this preliminary project plan can be used to explain the project's scope to the director of telecommunications, project manager candidates, prospective team members, or anyone else who is interested in project details.

Figure 14–5a. Year 2003 calendar.

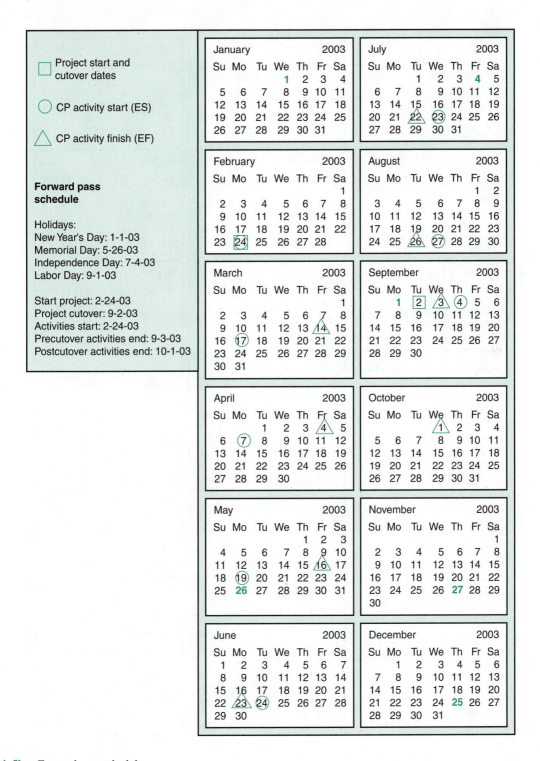

Figure 14–5b. Forward pass schedule.

Project start and cutover dates

○ CP activity start (ES)

△ CP activity finish (EF)

Backward pass schedule

Holidays:
New Year's Day: 1-1-03
Memorial Day: 5-26-03
Independence Day: 7-4-03
Labor Day: 9-1-03

Start project: 2-24-03
Project cutover: 9-2-03
Activities start: 2-20-03
Precutover activities end: 8-29-03
Postcutover activities end: 9-29-03

January						2003
Su	Mo	Tu	We	Th	Fr	Sa
			1	2	3	4
5	6	7	8	9	10	11
12	13	14	15	16	17	18
19	20	21	22	23	24	25
26	27	28	29	30	31	

July						2003
Su	Mo	Tu	We	Th	Fr	Sa
		1	2	3	4	5
6	7	8	9	10	11	12
13	14	15	16	17	18	19
20	21	22	23	24	25	26
27	28	29	30	31		

February						2003
Su	Mo	Tu	We	Th	Fr	Sa
						1
2	3	4	5	6	7	8
9	10	11	12	13	14	15
16	17	18	19	20	21	22
23	24	25	26	27	28	

August						2003
Su	Mo	Tu	We	Th	Fr	Sa
					1	2
3	4	5	6	7	8	9
10	11	12	13	14	15	16
17	18	19	20	21	22	23
24	25	26	27	28	29	30

March						2003
Su	Mo	Tu	We	Th	Fr	Sa
						1
2	3	4	5	6	7	8
9	10	11	12	13	14	15
16	17	18	19	20	21	22
23	24	25	26	27	28	29
30	31					

September						2003
Su	Mo	Tu	We	Th	Fr	Sa
	1	2	3	4	5	6
7	8	9	10	11	12	13
14	15	16	17	18	19	20
21	22	23	24	25	26	27
28	29	30				

April						2003
Su	Mo	Tu	We	Th	Fr	Sa
		1	2	3	4	5
6	7	8	9	10	11	12
13	14	15	16	17	18	19
20	21	22	23	24	25	26
27	28	29	30			

October						2003
Su	Mo	Tu	We	Th	Fr	Sa
			1	2	3	4
5	6	7	8	9	10	11
12	13	14	15	16	17	18
19	20	21	22	23	24	25
26	27	28	29	30	31	

May						2003
Su	Mo	Tu	We	Th	Fr	Sa
				1	2	3
4	5	6	7	8	9	10
11	12	13	14	15	16	17
18	19	20	21	22	23	24
25	26	27	28	29	30	31

November						2003
Su	Mo	Tu	We	Th	Fr	Sa
						1
2	3	4	5	6	7	8
9	10	11	12	13	14	15
16	17	18	19	20	21	22
23	24	25	26	27	28	29
30						

June						2003
Su	Mo	Tu	We	Th	Fr	Sa
1	2	3	4	5	6	7
8	9	10	11	12	13	14
15	16	17	18	19	20	21
22	23	24	25	26	27	28
29	30					

December						2003
Su	Mo	Tu	We	Th	Fr	Sa
	1	2	3	4	5	6
7	8	9	10	11	12	13
14	15	16	17	18	19	20
21	22	23	24	25	26	27
28	29	30	31			

Figure 14–5c. Backward pass schedule.

What If . . . ?

What if the development manager did not have the necessary skills to develop the technical schedule that becomes the basis for developing the administrative (project organization) plan?

In this case, managerial judgment must be exercised by delegating the technical plan development task to someone who has the necessary skills. This could be someone in the telecommunications department (Figure 14–2) or someone hired from the outside. If the development

CHAPTER 14

TABLE 14–5 Headquarters LAN Technical Schedule

	System Cutover: September 2, 2003 (Tuesday)					
CP	*Activity*	*Duration*	*ES*	*EF*	*LS*	*LF*
X	**Organize project**	**15**	**2–24–03**	**3–14–03**	2–20–03	3–12–03
X	**Develop requirements**	**15**	**3–17–03**	**4–4–03**	3–13–03	4–2–03
X	**Design network**	**30**	**4–7–03**	**5–16–03**	4–3–03	5–14–03
X	**Select equipment**	**25**	**5–19–03**	**6–23–03**	5–15–03	6–19–03
	Plan cutover	12	**6–24–03**	7–10–03	8–14–03	**8–29–03**
X	**Install premises wiring**	**20**	**6–24–03**	**7–22–03**	6–20–03	7–18–03
	Order & receive equipment	18	**6–24–03**	**7–18–03**	6–24–03	7–18–03
	Order & install WAN circuits	10	**6–24–03**	**7–8–03**	7–7–03	7–18–03
X	**Install equipment**	**25**	**7–23–03**	8–26–03	7–21–03	**8–22–03**
X	**Cutover preparation**	**5**	8–27–03	9–3–03	**8–25–03**	**8–29–03**
X	**Postcutover activities**	**20**	9–4–03	10–1–03	**9–2–03**	**9–29–03**
	Activity CP total	**155**				

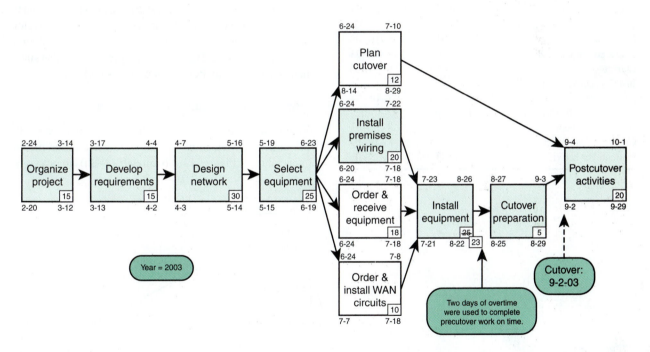

Figure 14–6. Headquarters LAN project technical schedule.

manager is a 50%/50% manager—someone who has strong skills in management (business and technology) and telecommunications technology—there is a strong likelihood that the task of carrying out detailed planning can be done on a personal basis. If not, it will be necessary to obtain the necessary skills from someone else so that the administrative plan can be completed.

Plan *v.* Actual Summary

The development manager's original objectives were to:

1. provide a project framework for directing the efforts of project team members. This project framework would provide guidelines for the project manager and project team members.

2. provide a calendar of events to use when giving an overseer managerial control of the LAN project. This will require the identification of key project dates, including project postcutover activities, and specifying milestone events for these dates.

Examination of the project administrative plan (Table 14–1) and the preliminary project plan information will show that the development manager has met the initial objectives. In addition, the work effort also provided a preliminary schedule for the corporate construction department's request.

TABLE 14–6   Headquarters LAN Final Schedule

System Cutover: September 2, 2003 (Tuesday)		
Activity	*Start*	*Finish*
Organize project	2–24–03	3–14–03
Develop requirements	3–17–03	4–4–03
Design internetwork	4–7–03	5–16–03
Select equipment	5–19–03	6–23–03
Plan cutover	6–24–03	8–29–03
Install premises wiring	6–24–03	7–22–03
Order & receive equipment	6–24–03	7–18–03
Order & install WAN circuits	6–24–03	7–8–03
Install equipment	7–23–03	8–22–03
Cutover preparation	8–25–03	8–29–03
Postcutover activities	9–2–03	9–29–03

CORPORATE CONSTRUCTION SCHEDULE

In the HealthProd case study, it is now January 17 (Table 14–1) and the development manager has completed the project administration plan, which includes a preliminary project plan schedule.

It is still necessary to provide the corporate construction department with a project schedule for the headquarters LAN project, and the appropriate format for completing this assignment would be to draft a memo containing the schedule. Because the memo will be sent to the VP of engineering, the development manager believes that the director of telecommunications should approve the letter before it is sent. In addition, it would be a good time to update the director of telecommunications about the project's scope and get approval (or change recommendations) for the preliminary plans. Therefore, the development manager plans on reviewing two deliverables with the director of telecommunications: 1) the corporate construction schedule memo and 2) a PowerPoint presentation that summarizes the headquarters LAN project's preliminary plan.

The Corporate Construction Letter Deliverable

Figure 14–8a shows the letter that will be reviewed with the director of telecommunications. Note that the memo "appendices" (Figures 14–8b through 14–8h) are in a word

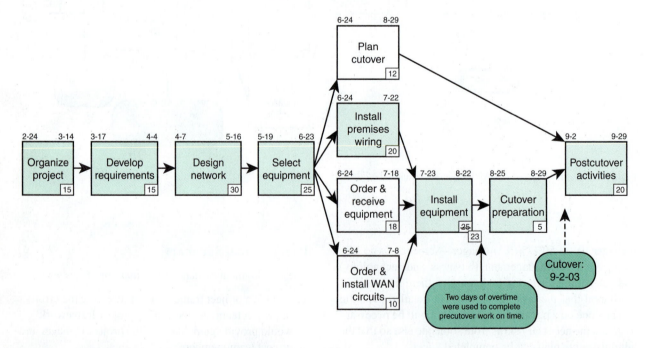

Figure 14–7.   Headquarters LAN project final schedule.

Date: January 22, 2003

To: Director of Telecommunications
From: Development Manager
Subject: Headquarters LAN Project Schedule

Attached is the headquarters LAN project schedule information requested by the vice president of corporate construction. It provides project schedule information so that the LAN project can be coordinated with the overall headquarters construction schedule.

Background Information
The new headquarters location is scheduled to begin operations on September 2, 2003, and the telecommunications project will be installing a 1,200 workstation LAN for corporate employees. The LAN is scheduled for completion on Friday, August 29 so that it will be fully tested and operational for headquarters employees on Tuesday, September 2.

Project Schedule
The project schedule was developed with CPM calculations—the planning management procedures being used by the construction department for their project planning efforts. The LAN schedule is as follows:

Activity	Start	Finish
1. Organize project	2-24-03	3-14-03
2. Develop requirements	3-17-03	4-4-03
3. Design internetwork	4-7-03	5-16-03
4. Select equipment	5-19-03	6-23-03
5. Plan cutover	6-24-03	8-29-03
6. Install premises wiring	6-24-03	7-22-03
7. Order & receive equipment	6-24-03	7-18-03
8. Order & install WAN circuits	6-24-03	7-8-03
9. Install equipment	7-23-03	8-22-03
10. Cutover preparation	8-25-03	8-29-03
11. Postcutover activities	9-2-03	9-29-03

Items 6 through 9 will require close coordination with the construction department to ensure that the facilities are ready for the LAN installation work.

Appendices A through C provide the technical CPM scheduling details for Corporate Construction department personnel and will allow them to incorporate LAN Project information into the overall construction project schedule.

Weekend Accessibility
While the LAN project will be done primarily during normal working hours (8 a.m. to 5 p.m., Monday through Friday), it will be necessary to have facility access during the weekends of July 26/27 and August 2/4 to work overtime so that the necessary LAN project work can be completed on time. Preliminary discussions with the Construction department have indicated that the facilities will be ready for the weekend LAN installation work.

Conclusions/Next Steps
This memo and attachments should provide the Construction department with the information they requested. Please forward the memo to Corporate Construction by January 24 (Friday)—the deadline established by the VP of engineering for receiving the LAN schedule information.

Figure 14–8. Example corporate construction letter.

Attachments:

Appendix A. LAN Project Schedule

Appendix B. WBS Worksheet

Appendix C. Critical Path Calculations

Year 2003 Calendar

Figure 14–8. (continued)

processing format – not in the original spreadsheet used to create them. The memo is intended to be a polished document suitable for review by upper management. The memo body avoids technical jargon while indicating that technical details are attached for corporate construction personnel who are knowledgeable about CPM. A document in this format has a much better chance of being forwarded to and understood by upper management.

This letter would be sent to the director of telecommunications in advance of the letter's due date (January 22) referenced in the memo. The director would have the option to forward it if there were no questions. On the other hand, the January 24 meeting will provide the director with the opportunity to bring up any questions, while still providing the development manager with time to react to any change requirements.

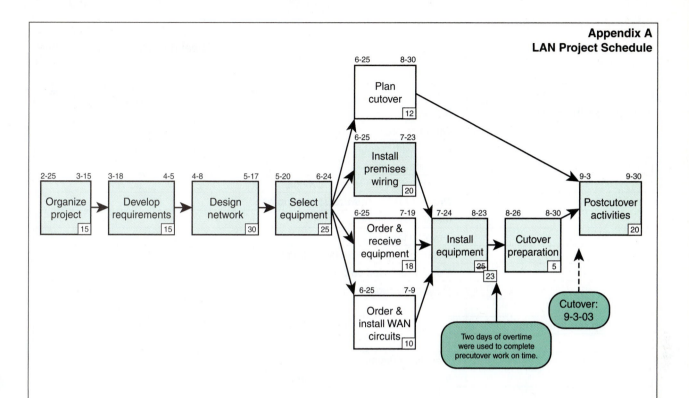

System cutover: September 2, 2003 (Tuesday)

Activity	Duratn	ES	EF	LS	LF
Organize project	15	2-24-03	3-14-03	2-20-03	3-12-03
Develop requirements	15	3-17-03	4-4-03	3-13-03	4-2-03
Design network	30	4-7-03	5-16-03	4-3-03	5-14-03
Select equipment	25	5-19-03	6-23-03	5-15-03	6-19-03
Plan cutover	12	6-24-03	7-10-03	8-14-03	8-29-03
Install premises wiring	20	6-24-03	7-22-03	6-20-03	7-18-03
Order & receive equipment	18	6-24-03	7-18-03	6-24-03	7-18-03
Order & install WAN circuits	10	6-24-03	7-8-03	7-7-03	7-18-03
Install equipment	25	7-23-03	8-26-03	7-21-03	8-22-03
Cutover preparation	5	8-27-03	9-3-03	8-25-03	8-29-03
Postcutover activities	20	9-4-03	10-1-03	9-2-03	9-29-03
Activity CP total	155				

Figure 14–8.   (continued)

Activity/Phase	Task description	Days
Organize the project	Set project objectives.	**15**
	Organize project team.	
	Hold kickoff meeting.	
	Set cutover dates.	
	Schedule project team meetings.	
	Project team organization complete.	
	Identify constraints.	
	Develop task list.	
	Develop project network diagram.	
	Develop detailed cutover schedule.	
	Project schedule complete.	
Develop requirements	Identify applications that will run over the network.	**15**
	Identify need for mainframe connectivity.	
	Identify workstation locations.	
	Identify workstation requirements.	
	Identify printing requirements.	
	Identify LAN remote access requirements.	
	Requirements completed.	
Design network	Select LAN architecture.	**30**
	Select network operating system.	
	Select workstation operating system.	
	Select backbone architecture.	
	Select backbone protocol (Ethernet, FDDI, etc.).	
	Select network transmission medium.	
	Calculate bandwidth requirements.	
	Estimate network load.	
	Identify network management requirements.	
	Determine UPS requirements.	
	Determine hub configuration.	
	Determine switching requirements.	
	Design hub hierarchy.	
	Provide space for hubs.	
	Determine NMS workstation requirements.	
	Determine network security requirements.	
	Determine internetworking requirements.	
	Design IP addressing system.	
	Design subnet architecture.	
	Design domain name and IP addressing structure.	

Figure 14–8. (continued)

Activity/Phase	Task description	Days
	Establish computer names.	
	Develop a security plan for the file server.	
	Select type of public network facilities.	
	Identify file server requirements.	
	Design the directory structure.	
	Determine specialized server requirements.	
	Identify outside support requirements.	
	Establish workstation software standards.	
	Determine station wiring requirements.	
	Specifications completed.	
Select equipment	Prepare request for proposals (RFPs).	**25**
	Issue RFPs.	
	Identify product selection criteria.	
	Receive LAN proposals.	
	RFP responses received.	
	Review LAN proposals.	
	Select vendor.	
	Equipment selected.	
Plan cutover	Develop network cutover plan.	**12**
	Develop network testing plan.	
	Develop backup strategy.	
	Develop training plans.	
	Cutover planning complete.	
Order & receive equipment	Order network hardware.	**18**
	Order network operating system.	
	Order server.	
	Equipment ordered.	
	Deliver network hardware.	
	Deliver network operating system.	
	Deliver server.	
	Equipment on site.	
Order & install WAN circuits	Order public network (WAN) circuits.	**10**
	Install WAN circuits.	
	WAN circuits Installed.	
Install premises wiring	Install backbone cabling.	**20**
	Install horizontal and station wiring.	
	Wiring installed.	

Figure 14–8. (continued)

Activity/Phase	Task description	Days
Install equipment	Install network hardware.	**25**
	Install internetworking equipment.	
	Install hubs and switches.	
	Install server.	
	Install network operating system.	
	Install directory structure.	
	Transfer files to the file server.	
	Set up users on servers.	
	Install security on servers.	
	Configure network printers.	
	Install network management system.	
	Configure network management system.	
	Create user environment.	
	Install network printers.	
	Install workstations.	
	Test network operations.	
	Installation complete.	
Cutover preparation	Train users.	**5**
	Set up help desk.	
	Cut over network.	
	Complete cutover preparation.	
Postcutover activities	Provide ad hoc user training.	**20**
	Provide cutover support services.	
	Audit and accept PBX system.	
	Obtain end-user operational approvals.	
	Complete operations documentation.	
	Complete project documentation.	
	Close out project.	
	Total workdays	**195**

Figure 14–8. (continued)

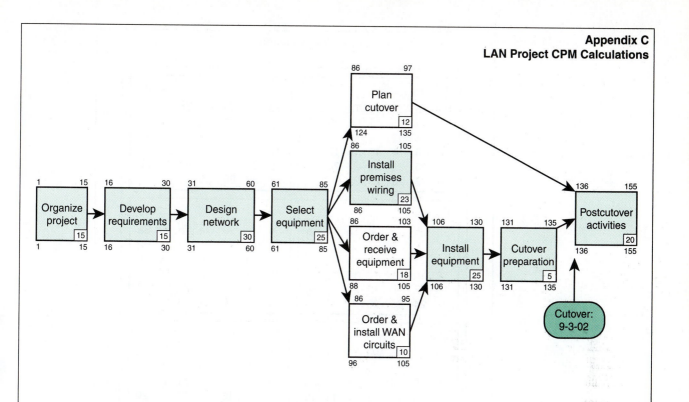

System Cutover: September 2, 2003 (Tuesday)

CP	Activity	Duration	ES	EF	LS	LF
X	**Organize project**	**15**	**1**	**15**	**1**	**15**
X	**Develop requirements**	**15**	**16**	**30**	**16**	**30**
X	**Design network**	**30**	**31**	**60**	**31**	**60**
X	**Select equipment**	**25**	**61**	**85**	**61**	**85**
	Plan cutover	12	86	97	124	135
X	**Install premises wiring**	**20**	**86**	**105**	**86**	**105**
	Order & receive equipment	18	86	103	88	105
	Order & install WAN circuits	10	86	95	96	105
X	**Install equipment**	**25**	**106**	**130**	**106**	**130**
X	**Cutover preparation**	**5**	**131**	**135**	**131**	**135**
X	**Postcutover activities**	**20**	**136**	**155**	**136**	**155**
	Activity CP total	**155**				

Figure 14–8. (continued)

Figure 14–8.
(continued)

2003 Calendar

January						2003
Su	Mo	Tu	We	Th	Fr	Sa
			1	2	3	4
5	6	7	8	9	10	11
12	13	14	15	16	17	18
19	20	21	22	23	24	25
26	27	28	29	30	31	

July						2003
Su	Mo	Tu	We	Th	Fr	Sa
		1	2	3	**4**	5
6	7	8	9	10	11	12
13	14	15	16	17	18	19
20	21	22	23	24	25	26
27	28	29	30	31		

February						2003
Su	Mo	Tu	We	Th	Fr	Sa
						1
2	3	4	5	6	7	8
9	10	11	12	13	14	15
16	17	18	19	20	21	22
23	24	25	26	27	28	

August						2003
Su	Mo	Tu	We	Th	Fr	Sa
					1	2
3	4	5	6	7	8	9
10	11	12	13	14	15	16
17	18	19	20	21	22	23
24	25	26	27	28	29	30

March						2003
Su	Mo	Tu	We	Th	Fr	Sa
						1
2	3	4	5	6	7	8
9	10	11	12	13	14	15
16	17	18	19	20	21	22
23	24	25	26	27	28	29
30	31					

September						2003
Su	Mo	Tu	We	Th	Fr	Sa
	1	2	3	4	5	6
7	8	9	10	11	12	13
14	15	16	17	18	19	20
21	22	23	24	25	26	27
28	29	30				

April						2003
Su	Mo	Tu	We	Th	Fr	Sa
		1	2	3	4	5
6	7	8	9	10	11	12
13	14	15	16	17	18	19
20	21	22	23	24	25	26
27	28	29	30			

October						2003
Su	Mo	Tu	We	Th	Fr	Sa
			1	2	3	4
5	6	7	8	9	10	11
12	13	14	15	16	17	18
19	20	21	22	23	24	25
26	27	28	29	30	31	

May						2003
Su	Mo	Tu	We	Th	Fr	Sa
				1	2	3
4	5	6	7	8	9	10
11	12	13	14	15	16	17
18	19	20	21	22	23	24
25	**26**	27	28	29	30	31

November						2003
Su	Mo	Tu	We	Th	Fr	Sa
						1
2	3	4	5	6	7	8
9	10	11	12	13	14	15
16	17	18	19	20	21	22
23	24	25	26	**27**	28	29
30						

June						2003
Su	Mo	Tu	We	Th	Fr	Sa
1	2	3	4	5	6	7
8	9	10	11	12	13	14
15	16	17	18	19	20	21
22	23	24	25	26	27	28
29	30					

December						2003
Su	Mo	Tu	We	Th	Fr	Sa
	1	2	3	4	5	6
7	8	9	10	11	12	13
14	15	16	17	18	19	20
21	22	23	24	**25**	26	27
28	29	30	31			

PRELIMINARY PLAN PRESENTATION

The development manager intends the preliminary plan presentation (Figures 14–9a through 14–9g) to provide an informal status update for the telecommunications director and will limit the number of presentation slides to seven—including the title page. The slide topics are open ended and the manager can react to the director's areas of interest while the limited number of slides should ensure a relatively brief update. A long, detailed status update will not be appropriate until the project team is in place.

HealthProd
Headquarters LAN
Project

January 24, 2003

Figure 14–9a. Telecommunications director presentation (slide 1 of 7).

Agenda

- Project description
- Project framework
- Project network diagram
- Preliminary project schedule
- Project organization status

Figure 14–9b. Telecommunications director presentation (slide 2 of 7).

Project Description

- 1,200 workstation LAN at headquarters
- Cutover: September 2, 2003 (Tuesday)
- Project start date: February 24, 2003
- CPM scheduling
  —Also used by corporate construction
- Project management
  —CPM software
  —Plan *v.* actual

Figure 14–9c. Telecommunications director presentation (slide 3 of 7).

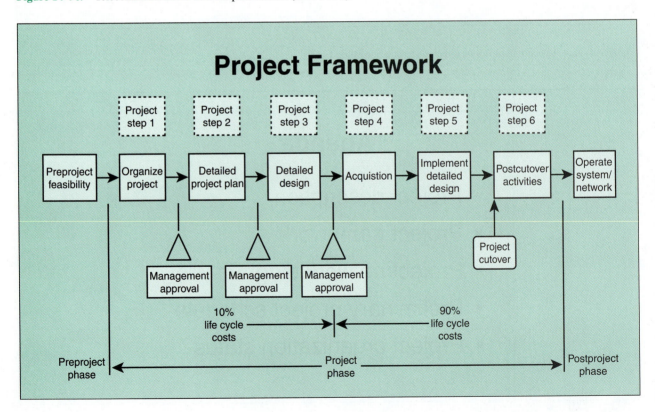

Figure 14–9d. Telecommunications director presentation (slide 4 of 7).

Project Diagram

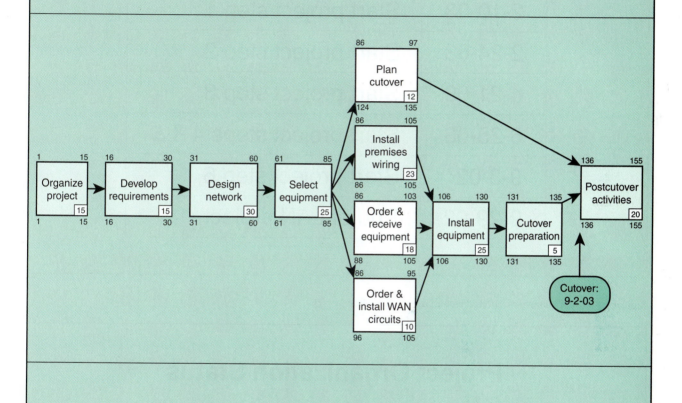

Figure 14–9e. Telecommunications director presentation (slide 5 of 7).

Preliminary Project Schedule

Date	Description
2-10-03	Start project step 1
2-24-03	Start project step 2
4-21-03	Start project step 3
6-25-03	Start project steps 4 & 5
9-3-02	Start project step 6
9-29-02	End of LAN project

Figure 14–9f. Telecommunications director presentation (slide 6 of 7).

Project Organization Status

- Dedicated project manager (100%)
  —Potential candidates
- Project manager selects team members
- Project manager selection process
  —Intial interviews: Jan 20
  —Complete interviews: Feb 4
  —Review selection with VP: Feb 7

Figure 14–9g. Telecommunications director presentation (slide 7 of 7).

SUMMARY

The case study provides an example of how the different topics contained in Parts 2 and 3 can be applied to a real world problem. The ability to effectively meet real world project situations will be based on an individual's personal skills and experience. If the conceptual details are worked out during the early stages of a project, they are available for management updates and for directing the efforts of personnel assigned to the project. The information presented in the memo (Figure 14–8) and slide presentation (Figure 14–9) examples were based on the original preliminary planning effort and required only a short period of time to prepare.

Where possible, tools and techniques should be used to minimize the work effort. The example illustrated in this chapter is based on having good PC-application skills in Word, Excel, and Visio. Without PC skills, it is unlikely that a good administrative plan could have been developed for the headquarters LAN project. In addition, basic skills in reading, writing, and mathematics were needed to compile the documentation provided in this chapter.

The bottom line is that the development of personal skills is a direct responsibility of the individual, but gaining experience normally requires the cooperation of an employer. However, individuals are accountable for selecting employers that provide the opportunity to gain good experience.

Note: This chapter developed a project schedule by using manual calculations. In the real world, it is unlikely that someone would subject themselves to the tedious, error-prone manual calculation process when PC software tools are available. The manually computed project schedule has also been computed by: 1) using Microsoft Excel's Workday and Net Workday functions, and 2) by using Microsoft Project.

The Excel solution is shown in two places: 1) in the Excel case study solution provided with the text's CD and 2) in Appendix A, which discusses the use of Excel's functions.

The Microsoft project solution is given in Appendix B, which provides a detailed step by step solution. The software solution should take someone who has a basic knowledge of Microsoft Project less than fifteen minutes to complete.

4

OPERATIONS
MANAGEMENT

The topics covered in Parts 2 and 3 focused on the various tools and techniques that a telecommunications manager could use to plan, develop, and implement a telecommunications technology infrastructure to provide business communication. Successful application of the tools and techniques introduced and discussed in Parts 2 and 3 would create a technology infrastructure consisting of LANs, WANs, internetworks, telephone systems, and WWW facilities.

Part 4 addresses the need to manage a telecommunications technology infrastructure after it has been implemented. Project-oriented activities are the proverbial tip of the iceberg when the operating life (LCA) of telecommunications products and services is considered. Projects occupy only a relatively small period of time in a network or system's useful life, while the telecommunications operations department has responsibility for it during most of its life. Operations departments are the caretakers of implemented telecommunications products and services and will have the greatest impact on lifetime expenses and operating performance. A strong operations department can compensate for a poorly installed equipment infrastructure. On the other hand, the reputation of an outstanding

equipment installation can quickly be tarnished when a weak operations department runs the facilities.

Telecommunications technology is complex and ever changing, and the problems associated with change must be managed effectively. Telecommunications operations departments have the responsibility for making sure that existing telecommunications technology meets current business needs. To fulfill this responsibility, an operations manager may need to use internal personnel to operate the equipment or may hire outside services to provide internal communication services.

Telecommunications operation departments are a critical element in a telecommunications organization in terms of providing high quality business communication services and controlling expenses.

PART 4, OPERATIONS MANAGEMENT TOPICS

The telecommunications operations department is responsible for:

1. maintaining existing telecommunications equipment so that it continues to meet initial performance standards

2. installing equipment to meet new capacity and performance requirements

3. providing a customer-oriented interface to ensure the effective use of telecommunications services by users

4. controlling operating costs through ongoing cost reduction initiatives

Part 4 will use the managerial methods and techniques discussed in Parts 2 and 3 and will apply them within the operations management context. Part 4 topics will include operations management organization design, carrying out department management responsibilities, a telecommunications manager's supervisory responsibilities, and other real world managerial topics. The ISO X. 700 network management model framework will be discussed from a managerial perspective and as an operating model for managing a network-centric telecommunications technology environment.

Part 4 consists of four chapters:

Chapter 15: What is Operations Management?

Chapter 16: Developing an Operating Plan

Chapter 17: Managing Operations

Chapter 18: Operations Management: A Case Study

Chapter 15: What is Operations Management?

A telecommunications operations management department has three basic responsibilities: 1) ensure that telecommunications products and services are available and operating properly, 2) effectively control the financial investments and operating costs used to create and maintain the technology infrastructure, and 3) provide a user friendly interface that resolves problems quickly and provides support services to service users. From an organization design viewpoint, a single department or multiple departments may handle these three functions. If separate departments were used, the generic titles would be operations, administrative services, and help desk.

Chapter 15 examines the day to day managerial responsibilities of running operations departments—including a manager's responsibility for employee hiring, development, performance appraisals, salary administration, and organizational communication. A department budget model is examined and the use of expense codes and expense variance control are reviewed. A three-level help desk escalation organization process is discussed and the ISO X. 700 network management model is presented as an operations management tool.

Chapter 16: Developing an Operating Plan

Operating plans provide the funding and resources needed to maintain and operate a telecommunications technology infrastructure. Chapter 16 reviews the telecommunications operations manager's role in establishing department (organization) and technology budgets within the overall framework of a business operating plan. Unless the department's operational budget has been carefully prepared, an operations manager can be saddled with a no-win situation in which inadequate resources and funding have been provided to carry out critical operations responsibilities.

As part of the operations planning process, department managers must identify the resources needed to run a department, maintain equipment and services, and provide support to network customers. These requirements must be translated into a budget format and approved during the year prior to being implemented. Once the budget is approved, it becomes the operating standard by which a telecommunications manager is evaluated. The manager's primary focus is one of living within the budget's parameters while delivering quality telecommunications services.

Chapter 16 discusses expense forecasting techniques, the use of telecommunications chargeback systems to control internal costs, and the accounting mechanics of establishing and managing budgets. A case study is provided to illustrate the concept of a budget *v.* actual operating environment and expense variance control procedures are described. Examples of department expense forecasting and telecommunications technology expense forecasting are provided.

Chapter 17: Managing Operations

Chapter 17 describes the day to day activities that must be carried out by a telecommunications operations manager. These responsibilities include business management, technology management, and budget management. Managerial responsibilities require the application of the managerial tools and methods reviewed in Parts 2 and 3 as operations management functions.

A review of telecommunication disaster planning is provided. The objective of disaster planning activities is to: 1) minimize the potential for telecommunications service outages that disrupt business activities and 2) provide rapid restoration of critical business communications facilities when outages occur.

Chapter 18: Operations Management: A Case Study

The Chapter 18 case study describes a planning process for establishing an operations department budget within the context of a typical enterprise annual planning cycle. The current year and future year planning process is described in detail and applies the information provided in Chapter 16.

15

WHAT IS OPERATIONS MANAGEMENT?

LEARNING OBJECTIVES

1. Understand the impact that upper management's viewpoint of the telecommunications department can have on the operations management department.

2. Understand the three basic functions provided by operations management.

3. Understand the role of operations management within the telecommunications department.

4. Understand the common organization management responsibilities that operations management managers have.

5. Understand the scope of help desk department responsibilities.

6. Understand the scope of operations department responsibilities.

7. Understand the scope of administrative services responsibilities.

8. Understand the need for disaster prevention and recovery planning.

9. Understand the role of ISO X. 700 standards in operations management functions.

10. Understand the operations department's role in implementing projects.

11. Understand the importance of managing operating expenses.

12. Understand how accounting concepts are used to control operating expenses.

WHAT IS OPERATIONS MANAGEMENT?

Parts 2 and 3 of the text addressed the planning and implementation aspects of telecommunications. Once the telecommunications product or service has been implemented, the operations management department is responsible for managing the daily operations that provide telecommunications products and services to the business enterprise. The telecommunications operations management department has ownership responsibility for telecommunications products and services during their entire operating life and must maintain the technology's performance. Opinions regarding the effectiveness (or ineffectiveness) of internal telecommunications departments will be based on the performance of the operations department. If internal and external customers perceive enterprise telecommunications products and services to be of high quality and always available, the entire telecommunications department will be viewed as being highly effective. On the other hand, if a negative opinion is held about enterprise telecommunications services, the entire telecommunications department will be seen as being ineffective.

From a business perspective, the value received from telecommunications products and services are in their use, not the design and implementation phases. These preoperations phases are simply necessary steps for obtaining the desired objective—strong internal and external business communication capabilities. The opinion that upper management has toward its internal telecommunications department will be a direct reflection of the effectiveness of the telecommunications operational management departments that have the responsibility for maintaining, operating, and supporting the business telecommunications infrastructure.

Three Views of Telecommunications

The size and scope of an internal telecommunications department will be a strong indicator of upper management's opinion of telecommunications as a business resource. There are three basic philosophical viewpoints that upper management can have regarding an internal telecommunications department:

1. an overhead expense to be minimized
2. an operating resource to improve internal productivity
3. a strategic resource to gain competitive advantage (Figure 15–1)

The listing portraying these viewpoints is a hierarchical listing. Upper management is unlikely to hold a high opinion without having migrated through the lower stages. Prior to the 1980s, all telecommunications services—primarily voice-based services—were seen as an **overhead expense** to be reduced (a necessary evil whose usage and cost should be minimized). The operations management department also determines how effective productivity tool and strategic resource initiatives will be. The maturing of computer technologies fostered an initial need for mainframe computer-to-mainframe computer communications that eventually evolved into an any-to-any requirement between mainframe computers, PCs, WWW sites, and LANs.

Business management found that voice and data communication could be used to link internal organizations so that issues of centralization and decentralization were no longer linked to a geographical deployment strategy. The use of 800-services could make a central site appear to be a local entity—particularly when computer applications provided telephone representatives with access to a customer's entire database, including buying history and buying preferences. Small companies that have a well-designed Web page can look as impressive as the largest corporations. Telecommunications became the wizard behind the magic curtain, and business management began to see telecommunications as a business support tool that could be used to minimize internal and external expenses and provide value-added features for marketing an enterprise's products and services.

Regardless of which management viewpoint exists, the primary responsibility for the telecommunications department's effectiveness when meeting business management expectations will fall on the telecommunications **operations management** department.

Operations Management Context

Telecommunication operations management will determine the role that telecommunications has within a business organization. In the cost to be minimized stage, telecommunications operations was primarily concerned with controlling costs. In the **productivity tool** stage and the **strategic resource** stages, telecommunications operations is the key resource used to determine how well the telecommunications function performs in these areas. While telecommunications planning and development activities

Figure 15–1. Telecommunications department evolution.

are more glamorous, the day to day telecommunications operation department is the final delivery mechanism for all telecommunications products and services.

Figure 13–1 on page 341, the telecommunications **project life cycle** model, provided the context for operations management—the key player in the postproject phase of the project life cycle.

Planning and development activities are relatively short time periods in the life cycle of a telecommunications system or network. The operations function is directly accountable for operations performance during the majority of an asset's (system, network, or equipment) life cycle.

TELECOMMUNICATIONS OPERATIONS ORGANIZATION

The structure of the telecommunications operations should mirror the business organization structure (functional, divisional, matrix, or team). These organization design options were discussed in Chapter 8, *Business Management Skills*. For discussion purposes, it will be assumed that the business enterprise utilizes a functional organization structure. A generic example of a functional business organization was provided in Figure 13–5, on page 352. This generic model will be used to describe the telecommunications function and provide a context for discussing telecommunications operations management responsibilities.

The telecommunications department is shown as being a management board level department in Figure 13–5. While the actual departmental organization structure would vary for different businesses, the departmental organization approach would conceptually resemble the one shown. Figure 15–2 provides additional details about the telecommunications department's organization.

The telecommunications structure and staffing will vary depending upon upper management's assignment of responsibilities to the telecommunications department. If the telecommunications department is viewed as an unavoidable overhead cost that should be minimized, only one department may exist—the operations department—which would have the responsibility for providing planning, development, administrative services, and help desk services. If the telecommunications department is seen as both a productivity tool and a strategic resource, a full service telecommunications department may exist where planning, development, operations, **administrative services,** and **help desk departments** operate as organizational peers within the telecommunications department.

Operations Management Functions

In Figure 15–2, the operations, administrative services, and help desk departments provide operations management functions. These departments represent activities that must be provided in any operations management environment that has the responsibility for providing telecommunications products and services to the business. The operations department has direct responsibility

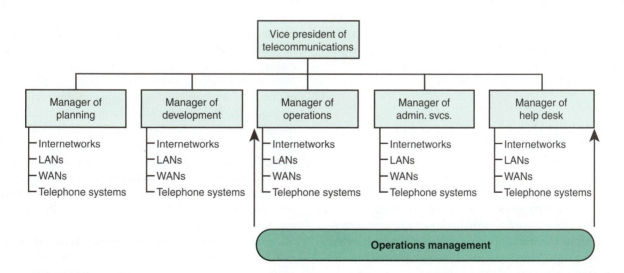

Figure 15–2. Functional telecommunications organization structure.

for the technical operating performance of system and network services. The administrative services department would provide the customer services, which would typically include usage and billing reports, directory services, account services, and providing an accounts payable interface for outside service expenses. The help desk department's role would be to provide a single point of contact for internal and external customers of the products and services operated by the operations department.

The use of a separate help desk department is recommended when the telecommunications operational activities are large enough to justify a separate help desk function. Although a help desk department is a peer organization of the operations department, its primary accountability should be to the customers of the operations department. The help desk department should operate as an ombudsman organization that represents customer interests. This ombudsman role would be in conflict if the help desk responsibility were given to an operations department, which also has the primary responsibility for the technical operating performance of systems and networks. If an operations department's help desk function acknowledges that customer problems exist, the help desk function is acknowledging poor performance exists within the operations department—an uncomfortable position for most employees. A customer-oriented, separate help desk department's advocacy of the customer's viewpoint will be seen as good performance. While the use of separate help desk and operations departments has the potential for creating an adversarial interface between the help desk and operations departments, it has a better chance of ensuring that technical performance meets customer needs than establishing an operations department help desk organization.

In smaller organizations, the operations department may be responsible for providing operations, administrative services, and help desk functions.

OPERATIONS MANAGEMENT RESPONSIBILITIES

The previous section described the operations management role in terms of organizational structure. Another perspective can be gained by examining the managerial responsibilities assigned to operations management personnel. Operations managers are responsible for managing the operating departments (organization management) and for managing telecommunications technology (technology management).

Organization Management

Operations, administrative services, and help desk managers are operations management managers. The following discussion identifies the different responsibilities for these three positions.

Common Organization Management Responsibilities

The following describes common business management responsibilities carried out by the operations, administrative services, and help desk managers for their respective departments.

IMPROVING PERSONNEL PRODUCTIVITY. Telecommunications managers are responsible for developing and maintaining a productive organization. The managerial tools for increasing productivity include organizational design and structure, job design and documentation, employee hiring, employee training, employee development plans, employee performance appraisals, salary administration, and ongoing departmental communications. Department operating budgets provide the funds for employee-oriented activities and specific expense categories are shown on separate expense code line items in the budget. When budgets do not provide adequate funding for training, there is a low likelihood that the operations management department will be run efficiently and effectively. A key managerial responsibility is to ensure that the appropriate funding exists for training purposes.

OUTSOURCING V. INSOURCING. Staffing is an area of concern in most organizations because of the high cost and limited flexibility involved with maintaining a large number of employees. In recent years, many organizations have been using *outsourcing* to significantly reduce internal staffing levels and to provide a higher level of flexibility when responding to competitive pressures for cutting costs. Outsourcing refers to the use of third party outside services for functions that historically had been handled internally. The term *insourcing* refers to the use of internal staffing to provide services that could be performed by outside sources. A responsibility of operations management is to evaluate the operations, administrative services, and help desk departments periodically from an outsourcing *v.* insourcing perspective.

When comparing outsourcing and insourcing alternatives, it is necessary to have a common standard of measurement to avoid the trap of using one set of measurement standards for one option and a different set for the other.

To ensure that a common set of standards is used when comparing outsourcing and insourcing options, the deliverables for both options should be the same. The establishment of common deliverables requires the establishment of a detailed listing of the telecommunications products and services that must be provided to the business. If this is done, an apples-to-apples comparison will exist for both alternatives and an equitable comparison can be made.

The process described in the previous paragraph is effectively a description of benchmarking, where metrics (typically costs, time, and labor measurements) are assigned to standard units of work output (the deliverables). Benchmarking provides a way to objectively measure different alternatives. When telecommunications functions are provided by internal personnel, ongoing comparisons should be made with the outside service alternatives to assess the effectiveness of internal operations. If the external service alternative can perform the internal function in a more productive manner (at a lower cost), the internal service must be reengineered to become as efficient as the external option—or serious consideration should be given to replacing the internal function with an outsourcing alternative.

A telecommunications manager is responsible for periodically benchmarking internal services and quantifying the results by using a metrics-based assessment of deliverables and service level performance. The use of accurate benchmarking metrics will allow an objective evaluation to be made between external and internal service alternatives and will provide an accurate comparison. Outsourcing *v.* insourcing decisions, based on the use of benchmarking practices, will result in good operations management decisions.

ORGANIZATION DESIGN AND STRUCTURE. Different telecommunications organization design options were discussed in Chapter 8, *Business Management Skills*. The selected telecommunications organization structure would vary according to the business enterprise's organizational philosophy. That structure will determine the scope of responsibilities assigned to different telecommunications departments. If the business design is customer-oriented, department-oriented, or location-oriented, the overall telecommunications department design should reflect the same philosophy. Once the appropriate telecommunications department structure is selected, internal telecommunications functions should be integrated within the structure to ensure that enterprise goals drive telecommunications efforts. This same philosophy would apply to designing the structure used within the operations man-

agement department for the operations, administrative services, or help desk functions.

JOB DESIGN AND DOCUMENTATION. Job design is closely related to business design. Departments are created to increase employee efficiency by consolidating employee skills so that employees in the department have an opportunity to develop skills from entry level positions to senior technician positions. The consolidation of similar skills also provides the department manager with the ability to select the appropriate level of skill(s) for any given department activity or project. Employee job responsibilities are documented by establishing job description documents that identify work responsibilities for different jobs and the relationships among different job positions.

Job documentation is a key component of the personnel development and employee appraisal process. An ongoing responsibility of an operations management manager is to ensure that accurate, up to date job descriptions exist for each position in the department. These job descriptions will be the basis for determining fair compensation levels and setting employee performance goals during the performance appraisal process. The process of establishing and maintaining job descriptions is a dual responsibility of telecommunications management and the human resources department.

Appendix C, *Job Descriptions and Performance Appraisals*, provides a detailed discussion of the process used to develop job descriptions. It also provides a job description for a voice communications manager.

EMPLOYEE HIRING. A telecommunications manager has a very important decision to make whenever the opportunity to hire an employee exists. Just as manufacturing a high quality product depends upon the use of high quality raw materials, the development of highly productive employees is made significantly easier by hiring employees who are good "raw materials." Hiring good "raw materials" means that hired employees have strong enabling skills (see Figure 7–1, page 130) and a positive attitude toward applying these skills to job responsibilities.

An employee who has strong skills and a good attitude will provide a triple benefit compared to employees who have weak skills and poor attitudes. A good employee will do the job correctly the first time, but poor employees will do the job incorrectly (an event frequently requiring someone else's time to correct). When this occurs, a triple loss will be incurred. The organization has lost the unproductive time spent to do the work incorrectly, loses the time needed by someone else to correct the problem, and

outlet. Then the need for client-supported network management activities will disappear into the background. However, this is not likely in the foreseeable future because new communication technology continues to be generated at mass-production speeds.

> The ISO X. 700 Network Management Standard can be used as a conceptual framework for managing any technology infrastructure. It addresses both the technical and managerial concerns of operations management functions.

X. 700 Technology Issues

Internetworking technologies are used to combine multiple heterogeneous technologies and networks into a single, homogeneous operating network. Internetworks consist of many different vendor products and disparate network technologies that require custom built interfaces between different products and services. Interoperability—the ability to make individual network elements appear as a single, homogeneous network—is easy to state conceptually but difficult to achieve practically. The practical reality is that problems continually occur in today's networking environment. Network management technology is used to automatically correct problems, to correct potential problems before they become real problems, and to escalate real problems to the appropriate repair source. In the second case, the problem repair activity has been started at the earliest possible time.

Managing network requirements i.e, (planning, organizing, operating, and controlling networking facilities) has become increasingly complex as communications technology evolves. Most communications products are proprietary products, and this multivendor environment must be managed effectively at an enterprise level to ensure enterprise level interoperability. During the 1980s, many companies offered enterprise **network management systems (NMSs).** However, today there are only a few survivors. Hewlett Packard provides an enterprise network management system as part of its OpenView product line, and Sun Microsystems offers a Solstice Enterprise Manager product. Most other major systems that are offered today are derivatives of these two products. This scarcity in network management system alternatives is a good indication of the technical and financial difficulties involved with developing

a viable enterprise NMS in today's complex, continually changing, computer networking environment.

Understanding the hardware and software operating requirements of an NMS is a technology topic and is beyond the scope of a management text. However, the architectural concepts associated with a modern enterprise network management can be explained without the use of technical terms. These architectural concepts will be discussed prior to examining the X. 700 standard.

Manager/Agent Network Management Model

In the centralized mainframe architecture environment established during the 1950s, network management was a proprietary function. The purchase of a vendor's computer system also included an implicit agreement for using the supplier's network management products. This approach made sense when computer and communication options were limited. However, by the 1980s, a large number of high quality computer and communication products were available. IBM dominated the mainframe computer marketplace and provided both computer and communication products for use with its equipment. As is currently the case with IBM-compatible PCs, many computer and communication suppliers began to offer equipment that was IBM compatible and could be used with IBM mainframe computer systems. As computer and communication technologies advanced, no single vendor (including IBM) had the best solution for all computer and communication applications. The ISO 7-Layer OSI Model provided a conceptual approach for allowing computer communication interoperability between different vendor products, but this created a network management problem. While proprietary systems allowed individual vendor products to be monitored and controlled, these same systems could not "see" nonproprietary devices. As a result, the corporate computer departments found that they were operating a multivendor computer and communication environment without a good set of multivendor network management tools.

Mainframe computer and communication device suppliers provided proprietary network management products tools to allow their customers to manage their own products. In this post-OSI Model environment, a product might be interoperable with another vendor's hardware and software but not necessarily with the other vendor's network management system. Multivendor products based on OSI concepts worked well with each other as long as the system or network that contained the products didn't experience a component failure. When this occurred, the identification of problem areas became very difficult because one vendor's network management system could not understand the network management information generated by another vendor's products.

A network management architecture that would allow proprietary network management products to be interoperable, while also allowing a single enterprise network management system to see all of the proprietary network management products that a business organization may have installed, was needed. This need led to the development of the manager/agent network management architecture contained in ISO X.700. As is the case with many technology areas, the manager/agent concept is simple but difficult to implement. It is based on installing translator network management software on proprietary products to translate the proprietary network management protocols into ISO X.700 protocols. These ISO protocols are then used by a central system to provide a standardized, high-level view of all network elements.

Figure 15–4 provides an illustration of the X.700 manager/agent network management architecture.

NETWORK MANAGEMENT MANAGER (NMM). In the integrated network management environment, telephone systems (PBXs), LANs, WANs, or internetworking devices are all considered elements within a network infrastructure. Each element is monitored, and important device status information is forwarded to the **network**

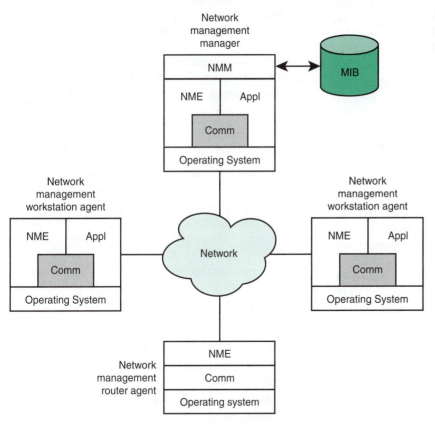

Figure 15–4. The enterprise manager/agent network management model.

NMM:	Network management manager application software
MIB:	Management information base
NME:	Network management entity application software
Comm:	Communications software
Appl:	Other application software

management manager (NMM) system. NMM software that is implemented at the enterprise level provides a standard view of all network elements, typically in a graphical map format. Elements functioning normally are shown in green, elements functioning below designated threshold levels are shown in yellow, and elements that have failed are shown in red. An audible warning is normally used when a red condition occurs.

The advantage of using an NMM is that a standard enterprise-level view of all network elements is provided, and NMS operators are not required to understand the technology details of individual network devices. The NMM station also includes: 1) a management information database (MIB) and 2) **network management entity (NME)** software that provides a standard software interface to the various devices being monitored by the NMS. The MIB stores information received from various network elements and has a database that contains details about the network topology and the components that make up the network. NMS operators can access the MIB to retrieve information and obtain operating details about individual devices.

The NME software converts the proprietary network management information of network elements into the NMM format. Therefore, as proprietary devices are added to a network, the NME conversion software must be obtained from the supplier of the device by operations management and installed on NMM and NME elements.

NETWORK MANAGEMENT ENTITY (NME).

The individual network elements that are monitored in a manager/agent network management environment are called agents, and each agent contains NME software that translates the device's proprietary network management protocol information into the NMM format. The NME software is able to communicate with the master station's NME software, and this allows a steady stream of intelligible NMS information to be made available to the NMM. To minimize network traffic, the NME contains sufficient storage and intelligence to store noncritical information, and will transmit routine information to the NMM during low traffic periods. However, during emergencies (failures or potential failure conditions), the NME initiates immediate contact with the NMM to inform the enterprise system of problems and potential problems.

The NME software in each monitored agent performs the following tasks:

- collects statistics of communications and network-related activities and stores the data locally
- responds to commands for the master NME, such as:

- transmit collected statistics NMM station
- change local parameters, as specified
- provide immediate status information
- generate test traffic data to perform local tests
- sends messages to the master station when local conditions deviate from standard conditions (failure conditions)

Under the manager/agent approach, the only NMS requirement is that the agent device's proprietary software can interface with NME application software. This distributed system approach minimizes the need for central control while providing individual locations with access to local and centralized network information.

There are many proprietary network management systems currently being used by different organizations in different locations. From an enterprise NMS perspective, the only requirement for establishing an interface to a proprietary network system is that the proprietary system's master station must have the NME software needed to translate information into a format suitable for the NMM station.

ISO X. 700 Network Management Standard

Effective network management must be able to meet the needs of a broad range of communication technologies (voice, data, internetworking, video, telemetry, messaging, etc). As a result, there are many network management definitions available, each from a different technology perspective. The ISO's X. 700 subcommittee has established a framework for defining network management, and this framework identifies five areas that should be addressed by any enterprise network (or system) management structure:

1. **fault management:** detecting and fixing problems
2. **configuration management:** changing network hardware and software
3. **performance management:** meeting user expectations
4. **security management:** protecting critical information assets
5. **accounting management:** managing the network investment

Another area that must be addressed but is not included in the X. 700 standard is the operations management organization needed to implement and operate any enterprise network/system management system, (the people part of the network management equation). This topic was discussed previously in the *Operations Management Responsibilities* section.

FAULT MANAGEMENT.   Fault management identifies problems, or potential problems, and restores normal communication as soon as possible when problems cause service disruptions. If a system or network is critical for maintaining business operations, redundant components can be installed. These standby components can be configured to automatically cut in when service disruptions occur or when a network monitoring function detects substandard network performance. Typically, there is a cost associated with installing redundant components. The benefits of using this approach must be balanced against the costs that are incurred.

From a technical perspective, the following steps must be carried out to restore services:

1. Determine the fault's location and magnitude.
2. Isolate the fault problem from other parts of the network.
3. Repair or replace the failed component(s).
4. Restore the network to its original condition.

An Enterprise network management system that uses the principles described in the manager/agent NMS model will handle the technical requirements associated with monitoring network performance and restoring services when service disruptions have occurred.

PERFORMANCE MANAGEMENT.   Communication networks rely heavily on the interoperability of many different components and sharing common network resources. If traffic loads change, bottlenecks in one subnetwork could cause slower response times in other subnetworks. Therefore, it is necessary to have knowledge of all subnetworks and their component elements and still understand the impact that individual networks have on overall end-to-end performance.

Performance management consists of two broad functions: 1) monitoring performance and 2) modifying network resources to meet standard performance standards. Performance management activities include:

1. keeping track of capacity utilization trends
2. monitoring peak traffic loads
3. identifying unacceptable deviations from standard levels
4. identifying traffic bottlenecks

5. measuring end user response times
6. changing the network configuration to improve performance

The MIB discussed previously would be the repository for performance management information. While network performance is an operational responsibility, performance information should also be available to the help desk and planning departments. If the help desk is aware of conditions that will adversely impact performance, they will be able to respond to user problem reports in a proactive manner. The planning function must also be aware of potential performance bottlenecks and capacity issues so that they can incorporate them as design change requirements during telecommunications strategic and tactical planning activities.

CONFIGURATION MANAGEMENT.   Communication networks and systems are made up of many elements that include subsystems used by other systems and subsystems. These subsystems may be highly complex, and changing the configuration of subnetwork elements can have a major impact on overall enterprise network capacity and performance.

Configuration management performs the following functions:

1. starting up individual subnetworks or the entire network
2. gracefully shutting down subnetworks or the entire network
3. maintaining, adding, deleting, or modifying network elements
4. restoring subnetworks or the entire network after failures

Starting up a network requires hardware and software parameters to be set up, based on the appropriate design specifications. This startup process requires an initialization period similar to that carried out by a PC when it is turned on (the boot up process). Configuration management activities require access to a detailed inventory of network components (data links, hardware, and software) and the parameters needed to use their capabilities. This control information is stored in an information database (typically the MIB).

SECURITY MANAGEMENT.   Security management protects telecommunications technology assets and protects the confidentiality of the information that is available to networked users. Concerns about protecting assets are addressed by maintaining an inventory of network assets, storing assets in a secure environment, and limiting access to them. Information security concerns are primarily addressed by limiting information access to authorized personnel.

The ISO X.700 security management recommendations for organization information addresses four main areas:

1. **access**: What form of access will be provided? Will PCs, telephones, remote, local, etc. be the primary access vehicle(s)?

2. **authentication:** Once an access connection has been established, what procedures will be used to authenticate the identification of the individual requesting access? Will passwords, card access, physical identification methods, etc. be used?

3. **authorization**: After the authentication process is completed, what access rights will be granted to computer files or applications? How will this authorization be communicated to the various files and applications existing within a distributed processing environment?

4. **auditing**: How will ongoing security activities be monitored and recorded so that it is possible to evaluate successful and unsuccessful attempts to breach security? Who will perform the auditing function, and who will be responsible for plugging security breaches?

In today's world of distributed applications and databases, the network management function becomes the gatekeeper to many information areas that had previously been stored in closely monitored central databases. Under the centralized mainframe environment, a single security gate could be established at the central mainframe site. In a distributed PC environment, each PC has processing information storage capabilities that had formerly been available only on mainframe computers.

Protecting data is an equipment- and people-intensive activity. As a result, securing network information is an expensive activity. A delicate balance exists between the need for confidentiality and the cost for installing a protection system that is easy to use. Limiting access to needed information can generate as many problems as having critical information disseminated to unauthorized personnel. It is important to protect only the information that has enough importance to warrant the cost of protecting it. The potential downside of authorized users having difficulty in accessing needed information should be considered. The risk involved with the loss of information should be weighed against the cost of protecting it. A cost must be assigned to the value of in-

formation by assigning a dollar value to the information. The greater the protection provided by a security system, the higher the initial and operating costs of the protection system.

NETWORK/SYSTEM ACCESS. The first rule of network security is that "if information must be kept confidential, don't provide network access to that information." If information is to be shared, the first line of security is to limit physical access to devices that have the capability for accessing the information.

When access is distributed and the access to secured information is based on accessing a network, network access passwords, terminal IDs, and callback procedures provide a measure of access control. However, distributed access control to critical information is an oxymoron because the term "distributed" implies open access to network users, while "access control" implies limitations on access to the desired information.

INDIVIDUAL AUTHENTICATION. Authentication procedures are used to validate the authenticity of an individual requesting access to secured information. The authentication information is then used to determine the level of security with which the network user has been provided. User passwords, electronic badges, and physical characteristic may be used to validate the requester's identity.

The authentication method and maintenance of the associated security access information is a task performed by network security personnel—an administrative activity that is reviewed periodically by an internal auditing department. Authentication is a potential weak link in the security management function because it typically relies on devices (passwords, physical media, etc.) that can be replicated through a trial and error hacking process or can be obtained by using criminal activities that involve theft and espionage. Ideally, authentication should be based on a process that only the individual being authenticated could pass. (Perhaps the secret agent approach to using finger prints or retinal eye scans to ensure a person's identity may become economically viable in the future.)

FILE/APPLICATION AUTHORIZATION. After an individual's identity has been authenticated, the individual's file/application access privileges determine the level of access that will be allowed. Access privileges are maintained by network security administrators, and changes to access files require the appropriate approvals by the security personnel authorized to grant access privileges. In today's distributed environment, this task becomes difficult.

AUDIT TRAIL. The term *audit trail* refers to the practice of keeping a record of all attempts to access information stored in secured files. Audit trail information would provide details of access attempts, including user names, passwords, access location, etc. NME agents manager/agent NMM may be asked to store large amounts of data to fulfill audit trail requirements, and the MIB database storage capability must be quite large if large volumes of audit data will be stored. This need for additional network or database capacity translates into higher purchase and operating costs and, again, a cost *v.* benefit evaluation is needed to determine the tradeoff between information value and the cost for keeping it secure. Audit trail data collection requirements should be based on the value of the protected data. This is done by: 1) collecting more audit information (at higher cost) when access to critical data is attempted, and 2) collecting less information when access is attempted to noncritical data.

Storing audit trail information is largely a technical process. However, the review and analysis of audit trail information is normally a very labor intensive process. Someone must manually review and evaluate audit trail information. The administrative effort (and cost) of reviewing audit trail information can be very high in large corporations. After the collected information has been reviewed and the attempted (or successful) security breaches are identified, someone must recommend changes to existing procedures and be responsible for implementing them. This role is typically assigned to a corporate auditing function.

SECURITY IN A DISTRIBUTED SYSTEM ENVIRONMENT. Earlier security management systems (pre-1990s) focused on a centralized mainframe environment that incorporated physical and centralized access checkpoints at the mainframe computer's data center site. Security equipment and personnel could be consolidated at one location, and a set of uniform procedures could be used. A single corporate database existed at the data center, and requests for database access were addressed by using a single data center security checkpoint.

In today's distributed environment, a corporate database may be replicated on several network servers and distributed across wide geographic areas. Access requests can be generated from any location that has access to a network used to provide access to the database. Two conflicting needs emerge when security requirements are evaluated: 1) the ease of access required for a highly mobile workforce and 2) the need to avoid providing unauthorized access to key files and databases. One approach for handling distributed network access is to generate a security token after authentication, then send this token to the authenticated workstation. When the authenticated workstation requires access to applications and files, the security token is sent as part of the request for services. After receipt of the service request and the token, the application or file software accesses a security server to determine what access rights should be granted based on the token's security information. Based on the security server information, the request for access is accepted or denied. The security token is normally given a limited lifetime, so that it disappears at the end of its life to minimize the potential for someone to access the network at a later time when the original user fails to log off.

ACCOUNTING MANAGEMENT. Accounting management provides the capability to extract network transaction information and develop cost-oriented data to assist in the business management of the network resource. The previous areas—fault, configuration, performance, and security management—focused on the technical aspects of network management and are important for ensuring the operational effectiveness of the network resource. The network management accounting function provides the budget management tool that identifies where costs are being incurred and who is using network facilities. The accounting management database can be used to develop a chargeback system in which the costs of operating a network can be allocated back to network users. The use of chargebacks to manage network facilities provides two advantages: 1) it provides a means of identifying usage at the user level and 2) it places accountability for the cost of telecommunications services on the end user of the service.

The accounting management area translates network technical database information into network costs and also identifies the consumers of network resources. The information provided as part of accounting management may include fixed asset, network operating costs, network chargeback, network directory services, and budget *v.* actual financial information.

OPERATIONS DEPARTMENT PROJECTS

In Part 3, Project Management, the management of administrative (nontechnology) and technology projects was discussed and examples were provided for both types of projects. Consult the telecommunications project life cycle model (Figure 13–1 on page 341).

While the operations management role takes place during the postproject phase, the reality is that there is a need to continuously upgrade system and network investments during their functional lifetime. Major modifications may be implemented by the telecommunications development department (Figure 15–2) as part of a project phase, but the operations department normally implements many technology upgrades on an ongoing basis. In this role, the operations department budgets for upgrades and implements them as miniprojects.

While all operations management (operations, help desk, and administrative services departments) managers have responsibility for successfully completing administrative projects, the operations manager must also have strong skills in **technology management** to meet the operational responsibilities associated with maintaining system and network performance. The operations manager must be highly skilled at carrying out project steps 1 through 6, while also being able to operate systems and networks efficiently and effectively during the postproject phase.

MANAGING OPERATING EXPENSES

In the project life cycle model, 90% of a telecommunications asset's costs are incurred after the project is implemented. Actually, the majority of this expense is incurred during the postproject phase. The operations manager has the greatest impact on controlling the costs associated with providing telecommunications products and services to the business enterprise. Expense control is a key measurement tool used to evaluate operations management (operations, help desk, and administrative services). Operations managers must monitor telecommunications expenses on an ongoing basis and actively seek less expensive service alternatives to minimize the rates being paid for telecommunications services. In addition, the administrative services function may provide chargeback systems to provide internal departments with the tools they need to manage their telecommunications costs. In a chargeback environment, the telecommunications operations department focuses on getting the best rates for the products and services used to provide telecommunications services, and the administrative services department generates the chargeback system information that allows internal departments to monitor and control their use of these services.

Accounting: The Language Of Business

The **cash drawer management** approach used by mom and pop stores of the past is no longer possible or practical if it is based on examining cash assets. Plastic has largely replaced cash for consumer transactions, and accounting transactions take the place of cash within a business enterprise. Looking in the department cash drawer of today's business environment means looking at accounting transactions in a report format and being able to translate the accounting information. Accounting is the language of management, and dollars is the standard business measurement unit displayed on accounting reports. Department managers must understand both the terminology and definitions used on the accounting reports they receive and should have the ability to translate accounting numbers into meaningful managerial actions.

Department budgets are the focus for managing overall telecommunications expenses because departmental budgets are relatively simple and easy to understand when compared to enterprise level telecommunications budgets. Department budgets can be managed by using a mom and pop philosophy, in which department managers can be seen as the proprietors of the department and can be held accountable for the expenses they incur. Under this philosophy, if all departments manage their individual budgetary goals effectively, enterprise budgetary goals will be met.

DEPARTMENT BILLING. Department expense charges are listed on a department's monthly budget v. actual (BVA) report. Different names may be used by different organizations, but the format and content will be similar to the BVA report description that follows. The internal financial organization receives bills in its accounts payable department, matches the billing to the appropriate expense category coding information, identifies the departments that have incurred the expenses, and forwards the actual expense information for inclusion in the department's monthly BVA report.

DEPARTMENT CODES. Each department is assigned a unique identification code by the finance department, and this numeric identifier is used to assign expense (actual) and budget information to individual departments. Department coding schemes vary from company to company and the following one provides one example. In a three level coding scheme—company/division/department—the equivalent data format could be CC.DDD.XXX, where

CC is a two-digit company code

DDD is a three-digit division code

XXX is a three-digit department code

For example, the department code 01.080.005 could be interpreted as ABC company/telecommunications division/operations department. The digital-to-name conversion would be based on the information that is contained in the finance organization's database. As bills are received for the telecommunications operations department, the actual expenses would be allocated to the 01.080.005 department code. Internal expenses that are allocated to departments would also use the same department coding scheme to allocate costs to different departments.

Expense Codes

A standardized expense coding scheme is essential, whether department expenses are assigned to various departments or consolidated to calculate enterprise level expenses. The finance department establishes a list of expense codes that will be used in the organization's BVA reports, and will add new codes when other departments require new expense categories. All departments use the same expense codes during the annual expense forecasting (budgeting) cycle. Table 15–1 provides a hypothetical expense code structure that is based on using three digits to identify expense categories. These codes would be used to forecast expenses and to assign expenses (actuals) to a department's BVA report.

Table 15–1 separates expense codes into two categories: **controllable** and **noncontrollable expenses.** Controllable expenses are a category of expenses where the department manager has the option of taking action to eliminate or reduce the expense. Noncontrollable expenses have been allocated to the department by the finance department and individual department managers cannot take action to eliminate or reduce expenses listed under this category. Noncontrollable expenses typically include expenses that are generated by internal departments for services that they provide to other departments. For example, the cost for a human resources department may be allocated to organization departments based upon the number of employees in each department, and this charge would show up as a noncontrollable charge.

Department managers can reduce salary expenses (a controllable expense) by terminating existing personnel or by not filling open positions. However, they would be unable to change noncontrollable expense categories because they are allocated expenses that are controlled by the finance department. Note the existence of code 909—telecommunications expenses—an expense code that can be used to charge telecommunications costs to individual departments and make department managers accountable for controlling their telecommunications expenses in the same way they control other department expenses.

Telecommunications Expenses

Expenses are incurred by the telecommunications organization for the products and services they provide to other in-

TABLE 15–1   Generic Department Expense Codes

Code	Description
Controllable expenses	
001	Salaries
008	Overtime
009	Shift premium
010	Wages
013	Overtime premium
027	Special compensation
029	Severance pay
099	Recreation/general welfare
100	Travel expense
124	Employee training
140	Company meetings
160	Petty cash
180	Employee moving expenses
190	Dues, fees, subscriptions
300	Supplies
304	Printing and duplicating
310	Equipment purchases
330	Equipment rental
401	Repairs and maintenance
449	Outside services
687	Express courier service
688	Miscellaneous freight
689	Miscellaneous postage
909	Telephone
Noncontrollable expenses	
025	Other compensation (vacation)
040	Payroll taxes
050	Group insurance
060	Retirement plan
070	Savings plan
520	Depreciation & amortization
900	Fixed charges
910	Redistributed telephone operator
911	Office services
912	Floor space
913	Personnel
915	Other redistributed expenses
925	Building costs
926	Redistributed personnel expenses

ternal departments. As a result, the telecommunications department is in the position of having managerial accountability for expenses whose cost magnitude is determined by users that are outside the control of the telecommunications department. Telecommunications, effectively a reseller of telecommunications services, uses a variety of products and services to fill this role. When outside services are used, the telecommunications department's role is one of quality assurance and cost control. When facilities are operated and maintained internally by the telecommunications department, the process becomes more complex.

Historically, regulated service providers—AT&T Long Lines, Bell Operating Companies, and non-Bell Operating Companies—were responsible for providing telecommunications services and equipment to all businesses. The January 1, 1984, implementation of the Department of Justice's 1982 AT&T Consent Decree immediately deregulated communications equipment and set the stage for deregulating all regulated telecommunications services. Currently, many of the previously regulated telecommunications services have been deregulated, and the deregulation of the remainder is well underway.

In the post-1984 environment, a plethora of new services has emerged. Computer communications technologies are now the dominant form of telecommunications technology. Telecommunications systems and services—telephone systems, WANs, LANs, internetworks, and the Web—are implemented in many ways. Some enterprises use an in-house resource to install and operate systems and networks, while others rely on purchasing outside services from providers of systems and networks. Regardless of whether systems and networks are provided based on internally or externally provided services, the enterprise telecommunications department has the responsibility for ensuring the availability of cost-effective, high quality services to internal departments.

The preceding section discussed department expenses and the use of the BVA cash drawer concept to control department expenses. However, what about the bills received by a telecommunications operations department for telecommunications services provided to internal departments? Does the operations department simply pay the bills and reflect the cost in one of its expense categories? If this is done, how will the operations department control telecommunications charges incurred by other departments? The bottom line is, how will the telecommunications operations department respond to questions asked by upper management about large, rapidly escalating telecommunications charges?

There is no simple answer to these bottom line questions. The quandary can be summarized in the following statement: "Management always wants simple answers to complex questions, but there are few simple answers."

CONTROL OF EXTERNAL TELECOMMUNICATIONS EXPENSES.

The common ways of controlling outside telecommunications costs is by auditing bills, installing call accounting systems on PBX telephone systems, and negotiating lower rates with telecommunications service providers. These alternatives will be discussed further in Chapter 17, *Managing Operations*.

CONTROL OF INTERNAL TELECOMMUNICATIONS EXPENSES.

When systems and services are provided by internal organizations, two mechanisms exist for controlling internal costs: 1) the chargeback of telecommunications services to the end user and 2) the use of benchmarking to ensure that internal costs are competitive with other telecommunications service options.

This topic will be discussed further in Chapter 16, *Developing An Operating Plan*.

SUMMARY

This summary is organized to correspond with the learning objectives found at the beginning of the chapter.

1. Upper management's view of an enterprise telecommunications department can be: 1) an overhead cost to be minimized, 2) an operating tool for improving internal productivity, or 3) a strategic tool for increasing product sales. The higher level viewpoints cannot be achieved without achieving positive results in lower level categories. If the primary concern is cost, the operations management staffing will be minimized and there is strong likelihood that only an operations department will exist. As upper management's interest for using telecommunications as a productivity tool and strategic asset increases, the operations management function will become more diverse, with a heavier emphasis on customer service and the effective use of telecommunications. In addition, other telecommunications department units (planning and development) will increase in importance and play a larger role in the enterprise telecommunications department.

2. Operations management departments fall into three major categories: 1) the operation of telecommunications systems and networks, 2) providing a customer-oriented problem resolution resource, and 3) providing value added information to system and network customers to allow them to use telecommunications products and services more effectively. When separate operations management departments are established in

these three areas, they are usually the operations, help desk, and administrative services departments. A balance of insourcing and outsourcing options may be used to provide operations management departments with the primary responsibility for efficient and effective performance being largely an operations function responsibility.

3. The operations management department has the greatest responsibility within an enterprise telecommunications organization, because operating expenses account for the majority of all enterprise telecommunications expenses. Telecommunications cost control consists of ensuring that the lowest price is paid to obtain quality services and that internal departments use the telecommunications resource effectively and efficiently. The operations management has two basic responsibilities: 1) provide 100% availability of the appropriate telecommunications services and 2) control the associated costs to ensure that the expenses incurred by the business enterprise are justified by the business benefits obtained by using telecommunications services.

4. Operations managers have the same organization management responsibilities required of managers working within a business enterprise environment. These responsibilities include accountability for maintaining high personnel productivity levels, implementing an effective organization design, hiring skilled personnel that will develop into assets for the organization, providing training to employees, "grooming" employees for higher skill positions, administering salaries equitably and based on performance, and promoting good communication between department employees and between managers and subordinates.

5. The help desk department's primary responsibility is to provide a single point of contact for enterprise telecommunications users to resolve problems and perceived problems. This is done by providing an easy to use interface (typically a telephone call) and a problem escalation process that is transparent to service users. Help desk representatives resolve simple problems and forward more complex problems to the appropriate technical resource while continuing to have primary responsibility for keeping the problem originator informed of problem resolution activities. Help desk representative will close the incident when the problem originator indicates that the problem has been satisfactorily resolved.

6. The operations department has direct responsibility for ensuring that telecommunications services are available to internal users and that the costs for these services are controlled effectively. The daily activities carried out by operations personnel include monitoring and resolving operating problems, adding and removing service users, upgrading the technology infrastructure to accommodate new requirements, ensuring that the telecommunications asset is protected from physical and logical damage, and maintenance of operating records used to identify problem trends and capacity utilization levels.

7. Administrative service responsibilities are focused on providing internal telecommunications service users with the information they need to utilize services effectively and efficiently. The activities performed to meet this primary objective may include providing telephone and e-mail directory services, centralized telephone operator services, an accounts payable role for telecommunications related bills, and chargeback reports. Chargeback systems provide usage and expense information to internal department managers, which allows them to monitor and control the use of telecommunications services in their departments.

8. A business "disaster" occurs when normal business activities are disrupted or shut down. In today's business environment, computer and telephone communication services are essential for conducting everyday business activities. Without telecommunications services, orders could not be entered, product inventory could not be allocated, money could not be collected, etc. The role of operations management is to: 1) minimize the potential for incurring telecommunications service disruptions and 2) rapidly restore communication services when disruptions do occur. The planning processes associated with disaster planning are disaster prevention planning and disaster recovery planning.

9. The ISO has issued many communications standards, with the underlying purpose of promoting the interoperability of proprietary vendor products and services. In 1992, ISO issued the X. 700 standard, which described the network management architecture required to maintain effective network performance in a multivendor technology environment. X. 700 standards identify the requirements for collecting status information from any device that is connected into a network infrastructure. A centralized network management organization is utilized to monitor, identify, and resolve device problems. While the X. 700 standard describes the various technical interfaces to provide effective network management services, there are five categories of operating information provided as a byproduct of the technical procedures:

fault management, configuration management, performance management, security management, and accounting management. Examination of these standard areas will show that they provide the information needed to effectively and efficiently operate a telecommunications technology environment.

10. The operations department has a major role in implementing telecommunications projects. Although large projects may utilize personnel from separate internal telecommunications departments (planning and development departments), the operations department carries out project activities on an ongoing basis. Equipment is replaced to resolve operating problems, and modifications are normally required during a system over a network's operating lifetime. Operations personnel normally implement these projects. Project management skills are key requirements for managerial and technical operating personnel, who account for a major part of the operating budget. An operations manager must identify the need for equipment replacement and upgrades in the budgeting process to ensure that the necessary funding is available for any given budgetary period.

11. Operating expenses are those expenses that are incurred after a telecommunications technology infrastructure has been developed and implemented. The design and implementation efforts associated with developing and implementing telecommunications products and services account for a relatively short part of their useful lifetime. Telecommunication products are normally used for five or more years, and most of this time is spent in an operations mode. Over 80% of a telecommunication asset's life cycle costs are incurred during the operating phase. As a result, the effectiveness and efficiency of the operations function have a greater influence on the telecommunications budget than any project activity. Sound operations management practices will minimize costs while ensuring the availability of telecommunications services.

12. The BVA concept is a key factor in managing operating budgets and is based on identifying variances (variance = budget$ − actual$) between forecast expenses and actual expenses. Operations management is responsible for identifying budget requirements to maintain a telecommunications environment and to operate within the budget. The operations management department's role is to ensure that the lowest price is paid for quality telecommunications equipment and services while monitoring the use of these services by internal users to ensure that they are used effectively and efficiently. The BVA approach is used to control external telecommunications costs and their use by internal departments.

KEY TERMS AND CONCEPTS

Descriptions of the following terms can be found in the chapter and in the text glossary.

Accounting Management	Fault Management	Performance Management
Administrative Services Department	Help Desk Department	Productivity Tool
Cash Drawer Management	Incident Reporting System (IRS)	Project Life Cycle
Configuration Management	Network Management Entity (NME)	Security Management
Controllable Expenses	Network Management Manager (NMM)	7-Layer OSI Model
Disaster Prevention	Network Management System (NMS)	Strategic Resource
Disaster Recovery	Noncontrollable Expenses	Technology Management
Escalation Procedures	Operations Management	X. 700 Network Management Standard
Expense Codes	Overhead Expense	

REVIEW

The following questions are open-ended—predefined answers are not included as part of the text. The purpose of these questions is to allow the readers to test themselves on the chapter material.

1. Describe the three basic viewpoints that upper management can hold about internal telecommunications and why each viewpoint cannot be viewed as a standalone option.

2. Explain the role of telecommunications operations management departments in the telecommunications project life cycle model.

3. List and describe the three basic functions provided by telecommunications operations management.

4. How should telecommunications management address the issue of outsourcing *v.* insourcing?

5. Why is the employee hiring process so critical to the formation of a high quality, well performing organization?

6. Describe the relationships among employee development plans, employee performance appraisals, and salary administration.

7. Describe three-level help desk procedures and how timely resolution of incidents are addressed.

8. What is the difference between natural disasters and business disasters?

9. Summarize the five network management areas in the X.700 Network Management standard.

10. Why are chargeback systems used and what is their value to the telecommunications department?

11. In the postproject phase of the telecommunications project life cycle model, how are major upgrades or modifications to the system or network handled?

MULTIPLE CHOICE

1. Operations management is accountable for maintaining the performance of telecommunications products and services for _____ of the product life cycle.
   a. 10%
   b. 20%
   c. 40%
   d. 50%
   e. 90%

2. Three upper management philosophical viewpoints of an internal telecommunications function's role are _____. (Select all that apply.)
   a. an overhead expense
   b. a technology asset
   c. a leading edge concept
   d. a productivity tool
   e. a strategic resource

3. Outsourcing analysis is best accomplished by _____.
   a. BVA reporting
   b. strategic planning
   c. tactical planning
   d. benchmarking
   e. employee development planning

4. Three operations management functions are _____.
   a. development
   b. operations
   c. administrative services
   d. planning
   e. help desk

5. Job descriptions are used to_____.
   a. identify employees who have promotion potential
   b. evaluate employee performance
   c. determine compensation levels
   d. improve productivity
   e. strategic planning

6. A key strategy for improving employee productivity is _____.
   a. to hire employees with strong enabling skills
   b. to write better job descriptions
   c. to conduct employee appraisals more frequently
   d. to increase salary levels
   e. to promote employees

7. When hiring new employees, two key attributes to look for are _____. (Select all that apply.)
   a. salary levels
   b. education
   c. enabling skills
   d. outsourcing
   e. attitude

8. Conducting employee performance appraisals is a _____ responsibility.

a. tactical planning

b. tactical mangement

c. technology management

d. organization management

e. project management

9. In a performance-driven organization, salary increases are heavily influenced by _____.

a. employee development plans

b. employee performance appraisals

c. employee job descriptions

d. medical benefits

e. human resources

10. The _____ department provides a single point of contact for user problems.

a. technical resource

b. development

c. administrative services

d. help desk

e. directory services

11. An effective end user problem resolution procedure relies on _____ to ensure a quick resolution of user problems.

a. X.700 manager/agents

b. personnel productivity initiatives

c. multilevel escalation procedures

d. an incident reporting system

12. Disaster planning addresses two areas: _____. (Select all that apply.)

a. natural disasters

b. unnatural disasters

c. disaster prevention

d. business operations

e. disaster recovery

13. The X.700 technical solution for providing network management of proprietary communication is based on the _____ concept.

a. MIB

b. manager/agent

c. accounting management

d. disaster prevention

14. The X.700 Network Management framework includes _____ standards. (Select all that apply.)

a. technology management

b. configuration management

c. organization management

d. performance management

e. technical management

15. X.700 _____ is concerned with gracefully shutting down network elements.

a. technology management

b. configuration management

c. security management

d. fault management

e. performance management

16. Enterprise network management systems allow _____ to be monitored and managed from a central network control center. (Select all that apply.)

a. WANs

b. LANs

c. internetworking

d. telephone systems

e. All of the above.

17. Noncontrollable expense budgets are established by _____.

a. operations

b. administrative services

c. accounting

d. help desk

e. salary administration

18. Chargeback systems are used by a telecommunications department to _____.

a. pay bills

b. identify service usage

c. escalate problems

d. install NMEs

e. consolidate technologies

19. External telecommunications expenses are controlled by _____.

a. establishing budgets

b. selecting the appropriate expense codes

c. authorizing payment

d. auditing bills

16

DEVELOPING AN OPERATING PLAN

1. Understand the responsibilities of an operations management department.

2. Understand the ISO X.700 Network Management Standard's importance to the operations management department.

3. Understand the role of operations management in the telecommunications project life cycle model.

4. Understand the need for the accurate forecasting of operations management needs.

5. Understand the theoretical forecasting elements and the underlying assumptions of quantitative forecasting methods.

6. Understand practical forecasting elements, the need to address financial issues, and the basic tools and skills needed to manage the process.

7. Understand the department expense forecasting process and the deliverables needed to complete the process.

8. Understand the basic cost allocation concepts used to charge telecommunications expenses back, as well as its advantages and disadvantages.

9. Understand the makeup of telephone system expenses and the three factors that must be addressed when forecasting them.

10. Understand the basic telephone expense forecasting process and the deliverables needed to carry it out.

11. Understand the next step's requirements after the department and telecommunications expense forecasts have been developed.

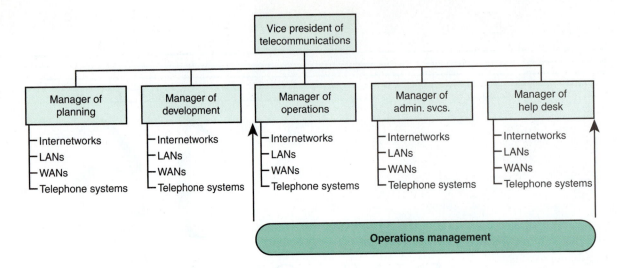

Figure 16–1. Telecommunications operations functions.

Telecommunications operation departments have a responsibility to provide high quality, cost effective telecommunications products and services to support the activities of the business. As part of their charter, **operations management** departments (Figure 16–1) may operate on-site systems and networks to provide services or may purchase various telecommunications services from an external organization. In both instances, expenses are generated and the operations management department would receive bills, approve them for payment, and evaluate them to identify cost saving opportunities.

Telecommunications operating expenses for internal and external resources normally account for over 80% of the total telecommunications budget. (The other 20% is for planning and development activities. As new projects are implemented to install additional technology components or purchase new services, these costs are transferred into the telecommunications operational budget. In an unchanging business environment, telecommunications expenses would be stable, and any cost increases for external telecommunications services would be driven by rate increases from product and service providers. In a stable environment, the prevailing management concern would most likely be a desire to minimize telecommunications costs, as was the case prior to the implementation of the 1984 AT&T divestiture.

However, that was then and this in now. In today's business and technology environment, business communication needs are constantly changing and the telecommunications department must also react to these changes by introducing new products and services while continuing to maintain existing services. From an operations planning perspective, there are two major elements that must be addressed in today's operating environment:

- manage the technology
- manage the cost of technology

The following will address both areas.

THE OPERATIONS PLANNING PROCESS

The primary responsibility for operations management is to maintain the telecommunications technology infrastructure that was implemented previously in various projects. This responsibility includes maintaining the performance and capacity levels designed into systems and networks and initiating corrective action when network requirements change because of new business communication requirements or increased traffic loads.

Maintaining existing telecommunications and systems is an operational management department responsibility, but initiating major upgrades or replacements of existing systems and networks are planning department and development department responsibilities. However, operations managers will be measured on how well business communication services perform. This responsibility means that an operations manager must understand the strategic, tactical, and operational planning process in order to provide input at the appropriate planning stage to ensure the ongoing viability of an enterprise's communications resource.

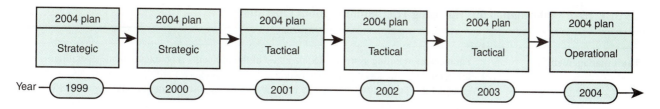

Figure 16–2. Enterprise planning process overview.

Figure 16–2 illustrated the enterprise planning process model used for business and technology planning. The figure illustrates how the plan for a given year (in this case, the year 2004) changes planning categories as the plan year approaches. When planning for the year 2004 was originally begun in the year 1999, it was categorized as a **strategic plan** (a future planning window of more than three years). It was then was categorized as a **tactical plan** during the 2001 to 2003 time period (a future planning window of one to three years). In the last year of its tactical planning phase, the 2004 plan year budget is finalized. This budget becomes the operating plan in the year 2004. The planning cycle for 2004 is now completed and has run the full cycle from concept (strategy) to implementation (operational).

From a planning perspective, operations management is primarily concerned with an operational budget that provides the ability to effectively maintain and operate existing telecommunications products and services. This operational budget would be developed in the previous year as a final tactical plan budget, and the viability of the operational budget will be based on the accuracy of the tactical planning phase. Earlier strategic plans and tactical plans (two to three years before the operational phase) are primarily a concern of the telecommunications planning and development departments and would be used to identify funding requirements for: 1) new products and services and 2) major upgrades or expansion of existing products and services.

The need for new business communications services would largely be driven by growth (the addition of new company locations) or the introduction of new technologies, while the need for major upgrades to existing facilities would be driven by capacity and performance shortcomings of existing systems and networks. Business plans provide the primary source for identifying new service needs while operating statistics (user response time, percent capacity utilization, equipment breakdown statistics, etc.) would provide the information used to identify the need for upgrades or expansions. For large projects, the telecommunications development department would im-

plement the effort. For smaller projects, the operations department would implement the effort.

However, it is important for operations management to be familiar with long-range telecommunications planning efforts to ensure that budgetary allowances are made for the postproject maintenance needs. It is equally important that operations management identify problem trends or ongoing problems to the telecommunications planning and development departments so that sufficient lead time is allowed for obtaining the necessary funding through the normal annual planning cycle.

MANAGING THE TECHNICAL ENVIRONMENT

In Chapter 15, *What is Operations Management?* the ISO **X.700** Network Management standard was discussed. While the initial impetus for developing technical ISO standards was driven by the need to standardize the technical elements of networking, the X.700 standard goes beyond technical design considerations by identifying the type of information needed to effectively and efficiently manage systems or networks. X.700 identifies five information categories that must be managed by an operational management function:

1. **fault management:** detecting and fixing problems

2. **configuration management:** changing network hardware and software

3. **performance management:** meeting user expectations

4. **security management:** protecting enterprise information

5. **accounting management:** managing the network investment

These five information areas must be managed effectively to provide high quality telecommunications services. The control information may be maintained in manual or computerized databases, depending upon the

TABLE 16–1   Information for Managing Telecommunications Operations.

Information Category	Status Information
Fault management	An incident reporting system (IRS) database of the problems encountered while operating telecommunications systems and networks is used to categorize problem types, trends, and their eventual resolution. It would include a history of service disruptions and substandard performance periods and a diagnosis of their causes.
Configuration management	A configuration database would be used to provide existing hardware and software technical specifications, their location and operating history, and list the version levels for various system and network software applications. This information is used to start up or shut down different systems or networks and restore normal services quickly and minimize the inconvenience of its users. The database would include an inventory of maintenance parts maintained for repair and disaster recovery purposes.
Performance management	Operational response times, capacity, and throughput for system and network elements are contained in the performance database. The database would track capacity utilization trends, peak traffic volumes, equipment bottlenecks, and end-user response times for different operating periods.
Security management	The security management database would maintain an audit trail of unauthorized attempts to access system and network information whose access is restricted by security software. Security attempts and breaches of security require a proactive response that may require the installation of additional security hardware and software.
Accounting management	This database is cost oriented and provides information that can be used to identify the resource usage of individuals and departments. It can be used to develop chargeback systems for different system or network services provided by the telecommunications department or to identify cost elements for use in the operations budgeting process.

specific operating environment. It becomes the basis for managing the technical operating environment. When problem conditions are detected in the control system, the appropriate technical and administrative actions are initiated to return operations to normal levels. Table 16–1 describes the type of information needed to assess the status of each X.700 category area.

While the effort for developing the X.700 database information is a technical process that requires technical specialists who have appropriate skills, it is a price that must be paid to create a manageable technical operating environment. The management category elements in Table 16–1 must be given the appropriate measurement standards so that the performance of system or network components can be measured quantitatively and monitored continually. Deviations from standards would be highlighted for follow up by a suitable problem escalation source.

Note: The concept of addressing only problems or potential problems is an example of management-by-exception, where management time is spent addressing exceptions and not activities that are operating normally.

The standard state of any given system or network effectively becomes the "plan" element in the POLC Model and is also the criterion used by operations management to determine whether operating problems actu-

ally exist. Once a problem is detected, it can either be fixed permanently or temporarily. When a permanent solution cannot be implemented immediately to correct a problem, the temporary solution's purpose is to minimize the impact of the operating problem while a long term corrective action is being carried out. When the long term solution requires the purchase and installation of new equipment, the temporary fix must provide the lead time needed to acquire and install the equipment.

Responding to Technical Problems

In an X.700-based network management environment, technical deviations from normal operating levels can be identified quickly. While advanced network management systems may use some form of embedded maintenance logic to correct operating problems by initiating problem fixes automatically, all operating problems eventually create operating expenses. The cost savings, generated when operating problems are fixed, frequently pay for corrective action initiatives—technical specialist labor costs, equipment repair and purchase expenses, and/or administrative overhead expenses associated with the corrective action.

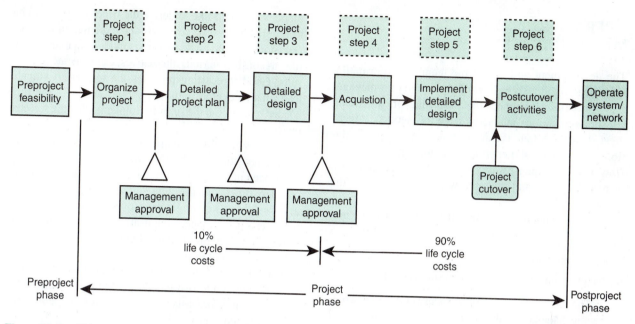

Figure 16–3. Telecommunications project life cycle overview.

Operations management uses two measurement tools to determine the magnitude of operating problems:

- technical information provided by monitoring devices
- expense information provided on **BVA** reports

Large operating problems are those whose corrective action response creates an operating expense impact that is not normal (it has not been allowed for in the operating budget). When this occurs, it may be necessary to involve the planning and development departments in a crisis mode to obtain both the labor and funding resources. However, the operations function will normally be expected to handle most operating problems—including many big problems—as part of its normal responsibilities. The corrective action for operating problems may require establishing ad hoc projects to implement new equipment and services. Many ad hoc projects will be initiated by the operations manager and operations management personnel brought in to provide the necessary project management and technical specialist skills.

PROJECTS INITIATED BY OPERATIONS DE-PARTMENTS. When long term corrective action is required in a technical operating environment, it frequently means that equipment must be modified, replaced, or added. For a significant effort (a large number of labor hours and expense dollars), the operations department must go into a project management mode and apply the project management processes described in Part 3, *Project Management*.

Figure 16–3 shows the **telecommunications project life cycle model.** Operations projects will go through the same project steps that were described previously. However, operations management does not have the luxury of employing long range planning processes and must compress the preproject phase into either this year's or next year's budget.

It should not be surprising that ad hoc projects initiated during the current year are not viewed favorably when the current operating budget does not provide the funding needed to carry them out. When this occurs, it may require a special effort to find the necessary funding, and the operations manager will be placed in the uncomfortable position of having to explain why the need for the ad hoc project was not forecast during the previous annual planning cycle.

Assuming that the project funding effort is resolved by having the money in either the current operating budget or through a special budget authorization process, the operations management department will follow the six step planning process in Figure 16–3. As was the case for any project, the project initiator (typically the operations manager) will be held accountable for the results and the costs.

OPERATING EXPENSE MEASUREMENTS

The development and use of the technical information referenced previously is beyond the scope of a managerial text. It is assumed that aspiring or practicing telecommunications managers have the necessary technical skills to initiate the development and implementation of a technical network management framework. However, the expense side of managing operations is a managerial topic and this area will be discussed in the following section.

Telecommunications **operating expenses** fall into two major expense categories:

- department budget expenses
- telecommunications product and service expenses

The first expense category focuses on the telecommunications manager's department budget, and the second focuses on expenses associated with providing telecommunications services to the business enterprise. Operations management establishes budgets for both areas and is responsible for accurately forecasting them. Operational forecasting has a planning horizon of one year, and a variety of forecasting techniques are available. Forecasting techniques include: 1) **quantitative methods** that are based on mathematical theory, and 2) **qualitative methods** that provide educated guesses through the application of mathematical forecasting techniques. An underlying assumption for quantitative forecasting is that historical data trends will remain the same in the future. This is an assumption that is not necessarily valid when a business environment changes quickly or when the historical data is inaccurate. When forecasting expenses, the best approach is to use simple forecasting techniques and good judgment.

WHY FORECAST EXPENSES?

Knowing the outcome of a horse race before it has begun has obvious advantages for the serious gambler. While most businessmen would not classify themselves as gam-blers, they would like to derive the benefits of being able to accurately forecast revenues and expenses in advance. Decisions that are made in a crisis mode, when there is no time to consider various alternatives, can generate poor results. Good forecasting provides the forecaster with the lead time to explore multiple options and have the time needed to carry out the steps for implementing the selected option.

Clearly, telecommunications managers who have good forecasting capabilities would achieve the benefits mentioned in the preceding paragraph. The ability to forecast department and telecommunications service expenses accurately is a key component of a telecommunications manager's performance appraisal and is a key tool for surviving in a changing technical environment. Good forecasting will result in small deviations (variances) between expense forecasts and actual expenses. Small variances are considered a measurement of good performance. Accurate expense forecasts also give upper management the data they need to develop accurate enterprise profitability forecasts and ensure the long-term viability of the business enterprise.

Therefore, there is a strong need for telecommunications managers to know how to establish accurate telecommunications expense forecasts. The only issue is whether it is possible. If it is possible, how is it done?

THEORETICAL FORECASTING

Forecasting techniques range from simple mathematical calculations to those requiring advanced mathematical skills in probability and statistics. The following will discuss only the quantitative forecasting process (and not the qualitative process) because it is most likely the approach to be used in expense forecasting. At the conceptual level, quantitative forecasting is a five step process involving: 1) problem definition, 2) data collection, 3) exploratory analysis and decomposition, 4) selecting a forecasting model, and 5) using the selected forecasting model(s) to generate forecasts. These steps are illustrated in Figure 16–4.

The complexity of each step will depend on the nature of the forecasting problem. Simple problems need sim-

Figure 16–4. The five step forecasting process model.

ple solutions. The work effort associated with complex problems can be extensive, and a formal or informal cost v. benefit assessment may be appropriate before undertaking a complex forecasting project. Quantitative forecasting is a technique that is most effective for situations in which the historical data profile will match the future data profile.

Problem Definition

This step is the most critical phase of the forecasting process, because the problem definition elements will become the basis for selecting the appropriate forecasting model. An accurate problem definition requires a good understanding of the situation to which the forecasting tools will be applied exists. When **forecasting** specialists are asked to establish forecasts, they will rely upon individuals who are familiar with the situation to explain their needs and help them develop a forecasting model to address the situation. The understanding must include knowledge of the validity and quality of historical data, the tolerance range for forecast errors, and the likelihood of creating a reliable forecast simulation when historical data is being used.

Some forecasting techniques are of such mathematical complexity that any feasibility step requires the use of a professional forecaster—someone who understands how to perform various quantitative and qualitative forecasting techniques and understand their limitations. When a professional forecaster is required for the feasibility analysis phase, the role of a telecommunications manager is one of assessing the cost v. benefit feasibility of using formal forecasting alternatives. The viability of forecasting proposals is determined by applying common sense to the preliminary output generated by forecasting models. Managers should maintain the same professional skepticism, when evaluating formal forecasting project proposals that would be used when making decisions in technical or organizational management situations.

The problem definition phase is the most difficult step because it requires problem solving skills in a broad range of topics. When applying forecasting techniques to real world business problems, a blend of business knowledge, problem solving skills, and forecasting skills is required. If only one of these skill elements exists, the wrong problem may be defined. It may also be defined improperly, or it may be defined in such a way that makes the forecasting model selection process extraordinarily difficult. It is at this stage that a decision should be made regarding the viability of using quantitative forecasting methods for the operations forecasting application that is being evaluated.

Information Gathering

The problem definition stage provided the opportunity to review the existing data and determine its viability for various forecasting techniques. If sufficient historical data of the correct type and quality is readily available, the information-gathering step is one of converting existing information into a format appropriate for use with a forecasting model.

When good input data is not available, a data retrieval and consolidation step may be required. However, if good historical data cannot be obtained, it may be necessary to make educated guesses or begin to establish a database. Forecasters legitimize this technique by classifying it as a qualitative forecast that uses a "jury of opinion" method, while business managers are more likely to refer to them as educated guesses—a description that more accurately reflects their source. When the application is a good candidate for applying forecasting techniques but historical data is not available, it will be necessary to 1) set up a procedure that begins to collect historical data in the proper format and 2) use educated guesses until a reliable historical database has been established.

Exploratory Analysis

This step examines the historical data and identifies how it should be used with quantitative forecasting method(s). Data elements may be broken down or consolidated, and trends may be identified to assist in the evaluation of different forecasting models. Exploratory analysis also includes determining the relationships among the variables that will become part of the selected forecasting method. It is an activity relegated to individuals who have strong mathematical forecasting skills. These are not skills that the average telecommunications manager would have.

Selecting a Forecasting Model

Using the historical information obtained from the previous steps, the appropriate forecasting model(s) will be selected and the technical details will be worked out to provide preliminary examples. Normally, one or two leading forecasting model contenders would be available for the last step.

Each forecasting model's implicit and explicit assumptions should be known and compared to the forecasting application under consideration. The forecasting model(s) that provides the best fit would be the one that is selected.

Using the Forecasting Model

In this final step, forecasts are created and individuals who are familiar with the application are requested to determine the validity of the generated forecasts. One way of testing the validity of forecasts is to use a historical database that contains actual results for a number of years. The forecasting model can be used with data from an earlier year, and its results can be checked against the actual results of the following period. While this may not necessarily reflect the current environment, it provides a tool for honing the effectiveness of the selected forecasting model.

Managerially, the focus should be on evaluating the forecasting results. The burden of establishing good forecasts is placed on the technical forecast developers. Of course, if managers create their own forecasts, they should hold themselves accountable for the results obtained and they should apply the same performance standards they would use to measure the performance of others.

Forecasting Reliability Comments

The theoretical forecasting discussion was presented to describe the complexity that is involved when applying theoretical forecasting concepts to forecasting operations expenses. If it were simple to apply theoretical forecasting to business expense forecasting, expense forecasting would be a standardized operating procedure. It is not.

Prophecies are predictions of the future and have little relevence to the current environment. However, unlike a prophecy, a forecast requires a knowledge or estimate of past events so that it can be used to predict future events. These past events—actual or estimated—are mathematically manipulated to establish trends. The trends based on historical information are then used to provide estimates of the future.

Historical information may also be stored in the memories of individuals, and some individuals have the innate ability to accurately forecast future events without the use of mathematical forecasting tools. When the historical data used in a quantitative forecasting process are developed by expert opinion, the quantitative forecasting process effectively becomes a qualitative forecasting process with all of its inherent vagueness. Regardless of how the forecasting process is carried out, there is always an element of uncertainty about the results. Mathematically based forecasting tools can always generate a forecast. However, accurate forecasting is possible only when the database used to develop the forecast is accurate and when the forecasting model is designed to use the data accurately.

PRACTICAL FORECASTING

The preceding section provided an overview of the forecasting process commonly used by forecasting specialists. This section will introduce procedures that eliminate theoretical forecasting techniques in favor of techniques that rely on the use of spreadsheet calculations and simplifying assumptions. In some respects, **practical forcasting** can be considered a pragmatic summary of quantitative and qualitative forecasting techniques.

When mathematics is used in business calculations, spreadsheet software is faster and more accurate than performing repetitive manual calculations on a handheld calculator. Although there is an initial time investment for acquiring the knowledge needed to develop spreadsheets, the subsequent productivity increases should easily justify the effort. Microsoft's Excel is used for the examples in this chapter. Using any spreadsheet software typically requires an investment of time to build the skills necessary to be effective and efficient in using it. However, unless one has good enabling skills in mathematics, the ability to use any spreadsheet software will be limited.

Department Cost Centers

In a business, each department is seen as a cost center that is accountable for the expenses used to maintain and operate the department. The assumption is that if all department managers manage their expenses effectively, the business will also manage its expenses effectively. The profit center concept is implemented by holding individual department managers accountable for the expenses they generate—both direct and overhead expenses. If a department is able to generate revenues, revenues will also be shown on department reports.

Departments incur charges directly for salaries, the use of outside services, and the expense required for operating the department. The department may also be assigned costs by the finance department for facilities they share with other departments. These shared charges include costs associated with housing, utilities, shared corporate resources (e.g., the personnel and law departments, LANs, etc.), personnel benefits, and depreciation expenses. Because a department manager has the ability to control the quantity of direct charges used, they are sometimes referred to as **controllable expenses** while the shared overhead costs are referred to as **noncontrollable expenses.** These charges are presented separately in the typical BVA reports issued to department managers.

BVA Measurements

To provide business management with a profit center performance measurement tool, a BVA process is used. In the BVA process, an organization plan (forecast or budget) is established for the future. This forecast contains an estimate of all the direct and allocated expenses needed to maintain and operate the organization. Enterprise forecasts also contain revenue projections so that financial reports—income statements, profit and loss statements, and balance sheet forecasts—can be developed. These future period forecasts are used as a reference standard when expenses and revenues are actually incurred. When deviations exist between forecasts and actual performance, steps are taken to bring actual performance in line with forecast estimates.

As part of this enterprise planning process, department forecasts are established and similar performance measurement tools are used at the department level. The enterprise forecast that is developed is actually the sum of all the department forecasts generated within the business.

Forecast (Budget) Preparation

A business's budget preparation process is driven by the fiscal calendar. Most companies employ a January to December calendar, but there are some that use different time spans, such as July to June. Annual forecast planning efforts are started at least six months in advance of the plan year under consideration. For example, the development of a 2003 forecast using a January to December fiscal year would typically begin during July, 2002, and would be completed during the third quarter of 2002. Financial forecasts are also called budgets.

The objective of a company's annual planning cycle is to allocate funds for capital and operating expenses based on the budgeted revenues. If capital and operating expense forecasts exceed revenue forecasts and the company would lose money, adjustments must be made to the forecast elements. Unless there are errors in the revenue forecast or new revenue sources are identified, these adjustments involve a reduction of expense budgets to the level where desired profitability objectives can be achieved.

When an acceptable balance is achieved between revenue forecasts and expense forecasts, the annual forecast is finalized. It provides a financial baseline that becomes the game plan for the future time period. A key objective of annual planning activities is to ensure that future revenue streams can support planned expenditures. If forecast revenues cannot cover forecast expenses, the plan must be modified to establish revenue and expense budget values that meet the desired company profit objectives.

Budget Variances

BVA reports provide variance information in a format that allows budget deviations to be identified quickly, where:

$$Variance\$ = Budget\$ - Actual\$$$

Conceptually, budgets can be considered cash. A department manager has been given a cash bank account to spend on the annual expenses incurred for running the department. A negative variance indicates that the manager has spent more money than is available in the bank account and managers are expected to take the appropriate actions to correct overspending conditions. A positive variance is normally viewed positively, although there are circumstances when this may not be true.

Large negative variances are red flags that normally require mangers to explain the variances to his or her boss. Positive variances tend to receive less attention, but should also be analyzed to understand the reason. Large positive variances may be an indication of poor forecasting on the part of the manager. Typically, negative **variances** are highlighted on BVA reports by using parentheses instead of using a minus sign:

$$forecast = 100; actual = 120$$
$$variance = 100 - 120 = (20)$$

Parentheses do a much better job of emphasizing the negative variance than negative signs because parentheses are much more prominent when printed on a report or seen on a display screen.

Practical Expense Forecasting Process

The practical managerial forecasting process consists of four steps:

1. identify appropriate expense categories
2. store expense history by expense category
3. estimate current year actual expenses
4. develop a future year forecast

This general process will be used and modified as needed to develop both department expense and telecommunications expense forecasts. The procedure is shown as a **pragmatic expense forecasting model** in Figure 16–5. The expense codes will be the means for identifying expense categories; **expense codes** are maintained by the accounting department of a business.

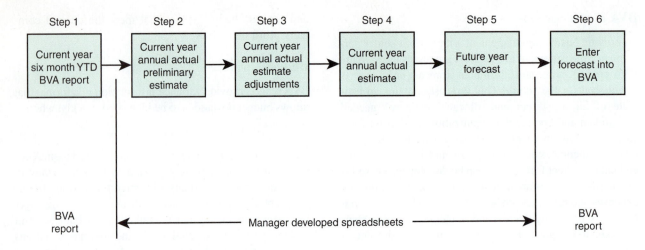

Figure 16–5. A pragmatic expense forecasting model.

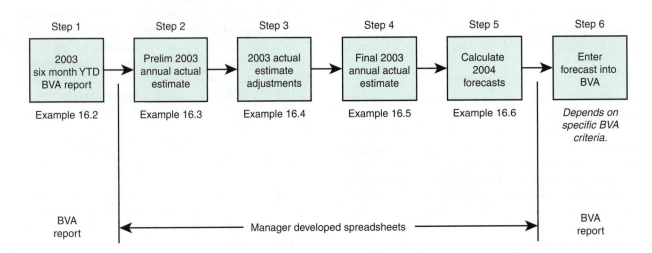

Figure 16–6. Operations department forecast preparation process.

DEPARTMENT EXPENSE FORECASTING EXAMPLE

The following reviews the expense forecasting (budgeting) process associated with the business management responsibilities of telecommunications operations management departments. Department expense forecasting is a generic management skill—all department managers in a business must go through the same process and develop the forecast in accordance with guidelines issued by the finance department.

The process shown in the forecasting model in Figure 16–5 will be used to establish an expense forecast for a telecommunications operations department. The operations department has been in place for a number of years and, therefore, a historical database is available in the enterprise organization's BVA system, which is maintained by the organization's accounting department. The six month year-to-date (YTD) report summarizing the current year actuals contained in the BVA system will be used as the expense forecast database for the operations department forecast.

The operations manager has developed a personal spreadsheet to assist in the operations department expense forecasting process and will use the information that is on the six month BVA report. (In the absence of an electronic interface, it is always possible to use manual input.) The operation manager's procedures are summarized in Figure 16–6. The tables referenced in Figure 16–6 refer to the tables that will be used to show the results of a PC-based forecasting process.

Expense Code Categories

For our department expense forecast example, we will use the generic department codes described previously in Chapter 15, *What is Operations Management?* These codes are listed in Example 16–1. For the forecasting example, it will be assumed that the current year is the year 2003 and the future year is 2004.

Expense History By Expense Category

In the example, the finance department has stored historical department data for the expense categories shown in Example 16–1 and they have given a six month history report to the telecommunications operation manager (Example 16–2). The report provides YTD forecast and actual expense information. The manager will use this report to establish 2004 budget forecasts.

Only controllable expenses have been shown on the six month history report because department managers cannot change noncontrollable expense information. Noncontrollable expenses are allocated to individual departments by the finance department after all approved department expense forecasts have been returned to them. The finance department calculates noncontrollable expenses after they have received department forecasts and submits the controllable and noncontrollable expense items to upper management for the approval of all budget categories. If finance has questions regarding controllable forecast information, they will contact the department managers directly and resolve the issue.

> If existing expense codes do not adequately describe department expenses, the finance department will add additional expense categories upon request.

Example 16–2 provides the 2003 annual forecast and six months of actual expenses that appeared in the monthly department BVA reports. The variances shown in Example 16–2 are based on comparing half the annual forecast value against the YTD actual values.

Current Year Actual Expense Estimate

Example 16–2 provided the year 2003 six month YTD estimate information that will become the basis for de-

Code	Description
Controllable	
001	Salaries
008	Overtime
009	Shift premium
010	Wages
013	Overtime premium
027	Special compensation
029	Severance pay
099	Recreation/general welfare
100	Travel expenses
124	Employee training
140	Company meetings
160	Petty cash
180	Employee moving expenses
190	Dues, fees, subscriptions
300	Supplies
304	Printing and duplicating
310	Equipment purchases
330	Equipment rental
401	Repairs and maintenance
449	Outside services
687	Express courier services
688	Miscellaneous freight
689	Miscellaneous postage
909	Telephone
Noncontrollable	
025	Other compensation – vacation
040	Payroll taxes
050	Group insurance
060	Retirement plan
070	Savings plan
520	Depreciation & amortization
900	Fixed charges
910	Redistributed telephone charges
911	Office services
912	Floor space
913	Personnel
915	Other redistributed expenses
925	Building costs
926	Redistributed personnel expenses

Example 16–1. Generic department expense codes.

veloping both the current year (2003) **actual operating expense estimate** and the future year (2004) forecast. The operations manager transferred the Example 16–2 information onto spreadsheets that are used to calculate 2003 actual estimates and 2004 forecasts. To simplify the calculation of forecasts, it will be assumed that the

Department ID: 12.69.10   7/31/03

Code	Expense Description	Annual FC	Actual	Variance$	Variance%
001	Salaries	$600,000.00	$294,000.00	$6,000.00	1.0%
008	Overtime	$24,000.00	$13,680.00	($1,680.00)	–7.0%
009	Shift premium	$30,000.00	$15,450.00	($450.00)	–1.5%
010	Wages	$300,000.00	$163,500.00	($13,500.00)	–4.5%
013	Overtime premium	$30,000.00	$13,800.00	$1,200.00	4.0%
027	Special compensation	$18,000.00	$9,000.00	$0.00	0.0%
029	Severance pay	$0.00	$6,000.00	($6,000.00)	-
099	Recreation/general welfare	$1,500.00	$1,125.00	($375.00)	-25.0%
100	Travel expenses	$3,000.00	$1,800.00	($300.00)	–10.0%
124	Employee training	$8,400.00	$4,284.00	($84.00)	–1.0%
140	Company meetings	$1,800.00	$792.00	$108.00	6.0%
160	Petty cash	$2,820.00	$1,395.90	$14.10	0.5%
180	Employee moving expenses	$0.00	$0.00	$0.00	0.0%
190	Dues, fees, subscriptions	$660.00	$313.50	$16.50	2.5%
300	Supplies	$1,920.00	$979.20	($19.20)	–1.0%
304	Printing and duplicating	$1,200.00	$606.00	($6.00)	–0.5%
310	Equipment purchases	$2,640.00	$990.00	$330.00	12.5%
330	Equipment rental	$3,600.00	$1,854.00	($54.00)	–1.5%
401	Repairs and maintenance	$6,000.00	$3,090.00	($90.00)	–1.5%
449	Outside services	$55,200.00	$33,120.00	($5,520.00)	–10.0%
687	Express courier services	$1,500.00	$480.00	$270.00	18.0%
688	Miscellaneous freight	$0.00	$0.00	$0.00	0.0%
689	Miscellaneous postage	$600.00	$336.00	($36.00)	–6.0%
909	Telephone	$30,000.00	$14,550.00	$450.00	1.5%
	Controllable expense totals	**$1,122,840.00**	**$581,145.60**	**($19,725.60)**	**–3.5%**

Variance$ = (annual FC/2)–actual
Variance% = variance$/(annual FC/2)

Example 16–2.   YTD forecast and actual information for July, 2003.

six month actual values represent one half of the estimated actual expenses for the current year. If this were not the case because of special circumstances, the manager would make adjustments to the estimated 2003 annual actual values.

Example 16–2 contains all the information needed to develop practical forecasts. If real world reports do not provide all of the information shown, the telecommunications manager would need to develop additional spreadsheets and manually incorporate any missing information needed to calculate current year actual expenses. The spreadsheet tool is a major asset when developing forecasts and the only limiting factor is the imagination and the skill of the individual preparing forecast information.

Example 16–3 shows the telecommunications manager's spreadsheet for a preliminary calculation of 2003 estimated actual expenses. The EstActual value was calculated by doubling the 2003 YTD actual values.

CURRENT YEAR ACTUAL EXPENSE ESTIMATE ADJUSTMENTS.   The telecommunications manager reviewed the Example 16–3 results and saw that some of the preliminary annual actual estimates were unreasonable. This judgment can be made when he or she has been managing the costs closely and the statement is based on his or her expert knowledge.

Adjustments were needed and they were noted in the Example 16–4 spreadsheet by showing the adjusted change (AdjActual) and noting the cause for the change (Reason).

2003 Preliminary Actual Operating Expense Estimate
Telecommunications Operations Department

Department ID: 12.69.10

Code	Expense Description	Annual FC	EstActual	Variance$	Variance%
001	Salaries	$600,000.00	$588,000.00	$12,000.00	2.0%
008	Overtime	$24,000.00	$27,360.00	($3,360.00)	–14.0%
009	Shift premium	$30,000.00	$30,900.00	($900.00)	–3.0%
010	Wages	$300,000.00	$327,000.00	($27,000.00)	–9.0%
013	Overtime premium	$30,000.00	$27,600.00	$2,400.00	8.0%
027	Special compensation	$18,000.00	$18,000.00	$0.00	0.0%
029	Severance pay	$0.00	$5,000.00	($5,000.00)	-
099	Recreation/general welfare	$1,500.00	$2,250.00	($750.00)	–50.0%
100	Travel expenses	$3,000.00	$3,600.00	($600.00)	–20.0%
124	Employee training	$8,400.00	$8,568.00	($168.00)	–2.0%
140	Company meetings	$1,800.00	$1,584.00	$216.00	12.0%
160	Petty cash	$2,820.00	$2,791.80	$28.20	1.0%
180	Employee moving expenses	$0.00	$0.00	$0.00	0.0%
190	Dues, fees, subscriptions	$660.00	$627.00	$33.00	5.0%
300	Supplies	$1,920.00	$1,958.40	($38.40)	–2.0%
304	Printing and duplicating	$1,200.00	$1,212.00	($12.00)	–1.0%
310	Equipment purchases	$2,640.00	$1,980.00	$660.00	25.0%
330	Equipment rental	$3,600.00	$3,708.00	($108.00)	–3.0%
401	Repairs and maintenance	$6,000.00	$6,180.00	($180.00)	–3.0%
449	Outside services	$55,200.00	$66,240.00	($11,040.00)	–20.0%
687	Express courier services	$1,500.00	$960.00	$540.00	36.0%
688	Miscellaneous freight	$0.00	$0.00	$0.00	0.0%
689	Miscellaneous postage	$600.00	$672.00	($72.00)	–12.0%
909	Telephone	$30,000.00	$29,100.00	$900.00	3.0%
	Controllable expense totals	**$1,122,840.00**	**$1,155,291.20**	**($32,451.20)**	**–2.9%**

EstActual = 2 × six month actual

Example 16–3. Preliminary 2003 annual actual estimate.

The round up notation was used to show that the preliminary annual estimates were rounded up or down to the nearest tens or hundreds position. The rounding of calculated annual expense values is a matter of personal taste. Listing numbers to the nearest dollar and cents implicitly implies an accuracy level to the penny, which is not the case.

Example 16–4 required a detailed knowledge of the department's forecast and actual expense history during the year—knowledge the department manager should have if a good job of monitoring and controlling monthly department expenses has been done.

Example 16–5 is the 2003 final actual estimate that the manager will use for calculating 2004 forecasts. It incorporates the Example 16–4 information and shows the final estimate calculation for 2003 actual expenses. The final 2003 actual expense estimate (Example 16–5) be-comes the information database that will be used to develop future year (2004) forecasts. If the year 2003 actual expense estimate were not modified to reflect real world happenings (Example 16–4), the 2002 forecasts could have built-in inaccuracies. Comparing the preliminary and final year 2003 actual expense estimates shows this adjustment difference to be $5,281.20 ($1,155,291.20 – $1,150,010.00). If the adjustments had not been made, the database used for calculating 2002 forecasts would have been overstated by $5,281.20.

Future Year Forecast

Without making any changes, the adjusted annual actual operating expense estimate would become the future year forecast. However, in the real world there are

2003 Annual Adjustment Information
Changes to Preliminary Actual Operating Expenses
Telecommunications Operations Department

Department ID: 12.69.10   8/5/03

Code	Expense Description	AdjActual	Reason
001	Salaries	$600,000.00	Delays in hiring staff replacements.
008	Overtime	$25,000.00	Overtime due to hiring delays.
009	Shift premium	$30,900.00	
010	Wages	$327,000.00	
013	Overtime premium	$27,600.00	
027	Special compensation	$18,000.00	
029	Severance pay	$0.00	$5,000 was a one-time expense.
099	Recreation/general welfare	$2,250.00	
100	Travel expenses	$3,600.00	
124	Employee training	$8,600.00	Round up.
140	Company meetings	$1,600.00	
160	Petty cash	$2,800.00	
180	Employee moving expenses	$0.00	
190	Dues, fees, subscriptions	$660.00	Round up.
300	Supplies	$2,000.00	Round up.
304	Printing and duplicating	$1,200.00	Round down.
310	Equipment purchases	$2,500.00	Includes new equipment needs.
330	Equipment rental	$3,900.00	Revision.
401	Repairs and maintenance	$5,500.00	Scrapping high maintenance unit.
449	Outside services	$55,200.00	Spending pattern skewed to first 6 months.
687	Express courier services	$1,000.00	Round up.
688	Miscellaneous freight	$0.00	
689	Miscellaneous postage	$700.00	Round up.
909	Telephone	$30,000.00	Round up.
	Totals	**$1,150,010.00**	

Example 16–4. Adjustments to the preliminary 2003 annual actual estimate.

always changes—staffing additions/deletions, new purchases, rate increases for existing services, etc. In a period of high inflation, it may be prudent to use an inflation factor to reflect the expected price increases. The finance department normally provides guidelines for department forecasting, and this would include raise percentage guidelines for salaried and wage personnel pay raises. In many annual planning cycles, staffing is reviewed as a separate planning effort that provides input into the appropriate department's salary-related expense categories.

In Example 16–6, it will be assumed that salary increases of 4% will be applied to all salary and wage categories. All other noncategories will use the estimated 2003 final actual expense estimates.

When staffing changes are planned, the impact on personnel-related operating expense categories would also have to be determined. Because most department budget operating expenses are based on staffing levels, it would require an assessment of every expense category contained on the BVA report. In our example, staffing will remain the same for the future year. Refer to Example 16–6 for the final future year department operating expense forecast.

At the summary level, Example 16–7 shows that there has been an overall increase of 3.1% between the current year actual and future year forecast operating expenses. The budget in Example 16–7 is one that has a minimal expense forecast increase compared to the estimated actuals of the prior year. The only expense cate-

2003 Final Adjusted Annual Actual Estimate
Telecommunications Operations Department

Department ID: 12.69.10   **8/5/03**

Code	Expense Description	EstActual	AdjActual	Variance$	Variance%
001	Salaries	$588,000.00	$600,000.00	($12,000.00)	–2.0%
008	Overtime	$27,360.00	$25,000.00	$2,360.00	8.6%
009	Shift premium	$30,900.00	$30,900.00	$0.00	0.0%
010	Wages	$327,000.00	$327,000.00	$0.00	0.0%
013	Overtime premium	$27,600.00	$27,600.00	$0.00	0.0%
027	Special compensation	$18,000.00	$18,000.00	$0.00	0.0%
029	Severance pay	$5,000.00	$0.00	$5,000.00	-
099	Recreation/general welfare	$2,250.00	$2,250.00	$0.00	0.0%
100	Travel expenses	$3,600.00	$3,600.00	$0.00	0.0%
124	Employee training	$8,568.00	$8,600.00	($32.00)	–0.4%
140	Company meetings	$1,584.00	$1,600.00	($16.00)	–1.0%
160	Petty cash	$2,791.80	$2,800.00	($8.20)	–0.3%
180	Employee moving expenses	$0.00	$0.00	$0.00	0.0%
190	Dues, fees, subscriptions	$627.00	$660.00	($33.00)	–5.3%
300	Supplies	$1,958.40	$2,000.00	($41.60)	–2.1%
304	Printing and duplicating	$1,212.00	$1,200.00	$12.00	1.0%
310	Equipment purchases	$1,980.00	$2,500.00	($520.00)	–26.3%
330	Equipment rental	$3,708.00	$3,900.00	($192.00)	–5.2%
401	Repairs and maintenance	$6,180.00	$5,500.00	$680.00	11.0%
449	Outside services	$66,240.00	$55,200.00	$11,040.00	16.7%
687	Express courier services	$960.00	$1,000.00	($40.00)	–4.2%
688	Miscellaneous freight	$0.00	$0.00	$0.00	0.0%
689	Miscellaneous postage	$672.00	$700.00	($28.00)	–4.2%
909	Telephone	$29,100.00	$30,000.00	($900.00)	–3.1%
	Controllable expense totals	**$1,155,291.20**	**$1,150,010.00**	**$5,281.20**	**0.5%**

Example 16–5. 2003 final estimated actual values.

gories showing an increase are the salary categories. The increase is due to following the finance department's guidelines for providing wage and salary increases. The largest category of expenses is for the compensation categories, which is not unusual. It is one of the reasons why serious expense reduction efforts frequently target staffing reductions.

The final results (Example 16–7) indicate that a modest budget increase of $35,420 (3.1%) is being forecast. Except for the compensation categories, which received a 4% increase, and the elimination of the one time 2001 severance pay entry, all other categories were budgeted to receive the same funding level as the previous year.

When the number crunching phase of budget preparation has been completed, the implications of the new budget should be summarized in a letter to the telecommunications manager's management. This would include a translation of numbers into projects and other department related activities.

> Budget preparation can be a time-consuming, tedious task that someone with good mathematical and PC spreadsheet skills can simplify. While not as impressive as giving orders or making presentations, it sets the stage for measuring future year performance and is a very important job skill.

The spreadsheets used for this forecast example is contained on the CD that accompanies the text.

Year 2004 Department Forecast
Telecommunications Operations Department

Department ID: 12.69.10		8/15/03
Code	Expense Description	Forecast$
001	Salaries	$624,000
008	Overtime	$26,000
009	Shift premium	$32,136
010	Wages	$340,080
013	Overtime premium	$28,704
027	Special compensation	$18,000
029	Severance pay	$0
099	Recreation/general welfare	$2,250
100	Travel expenses	$3,600
124	Employee training	$8,600
140	Company meetings	$1,600
160	Petty cash	$2,800
180	Employee moving expenses	$0
190	Dues, fees, subscriptions	$660
300	Supplies	$2,000
304	Printing and duplicating	$1,200
310	Equipment purchases	$2,500
330	Equipment rental	$3,900
401	Repairs and maintenance	$5,500
449	Outside services	$55,200
687	Express courier services	$1,000
688	Miscellaneous freight	$0
689	Miscellaneous postage	$700
909	Telephone	$30,000
	Controllable expense totals	**$1,190,430**

Example 16–6.   Year 2004 department budget forecast.

TELECOMMUNICATIONS OPERATING EXPENSES

The other half of the budgeting process for operations managers is to forecast expenses for telecommunications products and services. When a chargeback system is used, it involves forecasting the costs that will be charged to individual departments.

Telecommunications technologies—telephone services, WAN services, LAN services, internetwork services, the WWW—are used throughout businesses. Some departments, such as an order processing department that receives calls from customers, could not operate without computer and communication technologies. WWW services are being used for e-commerce functions, and a company that does not have a website is not communicating effectively with customers, stockholders, or the public.

Telecommunications services are expensive resources, and the associated equipment is complex and diffi-

cult to operate. Internal telecommunications departments are responsible for controlling costs and acting as a liaison between the telecommunications technology infrastructure and the using departments. The telecommunications department may act as the service provider for various telecommunications services, or as a facilitator that is responsible for implementing and managing the externally provided services. Regardless of the telecommunications department's technical role, business management will expect it to manage the telecommunications resource effectively, control expenses, and answer any questions relating to them.

When telecommunications expenses are relatively small compared to other operating expenses, it is not unusual for them to be treated as a cost of doing business and to be paid for as an administrative expense at the corporate level. However, at some point in time, telecommunications expenses will become large enough to cause upper management to raise the question, "Why are telecommunications expenses so high and increasing so rapidly?" A normal response in a no control environment will typically be, "We don't know," and a flurry of activity takes place in an attempt to answer the question.

Controlling expenses has a cost associated with it. The cost is directly related to the level of control exercised. The cost of establishing tighter controls over telecommunications costs should continually be weighed against the benefits being derived from the cost control function. If $10,000 per year is being spent on controlling $10,000 per year in telecommunications expenses, poor judgment is being used. On the other hand, if $30,000 per year is being used to control $1,000,000 per year and auditing information identifies a 15% savings benefit ($150,000) being attributed to the control function, good managerial judgment is being exercised. Good judgment remains the primary criterion for determining what level of cost control measures should be used and the degree to which it is deployed. Cost control is a tool and telecommunications managers are responsible for using the tool effectively.

One of the common ways to control telecommunications costs is by establishing a **chargeback** system, where users of services receive bills for their usage. The chargeback system should identify the individuals who use telecommunications services and should allocate costs based on the quantity of the service being used and the rate assigned to the service.

Cost Allocation Concepts

An underlying philosophy of the business profit center concept is that department managers are accountable for department expenses. Where possible, costs (expenses) are charged directly to the individual or department using

2003 Final Actual Estimate v. 2004 Forecast
Telecommunications Operations Department

Department ID: 12.69.10   8/19/03

Code	Expense Description	2003 YrActEst	2004 YrFC	Difference$	Difference%
001	Salaries	$600,000.00	$624,000.00	$24,000.00	4.0%
008	Overtime	$25,000.00	$26,000.00	$1,000.00	4.0%
009	Shift premium	$30,900.00	$32,136.00	$1,236.00	4.0%
010	Wages	$327,000.00	$340,080.00	$13,080.00	4.0%
013	Overtime premium	$27,600.00	$28,704.00	$1,104.00	4.0%
027	Special compensation	$18,000.00	$18,000.00	$0.00	0.0%
029	Severance pay	$5,000.00	$0.00	($5,000.00)	-100.0%
099	Recreation/general welfare	$2,250.00	$2,250.00	$0.00	0.0%
100	Travel expenses	$3,600.00	$3,600.00	$0.00	0.0%
124	Employee training	$8,600.00	$8,600.00	$0.00	0.0%
140	Company meetings	$1,600.00	$1,600.00	$0.00	0.0%
160	Petty cash	$2,800.00	$2,800.00	$0.00	0.0%
180	Employee moving expenses	$0.00	$0.00	$0.00	0.0%
190	Dues, fees, subscriptions	$660.00	$660.00	$0.00	0.0%
300	Supplies	$2,000.00	$2,000.00	$0.00	0.0%
304	Printing and duplicating	$1,200.00	$1,200.00	$0.00	0.0%
310	Equipment purchases	$2,500.00	$2,500.00	$0.00	0.0%
330	Equipment rental	$3,900.00	$3,900.00	$0.00	0.0%
401	Repairs and maintenance	$5,500.00	$5,500.00	$0.00	0.0%
449	Outside services	$55,200.00	$55,200.00	$0.00	0.0%
687	Express courier services	$1,000.00	$1,000.00	$0.00	0.0%
688	Miscellaneous freight	$0.00	$0.00	$0.00	0.0%
689	Miscellaneous postage	$700.00	$700.00	$0.00	0.0%
909	Telephone	$30,000.00	$30,000.00	$0.00	0.0%
	Controllable expense totals	**$1,155,010.00**	**$1,190,430.00**	**$35,420.00**	**3.1%**

Example 16–7. Comparison of 2003 final actual estimate *v.* 2004 forecast.

the resource. This cost allocation process is typically called a chargeback, and chargebacks may be **direct** or **shared.** Direct chargebacks are used when the individual or department using a resource can be identified. If this is not possible, a shared chargeback may be employed. Shared chargebacks allocate the cost of using a resource back to its users by establishing some equitable allocation scheme. A common approach is to divide a shared resource equally between all the users by calculating a per user cost rate.

The concept of chargebacks assumes that the end user of the service incurring the cost should manage and control the use of the service. The chargebacks are incorporated into department budgets and department managers are expected to monitor the use of telecommunications services by department members. The alternative to using chargebacks is to pay expenses at the company level and

not be able to identify the use—or misuse—of telecommunications services.

SHARED CHARGE ALLOCATION MECHANICS. A shared charge allocation approach is used when the usage of telecommunications products or services cannot be assigned directly to individual users. A typical shared charge calculation process requires four steps:

1. Establish shared charge categories.
2. Consolidate shared charge expenses.
3. Calculate a per user charge rate.
   - total shared charges ÷ number of users
4. Allocate shared charges to users of the shared facilities.

Shared Charge Calculation Example for Calculating Basic Telephone Rates

Basic Charge Information	
Description	*Monthly$*
PBX maintenance	$6,000
Administrative support	4,000
Shared network charges	2,000
Total basic Charges	**$12,000**
Number of sharing extensions	200
Basic charge rate	**$60/Extn**

Assuming a department has twelve telephone extensions and is a user of the basic services, the department's charge would be $720.00 (12 extensions × $60/extension).

Chargeback Systems

In a business environment, department managers are accustomed to receiving monthly BVA reports to help them manage expenses. When a telecommunications chargeback system is used, a mechanism must link these chargebacks to the BVA reports issued by the finance department. Linkage to the BVA reporting system is implemented by establishing a telephone controllable chargeback expense code for this purpose, such as the 909 code listed in Example 16–1.

However, chargebacks would appear as a single line item on a BVA report, which is not enough information when the expense is a major department expense. Chargeback systems must provide additional information to users of internally or externally provided services to allow department managers to control their charges. Chargeback systems may be complex or simple, depending upon the business. If a chargeback system is required to control telecommunications costs, the telecommunications manager assumes the primary responsibility for taking the appropriate actions to create it. This may involve purchasing a software application or developing one internally.

Call Detail Reporting (CDR) Systems.
There are two types of telephone systems commonly used by large business customers: Centrex and PBX telephone systems. Centrex system equipment is housed in the telephone company's CO, and Centrex customers pay service fees for the use of the equipment. The telephone company will offer different reporting options to the Centrex customer and will explain the Centrex expense charges at the telephone extension (individual user) level. On the other hand, PBX system equipment is installed at a customer's locations and is han-

dled as a fixed asset purchase. From a local call or long distance call perspective, a PBX system looks like a single telephone number (the location's main number) because the PBX system routes calls to and from individual extensions. As a result, the local call provider (normally the telephone company) or the interexchange carrier cannot provide billing at the telephone extension level, and all local and long distance charges are levied against the main telephone number without any supporting details.

Fortunately, PBX systems have a feature that records calls by generating call detail records (CDRs). (The CDR is also known as a **station message detail record** (SMDR). A PBX CDR record is generated for every call (local, long distance, or intercom) and identifies the calling number, called number, time of day, call duration, start time, etc.) A CDR contains the same information used by local and long distance carriers to determine customer charges for local or long distance calls.

Therefore, the extension call costs of a PBX system can be identified by using CDR cost calculation software to calculate calling charges in the same way that the local or long distance call suppliers do. Using the CDR information to determine call lengths and then applying the service provider rates allows local and long distance call costs to be calculated. This information can then be placed into a chargeback report that is similar in format to that received by local telephone company subscribers. If the CDR process is carried out properly and covers the same time period as the service provider's bill, the total cost of all CDR calls should match the service provider's billing. CDR cost calculation software has a range of options (at different costs) to provide internal chargeback features. It typically provides the capability to:

1. calculate telephone extension long distance and local call costs
2. validate local and long distance service provider billing
3. provide chargeback information reports for telecommunications users

TELEPHONE EXPENSE FORECASTING EXAMPLE

Forecasting telephone expenses utilizes different forecasting techniques than those used when forecasting department expenses. Future telephone expenses are strongly influenced by:

- vendor rate changes
- service usage patterns
- staffing changes

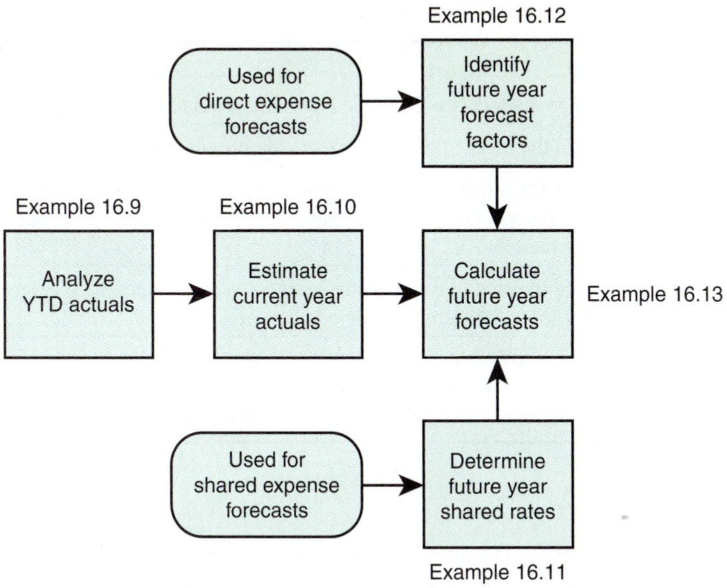

Example 16.12

Example 16.9   Example 16.10

Example 16.13

Example 16.11

Figure 16–7. Telephone system forecasting process.

Rate changes for different telecommunications services are ongoing and can have a significant impact on future expenses in either a positive or negative direction. A general pattern of increasing rates with existing vendors may be offset by renegotiating an existing contract or by finding alternative supplier sources. Usage patterns of communications are constantly increasing as businesses provide free communications access to their services by using 800-services and other dedicated access services. Businesses continue to provide free communication access services to their customers. However, the price for successfully attracting new customers by providing 800-services may result in a major increase in telecommunications expenses for the business. In addition, an aggressive telemarketing organization would view an increase in outgoing call volumes as a measure of success at an increased cost. Finally, an organization that has more employees will normally generate higher costs than one that has fewer employees.

The process that will be used to develop telephone expense forecasts in this section is summarized in Figure 16–7.

Figure 16–7 shows two major forecasting expense categories, direct expenses, and shared expenses, and different forecasting approaches will be used for each category. Direct expenses include those telephone expense charges whose user can be identified directly from either the vendor's billing information or by having an internal CDR application system that can identify usage and allocate costs. Shared expenses include those telephone expenses whose usage cannot be easily identified to individual users. Table 16–2 summarizes the different direct and shared telephone expense categories that will be used in this example.

The following will assume the use of a hypothetical telephone expense chargeback system that has been developed by the telecommunications department. Spreadsheet software will be used to generate the text's chargeback system reports, but the format and content could easily be replicated by writing a software application.

Telephone Billing

Telephone billing is complex and difficult to understand for the average person, and it is not unusual for the telecommunications department to receive bills directly from the service providers and screen them before passing them onto an accounts payable department for payment. Telecommunications administrative services personnel would validate the billing charges, enter the expense information into a telephone chargeback system database, approve the bills for payment, and forward the bills to accounts payable for vendor payment.

Telephone Expense Chargeback System

Our hypothetical telephone expense chargeback system will generate monthly reports that are distributed to telephone system users. Example 16–8 is an example of the basic report that would be sent out to department managers and Table 16–3 provides a description of the various heading

TABLE 16–2   Telephone System Direct and Shared Charge Expenses

Charge Category	PBX System Charge	Description
Direct charges	Long distance calls	Calls made outside the local calling area. Normally provided by an IXC.
	Local calls	Calls made within the local calling area. Normally provided by an LEC.
	OCC	Other charge or credit. Charges incurred by moves, adds, changes (MAC) activity for telephone equipment. The provider of telephone system maintenance services supplies this information.
	Miscellaneous	Direct charges not covered in the previous categories. It may include special equipment, department 800-number services, etc.
Shared charge	Basic charges	Includes charges for maintaining the telephone system, providing access to the telephone CO, and the cost for internal personnel used to provide system services (directory services, repair coordination, telephone operator services, etc.).

TABLE 16–3   Telecommunications Expense Report Headings (Example 16–8)

Heading	Description
Basic$	Shared charges allocated to individual telephone extensions by multiplying the number of extensions in a department by a basic rate. For telephone systems, shared charges typically include telephone system maintenance, administrative support personnel, shared network, telephone expense reporting system, and common equipment depreciation charges.
Eqpt$	Equipment charges for the telephone equipment (a.k.a. station equipment) connected to the telephone line.
Local$	Local call charges. For a PBX telephone system, these are calculated with CDR reporting system software.
LD$	Long distance call charges. For a PBX telephone system, these are calculated with CDR reporting system software.
OCC$	Other charges and credits. These are one-time charges incurred when telephone station equipment is moved, added, or changed.
Misc$	Miscellaneous charges. A general charge category used for charges not covered by the other categories. It may be used for 800-services, home phones, modems, etc.
Total$	The sum of Basic$, Eqpt$, Local$, LngDst$, OCC$, and Misc$ charges.
Basic Rate	The charge allocated to each individual telephone extension for shared services.

categories contained on the report. In addition, a CDR-based report would also be sent to the department managers to provide backup for the call cost information summarized in the chargeback system report.

When the telecommunications department utilizes chargeback systems, they must maintain and control the different telecommunications expense categories independently of the finance department and provide the finance department with summary telephone expense entries for the monthly BVA reports. In our example, the 909 code (telephone expenses) will be used to charge back telecommunications costs on monthly department BVA reports. The finance department will receive a copy of the monthly

charges developed in the chargeback system and enter the department total on the department's BVA report. The department managers would also receive department telephone expense chargeback system reports from the telecommunications department so they could review the details that make up the 909-code telephone expenses in their BVA reports.

In Example 16–8, the monthly charge for the human resources department was $2,249.86 and the different charge elements are shown on the report. Budget variance information has been provided in the chargeback report and the human resources manager would see that the department has a negative variance of $369.86 for July, 2003.

Department: Human Resources

A/C	XCH	EXTN	Total$	Basic$	Equiptment Description	Eqpt$	Local$	LD$	OCC$	Misc$
732	765	3200	331.98	39.67	Display phone	125.00	20.50	146.81		
		3201	560.60	39.67	Feature phone	55.00	16.22	129.71	320.00	
		3202	141.79	39.67	Single line phone	20.00	8.99	73.13		
		3203	136.46	39.67	Two line phone	25.00	7.02	64.77		
		3204	116.73	39.67	30 button call director	45.00	3.81	28.25		
		3205	327.99	39.67	Feature phone	55.00	12.71	220.61		
		3206	163.63	39.67	Two line phone	25.00	11.03	87.93		
		3207	106.36	39.67	Two line phone	25.00	9.84	31.85		
		3208	158.16	39.67	Single line phone	20.00	11.88	86.61		
		3209	105.74	39.67	Two line phone	25.00	10.87	30.20		
		3210	100.38	39.67	Two line phone	25.00	9.45	26.26		
	Actual	**11**	**2,249.86**	**436.41**		**445.00**	**122.32**	**926.13**	**320.00**	**0.00**
	Forecast	**12**	**1,880.00**	**450.00**		**500.00**	**110.00**	**820.00**	**0.00**	**0.00**
	Variance	**1**	**(369.86)**	**13.59**		**55.00**	**(12.32)**	**(106.13)**	**(320.00)**	**0.00**

2003 basic rate: $45.36

Example 16–8. Telecommunications chargeback expense report example.

The human resources manager would quickly see that $320 of the negative variance amount was due to OCC$—a category used when telephone equipment is moved, added, or changed (refer to Table 16–3). The negative variances under the local and long distance categories could also be evaluated by examining the CDR report that lists the detailed call information.

> The telecommunications department is responsible for initiating the selection, implementation, and operation of any chargeback systems used to support internal telecommunications services. The telecommunications department would provide billing information input for the chargeback system and is accountable for ensuring its accuracy.

The following sections will complete the five different forecasting activities identified in the Figure 16–4 forecasting model:

1. Analyze YTD actual expenses.
2. Estimate current year actual expenses.
3. Calculate future year shared expenses.
4. Calculate future year direct expenses.
5. Forecast future year telephone expenses.

Analyze YTD Actual Expenses

The charge categories used in our telephone expense chargeback system are similar to those seen by residential telephone customers. A description of the telephone expense categories was provided in Table 16–3:

1. basic telephone (Basic$)
2. equipment (Eqpt$)
3. local calls (Local$)
4. long distance calls (LD$)
5. other charges and credits (OCC$)
6. miscellaneous (Misc$)

Our hypothetical telephone expense chargeback system generated the six month department summary telephone expense information shown in Example 16–9, which will be used for the initial analysis of current year (2003) telephone expenses. It is a summary-level report, where only one line of information is shown for each department and the report has been specially formatted for

use in the forecasting process. It shows six months of current year history. A similar report that contains current month information would be issued monthly. The finance department would use it to post summary-level 909 code charges to each department's BVA report.

Example 16–9 shows that a YTD negative variance of $16,263 has been generated against a forecast of $263,208 (a 6% negative variance). The causes for this variance must be determined, and any necessary adjustments must be made to the 2003 Actual Expense Estimate. The variance analysis would require looking at department reports (Example 16–8) and may require discussions with the department managers generating these variances to understand if the root cause is a one-time occurrence or is permanent. If the variance was expected to be ongoing, its impact would be incorporated into the forecast. Otherwise, it would be treated as a one-time anomaly.

Estimate Current Year Actual Expenses

With the Example 16–9 report providing the basic forecasting input, the telecommunications manager would generate spreadsheets as worksheets for the forecasting process. (These worksheets could have been generated by our hypothetical telephone expense chargeback system, but only after the approach has been validated in an easy to create format.)

The initial spreadsheet is shown in Example 16–10, which provides an estimate of the annual 2003 actual telephone expenses for shared expenses (Basic$) and direct expenses (Eqpt$, Local$, LngDst$, OCC$, and Misc$).

2003 Telecommunications Expenses
Six Month YTD Department Summary

Department	#Extns	Total$	Basic$	Eqpt$	Local$	LD$	OCC$	Misc$
Accounting	20	15,633	5,442	3,900	734	5,557	0	0
Executive	12	21,090	3,264	3,750	684	6,162	3,780	3,450
Legal	14	16,278	3,810	4,200	912	7,356	0	0
MIS	11	13,872	2,994	2,670	732	5,556	1,920	0
Sales	110	172,056	29,940	22,200	6,384	65,532	0	48,000
Service	53	40,542	14,424	9,900	8,244	7,974	0	0
Six month YTD actual	**220**	**279,471**	**59,874**	**46,620**	**17,690**	**98,137**	**5,700**	**51,450**
Six month YTD budget	218	263,208	56,400	42,720	18,600	90,000	4,920	50,568
Variance	**(2)**	**(16,263)**	**(3,474)**	**(3,900)**	**910**	**(8,137)**	**(780)**	**(882)**
Variance %	-1%	-6%	-6%	-9%	5%	-9%		-2%

2003 basic rate: $45.36

Example 16–9. July, 2003 department summary report example.

These estimates were calculated by doubling the six month actual expense values shown in the Example 16–9 report. The annual basic rate is twelve times the monthly rate shown in Example 16–9.

With the creation of Example 16–10, a current year (2003) database exists. This information will be the basis for developing next year's (2004) telephone expense forecasts.

Calculate Future Year Shared Expenses

To develop future year *shared expense* forecasts, the year 2004 basic rate (shared rate) must be calculated. Example 16–11 provides a chargeback system report displaying shared charge information that is stored in the chargeback system. The system stores the monthly shared charges (PBX maintenance, administrative support, network services, and SMDR services) that are being allocated to users and the number of users (extensions) sharing these charges. Both annual and monthly shared charge rates are calculated and used in the appropriate reports.

Example 16–11 shows that there will be thirty additional extensions needed in 2002, due to a staffing increase. As a result of the staffing increase and minimal shared charge category increases, the annual basic rate will be $16.32 lower in 2004 ($528.00) than it is in 2003 ($544.32) (a "good news" item that should be pointed out to business management during 2004 budget reviews).

To calculate the 2004 Basic$, the number of department extensions will be multiplied by the appropriate 2004 basic rate (annual or monthly, as is appropriate for the specific report).

Calculate Future Year Direct Expenses

To forecast 2004 direct telephone expenses (Eqpt$, Local$, LD$, OCC$, and Misc$), the 2003 annual actual estimate of direct expenses will be used as the **forecast factor** (**FF**). However, telecommunications direct expenses in the future year will be subject to two factors that should be included in the calculated forecast:

1. rate changes

2. staffing changes

The input for the rate adjustments is obtained by contacting the provider of the products and services. Any planned 2004 rate changes that will affect 2004 expenses will be used in the forecasting process. Staffing changes can be identified from the staffing change information that is made available for the business's annual planning cycle. The approach used to adjust forecasts for these two items will be to identify percentage increase expected and adjust the 2003 estimated direct actual expenses by this percentage. For example, if the telecommunications expense were $10,000 for a given department and the increases are forecast:

- rate change: −4% (a rate reduction)

- staffing change: 14%

An overall increase of approximately 9% ($944) would be expected, and next year's forecast would be $10,944 ($1,000 + $944). (If decimal values occur, the calculation would be rounded to the nearest dollar, because dollars are the standard unit for BVA systems.) Negative or positive changes are possible for these adjustments.

The mathematical basis for making these adjustments is straightforward, and the following will provide a minitutorial of the calculation process. If the adjustments are considered individually:

$$2004 \text{ rate impact} = 96\% \ (100\% - 4\%) \text{ to reflect the rate reduction}$$

$$2004 \text{ rate adjusted forecast} = .96 \times 10,000 = \$ 9,600$$

2003 Annual Telephone Actual Expense Estimate
Department Summary

Department	#Extns	Total$	Basic$	Eqpt$	Local$	LD$	OCC$	Misc$
Accounting	20	31,267	10,886	7,800	1,468	11,114	0	0
Executive	12	42,184	6,532	7,500	1,368	12,324	7,560	6,900
Legal	14	32,556	7,620	8,400	1,824	14,712	0	0
MIS	11	27,744	5,988	5,340	1,464	11,112	3,840	0
Sales	110	344,107	59,875	44,400	12,768	131,064	0	96,000
Service	53	81,085	28,849	19,800	16,488	15,948	0	0
2001 annual actual	**220**	**558,943**	**119,750**	**93,240**	**35,380**	**196,274**	**11,400**	**102,900**

2003 basic rate: $544.32

Example 16–10. Estimated 2003 annual telephone expenses.

Basic Charge Calculation Worksheet

Description	2002	2003	2004	2004Diff$	2004 Chg%
PBX maintenance	$32,500	$35,000	$41,000	$6,000	17%
Administrative support	$55,000	$56,750	$60,000	$3,250	6%
Network services	$14,000	$15,000	$17,000	$2,000	13%
SMDR services	$12,000	$13,000	$14,000	$1,000	8%
Annual total	**$113,500**	**$119,750**	**$132,000**	**$12,250**	**10%**
Number of sharing extensions		220	250	30	14%
Annual basic rate		$544.32	$528.00	($16.32)	-3%
Monthly basic rate		$45.36	$44.00	($1.36)	-3%

basic monthly rate = monthly total/#total sharing extensions

Number of Extensions

Department	2003 Act	2004 FC	Difference	%Change
Accounting	20	22	2	10.0%
Executive	12	12	0	0.0%
Legal	14	15	1	7.1%
MIS	11	13	2	18.2%
Sales	110	125	15	13.6%
Service	53	63	10	18.9%
Total	**220**	**250**	**30**	**13.6%**

Example 16–11. Chargeback system basic charge calculation worksheet.

The 2004 rate forecast can also be calculated by: 1) identifying the rate effect and 2) subtracting it from the 2003 actual estimate value.

2004 rate effect $= -.04 \times 10,000 = -\$400$

2004 rate forecast $= \$1,000 + (-\$400) = \$9,600$

If the staffing had remained the same, the final 2004 forecast would have been $9,600. However, there was a 14% staffing increase and the rate-adjusted forecast must be modified to reflect the staffing increase. The final 2002 forecast is calculated by increasing the rate-adjusted forecast to reflect the staffing increase:

$9,600 \times 1.14 = \$10,944 = $ 2004 final forecast

Note: The staffing increase factor (1.14) could also have been calculated directly by dividing next year value by the current year value (114 ÷ 100).

This somewhat akward, multistage calculation process could have easily been completed in one step.

2004 final forecast $= (100\% - 4\%) \times (114/100) \times \$10,000$

or

$.96 \times 1.14 \times 10,000 = \$10,944$

To establish a method for calculating direct expense forecasts, the two adjustment factors—rate and staffing—will be designated as forecast factors (FF) used to adjust the base year's annual actual estimate. When the two forecast factors (**RateFF** and **StaffingFF**) are multiplied by the base year annual actual estimate, the result will be the annual forecast.

NetFF = RateFF × StaffingFF

where, rateFF = 100% +/− rate change% and

staffingFF = 100% +/− rate change%

If we apply this approach to the previous example:

NetFF $= .96 \times 1.14 = 1.0944$ (or 1.09440%)

where, rateFF = 100% − 4% = 96% or .96 and

staffingFF = 100% + 14% = 114% or 1.14

The decimal version will be used in calculation because it is easier than using percentages when using a calculator. Calculator forecast factors will be carried out to five decimal places to maintain the accuracy of the calculation. The accuracy when using spreadsheet software will

2004 Rate Forecast Factors

| | 2003 | | 2004 | |
Charge Category	Rate%	RateFF	Rate%	RateFF
Local Calls	0%	1.00000	3.0%	1.03000
Long Distance Calls	5%	1.05000	-8.0%	0.92000
Equipment	0%	1.00000	0.0%	1.00000
Miscellaneous	5%	1.05000	-8.0%	0.92000
OCCs	0%	1.00000	0.0%	1.00000

2004 Staffing Forecast Factors

| | StaffingFF | |
Department	2003	2004
Accounting	1.05263	1.10000
Executive	1.09091	1.00000
Legal	1.00000	1.07143
MIS	1.00000	1.18182
Sales	1.02804	1.13636
Service	1.06000	1.18868

Example 16–12. Forecast factor tables.

be greater because the software keeps track of more than five decimal places during calculations.

Example 16–12 summarizes the forecast factor information that will be used to calculate forecasts for the Example 16–10 2003 annual telephone expense estimate.

Example 16–12 2004 RateFFs were calculated by adding 100% to the 2004 Rate% changes while StaffingFFs were calculated based on the information contained in Ex-

ample 16–11. The 2004 StaffingFF for accounting was calculated by dividing the 2004 number of extensions (Staffing) by the 2003 value. (The 2003 StaffingFFs were calculated the same way by using the Example 16–11 2003 and 2002 extension values.)

Forecast Future Year Telephone Expenses

The telecommunications manager now has all the elements required to forecast telephone expenses for the future year (2004). Shared charge rates have been calculated (Example 16–11), direct charge increases have been identified (Example 16–12), and a 2003 estimated actual database (Example 16–10) has been established.

A new spreadsheet, Example 16–13, will be created and used to complete the 2004 telephone expense forecasting process.

YEAR 2004 SHARED TELEPHONE EXPENSE FORECASTS (BASIC$). Shared telephone expense forecasts were developed in Example 16–13 by multiplying the #Extns time the 2004 annual basic rate ($528.00). The total Basic$ value ($132,000) in Example 16–13 is the same as the annual total ($132,000) basic charges being allocated to system users (Example 16–11). Therefore, all of the forecast 2004 shared costs have been allocated to users of the services.

YEAR 2004 DIRECT TELEPHONE EXPENSE FORECASTS. Multiplying the department level annual actual estimate value (Example 16–10) by the RateFFs and StaffingFFs developed in Example 16–12 calculate the direct telephone expense forecasts.

2004 Annual Telephone Expense Forecast
Department Summary

2004 Annual Forecast

Department	#Extns	Total$	Basic$	Eqpt$	Local$	LD$	OCC$	Misc$
Accounting	22	33,106	11,616	8,580	1,663	11,247	0	0
Executive	12	40,491	6,336	7,500	1,409	11,338	7,560	6,348
Legal	15	33,435	7,920	9,000	2,013	14,502	0	0
MIS	13	31,577	6,864	6,311	1,782	12,082	4,538	0
Sales	125	368,784	66,000	50,455	14,944	137,021	0	100,364
Service	63	94,427	33,264	23,536	20,187	17,440	0	0
2004 annual forecast	250	601,820	132,000	105,381	41,998	203,631	12,098	106,712

Annual basic rate: $528.00

Example 16–13. 2004 annual telephone expense forecast example.

2003 actual estimate for sales
department long distance calls   = $131,064

Sales department StaffingFF   = 1.13636

LD RateFF   = .92000

then, 2004 long distance forecast for the sales department:

$$= 131{,}064 \times 1.13636 \times .92000 = \$137{,}021$$

These calculations can be done with a calculator but are much simpler to do by using spreadsheet software. When spreadsheet software is used, the accuracy and rounding can be controlled in a spreadsheet formula. In addition, the spreadsheet worksheet results can easily be copied and placed into word processing documents by using Microsoft's OLE (Object Linking and Embedding) software. The final result of these calculations is provided in Example 16–13, and the total 2004 annual telephone expense forecast is $601,820.

Example 16–14 provides a monthly version of the same forecast information. The monthly expense values shown in Example 16–14 were obtained by dividing the annual values of Example 16–13 by twelve.

2003 *v.* 2004 Telephone Expense Comparison

The last step in the forecasting process is to provide a reference point for the Example 16–13 telephone expense forecast: Is it high? Is it low?

The normal format used is to provide a comparison of the forecast against previous year information and explain any differences. Example 16–15 was developed by the telecommunications manager for this purpose, and compares 2003 estimated actual expenses to 2004 forecast expenses.

The information contained in Example 16–15 is highly favorable. Although staffing increased by almost 14% (30 extensions), the overall increase was only 7.7% ($42,877) compared to the 2003 estimated actual level.

2004 Monthly Telephone Expense Forecast

Department Summary

Department	FCxtn	Total$	Basic$	Eqpt$	Local$	LD$	OCC$	Misc$
Accounting	22	2,759	968	715	139	937	0	0
Executive	12	3,374	528	625	117	945	630	529
Legal	15	2,786	660	750	168	1,208	0	0
MIS	13	2,631	572	526	149	1,007	378	0
Sales	125	30,732	5,500	4,205	1,245	11,418	0	8,364
Service	63	7,869	2,772	1,961	1,682	1,453	0	0
2004 monthly forecast	**250**	**50,152**	**11,000**	**8,782**	**3,500**	**16,969**	**1,008**	**8,893**

Monthly basic rate: $44.00

Example 16–14.   2004 monthly telephone expense forecast example.

2003 Actual Estimated *v.* 2004 Forecast Comparison
Company Summary

Annual Comparisons

Department	#Extns	Total$	Basic$	Eqpt$	Local$	LD$	OCC$	Misc$
2004 annual forecast	250	601,820	132,000	105,381	41,998	203,631	12,098	106,712
2004 basic rate	$528.00							
2003 annual actual est.	220	558,943	119,750	93,240	35,380	196,274	11,400	102,900
2003 basic rate	$544.32							
2004 FC–2003 actual	30	42,877	12,250	12,141	6,619	7,357	698	3,812
% Difference	13.6%	7.7%	10.2%	13.0%	18.7%	3.7%	6.1%	3.7%
2004 basic–2003 basic	($16.32)							
% Difference	-3.0%							

Example 16–15.   2003 actual expense estimate *v.* 2004 forecast example.

This was made possible by savings generated in the shared charge (Basic$), miscellaneous charge (Misc$), and long distance charge (LD$) categories, which kept the increase in these areas well below the 14% expense increase due to the staffing addition. This information should be included in the memo forwarding the budget information to the manager's boss for the opportunity to gain recognition for developing a good budget.

CLOSING COMMENTS

Operational planning is a tough, tedious process that requires a strong focus on details. The department and tele-phone planning process described in this chapter is the proverbial tip of the iceberg, and an effective operations manager must have a broad set of skills in business management, telecommunications technology, accounting, and spreadsheet software. Without good PC skills, the budgeting process can easily overwhelm managers and force them to either rely on someone else's budgeting skills or "wing it" and hope for the best. There is little likelihood of enjoying the detailed planning process that is needed to effectively manage a telecommunications operation environment, but a strong set of skills in key areas can minimize the pain of performing a necessary function.

SUMMARY

This summary is organized to correspond with the learning objectives found at the beginning of the chapter.

1. An operations management department is responsible for providing high quality, cost effective services that support the business activities of their business. These activities may include operating systems or networks, providing administrative services that improve the usability of telecommunications services, and help desk services to resolve operating problems and provide customer-oriented support. Telecommunications operations activities typically account for 80% of the total telecommunications department activities, and an effective operations management department is the critical component that ensures that enterprise telecommunications investments maintain their value.

2. The ISO X.700 standard defines the technical network management architecture needed to support a complex communications system and network infrastructure. The standard also identifies the information elements needed to manage a networked environment in five key areas: fault management, configuration management, performance management, security management, and accounting management. Because most telecommunications devices utilize network connectivity, the X.700 information architecture is applicable to the telecommunications infrastructure managed by the operations management department. Knowledge of X.700 concepts provides a design framework that can be modified to fit a broad range of technology environments.

3. The telecommunications project life cycle model describes the preproject, project, and postproject activities used to implement telecommunications systems and networks. Operations management assumes responsibility for implemented systems and networks during the transition from the project phase to the postproject phase. Eighty percent of an asset's life cycle costs are incurred during its postproject (operational phase). While larger telecommunications projects may be implemented by different internal or external organizations, the operations department is responsible for effectively administering smaller projects on an ongoing basis to resolve problems and improve operating performance. In a crisis mode, the operations department may need to coordinate the implementation of major system and network projects while maintaining normal operations.

4. Accurate operations management forecasting means that the appropriate funding and associated resources are available to maintain the technology investment in telecommunications products and services. From a managerial perspective, accurate forecasting also provides a positive measure of managerial capability by demonstrating an understanding of both the business and the technical aspects of the telecommunications environment. Accurate forecasting also helps upper management to achieve profitability objectives that are based on the revenue and expense budgets developed during the financial planning process.

5. Theoretical forecasting is a mathematical, statistically oriented activity that requires specialized skills. Quantitative forecasting methods are based on applying historical data trends to future events, while qualitative forecasting methods rely more heavily on expert judgment to assign probabilities to potential future scenarios. Quantitative methods work best in a stable environment, in which long term trends are consistent. Qualitative methods are applicable to environments that have inconsistent data patterns. A blend of forecasting skills and business knowledge is needed to effectively apply theoretical forecasting methods in

business situations. Regardless of the methods used, forecast results should be subject to constant scrutiny to ensure that the input assumptions they utilize continue to be reflected by the business environment.

6. In the practical forecasting approach, the intent is to find a situational forecasting approach that takes advantage of job knowledge and PC skills (particularly spreadsheet skills) to provide good forecasts. The job knowledge element includes business management skills, technology management skills, and accounting skills, and these elements must be creatively blended to provide accurate forecasts that are compatible with business accounting standards. Practical forecasting comes into play during the annual financial planning cycle, and must meet planning deadlines while providing the appropriate input to financial budgets.

7. Operations management department forecasting identifies the budget needs for operations, administrative services, and help desk departments. The forecast information must be in a budget format, in which expense and revenue code definitions drive the format of forecast information. A typical department budget consists of thirty or more expense code categories that require individual forecasts. In the budget year, budgets become the measurement standard in a BVA report, which identifies operating deviations from budget standards as variances. Managers are held accountable for meeting the budget values they have established during the annual planning cycle.

8. Cost allocation procedures are used by business enterprises to provide accountability at the department level. Department managers are given the responsibility for managing the use of various resources in their departments. Cost allocation procedures are used to identify the cost of department resources used by the department. In telecommunications, cost allocation procedures are coupled with chargeback systems to allocate telecommunications costs to individuals and departments that use the services. When cost allocation and chargeback procedures are used, the department manager has the usage and cost information needed to manage the use of telecommunications services. He or she would be responsible for budgeting and controlling telecommunications expenses (with the assistance of the telecommunications administrative services department).

9. Voice-based telephone services are normally a significant business expense. Telephone expense elements include equipment, long distance calling, local service calling, maintenance, and service charges. From a telecommunications chargeback perspective, these expenses fall into two categories: direct and shared charges. Direct charges are those expenses that can be assigned directly to the individual or department using the service. Shared charges are used when individual users of services cannot be easily identified. A cost allocation scheme is established for shared charges, and this scheme typically consolidates charges and calculates a per-user rate that is applied to individual service users.

10. The basic telephone expense forecasting process consists of five steps: 1) analyze current year actual expenses, 2) estimate current year annual expenses, 3) calculate future year shared expenses, 4) calculate future year direct expenses, and 5) consolidate the future year calculation information to provide a future year forecast. The deliverables are typically prepared in a spreadsheet and would include shared rate calculations, direct charge estimates of staffing, rate, and usage percentage changes, and input for the financial budget system of the business. The overall telephone forecasting process assumes that the forecaster has been monitoring and evaluating current year charges (actuals) and has a good understanding of the total enterprise telephone expense environment.

11. After department and telecommunications forecasts have been developed and translated into the business's financial budget format, the outcomes should be compared to the previous year's actual expenses. This allows business management to understand the proposed budget recommendation in light of the previous year's budget. The overall expense patterns of each budget should be evaluated and comparisons should be made to identify inconsistencies, improved performance, or areas for improvements. This phase provides an opportunity for the telecommunications manager to demonstrate his or her competence as a business manager by focusing on budget results and performance—an area of ongoing interest for upper management.

KEY TERMS AND CONCEPTS

The language of telecommunications management is multifaceted and includes words and phrases from managerial, technological, accounting, regulatory, and other business areas. The definitions of these key terms and concepts can be found within the chapter and in the text glossary.

Accounting Management
Actual Operating Expense Estimate
BVA
Call Detail Reporting (CDR) System
Chargeback
Configuration Management
Controllable Expenses
Direct Expenses
Expense Codes
Fault Management
Forecast Factor (FF)
Forecasting

Moves, Adds, Changes (MAC)
Noncontrollable Expenses
Other Charge or Credit (OCC)
Operating Expenses
Operations Management
Performance Management
Practical Forecasting
Pragmatic Expense Forecasting Model
Qualitative Forecasting Methods
Quantitative Forecasting Methods
RateFF
Security Management

Shared Expenses
Station Message Detail Record (SMDR)
Staffing FF
Strategic Plan
Tactical Plan
Telecommunications Project Life Cycle
    Model
Variances
X.700

REVIEW

The following questions are open-ended—predefined answers are not included as part of the text. The purpose of these questions is to allow the readers to test themselves on the chapter material.

1. Describe the operations management department and the size of its operating costs and compare those costs to the telecommunications planning and development departments' costs.

2. Describe the role of the operations department relative to the strategic, tactical, and operational planning process.

3. List the five standard categories that are used in the X.700 Network Management Standard to define the management requirements for communications products and services. Provide a brief description of each.

4. What is the value of forecasting telecommunications expenses (for departments, products, and services)?

5. What are budget variances? What are variances used for?

6. Describe the department forecasting process.

7. Describe the telecommunications expense forecasting process.

8. What is the value of using telecommunications chargeback systems?

9. Describe the process for charging back direct and shared expenses.

10. What are SMDR (CDR) records, and how are they used for chargeback purposes?

11. Describe the forecasting process shown in Figure 16–7.

12. What is the normal context used to explain forecasting results?

13. Describe the role that the operations department plays in initiating and implementing telecommunications projects.

MULTIPLE-CHOICE

1. From an operations management perspective, the two major areas to be managed are _____.

   a. organization costs

   b. planning

   c. development

   d. technology

2. X.700 Fault Management responsibilities include _____.

   a. maintaining an audit trail

   b. measuring user response times

   c. gracefully shutting down devices

   d. tracking capacity utilization trends

   e. maintaining IRS data

3. Telecommunications operations management functions typically account for _____ of the total telecommunications department budget.

   a. 20%

   b. 40%

   c. 60%

   d. 80%

   e. 100%

4. Telecommunications operating expenses fall into two major expense categories: _____ and _____.
   a. department budgets
   b. X.700
   c. office supplies
   d. product and services
   e. forecast

5. Quantitative forecasting techniques rely heavily on _____.
   a. jury of opinion
   b. expert opinion
   c. historical data
   d. products and services

6. Department cost centers _____.
   a. are not used in operations management
   b. are accountable for managing their expenses
   c. cannot generate revenues
   d. charge their expenses back

7. The variance formula is _____.
   a. budget – expenses
   b. expenses – budget
   c. zero based
   d. BVD
   e. incremental accounting

8. _____ variances are normally desirable.
   a. Large
   b. BVA
   c. Incremental
   d. Negative
   e. Positive

9. Expense codes are used to _____.
   a. calculate expenses
   b. identify expense categories
   c. highlight revenues
   d. identify departments
   e. identify divisions

10. When a chargeback system is used to allocate telecommunications expenses, the using department sees telecommunications charges as _____
    a. fixed asset expenses
    b. overhead expenses
    c. controllable expenses
    d. noncontrollable expenses
    e. shared expenses

11. Chargeback systems are used when telecommunications expenses are _____.
    a. large
    b. small
    c. zero
    d. corporate overhead costs
    e. shared expenses

12. _____ charges are allocated among all system users.
    a. Corporate overhead cost
    b. Direct
    c. Shared
    d. Controllable
    e. Noncontrollable

13. CDRs are _____.
    a. computer tokens generated by LAN servers
    b. computer tokens generated by telephone systems
    c. computer tokens generated by WAN servers
    d. secondary budget items

14. _____ charges are examples of direct expenses.
    a. Telephone system maintenance
    b. Centralized directory services
    c. Lines to COs
    d. Long distance call

15. OCCs are generated when _____.
    a. telephone sets are moved
    b. long distance calls are made
    c. local calls are made
    d. SMDR records are examined

PRACTICE

The following is a forecasting problem that uses the same procedures as the telecommunications forecasting problem described in this chapter. All necessary information (future year staffing, rate changes, and shared charge expenses) is provided and the ability to correctly solve this problem shows an understanding of the chapter's forecasting process.

The solutions are highlighted to allow the reader to check his or her results.

1. Practice problem:

2003 avg Monthly Actual Estimate: Round Calculations up to Nearest Integer

Department	#Extns	Total$	Basic$	Eqpt$	Local$	LD$	OCC$	Misc$
Executive	8	1,575	320	430	75	710	40	0
Finance	13	2,120	520	450	85	640	65	360
Human resources	10	1,875	400	480	105	840	50	0
Manufacturing	50	3,120	2,000	260	270	555	35	0
Totals	**81**	**8,690**	**3,240**	**1,620**	**535**	**2,745**	**190**	**360**

2003 mo. basic rate: $40.00

2003 Annual Actual Estimate

Department	#Extns	Total$	Basic$	Eqpt$	Local$	LD$	OCC$	Misc$
Executive	8	18,900	3,840	5,160	900	8,520	480	0
Finance	13	25,440	6,240	5,400	1,020	7,680	780	4,320
Human resources	10	22,500	4,800	5,760	1,260	10,080	600	0
Manufacturing	50	37,440	24,000	3,120	3,240	6,660	420	0
Annual actual	**81**	**104,280**	**38,880**	**19,440**	**6,420**	**32,940**	**2,280**	**4,320**

Curr. r. basic rate:$480.00

2004 Staffing Forecast Factors: Calculate FF to Five Decimal Places

Department	2003 Act	2004 FC	Diff	%Diff	StaffFF
Executive	8	8			
Finance	13	14			
Human resources	10	10			
Manufacturing	50	54			
Total					

2004 Rate Forecast Factors: Calculate FF to Five Decimal Places

	2003		2004	
Charge Category	Rate%	RateFF%	Rate%	RateFF%
Equipment	0%		0%	
Local calls	0%		3%	
Long distance calls	5%		-6%	
OCC	0%		4%	
Miscellaneous	5%		-5%	

Calculate Rates to Two Decimal Places

Description	2003
PBX maintenance	$9,500
Administrative support	$10,000
Network services	$13,000
SMDR services	$9,500
Annual total	
#Sharing extns.	
Annual basic rate	

2004 Annual Forecast

Department	#Extns	Total$	Basic$	Eqpt$	Local$	LD$	OCC$	Misc$
Executive		18,502	3,907	5,160	927	8,009	499	0
Finance								
Human resources		22,041	4,884	5,760	1,298	9,475	624	0
Manufacturing		40,579	26,372	3,370	3,604	6,761	472	0
2004 forecast								

2004 basic rate: $488.37

Comparison of 2003 Estimated Actual$ and 2004 Forecast$: Calculate Percentages to One Decimal Place

Department	#Extns	Total$	Basic$	Eqpt$	Local$	LD$	OCC$	Misc$
2004 Annual F/C Summary								
2003 Annual Est Summary	81	104,280	38,880	19,440	6,420	32,940	2,280	4,320
Diff$								
Diff%								

The primary justification for business management's investment in a telecommunications department is to obtain the benefits derived from using telecommunications products and services to help the business achieve its objectives. From a business perspective, there would be no need to have a telecommunications department within the organization if products and services were as readily available as public utilities. However, the reality is that unless business and technical expertise is used in the selection, implementation, and operation of telecommunications services, the investment in telecommunications products and services can be a money pit that absorbs large quantities of money without providing tangible business benefits. As a result, telecommunications departments have become part of a business organization, based on the value of the services. The role of telecommunications management is to manage the telecommunications function as a business resource and ensure that the technology investments make business sense.

Operations management is responsible for ensuring that the correct telecommunications products and services are available to meet business communication needs. They are also responsible for keeping pace with technology developments and constantly evaluating them on a cost *v.* benefit profile. This is analogous to saying that a manufacturing business must produce a desirable, high quality, cost effective customer product to ensure the success of the business. The intelligent use of telecommunications products and services can result in increased internal productivity and can improve customer access to products and services.

From a top-down management planning perspective, there are three primary factors needed for establishing and maintaining an effective operations management function:

1. philosophy
2. tools
3. execution

HOW ARE OPERATIONS MANAGED?

Managing activities means using **POLC Model** concepts (Figure 17–1) and executing them intelligently by:

- setting goals
- developing a plan
- organizing (obtaining) resources
- leading (directing) the use of resources
- controlling activities (to achieve goals)

Managing operations involves executing all POLC Model elements and using the feedback obtained during the execution process to ensure that activities continue to be directed toward achieving the desired goals. When gaps exist between the plan and the actual results achieved, managerial action is needed to close the gap by modifying the activity or the plan to ensure that the desired objectives are achieved.

The alternative to managing a department is to employ a *laissez faire* philosophy when carrying out organization activities and hope for the best—an approach that is unlikely to achieve success in a constantly changing, highly competitive business environment. The telecommunications operations department is managed by assigning managerial responsibility to department managers and holding these managers accountable for carrying out the necessary POLC Model elements needed to achieve the primary goal of a telecommunications organization—the effective and efficient use of telecommunications products and services.

Operations Management Environment

In Chapter 16, *Developing an Operating Plan*, the planning role of telecommunications operations management departments was described as consisting of three primary activities: operations, administrative services, and a help

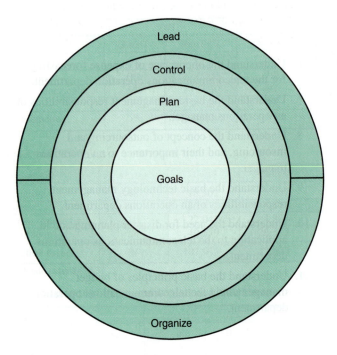

Figure 17–1. The POLC model.

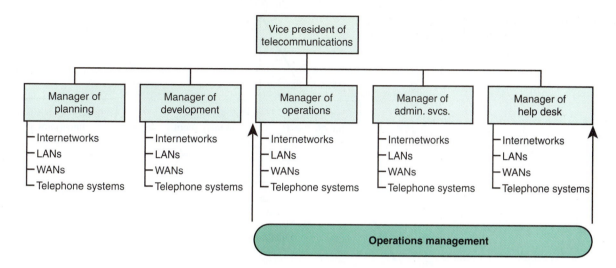

Figure 17–2. Telecommunications operations management organization.

desk function. These activities may be provided by separate departments (Figure 17–2), a single department, or by some other combination of departments. The specific organization structure may vary, but the same basic functions will be provided.

Chapter 16 also described the planning and budgeting processes used to develop budgets for telecommunications business and technology management needs. Telecommunications budgets will vary from organization to organization in terms of complexity, size, and cost. However, they always have the underlying objective of supporting business management goals. This chapter will describe the managerial activities involved with implementing the plans and budgets developed during the tactical planning phase—managing the operations departments.

MANAGERIAL TOOLS AND TECHNIQUES

The following provides an overview of the managerial tools and techniques discussed in previous chapters that would be applied in an operations management context when managing an operations department. The assumption is that the reader understands how these elements are used and the purpose of listing them again is to provide a reminder that management tools are to be used—not to be placed into a toolbox that is not opened after a chapter has been read. It also assumes that the reader has the knowledge base of the appropriate **telecommunications management**

skills, project management skills, and **enabling skills** (Figure 17–3) to react to new situations, evaluate their context, and apply the appropriate managerial tools and techniques intelligently.

Tool Selection

In Chapter 6, *What is Enterprise Planning?*, a history of managerial theory was provided with the closing comment that current managerial theorists had concluded that a situational approach should be used to manage a business. The situational approach calls for selecting the management theory (tool) that is appropriate for a given managerial situation and applying the tool. If the situation changes, a different set of tools may be needed. This concept is illustrated with a basic input/method/output model in Figure 17–4.

Managerial judgment is required to select the appropriate tool or method, and good managers do a good job of selecting the right tools; mediocre managers do a poor job. Managers who have good judgment typically have a common set of characteristics, including strong **business management skills** and **technology management skills,** and the experience needed to use their skills effectively.

The Telecommunications Project Life Cycle Model

In Part 3, *Project Management*, a **telecommunications project life cycle model** was used to describe a process of developing telecommunications products and services that incorporates technology and business planning elements

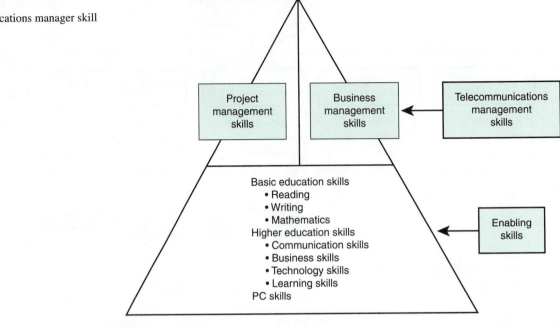

Figure 17–3.
Telecommunications manager skill requirements.

Figure 17–4. Management method selection process model.

(Figure 17–5). This model identified the need to forecast life cycle costs and to periodically reexamine initial project justification assumptions when a project effort is being carried out to ensure that the desired project goals can still be achieved and that the project has remained viable. It also provided a timeline that showed how a project evolved from a **strategic planning** phase to an **operational planning** phase.

Microthinking Concepts

The previous discussion regarding tools and techniques requires the application of basic microthinking skills while using various tools and techniques. In technology and engineering programs, the scientific method is taught, and the individual seeking to solve scientific problems is taught a system of formulating questions, collecting data through observation and experiments, and then testing hypothetical solutions. Chapter 7, *Managerial Tools and Techniques*, discussed two variations of the scientific

method: 1) a problem analysis process and 2) a decision making process. The flowcharts in Chapter 7 have been reproduced in Figures 17–6 and 17–7.

Operations managers need to be highly skilled in using the problem solving, decision making, and analytical thinking processes discussed in Chapter 7.

PROFIT CENTER PHILOSOPHY

Mom and pop stores were the small, family-owned businesses that preceded today's corporate business environment. The concept of chain stores—a single firm owning and operating multiple retail stores that sell the same type of merchandise—is credited to George F. Gilman and George Huntington Hartford. Gilman and Hartford founded the Great Atlantic and Pacific Tea Company (A & P) in 1859 and opened a chain of A & P grocery stores nationwide to sell food. Prior to 1859, each grocery store was individually owned and operated, and each owner made independent decisions regarding the goods they carried, stocking levels, and the suppliers they dealt with. Operating times, product displays, packaging, extending credit, and all other basic managerial decisions were made by the owner of the grocery store.

Since their origin, chain grocery stores have dominated the grocery business in terms of market share and sales volume, despite the fact that there are still many more mom

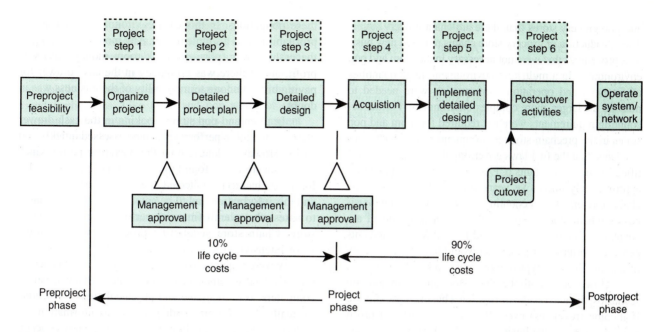

Figure 17–5. Telecommunications project life cycle model.

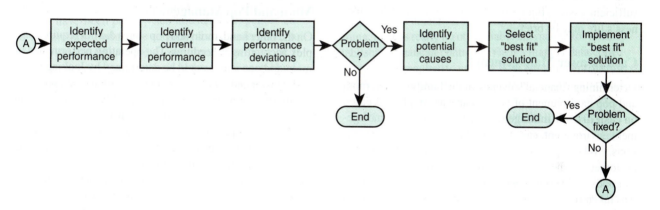

Figure 17–6. A problem solving approach.

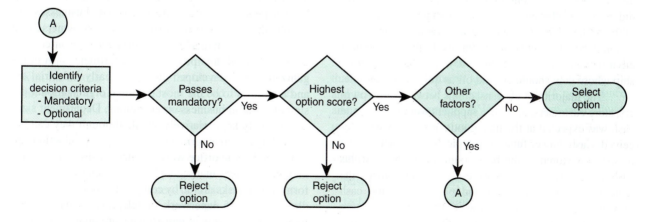

Figure 17–7. A decision making approach.

Operations Projects

Technology management involves selecting equipment, designing systems and networks, implementing the design plan, and operating implemented systems and networks. A key for managing technologies is a firm grasp of the **project management skills** discussed in Part 3, *Project Management*. Figure 17–5 provided a graphical view of the project management process when telecommunications equipment (fixed assets) is purchased and implemented in a business. Large telecommunications projects may be implemented by another telecommunications department (the development department shown in Figure 17–2), but the operations department also implements projects as an ongoing activity. They are triggered by the need to replace defective equipment or to improve performance levels that have dropped below acceptable levels. Unless some catastrophic event has occurred, most operations projects operate within the operations department budget. Larger projects have their own implementation budgets.

Operations managers must have the technical and project management skills necessary to direct the technical specialists needed in operations departments. This knowledge will be used to manage technology elements, but is also an essential factor for effectively creating employee development plans, identifying training needs, and conducting employee performance appraisals.

Disaster Prevention & Recovery

The dictionary defines a disaster as an event that causes serious loss, destruction, hardship, unhappiness, or death. From a business viewpoint, a disaster is any event resulting in the accidental or intentional destruction of information, equipment, or facilities that can interrupt the normal flow of business activities. A disaster can take many forms ranging from acts of God, such as a tornado or a flood, to a fire or intentional sabotage.

Telecommunications is an integral part of modern business activities, and disruption of telephone, LAN, internetworking, or a WWW services has the potential for severely disrupting normal business functions. A key responsibility of telecommunications management is to have plans in place that: 1) reduce the potential for having telecommunications service disruptions and 2) minimize the business impact of any telecommunications service disruptions that do occur. A benefit associated with effective disaster planning is obtaining time needed for implementing solutions that cannot be implemented quickly when a problem is actually encountered.

Disaster planning addresses two areas: 1) disaster prevention and 2) disaster recovery. The focus of disaster prevention activities is to proactively avoid having disasters while the focus of the disaster recovery activities is to get back in business as quickly as possible once a service disruption has taken place.

Disaster Prevention

Events that have the potential for creating telecommunications systems outages include equipment failure, electricity outages, water damage, storms, fire, earthquakes, vandalism, and sabotage. If action can be taken to minimize the potential for these events occurring or to minimize their impact, service disruptions can be avoided or minimized. The best prevention plan for most business disaster situations typically involves implementing better physical security or installing redundant equipment facilities.

EQUIPMENT FAILURE. Equipment failures can be prevented by implementing an effective maintenance program or by installing redundant equipment. Wide ranges of solutions exist within each area. The selection of the best option is a situational decision, where the investment allocated to prevent equipment failures would depend upon the criticality of the telecommunications department for maintaining normal business operations. The New York Stock Exchange (NYSE) maintains a fully redundant communications network. In the event that equipment or communications services are disrupted, the NYSE is still open for business and fully operational. The existence of 100% redundancy in this case is not a matter of good management or a personal choice. SEC regulations governing the stock exchange require 100% backup of key facilities. The only question is how to minimize the cost for obtaining it. While most businesses are not subject to the stringent requirements that the stock exchange is under, few organizations could tolerate being without telephone or computer communications for more than one business day. Some businesses could not tolerate a one-hour outage. In some cases, companies view their computers and communications resources as being so critical to business operations that they maintain **hot sites**—locations where a third party maintains fully operational standby computer and communications facilities in a separate location. Maintaining hot sites is expensive, but many corporations maintain contracts with firms that specialize in providing hot sites so that business operations will continue at the hot site if key business locations are damaged or destroyed. Hot sites may provide allowances for housing order processing, customer service, and other customer-oriented departments that will use the hot site's computers and communications infrastructure.

Telecommunications management is responsible for identifying potential service disruption causes and for identifying solutions that eliminate or minimize the potential for service disruptions. The final authority for making investments in redundant equipment or maintaining a hot site facility is upper management.

ELECTRICITY OUTAGES. Electricity outages occur because of breakdowns in the public utility infrastructure: downed power lines, damaged transformers, etc. Short-term (less than 1/2 hour) outages can be handled effectively by using uninterruptible power sources (UPSs) that provide battery power as the backup power source. However, because battery backup is expensive, its use is frequently limited to providing short-term power to critical computer-based equipment where a loss in power can disrupt equipment's software or database functions. Disrupting software or database operations can require long time periods to rebuild databases, but a battery backup that cuts over instantaneously to maintain computer processing would allow the equipment to be turned off in a normal shutdown mode, thus avoiding data loss.

Battery backup is not suitable for providing power to utility functions (lighting, air conditioning, heating). In addition, the amount of time that battery power can be provided economically is also limited. Gas or diesel generators can be installed to provide power for extended equipment outages when equipment battery backup time periods are exceeded, and to provide power for utility functions. As was the case when equipment redundancy decisions had to be made, the level of investment to protect against power outages would be based upon: 1) the likelihood of having electrical outages and 2) the impact that such an outage would have on business operations. The cost of a 100% electricity backup facility using batteries and electric generators is high and must be balanced against the business impact of potential electrical outages.

WATER DAMAGE. Floods, storms, and broken water pipes may cause water damage. This is an area where an ounce of prevention goes a long way in preventing major problems. Telecommunications equipment should not be located in the low point of a building, particularly if the low point is below ground level and a high water table exists. Telecommunications equipment should be housed in an area where there is a low potential for water damage due to floods, storms, and broken water pipes. Disaster prevention planning would include not placing a data center in an area that is prone to flooding and placing the equipment above potential flooding

levels. Another simple way to avoid the potential for water damage is to make sure that building water supply lines do not run near areas that house telecommunications equipment.

Good judgment can minimize the potential for water damage. Prevention activities require a relatively low effort or expense if they are implemented when the building is under construction or when the location is initially occupied by the business.

STORM DAMAGE. The previous topic covered the water aspect of storms. What about storms that generate high winds that have the potential for felling large trees that can fall onto a building or tear off exterior sections of a building? A simple approach for this type of damage is to remove any large trees that have the potential for creating major damage. In addition, telecommunications equipment and cabling should be kept away from exterior walls so that if damage occurs to the exterior walls of a building, the potential for damage to the equipment and wiring is minimized. If it is necessary to place equipment near exterior walls, the walls can be heavily reinforced to minimize the potential for internal storm damage.

FIRE DAMAGE. Most local ordinances require fire sprinklers to be installed in commercial buildings, and the area housing telecommunications equipment may have sprinklers installed to avoid fire damage. However, what about the potential for water damage to the telecommunications equipment if the sprinklers go off unnecessarily? Again, it is a matter of designing the environment in advance. Use of appropriate waterproof shielding on the top of the equipment and placing wiring in watertight conduits would minimize the potential for water damage from fire sprinklers. Careful planning will allow the benefits of fire protection to be enjoyed without incurring the downsides of having water damage to equipment and cabling.

EARTHQUAKE DAMAGE. There are two basic approaches for avoiding earthquake damage: 1) don't build in earthquake areas or 2) design the building structure to be earthquake resistant in accordance with area building codes. Earthquake resistant standards should also be applied to the installation of the equipment and wiring infrastructure within the building location.

VANDALISM. The first line of defense against vandalism is physical security. This includes the use of high fences, electrified fences, and installing equipment in rooms without windows. Special access doors, alarm systems, locks, and many other options can be used to keep people away from a high-security area. If telecommunications equipment is housed in a secure area, vandals cannot easily access the area to damage equipment or wiring. Vandalism may also be information-oriented—**hackers** planting viruses or extracting information from corporate databases for ulterior motives. Protecting information against hackers requires the attention of someone who is highly skilled in computer and communications technologies, and it may be necessary to use outside consulting assistance on an interim or long-term basis.

SABOTAGE. Sabotage refers to the deliberate damaging or destruction of property or equipment. Sabotage may be carried out by disgruntled employees or by outsiders who have their own agendas. The damage inflicted by internal or external saboteurs may be physical or logical in nature, and the physical line of defense for sabotage damage is similar to that described under vandalism damage. Logical damage (typically computer file or network-oriented hacking) is much more complicated. Logical damage may involve the intentional destruction or corruption of data. Information damage could also involve the theft of critical business information by competitors to gain competitive advantage by obtaining a competitor's product development or marketing plans.

The destruction or corruption of computer- or network-based information requires an advanced level of expertise, and protecting against information damage also requires specialized skills. If the expertise does not exist internally, the use of outside consulting assistance is appropriate.

Disaster Recovery

A business disaster takes place when—despite the implementation of good disaster prevention procedures—normal business operations stop (otherwise, it isn't a business disaster). The focus of disaster recovery is on restoring normal or operationally acceptable business services to allow the continuation of customer-related activities. In some cases, this may require transporting files and personnel to a hot site and being able to resume business operations in a matter of hours. The hot site would be equipped with the computer and networking facilities needed to carry out business activities and may also provide people facilities for the employees using the equipment. The level of support provided at a hot site location will be based on the investment levels that business management is willing to make.

Depending upon a company's business, it may be possible to operate in a manual mode for some period of time until regular automated procedures become available,

or manual operations may be unacceptable for any period of time. The specific plan of action for any given disaster recovery is situational and depends on the importance that upper management places on resuming normal business operations. From a telecommunications perspective, the primary issue is one of identifying a range of technical options that may be deployed. Upper management will have to decide the level of investment they are willing to make to shorten downtime due to a telecommunications-based disaster. Normally, the cost of disaster recovery options are directly related to their effectiveness in reducing business downtime. Fast recovery options typically cost more than options that recover business operations over a longer period of time.

BUSINESS-DRIVEN DISASTER RECOVERY PLAN. The first step in disaster recovery is to define a business disaster from a business management perspective. The manager must identify the maximum length of time that internal customer-oriented departments can shut down without affecting normal business operations. A two step disaster recovery plan definition that includes two major parts would be created: 1) a short-term disaster recovery plan and 2) a long-term disaster recovery plan. Disaster recovery documentation would specify the criteria that will be used to classify the required disaster recovery response as short term or long term. Short-term procedures would be used to provide an initial response when business operations are disrupted and may be the only required response if the cause of the downtime can be identified and rectified quickly. Long-term procedures are initiated if the expected downtime duration cannot be addressed adequately by using short-term procedures. In the worst-case scenario, when a building facility is destroyed, the rebuilding process will be a long-term activity, and a long-term disaster recovery plan will be needed. The long-term disaster recovery response may require a significant investment for interim office space and the installation of an interim technology infrastructure at the temporary location.

The definitions of short-term and long-term disasters are business-driven definitions, not technology-driven definitions. A business-oriented definition will define the impact that any interruption of business activities will have on enterprise customers, suppliers, and other external entities. When a telecommunications disaster recovery plan is being created, each department should be asked to identify the telecommunications services needed to operate normally and asked if manual methods can be used as a temporary measure. The final decision about the investment levels to make for telecommunications disaster recovery efforts will be based upon upper management's assessment of the cost of recovery options against the business losses incurred because of reduced operations.

A good disaster recovery plan will document recovery procedures, which should be tested periodically to make sure they work as designed. Elements of a good disaster recovery plan include:

1. personnel evacuation procedures
2. notification of key personnel
3. evaluation of the disaster's scope
4. selection of the appropriate recovery response
5. implementation of the selected response

BUDGET MANAGEMENT

Chapter 16, *Developing an Operational Plan,* discussed the procedures for establishing a final tactical budget the year before it becomes an operational budget. While **tactical planning** and operational planning activities have the greatest impact on operations management, operations managers must understand the entire enterprise financial planning process (Figure 17–8), including the strategic planning process, and be prepared to support planning activities in any phase of the planning cycle.

Operations management input is essential for identifying the need for major investments in equipment and services, and they are in the best position to know when existing systems and networks are unable to handle business communications needs. When there is a need for a major equipment upgrade and the investment requirement is very large, it is critical to identify this need as early as possible in the overall planning process to provide upper management with the time it needs to evaluate the business impact and allocate the necessary funds.

What is Budget Management?

The telecommunications manager's ability to manage personnel and technology resources effectively will be strongly influenced by their ability to develop good budgets. An effective manager must understand the relationship between delivering the telecommunications services and the personnel, technology, and budgetary support requirements associated with them. This knowledge is essential to the selection of the right areas to include in a budget, because budgets are translations of personnel and technology elements into a financial format (the operating budget).

Once the budget line items needed to do the right things have been identified and placed into a financial format, budgetary control issues are required and the concept of budget **variances** is utilized. Budget variances—or simply *variances*—are defined as:

$$\text{variance\$} = \text{budget\$} - \text{actual\$}$$

Negative variances indicate that actual expenses (actual\$) have exceeded the budgeted expenses (budget\$). The department manager has spent more money than was in the budget. When negative variances are generated at the department level and additional budget dollars are needed to provide essential enterprise services, the money to pay for budget shortfall must be taken from other budget areas of the enterprise.

The relationship between budget variances and enterprise profitability is a direct one:

$$\text{profitability\$} = \text{revenue\$} - \text{expense\$}$$

Negative department budget variances indicate that the actual expenses incurred are higher than originally forecast. This will have a negative impact on profitability, because any increase in enterprise expenses—and the department is part of the enterprise—will reduce enterprise profitability. If all departments generate negative variances, the enterprise's profitability and long-term viability are under attack. Hopefully, if one department incurs negative variances, another department(s) will generate a positive variance that can be used to offset the negative performance. Another option is that the revenues have increased sharply and that the increased expenses are due to the need for supporting the sales effort. In this case, the

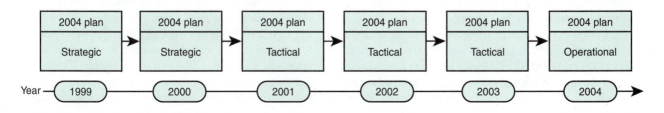

Figure 17–8. Enterprise financial planning cycle.

additional revenues should offset the additional expenses and should explain department budget variances.

Upper management is responsible for meeting profitability objectives. Depending upon the magnitude of projected profitability decreases during any fiscal period, they may be required to take drastic steps, such as mandating across-the-board budget or staffing reductions.

Although the telecommunications operations department is responsible for providing telecommunications services, they normally have little direct control of its use by internal users. In a worst-case scenario, operations management could provide high quality services at very low rates compared to any service alternative, but the end users of these services could use the resource wastefully or for personal purposes. In this case, upper management would see high telecommunications expenses while the telecommunications department was publicizing its effectiveness in controlling costs—clearly, an oxymoron to upper management because "you can't be doing a good job of controlling costs when expenses are so high."

Chargeback systems are one of the managerial tools that can be used to make end users of a service accountable for their use of the service. Chargeback systems identify the cost at the individual user level, allocate service costs to them directly, and provide users with the reporting information needed to identify usage and cost details. In an effective **chargeback** environment, the end users of telecommunications services assume responsibility for managing their use of services and are also provided with the information needed to control usage. End users must answer any questions regarding the quantity (and cost) of the service that is being used.

A chargeback system is one of the tools that can be used by operations management to control telecommunications costs by making the end user accountable for the use and cost of services.

Common Sense Budgeting

Department budgets, like personal budgets, should be administered rationally with a large dose of common sense. While they do require attention, large variances are not necessarily bad, but may reflect timing differences between the budget and actual expenditure. For example, a budget line item may show a large negative variance for outside services because consulting services were used earlier than expected. The budgeted line item is still under control but this control will not be apparent until a later report when more of the available budget is shown. In the same way, a large positive variance may appear on the salary line if it takes longer to find a good candidate for an open position than shown in the budget. It is necessary to understand the reasons for negative and positive variances to determine whether they are good or bad variances.

Telecommunications operations management departments frequently maintain separate internal budgets to identify the cost of providing telecommunications services because the BVA accounting process does not contain a sufficient level of detail for managing telecommunications products and services. This separate database may also be used to generate chargeback information for internal departments that use telecommunications services. Regardless of whether chargebacks are utilized, the telecommunications manager is responsible for ensuring that telecommunications expenses are monitored continually and that there are ongoing efforts to improve service levels and reduce costs.

While variance control is important to a manager, a balanced approach to variance control is required and the telecommunications manager must continually evaluate the final end of year results to identify real problems. If end of year results include large negative variances, a problem probably exists unless the negative variance has been caused by a direct request from upper management to increase enterprise telecommunications activities or by a heavy increase in revenue-generating sales activities. If the end of year projections indicate a small positive variance with relatively modest variances (less than 5%) at the line item level, this result is normally seen as positive and is viewed with favor by the manager's boss and by upper management.

Padding The Budget

"Padding the budget" is the practice of over-inflating the budget by placing unnecessary costs in a department budget to achieve positive variances and provide the perception of good performance. Padding the budget has two major downsides: 1) large positive variances are actually an indication of poor managerial performance and 2) padding the budget is unacceptable from an enterprise planning perspective.

POOR PERFORMANCE INDICATOR. When individual budget line items are padded, the end result inevitably includes large variances for some of the budget's line items. If this is not the case, then the forecaster has found a means to forecast accurately. A competent supervisor will review both the total department variance and individual line items variances. A BVA report showing a minor variance at the department level but major variations in the individual line item values indicates either poor budgeting or a series of unusual, explainable circumstances. Department managers should be able to explain large variances and—if they can't—it may be an indication that padding was involved and that the manager's budgeting skills need improvement.

ENTERPRISE ISSUES.   During the annual planning cycle, all departments develop revenue and expense estimates for various planning periods. This process establishes profitability goals and sets aside funding for the different programs and projects that were evaluated during the planning period. When individual department expense budgets are padded, future year expense estimates will be larger than the actual expenses that will be incurred. On the surface, it may appear that the only impact would be to increase profitability estimates (profitability = revenues – expenses) by the amount of the department budget's padding factor. However, poor expense forecasts can also adversely affect investment decisions made for other programs and projects planned for future years. When padding is pervasive in an enterprise, there is a strong likelihood that key programs and projects may not be underwritten, because expense budgets were overstated and the initial profitability shortfall estimates caused upper management to reduce budgeted expenses. If high payback projects were eliminated because normal operating expense estimates were overstated, the padding factor would have eliminated their consideration by upper management during the fiscal planning cycle. As a result, the enterprise will not be able to gain the benefits associated with implementing high payback projects.

A telecommunications manager's goal should be to develop accurate budgets that provide the appropriate level of funding needed to complete all programs and projects covered by budgeted money. If the budgeting process is implemented effectively, the issue of variances is irrelevant.

Each telecommunications department manager has been assigned an operating budget and a charter—implicit or explicit—to efficiently and effectively utilize the department budget for providing high quality services to internal departments and external customers. From an enterprise management perspective, all department budgets were established to assist the enterprise in meeting its operating mission—supplying products and services to its customers while providing enterprise stockholders with a fair return on their investment.

The career advancement potential of managers will be based on their ability to develop budgets that use limited enterprise operating dollars effectively and manage their areas of responsibility within those budgetary limits. The long-term incentive for good budgeting skills is career advancement within the business and the short-term incentives include salary increases, performance bonuses (cash or stock), promotions, and increased authority. As with any job, providing incentives for good performance has a downside. Failure to demonstrate managerial effectiveness in using budget funds or in controlling budget expenses is reflected in poor performance ratings, which will result in reduced compensation. In a worst-case scenario, it could mean the termination of a manager's employment.

MANAGING NEGATIVE VARIANCES.   An operations manager has responsibility for two types of budgets: 1) department operating budgets and 2) telecommunications expense budgets. Department budgets provide expense information for internally managed personnel, while telecommunications service budgets provide expense information for external telecommunications services (or its internal equivalent if the operations department handles the telecommunications service).

The control process for both budget types is similar: 1) identify major expense code variances, 2) analyze the reasons for their occurrence, and 3) take the appropriate corrective action.

Managing Department Expense Budgets

Understanding the department budgeting process requires knowledge of internal accounting procedures and knowledge of people management needs. Because the operations manager is responsible for developing budgets, a prerequisite is to have the necessary skills for evaluating variances and identifying the reasons for them. If budget variances are low (within 5%), they may be tolerable in a profitable organization. However, when budget shortfalls are large, the manager is confronted with a problem.

When the budget shortfall is due to poor forecasting, the manager will be placed in the position of having to reduce other budgeted expenses to cover the shortfall or risk the adverse reaction that will be generated if additional funding is sought. When the budget shortfall is caused by uncontrolled conditions, the manager must clearly and objectively document the supporting details that caused the problem and look for relief outside of the department budget. In either case, the aftermath of explaining significant variances is likely to be an unpleasant experience for the manager.

Handling negative variances found in department BVA reports is largely a matter of common sense. When an operations manager has developed a budget and actual expenses are more or less than the budgeted value, it becomes a matter of returning to the original forecasting process to identify the assumptions made when the forecast was

6. Expense forecasting is a key element in the BVA approach to managing business departments. A realistic, accurate budget provides a good measurement tool for evaluating a department's performance by comparing budgeted expenses to actual expenses. This measurement provides a way for managers and their bosses to assess managerial performance. In the telecommunications operations area, expense forecasting techniques are also used to determine the impact that staffing, supplier rate changes, and usage changes will have on the need for telecommunications services. Good expense forecasting identifies changing trends and provides the lead time needed to initiate the appropriate response in a planning mode. The alternative is to react in a crisis mode when expenses reach unacceptable levels—a situation where solution lead times may limit the options available to an operations manager.

7. Basic department management responsibilities for an operations manager are the same as for any business manager. The primary focus for department management activities is to support a department infrastructure. The manager is responsible for hiring, directing, supervising, developing, training, appraising, and providing administrative services for department employees. These basic responsibilities must be applied to the individual situational environment found in different operations management departments—help desk, administrative services, and operations—based upon the needs in the individual environment.

8. Outsourcing refers to the use of outside contractors to perform tasks and functions that can be carried out by company employees. Outsourcing has become a very popular option for business management since the early 1980s. The computer and communications departments are areas where outsourcing has been used by many organizations. The primary justification for outsourcing is frequently cost based, where business management views the move to outsourcing as a major expense reduction initiative. Insourcing is a term that has emerged as the opposite of outsourcing. It means internal personnel will be used to provide functions and services. The operations manager should continually evaluate outsourcing options in the telecommunications operations areas to use as a comparison to any insourcing operations. If the outsourcing option has significant advantages, the operations manager must make the insourcing option competitive or seriously consider the outsourcing option for the task or function.

9. An operations manager's responsibilities in the technology management area include operating or monitoring the external services operation of LANs, WANs, internetworks, telephone systems, WWW facilities, and different application specific communications equipment. The operations manager should be knowledgeable of the selection, design, implementation, and operations requirements associated with his or her operating environment. Operations managers are accountable for providing high quality telecommunications services by monitoring and resolving problems, adding equipment for new user needs, and initiating the appropriate project to maintain a viable telecommunications technology infrastructure. An operations manager must have the technical skills to effectively direct the efforts of technical specialists.

10. A primary responsibility of the operations management department is to ensure the ongoing availability of telecommunications services to support the business needs of the business. From a telecommunications perspective, a disaster is when communications services are disrupted and are not available for supporting business operations. Telecommunication service outages can stop all business transactions, and disaster planning is concerned with ensuring the ongoing availability of telecommunications services to the business. Disaster planning addresses two areas: 1) disaster prevention and 2) disaster recovery. Disaster prevention focuses on eliminating those conditions that could trigger a service outage, and disaster recovery planning efforts addresses situations in which a service outage has occurred. Disaster recovery efforts focus on restoring services as quickly as possible. Operations managers should have realistic plans that address disaster prevention and disaster recovery issues.

11. For telecommunications operations managers, budget management is primarily concerned with ensuring that financial plan (the budget) objectives are met during the operation phase. While the trigger mechanism is variance-based, the actual response to variances is the most important aspect of budget management. When the assumptions used to create the budget are valid, the operations manager must evaluate his or her forecasting performance. If operating environment changes invalidate forecasting assumptions, the operations manager must recast the plan to achieve operational objectives. An operations manager is responsible for managing department budgets and telecommunications technology budgets (projects and outside services).

KEY TERMS AND CONCEPTS

The language of telecommunications management is multifaceted and includes words and phrases from managerial, technological, accounting, regulatory, and other business areas. The definitions of these key terms and concepts can be found within the chapter and in the glossary.

Benchmarking
Business Management Skills
BVA Cash Drawer
Cash Drawer Management
Chargeback System
Chargebacks
Disaster Planning
Enabling Skills
Hacker

Hot Site
Insourcing
Mom and Pop
OCC
Operational Planning
Operations Management
Outsourcing
POLC Model
Productivity

Profit Center
Project Management Skills
Strategic Planning
Tactical Planning
Technology Management Skills
Telecommunications Management Skills
Telecommunications Project Life Cycle
   Model
Variance

REVIEW

The following questions are open-ended—predefined answers are not included as part of the text. The purpose of these questions is to allow the readers to test themselves on the chapter material.

1. What role(s) does operations management have in the telecommunications project life cycle model?

2. Describe the mom and pop management philosophy.

3. Explain the problem solving approach shown in Figure 17–6.

4. Explain the decision making approach shown in Figure 17–7.

5. What is the profit center philosophy?

6. Explain the principles behind the BVA cash drawer management concept.

7. If a BVA database does not exist, how would a telecommunications manager go about setting up an expense forecasting database?

8. Describe the people management responsibilities that an operations manager would have.

9. How should an operations manager address the outsourcing issue?

10. Define *disaster prevention* and *disaster recovery*, and explain the differences between them.

11. What is a hot site and when is it used?

12. What are the benefits of using a chargeback system for telecommunications services?

13. What are some of the negative aspects of padding budgets?

14. Describe the process of reviewing a BVA report to identify items for additional investigation. How would investigation items be prioritized?

15. What responsibilities does a telecommunications department have in explaining budget variances when a chargeback system is used?

16. How can benchmarking activities be used to manage internal telecommunications expenses?

MULTIPLE CHOICE

1. The mom and pop operating model is analogous to the _____ model.

   a. organization management

   b. technology management

   c. telecommunications management

   d. profit center

   e. chargeback

2. In a BVA environment, the _____ is equivalent to cash in a cash drawer operating environment.

   a. expense actuals

   b. expense budget

   c. petty cash

   d. direct expenses

   e. shared expenses

3. The three general responsibility areas for operations managers are _____, _____, and _____.

   a. business management

   b. technology management

   c. mom and pop management

   d. budget management

   e. asset management

4. A primary measure of the effectiveness rating of an operations manager will be his or her _____.

   a. organization management skills

   b. personal skills

   c. department management skills

   d. technology management skills

   e. operational results

5. The use of outsourcing is frequently utilized to _____.

   a. develop core competencies

   b. increase costs

   c. achieve cost savings

   d. develop operating budgets

6. Analysis of outsourcing options is aided with the appropriate _____ information.

   a. BVA

   b. benchmarking

   c. technology management

   d. business management

7. The primary objective of disaster planning activities is _____.

   a. disaster planning

   b. disaster recovery

   c. zero variances

   d. maintaining business operations

8. An example of a business disaster is _____.

   a. disaster planning

   b. fire

   c. traffic jams

   d. flooding

   e. a PBX telephone system outage

9. On a BVA report, if actual expenses are $1,100 and the budget is $1,200, the variance is _____.

   a. disaster planning

   b. +$100

   c. -$100

   d. -$1,200

   e. +$2,300

10. Padding the budget refers to _____.

   a. overestimating budget line items

   b. underestimating budget line items

   c. a large budget

   d. large negative variances

11. From a business perspective, accurate forecasts are important for _____.

   a. accurately estimating future expenses

   b. accurately estimating future revenues

   c. accurately estimating future profitability

   d. calculating negative variances

   e. calculating positive variances

12. Budget management for telecommunications management involves two types of budgets: _____ and _____.

   a. salary budgets

   b. department operating budgets

   c. service budgets

   d. telecommunications expense budgets

   e. BVA

13. With chargeback systems, the primary responsibility for controlling telecommunications service rates is a _____ responsibility.

   a. telecommunications management

   b. end user management

   c. business management

   d. technology management

18

OPERATIONS MANAGEMENT: A CASE STUDY

There is one basic learning objective for this chapter: To demonstrate an understanding of the information reviewed in Chapters 15, 16, and 17, and apply it to a hypothetical real world case study requiring the development of a 2004 telecommunications operations department budget. The department expense forecasting example section in Chapter 16, *Developing an Operating Plan,* provided de-

tailed examples of developing operations department and telephone expense budgets. The reader should examine the basic information at the beginning of this chapter and develop a 2004 department forecast based on the Chapter 16 guidelines. Results can then be checked against the case study solution.

INTRODUCTION

This chapter's case study provides the basic information needed to develop a future year (2004) department forecast for a telecommunications operations department. It is assumed that the forecasting process takes place during the third quarter of the previous year (2003) and that the accounting department has issued a six month summary of actual expenses for all departments in the enterprise organization. Forecast guidelines for 2004 have also been distributed and the operations manager must develop a 2004 forecast baseline: the 2003 annual estimated actual expenses. As was the case in Chapter 16, the operations manager will use software spreadsheets to develop a personal computing forecast and will use the spreadsheet results as input for the organization's annual planning cycle requirements. (Refer to Figure 18–1, which replicates the spreadsheet-based forecasting process used in Chapter 16. It has been modified to reflect the Chapter 18 forecasting requirements.)

Commentaries will be given for each step during the manual forecasting process.

COMMON SENSE BUDGETING GUIDELINES

> **Common sense:** sound, practical judgment derived from experience rather than study.

The phrase, "You don't have any common sense," is typically used when someone has made an error in judgment that a more experienced individual would not make. Individuals who make the comment to someone else are using their experience factor to belittle someone else's lack of experience. However, there is another side to the common sense comment. Some individuals acquire common sense (experience) more quickly than others, and an examination of the reasons for this frequently shows that those who quickly benefit from experience see common sense elements as logical solutions for a given problem or set of problems. This rapid learning means that they have mentally established a relationship between the solution and the situation to which it is being applied. In mathematical terms, they intuitively see a cause and effect relationship between the different variables in various situations.

The following discusses common sense guidelines for carrying out the department forecasting process by showing that many expense code categories (Table 18–1) used in department budgets are variables driven by staffing levels. Just as staffing was a driving element during the technology planning process described in Chapter 9, *Technology Management Skills,* staffing levels drive many elements contained in department budgets. The staffing level can be viewed mathematically as an independent variable that drives other dependent variables. In some instances, total staffing may drive the dependent variable value. In other instances only a subset of the staffing total will drive the dependent variable. For ex-

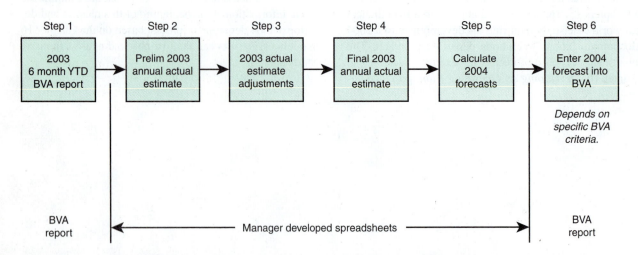

Figure 18–1. Operations department forecasting process.

TABLE 18–1   Controllable Budget Expense Codes

Code	Description
Controllable	
001	Salaries
008	Overtime
009	Shift premium
010	Wages
013	Overtime premium
027	Special compensation
029	Severance pay
099	Recreation/general welfare
100	Travel expenses
124	Employee training
140	Company meetings
160	Petty cash
180	Employee moving expenses
190	Dues, fees, subscriptions
300	Supplies
304	Printing and duplicating
310	Equipment purchases
330	Equipment rental
401	Repairs and maintenance
449	Outside services
687	Express courier service
688	Miscellaneous freight
689	Miscellaneous postage
909	Telephone

ample, if a department has a staff of thirty employees but only two employees need to use their cars for making trips on behalf of the business organization, it is likely that only the two employees will need petty cash for car trips. On the other hand, if all employees use their personal cars for business purposes, then all department members are likely to submit petty cash vouchers for reimbursement purposes. The key for budgeting, in this situation, is to have the common sense (experience) of knowing which employees require reimbursement—or obtain common sense by asking and answering the right questions when preparing the budget.

Note: Question-asking is an important activity for acquiring managerial common sense (Table 18–2).

If the reader finds that Table 18–2 appears simplistic and trivial, welcome to the world of common sense. The key element in using common sense is to develop and place a mental standard in memory and modify it, as needed, based on experience.

CONSUMERPROD CASE STUDY DESCRIPTION

The telecommunications operations department provides business telecommunications services for the Consumer-Prod Company, a major distributor of sports equipment. The operations department, housed in the corporate headquarters location, provides LAN and telephone services for 1,600 employees. ConsumerProd owns and operates six regional distribution centers and utilizes a private data network to communicate between headquarters, the regional distribution centers, customers, and suppliers. The telecommunications operations department operates a network control center in the headquarters location and provides 24/7 network center coverage. Figure 18–2 shows the organization chart for the headquarters location.

The lower level departments shown in Figure 18–2 are each headed by a director who, depending upon the specific department, may have multiple managers reporting to him or her.

The information services department provides computer and communications services for all ConsumerProd locations. A minimal computer and communications staff is maintained at the smaller locations, while the corporate function has primary responsibility for handling the information technology needs of the entire corporation. A director of telecommunications heads up the telecommunications department, which is shown in Figure 18–3.

There are sixty-three employees in the telecommunications department, and it is made up of five departments: planning, development, operations, administrative services, and help desk. They provide 24/7 network services to all locations and online Web-based access services to ConsumerProd customers.

The development manager has primary responsibility for implementing new telecommunications products and services, and then transfers the operating responsibility for the new equipment to the operations manager. The help desk manager maintains an IRS that is used to log information for all telephone system and network operating problems reported by ConsumerProd network users. The administrative services manager is responsible for adding and maintaining network users, providing corporate directory services, generating end of month cost allocation

TABLE 18–2   Common Sense Guidelines for Controllable Expenses

Code	Description	Common Sense Guidelines
001	Salaries	Based on existing salaries and financial guideline for salary% increases.
008	Overtime	Perform detailed estimates for employees who are eligible and likely to receive overtime pay.
009	Shift premium	Perform detailed estimates for employees who are eligible and likely to receive overtime pay.
010	Wages	Same guidelines as 001
013	Overtime premium	Same guidelines as 008
027	Special compensation	Use guidelines provided by human resources and accounting.
029	Severance pay	Use guidelines provided by human resources and accounting.
099	Recreation/general welfare	Assume a $/employee and add, or modify prior year budgets.
100	Travel expenses	Perform detailed estimates based on an estimate of "likely trips," using past experience.
124	Employee training	Assume a $/employee and add or modify prior year budgets.
140	Company meetings	Identify the number of employees who will attend and use a $/attendee estimate for the budget.
160	Petty cash	Use the prior year's budget value and modify as appropriate.
180	Employee moving expenses	Unlikely except for special cases.
190	Dues, fees, subscriptions	Use prior year's budget value and modify, as appropriate.
300	Supplies	Use prior year's budget value and modify, as appropriate.
304	Printing and duplicating	Use prior year's budget value and modify, as appropriate.
310	Equipment purchases	Develop a detail level estimate based on existing information and modify as required.
330	Equipment rental	Develop a detail level estimate based on existing information and modify as required.
401	Repairs and maintenance	Develop a detail level estimate based on existing information and modify as required.
449	Outside services	Use prior year's budget value and modify as appropriate.
687	Express courier service	Use prior year's budget value and modify as appropriate.
688	Miscellaneous freight	Use prior year's budget value and modify as appropriate.
689	Miscellaneous postage	Use prior year's budget value and modify as appropriate.
909	Telephone	Use prior year's budget value and modify as appropriate.

reports for telephone system and network users, and authorizing the payment of bills for all corporate telecommunications expenses.

2003 BUDGET PROJECT ADMINISTRATION

It is July 7, 2003, and the operations manager is reviewing the June BVA and 2003 YTD BVA reports (Examples 18–1 and 18.2) for the operations department. The manager had already reviewed the June BVA and identified the reasons for the two large negative variances: travel expense and outside services. The overall June BVA performance was good—a positive variance of $2,357—and this positive result is also reinforced by the six month YTD information (Example 18–2), which shows a YTD positive variance of $19,427 (3.3%).

The annual planning cycle instructions issued by the finance department established a due date of September 12, 2003, for submission of department budget recommendations.

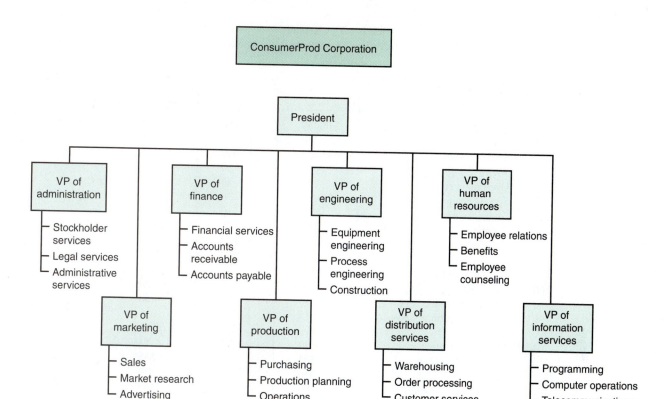

Figure 18–2. ConsumerProd corporate headquarters organization.

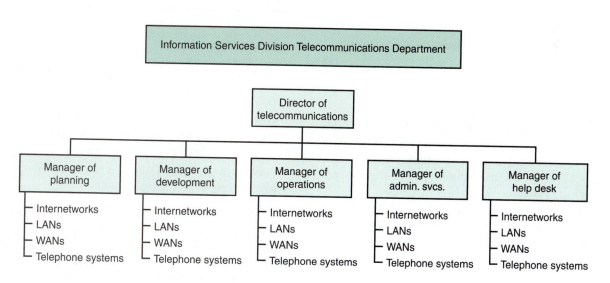

Figure 18–3. ConsumerProd telecommunications department.

Monthly BVA Report
Telecommunications Operations Department
June, 2003

Department ID: 12.69.10   **6/30/2003**

Code	Expense description	Forecast	Actual	Variance
001	Salaries	$76,250	$75,130	$1,120
008	Overtime	$1,440	$1,550	($110)
009	Shift premium	$2,125	$2,000	$125
010	Wages	$0	$0	$0
013	Overtime premium	$0	$0	$0
027	Special compensation	$3,125	$0	$3,125
029	Severance pay	$0	$0	$0
099	Recreation/general welfare	$183	$120	$63
100	Travel expenses	$6,750	$7,800	($1,050)
124	Employee training	$1,283	$590	$693
140	Company meetings	$275	$0	$275
160	Petty cash	$200	$320	($120)
180	Employee moving expenses	$0	$0	$0
190	Dues, fees, subscriptions	$75	$150	($75)
300	Supplies	$150	$250	($100)
304	Printing and duplicating	$230	$225	$5
310	Equipment purchases	$65		$65
330	Equipment rental	$50	$0	$50
401	Repairs and maintenance	$1,200	$1,250	($50)
449	Outside services	$2,300	$4,000	($1,700)
687	Express courier services	$100	$45	$55
688	Miscellaneous freight			$0
689	Miscellaneous postage	$125	$100	$25
909	Telephone	$2,640	$2,680	($40)
	Controllable expense totals	$98,567	$96,210	$2,357

Example 18–1. June 2003 BVA report.

2003 Budget Project Game Plan

The operations manager prepared a document (Table 18–3) that identified key milestone events and provided target dates for completing them. Meeting the milestone event schedule would ensure that the finance department's due date of September 12 would be met.

This table is considered a working document where additional entries will be inserted, as needed, based on any new information that is uncovered during the 2004 budget preparation process. The key milestone events that were entered include:

- the 2004 budget recommendation due date
- a meeting with the telecommunications director so that budgetary approval could be received prior to submitting the information to the finance department.

This meeting will be held a week prior to the budget submission date to provide flexibility for scheduling the meeting and allow time for making any budget revisions the director may recommend.

- a review of the final 2003 budget recommendations with the operations manager's staff

The budget preparation process is one of the normal administrative projects that are carried out by managers. The operations manager will complete most of the budget preparation effort personally and will utilize the time of other department members in an ad hoc manner. The preliminary timetable (Table 18–3) provides a seven week period for this process. On the surface, this appears to be a large amount of time. However, the reality is that there is less time than it seems. This is also the time

Department ID: 12.69.10   **7/12/2003**

Code	Expense description	Annual FC	6-MosFC	6-MosActual	6-MosVar$	6-MosVar%
001	Salaries	$915,000	$457,500	$450,780	$6,720	0.7%
008	Overtime	$17,280	$8,640	$8,268	$372	2.2%
009	Shift premium	$25,500	$12,750	$13,000	($250)	-1.0%
010	Wages	$0	$0	$0	$0	-
013	Overtime premium	$0	$0	$0	$0	-
027	Special compensation	$37,500	$18,750	$0	$18,750	50.0%
029	Severance pay	$0	$0	$0	$0	-
099	Recreation/general welfare	$2,200	$1,100	$1,320	$220	-10.0%
100	Travel expenses	$81,000	$40,500	$34,500	$6,000	7.4%
124	Employee training	$15,400	$7,700	$8,000	($300)	-1.9%
140	Company meetings	$3,300	$1,650	$2,500	($850)	-25.8%
160	Petty cash	$2,400	$1,200	$1,920	($720)	-30.0%
180	Employee moving expenses	$0	$0	$0	$0	0.0%
190	Dues, fees, subscriptions	$900	$450	$425	$25	2.8%
300	Supplies	$1,800	$900	$880	$20	1.1%
304	Printing and duplicating	$2,760	$1,380	$1,450	($70)	-2.5%
310	Equipment purchases	$780	$390	$550	($160)	-20.5%
330	Equipment rental	$600	$300	$220	$80	13.3%
401	Repairs and maintenance	$14,400	$7,200	$7,140	$60	0.4%
449	Outside services	$27,600	$13,800	$24,000	($10,200)	-37.0%
687	Express courier services	$1,200	$600	$390	$210	17.5%
688	Miscellaneous freight	$0	$0	$0	$0	0.0%
689	Miscellaneous postage	$1,500	$750	$730	$20	1.3%
909	Telephone	$31,680	$15,840	$15,900	($60)	-0.2%
	Controllable expense totals	**$1,182,800**	**$591,400**	**$571,973**	**$19,427**	**3.3%**

Example 18–2.   June 2003, six month YTD report.

TABLE 18–3   Initial 2004 Budget Preparation Timetable

Date	Activity
7–7–03 (Monday)	Review six month YTD BVA Develop timetable for developing the 2003 operations forecast Set up budget spreadsheets
8–29–03 (Friday)	Finalize budget spreadsheet information
9–3–03 (Wednesday)	Review 2004 budget with operations department staff
9–5–03 (Friday)	Complete budget recommendation documentation for telecommunications Director review meeting
9–8–03 (Monday)	Review operations department budget recommendations with telecommunications director
9–12–03 (Friday)	Submit operations department budget recommendations to finance department

when: 1) current year employee performance appraisals must be completed, 2) next year employee performance appraisal forms must be created, 3) vendor contracts and rates need to be reviewed, 4) salary increase recommendations must be established, 5) promotion recommendations are due, and 6) normal operations must be maintained. In addition, this is the time of year when many department members, including the operations manager, take vacations.

The next section will describe the budget changes that the operations manager will incorporate into the 2004 budget forecast.

2004 Budget Changes

ConsumerProd relies heavily upon communications services to communicate with its employees, customers, and suppliers. In 2003, a major addition was added to ConsumerProdNet—ConsumerProd's private data communications network. As a result of this expansion, the operations department has been authorized to add three more technicians to its network control center staffing in 2004. This addition will free up time from three senior network technicians who are traveling to the smaller ConsumerProd locations. The three senior network technicians address complaints that service levels for corporate telecommunications support activities had deteriorated significantly in recent months.

The salary allowance for the three new positions is $120,000 and they will be hired during the latter part of the fourth quarter. The total staffing for the network control center (NCC) is currently eighteen, including three shift supervisors. All NCC personnel are provided a shift premium of 10% when they work the third shift (12 midnight to 8 AM). Most of the operations department overtime budget is for NCC personnel. A 4% salary increase allowance should be included in the 2003 budget for salary expenses, except for the three new additions whose 2004 salary increases are included in the $120,000 salary pool.

An outside services expense budget line is used by the operations manager to hire outside consultants for supplementing the internal staff. (Outside consultants are used when special skills are needed or when peak workload conditions require the temporary addition of staff.) The 2003 budget includes a normal allowance for outside services, but in 2004 the operations department will make major modifications to the data network. An additional $10,000 (above 2003 budget levels) should be added to the outside services budget category.

The Budgeting Approach

Budget preparation is not an exact science, which is frequently the case for many managerial areas. It requires the use of common sense and reasonable assumptions. The following will assume that no additional information is available and that the only hard information available to the operations manager is what is shown in Example 18–1, Example 18–2, and in the case study background information description.

The operations manager will utilize the common sense budgeting guidelines provided as part of the precase study introduction. The Figure 18–1 forecasting process will be followed and will be used to describe the forecasting details.

The basic requirements for developing the 2004 budget forecast are: 1) estimate current year (2003) actual expenses and 2) develop a future year (2004) forecast that incorporates the addition to staffing (salaries = $120,000) and the additional outside services requirements (estimate = $10,000). The baseline history established for the 2003 actual estimate would become the basis for calculating 2004 forecast requirements—except for the new requirements ($120,000 + $10,000).

CHAPTER 16 REFRESHER. In Chapter 16, *Developing an Operating Plan,* a department forecast preparation process was described. This same basic process will be followed, and Figure 18–4 provides a version of Figure 18–1, modified to reflect the specific 2003 forecasting situation in the case study.

The operations manager generated a series of spreadsheets (Examples 18–2 through 18–8) and their context in the forecasting process is shown in Figure 18–3. Copies of these spreadsheets will be provided during the forecasting discussion, and the common sense adjustment discussed earlier will be applied to the forecasting process.

In addition to generating an expense forecast, it is necessary to place the new forecast in its proper context. Therefore, Example 18–8 (see Example 18–4) provides a 2003 estimated actual *v.* 2004 forecast report to indicate the context of the forecast against the actual expense estimate for the previous year. It will become a key element in the operations manager's memo to the telecommunications director.

2003 BUDGET PREPARATION

The operations manager previously identified five spreadsheet worksheets that will be used to establish 2004 fore-

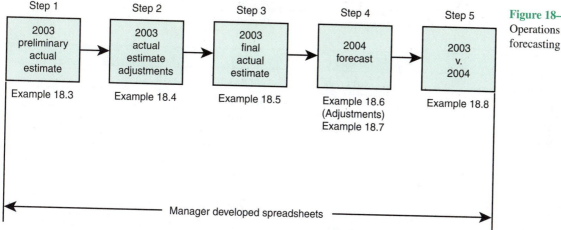

Step 1 → Step 2 → Step 3 → Step 4 → Step 5

Step 1: 2003 preliminary actual estimate — Example 18.3

Step 2: 2003 actual estimate adjustments — Example 18.4

Step 3: 2003 final actual estimate — Example 18.5

Step 4: 2004 forecast — Example 18.6 (Adjustments) Example 18.7

Step 5: 2003 v. 2004 — Example 18.8

← Manager developed spreadsheets →

Figure 18–4.
Operations department forecasting process.

cast information. These worksheets will be developed using spreadsheet software:

1. a 2003 preliminary actual estimate (Example 18–3)
2. a 2003 actual expense estimate adjustments (Example 18–4)
3. a 2003 final actual expense worksheet (Example 18–5)
4. a 2004 forecast adjustment worksheet (Example 18–6)
5. a 2004 final forecast (Example 18–7)
6. a 2003 annual expense estimate v. 2004 expense forecast (Example 18–8)

The final 2004 forecast values are shown in the Example 18–7 and 18–8 spreadsheets.

2003 Preliminary Actual Expense Estimate

Example 18–3 shows the preliminary actual expense estimate worksheet that the operations manager developed, based on the information shown in the six month YTD BVA (Example 18–2). The EstActual values shown in Example 18–3 were calculated by multiplying the six month YTD actual expense information shown on Example 18–2 by two to provide a preliminary annual estimate.

Based on the Example 18–3 worksheet, a positive variance of $38,854 is generated compared to the annual 2003 forecast (AnnualFC). The operations manager will review the Example 18–3 worksheet and apply judgment (common sense), assumptions, and knowledge of 2003 expenses to adjust these values, as needed, to develop a realistic final actual estimate for 2003.

Example 18–4 lists the adjustments identified by the operations manager, and these adjustments were applied to

the Example 18–3 spreadsheet to generate the 2003 final adjusted annual expense estimates shown in the Example 18–5 worksheet.

The next section discusses the 2003 actual estimate adjustments in detail.

2003 Final Adjusted Annual Expense Estimate

Example 18–4 shows the worksheet adjustments used to develop the final 2003 annual expense estimate. The values shown on this worksheet would replace the values shown in Example 18–3 when differences exist between the two. The following summarizes some of the reasons for making these changes. Knowledge of YTD expenses and experience will be used.

> **Original FC** indicates that the manager felt that second half of the year spending would result in the meeting the original forecasts. The preliminary calculated estimates were overridden.

> **Special compensation** values are not used until year end, when bonuses are calculated. Therefore, the money will not be spent until bonus time, and the initial forecast value of $37,500 should still be used.

The remainder of the notation information shown in Example 18–4 is straightforward. The values shown in Example 18–4 are the 2003 final annual expense estimates and will be entered in the next worksheet (Example 18–5), the final 2003 actual expense estimate worksheet.

Department ID: 12.69.10

Code	Expense Description	AnnualFC	EstActual	Variance$	Variance%
001	Salaries	$915,000	$901,560	$13,440	1.5%
008	Overtime	$17,280	$16,536	$744	4.3%
009	Shift premium	$25,500	$26,000	($500)	-2.0%
010	Wages	$0	$0	$0	-
013	Overtime premium	$0	$0	$0	-
027	Special compensation	$37,500	$0	$37,500	100.0%
029	Severance pay	$0	$0	$0	-
099	Recreation/general welfare	$2,200	$2,640	($440)	-20.0%
100	Travel expenses	$81,000	$69,000	$12,000	14.8%
124	Employee training	$15,400	$16,000	($600)	-3.9%
140	Company meetings	$3,300	$5,000	($1,700)	-51.5%
160	Petty cash	$2,400	$3,840	($1,440)	-60.0%
180	Employee moving expenses	$0	$0	$0	0.0%
190	Dues, fees, subscriptions	$900	$850	$50	5.6%
300	Supplies	$1,800	$1,760	$40	2.2%
304	Printing and duplicating	$2,760	$2,900	($140)	-5.1%
310	Equipment purchases	$780	$1,100	($320)	-41.0%
330	Equipment rental	$600	$440	$160	26.7%
401	Repairs and maintenance	$14,400	$14,280	$120	0.8%
449	Outside services	$27,600	$48,000	($20,400)	-73.9%
687	Express courier services	$1,200	$780	$420	35.0%
688	Miscellaneous freight	$0	$0	$0	0.0%
689	Miscellaneous postage	$1,500	$1,460	$40	2.7%
909	Telephone	$31,680	$31,800	($120)	-0.4%
	Controllable Expense Totals	**$1,182,800**	**$1,143,946**	**$38,854**	**3.3%**

EstActual = 2 × six-month actual
variance = AnnualFC – EstActual

Example 18–3. 2003 preliminary actual expense estimate worksheet.

2003 Final Annual Actual Expense Estimate

The Example 18–5 worksheet shows the 2003 final actual expense values (AdjActual) and compares them to the 2003 annual forecast (AnnualFC) values. The total variance is a positive value ($17,930), primarily due to high positive variances in the salaries and travel accounts. The 1.5% positive variance is unlikely to raise any questions by the telecommunications director, and the 2003 forecasting effort of the previous year would be rated as being "good." If unexpected expenses are incurred during the fourth quarter of 2003 because of the early hiring of the 2003 headcount additions, the $17,930 can be used to absorb those expenses and the department will still meet the original 2003 forecast.

The $1,164,870 controllable expense total would be the manager's 2003 final annual actual estimate used for calculating the 2004 budget.

CHAPTER 18

2003 Final Annual Expense Adjustments
Changes to 2003 Preliminary Actual Expense Estimate

Department ID: 12.69.10

Code	Expense Description	AdjActual	Reason
001	Salaries	$901,560	
008	Overtime	$17,280	Original FC
009	Shift premium	$26,000	
010	Wages	$0	
013	Overtime premium	$0	
027	Special compensation	$37,500	Bonus allocation used @ EOY
029	Severance pay	$0	
099	Recreation/general welfare	$2,500	Higher costs than originally forecast
100	Travel expenses	$78,000	EOY travel to company locations
124	Employee training	$15,400	Orginal FC
140	Company meetings	$3,300	Orginal FC
160	Petty cash	$2,400	Orginal FC
180	Employee moving expenses	$0	
190	Dues, fees, subscriptions	$1,050	Adding new DataPro reference
300	Supplies	$1,800	Orginal FC
304	Printing and duplicating	$2,900	EOY user manual increases
310	Equipment purchases	$780	Orginal FC
330	Equipment rental	$600	Orginal FC
401	Repairs and maintenance	$13,500	Scrapping high maintenance unit
449	Outside services	$26,000	Lower than expected needs
687	Express courier services	$1,000	Lower than expected needs
688	Miscellaneous freight	$0	
689	Miscellaneous postage	$1,500	Orginal FC
909	Telephone	$31,800	Slight increase
	Totals	**$1,164,870**	

Example 18–4. 2003 actual expense estimate adjustment worksheet.

2004 Annual Forecast Adjustments

Example 18–6 shows the worksheet used by the operations manager to identify adjustments that would be made for the 2004 forecast to allow for new 2004 requirements.

The basic approach for creating the 2004 budget is to utilize the 2003 final actual expense estimates unless reasons exist (Example 18–6 2004 forecast adjustments) to change them.

Two major adjustments are shown on Example 18–6:

- changes due to the new 2004 staffing
- the operations upgrade project

Some other minor changes are also shown, along with their reasons.

Note: Staffing addition adjustments were made to all codes related to employees—not just the salaries code.

Department ID: 12.69.10

Code	Expense Description	AnnualFC	AdjActual	Variance$	Variance%
001	Salaries	$915,000	$901,560	$13,440	1.5%
008	Overtime	$17,280	$17,280	$0	0.0%
009	Shift premium	$25,500	$26,000	($500)	-2.0%
010	Wages	$0	$0	$0	-
013	Overtime premium	$0	$0	$0	-
027	Special compensation	$37,500	$37,500	$0	0.0%
029	Severance pay	$0	$0	$0	-
099	Recreation/general welfare	$2,200	$2,500	($300)	-13.6%
100	Travel expenses	$81,000	$78,000	$3,000	3.7%
124	Employee training	$15,400	$15,400	$0	0.0%
140	Company meetings	$3,300	$3,300	$0	0.0%
160	Petty cash	$2,400	$2,400	$0	0.0%
180	Employee moving expenses	$0	$0	$0	0.0%
190	Dues, fees, subscriptions	$900	$1,050	($150)	-16.7%
300	Supplies	$1,800	$1,800	$0	0.0%
304	Printing and duplicating	$2,760	$2,900	($140)	-5.1%
310	Equipment purchases	$780	$780	$0	0.0%
330	Equipment rental	$600	$600	$0	0.0%
401	Repairs and maintenance	$14,400	$13,500	$900	6.3%
449	Outside services	$27,600	$26,000	$1,600	5.8%
687	Express courier services	$1,200	$1,000	$200	16.7%
688	Miscellaneous freight	$0	$0	$0	0.0%
689	Miscellaneous postage	$1,500	$1,500	$0	0.0%
909	Telephone	$31,680	$31,800	($120)	-0.4%
	Controllable expense totals	**$1,182,800**	**$1,164,870**	**$17,930**	**1.5%**

Example 18–5.   Final 2003 actual expense worksheet.

Salary-related adjustments are identified with a reason statement. Although not shown as a worksheet, the operations manager utilized a worksheet containing the salaries of all employees. (Because this is confidential information, it is not shown.)

Example 18–6 shows that an adjustment of + $156,125 will be made to the 2001 final actual estimate expense. In addition, the initial budgeting guidelines provided to the operations manager stated that a 4% salary increase

guideline should be incorporated into the salary-related accounts for the 2003 forecast, and this has been done.

2004 Annual Forecast

The Example 18–7 worksheet shows the final 2004 annual forecast. Each salary related account (001, 008, 009, 027) provides a 4% increase above the 2003 final actual expense estimate, plus any adjustments from the Example 18–6 2004 forecast adjustments worksheet.

Year 2004 Annual Adjustment Information
Changes to 2004 Final Actual Operating Expenses

Department ID: 12.69.10

Code	Expense Description	Adjustment	Reason
001	Salaries	$120,000	Staff addition (3)
008	Overtime	$2,880	Staff addition (3)
009	Shift premium	$12,000	Staff addition (3)
010	Wages	$0	
013	Overtime premium	$0	
027	Special compensation	$0	
029	Severance pay	$0	
099	Recreation/general welfare	$375	Staff addition (3)
100	Travel expenses	$1,500	Staff addition (3)
124	Employee training	$1,000	Staff addition (3)
140	Company meetings	$360	Staff addition (3)
160	Petty cash	$540	Staff addition (3)
180	Employee moving expenses	$0	
190	Dues, fees, subscriptions	$0	
300	Supplies	$500	Increased documentation estimates
304	Printing and duplicating	$400	Increased documentation estimates
310	Equipment purchases	$0	Orginal FC
330	Equipment rental	$500	Binding equipment
401	Repairs and maintenance	$780	Staff addition (3)
449	Outside services	$10,000	Operations upgrade project
687	Express courier services	$0	
688	Miscellaneous freight	$0	
689	Miscellaneous postage	$0	
909	Telephone	$5,290	3% increase forecasted + headcount addition
	Totals	**$156,125**	

Example 18–6. 2004 forecast adjustments to 2004 final expenses.

The calculations described previously are relatively simple for individuals who have a good understanding of spreadsheet software and algebra. A manual approach could wind up as a tedious, error-prone task unless extreme care is taken. The spreadsheet version allows each element (cell) to be evaluated easily. The use of links between cells eliminates the possibility of transcription errors.

2003 Actual Estimate v. 2004 Forecast

The final 2004 annual forecast ($1,386,237) provides a 17.2% ($203,437) increase over the 2003 annual forecast ($1,182,800)—an increase that is significant. This information is shown in Example 18–8.

Analysis of Example 18–6 (2004 forecast adjustments for new requirements) shows that over 90% of 2004 forecast increases are due to the staffing increase of three

2004 Annual Forecast
Telecommunications Operations Department

Department ID: 12.69.10

Code	Expense Description	2002 YrFC
001	Salaries	$1,071,600
008	Overtime	$20,851
009	Shift premium	$38,520
010	Wages	$0
013	Overtime premium	$0
027	Special compensation	$39,000
029	Severance pay	$0
099	Recreation/general welfare	$2,663
100	Travel expenses	$85,740
124	Employee training	$17,016
140	Company meetings	$3,792
160	Petty cash	$3,036
180	Employee moving expenses	$0
190	Dues, fees, subscriptions	$936
300	Supplies	$2,372
304	Printing and duplicating	$3,270
310	Equipment purchases	$811
330	Equipment rental	$1,124
401	Repairs and maintenance	$15,756
449	Outside services	$38,704
687	Express courier services	$1,248
688	Miscellaneous freight	$0
689	Miscellaneous postage	$1,560
909	Telephone	$38,238
	Controllable expense totals	**$1,386,237**

Example 18–7.   2004 final forecast worksheet.

technicians. If the expenses associated with the staffing increase are subtracted from the 2003 forecast, it would be seen that the net increase before the staff is added is approximately $18,000, or a 1.5% increase—a very nominal increase in view of the 4% salary increases that are part of the 2004 forecast guidelines.

FINAL 2004 FORECAST RECOMMENDATIONS

Although the operations manager has completed the actual department forecasting process, there is still the remaining task of formally recommending the budget to the director of telecommunications and requesting that it be forwarded to finance for inclusion in the enterprise level 2004 budgets. Managers are accountable to their managers, and the role of a manager of managers is to review the budget recommendations of subordinates and approve them prior their submission as formal recommendations.

Example 18–9 is a typical memo that communicates the budget recommendation to the direc-tor of telecommunications. It is included as a generic example.

2003 Actual Estimate v. 2004 Forecast
Telecommunications Operations Department

Department ID: 12.69.10

Code	Expense Description	2003 YrAct	2004 YrFC	Difference$	Difference%
001	Salaries	$915,000	$1,071,600	$156,600	17.1%
008	Overtime	$17,280	$20,851	$3,571	20.7%
009	Shift premium	$25,500	$38,520	$13,020	51.1%
010	Wages	$0	$0	$0	-
013	Overtime premium	$0	$0	$0	-
027	Special compensation	$37,500	$39,000	$1,500	4.0%
029	Severance pay	$0	$0	$0	-
099	Recreation/general welfare	$2,200	$2,663	$463	21.0%
100	Travel expenses	$81,000	$85,740	$4,740	5.9%
124	Employee training	$15,400	$17,016	$1,616	10.5%
140	Company meetings	$3,300	$3,792	$492	14.9%
160	Petty cash	$2,400	$3,036	$636	26.5%
180	Employee moving expenses	$0	$0	$0	0.0%
190	Dues, fees, subscriptions	$900	$936	$36	4.0%
300	Supplies	$1,800	$2,372	$572	31.8%
304	Printing and duplicating	$2,760	$3,270	$510	18.5%
310	Equipment purchases	$780	$811	$31	4.0%
330	Equipment rental	$600	$1,124	$524	87.3%
401	Repairs and maintenance	$14,400	$15,756	$1,356	9.4%
449	Outside services	$27,600	$38,704	$11,104	40.2%
687	Express courier services	$1,200	$1,248	$48	4.0%
688	Miscellaneous freight	$0	$0	$0	0.0%
689	Miscellaneous postage	$1,500	$1,560	$60	4.0%
909	Telephone	$31,680	$38,238	$6,558	20.7%
	Controllable expense totals	**$1,182,800**	**$1,386,237**	**$203,437**	**17.2%**

Example 18–8. 2003 actual expense estimate v. 2004 forecast worksheet.

SUMMARY

The case study in Chapter 18 shows how the information in Chapter 16, *Developing an Operating Plan*, would be applied to a real world department budget preparation activity. While there is a definite advantage in knowing budget details, there is a bigger advantage in knowing budget details, there is a bigger advantage in understanding how to develop estimates based on common sense and good judgment. This includes estimating per employee charges for employee-related accounts and using this value when new employees are added.

Date: September 6, 2002

To: Director of telecommunications
From: Operations manager
Subject: Year 2003 operations department forecast

A preliminary 2003 telecommunications forecast has been developed for the six ABC Company departments. The following summarizes the process and final results of the 2003 forecasting process.

2002 operations department budget forecast

The 2002 monthly telecommunications expense forecasts have been completed for the operations department in accordance with the finance department's annual planning instructions. The six month BVA report was used as the primary input for the forecast, and a completed finance forecast form is attached.

The net result is that the operations department's 2003 budget will increase by 17.2% over 2002 estimated actual expenses. Over 90% of this increase is due to the costs of adding three new network control center technicians to the department staff. This staffing recommendation and the associated budget increase was approved in May. Appendix A provides a spreadsheet that compares the 2003 budget forecast against 2002 estimated actual expenses.

If the headcount addition effect is removed, the overall increase to the 2001 estimated annual expenses would be $18,746 (1.6%).

Next steps

A meeting has been set up for tomorrow at 10 a.m. to review the 2002 budget and answer any questions that you may have.

Example 18–9a. Cover memo to the director of telecommunications.

2003 Estimate Actual v. 2004 Forecast
Telecommunications Operations Department

Department ID: 12.69.10

Code	Expense Description	2003 YrAct	2004 YrFC	Difference$	Difference%
001	Salaries	$915,000	$1,071,600	$156,600	17.1%
008	Overtime	$17,280	$20,851	$3,571	20.7%
009	Shift premium	$25,500	$38,520	$13,020	51.1%
010	Wages	$0	$0	$0	–
013	Overtime premium	$0	$0	$0	–
027	Special compensation	$37,500	$39,000	$1,500	4.0%
029	Severance pay	$0	$0	$0	–
099	Recreation/general welfare	$2,200	$2,663	$463	21.0%
100	Travel expenses	$81,000	$85,740	$4,740	5.9%
124	Employee training	$15,400	$17,016	$1,616	10.5%
140	Company meetings	$3,300	$3,792	$492	14.9%
160	Petty cash	$2,400	$3,036	$636	26.5%
180	Employee moving expenses	$0	$0	$0	0.0%
190	Dues, fees, subscriptions	$900	$936	$36	4.0%
300	Supplies	$1,800	$2,372	$572	31.8%
304	Printing and duplicating	$2,760	$3,270	$510	18.5%
310	Equipment purchases	$780	$811	$31	4.0%
330	Equipment rental	$600	$1,124	$524	87.3%
401	Repairs and maintenance	$14,400	$15,756	$1,356	9.4%
449	Outside services	$27,600	$38,704	$11,104	40.2%
687	Express courier services	$1,200	$1,248	$48	4.0%
688	Miscellaneous freight	$0	$0	$0	0.0%
689	Miscellaneous postage	$1,500	$1,560	$60	4.0%
909	Telephone	$31,680	$38,238	$6,558	20.7%
	Controllable expense totals	**$1,182,800**	**$1,386,237**	**$203,437**	**17.2%**

Example 18–9b. Appendix included with cover memo.

5

ACQUISITION MANAGEMENT

Parts 2,3, and 4 provided a telecommunications-oriented discussion of managing the organizational and technical responsibilities associated with running a telecommunications department. Part 5 describes a nontelecommunications skill—the purchase of equipment and services—that is essential for telecommunications managers. Unless telecommunications managers are able to buy the right equipment and services at the best price, they will not manage telecommunications expenses effectively.

Generally, purchasing in a telecommunications context can be described as getting something by paying money, or using money or its equivalent to obtain the equipment or services required to establish or maintain a business communication infrastructure. Purchasing telecommunications equipment and services requires a good understanding of the purchasing department's procedures and good telecommunications management skills. Business purchasing methods and procedures will be reviewed in Part 5 and—as has been the case throughout this text—the topics covered in Parts 2, 3, and 4 will provide

the managerial tools needed to customize the equipment and service acquisition process to meet telecommunications needs.

PART 5: ACQUISITION MANAGEMENT TOPICS

Telecommunications products and services are a major expense item for most corporations, and the effectiveness of telecommunications managers in handling acquisition (purchasing or leasing) requirements will be dependent upon their general management and technology management skills.

Part 5 consists of four chapters:

Chapter 19: *Purchasing Process Overview*

Chapter 20: *Purchasing Products and Services*

Chapter 21: *Evaluating Acquisition Options*

Chapter 22: *Acquisition Management: A Case Study*

CHAPTER 19: PURCHASING PROCESS OVERVIEW

Chapter 19 reviews the general purchasing process used by businesses to purchase products and services. This discussion includes a detailed examination of the generic purchasing process found in many corporations and introduces a seven step telecommunications acquisition model that is used as the basis for subsequent discussions. The model is a complementary addition to the project life cycle model discussed in Part 3, *Project Management*.

Chapter 19 discusses the accounting implications of purchasing equipment, including the IRS's depreciation allowance process and its importance in managing telecommunications projects. The chapter also provides an overview of the Electronics Industry Association/Telecommunications Industry Association (EIA/TIA) 568 Premises Cabling Standard. While this standard may be thought of as a technical standard and not a managerial concern, the discussion focus will be on the managerial advantages gained when using a mature technical standard. The 568 standard provides a full set of technical and operating standards that will ensure the long-term viability of a cabling infrastructure investment and, from a managerial perspective, it is primarily a matter of ensuring that cabling installations and changes conform to the 568 standards.

CHAPTER 20: PURCHASING PRODUCTS AND SERVICES

Chapter 20 reviews the existing methods and procedures used in the acquisition process: RFIs, RFQs, and RFPs. It discusses their use within the context of the seven step acquisition model introduced in Chapter 19. The primary focus of Chapter 20 is on acquisition model steps 1 through 4:

1. define business requirements
2. create technical specifications
3. identify purchase selection criteria
4. issue purchase documentation to vendors

Acquisition model steps 5 through 7 are covered in Chapter 21.

CHAPTER 21: EVALUATING ACQUISITION OPTIONS

Telecommunications equipment purchases are long-term investments that will normally be used for many years. Once the technical and business requirements for a telecommunications acquisition have been identified, a telecommunications manager typically obtains several bids and then goes through a selection process to determine which purchase alternative is best. Bid responses normally include a large quantity of diverse technical and financial information that is difficult to evaluate objectively.

Chapter 21 describes the use of a decision-making method that is based on evaluating mandatory requirements and optional requirements criteria. This method clearly highlights both the decision process and the results that are obtained from the decision process. The outcomes of the decision process are suitable for presentation to technical or nontechnical personnel and provide a mechanism for translating technical criteria into terminology that can be understood by nontechnical business managers.

The LCA/NPV financial model discussed in previous chapters is used to evaluate different purchase options, purchase costs, and operating expenses within a common financial framework. The proper use of the LCA/NPV model allows telecommunications managers to avoid the mistake of purchasing low-cost equipment that will be a high-cost, long-term maintenance liability.

CHAPTER 22: ACQUISITION MANAGEMENT: A CASE STUDY

The Chapter 22 case study applies the seven step acquisition model to a project during which a large telephone system is being acquired. A detailed description of the technical and financial criteria evaluation process (model steps 5 through 7) is given.

Because this is not a technical text, a set of technical decision criteria has been preselected for the evaluation process. The technical side of the telecommunications acquisition process requires a high level of technical expertise, and discussing the basis for selecting technical criteria is outside the scope of this management-oriented text. The technical elements are introduced to underscore the need for having a balance of technology and managerial skills if a telecommunications department is to be managed effectively.

19

PURCHASING PROCESS OVERVIEW

1. Understand the seven step telecommunications acquisition model.

2. Understand the use of RFIs, RFQs, and RFPs in the acquisition process.

3. Understand the relationship of the telecommunications acquisition model to the telecommunications project life cycle model.

4. Understand the need for postacquisition meetings with suppliers who have not been selected during a competitive bidding situation.

5. Understand the role of the telecommunications department in the purchasing process.

6. Understand the responsibilities associated with telecommunications purchasing activities.

7. Understand the accounting procedures associated with purchasing fixed assets, and purchasing's

relationship to the telecommunications acquisition process.

8. Understand the difference between technical and functional obsolescence and their effects on telecommunications acquisition decisions.

9. Know how to perform straight line depreciation method calculations and understand the meaning of the elements in the straight line formula.

10. Understand leasing concepts and the advantages and disadvantages that the leasing option offers business organizations.

11. Understand the concept of outsourcing and its implications for a telecommunications manager.

12. Understand the managerial advantages provided by the ANSI/TIA/EIA 568A premises cabling standard.

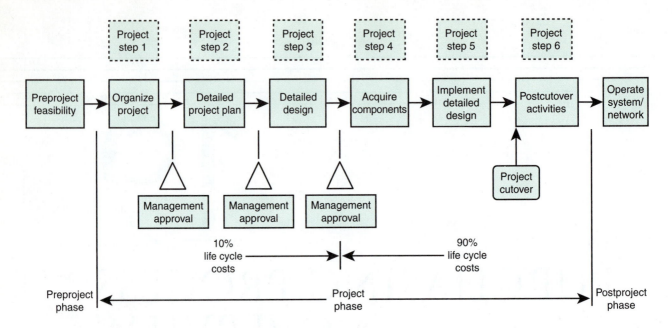

Figure 19–1. Telecommunications project life cycle model.

In earlier technology management chapters, the **telecommunications project life cycle model** (Figure 19–1) was the focus of discussion. The implementation of a telecommunications infrastructure (LANs, WANs, internetworks, telephone systems, etc.) for all projects, large and small, will follow the six step process shown in Figure 19–1.

A telecommunications project is a mechanism for implementing telecommunications products and services in a business. Project activities include the design, **purchase (acquisition),** and implementation of the technology elements needed to build telecommunications systems and networks. Step 4 in the telecommunications project life cycle is the project's acquisition phase and it is at this point in the project's life cycle that equipment purchases are made for projects. In a project, the acquisition phase is simply a natural end result of the project activities preceding the actual purchase.

The Chapter 11, *What is Project Management?*, discussion identified five deliverables that are generated as part of project step 3 (detailed design) efforts:

1. a summary evaluation of acquisition alternatives
2. recommended supplier(s)
3. a five year financial plan
4. an implementation schedule
5. final recommendations

Items 1, 2, 3, and 5 are the primary focus of Part 5, *Acquisition Management*, topics and discuss the acquisi-

tion process within the context of the project life cycle model in Figure 19–1.

Project step 4 (acquisition) will be the implementation phase of the purchase recommendations. This is when project step 3 recommendations will be carried out and project products and services will be acquired.

THE TELECOMMUNICATIONS ACQUISITION PROCESS

The purchasing process for acquiring telecommunications technology requires: 1) technology management skills and 2) purchasing process skills. Technology management skills are needed to identify and select the right products and services for a specific business environment. Purchasing process skills are needed to obtain the product at the best life cycle cost, where the life cycle cost refers to all the costs incurred from the time of the initial purchase to the time an asset is retired or replaced with new products.

There are four requirements that must be incorporated into the purchase planning process to ensure that a selected product or service provides the best life cycle pricing:

1. The selected product is backed by a viable business that will be in business during the product's life cycle and will continue to improve the product.

2. The product has a track record that indicates it will function as designed during its entire life cycle.

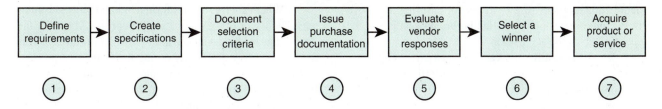

Figure 19–2. Seven step telecommunications acquisition model.

3. Quality maintenance support will be available during the product's entire life cycle.

4. The total life cycle cost of the selected product is better than, or as good as, other acceptable product alternatives.

If any of these implications are not met, the product selection process must be reexamined and adjusted.

When a telecommunications manager purchases telecommunications equipment and services for a business, the business's purchasing procedures must be followed. While purchasing procedures may vary from business to business, they will typically contain many common elements. Internal departments involved with the purchasing process include: 1) the purchasing department, 2) the accounting department, and 3) the legal department. Telecommunications products and services may be purchased, **leased,** or **rented,** and each option may have specific company guidelines that must be followed. Individual businesses may have biases that favor different acquisition modes (purchase, lease, or rental), and the purchasing process will incorporate these biases into the procedures.

One of the requirements associated with being an effective telecommunications manager is to have a good understanding of the business's purchasing, accounting, and legal procedures. A manager also requires a good understanding of the business and technical criteria used to select specific telecommunications products and services from different purchasing options.

In summary, a telecommunications manager must select products and services that best meet the business and technology needs of the business while conforming to any purchasing, accounting, or legal policies used to manage the business's purchasing process.

These requirements can be summarized into a **seven step telecommunications acquisition process** that incorporates required organizational acquisition elements:

1. Define and document business requirements.

2. Translate business requirements into technical specifications.

3. Develop and document acquisition selection criteria.

4. Issue acquisition specifications to the appropriate vendors.

5. Evaluate vendor responses $v.$ acquisition selection criteria.

6. Select a specific vendor's product or service.

7. Acquire the selected product or service.

These seven steps will collectively be referred to as the telecommunications acquisition model, which is shown in Figure 19–2. The model will be the focus for discussions in Chapters 19, 20, 21, and 22. During the acquisition phase of the project life cycle (Figure 19–1), acquisition activities are integrated into the overall project fabric, but they may also be implemented outside of a project environment. Figure 19–2 shows the telecommunications acquisition model as an independent set of activities that incorporate some of the elements used in the telecommunications project life cycle model.

When the acquisition model is used as part of the project life cycle model, the project model's activities would satisfactorily meet the equivalent acquisition model activity requirements. However, if a product acquisition were made independently of a project process, the acquisition model's seven steps should be used.

The following describes the seven steps of the acquisition model.

Step 1: Define and Document Business Requirements

Whether the acquisition process is carried out as part of a project or independently, business requirements should be clearly identified at the start of the project process and should be used as the criteria for developing technical specifications. When the acquisition process is carried out within a project context, project management activities will generate business requirements as part of the preproject phase. When the acquisition process is performed independently of a project process, the initiator of the acquisition assumes responsibility for ensuring that business requirements are identified before proceeding to the second step of the acquisition model.

Business justifications address cost savings opportunities, increased internal productivity efforts, or the use of telecommunications products and services to support efforts that will generate revenues. As with any business investment, the telecommunications purchase justification should be a measurable one. The benefits must be weighed against the investments needed to obtain these benefits. Standard analysis tools like ROI, IRR, or LCA/NPV may be utilized for the cost justification analysis.

Step 2: Translate Business Requirements into Technical Specifications

Telecommunications products and services are technology-based, and it is essential that business requirements are translated into a technical design that is compatible with existing enterprise telecommunications technology. In a project mode (Figure 19–1), step 3 (project design) would generate the specification information. If the acquisition process is performed independently, the project design activities must be based either on previous project designs or performed as an independent step that provides the equivalent of project step 3 deliverables. (If necessary, refer back to Chapter 11, *What is Project Management?* for a discussion of the project model deliverables in the various project steps.)

Technical specifications provide a standard against which alternative vendor products or services can be measured. When competitive bidding is involved, a preliminary evaluation step is inserted during the acquisition selection process (step 5 in Figure 19–2) to ensure that all vendor offerings meet the technical specifications before the evaluation phase begins. Buyer-prepared specifications are the best way to address the technical requirements area, and telecommunications management is responsible for ensuring that the appropriate technical information is provided when telecommunications products and services are being acquired.

Step 3: Develop and Document Acquisition Selection Criteria

Acquisition selection criteria refers to those attributes against which vendor proposals will be evaluated. The criteria will identify the mandatory and optional requirement evaluation criteria discussed in the Chapter 7 *Decision Making* section. This decision-making method provides a way for objectively evaluating different choices and is used throughout Part 5 discussions.

Whether a formal or informal bidding process is initiated, the issuer of the bidding document should specify the format that the bidder should use to submit information. This is done to allow objectivity during the evaluation process, because each bidder will be required to submit information in a standard format. In addition, the use of a common format by all bidders eliminates the need for the evaluator to convert bidder information into a standard format when comparing vendor options. The use of a buyer-specified format simplifies the buyer's evaluation process and requires the bidders to use common terminology and definitions to explain their proprietary products. Each vendor's product will have different names, models, and technical specifications that will be used to respond to a purchaser's specifications. The use of a common format will require the vendors to translate their offerings into the buyer's terminology. Vendor market share and history of performance may also vary widely, and it is easy to have the acquisition decision influenced by a professionally orchestrated multimedia show presented by skilled players. Telecommunications equipment is unemotional (computers don't laugh unless programmed to do so) and equipment capabilities can best be evaluated in technical terms. Reviewing public records and contacting user groups of peer telecommunications professionals provides a means for validating equipment and vendor maintenance performance claims submitted by vendors.

Prior to issuing formal or informal acquisition specifications to qualified vendors, the issuer of the specifications should develop a matrix of decision criteria that will be used to select the winner of a bidding process. Preparing a decision matrix in advance assists the buyer during discussions with potential bidders and also helps quantify an evaluation process that has the potential for becoming very personal and emotional for both the buyer and the seller. (Sales personnel do not normally respond well to situations where they have expended a great deal of time and effort but are not selected to provide the product or service requested by the purchaser.)

Step 4: Issue Acquisition Specifications to the Appropriate Vendors

This step in the acquisition process translates the business and technical information developed during the create-specifications step into a format suitable for distribution to suppliers of telecommunications services and products. The documentation issued to prospective suppliers should contain information that clearly defines buyer needs and can be used to generate a response showing how a supplier's product(s) can meet the purchaser's requirements.

Purchase documentation would be sent to qualified suppliers that have an interest in responding to the buyer **RFP.**

In the acquisition process, an RFP is used to define technical product requirements to bidders. The RFP is commonly used for purchasing systems and networks, particularly if the purchase is large, costly, or technically complex. Formal RFPs are used when a formal, competitive bidding process is desired. A formal RFP is a legal contract that requires specific actions on the part of both the issuer of the RFP and the winner of an RFP bidding process. Many desirable elements of the RFP process can be applied in a looser, less binding format by using an informal RFP process. There are many advantages to using the informal approach.

RFI, RFQ, and RFP documentation and processes are used in the acquisition phase and will be discussed in Chapter 20 (*Purchasing Products and Services*).

Step 5: Evaluate Vendor Responses *v.* Acquisition Selection Criteria

Purchase documentation should contain deadlines for the submission of bid proposals and should specify the buyer's timeframe for generating a purchase decision. After bid responses have been received, it will be necessary to evaluate the various proposals and select a winner. The buyer can simplify the evaluation process by documenting evaluation criteria requirements during step 3 in the acquisition model. Step 5 will use an objective, quantifiable method to clarify the decision process and highlight the information used to generate final decisions.

Step 6: Select a Specific Vendor's Product or Service

The selection of a winner during the acquisition process is a byproduct of the evaluation performed in acquisition step 5. The step 6 topic is presented separately to focus on the importance of communicating the decision to both the winners and losers when a bidding process is used. If the selected supplier is the only supplier submitting a proposal, the following comments are not applicable. In a bidding environment, the buyer invites multiple suppliers to bid on a proposal prepared by the buyer. There is a significant work effort involved when responding to RFPs, and suppliers will respond only if they believe that they have a reasonable chance of winning the bid. Therefore, when they are not selected as the winner, bidders have a strong interest in learning why they were not selected—an explanation process that can be painful and emotional if executed poorly. The winner typically does not need much of an explanation, although it should be easy to provide one. It is more important that bidders whose proposals were not selected understand the reason(s) they were not selected. If a bid solicitor (the buyer) is perceived to be unreasonable or to have actually selected a winner in advance of the bidding process, fewer bids may be received the next time a bid is solicited. Bid participants will participate in a bidding process only if they believe they have an opportunity to win the bid, and they must perceive the treatment they receive during the acquisition process as being fair and above board.

When a contract is not involved, the acquisition will be implemented based on the receipt of a purchase order from the buyer. Purchase order requirements are reviewed in this chapter's *Enterprise Purchasing Procedures* section.

Step 7: Acquire the Selected Vendor's Product or Service

In the bidding process, a contract is normally signed with the winning supplier. Once a contract is signed, the bid solicitor should assemble a project team to manage the vendor interface and to ensure that both parties (bidder and bid initiator) meet the contract terms. The successful bidder will typically provide members for the implementation effort to create a coordinated, cooperative climate during the postacquisition phase.

When a purchase order has been used instead of a contract, the product or service will be delivered in accordance with the purchase requisition terms.

Operate the Implemented System/Network

While not shown on the acquisition model in Figure 19–2, the last step in acquiring telecommunications products is to use the product or services. Regardless of whether the acquisition effort was part of a project or was carried out independently, the acquisition team has the responsibility for documenting procedures that describe the operational requirements for the equipment. Normally, operations management would be part of the implementation team, and the operations manager would agree to accept operational responsibility for the acquisition only if the necessary documentation and training has been provided to operations personnel. For smaller projects carried out as part of normal operations activities, the operations department may handle the project acquisition process.

ENTERPRISE PURCHASING PROCEDURES

Purchasing procedures will vary for different businesses. It is the responsibility of the telecommunications managers to understand the purchasing requirements of their businesses. The preceding acquisition process discussion assumed that the telecommunications manager would follow the business's purchasing policies. Figure 19–3 provides a general flowchart of a typical purchasing process found in a business.

If the flowchart looks complicated, it is because the purchasing process is complicated. *It should be*. The use of funds for purchasing equipment and services is a process that must be tightly controlled to minimize the potential for misusing funds. The purchasing, legal ser-

vices, receiving, accounts payable, and telecommunications departments shown in Figure 19–3 are internal departments.

The telecommunications department has responsibility for identifying the viable suppliers for different telecommunications products and services, and must use a selection process based on the technical and business criteria highlighted by the design and selection process in Figure 19–3. To purchase equipment or services, the telecommunications department would send a purchase requisition to the purchasing department, and the purchasing department would send a purchase order to the supplier and inform the accounts payable department of the purchase. The accounts payable department provides the auditing and control function over purchases and ensures that

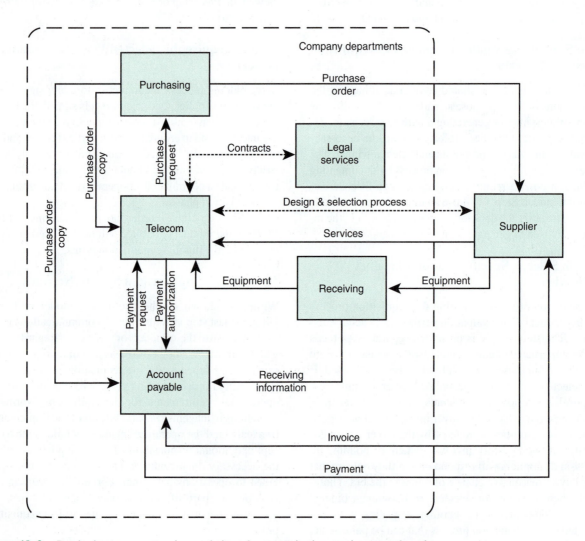

Figure 19–3. Purchasing process overview: ordering telecommunications equipment and services.

TABLE 19–1   Generic Purchase Order Process Description

Activity	Description
Purchase requisition preparation by the originator	The originator of the purchase requisition must fill in all required information on the form and obtain the necessary approval signatures—the number of signatures is dependent on the size of the purchase. The purchase requisition is then forwarded to the purchasing department.
	Spending levels are controlled by the finance department. The spending level authorization is based on managerial level and the job requirements of the position. If the purchase requisition amount exceeds the manager's approval limit, the appropriate approval level signatures must be obtained to authorize the purchase order.
Purchasing department	After verifying that all the required information and approvals have been included, a purchase order number is assigned and the purchase requisition becomes an active purchase order (PO).
	The purchasing department will return PO copies to: 1) the originator, 2) accounts payable (A/P), 3) receiving, and 4) the supplier.
Supplier	Upon receipt of the PO, the vendor will initiate the paperwork needed to send the product and/or install the service. Once the product is sent or the service is installed, the supplier will send a bill to the A/P department.
Receiving	If the PO item is delivered to the receiving dock (equipment), the receiving dock enters the information into a database that is used by A/P to initiate a payment authorization from the PO originator.
	If a service is acquired, the PO originator has the responsibility for coordinating installation requirements.
Accounts payable	A/P will initiate a request for bill payment after the bill is received from the supplier and its receipt, for a hard goods item is acknowledged by the receiving department.
	Upon receipt of the payment approval from the originator, A/P pays the bill and informs purchasing that the PO activity has been completed.

enterprise funds are used appropriately and vendors are paid only for products and services that have been received.

While some of the specific procedures in Table 19–1 may differ in different companies, all acquisitions activities referenced in the table are needed to order standard items with purchase orders. For large acquisitions (e.g., telecommunications networks and systems), these procedures are modified in accordance with the business's guidelines established for large acquisitions.

If a telecommunications purchase requires the establishment of a formal contract between the supplier and the business, the telecommunications manager is responsible for documenting these requirements, enlisting the assistance of the legal services department, obtaining the necessary company and supplier authorization signatures, and including the contract information with the purchase requisition.

Once the supplier has received a purchase order, the product (typically equipment) or service is delivered to the enterprise. Equipment would be delivered to the receiving department, which would deliver the equipment to the telecommunications department and would also inform the accounts payable department of the equipment delivery. Services (long distance call or local call services) would be delivered to the business and the supporting details would be sent to the telecommunications department by the supplier. The telecommunications department would review the service billing details, ensure their accuracy, and approve the service invoice for payment by accounts payable.

Telecommunications Purchasing Responsibilities

In a large business, ordering telecommunications products and services is a major activity that involves significant cash flow, and the telecommunications purchasing activity may be distributed throughout the telecommunications department. Figure 19–4 shows the generic telecommunications department chart discussed previously in Chapter 15, *What is Operations Management?* The following discussion reviews telecommunications purchasing responsibilities within the context of Figure 19–4.

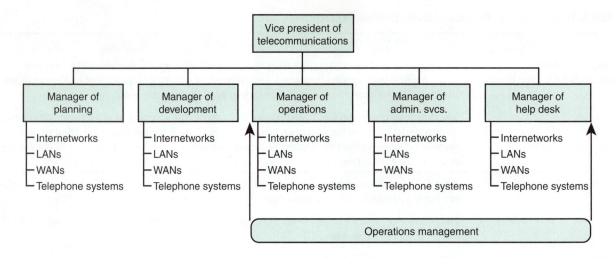

Figure 19–4. An example of a generic telecommunications department.

Most of a business's telecommunications purchases are handled by the operations management department. They have the direct responsibility for providing services to the business, and they receive and approve the bills from external telecommunications suppliers for business communications products and services. Annual purchase requisitions may be established by operations management departments for standard services supplied by telecommunications service providers to ensure that the service billing process conforms to purchasing control standards. In Figure 19–4, the administrative services department would review the service billing details and give the necessary payment approvals to the accounts payable department.

Equipment purchases are initiated by the department that needs the equipment—typically the development or operations departments. The operations department would order equipment for repairs, upgrades, and spare parts, activities that are ongoing and carried out within the context of the department's operating budget. Operations would approve payment for equipment purchases once they have received the equipment.

For large projects that add new facilities or significantly modify existing systems and networks, the development department would originate the necessary equipment purchase requisitions. There is a strong likelihood that RFPs will be used for large projects and that contracts will be required. The development department would use the legal services department to establish contracts and is directly responsible for carrying out contract administration activities for any projects they initiate. As part of the project management process, the development

department may also negotiate long-term pricing for telecommunications products and services that are needed for the project. At the completion of the project, these contractual maintenance and payment responsibilities would be transferred to the appropriate operations management department.

ACQUISITION PAYMENT OPTIONS

There are three basic payment modes available for the acquisition of telecommunications products and services: 1) a payment of cash, 2) leasing, and 3) rental. When asset purchases are involved, Internal Revenue Services (IRS) accounting procedures must be followed to convert asset costs into tax deductible expenses (the depreciation process). For other types of purchases, a tax deductible expense is generated immediately. In either case, the telecommunications manager should have an understanding of the accounting methods used by the finance department to handle assets and expenses and follow the appropriate company accounting policies and procedures.

Cash Payment

Cash payments (this actually consists of mailing checks) may be used to purchase telecommunications products and services. When a fixed asset is purchased, the depreciation expense accounting procedures would be followed. (For text problems, the **straight line method of depreciation** will be used.) For other purchase modes, normal expense analysis procedures should be used.

Lease Payment

A lease is a legal rental contract that gives somebody (the lessee) exclusive possession and use of another's property (the lessor) for a specific length of time in return for regular payments being made to the lessor during the time span of the lease. The lease contract between the lessor and lessee documents the payment schedule and outlines the responsibilities assumed by the lessee for use of the lessor's property. Unless stipulated otherwise in the lease contract, a lessee is responsible for any operating costs associated with using the asset. The lease contract may also specify the standard level of usage that the lessee can exercise during the lease time period and penalties if the usage exceeds contractual limits. (This latter constraint is commonly found when automobiles are leased.)

For example, a business may lease a car from an automobile leasing company for a three-year period at a cost of $550 per month, with the stipulation that the annual mileage cannot exceed 15,000 miles. If the mileage is greater than 15,000 miles per year, the lessee will pay a penalty for the additional mileage. At the end of the lease period, the lessee returns the leased asset to the lessor and the lessor may sell the asset or lease it to someone else.

WHY LEASE?   It is possible to lease virtually anything, including telecommunications equipment. The lessor receives a profit from the asset over the life of the asset and as long as this profit justifies the ownership role, the lessor will stay in business. Because the lease duration is typically a significant portion of the asset's life, the profit margin is predictable and the lessor receives payments on a regular schedule. The lessor's incentive is to make a profit on the leasing operation and ensure that a net positive cash flow (revenue) is generated when leasing assets are purchased and leased.

From a lessee viewpoint, the major difference between purchasing the asset directly and leasing the asset is in the treatment of lease costs. Lease costs are operating expenses that are written off during the time period they are incurred. Therefore, the lessee views leased asset costs as a pure operating expense without the need to use depreciations schedules or become involved with depreciation accounting requirements. With leasing, accounting requirements are simplified for the lessee, and there is no need to purchase or depreciate the asset.

The selection of a lease or purchase option is a finance department responsibility and is typically a matter of corporate policy that may vary for different asset categories. There is a bias toward leasing if computer equipment is involved, because the functional life is frequently shorter than the asset life allowed by the IRS.

Telecommunications managers should be familiar with both the philosophy and procedures used by the finance department when evaluating purchase versus lease options. Telecommunications equipment acquisitions may require the submission of lease and purchase options, or may simply involve following a mandated purchase or lease procedure.

LEASING   TELECOMMUNICATIONS   EQUIPMENT.   When telecommunications equipment is leased, the business (the lessee) assumes contractual responsibility for:

1. using the equipment for the length of the lease period
2. making lease payments as specified in the lease contract
3. using the asset as specified in the lease contract
4. paying the costs associated with the use of the equipment

Under ideal conditions, there would be no changes required to the leased asset. However, in the real world, it may be necessary to 1) have a major upgrade to the equipment to gain additional capacity or 2) terminate the lease prior to reaching the lease termination date. The following discusses these scenarios.

LEASED ASSET UPGRADE.   Because the lessor owns the equipment, any major upgrade must be initiated through the lessor to ensure that the upgrade conforms to their standards. Major upgrades increase the value of an asset, which will be reflected in a change in lease payments. A supplemental contract will be required, where the upgrade cost is incorporated into the lease payments made during the remainder of the lease.

EARLY LEASE TERMINATION.   Penalties are invoked when leases are terminated early. While the asset may be largely intact, the lessor may have other one-time costs that were allocated over the lease's time period and reflected in future lease payments. Early termination penalties should be specified in the lease contract and are typically higher during the early stages of a lease cycle than later in the cycle.

At the termination of the leasing contract, the lessee may be given the option of renewing the lease (typically under a reduced lease payment rate) or purchasing the asset. The financial analysis used to evaluate leasing options should be based on the company's finance department guidelines.

LEASING CAVEATS. Leases are legal contracts that commit the lessee to specified payments during a specified time period. Failure to meet monetary, time, or technical lease contract conditions is a breach of law and the lessor has the right to go to court to enforce the conditions of the lease or to receive penalty payments for contract nonconformance. Paying for contractual nonconformance always has the potential for involving additional penalty payments to compensate for any inconveniences created for the contract holder.

Leasing contracts are used extensively in the business world and the format is largely standardized. However, the reasonability of a lease contract is a matter of perspective, and lessors and lessees have varying definitions of *reasonability*. Lease contracts should be reviewed by the enterprise's legal department to ensure that the contract is reasonable from a lessee perspective. In addition, telecommunications technical specialists should review the technical support requirements to ensure that they are also reasonable.

If the lessee has identified usage requirements accurately over the lease period and has done a good job of technology planning, these elements should be incorporated into the leasing arrangement and both parties will benefit.

Rent Payment

The only conceptual difference between a lease and rental option is normally the length of the pricing commitment between the service provider and the service user. A lease provides price protection for the duration of the lease, while rental rates are normally variable from payment time period to payment time period. The service provider has the option of increasing service rates between time periods, and the service user has the option of terminating (normally without penalty) the use of services at the end of time periods. When a monthly billing cycle is used for telecommunications services, the lease or rental period would be expressed in months.

Leasing agreements are used by service users to obtain lower prices than are available with normal (rental) monthly rates. In return for these better rates, the service user commits to utilizing the services at the lease rate for the entire lease period. Early termination of the lease by the service user will normally require the payment of penalties that are spelled out in the leasing contract.

TELECOMMUNICATIONS SERVICE CONTRACTS

The acquisition process associated with obtaining telecommunications products and services requires knowledge of contract management procedures, because contractual agreements frequently must be established as part of the acquisition process. A relatively recent (circa early 1990s) contractual activity is **outsourcing,** the assignment of tasks and responsibilities formerly carried out by internal employees to outside organizations called outsourcers. The following section will discuss the general aspects of contract management and will discuss outsourcing and its antonym—**insourcing**—the use of internal employees to perform tasks or functions that could be performed by outsourcers.

Contract Management

Contracts are legally binding agreements established between the buyers and sellers of products and services. Contracts may be established for various telecommunications purchasing activities that involve:

- equipment purchases
- consulting services
- equipment installation and maintenance services
- long distance network services

Contracts are legally binding documents that place obligations upon both buyers and sellers of products or services. The contract terms typically specify the payment amount, a schedule of payments, the period of time over which payments are made, and any penalties that are applicable if the buyer or seller does not abide by the terms of the contract. Contracts for telecommunications equipment and services may also contain technical criteria that define the standards or performance measurements used to determine acceptability of the seller's equipment or service.

Telecommunications managers should employ the counsel of individuals who are familiar with contractual law and should follow their recommendations when costs are high or the potential risk of failure is high.

Equipment Purchases

A body of law exists—**Uniform Commercial Code (UCC)** —that applies to all equipment purchases in the U.S., except for the state of Louisiana. The UCC provides protection for buyers regarding merchantability and fitness for purpose. **Merchantability** is defined as the requirement that new equipment must conform to generally accepted industry standards, while **fitness for purpose** requires new equipment to be warranted to fulfill the purpose for which it was manufactured but not for other purposes that were not intended.

As a result, the UCC provides what can be called an *implicit warranty* that can be used if the equipment provider does not give an explicit, or written, warranty. When explicit warranties are given, they supersede the implicit UCC warranty. If equipment that does not meet the UCC merchantability or fitness of purpose criteria is purchased, the buyer can use the UCC provisions and attempt to recover the cost of the equipment through legal procedures. The legal process of using the UCC incurs litigation costs and the cost of winning must be evaluated against the value received.

The UCC covers only new equipment. Generally, used equipment is sold in an as-is condition unless the seller provides a separate written warranty. As-is equipment is subject to the warranty provided by the seller and there is no recourse to obtain UCC protection for used equipment. UCC provisions are not applicable to any services.

From a telecommunications manager's perspective, it is important that any equipment warranties are read and understood prior to acquiring equipment, and that copies of any warranties are kept on file in the event of equipment problems. In addition, because contracts are legally binding documents, it is important that telecommunications managers obtain legal counsel when significant equipment purchases are planned or being negotiated so that their business's interests are protected.

PURCHASE ORDERS V. SALES AGREEMENTS. When equipment is purchased, the buyer uses a purchase order to order the equipment and the seller issues a sales agreement for the equipment. Both documents typically have terms and conditions written on them, and each set of conditions protects the interests of the party who issued them.

A seller's sales agreements may include language that supersedes the purchase order terms, such as: "It is expressly agreed, however, that any terms and conditions on such a form that are contrary to the terms of this agreement, or which add terms or conditions beyond those contemplated in this agreement or its attachments, will be null, void, and of no effect. The rights and obligations of the parties as set forth herein may only be altered by written amendment or modification executed by both parties." In other words: "Let the buyer beware."

It is the responsibility of a telecommunications manager to understand the terms and conditions under which they will be buying equipment and to use legal counsel to ensure that they protect the interests of their employer.

NEGOTIATING PURCHASE CONTRACTS. When an RFP is used to purchase equipment, the RFP's terms and conditions may amend or supersede the seller's sales agreement. (RFPs will be discussed further in Chapter 20, *Evaluating Purchase Options.*) To ensure that the proper protection is provided when an RFP is being used, the telecommunications manager should utilize the appropriate legal and RFP preparation expertise.

Consulting Service Contracts

Consultants are used to provide specialized knowledge, and outside consulting services are typically used to fulfill five basic needs:

- to obtain specialized expertise
- to obtain a third party opinion
- to address temporary work overload conditions
- to gain internal credibility
- to act as a "lightning rod" in sensitive situations

A contract is normally written when consulting services are purchased, and the same issues discussed under the *Contract Management* section apply in this situation.

SELECTION CRITERIA. Selecting telecommunications consulting resources is a telecommunications management responsibility. The selection process is primarily one of asking the right questions and following up on the answers to ensure that the question responses were accurate. The easiest way to begin the consultant selection process is to list the general questions that should be asked:

1. What is the consultant's track record when providing consulting assistance for the activity for which they are being considered? The response should be backed up with documented project results.

2. Are there previous customers who have received consulting assistance that can be contacted to determine their level of satisfaction with the consultant's performance?

3. What are the qualifications of the project team members who would be assigned to the consulting project? The consulting business would respond to

The depreciation values for service years and salvage value are specified in IRS schedules, which must be followed when calculating depreciation values. The following section is an example of the straight line method calculation for a telephone system installation:

Straight Line Element	Value
Service life	Five years
Salvage value	10% of initial asset costs
Initial asset cost	Equipment cost: $850,000
	Shipping costs: $500
	Installation costs: $10,000

Calculations:

Description	Detail$
Equipment	$850,000
Shipping	$5,000
Installation	$10,000
Initial asset cost$	$865,000
Scrap value	$86,500
Depreciation ($/year)	$155,700

IRS Factors:

Straight Line	Value
Service life (years)	5
Salvage value	10%

In this example, the cost that will be depreciated is $865,000. Because the scrap value is 10%, the depreciation calculation will be:

$$155,700 = \frac{(865,000 - 86,000)}{5}$$

or

$$155,700 = \frac{(865,000 \times 90\%)}{5}$$

To demonstrate that the deprecation process recovers the cost of the asset, consider the following:

$$(5 \times 155,700) + 86,500 = 778,500 + 86,500 = 865,000$$

At the end of five years, the system is worth $86,500 (its salvage value), while $778,000 has been written off in depreciation expenses. The asset value of $86,500 indicates that this is either the remaining usefulness (functional life) or its scrap material value. Disposing of the asset for $86,500 would allow the business to recover all of the costs associated with owning the asset.

The business's financial department is responsible for managing the asset depreciation process and ensuring that IRS guidelines are followed. Each enterprise asset has a depreciation account that indicates the status of converting asset costs into operating expenses. At the end of the asset's useful life, the only cost that remains is the scrap value of the asset, which may be zero or some other residual amount. The accounting department maintains these records.

PREMISES CABLING STANDARD

Although this text primarily covers nontechnical topics, the **ANSI/TIA/EIA** 568A premises cabling standard warrants coverage as a text topic. A telecommunications manager is responsible for selecting technologies that conform to an overall technology architecture. Technology architectures identify the necessary protocols and network-oriented standards, but they typically ignore the mundane issue of **premises cabling.** Premises cabling problems are a common source of technical problems despite the fact that a standard—ANSI/TIA/EIA T568A—exists. Use of the ANSI/TIA/EIA standard will minimize the potential for cabling problems and will ensure the long-term viability of a premises cabling infrastructure investment.

The following will focus on the conceptual elements of the premises cabling standard and suggests that the ANSI/TIA/EIA standard should be viewed as an addendum to the managerial tools and techniques topics covered earlier in the text.

Introduction

In today's business environment, it is common for most employees to have both a telephone set and a PC on their desktop workspace and have access to other desktop equipment, including facsimile machines, desktop printers, etc. This type of office equipment requires attachment to central equipment or network facilities (e.g., PBX telephone systems, LANs, WANs) and the end-user devices are generically referred to as station equipment. Cable outlets are provided at user locations for an interface between different types of station equipment and the network facilities. The medium most commonly used for premises cabling is typically copper or fiber optics cable.

A structured wiring system provides a premises-based design that minimizes the need for adding, modifying, or removing telecommunications cabling when personnel (and their associated station equipment) are relocated during normal business operations. The use of premises cabling standards for the various cabling components provides a modular architecture that simplifies the addition, removal, or relocation of station equipment. Cross-connect facilities at key locations on the premises offer the capability to change cabling connections between station equipment outlets and central equipment and/or communications networks. Figure 19–5 illustrates a structured premises wiring system layout.

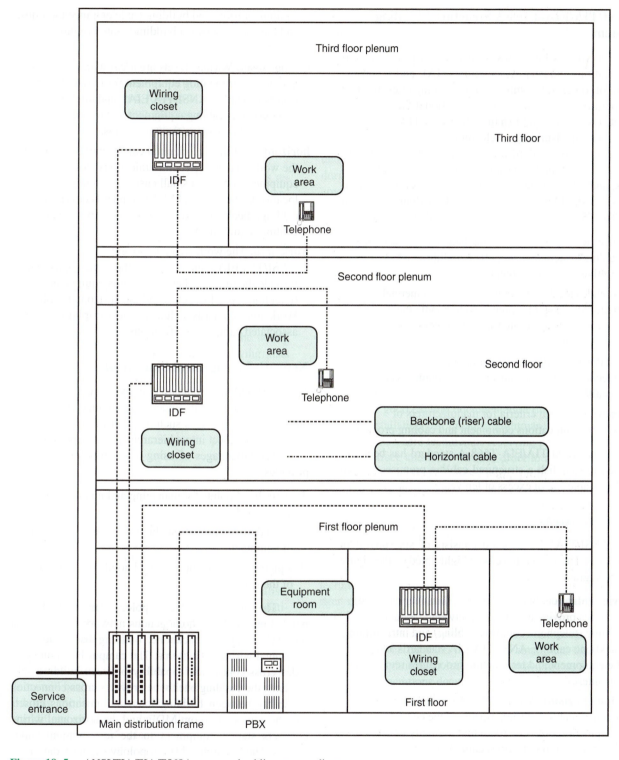

Figure 19–5. ANSI/TIA/EIA/T568A structured cabling system diagram.

11. Outsourcing is the use of outside contractors to perform tasks or functions that were traditionally performed by organization employees. Outsourcing of computer and communication functions started during the mid-1980s, and the use of outsourcing is now widespread as an alternative to maintaining an internal department. Prior to January 1, 1984, the Bell System provided all telecommunications products and services in the U.S.—all U.S. companies outsourced their telecommunications needs. The telecommunications manager should be aware of outsourcing alternatives to internally provided telecommunications services and should continually evaluate internal *v.* outsourcing options. The results of the evaluation should be used to improve internal operations or generate a recommendation to utilize the outsourcing option.

12. While the ANSI/TIA/EIA T568A premises cabling standard is a technical standard, the benefits it provides are managerial benefits. The use of the 568A standard results in a cabling infrastructure that is based on establishing a long-term (ten or more years) investment that handles both voice and data communication requirements and can be modified to meet a wide range of communication requirements. It provides the telecommunications manager with an architectural approach to premises cabling, while defining detailed specifications at the practical level for communications media, cable racks, cable entrance access, cable connectors, distribution frames, etc.

KEY TERMS AND CONCEPTS

The language of telecommunications management is multifaceted and includes words and phrases from managerial, technological, accounting, regulatory, and other business areas. The definitions of these key terms and concepts can be found within the chapter and in the glossary.

Acquisition	Lease	RFQ
ANSI/TIA/EIA	Merchantability	Seven Step Telecommunications
Asset Obsolescence	Outsourcing	Acquisition Model
Common Carrier	Premises Cabling	Straight Line Method Of depreciation
Disaster Planning	Purchase	System Integration
Facilities Management	Rent	Telecommunications Project Life Cycle
Fitness for Purpose	RFI	model
Insourcing	RFP	Uniform Commercial Code (UCC)

REVIEW

The following questions are open-ended,—predefined answers are not included as part of the text. The purpose of these questions is to allow the readers to test themselves on the chapter material.

1. Describe the four underlying requirements that should be built into the selection process when acquiring a new telecommunications product or service.

2. List and briefly summarize the seven steps used in the seven step telecommunications acquisition model.

3. Describe the processing environment shown in Figure 19–3.

4. Describe the steps in a generic purchasing cycle (reference Table 19–1).

5. What are the three different acquisition options for acquiring telecommunications products and services? What are the advantages and disadvantages associated with each?

6. Why are domestic long distance call tariffs not an issue today?

7. Describe the UCC and how a telecommunications manager would use it.

8. What is the difference between purchase orders and sales agreements?

9. When would outside consulting services be used? Describe the selection criteria that should be used to select consultants.

10. What is outsourcing? What is insourcing? What are their roles within a telecommunications context?

11. How does a fixed asset become obsolete?

12. Describe the straight line depreciation method and its cost recovery philosophy.

13. Describe the ANSI/TIA/EIA standards and their values from a managerial perspective.

MULTIPLE CHOICE

1. The acquire components phase of the telecommunications project life cycle model is _____.
   a. project step 1
   b. project step 2
   c. project step 3
   d. project step 4
   e. project step 5

2. The project step when the purchase recommendations are made is _____.
   a. project step 1
   b. project step 2
   c. project step 3
   d. project step 4
   e. project step 5

3. The _____ identifies the costs incurred for a fixed asset from the time of purchase until it is scrapped.
   a. present value factor
   b. project cutover
   c. return on investment
   d. project step 5
   e. life cycle analysis

4. Acquisition model step _____ evaluates the various bidder responses.
   a. 3
   b. 4
   c. 5
   d. 6
   e. 7

5. To simplify the vendor evaluation effort, the RFP should be in the _____ format.
   a. purchasing department's
   b. buyer's
   c. vendor's
   d. supplier's
   e. telecommunications project life cycle model's

6. The format used to convey complex, technical information for obtaining bids from suppliers is a(n) _____ format.
   a. RFI
   b. RFQ
   c. RFP
   d. telecommunications acquisition model
   e. purchase order

7. If a formal RFP is used to acquire equipment, the _____ identifies the equipment performance specifications.
   a. UCC
   b. legal department
   c. purchase order
   d. RFP
   e. RFQ

8. The telecommunications _____ department handles most of an enterprise's telecommunications purchases.
   a. planning
   b. development
   c. help desk
   d. accounting
   e. operations

9. When a fixed asset is _____, the associated expense will be recovered in future time periods.
   a. acquired
   b. leased
   c. subleased
   d. purchased
   e. rented

10. The _____ form of acquisition involves a contractual agreement.
    a. lease
    b. rental
    c. purchase
    d. hiring
    e. lending

11. A term used to describe the use of in-house employees to provide telecommunications products and services is _____.
    a. rightsizing
    b. contract management
    c. insourcing
    d. outsourcing
    e. reengineering

12. The warranty protection provided by the UCC is a(n) _____ warranty.
    a. explicit
    b. implicit
    c. lease
    d. service
    e. long range

13. The UCC applies to _____.
    a. services
    b. maintenance contracts
    c. used equipment
    d. new equipment

14. The abbreviation UCC stands for _____.
    a. Universal Commercial Code
    b. Uniform Code of Commerce
    c. Ultra Conservative Code
    d. Uniform Commercial Code
    e. merchantability

15. In the 2002 telecommunications environment, network services rates are determined by _____.
    a. Universal Commercial Code
    b. the FCC
    c. the PUC
    d. LECs
    e. contractual agreements

16. If straight line depreciation is used, the initial cost of an asset is $100,000, and its scrap value is $5,000, what is the depreciation per year assuming a five year asset life?
    a. $5,000
    b. $12,000
    c. $15,000
    d. $19,000
    e. $20,000

17. The ANSI/TIA/EIA standard area that specifies the interface between end users and the premises cabling system is the _____ standard.
    a. equipment room
    b. backbone cabling
    c. wiring closet
    d. horizontal cabling
    e. work area

20

PURCHASING PRODUCTS AND SERVICES

LEARNING OBJECTIVES

1. Understand the concept of best price as it applies to the acquisition of telecommunications products and services.

2. Understand the technology implications of documenting the acquisition selection criteria in acquisition step 3.

3. Understand the basic reasons that necessitate the acquisition of telecommunications products and services.

4. Understand the basic format requirements for establishing documentation for acquisition step 3 (selection criteria).

5. Understand the use of RFI procedures to identify potential vendors in the acquisition process.

6. Understand the use of RFQ and RFP procedures in requesting bids from vendors.

7. Understand the advantages and disadvantages of using a formal RFP process to acquire telecommunications products and services.

8. Understand the general format and content of an RFP.

9. Understand purchase authorization approval levels and how they are used when telecommunications products and services are acquired.

10. Understand the common sense control guidelines that should be applied to the telecommunications acquisition process.

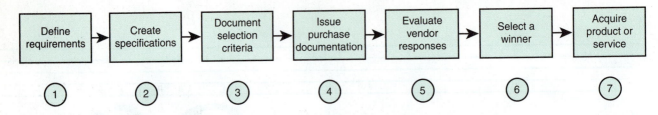

Figure 20–1. Seven step telecommunications acquisition model.

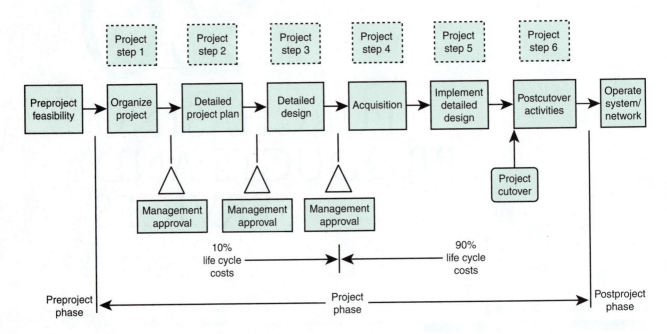

Figure 20–2. Telecommunications project life cycle model.

Telecommunications technologies are complex and, as a result, many of the acquisition decisions associated with the purchase of telecommunications products and services are also complex. In Chapter 19, *Purchasing Process Overview,* the overall acquisition process was examined and separated into seven individual activities shown as a flowchart diagram (Figure 20–1).

Telecommunications product and service acquisitions may be carried out independently (Figure 20–1) or within a project context, as shown in Figure 20–2.

When telecommunications products and services are acquired, it is an activity generated by the operating environment shown in Figure 20–3: a generic telecommunications department. This structure is typical, although the actual name given to the individual departments may differ. For large projects, the development department initiates and manages the acquisition process within the

project framework shown in the life cycle model. When operations management departments acquire telecommunications products and services, it is frequently in a non-project mode and the acquisition model would be used. While the acquisition costs associated with development projects is large, most of the dollars spent for telecommunications products and services flow through **operations management** to pay for maintenance contracts, network services contracts, local telephone company services, and numerous ad hoc operations projects that replace or upgrade equipment.

This chapter will thoroughly address two activities shown in Figure 20–1: acquisition steps 3 (document selection criteria) and 4 (issue purchase documentation). Chapter 21, *Evaluating Acquistion Options,* will discuss the activities included in acquisition steps 5 (evaluate vendor responses) and 6 (select winner) in detail.

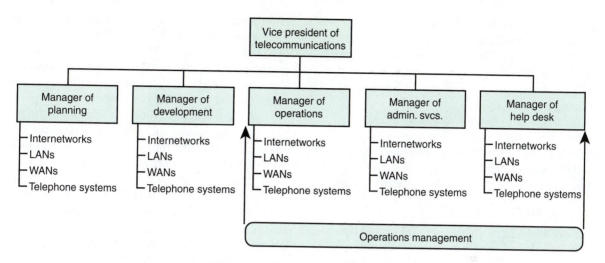

Figure 20–3. A generic telecommunications department structure.

WHAT WILL BE ACQUIRED?

The funding used to acquire telecommunications products and services originate from three sources:

1. They are outcomes of the normal financial planning process in which strategic plans have been converted into implementation budgets.

2. The need for funds is unexpected and arises when telecommunications operations needs unplanned acquisitions.

3. The need for funds is in unexpected responses required to support ad hoc business management requests.

Acquisitions that result from planned activities (item 1) have been identified during the organization's annual planning cycles, but the other two items are unplanned events.

The Rules of Acquisition

When the cost for individual pieces of equipment (fixed assets) exceeds levels defined by the IRS, the costs for these expenses must be recovered through the depreciation process. Therefore, the accounting department maintains an ongoing interface with ad hoc equipment purchases initiated by the operations department. When the equipment replacement cost is below the IRS expense threshold, the equipment expense will be recovered by using normal accounting expensing procedures. However, when the equipment replacement cost exceeds the expense threshold provided by the IRS, the acquisition costs must

be recovered through the depreciation process. The accounting department administers and controls the depreciation of all fixed assets, including telecommunications equipment.

Telecommunications managers need to be familiar with the criteria used by accounting to define normal operating expenses and those that must be recovered through the depreciation accounting process.

Planned Acquisitions

During the annual planning cycle when budgets are created, reviewed, and approved, capital expenditure forecasts are developed for telecommunications projects that require a major purchase of equipment and services. The funding for telecommunications project acquisitions is included within the project budget framework. The primary concerns of the telecommunications managers assigned to the project are 1) gaining sufficient funding and 2) the effective and efficient implementation of project activities.

In addition to planning for major project expenditures, the planning process provides funding for ongoing operations, which is reflected in department budgets. In telecommunications operations management budgets, allowances are provided for maintaining the existing telecommunications infrastructure elements (LANs, WANs, internetworks, telephone systems, etc.) and for ad hoc projects that will arise unexpectedly during the fiscal year. Many ad hoc projects cannot be specifically identified (otherwise they would be itemized in the budget) but will be generated in response to equipment breakdowns or unexpected needs for additional capacity. The operations department must provide a budgetary contingency for the cost of equipment replacements due to catastrophic failures and nonforecast traffic growth requirements. There is no simple way to predict that equipment will fail and require replacement—otherwise fail-proof equipment would have been purchased initially.

The best way to forecast equipment replacements in this category is based on history—an approach that has its limitations. In the case of equipment replacements caused by a need to increase equipment capacity, trend data may offer some information to forecast the replacement requirement, but system and network traffic growth is frequently unpredictable. The bottom line is that the experience and judgment of the operations manager will determine how accurate these estimates are. Even the best judgment will be unable to forecast major breakdowns or major increases in system or network traffic due to unforeseen events.

The operations budget should be sufficient to cover normal equipment replacement levels and obvious replacements to increase capacity. When the failure rate exceeds normal expectations, the acquisition process falls under the unplanned category and is covered later in the chapter (*Unplanned Operational Acquisitions*).

PLANNED PROJECT ACQUISITIONS. The justification process for planned projects takes place during the preproject phase, and as long as budgetary surprises are not encountered during the project's implementation, money and staffing should not be issues. Budgetary surprises refer to the unpleasant experience of discovering that expenses will be significantly higher (financial department guidelines address this range) than the original budget forecast. For example, if expenses exceed a 10% contingency guideline, it will be necessary to: 1) inform business management of the increased expense, 2) explain the reason for not accurately forecasting the requirements in the original budget, and 3) provide a detailed project financial plan to show that any request for additional funding will not be repeated during the remainder of the project.

For high cost projects, a lower deviation percentage guideline may exist. It is the job of the telecommunications manager to know how much leeway is allowed by the finance department.

Note: When the actual cost for a project is significantly higher than the funding forecast, the timing for requesting additional funding is a matter of managerial judgment. Delaying the request until the latter stages of the project has the advantage that the potential for encountering additional budgetary surprises is minimized because most of the project will be completed. Therefore, the work effort needed to complete the remaining phases will be more clearly understood. On the other hand, some business managers view early warning of potential budget problems as desirable. Which approach should be chosen? There are no right or wrong answers and personal judgment is the only available guideline.

While less traumatic, there is also the need to inform business management when the actual costs are significantly lower than the funding forecast for implementing the asset or service. In the telecommunications environment, cost reductions for equipment and services are not uncommon, because computer-based technologies continue the trend of providing more capabilities for fewer dollars. If this is the case, the explanation is relatively simple and all parties (business management and telecommunications management) should have a high level of comfort with the explanation if it has been presented clearly. However, if a telecommunications manager has an established track record of consistently requesting more funding than is used, budget surpluses will be seen as a sign of poor forecasting (a managerial accountability). Consistent poor budgeting is an outcome that, when detected, adversely affects the manager's performance rating and personal credibility. Companies have limited funds for investing in assets, facilities, and other areas. When forecast investment funds are not used, it means that other project areas were not funded even though the overall funding monies would have been available if budgets had not been inflated.

PLANNED OPERATIONAL ACQUISITIONS. As noted, an operating contingency is normally included in an operating budget to cover the cost for a reasonable level of unexpected equipment breakdowns, after which the equipment cannot be repaired and must be replaced. In addition, the operations budget may also show allowances for the planned replacement or addition of communication equipment to meet growth and technology planning needs. The budget typically includes cost increases over the previous year's budget to meet the projected increases in outside service costs.

Planned operations acquisitions are initiated by issuing standard purchase requisitions to telecommunications suppliers (refer to Chapter 19, *Purchasing Process Overview*). The original design specifications that were prepared when a system or network was installed become the technical specifications used to order services and equipment during its operational life. Larger operations projects would be handled as part of a formal project initiative, assuming that sufficient lead time has been provided to forecast the need in the operations budget. Otherwise, an unplanned operational acquisition may be required.

Unplanned Operational Acquisitions

If the normal replacement, upgrading, or addition of equipment is included in the operations budget, unplanned acquisitions are not issues unless the expense level exceeds budget limits. If this is the case, the operations manager must explain the reason for the budget shortfall and get approval for spending beyond the amount provided in the operating budget.

An operations manager who requires funding approval for an unplanned capital expenditure that cannot be handled within the operating budget is placed in the uncomfortable position of having to: 1) explain why the event was not forecast in the budget and 2) escalate the request for a special budget allocation through the management hierarchy. Major unplanned expenses are an unpleasant experience for everyone. The telecommunications manager must explain how it happened and what could have been done to prevent it from occurring, and the accounting department must find the money from a budget source other than the operation department's budget. If there is one managerial guideline to be followed regarding unplanned operating acquisitions, it is "avoid or delay them, if at all possible."

Unplanned Business-Driven Acquisitions

It is also possible that changing business conditions may generate a need for telecommunications assets and services to be acquired in an unplanned mode. The source that generates the acquisition need may be positive or negative. It could be triggered by the need to immediately add facilities and staffing because of unprecedented sales success (a positive reason) or having to acquire telecommunications products services to rebuild a communications infrastructure that was lost because of fire or water damage (a negative reason). In both cases, the business needs dictate the overriding mandate for adding or replacing telecommunications products and services. However, implicit in any business driven mandate is the expectation that telecommunications managers will generate the necessary financial paperwork to justify the required funding.

In all cases where the acquisition of telecommunications products or services is required—planned or unplanned—the planning process conducted by telecommunications managers is similar. The only difference is the time frame provided for generating the supporting paperwork and the climate under which the paperwork is prepared. By any measure, it is a more pleasant to have adequate time to prepare a budget in a planned mode than it is to have to react quickly to an equipment breakdown that must be fixed before communications can be restored.

HOW WILL IT BE ACQUIRED?

In Chapter 19, *Purchasing Process Overview,* three acquisition options were discussed: paying cash, leasing, or renting. In many organizations, the acquisition option that will be used for acquiring fixed assets will be set by the finance department and will be based on the financial philosophy of the business. If a need to conserve cash existed, the lease option would be the preferred method; if the corporation were cash rich, the purchase option may be preferred.

From a telecommunications management perspective, the acquisition method used is a secondary consideration in the product selection process, therefore enterprise guidelines will be used. However, a telecommunications manager continues to be responsible for ensuring the accuracy of all cost information used to initiate project or operations acquisition purchases so that the enterprise receives good value for its purchasing dollars—regardless of how or why telecommunications products and services are acquired.

ACQUISITION PROCESS STEPS 1–4

Documenting the business requirements, creating technical specifications, and documenting the selection criteria (Figure 20–1 steps 1 and 2; Figure 20–2 steps 1, 2, and 3) required for acquiring telecommunications products and services requires knowledge of telecommunications technology requirements and are activities carried out by technical specialists. Once the technical criteria have been identified, it becomes a matter of reformatting them into a documentation format suitable for distribution to vendors and suppliers. This purchasing documentation is developed in Figure 20–1 step 4 and Figure 20–2. step 3.

Creating purchasing documents when acquiring telecommunications products and services serves two purposes:

1. It clearly identifies the technical requirements a supplier's product or service must meet.

2. It provides a standard, buyer-formatted response that simplifies the evaluation of competitive bids that are received from suppliers.

Combining these two requirements in a single document provides the means for the buyer to control the acquisition process while obtaining pricing information for alternatives. The purchasing documentation options used for this purpose will be discussed in the *Purchase Documentation Development* section.

Acquisition process steps 3 and 4 are a primary focus of this chapter. Step 3 converts the business and technical needs into a decision document that will be used to evaluate acquisition alternatives and provide the decision criteria for making a selection. When multiple bids are received during the acquisition process, the winner will be the choice that best fits the selection criteria.

After step 3 is completed, step 4 is carried out and the purchase documentation is created. The purchase documentation will describe the technical and business requirements that must be met by suppliers and contains any terms and conditions that the buyer places on the acquisition process.

Acquisition Steps 1 and 2

In acquisition steps 1 and 2, the business and technical requirements used in designing system or network elements are identified. In a telecommunications project (Figure 20–2), project steps 1 through 3 provide this information. When a nonproject acquisition is required, the initiator has the responsibility for ensuring that the technical and business requirements are identified and documented prior to proceeding to acquisition step 3.

Acquisition Step 3

Acquisition step 3 (document selection criteria) requires a knowledge of the business and technical specifications established for the product and then identifying those criteria that are needed by suppliers. Technical specialists assigned to the project or operations personnel who have the required skills are needed to correctly identify the technical criteria. Step 3 selection criteria should be written in a format that is quantifiable and easily understood, and the decision making method discussed in Chapter 7 (*Managerial Tools and Techniques*), based on using mandatory and optional requirements, will be used for making acquisition decisions in the text.

MANDATORY REQUIREMENTS. From an administrative and business perspective, **mandatory requirements** would include meeting specific time schedules, cost constraints, or other management criteria. In a telecommunications acquisition, many mandatory requirements are technically driven requirements, such as data transmission speeds, response times, capacity, reliability, compatibility to existing equipment, and conformance to specific standards or protocols. Technical mandatory needs must be clearly highlighted in any documentation given to potential bidders.

If an acquisition alternative does not meet all mandatory requirements (technical, business, or administrative),

Mandatory Requirements
Cutover date: September 5, 2001
Operating line capacity: 400 lines
Wired line capacity: 450 lines
Remote maintenance capabilities
Voice mail messaging
Least-cost routing software
Beige [color] station equipment

Example 20–1. Mandatory requirements example.

it is eliminated from further consideration. Mandatory requirements should be used to screen vendor responses in the early stages of the evaluation process to eliminate unacceptable vendor alternatives as soon as possible. Example 20–1 is an example of a mandatory requirements listing for a telephone system acquisition.

OPTIONAL REQUIREMENTS. When a level of importance or desirability can be attached to a decision factor and it is not a mandatory requirement, it is designated an optional requirement. Optional requirements can be established for business or technical criteria. Example 20–2 provides a table of optional decision factors established for a telephone system acquisition.

In Example 20–2, the weights (the relative importance or desirability of the optional requirement) were established during acquisition Step 3. The ratings are assigned during acquisition Step 5, and the score (rating × weight) is calculated in step 5.

Example 20–2 shows the score calculation process for the initial cost optional requirement. The table provides an easy-to-read format for comparing different option scores and clearly highlights the various decision elements and the process used to calculate them. The identification of key options and assigning weights and ratings to them requires good business and technical judgment. It is unlikely that any single individual will have the depth and breadth of knowledge to develop an entire option listing and rate them. Fortunately, the option table format provides an excellent communications vehicle when using a team to originate weights and rates. The collaborative development of the final scores will result in a final recommendation that reflects a consensus of the team members while also allowing all team members to fully understand the viewpoint of other members in a quantifiable, metric-based format.

An optional evaluation table is also an excellent format to use with business management. When the option descriptions are written clearly and use descriptive terms that are understandable (no technical jargon allowed),

Optional Evaluation Factor	Weight	PBX A		PBX B		PBX C	
		Rating	Score	Rating	Score	Rating	Score
Initial cost	10	6	60	10	100	9	90
Annual operating cost	7						
Vendor viability*	10						
System reliability*	10						
Station equipment features*	6						
Voice messaging integration*	10						
Upgradability*	9						
Environmental requirements*	7						
Administrative tools*	9						
Totals							

*Technical assessment team items: 1 = Low; 10 = High
score = rating × weight

Example 20–2. Telephone system optional requirements example.

business management is in a position of being able to ask the right questions when they see differences between the weights of different **optional requirements** or the ratings given to different vendor alternatives.

At the conclusion of acquisition step 3, a mandatory listing table (Example 20–1) and an optional evaluation table with weights (Example 20–2) would have been completed. They can be used for reviewing project information with business management or for discussions with potential bidders. The mandatory and optional evaluation listings prepared in step 3 will be used in step 5 (evaluate vendor responses) to identify the best choice and select a winner. Information developed during step 3 may be incorporated into the purchasing documentation provided to the vendors (step 4) to highlight requirements they are being asked to address with their product proposals.

Acquisition Step 4 Introduction

During Acquisition Step 4, three activities are completed:

1. Qualified vendors are screened and selected.
2. Purchase documents are developed.
3. Qualified vendors are requested to provide bids.

Acquisition step 4 activities should be coordinated closely with the organization's accounting, purchasing, and legal departments to ensure that the purchase documentation issued to potential product and service providers conforms with enterprise purchasing policies.

Just as it was necessary to prepare the internal paperwork to obtain the funding needed to acquire telecommunications fixed assets and services, it is also necessary to prepare the external paperwork that will be sent to potential providers of products and services. The external paperwork must be in a format that is understandable to potential suppliers and allows them to accurately respond to requests for product and service pricing. Casually selecting a vendor from the local yellow pages directory and asking them to install a telephone system for handling 1,500 employees in six weeks is guaranteed to meet with failure. The request has not addressed four key areas: 1) what are the business and technical requirements the system must provide, 2) is the vendor qualified, 3) can the system or network be implemented in six weeks, and 4) how much will it cost?

If a telephone system is being purchased, a technical design process is needed to translate user functional needs into technical specifications that identify system capacity, features, and telephone set requirements. Once technical specialists have established the technical specifications, the specifications must be converted into a nonproprietary format that can be sent to suppliers that represent a variety of vendor products.

Three common purchasing-based procedures are used to answer the questions that have been raised:

1. **RFI** (Request for Information) procedures
2. **RFQ** (Request for Quotation) procedures
3. **RFP** (Request for Proposal) procedures

The following will discuss the use of RFI, RFQ, and RFP procedures to identify qualified suppliers, create the purchasing documentation, and request bids.

Acquisition Step 4: Vendor Selection

There are a limited number of qualified suppliers available to provide the telecommunications products and services used by businesses. These key suppliers are present at major trade shows, they advertise in trade and industry publications, and they support user groups where their customers meet to identify shared concerns and communicate directly with the supplier's marketing and technical departments.

The process used to identify qualified vendors and their products is called the RFI process. This term will be used in the text whenever a search is initiated to obtain information about a vendor's qualifications or products.

THE RFI PROCESS. The RFI process may be a highly complex or a relatively simple undertaking. The buyer may spend a great deal of time and effort to create a highly detailed requirement document and send it to prospective product suppliers or may simply make a telephone call to a supplier's sales organization and request brochures. Regardless of the level of complexity and detail used to obtain an RFI, the information provided by either the buyer or supplier is not binding for either party. It is neither a commitment by the requestor of information to purchase a product from a vendor nor a commitment by the vendor to provide a product that has performance and price characteristics of any RFI information that is given to the prospective buyer. RFIs are exactly what the letters stand for: request for information. The pricing commitment issues will be addressed by RFQ and RFP procedures.

The first issue that must be addressed when initiating an RFI process is to identify the vendors that should be contacted. Contacting too many vendors can result in a paper storm of irrelevant vendor material that requires time and effort to screen. Contacting too few vendors can prematurely screen out qualified vendors who have potential for satisfying acquisition objectives. Once qualified vendor(s) have been identified and selected, the buyer should provide these vendor(s) with the requirement information they need to configure and price their product offerings.

VENDOR INFORMATION. An experienced telecommunications manager attends trade shows, reads numerous trade publications, is a member of different vendor user groups, has surfed the Internet, and is a member of several professional organizations. If this is the case, the manager will have developed a personal information database (brochures, trade publication articles, etc.) about the products and services of different product vendors.

The telecommunications department in large companies will have ongoing relationships with multiple suppliers of telecommunications products and services, and the marketing departments of these suppliers will normally provide telecommunications personnel with a steady stream of product and service information.

Once a listing of qualified vendors has been created, it is necessary to identify the information that will be requested from the vendor. If an open-ended approach is used, there is a strong likelihood that the requestor will receive a mountain of irrelevant sales brochures. While a survey approach may be appealing and appropriate for inexperienced personnel, experienced telecommunications personnel would be interested in information that is selective and relevant to the specific acquisition. The type and quantity of information will be largely dependent upon the experience of the enterprise's telecommunications personnel. An experienced organization may require only an update about recent product developments or, in the extreme case, may not need any additional information prior to proceeding to the next step of using RFQ or RFP procedures to initiate the purchase decision process.

When a product or service is new to the telecommunications organization, the potential buyer can request the vendor to provide a presentation to describe the product or service. This can take place at either the vendor's site or at the buyer's location, depending upon the number of attendees and the magnitude of the potential sale. When the product is expensive and the vendor perceives that there is a good potential for getting the bid, there is little difficulty obtaining detailed information from vendors. They will gladly bring in the necessary technical and marketing support personnel to increase the odds of making a sale. Attending trade shows, user group meetings, or professional association meetings is one of the best ways to obtain vendor product information and develop a qualified vendor listing for various products.

NATIONAL ACCOUNTS. When a business is a major user of a specific vendor's products or services, it is a common practice for the vendor to dedicate a marketing group to the account. This dedicated resource is generically referred to as a national account. A national account manager (NAM) is assigned to the customer account, and he or she is evaluated on his or her effectiveness in meeting customer needs. (Not surprisingly, the primary measurement criterion for a NAM is the size of the revenue stream derived from the customer organization.) When a national account exists, there will be an ongoing flow of information between the vendor and the customer. Telecommunications personnel will be given ongoing product updates about technical, administrative, and pricing information.

RESEARCH SOURCES. Professional information subscription services such as Auerbach, DataPro, and the Gartner Group offer detailed descriptions of telecommunications vendors and their product offerings. Other sources of information that can be used to identify prospective suppliers include internal documentation about installed systems that are currently in use within the organization—particularly when a system is being replaced because of operating problems. (In the latter case, it may be a reason to bypass them from further consideration in the purchasing process.)

A listing of qualified vendors can be established by using the sources reviewed previously. The criteria for being listed would include the vendor's size, experience, range of product offering supplied, and historical performance record. Preliminary listing information should include the vendor's main location address and various telephone numbers for establishing an initial contact.

REQUESTOR INFORMATION. If a telecommunications organization has a good understanding of its requirements, they should be documented in a short summary requirements statement. This summary should be given to the vendors requested to provide RFI information. At this stage, the requirements documentation would be very general—e.g., the installation location, the number of users, the existing technology infrastructure, and the time frame for the acquisition, etc. This requestor information would be used to quickly screen out vendors that are unable to meet the basic capacity and time frame requirements while also providing qualified vendors with sufficient information so they can configure their product offerings to meet the requirements. Doing a good job of defining basic requirements can provide major time savings for both the buyer and the vendor.

Depending upon the business's culture, it may be appropriate to obtain feedback from upper management during the RFI process. If upper management has vendor biases (for or against) or if product appearance is important to them, identifying these issues at the start of the acquisition process can significantly reduce the time spent

on pursuing options that have a low likelihood of being approved by upper management.

Once a telecommunications department has identified the products and vendors that have the capability for meeting acquisition requirements, the next phase of acquisition step 4 can be addressed.

Acquisition Step 4: Purchase Documentation Development

This acquisition step 4 activity converts the technical requirements (acquisition steps 1 and 2) into a format that is suitable for the selected vendors to provide bids. Two existing procedures are available for addressing this requirement: RFQs and RFPs. The format for these procedures will vary depending upon the product or service and existing purchasing practices. Telecommunications products and services have been acquired for many years, and there is no need to start from scratch when developing RFQ or RFP documentation.

THE RFQ PROCESS. An RFQ is used to obtain formal price quotes from a supplier of commodity type products and commits the supplier to provide the product at the RFQ price within a specified period of time. A commodity type product is one that is commonly maintained in inventory by suppliers and whose technical specifications can easily be identified as part of the product description. When commodity type products are being purchased, the RFQ product information is provided to multiple suppliers and a request is made to obtain a pricing commitment that will be in effect for a time period specified by the potential buyer. The use of RFQs assumes the availability of multiple suppliers that can provide an identical product.

RFQ product specifications typically fall into two categories: 1) instances where a standard specification is used to identify product requirements and 2) when the brand name or model uniquely identifies the product. The former approach is commonly used by government agencies when they describe a standard government specification and request the supplier to identify different vendor products that meet these specifications. In the latter case, the brand and model information will uniquely identify the product specifications, and different product suppliers will be asked to provide pricing for the same vendor product.

RFQs place the buyer in the position of being able to identify several equivalent vendor offerings for which the only variable will be product pricing received from different bidders. Purchases can be made at the RFQ price during the time frame specified in the RFQ, and prospective buyers can issue RFQ requests periodically to identify the best deals on an ongoing basis. Purchasing departments frequently use a never-ending RFQ process to maintain a listing of the prices for products they commonly use, and RFQs provide a relatively simple mechanism for obtaining the best price when standard products are purchased. When the product complexity increases (systems and networks are complex products), the RFQ approach is unsuitable and an RFP approach will be required.

THE RFP PROCESS.

An RFP document is used to purchase expensive, complex products that are designed to meet specific buyer requirements. A formal or informal RFP approach may be used. A formal RFP is a legal document that contains binding contractual terms and conditions for both the buyer and the supplier. Failure to meet the RFP terms will have legal consequences for the party who violates the contractual terms. When using a formal RFP, a significant time investment by both the buyer and bidder must be made in order to perform required procedures. For large acquisitions, the preparation and issuance of an RFP can be a multiyear effort. A federal government agency can spend three or more years developing the RFP needed to acquire a communications network.

The formal RFP is used to obtain competitive bidding for large, complex projects. The RFP provides the technical specification information that vendors must meet (mandatory requirements) to deliver a system or network that will meet the buyer's performance requirements. The formal RFP becomes the vendor's specification. If the RFP specifications are accurate and the evaluation process is thorough, the buyer will get the right product at the best possible price—assuming that more than one bidder responds to the RFP.

LET THE BUYER BEWARE.

There is a potential downside for buyers who utilize a formal RFP process. If the RFP specifications are met and the purchased product doesn't work, the bidder has met his or her obligation and the fault is with the buyer. An alternative is to involve the vendor in the preparation of the specifications, but this approach is unacceptable in a formal, competitive bidding situation unless all potential suppliers are given the same opportunity. It is unlikely that bidders will make these investments unless the potential rewards were so great that bidders are willing to approach the project as if it were a research project that may or may not succeed. It is an approach that is not available for the average corporation, but is one that extremely large projects may employ.

RFP FORMAT AND DESCRIPTION.

A wide range of RFP formats are used in the RFP process. Selection of a specific format depends on: 1) the experience of the originator and 2) the formal or informal standards that exist for purchasing different types of equipment or services. Regardless of the format used, the basic intent of the RFP is to provide all bidders with a standard format (the originator's RFP format) that must be used for any bids that the vendor submits. Use of a buyer-oriented format simplifies the product comparison effort that is needed when multiple bids are received.

A key element in creating RFP documentation is to apply common sense in using them—a simple acquisition requires simple RFP documentation. Complex RFP documents should be used only for complex acquisitions. The following discussion framework will be for large, complex systems. If the RFP framework is used to develop an RFP for a simple acquisition, judgment must be applied to use those elements needed for the simpler requirements only.

The primary objective of an RFP is to clearly state buyer requirements to vendors who are being asked to submit bids. This primary objective should be the underlying objective for creating formal or informal RFPs. Despite differences in appearance, all RFPs have a similar basic content. The following outlines a generic RFP format where comparison of the generic version to any specific RFP documents would reveal many common elements.

The RFP should describe the buyer's requirements in sufficient detail so that the vendor has a clear, unambiguous understanding of the requirements. RFPs provide general and technical specification information about the buyer's requirements and request specific information from the vendors about their product pricing, equipment capacity, and references. The response to a formal RFP must be signed by an officer of the bidding business and will legally commit the bidder to fulfilling the RFP's contractual terms. Failure of a bidder to accept the buyer's RFP terms or to meet RFP submission deadlines automatically disqualifies the vendor from further consideration. Example 20–3 describes the generic RFP outline elements and Table 20–1 defines the terms.

RFP COMMENTARY.

Much of the information contained in a complex RFP is technical and requires a high level of technical knowledge to prepare. The RFP information may cover such a broad range of technology areas that multiple technical specialists are required to originate the specifications. The preparation of a complex RFP is a difficult, time consuming process that requires knowledge of the RFP process and the ability to translate

1. *Section 1.0: Procedures*
   - Executive summary
   - Terms & conditions to which the bidder must agree
   - Formal bidder acceptance of terms
2. *Section 2.0: System Description*
   - Technical overview
   - Floor plans
   - General standard requirements
   - Implementation requirements
3. *Section 3.0: System Hardware Technology & capacity; Operating features*
   - Generic/specific requirements
   - Tables
   - Equipment layouts
   - Five-year forecast estimates
4. *Section 4.0: System Software Technology & capacity; Operating features*
   - NOS/network environment overview
   - Generic/specific requirements
   - Tables
5. *Section 5.0: Vendor Information*
6. *Section 6.0: Pricing*
   Provides tables to be filled in for:
   - Hardware/software/cabling costs
   - Installation costs
   - Maintenance (Five year forecasts)
7. *Appendices*

Example 20–1. Generic RFP Outline

technical terms into a nonproprietary, generic format that is unambiguous and clear. If the RFP approach is appropriate, but the buyer lacks experience about the RFP process, the use of an outside consultant is recommended. The role of telecommunications managers is to assess the work effort in preparing an RFP against the benefits that are gained by using a formal RFP process.

Formal RFPs can fill multiple volumes of information for large, complex projects or may consist of relatively few (less than thirty pages) pages when the project is smaller. The acquisition of standard items can use the RFQ process to simplify the acquisition paperwork. Regardless of the RFP's length, the use of word processing software and word processing tables is recommended. Once a good RFP format has been developed and stored in a word processing format, it is a relatively simple process to use the original RFP as a template and modify it on an as-needed basis to establish new RFPs. Formal RFPs con-

tain a large amount of **boilerplate** terminology (stock language that is used repetitively in different RFPs) and the use of word processing simplifies the tedious task of replicating boilerplate information.

Except for regulatory agencies, the length of the RFP is of secondary importance. The important issues are to accurately and completely define the operational requirements for the system or network that is being purchased, and to provide sufficient information to the bidders so they are able to intelligently make recommendations on how their products can best meet the buyer's requirements. A five year equipment capacity forecast should be developed. This information should be converted into specifications that define both the initial system requirements and any upgrade requirements that are expected during the five year life.

FORMAL v. INFORMAL RFPs. The basic difference between formal and informal RFPs would be in the amount of legal language and requirements built into the RFP. Informal RFPs have minimal legal commitments built in and will also result in the establishment of a contract at the end of the RFP process. Informal RFPs are commonly used as a primary purchasing document once good relationships have been established between a buyer and prospective bidders.

While it gets easier with practice, the use of formal RFPs for the average business environment should probably be limited to large, expensive, complex, or mission-critical acquisitions for which failure to meet deadlines and performance expectations would seriously impact the business's customers. In these cases, the cost of using a formal RFP process would be outweighed by the protection it affords to the enterprise (and to the telecommunications manager).

If the vendors are known and experience exists with the product being acquired, an informal RFP process is easier on all parties and can achieve the same results as a formal process. In both cases, the accurate and complete definition of user requirements is necessary.

Once the RFP (formal or informal) is completed, it is sent to the selected vendors and a bid response is requested.

Acquisition Step 4: Request for Bids

The acquisition documentation (RFQs or formal/informal RFPs) is sent to the product vendors who have indicated an interest in bidding on the buyer's proposal. If the purchasing process is complex enough to warrant the use of an RFP, the buyer will schedule a meeting to take place within a week of the vendors' receipt of the RFP. The purpose of the meeting would be to provide prospective bidders with

TABLE 20–1   Generic RFP Description *(Refer to Generic RFP Outline)*

RFP Section	Description
Section 1.0: Procedures	This section contains an executive summary that describes the purpose for initiating the RFP and provides a high-level viewpoint of the "*big picture*" objectives that are to be satisfied by the selected system or network. This section includes: • the RFP originator's name • a formal contact for answering questions about the RFP • the date by which responses must be received • the required cutover date • buyer disclaimers • a formal bid acceptance form RFP recipients would have been informed in advance about the RFP and have agreed to participate in the RFP process. This first section provides an overview of the project and is oriented toward vendor management. The buyer disclaimers typically include wording to the effect that the vendor is not to receive any reimbursement for its effort in responding to the RFP and that the issuer of the RFP is not obligated to select any of the bidder responses. The bid acceptance form must be completed and signed by an officer of the vendor to acknowledge the formal acceptance of the RFP's technical and administrative terms. This is a key requirement because the contract may contain performance criteria that must be met prior to final payment and may contain penalty clauses for project delays.
Section 2.0: System Description	This section would summarize the overall technical standards to which the vendor product must conform. For example, if the RFP were being written to install a LAN at a new location, corporate standards for the network operating system and internetworking protocols would be specified to ensure compatibility of the new location with an existing networking environment. Performance criteria would be listed for systems and networks and any other appropriate interface standards required of the selected product. Floor plans would be provided to describe the equipment room, wiring closets, and user locations. These will allow the vendor to design the appropriate product configuration to meet RFP requirements. If any local restrictions exist, such as limited access or local labor rules, they would be described in this section.
Section 3.0: System Hardware	This section details the technical specifications for the various equipment components with tables and forms being provided for the vendor to fill in. Physical spacing, power, and air conditioning needs would be listed for each piece of equipment. The RFP originator should also provide a five year forecast of user requirements to allow the vendor to select the appropriate product models and identify any upgrades that would be the most cost effective way for addressing future capacity needs. The vendor would be requested to suggest alternative configurations other than those being requested by the RFP originator.
Section 4.0: System Software	This section lists the equipment software and provides comments regarding compatibility requirements for system or networking specifications (section 2.0) that have been itemized. Software versions should be specified and any unique capabilities should be identified, as well as any near-term capabilities that may become available during the next year. Tables would be included for the vendor to provide the software information.
Section 5.0: Vendor Information	This section provides the vendor with the opportunity to sell the viability of his or her organization for meeting the buyer's RFP requirements. Normally, a limit is placed on the number of pages the vendor can add (five or less) to avoid receiving every marketing brochure that is available.
Section 6.0: Pricing	The last section is the pricing section. Tables would list the hardware, software, cabling, and installation pricing for the proposed system or network. Maintenance costs would also be requested, along with requests for customer references that can be contacted to verify their satisfaction with the vendor's equipment performance and maintenance support. A five-year pricing schedule would be used to identify the costs of any upgrades required to meet the five-year forecast the buyer has provided to bidders. The pricing detail would be broken down into two major sections: 1) base system costs and 2) vendor recommendations for additions or deletions to the base system. The pricing format used by the originator of the RFP would be in a *contract ready format*, i.e., it would be in a format suitable for addition to a contract that would be issued to the selected vendor.
Appendices	All the various tables and forms requested in the various RFP sections would normally be placed in the appendix to minimize the clerical effort of consolidating them during the equipment selection phase. Because the RFP originator has established the format of required information (tables and forms), a common format is provided for the vendor selection phase of the acquisition process.

the opportunity to ask any questions they have regarding the proposal's content. It is also a chance for the bid participants to meet each other.

Once vendors fully understand the buyer's requirements, they assume the responsibility for designing a product solution that will meet the RFP requirements. As questions arise during response preparation activities, individual vendors may contact the buyer for clarification of information and the buyer's representatives must respond to these questions in a timely manner.

CONTROLLING TELECOMMUNICATIONS ACQUISITIONS

The telecommunications department is responsible for providing high quality, effective telecommunications services to the business enterprise. This responsibility also includes accountability for the acquisition process associated with purchasing telecommunications services.

Purchase Authorization Levels

Managers have different levels of authorization for approving purchases with spending limits, based on their managerial level and the nature of the department they manage. The financial organization has responsibility for assigning spending limits to managers and for monitoring acquisition activities to ensure that spending limits are enforced.

Telecommunications managers are typically assigned higher spending limits than peer organization managers because of the high cost of maintaining day to day telecommunications departments. To provide additional control, a hierarchical approval process exists where a multilevel approval process is required for large purchases. High level managers have larger spending limits assigned to them; as lower level managers exceed their spending limit, they must gain approval of the next management level. The maximum spending levels are assigned to management board managers. This multilevel approval process ensures that the appropriate management levels control the expenditure of budget money and that they are also aware of large expenditures within their areas of responsibility.

Managerial Control

Telecommunications managers are responsible for managing the organizational and technology expenses associated with managing a telecommunications department. This responsibility includes the relatively mundane activity of approving petty cash vouchers for department employees

who are being reimbursed for their out of pocket expenses (travel, mileage costs, tolls, technical publications, etc.). A petty cash spending limit is normally applied. For expenses exceeding $100, formal cash reimbursement forms must be filled out.

The two major budget categories controlled by telecommunications managers are department budgets and project budgets.

TELECOMMUNICATIONS DEPARTMENT BUDGETS. Except for an operations management department budget, most telecommunications department budgets address employee-oriented expenses that include compensation, recreation, travel, and office supplies, etc. (Refer to Chapter 16, *Developing an Operating Plan,* for additional details about the department budgeting process.) The department manager normally has the authorization needed for department level expenses and does not require higher level approval signatures to process any purchase requisitions for department expense codes.

In smaller organizations, the telecommunications department may consist of a single operations management department (Figure 20–3). For discussion purposes, it will be assumed that a single operations management department has the responsibility for paying the bills for telecommunications products and services used to support an enterprise's telecommunications infrastructure.

The operations management department will authorize bill payments to WAN service providers, the local telephone company, equipment suppliers, and other service providers. In a large corporation, this will require a multimillion dollar spending authorization at some level in the telecommunications management hierarchy. Lower level managers will recommend payments for purchase requisitions and higher level managers will approve the requisitions. The financial department has the responsibility for establishing and controlling the appropriate approval hierarchy that is needed to manage this approval process.

TELECOMMUNICATIONS PROJECT BUDGETS. The budgets for telecommunications projects are established in advance of the time when they will be implemented (Figure 20–2). Telecommunications managers are responsible for meeting the project's business and technical objectives, and this includes managing the acquisition requirements involved with project activities. The project management role may be filled directly by a telecommunications manager or may be delegated to a project manager for larger projects. However, the financial accountability for ensuring that the acquisition is carried out effectively and efficiently remains with the telecommunications manager, who has overall responsibility for the project.

If a development manager initiates the project (Figure 20–3), the manager must monitor and control the acquisition process described in Figure 20–1. This responsibility includes approving project purchase requisitions for payment. A project manager may recommend the bills for payment, but it is the development manager who will have the ultimate financial responsibility for approving and controlling project purchases.

Management of the project acquisition process consists of identifying who has been assigned the responsibility of completing different project tasks and monitoring their actual performance against the project's financial plan. The project manager's responsibility will be to ensure that project plan tasks are completed on time and within budget and the manager of managers has the responsibility for ensuring that project managers carry out their responsibilities effectively.

ACQUISITION CONTROL PROCEDURES. Normal project management procedures are used to control project acquisition activities (Chapter 11, *What is Project Management?*). A CPM-based project network diagram can be used to identify the project's acquisition deadlines and provide a mechanism to ensure that purchase process activities are completed on time. The project manager is responsible for incorporating the acquisition process elements into the project network diagram and using the project plan to control acquisition process activities. When BVA deviations occur, the project manager must initiate corrective actions to close the deviation gap and bring the acquisition process (and expenses) back under control.

COMMON SENSE CONTROL. The acquisition process can span days, months, or—for very large, complex projects—years. A formal acquisition process is appropriate when the selection process involves:

- a business critical application
- a very expensive product
- a technically complex, customized product
- competitive bidding is desired and is available

Another alternative to the formal acquisition approach is to select a *preferred supplier,* where the primary focus then becomes one of obtaining reasonable pricing. This assumes that the supplier's product can meet the buyer's needs and that a good working relationship exists between the two businesses. With familiarity, the planning process can be simplified for both parties, and the documentation work effort can be reduced substantially

by eliminating a significant portion of the structure needed to administer a formal RFP process. If an appropriate balance is achieved, the buyer receives a consistent, high-quality product at a fair price and the vendor is assured of a long-term relationship in which a fair profit will be made. Both parties must benefit when the preferred vendor approach is used or the relationship will not last. This typically requires good, ongoing dialogue between upper management levels of both organizations.

There are other benefits to be gained when using the preferred vendor mode. The preferred vendor derives the benefit of having a loyal customer who will support the vendor's user group activities in a positive manner and provide knowledgeable feedback to the vendor regarding the effectiveness of existing and planned products. The buyer derives the benefit of having insight into the vendor's long-range technology plans and knowing that the vendor will provide strong support for any operating problems the customer has with vendor products and services.

The primary benefit achieved with a formal acquisition process is that it requires the buyer to use detailed planning when preparing acquisition documents. These benefits can also be obtained by using an informal acquisition approach. The primary difference between the formal and informal approach is the degree of emphasis on contractual obligations. The formal acquisition process places contractual limitations on both the buyer and the seller; the informal acquisition process provides greater freedom for both the buyer and supplier and—in appropriate circumstances—may be a better method for both the buyer and the seller.

The acquisition process should be based on the needs of the acquisition. Simple acquisitions require simple procedures and complex acquisitions may require a complex set of procedures.

NEXT STEPS

The preceding discussion summarized acquisition steps 1 through 4; acquisition steps 5,6, and 7 must still be covered. These will be examined in Chapter 21 (*Evaluating Acquisition Options*). The following provides an overview of these "next step" topics.

Acquisition Step 5: Vendor Evaluation

A good acquisition process will identify the selection criteria in the early stages of a project. This information will be incorporated into acquisition documentation. Buyer selection criteria should be quantitative, so that it can be applied fairly and accurately across all vendor proposals. Using qualitative decision criteria should enter the decision process only when the quantitative process has not identified a clear winner. (This statement applies unless upper management makes the qualitative judgment, then, the qualitative view supersedes the quantitative view.) The next chapter will describe techniques that can be used to quantify decision criteria and will provide a process that maximizes the likelihood of making good decisions.

Acquisition Step 6: Product or Service Selection

This step involves the selection of a winner. It is important that telecommunications acquisition decisions are reviewed with business management prior to announcing which bid has been selected. As in any decision process, there are many viewpoints. It is imperative that commitments to spend large sums of money with any vendor are discussed with the funding source—upper management—prior to announcing the decision. While there is a low likelihood that a sound decision will be overridden by upper management if good communication exists between upper and lower management levels, it is important that upper management be given the opportunity to approve the selection prior to announcing the decision.

Once the selection is approved, the selected vendor should be notified and any necessary follow-up activities should be initiated—contracts, implementation planning, etc. At this point, the project emphasis with the selected vendor shifts from acquisition phase activities into implementation phase activities.

Acquisition Step 7: Acquire (Implement) Product or Service

This phase includes: 1) identifying a detailed implementation plan that meets the acquisition implementation schedule and 2) carrying out the plan. It normally requires a heavy involvement of time by telecommunications and vendor personnel. It is perhaps the most important phase because the perceived success or failure of the entire acquisition process will be reflected in how well it is implemented. If deadlines are met and everything operates smoothly, all internal departments will view it as a successful project; but if problems emerge and deadlines are not met, upper management will be quickly informed of these problems by internal clients. The implementation plan should receive the same attention to detail as the development of acquisition documentation.

SUMMARY

This summary is organized to match the learning objectives found at the beginning of the chapter.

1. When purchasing telecommunications products and services, selected products and services must first meet the business and technical selection criteria established for the acquisition. Once those selection criteria have been satisfied, the emphasis shifts to the pricing arena, and the product providing the best balance between meeting the business and technical selection criteria and price would normally be selected. Implicit in the process of establishing the business and technical criteria is that they will result in the acquisition of a high-quality, long-term product or service that provides excellent performance during its life cycle.

2. Telecommunications services can be only as effective as the technology infrastructure on which they are built. Once the business needs have been identified, technology decisions are the most important factor for determining the performance, capacity, and long-term viability of telecommunications acquisition investments. Therefore, it is essential that business and technical requirements drive the selection criteria that are established for the acquisition selection decision

process (acquisition step 3). In a decision framework, pricing should be a secondary consideration. It is relatively easy to obtain cheap telecommunications components that compromise the technical performance of a system or network investment. This outcome can be avoided by identifying the minimal level of technical performance in the selection criteria established for a telecommunications acquisition.

3. Ideally, major investments in telecommunications and services will be planned investments. This means that their need has been identified as part of the enterprise's annual financial planning process and the necessary time and planning has been invested in establishing the capital expenditure and operating expense budgets. When an unplanned event requires a major telecommunications acquisition to be made during a current operating period, there are normally two reasons: 1) a major equipment failure or 2) unexpected business-driven events. In either case, there will be heavy pressure on the financial department to find the money in other budgets and transfer the funds to the telecommunications budget. Finding ad hoc funding is normally difficult but becomes much easier to facilitate when upper management drives the decision.

4. The basic format requirement for establishing acquisition step 3 is to use a sound decision-making process. The process recommended is one in which two decision criteria categories are established: 1) mandatory requirements and 2) optional requirements. All mandatory requirements must be met for an acquisition alternative to be considered as a viable purchase option. Optional requirements provide a means for using desirable decision criteria with different importance levels and having them influence the final decision based on their importance. The final acquisition would be based on selecting a product that passes all mandatory requirement criteria and scores highest on meeting optional requirement criteria. As is always the case, managerial judgment can overrule decision calculations.

5. The RFI is used to obtain information about a vendor or vendor product prior to actively soliciting responses for meeting acquisition needs. RFIs are non-binding—they are basically informal and are not contractually binding for either the buyer or the vendor. The RFI process may be very broad and general or may be extremely comprehensive, where detailed requirement information is provided to prospective suppliers. There are two primary objectives for the RFI process: 1) identify qualified vendors to participate in the buyer's acquisition efforts and 2) identify the options that are available to meet the buyer's telecommunications needs.

6. RFQs and RFPs both have the same general objective of identifying the cost of a proposed acquisition. RFQs are used when the product or service being acquired can be identified by referring to a standard specification or by referring to a vendor product configuration. In these cases, the acquisition specifications have been defined and the only issue is pricing. RFQs are contracts to provide a specific price during a specified time period and the vendor issuing the RFQ is legally bound to provide the RFQ pricing. RFPs are used when the desired product or service requires a custom set of specifications to identify the acquisition requirements. The RFP information becomes the specifications used by the vendors, and are the basis for any pricing. Formal RFPs are contractual in nature (like the RFQ) and legally bind the vendor to provide the RFP product at a given price for a specified time period. The formal RFP also contains contractual terms and conditions, to which the vendor must agree. Informal RFPs contain the detailed specification information found in formal RFPs, but provide greater freedom for both the buyer and the vendor.

7. Formal RFPs are a time consuming, tedious effort whose overhead should be justified by the acquisition decision for which it is used. When business-critical applications are involved or when the technical complexity and costs are great, the formal RFP provides a measure of protection to the buying organization by allowing penalties to be built into the RFP's terms and conditions. A potential downside of the RFP process is that the buyer assumes responsibility for the operating performance of the RFP specifications. If the vendor meets all the specifications and the product or service does not meet the buyer's performance expectations, the responsibility for correcting the performance problem is the buyer's. The burden for correcting a formal RFP design flaw is the buyer's burden, at their cost.

8. RFPs are not standardized and are normally established by the buyer, based on the nature of the acquisition and the level of expertise they have. RFPs used for acquiring telecommunications products and services normally require a significant amount of technical specification information. A general format used for developing a telecommunications RFP would consist of six sections and the associated appendices: section 1, general procedures; section 2, system description; section 3, system hardware; section 4, system software; section 5, vendor information; section 6, pricing; and the appendices. RFPs vary in size, depending upon the application and business environment.

9. Purchase authorization levels used in a business determine the spending limits assigned to managerial personnel. The financial organization has responsibility for assigning, monitoring, and controlling spending authorization levels assigned to individuals. Different spending limits are assigned, based on a manager's level of responsibility and the functional organization they are in. Telecommunications is typically a high-cost area, and the spending levels assigned are quite significant. When a manager's spending authorization is not large enough to cover the cost of an acquisition, he or she will sign the purchase order/bill and obtain the necessary approval(s) of managers who have the appropriate spending limit authorization level.

10. Detailed, quantifiable procedures can be developed and administered when telecommunications products and services are being acquired. These procedures provide a means for managers to control the efforts of the acquisition process and minimize the risk of making poor decisions. The common sense

aspect of administering the telecommunications acquisition process is typically based on experience. Any quantitative process result should be evaluated in terms of common sense. This is another way of saying that there is no substitute for experience and intelligence, especially when nonstandard conditions are encountered.

KEY TERMS AND CONCEPTS

The language of telecommunications management is multifaceted and includes words and phrases from managerial, technological, accounting, regulatory, and other business areas. The definitions of these key terms and concepts can be found within the chapter and in the glossary.

Boilerplate
Mandatory Requirements
Operations Management

Optional Requirements
RFI

RFP
RFQ

REVIEW

The following questions are open-ended—predefined answers are not included as part of the text. The purpose of these questions is to allow the readers to test themselves on the chapter material.

1. List and explain the seven steps in the seven step telecommunications acquisition process model.

2. What is the role of a telecommunications manager during acquisition process model steps 1 and 2?

3. List and explain the six steps in the telecommunications project life cycle model.

4. Describe the generic telecommunications department structure and the role of each individual department in acquiring telecommunications products and services.

5. What are planned telecommunications acquisitions? Provide examples.

6. What are unplanned telecommunications acquisitions? Provide examples.

7. What options exist for a telecommunications operations manager when expensive equipment must be replaced but the operating budget does not have sufficient funding to cover its cost?

8. Describe the text's decision making process model, including the application of mandatory requirements and optional requirements. (If necessary, refer to Chapter 7, *Managerial Tools and Techniques*.)

9. List and describe the seven sections found in a RFP.

10. Explain the difference between formal and informal RFPs.

11. When would formal RFPs be used?

12. Why are spending level approvals required in a business.

13. What is a preferred vendor?

MULTIPLE CHOICE

1. The acquisition method (purchase, lease, or rental) used for acquiring assets is determined by _____.

    a. purchasing

    b. finance

    c. telecommunications

    d. project managers

2. Most telecommunications expenditures are provided by the _____ department budget.

    a. planning

    b. development

    c. operations

    d. help desk

    e. purchasing

3. The funding source for ad hoc miniprojects is the _____ department budget.

   a. planning
   b. development
   c. operations
   d. help desk
   e. administrative services
   f. purchasing

4. Examples of purchase documentation are _____. (Select all that apply.)

   a. RFI
   b. RFQ
   c. RFC
   d. RFP
   e. invoices

5. Acquisition process step 3 converts business and technical requirements into _____ documentation.

   a. problem solving
   b. RFQ
   c. RFC
   d. RFP
   e. decision making

6. Optional requirements used in the acquisition process are _____ criteria.

   a. mandatory
   b. RFQ
   c. problem solving
   d. weighted
   e. unimportant

7. When complex, expensive telecommunications equipment is purchased, _____ information will determine its cost.

   a. RFI
   b. RFC
   c. RFP
   d. RFQ
   e. invoice

8. When commodity type equipment is purchased, _____ information will determine its cost.

   a. RFI
   b. RFC
   c. RFP
   d. RFQ
   e. invoice

9. When a formal RFP is used to acquire equipment, the _____ specifies the equipment's performance metrics.

   a. purchase order
   b. sales agreement
   c. UCC
   d. RFP
   e. seller

10. RFP disclaimers are used to _____.

    a. specify equipment performance requirements
    b. limit the seller's liability
    c. limit the buyer's liability
    d. identify technical standards
    e. provide pricing tables

11. _____ are always required for large government purchases.

    a. RFIs
    b. RFCs
    c. RFPs
    d. RFQs
    e. Invoices

12. Spending authorization levels are established by _____.

    a. RFPs
    b. telecommunications
    c. project budgets
    d. finance
    e. managerial level

13. Preferred suppliers receive _____.

    a. RFPs
    b. RFQs
    c. general equipment requirements
    d. higher payments
    e. RFI bids

14. The primary advantage of the RFP process is that it _____.

    a. requires higher payments
    b. is expensive
    c. requires bids
    d. requires detailed level planning

15. The most important criteria used to measure success when acquiring telecommunications products and services are meeting _____ and _____ decision criteria.

    a. cost requirements

    b. business requirements

    c. staffing requirmentrs

    d. technical requirements

    e. scheduling requirements

16. The two decision criteria categories used to select telecommunications products and services are _____ and _____ decision criteria.

    a. mandatory

    b. cost

    c. technical

    d. optional

    e. mechanical

17. When a formal RFP process is used and the acquired product meets specification requirements but does not meet buyer expectations, the responsibility for fixing the problem falls on the _____.

    a. purchasing department

    b. end user

    c. buyer

    d. bidder

    e. legal department

18. Purchasing departments frequently use _____.

    a. RFCs

    b. RFIs

    c. RFPs

    d. RFQs

    e. RSVPs

19. The format used in an RFP should be established by the _____.

    a. manufacturer

    b. purchasing department

    c. bidder

    d. legal department

    e. buyer

20. The _____ department has the responsibility for setting spending approval authorization levels.

    a. purchasing

    b. financial

    c. legal

    d. telecommunications

    e. executive

21

EVALUATING ACQUISITION OPTIONS

1. Understand the relationship of the acquisition evaluation processes within the context of the seven step acquisition model diagram.

2. Understand the role of the technical and financial assessment steps as part of the acquisition assessment and selection process.

3. Understand the relationship of the acquisition process within the context of the telecommunications project life cycle model.

4. Understand the role of mandatory and optional requirement decision criteria in the acquisition assessment and selection process.

5. Understand the technical evaluation process for evaluating acquisition choices.

6. Understand the steps that should be followed to minimize the work effort associated with conducting the acquisition evaluation and selection process.

7. Understand the steps for setting up an LCA/NPV evaluation.

8. Understand the role of a project manager and a telecommunications manager in the final rating process.

9. Understand the phrase *technical jargon* and the role of project managers and telecommunications managers when it is used in technical documentation.

10. Understand how to apply the seven step acquisition model to a real world acquisition project.

INTRODUCTION

Selecting the best acquisition alternative when the selection involves comparing expensive, technically complex systems or networks can be a very difficult task. When a formal acquisition process that is based on competitive bidding has been used, the buyer will frequently be confronted with multiple options contained in each of the vendor options, which may include several pounds of paperwork to explain their unique merits. In addition, if the bidding has been active, the climate surrounding the acquisition evaluation process may be extremely tense. There is a high likelihood that those vendors who do not win the bid will want a good explanation of why their product was not selected.

This chapter will address these issues and will describe a process that is rational and objective. While it may not satisfy all subjective emotions, it should provide a reasonable, objective approach for reaching a decision and it should also provide a presentation format that clearly summarizes the decision rationale.

ACQUISITION MANAGEMENT OVERVIEW

In Chapter 19, *Purchasing Process Overview*, the overall acquisition process was examined and was separated into seven individual acquisition activities in a flowchart (Figure 21–1).

Chapter 20, *Purchasing Products and Services*, provided a summary overview of the entire process and a detailed discussion of acquisition steps 1 through 4. This chapter will complete the process of reviewing the **acquisition model** and will describe the activities of acquisition steps 5 (evaluate vendor responses) and 6 (select a winner). It will apply the tools and techniques discussed

earlier in the text and illustrate their use in a telephone system acquisition activity.

Technical and Financial Assessment

The assessment process used to select telecommunications products and services will be based on two primary criteria categories: 1) technical specifications and 2) product costs. A cursory technical assessment should be made at the beginning of the evaluation process to screen out any vendor choices that are unable to meet **mandatory technical requirements,** because failure to meet technical performance requirements will automatically eliminate the product or service from further consideration—regardless of how cheaply it can be purchased. A bargain exists only when a product is able to do the job for which it was acquired. Anyone who selects a product that is relatively low in cost but doesn't work is someone who exercises extremely poor judgment.

Acquisition choices that pass the **preliminary screening** process will undergo a more detailed technical analysis and cost assessment process as the remaining choices are evaluated to select a winner. Step 5 will format technical and cost decision factors into mandatory and optional requirement headings and will use this information to select the best choice. The use of multiple criteria also provides a balanced decision process, where each choice is evaluated against many technical and financial decision factors. Figure 21–2 provides a flowchart that was discussed in Chapter 7 and illustrates the technical/cost decision process that was just discussed.

The evaluation process is a managerial responsibility, even if various technical and financial assessment steps are delegated to others. When the acquisition phase is part of a large, technically complex project, the technical assessment would be carried out by technical specialists assigned to the project. The financial assessment could then be delegated to a member of the telecommunications

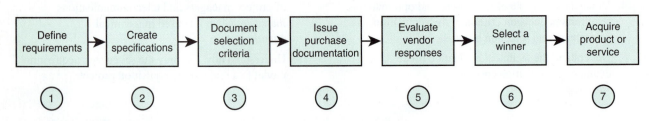

Figure 21–1. The seven step telecommunications acquisition model.

project team. For smaller projects or for nonproject acquisitions, a project manager or operations manager may be responsible for handling both the technical and financial assessment responsibilities.

Figure 21–3 duplicates the diagram of the **telecommunications project life cycle model** that has been used as a project framework throughout the text. Project step 4 shows the point in the life cycle when the project components will be purchased. The Figure 21–2 assessment and selections steps would be used in project steps 3 and 4 of the Figure 21–3 model or Step 3 of the project life cycle model.

The project manager is responsible for establishing the decision framework that will be used by project team members to purchase project equipment. For a project of any significant size, the final recommendation will require a consensus opinion when some team members may have strong biases and opinions that differ from those of other team members—particularly when technical issues are involved. The telecommunications manager or project manager who heads a project effort must have the facilitation skills needed to generate a consensus that can be supported by all project team members.

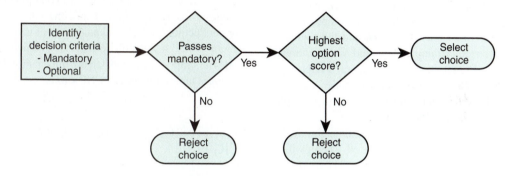

Figure 21–2. Acquisition assessment and selection process.

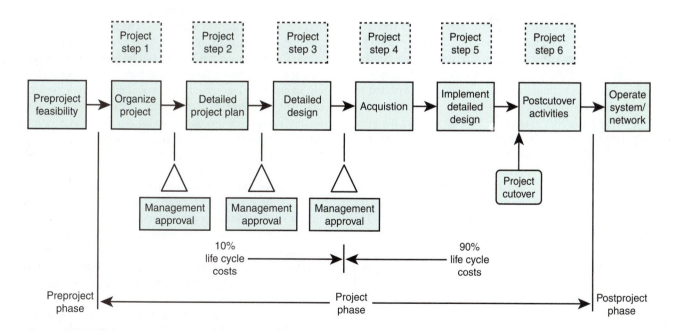

Figure 21–3. Telecommunications project life cycle model.

FINANCIAL ASSESSMENT CRITERIA

A key part of the acquisition evaluation is to identify the option that is the best choice—the one that is the most financially attractive and meets all mandatory requirements. A business's accounting department normally establishes internal policies that are used to evaluate the financial attractiveness of different investment choices. These criteria should be used for any telecommunications product or service acquisition.

Some of the more commonly used methods for evaluating the financial attractiveness of different investments include NPV, ROI, and investment payback methods. NPV procedures are arguably the most complete (and complex) form of investment analysis, and they will be used for the case study example at the end of this chapter. The LCA/NPV format was discussed in Chapter 9, *Technology Management Skills*. For the reader's convenience, some of the Chapter 9 information will be replicated as part of this section's discussion.

The telecommunications LCA/NPV financial model identifies all the costs that will be incurred when owning and operating an asset during its useful life. These costs—the LCA costs—include the expenses for designing, developing, implementing, and operating the telecommunications asset (typically a system or a network). LCA includes allowances for asset depreciation and annual inflation, and converts future costs to current year dollar values by applying a PV factor. The use of a standard base (current year dollars) provides a more meaningful financial assessment of a project that spans a period of years. The specific analysis that will be used in a business is a finance department responsibility, and telecommunications managers are expected to follow financial policies.

The LCA/NPV model can be used whether the asset is purchased, leased, or rented by eliminating the parts of the model that are not applicable. Example 21–1 demonstrates the **telecommunications LCA/NPV financial model,** and Tables 21–1 and 21–2 provide: 1) a description of the various data fields in the model and 2) a PV table for converting future year values into current year dollars. The LCA/NPV format will be the financial model used to evaluate acquisition choices.

In the optional requirements evaluation table, two basic cost measurements are normally shown: 1) initial investment costs and 2) life cycle operating costs. Example 21–1 provides a wide range of cost information, including initial investment and life cycle costs in a standard dollar (current year dollar) format. It also shows costs incurred in different time periods with a uniform measurement baseline. If other financial decision criteria are desired, the LCA/NPV model details can be examined and the necessary information can be extracted.

Information Source

The source for the information that is used to carry out the financial analysis is contained in the bid response information received from the bidders in either an **RFQ** or **RFP** format. In Chapter 20, *Purchasing Products and Services*, the generic RFP outline provided a section for obtaining pricing information including equipment, installation, and maintenance costs. If the team did a good job of identifying pricing information requirements, the information needed for conducting the financial analysis will have been conveniently placed into a table format. The financial analysis effort will simply mean transferring information from the bid response tables into an LCA/NPV pricing model.

TECHNICAL ASSESSMENT CRITERIA

Technical assessment criteria are an outgrowth of the technical design process, which normally includes a blend of business and technology criteria. The business factors would address the vendor's qualifications, such as financial solvency, long-term viability in the product/service market, service support facility locations, existing customer base, and range of product offerings. The project manager or telecommunications manager would be responsible for ensuring that this area is addressed as part of the technical decision criteria. Business criteria would also include project management elements such as time schedule constraints and unique working environment conditions. Business decision criteria are largely boilerplate criteria that can be reused for all acquisition initiatives. Obviously, the depth and scope of this boilerplate evaluation effort should be commensurate with the size and importance of the acquisition.

While a project manager or a telecommunications manager may establish the technical decision criteria directly, technical ratings are normally the responsibility of technical specialists—particularly for large or complex acquisitions. The technical specialists assigned to these projects have the primary responsibility for identifying the technical decision criteria that are important for the technology infrastructure, while the managerial responsibility would be to understand technical criteria concepts and integrate them with the business decision criteria. The final

ABC Company Case Study

Five Year Telecommunications Financial Plan
Uses Standard Economic Model Format & Assumptions

Fixed Asset Listing	Purchase
Product costs:	
LAN hardware/software	($602,750)
Structured cabling system	($28,984)
Physical networking	($30,200)
Internetworking devices	($12,250)
Telephone system	($143,000)
WAN	($1,000)
Total installed cost	**($818,184)**

Annual Costs:	
LAN maintenance	($53,350)
Physical network maintenance	($1,040)
Internetting maintenance	($850)
Telephone system maintenance	($19,000)
WAN maintenance	($28,900)
WAN—voice communication	($1,058,904)
WAN—data communication	($37,800)
Total depreciation (straight line)	$147,273
Total salvage value	$81,818

Common Cost Data	Item
Inflation%	4%
Annual inflation factor	104%
Cost of money	11%
Service life (years)	5
Salvage value	10%

Operating Costs

Description	Year 0	Year 1	Year 2	Year 3	Year 4	Total
Consolidated communication costs						
LAN maintenance	($53,350)	($55,484)	($57,703)	($60,011)	($62,412)	($288,961)
Physical network maintenance	($1,040)	($1,082)	($1,125)	($1,170)	($1,217)	($5,633)
LAN internet maintenance	($850)	($884)	($919)	($956)	($994)	($4,604)
Telephone system maintenance	($19,000)	($19,760)	($20,550)	($21,372)	($22,227)	($102,910)
WAN maintenance	($28,900)	($30,056)	($31,258)	($32,509)	($33,809)	($156,532)
WAN—voice communication	($1,058,904)	($1,101,260)	($1,145,311)	($1,191,123)	($1,238,768)	($5,735,366)
WAN—data communication	($37,800)	($39,312)	($40,884)	($42,520)	($44,221)	($204,737)
Total depreciation	$147,273	$147,273	$147,273	$147,273	$147,273	$736,366
Total salvage	$0	$0	$0	$0	$81,818	$81,818
Annual operating costs	**($1,052,571)**	**($1,100,565)**	**($1,150,478)**	**($1,202,388)**	**($1,174,556)**	**($5,680,558)**
PV factors	**1.0000**	**0.9009**	**0.8116**	**0.7312**	**0.6587**	
PV operating costs	**($1,052,571)**	**($991,500)**	**($933,754)**	**($879,176)**	**($773,717)**	**($4,630,717)**

Management Summary

Description	Year 0	Year 1	Year 2	Year 3	Year 4	Total
Consolidated communication costs						
Initial cost	$818,184					$818,184
Total PV operating cost	$1,052,571	$991,500	$933,754	$879,176	$773,717	$4,630,717)
Totals	**$1,870,755**	**$991,500**	**$933,754**	**$879,176**	**$773,717**	**$5,448,901**

Example 21–1. Telecommunications financial model example.

TABLE 21–1 Telecommunications Financial Model Description

Operation	Description
Example 21–1	**Common cost data** **Fixed asset costs** **Annual operating costs** The **common cost data** is normally provided by the accounting department. Asset cost information is based on the product's initial costs. The annual operating cost information is obtained from vendor information and operational records. (When an RFP is used, product information would be contained in the RFP.) *Depreciation and salvage value values are positive (+); All other values are expenses and are negative (–).* The following formulas are used for the various LCA calculations: 1. **inflation factor** = 1 + inflation% (e.g., 100% + 4% = 104% = 1.04) 2. total asset cost = sum of all the costs required to install the asset, i.e., product cost + installation costs 3. salvage value = total asset cost × salvage value% 4. straight line depreciation = $$\frac{\text{total asset cost} - \text{salvage value}}{\text{service life years}}$$ *All annual costs are shown as pretax values.* 5. floor space = sq. ft. × floor space rate 6. power & air cond. = KW × 24 × 365 × power$/KWHr
Operating Costs	The Example 21–1 worksheet provides a five year analysis (years 0 through 4). The designation of year 0 for the first year has been used to help students select present value factors. (The present factor table year values will match the corresponding worksheet year.) The annual cost information is linked to the operating expense year 0 column. 1. **Year 0 costs**: Copy the respective column cash flows from page 1 into the year 0 column. Year 0 is the first year of the NPV analysis. *First year maintenance charges for a new PBX are normally covered under warranty, but this will be ignored for this LAN example.* *Inflation Factor: Apply to all operating costs except depreciation, salvage value, and fixed contract costs—after year 0. It is equal to the previous year's cost × the Inflation Factor. The Inflation Factor is calculated on worksheet page 1 by adding 1 to the Annual Inflation%. <u>Depreciation, salvage value, and fixed contract costs (leases) are not subject to inflation.</u>* 2. **Year 1 costs**: maintenance cost = <u>PrevYr Cost × Inflation Factor</u> 3. **Year 2 costs**: = <u>PrevYr cost × inflation factor</u> 4. **Year 3 costs**: = <u>PrevYr cost × inflation factor</u> 5. **Year 4 costs**: = <u>PrevYr cost × inflation factor</u> When salvage value is present, the salvage value cash flow is entered only during the last year of the analysis. 6. **total annual costs** = sum of all costs in the column, keeping track of + and – signs 7. **PV factor** is based on a manual table look-up using the worksheet year and the cost of money interest rate. Refer to Table 12–3 on page 302. 8. **PV operating cost** = PV factor × annual operating cost 9. **initial costs** = total installed cost 10. **total PV operating cost** = sum of PV calculations for years 0 through 4 (5 years) 11. **total cost** = total installed cost + total PV operating cost

TABLE 21-2   Present Value Table

Present Value Of $1

PV Factors (DCF Factors)

Years	1%	3%	4%	5%	6%	7%	8%	9%	10%	11%	12%	13%	14%	15%	18%	20%
1	0.9901	0.9709	0.9615	0.9524	0.9434	0.9346	0.9259	0.9174	0.9091	0.9009	0.8929	0.8850	0.8772	0.8696	0.8475	0.8333
2	0.9803	0.9426	0.9246	0.9070	0.8900	0.8734	0.8573	0.8417	0.8264	0.8116	0.7972	0.7831	0.7695	0.7561	0.7182	0.6944
3	0.9706	0.9151	0.8890	0.8638	0.8396	0.8163	0.7938	0.7722	0.7513	0.7312	0.7118	0.6931	0.6750	0.6575	0.6086	0.5787
4	0.9610	0.8885	0.8548	0.8227	0.7921	0.7629	0.7350	0.7084	0.6830	0.6587	0.6355	0.6133	0.5921	0.5718	0.5158	0.4823
5	0.9515	0.8626	0.8219	0.7835	0.7473	0.7130	0.6806	0.6499	0.6209	0.5935	0.5674	0.5428	0.5194	0.4972	0.4371	0.4019
6	0.9420	0.8375	0.7903	0.7462	0.7050	0.6663	0.6302	0.5963	0.5645	0.5346	0.5066	0.4803	0.4556	0.4323	0.3704	0.3349
7	0.9327	0.8131	0.7599	0.7107	0.6651	0.6227	0.5835	0.5470	0.5132	0.4817	0.4523	0.4251	0.3996	0.3759	0.3139	0.2791
8	0.9235	0.7894	0.7307	0.6768	0.6274	0.5820	0.5403	0.5019	0.4665	0.4339	0.4039	0.3762	0.3506	0.3269	0.2660	0.2326
9	0.9143	0.7664	0.7026	0.6446	0.5919	0.5439	0.5002	0.4604	0.4241	0.3909	0.3606	0.3329	0.3075	0.2843	0.2255	0.1938
10	0.9053	0.7441	0.6756	0.6139	0.5584	0.5083	0.4632	0.4224	0.3855	0.3522	0.3220	0.2946	0.2697	0.2472	0.1911	0.1615

This table shows the PV of $1 received at a future time (FV). To use the table, select the interest rate from the top row and read down the column to the appropriate number of years. The PV factor is the intersection of the year row and interest rate column. The NPV of $1 received 10 years in the future discounted at 10% = $0.3855, i.e. FV = $1, NPV = $0.3855

Excel function: NPV(interest, value1, value2, . . .)

where Value 1 = FV of Year 1, Value 2 = FV of Year 2, etc.

e.g., NPV of $1 in Year 7 @ 7%: = NPV(.07,0,0,0,0,0,0,1) = 0.6227

e.g., @ i = 12%, FV1 = 235; FV2 = 250, FV3 =679: NPV(.12,235,250,679) = $892

TABLE 21–3 **Business and Technical Decision Criteria**

Decision Factor Category	Decision Factor Description
Mandatory	Must be implemented by XX/XX/XX
	Conforms to standard(s) XXXXXX
	Minimum capacity of XXXXXX
	Minimum speed of XXXXXX
	Service location with XX miles
	Ability for modular growth to XXXXXX size
	Network management interface standard XXXXXX
Optional	Administrative support features
	Maintenance support features
	Appearance
	Spare capacity
	Remote diagnostics capability
	Reliability track record
	Speed

decision-making format would consist of a two step decision process: 1) a set of mandatory requirements that provide a go/no go decision point for vendor choices and 2) a set of optional requirement decision factors that use a scoring system to identify the relative desirability of different vendor choices.

Table 21–3 provides an example of generic business and technical decision factors that can be applied to all telecommunications technology acquisitions. The Table 21–3 descriptions are open-ended, because the actual measurement criterion that is used would be based on the specific product or service that is being acquired. As was the case with business decision criteria, a standard (**boilerplate**) set of general technical criteria can be established for different acquisition categories and specific values can be established for each acquisition situation.

Information Source

The information used to carry out a technical assessment process will be found in bid response documents. The generic RFP outline in Chapter 20, *Purchasing Products and Services*, offered three sections for obtaining vendor technical information (*System Description*, *System Hardware*, and *System Software*). The project's technical specialists, who created the technical specifications and identified the key technical decision criteria to be used in selecting acquisition alternatives (acquisition steps 1 through 3), should have requested technical response information in a tabular format. When the technical special-

ists evaluate the various acquisition choices (acquisition step 5), the requested information should be readily available. The role of the technical specialists will be to validate the accuracy of vendor statements and then transfer the results into a decision making table.

If care was taken when the RFP's technical response format was established, the effort will be repaid many times over by how it simplifies the bid response comparison phase. This is an area where a buyer-oriented response form can be used to standardize response information and quickly highlight differences between vendor technologies.

ACQUISITION STEPS 5 AND 6

The primary objective of acquisition process steps 5 and 6 is to objectively and accurately select the best choice for satisfying acquisition requirements. A secondary objective is to minimize the work effort associated with the selection process.

Figure 21–4 shows the **decision-making process** that has been set up to minimize the time spent reviewing acquisition choices that do not meet mandatory requirements or are not competitive compared to the other bids. This figure provides a two level decision process, in which the preliminary screening takes place at the initial stage of acquisition step 5 and a more detailed evaluation takes place at the end of step 5.

At this point in the acquisition process, all bid responses have been received and a preliminary screening is preformed to ensure that all the bids meet the minimum acceptable requirements. If a bid does not meet the mandatory requirements, it is eliminated from further consideration. At this time, a preliminary screening of the optional requirements is done to see if the bid is competitive—particularly from a financial perspective. For example, if five bids pass the mandatory screening process and one bid is two times higher than the next highest bid, it would be set aside and eliminated from further consideration.

> Bids that have been rejected in the initial screening process can always be placed back into consideration if subsequent analysis shows that problems exist with the other bids that are under consideration in the final evaluation phase.

The acquisition evaluation process can be long and tedious—particularly when the bidding has been active

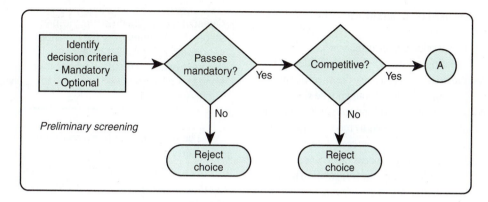

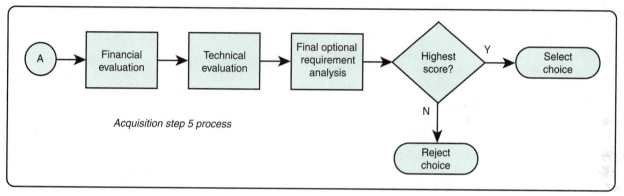

Figure 21–4. Acquisition step 5 (decision process) flowcharts.

and a large number of bids are received. The preliminary screening step shown in Figure 21–4 eliminates non-competitive bids early in the process and can provide significant time savings when compared to the time required to conduct a full evaluation for each bid that has been received.

As indicated in Figure 21–4, a complete financial and technical analysis is conducted for all bids that have passed the mandatory and preliminary optional requirement screening checks. Under normal circumstances, the acquisition choice that has the highest option score would be selected—but management judgment is always the determining factor for selecting the final winner.

The following section takes acquisition step 5 (evaluate vendor responses) and divides it into five areas, which are reviewed separately. These separate areas help to incorporate the decision-making process into the acquisition process.

1. evaluation documentation

2. preliminary screening

3. financial analysis

4. technical analysis

5. final optional requirements rating analysis

Acquisition Step 5: Evaluation Documentation

There is no right or wrong way to document the acquisition evaluation process. Any format is typically based on the judgment of the individual responsible for carrying out the process. To assist the reader, a worksheet format is shown in Example 21–2. It is not intended to imply that it is the only format that can be used to document the evaluation of acquisition choices. If the reader has an alternative format with which he or she is more comfortable, that format should be used.

When the bidding process is complex or formal (contractually binding), some form of documentation must be developed from the time bids are received until the final selection is made. Example 21–2 was developed for this purpose and it provides room for a wide range of comments. A benefit of being thorough when documenting the decision process is that it can be made part of the project documentation to be used by others when similar projects are undertaken.

The evaluation worksheet information can also be used during the debriefing sessions held with bidders who were not awarded the contract. However, the specific information used for rating other vendors should not be shared directly if it includes proprietary information that the vendor views as being confidential. The need to meet with bidders after a competitive bidding process is complete was discussed in Chapter 19, *Purchasing Process Overview*, and the evaluation worksheet should contain the information needed to explain the final selection decision process. The worksheet can also be used during meetings with upper management if questions arise regarding the evaluation process and the level of detail used during the evaluation phase.

The information contained on individual worksheets would be consolidated into a summary worksheet after the evaluation process has been completed (acquisition step 5, final optional requirements rating analysis).

Acquisition Step 5: Preliminary Screening

After all the bids have been received, each bid is reviewed to ensure that all the requirements listed in the original acquisition document have been met. Acquisition evaluation worksheets should be prepared (Example 21–2) for each vendor and the preliminary screening information should be filled in. When mandatory acquisition requirements have not been met, the vendor responses are placed in a reject file and will not require additional analysis. For those bids that meet the mandatory requirements, a cursory optional requirement rating is calculated by using the project's optional decision factors developed for acquisition step 3. A preliminary option rating score is calculated and a review is conducted to see if any significant deviations are found between the different bids. If extremely poor scores were calculated for any responses, these bids would also be placed in the reject file. Low score rejections may be recalled if subsequent rating efforts do not totally eliminate them from additional consideration.

At this point in the evaluation process, the surviving bids have passed the mandatory requirements and have preliminary optional requirement rating scores that make them competitive with each other. An LCA/NPV will be calculated for these proposals in the final LCA section. The cost information used for this analysis would be contained in the bid responses—assuming that purchase documentation was competently prepared and included a request for the necessary financial information. If any one bid is significantly higher than the others, a high cost note would be applied to it, and it would be placed into the reject file.

Questions may arise during the preliminary screening stage. These questions may not be resolved without vendor input. If this is the case, the bid is passed on to the next evaluation stage, where there is a high likelihood that all vendors will be called to clarify their bid response information.

The remaining bids are ready for an in-depth evaluation. Early elimination of noncompetitive bids can significantly reduce the evaluation effort and also allows full attention to be focused on bids that have a good potential for being selected.

Acquisition Step 5: Financial Analysis

The telecommunications LCA/NPV model in Figure 21–3 would be used to provide the financial evaluation information, and the following steps would be completed:

1. Establish the LCA study length.
2. Identify all current year product costs (capital and operating).
3. Identify the LCA/NPV inflation factor.
4. Identify the organization's interest rate for PV calculations.
5. Calculate LCA costs based on items 1–4.
6. Interpret the results and make a selection.

For our acquisition analysis, the study length will be seven years (required by our case study's hypothetical accounting department). All other parameters used in the model will be identified in the common cost data table portion of the model.

Acquisition Step 5: Technical Analysis

Technical specialist team members would carry out this step and conduct a detailed technical assessment of the proposals that survived the preliminary screening. Because the technical specialists created the technical specifications and the associated RFP information, they should be able to quickly and effectively validate each vendor's proposal. Their initial focus would be to ensure that all technical specification requirements (mandatory requirements) have been met. Then they would compare the relative merit of the technical solutions provided by each bidder to complete the acquisition evaluation forms. If questions arise during the technical assessment phase, the technical specialists would contact the vendors to clarify information and resolve any questions. When major technical

CHAPTER 21

Acquisition evaluation worksheet

Date: _____

Evaluator: _____

Project: _____

Vendor: _____

Preliminary screening: Mandatory requirements

Comments: _____

_____

Preliminary screening: Optional requirements rating	Total score
Comments: _____	_____
_____	_____

Preliminary screening: LCA	Costs
_____ Installed cost:	_____
_____ Five year operating cost:	
_____ Total cost:	

Final LCA	Costs
_____ Installed cost:	_____
_____ Five year operating cost:	
_____ Total cost:	

Final optional requirements rating	Total score
Comments: _____	_____
_____	_____

General comments: _____

_____

_____

_____

_____

_____

Example 21–2. Acquisition evaluation worksheet.

shortcomings that would disqualify the proposal are found, the reasons would be noted on the evaluation worksheet and the bid would also be placed in the reject file.

Acquisition Step 5: Final Optional Requirements Rating Analysis

As shown in Figure 21–4, after the financial and technical evaluations have been completed, a final optional requirements rating step is undertaken. Individuals may have been assigned specific areas in the evaluation process, and the final optional requirements rating step should be conducted in a meeting during which all team members have the opportunity to see the final evaluation results. If individuals prepare an initial evaluation, they must explain the ratings and scoring they used.

At the final meeting, all team members should be given the opportunity to provide input to any preliminary evaluation results. The intent is to develop a consensus for the final **optional requirement scoring.** The role of the meeting facilitator—the telecommunications manager or project manager—would be to resolve differences and, where necessary, develop compromise ratings. If the facilitation role is carried out effectively and the evaluation team members are rational, the final result will represent a consensus opinion. When strong opinions exist, it may be necessary for the manager to select a rating, while noting any dissension in the final rating results.

> **Facilitator**: someone who aids or assists in a process by encouraging people to find their own solutions to problems or tasks.

FINAL OPTIONAL REQUIREMENTS RATING TABLE. The rating table developed in acquisition step 3 becomes the basis to evaluate vendor responses. This table will be modified, as needed, if new information uncovered during the acquisition process changes rating information contained in the original table. The table prepared in step 3 may require additions, deletions, or modifications based on new information developed during the evaluation process.

This final **optional requirements rating** and scoring phase is the last opportunity for project team members to review the evaluation scoring results to make sure it contains the **optional requirements criteria** needed to accurately and objectively evaluate bid responses.

FINAL RATING PROCESS. Once the optional requirements rating and scoring table content is agreed to, the technical and financial factors for each vendor bid must be reviewed and a consensus rating must be established for each optional requirements rating element. The assigned optional requirements ratings are relative ones. The best rating given would be a 10. Other vendors would receive a rating relative to the one selected as the best. While this appears to be a heavily subjective process, good facilitation will allow the interaction of different viewpoints to converge on a consensus rating that will be surprisingly objective.

Table 21–4 is a sample optional requirements rating form that could be used for a telephone system project. It contains optional requirement factors that project members felt were important in the selection of a PBX telephone system.

TABLE 21–4   Sample Telephone Optional Requirements Table

Optional Decision Factor	Weight	Option A Rating	Option A Score	Option B Rating	Option B Score
Initial cost	6				
Annual operating costs	10				
Station equipment options	6				
Voice mail integration	10				
Upgradability	9				
Environmental requirements	7				
Administrative tools	5				
Totals					

1 = low; 10 = high; score = rating × weight

At the start of the final rating session, the only values that are filled in would be the optional decision factor description and the weight given to each factor. Using a consensus rating process, project team members would assign the ratings for the two vendor choices (A and B).

The optional requirements rating approach generates very good results if:

1. all pertinent decision factors are listed on the form
2. the weights accurately reflect the option factor's value
3. the ratings accurately reflect the relative strength of vendor offerings

Acquisition Step 6: Final Selection

At this point in the acquisition evaluation process, the selected bid would fulfill all mandatory requirements and would receive a significantly higher optional requirement rating score than the closest alternatives. If the optional requirements score gap is less than 5%, managerial judgment can be exercised without affecting the validity of the selection process, because any of the final bid choices will do the job equally well.

Regardless of rating scores, it is always necessary to stand back and view the decision from different viewpoints to see if the final calculated decision makes sense. The optional requirements rating approach helps to organize decision criteria so that it can be seen more clearly while providing a structured approach for quantifying subjective ratings—but no rating system is a substitute for good judgment.

ACQUISITION STEP 6: FINAL OPTIONAL REQUIREMENTS RATINGS. The steps to perform a final optional requirements rating evaluation are:

1. Review mandatory requirements.
2. Eliminate choices that do not meet mandatory requirements.
3. Rate vendor optional requirement factors.
4. Score the vendor's optional requirement factors.
5. Compare the vendors' optional requirement scores.

Table 21–5 provides a completed version of Table 21–4 to illustrate the final results of an optional requirement rating process.

Option B has scored 21 points higher (470–449) than option A. Unless other factors are uncovered, option B would be selected.

ACQUISITION CASE STUDY EXAMPLE

The following shows how the financial LCA and the optional requirements rating concepts are applied in an acquisition process case study. The decision-making procedures shown in Figure 21–4 will be followed.

Project Description

A 300-line PBX telephone system/voice messaging system is required for the HealthProd Corporation's midwest manufacturing facility. The project requirements are being handled by the telecommunications development

TABLE 21–5   Completed Version of Table 21–4

Optional Evaluation Factor	Weight	Option A		Option B	
		Rating	Score	Rating	Score
Initial cost	6	8	48	10	60
Annual operating costs	10	10	100	8	80
Station equipment options	6	8	48	10	60
Voice mail integration	10	8	80	10	100
Upgradability	9	8	72	9	81
Environmental requirements	7	8	56	7	49
Administrative tools	5	9	45	8	40
Totals			**449**		**470**

1 = low; 10 = high; score = rating × weight

Description	PBX A	PBX B	Diff$	Diff%
Initial costs	$294,650	$266,200	$28,450	
Total PV operating cost	$53,865	$10,896	$42,969	
Total LCA cost	**$240,785**	**$255,304**	**$14,519**	**6.0%**

Example 21–8. Summary comparison of PBX A *v.* PBX B in current year dollars.

Optional Evaluation Factors*	Weight	PBX A		PBX B	
		Rating	Score	Rating	Score
Vendor viability	10				
Reliability	10				
Station equipment options	7				
Voice mail integration	10				
Upgradability	9				
Environmental requirements	7				
Administrative tools	5				
Totals					

*Completed by technical assessment team

1 = low; 10 = high; score = rating × weight

Example 21–9. Final technical optional requirement rating table.

the final results—the total LCA cost. This single value can be compared to another evaluation to quickly compare life cycle costs.

> Example 21–7 results use negative/positive cash flow conventions. These conventions are needed for LCA/NPV calculations but should not be used in a memo format when describing costs to business management. An example of the necessary translation will be provided in the following discussion.

Technical Analysis

Technical specialist team members already completed this step and developed a final technical option requirements factor table that compared the two finalists. The final technical rating table is a consensus of the different technical specialists regarding the relative importance (weight) of the different technical criteria. These technical specialists are members of the project team that helped create the RFPs sent out to potential bidders.

Example 21–9 shows the preliminary optional requirements weights established by the technical specialists.

Example 21–9 will be used during the final optional requirements rating and scoring meeting, during which a consensus for ratings on all criteria used in the optional requirement rating table will be obtained. The technical specialists have already contacted the two finalists to resolve questions that arose during the technical analysis process.

Final Optional Requirements Evaluation

Once the individual technical and financial evaluations have been completed, the information must be consolidated into a single optional requirements rating table, which becomes the focus for completing the final evaluation used to determine which choice will be recommended for purchase. Example 21–10 is the consolidated optional requirements rating table. It contains the decision criteria discussed previously in the financial and technical evaluation sections.

It is now time to review both the financial analysis and technical analysis results and select the PBX telephone system that will be installed by the HealthProd telecommunications department. In this case study example, the telecommunications development manager did not participate in the technical assessment directly—a situation that is not uncommon for managers. Technical specialists nor-

Evaluation Factor	Weight	PBX A		PBX B	
		Rating	Score	Rating	Score
Initial cost	6				
Annual operating costs	10				
Vendor viability*	10				
Reliability*	10				
Station equipment options*	7				
Voice mail integration*	10				
Upgradability*	9				
Environmental requirements*	7				
Administrative tools*	5				
Totals					

*Completed by technical assessment team

1 = low; 10 = high; score = rating × weight

Example 21–10.   Final optional requirements rating table.

mally have a better understanding of technical issues than managers, and managers will play a facilitation role during technical assessment discussions. As a facilitator, managers will frequently find themselves in the position of obtaining a consensus opinion from individuals who have differing opinions. If the consensus negotiation process is handled effectively, the final result should be a valid indicator of the overall opinion of all participants.

The stage is now set for a final meeting, during which all team members who have participated in the project are present and have the opportunity to offer input into the final optional requirements rating table. During the final rating/scoring meeting, the project manager acts as the facilitator and negotiates for a consensus when one or more team members have divergent views.

Example 21–11 summarizes the consensus results obtained at the final evaluation meeting and shows the scoring for the telephone system options. The project's mandatory criteria are also shown in a table below the optional requirements table.

In the evaluation process for selecting the PBX telephone system, all viable acquisition options had to meet the criteria shown in the mandatory criteria listing. The optional requirements table is used only for systems that passed the mandatory requirements. The optional requirements factor table shows the weights used to indicate the relative importance of different nonmandatory decision criteria by using weighting factors. The assigned scores are based on selecting one of the choices as the best and then comparing the other choice to it using a 1 to 10 rating

scale. Different choices can receive the same weight and rating factors if they are considered equivalent.

The final scores show that PBX A received a slightly higher rating (712) than PBX B (688) and the optional requirements rating table provides an easy-to-understand summary of the decision-making process. While the difference of 24 points is only 3 1/2% compared to the PBX A point total, it can be seen that the technical and financial analysis indicated that PBX A received the highest ratings in four of five important factors. In the absence of other information that could have an impact on the decision, PBX A would be selected as the winner based on its final score and the consistent high ratings it received in key areas. PBX A also met all of the mandatory criteria that had been used to screen supplier options.

TRANSLATING TECHNICAL JARGON

Both the financial and technical evaluation processes are technically oriented processes from the viewpoint of business management. The technical terms may include words like bandwidth, Gbps, Mbps, ACD, FDDI, call waiting, DID, OWATS, INWATS, LCR, ARS, NOS, and DOS. On the financial level, terminology such as positive cash flows, negative cash flows, fixed assets, NPV, LCA, pretax, and posttax are examples of technical terms. For the average business manager, these terms are technical jargon—a language used by technical or financial specialists that has

Evaluation Factor	Weight	PBX A		PBX B	
		Rating	Score	Rating	Score
Initial cost	6	9	54	10	60
Annual operating costs	10	10	100	9	90
Vendor viability*	10	10	100	10	100
Reliability*	10	10	100	9	90
Station equipment options*	7	9	63	10	70
Voice mail integration*	10	9	90	10	100
Upgradability*	9	10	90	8	72
Environmental requirements*	7	10	70	8	56
Administrative tools*	5	9	45	10	50
Totals			**712**		**688**

*Completed by technical assessment team

1 = low; 10 = high; score = rating × weight

Mandatory Requirements
Implementation by 9/6/04
Operating line capacity: 250 lines
Wired line capacity: 300 lines
Remote maintenance capabilities
Voice mail messaging
Least cost routing software
Black (color) station equipment

Example 21–11. Final optional requirements rating table.

meaning for individuals who work in those areas only. For people outside the technical areas, technical jargon is gibberish—a spoken or written language that is incomprehensible to outsiders.

It is the responsibility of the telecommunications manager to translate technical gibberish into standard business English that can be understood by nontechnical management. Business English terms must be used in memos, reports, or presentations made to business managers—particularly to upper management. At presentations, the reaction to technical jargon is easy to spot if the presenter is able to recognize it. Typical reactions to technical jargon include rolling of the eyes, lack of interest in the presentation, and leaving the meeting before it is completed. The basic message never reaches the target audience because the presenter is speaking gibberish. The same reaction applies to written documents, except that the writer does not normally get to see the reaction of the reader.

SUMMARY

This summary is organized to correspond with the learning objectives found at the beginning of the chapter.

1. The seven step acquisition project model identifies the overall telecommunications acquisition process from the initial definition of *requirements* through the implementation of the products or services that have been purchased. The acquisition evaluation processes are found in two of the seven steps and are used to ensure that acquisition choices meet the business and technical specifications established for the products or services. The acquisition process identifies key

technical and business decision factors and uses them to measure the acquisition options and select the one that does the best job of meeting the decision factors.

2. Technical and financial requirements provide the two basic categories that are used to identify telecommunications product and service acquisition requirements. Technical requirements are established as part of the design process and will be used to document the technical performance standards that acquisition choices must meet. The financial evaluation process is applied to choices that meet the technical requirements only . For those choices that meet the technical requirements, a financial cost assessment process is initiated to identify the choice that offers the lowest cost. Conceptually, the technical and financial evaluation process consists of screening acquisition choices by carrying out a technical assessment process and then identifying the lowest cost choice.

3. The acquisition process may be carried out as an independent process or may be executed within the context of the telecommunications project life cycle model. During telecommunications projects, the acquisition process is part of the detailed design and acquisition phases. The model's acquisition phase is a critical step in the project process and provides a point of no return. The last management approval meeting is held to obtain the final approval for purchasing the equipment and services needed to implement the project. Prior to the acquisition phase, only a relatively small percentage of the system or network's life cycle cost has been expended (approximately 10%), and a decision to bail out has a small cost impact compared to total life cycle costs.

4. The acquisition and selection process consists of identifying the technical and financial decision criteria that will be used to evaluate acquisition choices. These criteria are separated into mandatory and optional requirement decision criteria. Failure to meet any mandatory requirements automatically rejects that choice. Optional requirements are given an importance level by assigning weight to factors on a 1 to 10 scale. A highly desirable decision factor would be given a weight of 10, and a 1 would be an extremely low level of importance. Acquisition options that pass the mandatory requirements would be rated and a score would be established based on the decision factor's weight and rating assignment. The acquisition choice that passes all mandatory requirements and has the highest total score for the optional requirements factors would normally be selected as the best acquisition choice.

5. The technical evaluation process for evaluating acquisition choices requires a strong knowledge of the specific technology being acquired. The job of identifying critical decision criteria and evaluating potential suppliers is a role best filled by technical specialists who have strong technical skills and appropriate experience levels. The managerial role will be to blend business criteria with the technical requirements so that the final technical evaluation process provides an assessment of the vendor's ability to meet technical specifications while also meeting the business criteria that make the selected vendor a desirable, long-term supplier. These business requirements include an assessment of the vendor's long-term viability in the market, financial resources, technology development track record, and customer support track record.

6. The evaluation process associated with selecting telecommunications products and services for large, complex projects can be an intricate, tedious process—particularly if a competitive bidding process is used to ensure that the best pricing is received. When a large number of bids are received, the overall effort to evaluate them can be minimized by discarding noncompetitive bids early in the evaluation process. A preliminary screening step is used, during which acquisition options are rejected if they do not meet mandatory requirements or are not competitive with the other bids that have been received. The bids that survive the preliminary screening step are then evaluated in detail against the technical and financial decision factors. The winner will be the bid that meets all mandatory requirements and has the highest score for optional requirements factors. The selected alternative should be the best choice of all acquisition options.

7. The LCA/NPV financial model summarizes the initial investment costs and life cycle operating costs incurred over the life of the telecommunications product or service that is being evaluated. The key steps in using the model are: 1) identify the LCA study length, 2) identify current year capital and operating costs, 3) identify the inflation factor for future year calculations, 4) identify the organization's cost of money that will be used for PV calculations, 5) calculate LCA costs for items 1 through 4, and 6) interpret the results to select the best financial option.

8. Identifying the best choice when purchasing telecommunications products and services requires a high level of technical, business, and financial expertise. Unless the technical requirements are met, the acquisition

process is flawed. Technical specialists are capable of assessing technical details, but in a project team environment, there are typically different viewpoints in the selection process. The role of project managers and telecommunications managers is to facilitate the decision-making process. If the facilitation process is done effectively, the final assessment results will have the support of all team members and will result in the selection of the best product or service. The selected product or service would best meet the overall technical, business, and financial criteria established for the acquisition.

9. Technical jargon refers to the language used by technical specialists. Jargon has little meaning for business management personnel. The use of jargon is essential for communication between individuals in a technical area, but it must be translated into a format that is understandable to business managers for meetings, conversations, or memos. Project managers and telecommunications managers have the primary responsibility for making this translation when communicating outside of the telecommunications department. Unless this step is taken, there is little likelihood that telecommunications will gain support from upper management to obtain the funding needed for telecommunications projects that could be a valuable business asset. Telecommunications managers have a primary business role and a secondary technology role within a business.

10. An understanding of how to apply the seven step acquisition model to a real world situation is best demonstrated by solving a case study. While the information can be presented in a text teaching format, only the reader will know if he or she understands the acquisition process. This can be demonstrated only by completing the documentation deliverables that show an understanding of the flowchart steps.

KEY TERMS AND CONCEPTS

The "language" of telecommunications management is multifaceted and includes words and phrases from managerial, technological, accounting, regulatory, and other business areas. The definitions of these key terms and concepts can be found within the chapter and in the glossary.

Acquisition Model
Annual Operating Costs
Boilerplate
Common Cost Data
Decision Making Process
Inflation Factor

LCA/NPV Model
Mandatory Technical Requirements
Optional Requirements Criteria
Optional Requirements Rating
Optional Requirements Score
Preliminary Screening

PV Factor
RFP
RFQ
Telecommunications Project Life Cycle
    model

REVIEW

The following questions are open-ended—predefined answers are not included as part of the text. The purpose of these questions is to allow the readers to test themselves on the chapter material.

1. List and explain the seven steps in the telecommunications acquisition model.

2. What is the relative importance of technical and financial assessment criteria when evaluating acquisition alternatives? Why?

3. Describe the general decision-making model shown in Figure 21–1, and describe the role of each element.

4. How are mandatory requirements and optional requirements used in the decision-making model?

5. How does the decision-making model allow subjective information to be used to evaluate acquisition choices?

6. Describe the rating and scoring processes used for evaluating optional requirements.

7. Describe the preliminary screening process and its purpose.

8. What is the value of performing an LCA when acquiring telecommunications products?

9. What is the purpose of PV factors?

10. What is the purpose of the final optional requirements evaluation process?

11. What is the relationship between the LCA results and the optional requirements rating process?

MULTIPLE CHOICE

1. The evaluate vendor responses acquisition activity is acquisition step _____.
   - a. 3
   - b. 4
   - c. 5
   - d. 6
   - e. 7

2. The primary criterion for selecting an acquisition option will be based on _____ factors.
   - a. RFI
   - b. technical
   - c. financial
   - d. managerial
   - e. administrative

3. In the text's decision-making model, an acquisition recommendation will be based on _____, _____, and _____.
   - a. sales agreements
   - b. managerial judgment
   - c. mandatory requirements
   - d. boilerplate requirements
   - e. optional requirements

4. The two major cost elements included in a typical financial attribute rating table are _____.
   - a. current asset costs
   - b. fixed asset costs
   - c. initial costs
   - d. development costs
   - e. operating costs

5. The highest score an attribute can receive in the text's decision-making model is _____.
   - a. 1
   - b. 5
   - c. 10
   - d. 100
   - e. insufficient information provided

6. Under straight line depreciation, a telephone system with an acquisition cost of $100,000, a salvage value of $10,000, and an asset life of 5 years is depreciated at a rate of _____ per year.
   - a. $15,000
   - b. $18,000
   - c. $20,000
   - d. $50,000
   - e. None of the above.

7. _____ selection criteria are criteria that alternatives must meet or they will be dropped from further consideration.
   - a. Obligatory
   - b. Desirable
   - c. LCA/NPV
   - d. Mandatory
   - e. Optional

8. Options A and B meet mandatory evaluation criteria and the desirability scores are 256 and 265, respectively. _____ would normally be selected.
   - a. Option A
   - b. Option B
   - c. Insufficient information has been provided.
   - d. Both options
   - e. None of the above

9. For the following matrix, the total score for option B is _____.
   - a. 221
   - b. 230
   - c. 239
   - d. 26
   - e. None of the above.

Factor	Weight	A Rating	A Score	B Rating	B Score
1	10	10		7	
2	9	10		9	
3	7	7		10	

10. The initial cost for a fixed asset is $90,000. Assuming a 5 year life and a 10% salvage value, the annual straight line depreciation would be _____ per year.
    - a. $15,200
    - b. $16,200
    - c. $18,000
    - d. $90,000

11. If the inflation% used for an LCA is 8%, a cost with a current year value of $15,000 will cost _____ in the third year of the analysis.
    - a. $15,000
    - b. $16,200
    - c. $17,496
    - d. $18,896
    - e. None of the above.

12. The salvage value for an asset with a 5 year life is taken in the _____ of a seven year financial analysis.

    a. first
    b. fourth
    c. fifth
    d. sixth
    e. seventh

13. Based on the following matrix, the best option is _____.

    a. option A
    b. option B
    c. option 1
    d. none of the above

Factor	Weight	A Rating	A Score	B Rating	B Score
1	10	10		7	
2	9	8		9	
3	7	9		10	

14. The initial cost for a fixed asset is $75,000. Assuming a 5 year life and a 5% salvage value, the annual straight line depreciation would be _____ per year.

    a. $13,500
    b. $14,250
    c. $15,000
    d. $75,000
    e. none of the above

15. If the inflation% used for an LCA is 3%, a cost with a current year value of $75,000 will cost _____ in the fifth year of the analysis.

    a. $87,739
    b. $75,000
    c. $84,413
    d. $81,955
    e. $86,946

16. Under straight line depreciation, a telephone system with an acquisition cost of $125,000, a salvage value of $11,000, and an asset life of 5 years is depreciated at a rate of _____ per year.

    a. $114,000
    b. $22,500
    c. $25,000
    d. $22,800
    e. $125,000
    f. $86,946

17. Option A's initial cost is $100,000 and it costs $12,250 per year to operate. Option B's initial cost is $115,000 and it costs $9,500 per year to operate. Using this information and life cycle analysis period of seven years, which option would you select?

    a. option A
    b. option B
    c. neither option
    d. either option

18. An option's cost is $1,060,000 and the operating cost is $79,500 per year. Over a 5 year period, the life cycle cost would be _____.

    a. $1,060,000
    b. $397,500
    c. $212,000
    d. $1,457,500
    e. none of the above

19. An option's cost is $775,000 and the operating cost is $60,500 per year. Over a 5 year period, the operating cost would be _____.

    a. $775,000
    b. $302,500
    c. $155,000
    d. $1,077,500
    e. none of the above

20. PV costs for future years when inflation is zero would normally be _____ than current year costs.

    a. higher
    b. lower
    c. the same
    d. none of the above

22

ACQUISITION MANAGEMENT: A CASE STUDY

LEARNING OBJECTIVES

There is one basic learning objective for this chapter. It is to understand and apply the information reviewed in Chapters 19, 20, and 21 to a hypothetical real world problem: A business enterprise is acquiring a new PBX telephone system. A case study format will be followed. The acquisition is for a new PBX telephone system that must be purchased to handle the voice communication requirements at a TransProd Corporation business location. The procedures used in the case study will be similar those followed in the case study example in Chapter 21, (*Evaluating Acquisition Options*).

It is recommended that the reader approach this chapter by reading the case study and developing a project plan that they would use to manage the PBX acquisition requirements. The reader's project plan should be used to develop a solution for which the primary emphasis is on developing the managerial procedures that would be used to acquire the system (the same format shown in the Chapter 21 example). Develop a plan that identifies the documentation needed to support an acquisition recommendation and compare your results to the case study solution in the chapter.

INTRODUCTION

In the case study, a telecommunications manager must make an acquisition recommendation for one of four PBX telephone system options. The system is a 400 line system that will be installed at a new location. The decision information (technical and financial) is contained in RFP responses prepared by four vendors. As was the case for the Chapter 21 example, there will be little discussion of how the technical decision factors were established, because this is a more appropriate topic for a technology-based text. The development of technical decision factors is an area that is outside the scope of this text and is a role normally assigned to technical specialists. This is a managerial project. The telecommunications manager: 1) develops an overall game plan to coordinate the required acquisition activities, 2) delegates the technical requirements to technical specialists, and 3) assumes direct responsibility for completing the financial and business documentation requirements. The managerial role will be discussed in detail, but the selection of the technical decision factors will be presented as a pro forma technical decision whose elements have been established by the project's technical specialists.

The case study will review the entire acquisition decision process from the preliminary screening stage to the selection of a winner (steps 1 through 6 in the acquisition model discussed in Chapters 20 and 21).

TRANSPROD CASE STUDY DESCRIPTION

The TransProd Corporation is a major manufacturer and distributor of parts for the automobile repair marketplace. Its headquarters location is in Los Angeles. Its manufacturing locations (in Los Angeles and Atlanta) fabricate, assemble, and store automobile parts for distribution throughout the U.S. The TransProd Corporation has experienced outstanding growth during the last fifteen years and now requires additional manufacturing capacity to keep pace with customer demands. The TransProd management board initiated a six month study to identify the best area of the U.S. for installing the new plant. The study's recommendation was that the plant should be located in Columbus, Ohio. A Columbus-based plant would be able to handle TransProd's midwest and east coast distribution requirements—an area where market growth has been particularly high. The new plant—referred to internally as the Columbus plant—will fabricate, assemble, and store automotive parts to be distributed to central and northeast U.S. distributor locations. In addition to housing manufacturing personnel, the new plant will have facilities for purchasing, engineering, production planning, sales, order processing, and customer service personnel. The plant is scheduled for occupancy in September, 2004.

TransProd Columbus Plant Organization

The organization chart for the new Columbus plant is shown in Figure 22–1. An initial staffing level of 400 is planned, which includes the staffing requirements for a satellite information services department to handle local information technology needs. The headquarters information services department will direct the information technology installation efforts of the plant and provide them with corporate data network support services—as it does for all other TransProd plant locations.

The Columbus plant's information services department will consist of two individual departments: 1) program services to handle software application requirements and 2) telecommunications to provide a help desk function that has operational responsibility for the Columbus plant telecommunications facilities. The telecommunications department is illustrated in Figure 22–2.

Telephone System Project

A 400-line PBX telephone system will be installed at the Columbus plant to handle the location's voice communication needs. The telephone system project was initiated by headquarters, which provided a project manager and technical specialists for the project. The Columbus telecommunications manager and telecommunications operations manager (Figure 22–2) were former members of the headquarters telecommunications department, and the telecommunications manager has overall managerial responsibility for all the telecommunications projects that will be implemented at the Columbus plant, including the PBX telephone system project. The headquarters project manager and technical specialists are accountable to the telecommunications manager and will return to the headquarters organization after the Columbus plant's telephone system project is completed.

The Columbus plant's telecommunications operations department has a staff of ten, who will provide on site technical support for telephone system, LAN, internetwork, and WAN services. Headquarters' telecom department will be the escalation resource if the local operations department requires assistance. The plant's help desk department provides a single point of contact for users of

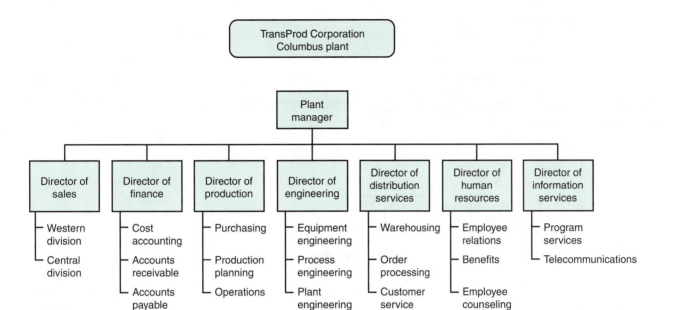

Figure 22–1. TransProd Columbus plant organization chart.

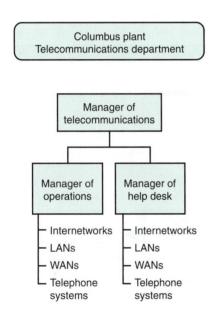

Figure 22–2. Columbus plant telecommunications department.

telecommunications services and also provides various support services functions, including maintaining and publishing a local telephone and LAN directory, authorizing local telecommunications bills for payment, and employee training for telephone and LAN services.

ACQUISITION PROJECT GAME PLAN

It is now June 11, 2004, and the Columbus telecommunications manager has just left a meeting held with the PBX system project team. The meeting was held to review the status of the acquisition process and initiate the activities for the final technical and financial review process.

The project team is following a baseline project schedule developed using MS-Project software. The plan's project activities are based on the project steps shown in the Figure 22–3 life cycle model. Key milestones from the baseline plan are summarized in Table 22–1. The Columbus telecommunications manager had been part of the project team that set up the MS-Project schedule and is familiar with all project plan elements.

Project Status Summary

During the detailed design phase (project step 3), the project team completed acquisition steps 1 through 4 (Figure 22–4) and obtained the vendor response information needed to complete acquisition step 5. The vendors had been working on the RFP responses for seven weeks.

The project team carried out the preliminary screening portion of acquisition step 5 (refer to Figure 22–5) for the four RFP responses that had been solicited and received. One bid was eliminated during the screening stage,

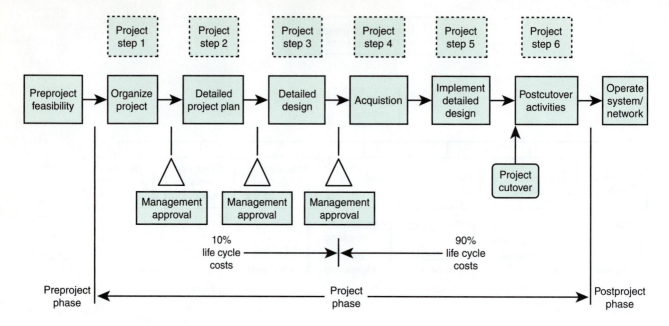

Figure 22–3. Telecommunications project life cycle model.

TABLE 22–1 Key PBX System Project Dates

Date	Milestone Event
June 10, 2004	Deadline date for receipt of vendor RFP responses.
June 23, 2004	Management approval checkpoint meeting: Present final PBX system acquisition recommendation.
June 25, 2004	Sign formal contract with selected PBX system vendor to allow sufficient lead time for manufacturing the system.
September 7, 2004	Cutover date for new Columbus plant PBX telephone system.

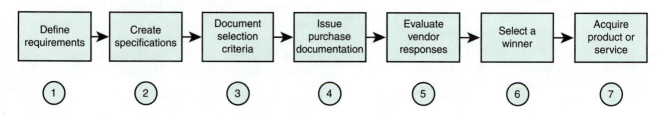

Figure 22–4. Telecommunications seven step acquisition model.

and detailed technical evaluations will be made of the three remaining bids.

Telecommunications Manager's Game Plan

The Columbus plant's director of information services (Figure 22–1) asked the telecommunications manager to prepare a final PBX telephone system recommendation in a format suitable for presentation to the Columbus plant management board (the plant manager and his or her direct reports). The meeting is scheduled for June 23, and the objective is to obtain final approval from the board for the system acquisition and get the necessary signatures on ac-

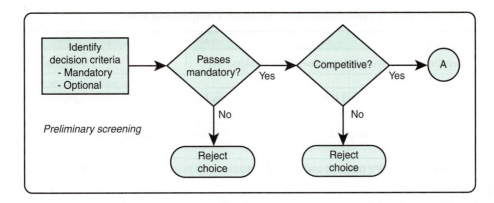

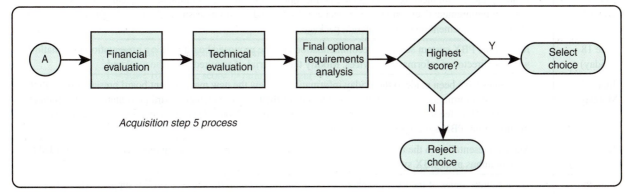

Figure 22–5. Acquisition decision process flowchart.

quisition contracts. The contracts must be signed by Friday (June 25) so that the project implementation schedule can be met.

The board meeting provides the telecommunications manager with the opportunity to obtain credibility with board members for the newly formed Columbus plant telecommunications department. It is important that the presentation information answer all potential questions that board members could ask to minimize the potential for project delays. Therefore, the telecommunications manager developed a detailed game plan that summarized the current status and clearly identified next-step requirements. He or she will use this information at the board meeting.

Table 22–2 is the document that the manager created to ensure that all the pieces come together for the management board presentation. (Because the manager has good PC skills, the use of a word processing table allows the table to be prepared as shown in the example. The date is June 11, 2004.)

The approach used by the manager for developing the acquisition plan (Table 22–2) was to identify critical dates and highlight those activities that must be

completed to meet this date. The focus of the manager's plan will be to identify the current status of the project, the system selection process and recommendations, and the activities needed to ensure that the contract is approved and signed by June 25—the date used with the vendors to ensure that the system is manufactured and delivered on time for the September 7 project cutover date. Table 22–2 provides a schedule for the work that must be done in a little over a week to finalize project step 3 (detailed design) and initiate the acquisition phase (project step 4).

The following discussion will convert the general statements in Table 22–2 into the various information elements that will be used to provide input for the June 24 management board meeting presentation package.

PBX SYSTEM ACQUISITION PHASE

The following summarizes the project-to-date acquisition information developed by the project team and completes acquisition steps 5 and 6.

Description	Year 0	Year 1	Year 2	Year 3	Year 4	Year 5	Year 6	Total
PBX A operating costs								
Lease costs	$0	$0	$0	$0	$0	$0	$0	
Maintenance	$0	($39,375)	($41,344)	($43,411)	($45,581)	($47,861)	($50,254)	($267,825)
Moves, adds, changes	($5,580)	($5,859)	($6,152)	($6,460)	($6,783)	($7,122)	($7,478)	($45,432)
Trunk costs	($24,000)	($25,200)	($26,460)	($27,783)	($29,172)	($30,631)	($32,162)	($195,408)
Software (1)	($600)	($600)	($600)	($600)	($600)	($600)	($600)	($4,200)
Floor space	($10,200)	($10,710)	($11,246)	($11,808)	($12,398)	($13,018)	($13,669)	($83,048)
Power & air conditioning	($1,822)	($1,913)	($2,009)	($2,109)	($2,215)	($2,325)	($2,442)	($14,835)
Depreciation	$77,751	$77,751	$77,751	$77,751	$77,751			$388,755
Salvage	$0	$0	$0	$0	$0	$0	$43,195	$43,195
Annual operating costs	**$35,549**	**($5,906)**	**($10,059)**	**($14,420)**	**($18,998)**	**($101,557)**	**($63,409)**	**($178,800)**
PV factors	**1.0000**	**0.9346**	**0.8734**	**0.8163**	**0.7629**	**0.7130**	**0.6663**	
PV operating costs	**$35,549**	**($5,520)**	**($8,786)**	**($11,771)**	**($14,494)**	**($72,408)**	**($42,252)**	**($119,682)**

PBX A initial cost ($431,950)
Total PV operating cost ($119,682)
Total LCA cost ($551,632)

(1) A fixed term contract was signed.

Description	Year 0	Year 1	Year 2	Year 3	Year 4	Year 5	Year 6	Total
PBX C operating costs								
Lease costs	$0	$0	$0	$0	$0	$0	$0	$0
Maintenance	$0	($37,275)	($39,139)	($41,096)	($43,150)	($45,308)	($47,573)	($253,541)
Moves, adds, changes	($5,580)	($5,859)	($6,152)	($6,460)	($6,783)	($7,122)	($7,478)	($45,432)
Trunk costs	($24,000)	($25,200)	($26,460)	($27,783)	($29,172)	($30,631)	($32,162)	($195,408)
Software (1)	($500)	($500)	($500)	($500)	($500)	($500)	($500)	($3,500)
Floor space	($7,800)	($8,190)	($8,600)	($9,029)	($9,481)	($9,955)	($10,453)	($63,508)
Power & air conditoning	($1,682)	($1,766)	($1,854)	($1,947)	($2,044)	($2,147)	($2,254)	($13,694)
Depreciation	$71,496	$71,496	$71,496	$71,496	$71,496			$357,480
Salvage	$0	$0	$0	$0	$0	$0	$39,720	$39,720
Annual operating costs	**$31,934**	**($7,294)**	**($11,209)**	**($15,319)**	**($19,634)**	**($95,662)**	**($60,700)**	**($177,884)**
PV factors	**1.0000**	**0.9346**	**0.8734**	**0.8163**	**0.7629**	**0.7130**	**0.6663**	
PV operating costs	**$31,934**	**($6,817)**	**($9,790)**	**($12,505)**	**($14,979)**	**($68,206)**	**($40,447)**	**($120,809)**

PBX C initial cost ($397,200)
Total PV operating cost ($120,809)
Total LCA cost ($518,009)

Example 22–5. PBX A *v.* PBX C operating costs.

Description	PBX A	PBX C	Diff$	Diff%
Initial Costs	$431,950	$397,200	$34,750	
Total PV Operating Cost	$119,682	$120,809	$ 1,127	
TOTAL LCA COST	**$551,632**	**$518,009**	**$33,623**	**6.10%**

Example 22–6. PBX A *v.* PBX C cost summary.

Optional Evaluation Factor	Weight	PBX A Rating	PBX A Score	PBX C Rating	PBX C Score
Initial cost	10	6	60	9	90
Operating costs	7	10	70	10	70
Vendor viability*	10	10	100	10	100
System reliability*	10	10	100	10	100
Station equipment features*	6	8	48	9	54
Voice messaging integration*	10	9	90	10	100
Upgradeability*	9	9	81	10	90
Environmental requirements*	7	10	70	9	63
Administrative tools*	9	9	81	10	90
Totals			**700**		**757**

* Technical assessment team items

1 = low; 10 = high; score = rating × weight

Example 22–7.   Final rating matrix for PBX A *v.* PBX C.

Seven Year Purchase *v.* Lease Evaluation of PBX C
Pretax Analysis; Includes Inflation Allowance
Uses Standard Economic Model Format & Assumptions

Description	PBX A	PBX C
Product costs:		
PBX	($340,300)	$0
Voice mail	($33,700)	$0
Spares	($2,450)	$0
Installation	($10,500)	$0
Software	($10,250)	$0
Total installed cost	**($397,200)**	**$0**

Common Cost Data	Item
Inflation%	5%
Annual inflation factor	105%
Power$/KWHr	$0.16
Cost of money	7%
Depreciation period (years)	5
Salvage%	10%
Floor space$ ($/yr/sq ft)	$24.00

Annual Costs:	Purchase	Lease
Lease	$0	($53,000)
Maintenance	($35,500)	$0
Moves, adds, changes	($5,580)	($5,580)
Trunk costs	($24,000)	($24,000)
Software upgrades	($500)	$0
Floor space (sq. ft.)	325	325
Floor space costs	($7,800)	($7,800)
Power & air cond. (KW/Hr)	1.20	1.20
Power & air cond. costs	($1,682)	($1,682)
Depreciation (straight line)	$71,496	$0
Salvage value	$39,720	$0

Example 22–8.   PBX C telephone system lease *v.* purchase analysis.

Description	Year 0	Year 1	Year 2	Year 3	Year 4	Year 5	Year 6	Total
Purchase operating costs								
Lease costs	$0	$0	$0	$0	$0	$0	$0	
Maintenance	$0	($37,275)	($39,139)	($41,096)	($43,150)	($45,308)	($47,573)	($253,541)
Moves, adds, changes	($5,580)	($5,859)	($6,152)	($6,460)	($6,783)	($7,122)	($7,478)	($45,432)
Trunk costs	($24,000)	($25,200)	($26,460)	($27,783)	($29,172)	($30,631)	($32,162)	($195,408)
Software (1)	($500)	($500)	($500)	($500)	($500)	($500)	($500)	($3,500)
Floor space	($7,800)	($8,190)	($8,600)	($9,029)	($9,481)	($9,955)	($10,453)	($63,508)
Power & air conditioning	($1,682)	($1,766)	($1,854)	($1,947)	($2,044)	($2,147)	($2,254)	($13,694)
Depreciation	$71,496	$71,496	$71,496	$71,496	$71,496			$357,480
Salvage	$0	$0	$0	$0	$0	$0	$39,720	$39,720
Annual operating costs	**$31,934**	**($7,294)**	**($11,209)**	**($15,319)**	**($19,634)**	**($95,662)**	**($60,700)**	**($177,884)**
PV factors	**1.0000**	**0.9346**	**0.8734**	**0.8163**	**0.7629**	**0.7130**	**0.6663**	
PV operating costs	**$31,934**	**($6,817)**	**($9,790)**	**($12,505)**	**($14,979)**	**($68,206)**	**($40,447)**	**($120,809)**

Purchase initial cost   ($397,200)
Total PV operating cost   ($120,809)
Total LCA cost   ($518,009)

(1) A fixed term contract would be signed.

Description	Year 0	Year 1	Year 2	Year 3	Year 4	Year 5	Year 6	Total
Lease operating costs								
Lease costs	($53,000)	($53,000)	($53,000)	($53,000)	($53,000)	($53,000)	($53,000)	($371,000)
Maintenance	$0	$0	$0	$0	$0	$0	$0	$0
Moves, adds, changes	($5,580)	($5,859)	($6,152)	($6,460)	($6,783)	($7,122)	($7,478)	($45,432)
Trunk costs	($24,000)	($25,200)	($26,460)	($27,783)	($29,172)	($30,631)	($32,162)	($195,408)
Software	$0	$0	$0	$0	$0	$0	$0	$0
Floor space	($7,800)	($8,190)	($8,600)	($9,029)	($9,481)	($9,955)	($10,453)	($63,508)
Power & air conditioning	($1,682)	($1,766)	($1,854)	($1,947)	($2,044)	($2,147)	($2,254)	($13,694)
Depreciation	$0	$0	$0	$0	$0			$0
Salvage	$0	$0	$0	$0	$0	$0	$0	$0
Annual operating costs	**($92,062)**	**($94,015)**	**($96,066)**	**($98,219)**	**($100,480)**	**($102,854)**	**($105,347)**	**($689,042)**
PV factors	**1.0000**	**0.9346**	**0.8734**	**0.8163**	**0.7629**	**0.7130**	**0.6663**	
PV operating costs	**($92,062)**	**($87,865)**	**($83,908)**	**($80,176)**	**($76,656)**	**($73,333)**	**($70,197)**	**($564,196)**

Lease initial cost $0
Total PV operating cost   ($564,196)
Total LCA cost   ($564,196)

Example 22–9.   PBX C purchase *v.* lease operating costs.

Description	Purchase	Lease	Diff$	Diff%
Initial costs	$397,200	$0	$397,200	
Total PV operating cost	$120,809	$564,196	$443,387	
Total LCA cost	**$518,009**	**$564,196**	**$46,187**	**8.9%**

Example 22–10. PBX C lease *v.* purchase cost summary.

Purchase *v.* Lease Evaluation Matrix

Evaluation Factor	Weight	Purchase Option		Lease Option	
		Rating	Score	Rating	Score
Initial cost	10	6	60	10	100
Annual operating cost	8	10	80	6	48
Vendor viability*	10	10	100	10	100
System reliability*	10	10	100	10	100
Station equipment features*	6	9	54	9	54
Voice messaging integration*	10	10	100	10	100
Upgradability*	9	10	90	10	90
Environmental requirements*	7	9	63	9	63
Administrative tools*	9	10	90	10	90
Totals			**737**		**745**

* Technical assessment team items

1 = low; 10 = high; score = rating × weight

Example 22–11. Purchase *v.* lease rating matrix for PBX C.

Example 22–10 summarizes the results of the lease *v.* purchase analysis for PBX C by summarizing the information in a single table.

The difference between the purchase and lease expenses over a seven year period is $46,187 (8.9%). This amounts to an average savings per year of about $6,600 in favor of the purchase option. While the telecommunications manager is biased toward the lower cost option (the purchase option), the final lease *v.* purchase decision will be left to the finance department.

Acquisition Summary

The telecommunications manager also prepared a mini-optional requirements comparison table between the lease and purchase option for PBX C (Example 22–11) to use if someone requests the information.

Because the same PBX system is used for both analyses, the difference is due to the financial evaluation factors. The finance department plans to recommend the lease option when it is presented to the midwest management board.

At this time, the Columbus plant has all the information needed to develop the management board presentation.

MANAGEMENT DOCUMENTATION

The Columbus plant's telecommunications manager put together a recommendation letter and a draft management board presentation for the June 23 meeting to be held with the director of information services. The manager plans to review both the letter and the presentation information with the director and modify them, as needed, as preparation for the management board meeting.

The midwest telecommunications manager's letter and presentation information are shown in Examples 22–12, and 22–13, respectively.

Date: June 21, 2004

To: Director of Information Services
From: Manager of Telecommunications
Subject: Columbus Plant Telephone System Recommendation

The following provides a telephone system selection recommendation for implementing a system at the Columbus plant. The recommendations have been reviewed with the finance department.

Background information
An RFP was sent to four telephone system suppliers that had the necessary qualifications for providing and maintaining a telephone system that could meet the needs of the Columbus location. The system will provide the voice communications and voice mail requirements for the 400 employees that will be housed at the Columbus plant. The plant will begin operations on September 2, 2004.

The RFPs contained the technical and administrative requirements for the new system and the vendors provided us with a bid response to our RFPs. A technical and financial evaluation has been completed for the four bids, and the [vendor C] choice has been selected as best meeting our requirements. Vendor C's system provides the best technical solution and is also the lowest priced system. The finance department has been involved with the telephone system selection process and agrees with our financial analysis results. They recommend that the new system should be acquired on a leased basis.

Evaluation process
The headquarters telecommunications department provided the technical personnel staffing for the Columbus plant telephone system project and they carried out the technical evaluation of the different systems. The financial analysis used the LCA/NPV format guidelines issued by the finance department and covers a seven year period. The technical and financial information used in the various analyses was provided from the vendors' bid responses.

One of the original bidders [vendor D] was eliminated early in the evaluation process because it was not technically or financially competitive with the other three bids. The proposals from the remaining three bids—vendor A, vendor B, and vendor C—were reviewed in detail. Vendor C's telephone system proposal was selected as having the best technical solution and also providing the lowest pricing of the three alternatives. The results of the evaluation analysis are summarized in Appendix A.

The lease *v.* purchase analysis for the vendor C telephone system is provided in Appendix B and has been reviewed by the Finance department. They recommend the lease option and will provide the information supporting the lease recommendation.

The total lease cost for the seven year period will be $371,000, and the total operating budget for this time period (including the lease costs) will be $564,196.

Next Steps/Recommendations
It is recommended that the vendor C telephone system be selected for implementation at the Columbus plant and that the leasing option be used.

The leasing agreements should be approved and signed by June 25 so that we can meet the September 7 start schedule.

Example 22–12a.   Page 1 of 4.

Comparison of three Columbus plant telephone system options

Evaluation Factor	Weight	PBX A		PBX B		PBX C	
		Rating	Score	Rating	Score	Rating	Score
Initial cost	10	6	60	10	100	9	90
Annual operating cost	7	10	70	8	56	10	70
Vendor viability*	10	10	100	8	80	10	100
System reliability*	10	10	100	8	80	10	100
Station equipment features*	6	8	48	10	60	9	54
Voice messaging integration*	10	9	90	8	80	10	100
Upgradability*	9	9	81	7	63	10	90
Environmental requirements*	7	10	70	9	63	9	63
Administrative tools*	9	9	81	9	81	10	90
Totals			**700**		**663**		**757**

*Technical Assessment Team Items
1 = Low; 10 = high; score = rating × weight

Example 22–12b. Page 2 of 4.

Seven year purchase v. lease evaluation for PBX C
Pretax analysis; Includes inflation allowance
Uses standard economic model format & assumptions

Description	Purchase	Lease
Product costs:		
PBX	($340,300)	$0
Voice mail	($33,700)	$0
Spares	($2,450)	$0
Installation	($10,500)	$0
Software	($10,250)	$0
Shipping	$0	$0
Trunk installation	$0	$0
Training	$0	$0
Total installed cost	**($397,200)**	**$0**

Common cost data	Item
Inflation%	5%
Annual inflation factor	105%
Power$/KWHr	$0.16
Cost of money	7%
Depreciation period (years)	5
Salvage%	10%
Floor space$ ($/yr/sq ft)	$24.00

Annual costs:	Purchase	Lease
Lease	$0	($53,000)
Maintenance	($35,500)	$0
Moves, adds, changes	($5,580)	($5,580)
Trunk costs	($24,000)	($24,000)
Software upgrades	($500)	$0
Floor space (Sq. Ft.)	325	325
Floor space costs	($7,800)	($7,800)
Power & air conditioning (KW/Hr)	1.20	1.20
Power & air conditioning costs	($1,682)	($1,682)
Depreciation (straight line)	$71,496	$0
Salvage value	$39,720	$0

Example 22–12c.   Page 3 of 4.

Description	Year 0	Year 1	Year 2	Year 3	Year 4	Year 5	Year 6	Total
Purchase operating costs								
Lease costs	$0	$0	$0	$0	$0	$0	$0	
Maintenance	$0	($37,275)	($39,139)	($41,096)	($43,150)	($45,308)	($47,573)	($253,541)
Moves, adds, changes	($5,580)	($5,859)	($6,152)	($6,460)	($6,783)	($7,122)	($7,478)	($45,432)
Trunk costs	($24,000)	($25,200)	($26,460)	($27,783)	($29,172)	($30,631)	($32,162)	($195,408)
Software (1)	($500)	($500)	($500)	($500)	($500)	($500)	($500)	($3,500)
Floor space	($7,800)	($8,190)	($8,600)	($9,029)	($9,481)	($9,955)	($10,453)	($63,508)
Power & air conditioning	($1,682)	($1,766)	($1,854)	($1,947)	($2,044)	($2,147)	($2,254)	($13,694)
Depreciation	$71,496	$71,496	$71,496	$71,496	$71,496			$357,480
Salvage	$0	$0	$0	$0	$0	$0	$39,720	$39,720
Annual operating costs	$31,934	($7,294)	($11,209)	($15,319)	($19,634)	($95,662)	($60,700)	($177,884)
PV factors	1.0000	0.9346	0.8734	0.8163	0.7629	0.7130	0.6663	
PV operating costs	$31,934	($6,817)	($9,790)	($12,505)	($14,979)	($68,206)	($40,447)	($120,809)

Purchase initial cost	($397,200)
Total PV operating cost	($120,809)
Total LCA cost	($518,009)

(1) A fixed term contract was signed.

Description	Year 0	Year 1	Year 2	Year 3	Year 4	Year 5	Year 6	Total
Lease operating costs								
Lease costs	($53,000)	($53,000)	($53,000)	($53,000)	($53,000)	($53,000)	($53,000)	($371,000)
Maintenance	$0	$0	$0	$0	$0	$0	$0	$0
Moves, adds, changes	($5,580)	($5,859)	($6,152)	($6,460)	($6,783)	($7,122)	($7,478)	($45,432)
Trunk costs	($24,000)	($25,200)	($26,460)	($27,783)	($29,172)	($30,631)	($32,162)	($195,408)
Software	$0	$0	$0	$0	$0	$0	$0	$0
Floor space	($7,800)	($8,190)	($8,600)	($9,029)	($9,481)	($9,955)	($10,453)	($63,508)
Power & air conditioning	($1,682)	($1,766)	($1,854)	($1,947)	($2,044)	($2,147)	($2,254)	($13,694)
Depreciation	$0	$0	$0	$0	$0			$0
Salvage	$0	$0	$0	$0	$0	$0	$0	$0
Annual operating costs	($92,062)	($94,015)	($96,066)	($98,219)	($100,480)	($102,854)	($105,347)	($689,042)
PV factors	1.0000	0.9346	0.8734	0.8163	0.7629	0.7130	0.6663	
PV operating costs	($92,062)	($87,865)	($83,908)	($80,176)	($76,656)	($73,333)	($70,197)	($564,196)

Lease initial cost	$0
Total PV operating cost	($564,196)
Total LCA cost	($564,196)

Description	Purchase	Lease	Diff$	Diff%
Initial costs	($397,200)	$0	$397,200	−100%
Total PV Operating Cost	($120,809)	($564,196)	($443,387)	367%
Total LCA cost	($518,009)	($564,196)	($46,187)	8.92%

Example 22–12d. Page 4 of 4.

**TransProd
Columbus Plant
Telephone System Project**

**Management Board Meeting
June 23, 2004**

Example 22–13a. Presentation example page 1 of 11.

Agenda

- Project overview
- Project description
- Project network diagram
- Project status
- System recommendation
- Telephone set policy
- Next steps

Example 22–13b. Presentation example page 2 of 11.

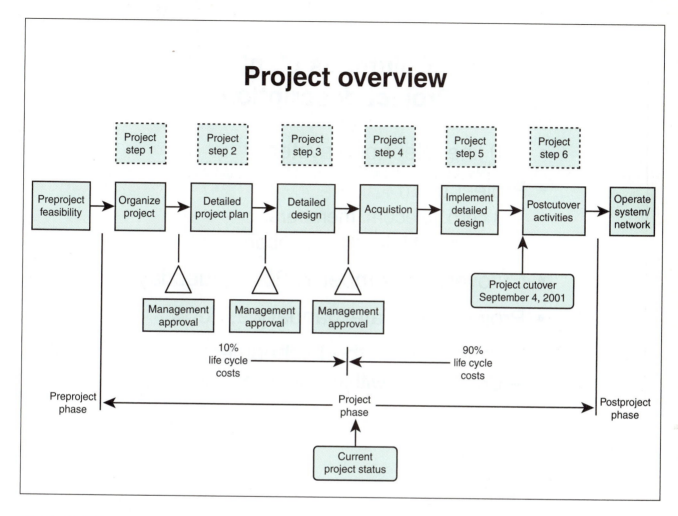

Example 22–13c. Presentation example page 3 of 11.

MANAGEMENT BOARD PRESENTATION

The telecommunications manager created a preliminary management board presentation that will be reviewed with the director of information services at the meeting on June 23. The presentation is shown in Example 22–13.

Example 22–13 was prepared for discussion purposes because the telecommunications manager was uncertain about the level of detail that would be most appropriate at a board meeting. The director will react to the basic presentation and, based on this reaction, the telecommunications manager can modify the presentation as required.

An incomplete telecommunications policy slide was included because to provide a detailed telephone standard in the absence of real world project information would be misleading and outside the context of the acquisition process.

Columbus plant
Project description

- 400 line telephone system
- Project team
  —3 corp. telecom. members
  —2 midwest telecom. members
- Cutover: September 7, 2004 (Tuesday)
- Project start date: January 2, 2004
- Critical path method schedule
  —Coordinated with construction schedule

Example 22–13d. Presentation example page 4 of 11.

Project status (slide 1 of 2)

- System design completed 4-16-04
  —Detailed technical specifications
- Purchase bids issued 4-23-04
  —Four qualified bidders
    - Bidder A, Bidder B, Bidder C, Bidder D

Example 22–13e. Presentation example page 5 of 11.

Project status (slide 2 of 2)

- Bid responses received 6-10-04
- Bid evaluation completed 6-16-01
  - —Bidder D eliminated
    - No technical advantages
    - 30% higher than next highest bid
  - —Detailed review of A, B, and C Options
    - Bidder C selected
      - —Best technical solution
      - —lowest cost

Example 22–13f. Presentation example page 6 of 11.

System recommendation: Selection criteria

Mandatory requirements
System cutover: September 7, 2004
Operating line capacity: 400 lines
Wired line capacity: 450 lines
Remote maintenance capabilities
Voice mail messaging
Least cost routing software
Beige (color) station equipment

Example 22–13g. Presentation example page 7 of 11.

System recommendation: Selection criteria

Evaluation factor	Weight	PBX A		PBX B		PBX C	
		Rating	Score	Rating	Score	Rating	Score
Initial cost	10	6	60	10	100	9	90
Annual operating cost	7	10	70	8	56	10	70
Vendor viability*	10	10	100	8	80	10	100
System reliability*	10	10	100	8	80	10	100
Station equipment features*	6	8	48	10	60	9	54
Voice messaging integration*	10	9	90	8	80	10	100
Upgradability*	9	9	81	7	63	10	90
Environmental requirements*	7	10	70	9	63	9	63
Administrative tools*	9	9	81	9	81	10	90
Totals			700		663		757

*Technical assessment team items
1 = low; 10 = high; score = rating × weight

Example 22–13h. Presentation example page 8 of 11.

System recommendation: Financial summary

Financial analysis has been reviewed
with finance department
Leasing the system is recommended

Description	Cost
Purchase cost	$0
Five year operating costs (1)	$518,009

(1) Future year costs converted to current year dollars

Example 22–13i. Presentation example page 9 of 11.

Telephone Set Policy

Job category	Telephone set type
Job A	Set 1
Job B	Set 2
Job C	Set 3
Job D	Set 4
Job E	Set 5

Telephone set color: beige

Example 22–13j. Presentation example page 10 of 11.

Next steps

- Lease approval required by 6-25-04
  to meet implementation schedule
  —Installation completed: 9-3-04
  —Columbus plant start date: 9-7-04
- Issue signed contract and down payment
  to vendor C on 6-25-04 (Friday)

Example 22–13k. Presentation example page 11 of 11.

SUMMARY

The case study illustrated how the information provided in Chapters 19, 20, and 21 would be applied to a hypothetical telecommunications acquisition project. While there is a definite advantage in knowing product life cycle and acquisition model concepts, there is a bigger advantage: to achieve real world project results and translate technical and financial information into a format that can be understood by business management. As has been stated throughout the text, there is no substitute for the use of common sense and good judgment—two factors that are typically an outcome of attitude, education, training, and experience.

PERSONAL COMPUTING FOR MANAGERS

INTRODUCTION

> **Catalyst**: A substance that increases the rate of a chemical reaction without undergoing any change to itself. **Managerial catalyst**: a tool or technique that increases both the effectiveness and efficiency of a manager.

Frederick Taylor's landmark 1911 publication, *Principles of Scientific Management*, began the new era of business management, from which come the underlying principles for all business, governmental, and nonprofit activities. Organizations that use good managerial practices flourish, but those that are managed poorly disappear "overnight." U.S. businesses embraced computers and communication as business tools during the 1970s in response to increased international competition, and technology tools have since become a competitive necessity. Companies that do not use the computers and communication technologies can't compete effectively.

The computer story began with the emergence of the mainframe computer during the 1950s—an expensive, cantankerous technical toy that evolved into the business necessity of the 1970s and spawned the "son" of mainframe, the personal computer (PC). Today's PCs have far more storage and processing capability than the largest mainframe of the 1970s at a cost of less than one ten-thousandth of a mainframe computer's cost. Complex word processing, spreadsheet, presentation graphics, technical graphics, Web browsers, e-mail, and project management software have become extremely user friendly and affordable. This combination of inexpensive hardware and high performance desktop software allows individuals to increase personal productivity and performance dramatically—if they have the necessary enabling and creativity skills. In this context, the PC is a managerial catalyst. It may do nothing or many things, depending upon the level of skills that the user has.

Just as businesses found it necessary to use computers and communication to remain competitive, it is necessary for telecommunications managers to use PC hardware and software effectively if they wish to be competitive.

Personal computing, the effective use of PC hardware and software to improve personal productivity, is critical for managers who have limited resources and time to do their jobs. The results achieved with personal computing, like many personal skills, are limited only by one's own skill and creativity in applying them.

THE PROBLEM WITH PC SOFTWARE IS . . .

The most commonly used PC software is word processing and spreadsheet software. Both of these products—regardless of the vendor providing them—are so complex and powerful that most users will never use more than 10% of the software's capabilities. Over the last fifteen years, PC software developers have continued to upgrade these products to meet the needs of an extremely diverse market. As a result, word processing and spreadsheet software contain many specialized features and options that can be accessed quickly via the keyboard or mouse. However, this also means that the software user is faced with a confusing array of features, and many of the features are not relevant to the task that is being addressed.

> PC desktop software is a far more powerful tool than most users need. However, this is analogous to saying that someone is overqualified for a given position—a wonderful luxury when responsibilities are expected to increase shortly. As a result, it is unlikely that the average user will outstrip the functional capability of the PC application they are using.

The following highlights features of commonly available PC software that was useful in developing managerial solutions in this text. While the discussion covers some basic software features, it is not intended to be a software tutorial, and it assumes that the reader has a basic understanding of the software that is being discussed.

DISCLAIMERS

One of the problems associated with discussing PC software features is that different vendors provide different software features. Appendix A focuses on the use of software products provided by Microsoft for IBM PCs. There are three reasons why the author has taken this approach: 1) Microsoft desktop software currently dominates the market and this discussion is intended to be relevant for the largest possible number of software users, 2) IBM PCs are the dominant PC platform, and 3) the author is familiar with the Microsoft software developed for IBM PCs. There are other vendors for Microsoft products, but fitting Appendix A discussions to other software products will be the responsibility of the reader.

This appendix is not intended to be a software tutorial. The reader should have basic knowledge of the software application that is being discussed—or should be able to learn on the fly. PC applications typically provide several ways to perform similar operations (keyboard, mouse, or shortcuts) and the author will discuss one way only of performing any given feature. In some cases, this is done because experience has shown that the selected technique has clear advantages over alternative techniques, while in other cases it may be simply be a matter of personal preference. If you choose to select a different technique, you are free to do so but you must accept accountability for your own results.

Finally, the following discussion is not intended to be a complete treatise that covers all the functional capabilities of the Microsoft software products discussed. Only selected functions and features will be reviewed, and the selection criteria will be based on the author's experience in using the product.

OVERVIEW

Appendix A will discuss the four Microsoft software products shown in Table A–1.

This appendix will review selected Word, Excel, Visio, and PowerPoint software features that were used to develop case study materials included with the text.

> Another strategic telecommunications management software product, Microsoft Project, will be discussed separately in Appendix B.

A good understanding of Table A–1 products or their competitive alternatives will provide a personal competi-

TABLE A–1   Microsoft PC Software

Microsoft Product	Primary Purpose
Word	Create word processing documents
Excel	Create spreadsheets
Visio	Create business drawings
PowerPoint	Create business presentations

Figure A–1. Telecommunications manager skill requirements.

tive advantage for an aspiring telecommunications manager and, in the author's opinion, is actually a competitive necessity for effectively carrying out managerial responsibilities. This assumes that the software user has the underlying enabling skills (Figure A–1) to allow the Table A–1 software to be used effectively.

PC software is a personal productivity tool, but the ability to productively utilize PC software will be directly related to the business, managerial, and technology skills that an individual possesses.

Learning By Doing

Reading about software application commands and features, or attending software classes, does not teach someone how to use PC software effectively. Simply learning software commands and functions is the same as learning the English language from a dictionary. Unless dictionary words are placed in the correct context within a document, effective communication will not take place between a reader and a writer. Someone who knows fewer words but combines them effectively will have a major advantage over someone who knows all the words in the dictionary but is unable to combine them in a way that is clearly understood by others.

The underlying objective for learning words is to be able to use them more effectively when communicating with others. In the same way, software application knowledge is useful only when it helps someone to accomplish real world tasks. Dictionaries are used as references when questions arise regarding the meaning of a word within the context of written or verbal communication, and words are more likely to be remembered when they are part of a person's vocabulary. In the same way, PC software commands and functions are more likely to be remembered within a usage context, and software will be used on a regular basis only if the user perceives that a benefit is obtained by using it. The level of ongoing usage required to retain PC software skills varies among individuals. The effective use of PC software requires two commitments: 1) the initial learning effort and 2) its ongoing use.

Pragmatically, there should be little need to justify the effort for learning Table A–1 PC applications in today's business environment. Word processing, spreadsheets, and presentation graphics have become the *lingua franca* of businesses, in which the use of non-PC software communication formats is viewed as a vestigial form of communication. The only real issue regarding the use of PC software is how well the user applies software capabilities.

The learning-by-doing approach is based on developing additional PC software knowledge to meet new needs. The objective should be to acquire a set of core skills that are supplemented on an as-needed basis by referencing new commands and features, applying them, and using them in the future. Fortunately, online documentation (the help function) provided with common software products is very good. In addition, there are also many excellent how-to books describing PC software functions. These can be used in the same way a dictionary is used to improve word skills. Some reference sources have been listed in the Bibliography.

This text was developed by using the four software products listed in Table A–1 and Microsoft Project, covered in Appendix B.

Compound Documents

In Appendix A, the term *compound document* refers to consolidating the output of two or more software products to create one final document. For example, a Word document may contain spreadsheet tables from Excel, drawings from Visio, or graphics from PowerPoint. This is possible because all of these products adhere to Microsoft's Object Linking and Embedding (OLE) protocol, which allows information to be shared between OLE-compliant applications. OLE allows the use of a simple copy-and-paste process to transfer information from one application to another. The effective use of tables, graphics, and drawings in a document improves the quality and intelligibility of business communication, and OLE provides the technical capability for doing this. Appendix A will describe the steps needed for creating compound documents in various PC application formats.

MICROSOFT WORD (MS-WORD)

MS-Word is a word processing application that can be used to create memos, faxes, e-mail, desktop publishing documents, and Web-oriented (HTML) text. From a managerial perspective, the ability to use word processing software effectively is arguably the most important PC software skill. The other strong candidate for the most important managerial software application is the spreadsheet application.

This section assumes that the reader has a basic understanding of MS-Word features, and will focus on how different features are used to improve word processing-based communications. The next section reviews the basic MS-Word features that the reader should know prior to reading the MS-Word notes.

Basic MS-Word Features

Before proceeding to the next section, the reader should have MS-Word skills that include knowing how to:

open and save documents

manage files

preview and print documents

work in the document window

use menus and shortcut menus

use toolbars

use templates and wizards

enter and edit text

find and replace text

formatting text (fonts, style, and paragraphs)

use bullets and numbering

create and modify tables

These features are considered basic features, and an understanding of them is assumed in subsequent discussions.

Tables

Tables are easy to use and provide an excellent vehicle for the communication of accounting and technical information in a concise, easy to read format—if the table creator made them concise and easy to read. In the author's opinion, Microsoft Word tables look better than Excel tables and are easier to modify. However, Excel tables (spreadsheets) are much better at performing calculations than MS-Word. The author has resolved this potential conflict by using Excel to generate calculation spreadsheets and then copying and pasting (OLE) the results into an MS-Word document. When this is done, MS-Word is used to reformat the table's appearance. With OLE, it is also possible to create a table in MS-Word, copy it into Excel, perform Excel calculations, and then copy the Excel table back into MS-Word.

MS-Word table features can be accessed by: 1) using the main menu or 2) selecting the table and right-clicking the mouse to access a shortcut menu. The main menu provides a full set of table features, while the shortcut menu has a limited set of features. The compromise is to use the shortcut menu where possible, because it is more convenient and quicker to access. Reserve the use of main menu commands for their unique features.

Tables are very important elements for inclusion in management documents, and the effective use of MS-Word's table feature can quickly be taught to someone who has a basic understanding of MS-Word. Basic table features accessed from the main menu and shortcut menu include: insert table, select table, entering/editing text (rows, columns, or cells), inserting rows or columns, and formatting cells (characters, paragraphs, borders, shading, and margins). A little time spent learning how to develop and modify tables will repay itself many times over when business documents are being prepared.

Different Document Views

View refers to the appearance of an MS-Word document when it is being created or modified. There are four document views in MS-Word.

1. Print Layout view
2. Outline view
3. Normal view
4. Web Layout view

The four view buttons are located on the left side of the horizontal scroll bar that is located at the bottom of the document display. A view can be selected by depressing the appropriate button. The author primarily uses two views: Print Layout view and Outline view, and uses the Print Layout view approximately 99% of the time. The Outline view is used only as a reference when writing long documents to ensure that the information structure (sections and paragraphs) are in the desired logical format. The Print Layout view is what used to be called a "WYSIWYG" view—What You See Is What You Get—and shows how the document will look when it is printed out.

To use the Outline view effectively, the user must have an understanding of headings and heading levels (one of the MS-Word basics). While it is relatively easy to write short documents without the Outline view, it is a good way of ensuring that the organization structure of long documents makes sense. Outline views can be collapsed or expanded to show different levels of detail.

Even if the Outline view is not used, it is recommended that the Print Layout view be used instead of the Normal view, because it provides a clearer picture of the final results that will be obtained when the document is printed.

Compound Documents

For the MS-Word discussion, the Word document will be considered to be the carrier for the compound document, i.e., information from other electronic applications will be copied and pasted (OLE) onto the Word document. Constructing a compound Word document allows text, tables, and graphics from other applications to be inserted at different locations in the document.

PARAGRAPH MARK (¶). A problem encountered when attempting to embed OLE information into a Word document is how to place it properly on a page of text. When paragraph marks (¶) are hidden, as they normally are, the document will appear to be a sheet of paper that contains text only. A paragraph mark indicates when the

Return key was pressed to provide a line break at the end of a sentence or paragraph. Pressing the Return key repeatedly without inserting text provides spacing between lines of text—a practice used to change the appearance of a text document. If the paragraph mark is shown, the line breaks are seen. If the paragraph mark is hidden, a blank space is seen between text lines. When paragraph marks are visible, the cursor can be placed next to a paragraph mark and OLE information can be entered at that point.

Note: If the cursor is not placed on the page, the OLE will appear where the cursor was located just before the OLE was initiated—an occurrence that can appear arbitrary and confusing to the user.

It is recommended that paragraph marks be made visible when OLE operations are being executed. Showing or hiding paragraph marks is controlled by the ¶ icon, which is located in the standard toolbar where it is normally positioned just below the menu bar. Press the More Buttons icon on the standard toolbar to find the ¶ button. Then press the ¶ button to allow the show/hide ¶ feature to be enabled or disabled. The author always shows paragraph marks—a habit that distracts some students when a document is projected during lecture periods.

MS-WORD OLE OVERVIEW. Used appropriately, compound documents are much more effective than using text only documents. The following summarizes the procedures for placing OLE information into MS-Word documents.

The "To" and "From" notation in the following table (Table A–2) refers to the use of the Copy [from] and Paste [to] function. When information is copied from one software application to another, it is transferred as text, a table (a special form of text), or as an object, depending upon the specific capabilities of the sending and receiving software. When compatibility exists between the sending and receiving applications, text can be modified with characters, table data, and borders, and objects can be reduced, enlarged, or cut by both applications. The following information transfers take

TABLE A–2   Summary OLE Transfers into MS-Word

From	From Format	To	To Format
Excel	Table (spreadsheet)	Word	A Word table
Visio	Drawing		An object
	Text only		Text
PowerPoint	Slide		An object

TABLE A–3   Guidelines for Creating A Compound Word Document

To" Document	"From" Document
To Word	It is recommended that you enable the "Show/Hide ¶" option before creating a compound document. The "¶" symbol will indicate where lines exist on the page and will allow you to select the location where the external information is to be pasted.
	From Excel: When an Excel table is being pasted into a Word document, it is necessary to select (highlight) the Excel information, copy it, open up the Word document, and paste the selection into the desired location.
	The Excel table will be converted into a Word table, and Word's Table function can be used to modify it. The table maintenance features are found on the Table menu. Rows and columns can be added or deleted, border lines can be erased or changed, the entire table can be selected, and table information can be converted into text.
	From Visio: When a Visio drawing is being pasted into a Word document, it is necessary to select (highlight) the Visio information and copy it, open up the Word document, and paste the selection into the desired location. The Visio drawing should be grouped before it is copied, because an ungrouped drawing may not reduce or enlarge uniformly.
	When the Visio drawing is pasted into Word, the drawing can be selected and enlarged or reduced in the same way a grouped Visio drawing can be resized. The Enter key can be used to insert lines and change the location of the drawing on the Word document page.
	From PowerPoint: Individual PowerPoint slides can easily be inserted into a Word document by placing the PowerPoint application in the Slide Sorter view and copying individual slides. The individual slide is selected, copied in the PowerPoint application, and pasted into the Word document. As was the case for a Visio object, the PowerPoint object can be resized as desired.

place when Excel, Visio, or PowerPoint information is pasted into MS-Word.

Table A–3 provides guidelines for embedding Excel, Visio, and PowerPoint into MS-Word and creating a compound document.

Business Memo Template

Business communication was discussed in Chapters 4 (*Criteria for Managerial Success*) and 5 (*Telecommunications Manager Skill Requirements*), and examples of business memos have been provided in the cases studies (Chapters 10, 14, 18, and 22).

While the content of business documents may vary depending upon the topic being addressed, there is a consistency of format (how it looks) and style (how it reads) in all business communications. The third variable—content (what is says)—will be dependent upon the topic being addressed. Style and content will be based upon the communications and technology skills of the writer, while format will normally be dictated by business environment standards. In the case studies that are part of the text, business memos must be written to explain the purpose of the assignment and describe its implications. To provide a consistent format for all case study solutions, an MS-Word

business memo template is included with the text's CD. The template provides a business memo example in a compound document format and should be used for all assignment memos. While style and content require expertise in communication skills and technology skills, the format can be applied without interpretation. Someone who is accustomed to following a standard format has less difficulty learning a new format in a different business environment.

Refer to the CD for both the Business Memo example and template.

MICROSOFT EXCEL

Excel is a mathematical analysis tool used to create accounting reports, perform ad hoc business analyses, create mathematical models, provide database functionality, and create various graphs and graphical displays. The original spreadsheet program was a PC software product called VisiCalc, and many historians credit VisiCalc as being the "killer" application that drove the development of PC technologies. Accounting departments found that they could use PC-based VisiCalc to perform ad hoc accounting analyses quickly and accurately. In the pre-PC environment, mainframe computers imposed many scheduling constraints on application users, and accountants found they were able to work around these scheduling constraints by running PCs equipped with VisiCalc. Excel is Microsoft's version of a spreadsheet application, and it has been enhanced significantly over the last fifteen years. It is unlikely that anyone uses more than a small percentage of Excel's total calculation and database capabilities.

From an analytical perspective, spreadsheet applications are the most widely used software applications. The case study material provided in this text is Excel-based. The author used Excel to create many tables for this text's rough draft, among them a telecommunications equipment forecasting model (Part 2), project management reports (Part 3), a BVA reporting and forecasting model (Part 4), and a matrix analysis and life cycle analysis model (Part 5).

As was the case for the MS-Word discussion, this section assumes that the reader has a basic understanding of Excel features and will discuss the specific Excel features used to complete the different managerial analyses provided in the text. The next section summarizes the basic Excel features that the reader should know prior to reading the Excel notes that follow.

Basic Excel Features

Before proceeding to the next topic, the reader should have good Excel skills, which includes knowing how to:

open and save workbooks

manage files

preview and print worksheets

work in the document window

use menus and shortcut menus

use toolbars

use the paste function and wizards

enter and edit text, values, and formulas

select, copy, and move text, values, and formulas

format text, values, and formulas

use borders and shading

add, insert, and delete columns and rows

work with cell ranges

use relative and absolute cell references

use the Paste Special function

create and use formulas

link cells in a worksheet, and between worksheets and workbooks

use Excel's functions

If the list looks long and complicated, it is because Excel is an extremely powerful application that has a broad range of capabilities.

Creating and Using Formulas

The primary purpose of Excel is to perform calculations. A formula is needed to define the desired calculation to Excel. Formulas use arithmetic operators to modify values (numbers), text, worksheet functions, and other formulas to generate calculation results. The values and text referenced in the formula can be located in other cells—a feature that makes it easy to change data in one place and observe the results in another.

WORKSHEET STRUCTURE. The files that Excel uses are called *workbooks*, and each workbook contains documents called *worksheets* or *spreadsheets*. Every worksheet consists of 65,536 numbered rows (1 through 65,536), starting at the top of a worksheet and ending at the bottom, and 256 lettered columns (A through IV) starting at the leftmost column and ending at the rightmost column. In a workbook window, the column and row identifiers are located at the top and left sides of the worksheet, respectively, as shown in Figure A–2.

Columns use two letter identifiers once the initial twenty-six alphabet letters (A–Z) have been used. After column Z comes column AA, and after column AZ comes column BA, etc. The intersection of a column and a row is called a *cell*. A cell's address consists of its column and row identifier. F6 is the cell that is highlighted in Figure A–2. The cell address F6 specifies the cell located at the intersection of column F and row 6, as shown. The advantage of using cell addresses is that the content of the cell can be changed without having to change the cell reference—an attribute that is used extensively when creating and using Excel formulas.

The Excel worksheet numbering scheme results in the creation of 16,777,216 individual cells per worksheet (256 columns × 65,536 rows) and, as a result, worksheets can contain an enormous quantity of information.

In Figure A–3, a table has been created in part of the worksheet, and the table has been formatted using Excel's border and shading options. Figure A–3 will be used to show how Excel can be used to carry out basic calculations in the same way that an electronic calculator does. The Excel calculations will be carried out with formulas that are created automatically when someone enters information into an "Excel Calculator." Simple Excel formulas can be created using the same techniques that are used to enter electronic calculator information.

Figure A–2. Excel worksheet.

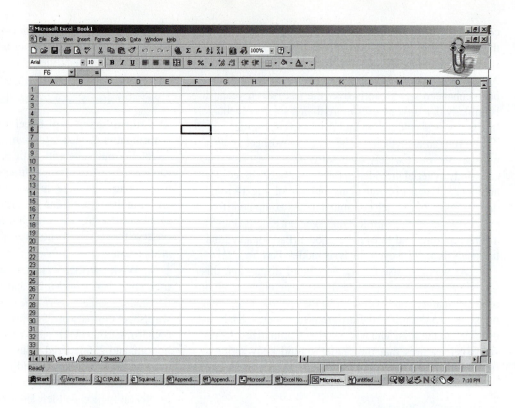

Figure A–3. Excel worksheet with pricing table.

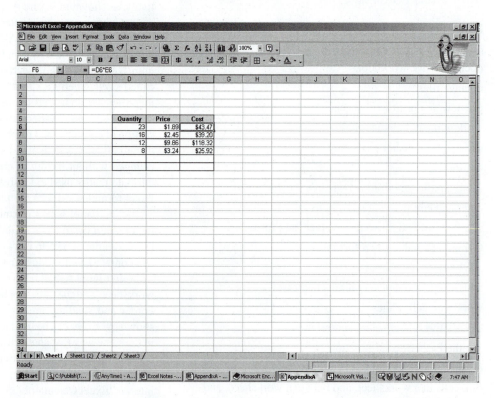

The Excel Calculator

The Figure A–3 table shows four rows that have cost calculation information based on the formula Cost = Quantity × Price. (Readers are invited to check out the Excel solutions with a calculator.)

If a calculator was used to develop the information contained in row 6 of the table, the calculator keyboard entries would have been

$$23 \times 1.89 =$$

and the result shown in the calculator display would have been

$$43.47$$

MATHEMATICAL OPERATORS. In mathematics, operators are symbols used to describe an operation. Multiplication (×) and subtraction signs (–) are operators. A calculator uses the operators +, –, ×, and ÷ to indicate addition, subtraction, multiplication, and division to the calculator's internal program. Excel uses a slightly different set of operator for the same functions: +, –, *, and /. As can be seen, the differences between the calculator and Excel operators is for the multiplication and division functions.

To calculate $23 \times 1.89 = 43.47$ with a calculator, the following steps would be followed:

1. enter 23
2. enter × (multiplication operator)
3. enter 1.89
4. enter =

The answer 43.47 would appear in the display.

To perform the same calculation shown in Figure A–3, the following steps would be carried out:

1. select cell F6 with the left mouse button
2. press =
3. select the Quantity cell (D6) with the left mouse button
4. type * (Excel multiplication operator)
5. select the Price cell (E6) with the left mouse button
6. press the Enter key

These operations will automatically create the Excel formula (=D6*E6). This formula building process can be observed in Excel's Formula bar display. The formula will automatically be entered into the cost cell (F6) and states [mathematically] that the F6 cell value will be calculated by taking the contents of cell D6 and multiplying it by the

contents of cell E6. In this case, D6 and E6 are 23 and 1.89. The Excel entry process is analogous to using the calculator, but the difference is that a formula (=D6*E6) is created and visually displayed in the Excel Formula bar, as shown in Figure A–3.

If the Excel process had to be repeated for each row in Figure A–3, there would be little—if any—advantage to using Excel other than creating an attractive printout (if the user knows how to format an Excel worksheet). The major advantage is that formulas can be used in similar calculations without requiring the creation of new formulas. If the input data (Quantity and Price) is put into Excel table rows, one Excel formula can be used for all the different row calculations. Excel's *relative addressing* feature provides the mechanism that allows formulas to be used repetitively.

RELATIVE ADDRESSING. The Figure A–3 calculation for row 6 centered on cell F6 – the Cost calculation cell. Cells D6 and E6—the elements of the formula in F6—have relative positions of two cells and one cell to the left of F6. If the F6 formula is copied and pasted into F7, Excel will change the formula's cell address information to a new value "=D7*E7". This new formula will multiply the values contained in the cells that have the same relative position to the new cost cell F7. Therefore, if the Figure A–3 table contained 100 row entries, the formula in the first row could be copied into the remaining 99 rows with a single copy and paste into the entire range of 99 Cost cells. Each row's calculation result in its Cost cell would contain the correct cost for that row.

With relative addressing, the cell formulas in each of the 99 rows will calculate a result based on its respective E ( ) and F ( ) cell values. If an Excel table is created with the appropriate Quantity and Price values for each desired cost calculation, a single formula can be created for the first row's Cost cell and can be copied into all the other rows in one operation. When multiple calculations are required, it is impossible for a calculator to match Excel's speed and accuracy.

EXCEL CALCULATOR CLOSING COMMENTS. Anyone who can use an electronic calculator can use the same skills to create simple Excel formulas. Simple formulas are those that do not require the use of parentheses to complete calculations correctly.

Parentheses are used in mathematical formulas to specify operation precedence when Excel calculations are performed. The correct use of parentheses normally requires an understanding of algebraic operations. In other words, you can't perform complex calculations unless you have the mathematical skills needed to understand how to

Figure A–4. Cost calculations including sales tax.

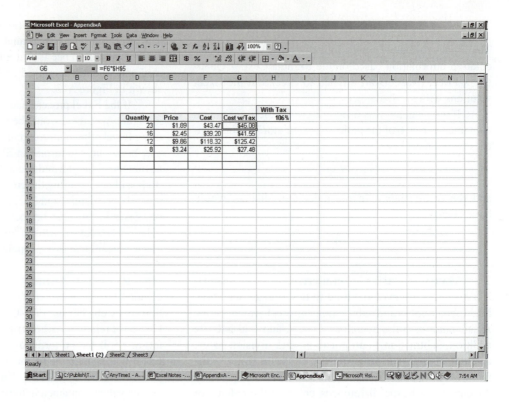

place parentheses correctly. However, in many applications for which only simple add, subtract, multiply, and divide operations are needed, the Excel formulas can be created by using the electronic calculator procedures described previously.

The text used complex Excel formulas, and the reader must have the necessary mathematical skills for understanding them to see how they are applied in a real world management environment.

Absolute Cell References

There are times when the Excel formula should access only the contents of a specific cell, and relative addressing would result in an erroneous calculation. For example, suppose that the Figure A–3 table must include a 6% sales tax in the cost (F column) calculation. While it is possible to enter the actual numeric (6%) in each cell formula, it would be simpler to incorporate this requirement into an Excel formula format. The mechanism for having a cell address fixed so that copied formulas always reference a specific cell is called an *absolute reference cell address*. When a formula contains an absolute cell address, the absolute value is placed into all copied formulas.

Absolute cell addresses are identified by the presence of a '$' sign in front of their column and row identifiers, such as H5. If H5 were in a formula, the copied formula would retain the absolute cell address. If the $ sign is not present, the copied formulas would only contain relative cell addresses.

Figure A–4 illustrates how the absolute reference would be used to include the sales tax in the Figure A–3 calculations. Cell H5 contains the value 106%, which, if multiplied by the existing Cost calculations, would add the 6% sales tax. A new column (G) has been added next to the Cost column (F)—Cost w/Tax. A new formula (=F6*H5) was created in the G6 cell, which is the equivalent of = 43.47 × 106% when using an electronic calculator. However, H5 is a relative address and must be changed to an absolute address. The relative address is changed to an absolute address by: 1) selecting H5 in the Formula bar, and 2) pressing the F4 key. One press of F4 will change H5 to H5. Note that the Figure A–4 cell formula for G6 (look in the formula bar) is =F6*H$5, and the value in the calculated value in cell G6 is $45.08. When this formula is copied into cells G7, G8, and G9 the 106% value (cell H5) will be accessed for each calculation.

TABLE A–4   Cell Reference Types

Example	Type
A1	Relative reference
A1	Absolute reference
$A1	Mixed reference (column letter is absolute)
A$1	Mixed reference (row number is absolute)

Note: While the F4 key was used to enter $ signs, they can also be entered manually on the keyboard.

Mixed Cell References

The absolute cell reference uses two dollar signs in its address (one for the column letter and one for the row number). Excel also allows either the row or column portion of the address to be preceded by the dollar sign. While the use of fixed column and fixed row references are not relevant to this discussion, Table A–4 illustrates the complete range of cell address references.

Depressing the F4 key after a cell address has been selected will toggle through the four reference types shown in the table. *This text uses relative and absolute cell references only in its examples.*

Linking Cells

Excel formulas offer the advantage that cell values may be changed, and their impact can be included in any formulas that use those cell addresses. However, copying formulas doesn't address the case where a nonformula cell value is used in several places: 1) within a worksheet, 2) between worksheets in the same workbook, or 3) between worksheets in different workbooks. If separate manual entries are made each time the value is needed, each cell must be changed when the value is changed. Linking provides a means for making only one manual entry and using this value for all other cells and formulas—regardless of the worksheet where the source cell is located.

Linking cells, or ranges of cells, sets the values of the linked cells (the linking source) to the cells they are linked to (the linking target). If care is taken when using common cell values, the manual entry will appear only once, and all other appearances of the cell value are based on links. The terms *source* and *target* will be used to designate the *from* and *to* relationships of cells that: 1) contain the desired information and 2) need access to the information.

LINKING CELLS WITHIN A WORKSHEET. When a value is first used on a worksheet, any other cells that need the information can easily be linked to the source cell by:

1. selecting the target cell by using the left mouse button
2. typing =
3. selecting the source cell
4. pressing the Enter key

The source cell's information will appear in the target cell. Examination of the target cell's contents (see the Formula Bar) will show the cell address of the source cell. Cells can link to the original cell or to cells linked to the original cell. When the original cell is changed, the value in all linked cells will automatically change.

LINKING CELLS BETWEEN WORKSHEETS IN THE SAME WORKBOOK. The previous technique used within a worksheet can also be used to link cell information between worksheets in the same workbook. In this case, it is necessary to locate the source cell on another worksheet, select it, and press the Enter key. Examination of the target cell's contents in the Formula bar would show that the *SheetName* has been added to the address and result in the address format: SheetName!CellAddress.

LINKING CELLS BETWEEN WORKSHEETS IN DIFFERENT WORKBOOKS. Again, the same technique that was used for linking cells within a worksheet or between worksheets can be applied to exchange information between workbooks. When the cells in two different workbooks are linked, the target cell's contents would contain an address with the format: [WorkbookName]SheetName!CellAddress.

PASTE SPECIAL LINKING. Excel's Paste Special function can be accessed from the main menu (Edit/Paste Special) or by using the shortcut menu accessed with the right mouse button. Paste Special linking is accomplished by:

1. selecting the source cell (left mouse button)
2. copying the source cell contents (Main Menu or Shortcut menu)
3. selecting the target cell (left mouse button)
4. selecting the Paste Special Function (Main Menu or Shortcut menu)
5. selecting the Paste Special "Paste Link" option

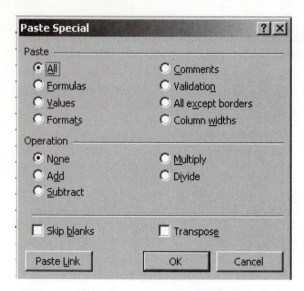

Figure A–5. Shortcut menu: paste special dialog box.

When this is done, the target cell's contents will show the address of the source cell as noted previously. Paste Special linking can be used within a worksheet, between worksheets in the same workbook, and between worksheets in different workbooks.

> The use of the Paste Special results in an absolute cell reference, while the = approach provides a relative address. There are advantages to both, and the cell addresses of each can be changed. However, it is a case where practical experience gained by using the linking option is the best teacher.

Copy/Paste Special

Copying and pasting are commonly used functions. The author has found that direct copying and pasting or dragging cell contents can frequently have an unwanted result: modifying table borders. It is distracting to a reader to see either missing borders or an inconsistent use of them, and this problem can be easily avoided by using the Excel's Paste Special function's Paste Formula option. The Paste Special function can be accessed by using the Main menu (Edit > Paste Special) or the shortcut menu (right mouse button) shown in the Figure A–5 dialog box. The Paste Formula option is then selected and OK is clicked. The formula or text will appear in the target cell without changing any borders.

The Paste Formula approach can be used for formulas, text, or number values and will paste the desired contents without affecting the borders. In addition, there are a number of other useful options provided by Paste Special, but their use is left to the reader's discretion and initiative.

Pasting Formulas into Noncontiguous Cells

It is a common occurrence to paste a formula from one cell to a group of cells that may be contiguous or noncontiguous cells. When the cells are contiguous, the range of cells can be highlighted and the source cell formula will be entered into all of the highlighted cells. However, when cells are not contiguous and a source cell formula must be copied into these cells, several copy and paste operations may be needed—unless the Alt key is used.

The procedure for simultaneously pasting a cell formula into a series of noncontiguous cells consists of:

1. Copy the source cell formula.
2. Paste the formula into the first block of contiguous cells.
3. Depress the Ctrl key.
4. Hold the Ctrl key down while highlighting groups of non-contiguous destination cells.
5. When all destination cells have been highlighted, place the cursor in a highlighted cell area and complete the desired Paste or Paste Special operation.

The highlighted destination cells will all receive copies of the source cell formula. This same approach can be used for any type of source cell information.

Compound Documents

Excel is not normally used as a final report deliverable, but the author has used OLE to incorporate Visio information onto Excel worksheets so that readers reviewing the electronic workbook can see the different diagrams used with labs and case studies. The worksheet containing the Visio diagram can also be printed for use as a worksheet or to allow a more detailed examination.

The author prefers to use Excel for calculations and MS-Word for formatting worksheets when the tables will be part of a report or text. When an MS-Word table is required, it can be developed by: 1) copying a worksheet table and pasting it into Word or 2) taking a Word table, copying it into Excel, applying Excel calculations, and repasting it back into Word. As with most tools, the use of the Word tools will be driven by the needs and creativity of the user.

TABLE A–5   Summary of OLE transfers into Excel

From	From Format	To	To Format
Word	**Text**	**Excel**	Text in single cell
	Table		An Excel table
Visio	**Drawing**		An object
	Text only		Text only
PowerPoint	**Slide**		An object

The following summarizes procedures for placing OLE information into Excel worksheets.

The *To* and *From* headings Table A–5 refer to the use of the Copy (From) and Paste (To) functions. When information is copied from a software application to another, it is transferred as text, a table (a special form of text), or an object, depending upon the specific capabilities of the sending and receiving software. When compatibility exists between the sending and receiving applications, text can be modified with characters, table data and borders can be changed, and objects can be reduced, enlarged, or cut by both applications. The following information transfers (in Table A–5) take place between Word, Excel, and Visio.

Table A–6 provides additional guidelines for adding Word and Visio information into Excel worksheets.

Excel Functions

Excel functions are predefined formulas that can be used in a stand-alone mode or incorporated into user-generated formulas. To use a function, it is necessary to select it from a list of functions and enter the necessary variable information needed to calculate results. There are approximately 400 functions that can be accessed in Excel, and they are grouped into nine categories:

1. database
2. date and time
3. engineering
4. financial
5. information
6. logical
7. lookup and reference
8. math and trig functions
9. text

The easiest way to become acquainted with Excel functions is to access Excel's help feature and browse through an extremely long list of function-specific references.

How to Use Functions

There are two ways to use functions: 1) enter the function formula manually or 2) use Excel's Paste Function dialog

TABLE A–6   Guidelines for Creating A Compound Excel Document

"To" Document	"From" Document
Excel	**From Word**: When text is being pasted into an Excel document, it is necessary to select (highlight) the Word information and copy it, open up the Excel Workbook, select the worksheet, and paste the selection into the desired location. The text format can be changed with the Excel functions.
	When a table is being copied from Word to Excel, the table should be selected and placed on a worksheet in the desired location. Once the table is pasted, it can be treated as an Excel worksheet table by using standard Excel features.
Excel	**From Visio**: When a Visio drawing is being pasted into an Excel document, it is necessary to select (highlight) the Visio information and copy it, open up the Excel workbook, select the worksheet, and paste the selection into the desired location. If it is being placed on a blank worksheet, it should be pasted into the leftmost top cell. After it appears on the worksheet, select the Print Preview button and then close the Print Preview dialog box. The size of the page will be shown on the worksheet and the Visio drawing size can be changed to match the space that is available.
Excel	**From PowerPoint**: Individual PowerPoint slides can easily be inserted into an Excel document by placing the PowerPoint application in the Slide Sorter view and extracting individual slides. The individual slide is selected, copied into the PowerPoint application, and pasted into the Excel document. As was the case for a Visio object, the PowerPoint object can be resized as desired.

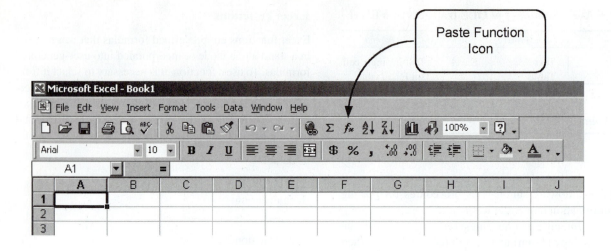

Figure A–6. The standard toolbar's paste function button.

box. The first option is one that is used when someone is constantly using a specific function and becomes so familiar with the function's format that the manual entry method is shorter than using the dialog box approach. The following will describe the Paste Function.

Pasting a Function

When the Paste Function approach is used, the Paste Function dialog box is accessed in one of three ways:

1. Select Insert/Function from the Main menu.

2. Click on the Standard toolbar's Paste Function button.

3. Press Shift + F3.

When the Paste Function is initiated, the Paste Function dialog box appears (Figure A–7) and the desired function can be selected by: 1) selecting the appropriate Function category (left side) and 2) selecting the desired Function name (right side). Figure A–6 shows the Standard toolbar's Paste Function Icon/Button, and Figure A–7 shows the Paste Function dialog box that appears when the Paste Function button is pressed.

Figure A–7. The paste function dialog box.

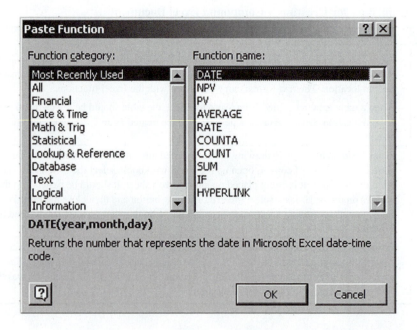

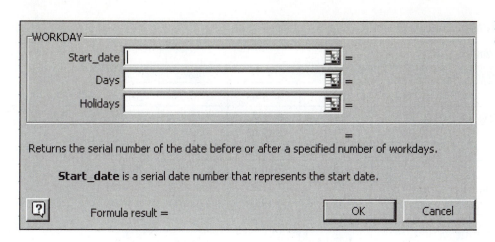

Figure A–8. Formula palette dialog box.

TABLE A–7   Excel Functions Used in the Text

Function Category	Function Name	Function	Case Study
Financial functions	Straight line depreciation Present value	SLN PV	Part 1
Date and time functions	Workday* Net workdays*	WORKDAY NETWORKDAYS	Part 2

* Only available when Excel's Analysis ToolPak add-in option is enabled. Worksheet functions are predefined.

If a Function name is selected, the associated Formula palette dialog box appears (Figure A–8). The Formula palette box describes the different variables (arguments) and prompts the user to enter the required variable information.

After the variable information has been entered and the OK button is pressed, Excel will calculate the results. Depending upon the function being used, the input requirements may be either simple or complex.

Functions Used in the Text

Table A–7 contains functions that were used in the text's case studies. An Example of the Workday and Net workday functions can be found in the text's electronic documentation provided.

WORKDAY FUNCTION EXAMPLE. In the Chapter 14 CPM case study, a forward and backward pass schedule was developed by using a calendar, and this information was used to create an acceptable project schedule. The manual technical schedule developed from these calendar schedules is shown in Table A–8.

It is assumed that the reader has completed the manual solution of the Chapter 14 case study and is familiar with the formulas used to calculate EF, ES, LS, and LF values:

ES
$$\text{Activity ES} = \text{EF}_{predecessor} + 1$$

Note: *The ES of an activity that has multiple predecessors is based on selecting the predecessor having the largest EF.*

EF
$$\text{Activity EF} = \text{ES} + (\text{activity duration} - 1)$$

LF
$$\text{Activity LF} = \text{LS}_{successor} - 1$$

Note: *The LF time of activities that have multiple successors is based on using the successor with the smallest LS.*

LS
$$\text{Activity LS} = \text{LF} - (\text{activity duration} - 1)$$

Referring to the original manual calculation procedures and the workday example in the Chapter 14 spreadsheet should enable the reader to apply the workday function effectively.

TABLE A–8   Chapter 14 CPM Technical Schedule

System Cutover: September 2, 2003 (Tuesday)

CP	Activity	Duration	ES	EF	LS	LF
X	**Organize project**	**15**	**2-24-03**	**3-14-03**	2-20-03	3-12-03
X	**Develop requirements**	**15**	**3-17-03**	**4-4-03**	3-13-03	4-2-03
X	**Design network**	**30**	**4-7-03**	**5-16-03**	4-3-03	5-14-03
X	**Select equipment**	**25**	**5-19-03**	**6-23-03**	5-15-03	6-19-03
	Plan cutover	12	**6-24-03**	**7-10-03**	8-14-03	**8-29-03**
X	**Install premises wiring**	**20**	**6-24-03**	**7-22-03**	6-20-03	7-18-03
	Order & receive equipment	18	**6-24-03**	**7-18-03**	**6-24-03**	**7-18-03**
	Order & install WAN circuits	10	**6-24-03**	**7-8-03**	7-7-03	7-18-03
X	**Install equipment**	**25**	**7-23-03**	8-26-03	7-21-03	**8-22-03**
X	**Cutover preparation**	**5**	8-27-03	9-3-03	**8-25-03**	**8-29-03**
X	**Postcutover activities**	**20**	9-4-03	10-1-03	**9-2-03**	**9-29-03**
	Activity CP total	**155**				

CP: Critical Path Activities; EF = LF

Bold dates show final schedule recommendation.

Figure A–9. Workday selection.

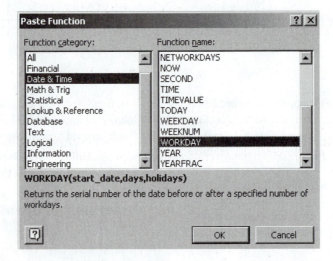

Excel's Workday function can be used to develop the Table A–8 technical schedule. The electronic Excel solution, found on the CD, for the Chapter 14 Case Study includes both the calendar and Workday function solution.

The first step in using the Workday function is to select it by using the Paste Function dialog box (Figure A–9). The Formula Palette dialog (Figure A–10) appears and identifies the information that is needed by the Workday function.

While it may be easy to look at Figure A–9 and decide that it is too confusing, the explanation for the dialog box is a mouse click away by using Excel's Help function. As indicated at the beginning of Appendix A, there is no substitute for learning by doing, and the combination of the Excel Help

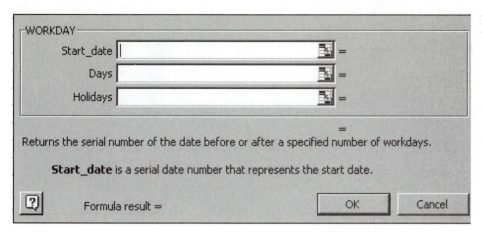

function and intelligent persistence are necessary ingredients for learning by doing. The following will describe how to use the Workday function. The reader will be given the responsibility of researching Help information, if required.

The Workday function will be used to identify the start and ending times for both CP and non-CP activities. Three inputs are identified in the Figure A-10 Formula Palette dialog box:

Start date

Days (activity duration)

Holidays

Table A–8 will be used to provide the start date and activity duration information, and the Chapter 14 case study holiday schedule will be used to identify nonworking days (holidays).

Note: The Workday function assumes that weekends are nonworking days. Holidays are entered into the Workday function by typing an Excel table with the dates and then specifying the table date range. Table A–9 shows the format of a table used to document the holiday schedule.

To use the Workday function to calculate a forward pass schedule, we will start on February 24—the project's start date—and use Table A–8 to obtain duration (Days) information. For example, the duration for the first activity, Organize Project, is 15 days. The Workday function will normally provide the first day of the next activity if the activity's duration is entered. Therefore, one day less will be entered: $15 - 1 = 14$. See Figure A–11.

> The Figure A.11 values are actual values from an Excel worksheet. Therefore, cell references are shown as input but their numeric value is shown to the right of the boxes – 37676, 14, and {37622; . . . }. (The target cell must be formatted with the appropriate Date format information.)

Some manipulation of the Day information is required, depending upon whether the calculated value is a finish value or the start value for the next activity. (This is part of the trial and error process of learning to use a new tool.) When all the appropriate dates and duration have been entered, the final result will be as shown in Table A–10.

Because both Table A–8 and A–10 are Word tables, the date information appears identical. Only the source document—the Excel worksheet—would show the function formulas in Table A–10.

MICROSOFT VISIO

Visio is used to create business drawings such as block diagrams, flowcharts, forms, charts, maps, network diagrams, office layouts, organization charts, and project schedules. Its primary value is as a supporting information element within a compound document, where a graphic or

TABLE A–9   Chapter 14 Case Study Holidays

Holidays	2003
New Years Day	1-1-03
Memorial Day	5-26-03
Fourth of July	7-4-03
Labor Day	9-1-03
Thanksgiving Day	11-27-03
Christmas Day	12-25-03

Figure A–11. Organize project activity input.

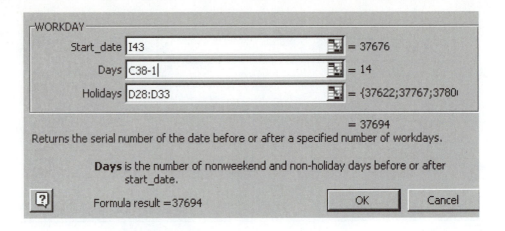

TABLE A–10 Network Workday Schedule for Chapter 14 Case Study. LAN Project Schedule: Based on Excel Workday Function

Holidays	2003
New Years Day	1-1-03
Memorial Day	5-26-03
July Fourth	7-4-03
Labor Day	9-1-03
Thanksgiving Day	11-27-03
Christmas Day	12-25-03

Precutover Work

Start date	2-24-03
End date	8-29-03

System Cutover: September 2, 2003 (Tuesday)

CP	Activity	Duration	ES	EF	LS	LF
X	**Organize project**	15	**2-24-03**	**3-14-03**	2-20-03	3-12-03
X	**Develop requirements**	15	**3-17-03**	**4-4-03**	3-13-03	4-2-03
X	**Design network**	30	**4-7-03**	**5-16-03**	4-3-03	5-14-03
X	**Select equipment**	25	**5-19-03**	**6-23-03**	5-15-03	6-19-03
	Plan cutover	12	**6-24-03**	7-10-03	8-14-03	**8-29-03**
X	**Install premises wiring**	20	**6-24-03**	**7-22-03**	6-20-03	7-18-03
	Order & receive equipment	18	**6-24-03**	**7-18-03**	6-24-03	7-18-03
	Order & install WAN circuits	10	**6-24-03**	**7-8-03**	7-7-03	7-18-03
X	**Install equipment**	25	**7-23-03**	8-26-03	7-21-03	**8-22-03**
X	**Cutover preparation**	5	8-27-03	9-3-03	**8-25-03**	**8-29-03**
X	**Postcutover activities**	20	9-4-03	10-1-03	**9-2-03**	**9-29-03**
	Activity CP total	**155**				

Preliminary est. completion date: 10/1/03

visual display will assist in the communication of business information. From a telecommunications management perspective, it is an excellent tool for creating network (LANs, WANs, and internetwork) drawings, organization charts, block diagrams, and flowcharts. The author used Visio to create the different drawings found throughout the text.

Conceptually, Visio provides an electronic alternative to using plastic drawing templates, where a pencil is used to trace various figures that have been cut out

TABLE A–11   Guidelines for Creating A Compound Visio Document

From	From Format	To	To Format
Word	Text	Visio	Text
	Table	Visio	If Visio's "Paste" function is used, the Word table will be pasted as unformatted text. However, by using Visio's "Paste Special/Microsoft Word Document" feature, it will be received as an object that looks just like the original table. This object can be resized and treated as a typical Visio shape. Double-clicking the object in Visio will also allow the object to be updated as a Word table.
Excel	Table (worksheet)	Visio	If Visio's "Paste" function is used, the Excel table will be received as unformatted text. However, by using Visio's "Paste Special/Microsoft Excel Worksheet" feature, it will be received as an object that looks just like the original table. This object can be resized and treated as a typical Visio shape. Double-clicking the object in Visio will also allow the object to be updated as an Excel table.
PowerPoint	Slide	Visio	By using PowerPoint Slide Sorter view, an entire PowerPoint slide can be copied and pasted into Visio as an object and treated as a typical Visio shape. This approach is useful for storing selected slides that will be used as attachment information for compound documents.

on the template. In Visio, the figures are called *shapes*, and hundreds of shapes are available on electronic Visio templates. While each Visio offering (Basic, Professional, and Enterprise) provides specific templates, additional templates can be found on the Microsoft website.

As was the case for previous discussions, this section assumes that the reader has a basic understanding of Visio and will address only Visio features used in this text.

Basic Visio Features

Before proceeding to the next topic, the reader should have good Visio skills that include knowing how to:

open and save documents

manage files

preview and print documents

work in the document window

use menus and shortcut menus

use toolbars

use stencil templates and wizards

enter and edit text

use Paste Special function for MS-Word and Excel

reformat shapes and text

use fundamental drawing tools

work with rulers, grids, and guides

Compound Documents

Someone who is familiar with word processing and spreadsheet software applications will find that using Visio is intuitive. Simple results can be achieved quickly, and the same basic procedures can be used to develop complex drawings.

Visio is not normally used to create a standalone deliverable, but it is used as a supporting element in compound documents. However, Visio is OLE-compliant and will accept input from other Microsoft applications.

The *To* and *From* notation in Table A–12 refers to the use of the Copy (From) and Paste (To) functions. When information is copied from a software application to another, it can be transferred as text, a table (a special form of text), or an object, depending upon the specific capabilities of the sending and receiving software. When compatibility exists between the sending and receiving applications, text can be changed with characters, table data and borders can be modified, and objects can be reduced, enlarged, or cut by both applications. The information transfers (Table A–11) take place between Word, Excel, and Visio.

MICROSOFT POWERPOINT

PowerPoint is used to create business presentations. While it incorporates a range of drawing tools, these tools are not as powerful as Visio drawing tools. It is also OLE compliant and will accept information from Microsoft Word, Excel, and Visio. From a telecommunications management perspective, it is an excellent tool for making presentations. Using the standard PowerPoint slide templates ensures that presentation material is suitably structured for oral presentations, because there is sufficient room on PowerPoint slides to contain summary-level information only in a bullet format.

The To and From notation in Table A–12 refers to the use of the Copy (From) and Paste (To) functions. When information is copied from a software application to another, it can be transferred as text, a table (a special form of text), or an object, depending upon the specific capabilities of the sending and receiving software. When compatibility exists between the sending and receiving applications, text can be changed with characters, table data and borders can be modified, and objects can be reduced, enlarged, or cut by both applications. Table A–12 summarizes the information transfers that take place between Word, Excel, and Visio.

CLOSING COMMENTS

The ability to use PC software effectively provides two benefits to the skilled user: 1) it saves time and 2) it looks good. Looking good means that computer-generated information has built-in credibility. A document that looks professional but contains inaccurate information has a much better chance for being approved by management than a document that has a mediocre appearance but contains excellent, accurate information. In today's media sensitive world, an ounce of professionalism is worth a pound of performance.

Unless good ideas are packaged properly, there is a low likelihood of them getting past the initial "how does it look" phase that business management employs as technique to save valuable time. On the other hand, knowing what looks good to business management and having good PC skills is a combination that allows a telecommunications manager to compete for limited investment dollars and get credit for good ideas.

TABLE A–12 Guidelines for Creating A Compound PowerPoint Document

From	"From" Format	To	"To" Format
Visio	Object	PowerPoint	Visio objects can be pasted onto PowerPoint drawings and resized as desired.
			By converting Word and Excel information into a Visio object (refer to the Visio discussion), a high level of flexibility of information displays can be achieved.

B

MICROSOFT PROJECT®— ANOTHER PERSONAL COMPUTING TOOL

INTRODUCTION

Possessing project management skills is an essential requirement for effectively managing and implementing telecommunications technology. In Part 3, Chapter 12 reviewed CPM and illustrated its application using manual calculations in the Chapter 14 case study, where the manual CPM approach was used to develop a schedule for implementing a 1,200 workstation LAN/internetwork project.

CPM and its sibling project management method, PERT, are project management tools whose viability is based on having computer processing capabilities to make calculations. Without a computer, the calculations are so intensive and tedious that CPM and PERT would probably exist as an interesting museum display relegated to specialized uses where cost and practicality issues are secondary considerations.

CPM calculations are simple, but the sheer volume of CPM calculations required for projects of any significant size increases exponentially as size increases. Prior to the introduction of today's computer-based electronic calculators, the combination of mechanical calculators coupled with the inconsistent human variable created problems.

The potential for human error is high when people are assigned repetitive, simple tasks, and it is necessary to include an administrative overhead to ensure that error-free calculations are the final result.

Microsoft Project® (MS-Project) is PC-based software that uses a CPM calculation engine to generate project management information. Unless a user has an understanding of both the CPM calculation process and project management concepts, the basis for the project information generated by an MS-Project application will not be evident. The next section provides an overview of key elements covered in Part 3. They are considered essential for the effective use of MS-Project.

PROJECT MANAGEMENT OVERVIEW

All projects have a beginning, a middle, and an end, which may also be described as:

- building a plan
- controlling a plan
- closing a plan

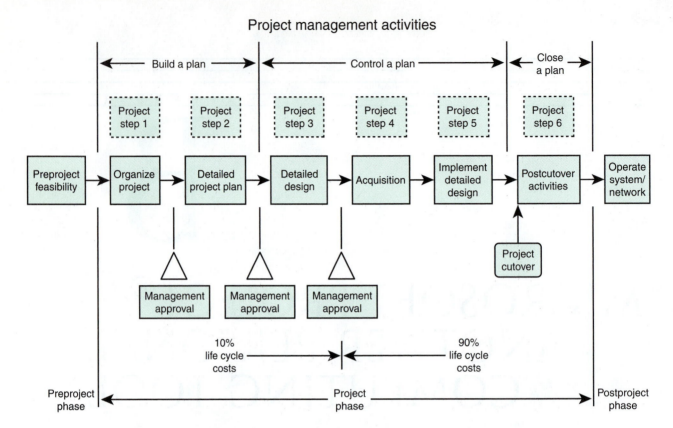

Figure B–1. Project management model.

TABLE B–1 Project Management Phases and Elements

Project Phase/Elements	Scope Management	Time Management	Cost Management
Building a plan	X	X	X
Controlling a plan	X	X	X
Closing a plan	X	X	X

Figure B–1 shows these descriptions as they relate to the text's telecommunications project life cycle model.

The text covered the building a plan phase in Chapter 12, and the elements contained have been summarized in Table B–1. Scope, time, and cost management elements are the major project management elements needed to plan and implement a project effectively. MS-Project is a software tool that can be used for all three elements.

Scope Management

Scope management includes: 1) the initial justification activities used as the basis for establishing the project, 2) the planning activities to implement the objectives on which the initial justification was based, and 3) translating conceptual goals into quantifiable deliverables that can be tracked and measured within a project management context. During the scope management process, project management personnel must be able to clearly show that proposed project deliverables will effectively meet the business goals used to justify the project. As part of this translation process, it is necessary to obtain agreement from business management that the proposed project deliverables will fulfill their expectations for the project.

Scope management also includes an ongoing verification of actual project costs, resources, and time frames, comparing them to baseline references established at the beginning of the project. Because the focus of scope management is on the project's goals, any project goal changes during the implementation of a project should be reflected in a change to the baseline information initially established for the project.

Time Management

Time management refers to those activities needed to ensure the timely completion of a project, including: 1) defining activities and tasks, 2) identifying the relationships among activities and tasks, 3) estimating activity and task durations, 4) developing activity, task, and project schedules, and 5) monitoring and controlling project activities to ensure that planned schedules are met.

Cost Management

Cost management activities address four major areas:

1. resource planning
2. cost estimating
3. cost budgeting
4. cost control

The knowledge required to carry out the cost management phase for telecommunications projects requires strong technical skills in the telecommunications technology being implemented. Technical specialists have these skills, and their input is essential for establishing viable cost management plans.

Summary

Scope, time, and cost management activities vary greatly in complexity and size, and each project can have a unique set of project management needs. CPM is not project management—it is simply a mathematical tool that can be used to develop project plans. Successfully implementing technical projects requires the application of strong technical skills, and CPM is not a substitute for technical skills or good managerial judgment.

While Microsoft Project (MS-Project) uses CPM and PERT calculations as a core calculation process, many of the tools other contained in MS-Project have been used for years to address project management needs.

MS-PROJECT INTRODUCTION

MS-Project is the leading project management software application package. However, its sister product—MS-Excel— is used even more frequently for various project management support activities. The solutions provided in the text used Excel for both documentation and calculation purposes.

MS-Project includes an extensive help facility that provides:

- a Quick Preview to MS-Project
- an Online Tutorial
- a Project Map
- an Office Assistant
- an Index
- a Table of Contents

The Quick Preview, Online Tutorial, and Project Map options are designed for users who are inexperienced in project management or in the use of MS-Project. The Online Tutorial is an excellent reference for using MS-Project but is (understandably) oriented toward the use of the MS-Project software. It is the responsibility of the user to determine how MS-Project can best be applied to a specific project management situation. The Index and Table of Contents information provided in MS-Project is similar in structure and format to that contained in other Microsoft Office applications.

The primary display used with MS-Project is the Gantt chart view—the default display screen seen by MS-Project users. The Gantt chart view can be activated by clicking on the Gantt chart icon in the left side View Bar or by accessing main menu features (View\Gantt Chart). Most MS-Project entries are made in the Gantt chart view. The right side of the display summarizes the status of project information in a Gantt chart format and the left side provides table information.

A first time user,[1] depending upon his or her learning style and experience, can either learn about MS-Project prior to using it or plunge directly into it and use the online documentation to answer questions as they arise. For those interested in taking the first approach (learning before doing), the MS-Project Table of Contents offers a step by step approach that includes the Quick Review, Online Tutorial, and Project Map information in a start-to-finish sequence for creating project documentation.

---

[1] Users should understand basic project management principles and the concept of the CPM project management technique before using MS-Project, or they will be faced with the challenge of understanding a complex software product that provides many data entry, project status, and database views of its project database. While these views will appear to have a logical relationship for individuals who understand project management basics and have a basic familiarity with using PC software, they can appear to be random displays of unrelated information for inexperienced users.

MS-PROJECT EXAMPLE: CHAPTER 14 CASE STUDY

The build a plan elements referenced in the *Project Management Overview* section include the following steps:

1. defining the project scope
2. identifying project work details (activities/tasks)
3. organizing project activities/tasks
4. establishing activity/task durations
5. establishing activity/task relationships
6. creating a project schedule
7. adjusting the schedule, if necessary
8. establishing a baseline schedule
9. assigning resources to activities/tasks
10. entering activity/task cost information

MS-Project provides the capability for managing all ten steps. Steps 1 through 8 are considered "primary" steps in establishing a project plan and would use either CPM or PERT. Steps 9 and 10—the resource assignment and cost assignment phases—assign costs to the project activities. Appendix B will address only steps 1 through 8.

As discussed previously, *project scope* activities consist of documenting project objectives, assumptions, and resource constraints (people, time, money). It is important that the requirements definition phase quantifies the project deliverables.

Deliverable A tangible, verifiable outcome of work used to produce a product or service. To be verifiable, the deliverable must meet predetermined standards for its completion, such as design specifications or a checklist of steps.

In both manual and MS-Project solutions, deliverables are represented by tasks and summary tasks (activities). Appendix B will "solve" the same case study presented in Chapter 14 by proceeding through the first eight steps in the build a plan list. If the reader has questions regarding MS-Project solution input details, it will be necessary to refer back to Chapter 14.

Step 1: Project Scope Definition

Because the cost management phase will not be included, human resource and budgetary resource constraints were not included as part of the scope definition. The following project description (Example B–1) was used in Chapter 14 and will be used as the basis for the MS-Project Solution.

MS-Project will receive the same input as was used for the manual process, and three ministeps will be used to enter the initial project scope information:

- set up project
- enter properties information
- enter work calendar information

SET UP THE PROJECT. An MS-Project project can be set up by using the main menu (File/New/Blank Project) or by clicking the New Blank Project button located on the left side of the standard toolbar. The display shown in Example B–2 will appear.

This display is called the Gantt Chart view, which is the default view provided by MS-Project. The left side of the Gantt Chart view consists of an Entry table for entering project task information, and the blank right side of Example B–2 will show Gantt Chart information after activity information has been entered. Different Table views can be selected for display on the left side of the Gantt Chart view.

Installation of a 1,200 Workstation LAN + Internetwork in a New HealthProd Headquarters Building Scheduled for Occupancy on September 2, 2003

Current date:	January 2, 2003
Project start date:	February 24, 2003
Cutover date:	September 2, 2003
Work days:	Monday through Friday, 8 AM to 5 PM
	Weekend overtime available
Holidays:	New Years Day, Memorial Day, July 4th, Labor Day,
	Thanksgiving, Christmas Day

Example B–1. Project (scope) description.

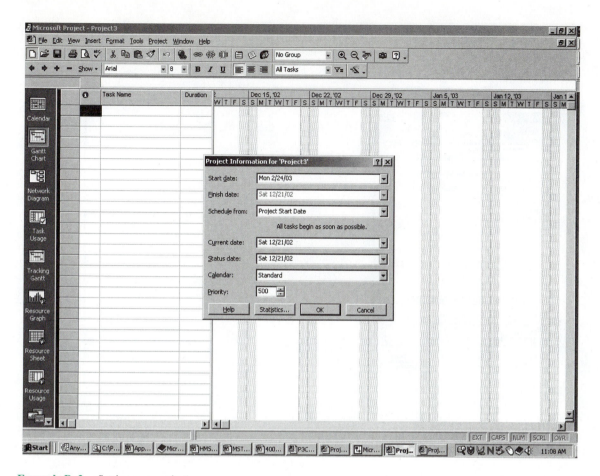

Example B–2. Setting up a project.

The first step will be to enter the desired Start Date into the "Project Information for Project X dialog box, where "X" is a numeric value assigned by MS-Project to indicate how many new project work sessions are being worked on concurrently during the user session. The "X" is a temporary number that disappears after a Project Title is assigned. The only required input is the desired project Start Date, because MS-Project will calculate the Finish Date based on the input data.

> Do not enter both 1) start and 2) finish date information when setting up project—*enter only the start date*.

After the start date is entered, click OK and the dialog box will disappear.

PROPERTIES INFORMATION. The next step is to enter a Title for the project, which includes the name of the author (you). The title information will appear on any reports that are printed for the project. Other information can also be entered into the Properties dialog box, but it is optional.

The Properties dialog box is activated through the main menu: File/Properties. After the Title and Author information has been entered, press OK and the dialog box will disappear. Example B–3 provides a completed example of the Properties dialog box for the Chapter 14 case study.

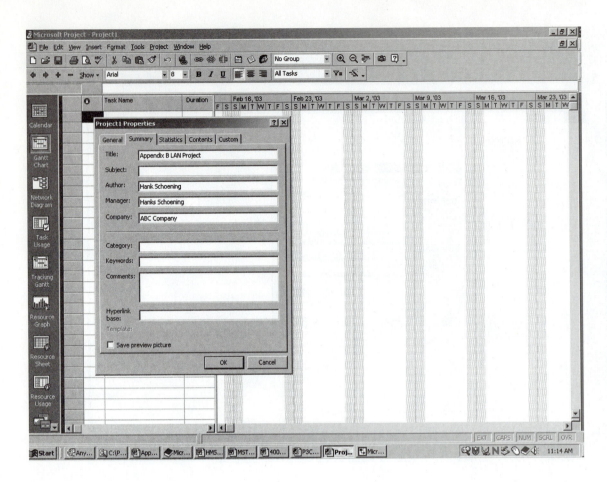

Example B–3. Enter MS-Project properties information.

WORK CALENDAR INFORMATION. MS-Project's default calendar provides for an 8-hour (8 AM to 5 PM), 5-day workweek. Any variations to this basic calendar must be entered into MS-Project through the main menu (Tools/Change Working Time) as shown in Example B–4, which entered the May 26 Memorial Day holiday as a nonworking date.

All holidays and standard work times that fall outside of the 8 AM to 5 PM time periods must be entered into the MS-Project work calendar using the Example B–4 maintenance display.

For the Chapter 14 case study, New Years Day (January 1), Memorial Day (May 26), Independence Day (July 4), and Labor Day (September 1) were entered as nonworking days in the MS-Project work calendar.

Step 2: Identifying Project Tasks

MS-Project's Gantt Chart's Entry (left side of the display) view is used to enter the various tasks and will use the same activity durations used in the Chapter 14 WBS worksheet.

Example B–5 shows the entries made to list the project's tasks. If this listing is compared to the Chapter 14 WBS, it will be seen that an additional task—the milestone task Project Cutover—was not on the Chapter 14 WBS. When tasks or activities are initially entered, a default duration value of **1 day**? is assigned by MS-Project. This default value will change when duration estimate information is added (Step 4). When milestone information is added, it is assigned an activity duration of 0 days.

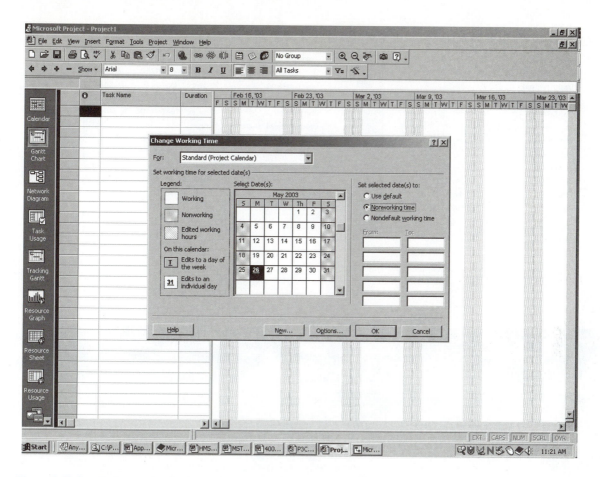

Example B–4. Project work calendar maintenance.

Steps 3 and 4: Organizing Tasks and Establishing Durations

When tasks are entered into the MS-Project list (Example B–5), they can be organized and structured by using of MS-Project's outlining capability. The top level tasks are called activity or summary tasks and are used to summarize the information contained in lower level tasks. Tasks can be indented (i.e., created at lower levels) as often as needed to reflect the organization of project tasks. Large, complex projects will have more task layers than simple projects.

In the case of the Chapter 14 case study, only the summary task level (activity) was shown, and MS-Project's outlining feature will not be used in the Appendix B solution so that both the manual and MS-Project solution contain the same information elements. Therefore, only activities are shown in Example B–6. If Example B–6 had contained summary tasks (activities), they would have been identified by positive (+) or negative (−) signs preceding them, and bold text would be used to highlight the text description.

Activity durations are entered directly onto the Gantt Chart Entry table and can be entered as minutes, hours, days, weeks, or months. The project's activity durations have been entered in Example B–6. Summary task duration values should not be entered, because their values will automatically be calculated once the dependency information is entered (the next section).

The activity entered for the Cutover Date was assigned a deadline date of August 29, as shown in Example B–7. (The deadline maintenance is accessed from the main menu: Project/Task Information/Advanced).

	❶	Task Name	Duration
1		Organize Project	1 day?
2		Develop Requirements	1 day?
3		Design Network	1 day?
4		Select Equipment	1 day?
5		Plan Cutover	1 day?
6		Order/Receive Equipment	1 day?
7		Order/Install WAN Circuits	1 day?
8		Install Premises Wiring	1 day?
9		Install Equipment	1 day?
10		Cutover Preparation	1 day?
11		Project Cutover	1 day?
12		Post-Cutover Activities	1 day?

	❶	Task Name	Duration	Start	Finish
1		Organize Project	15 days	Mon 2/24/03	Fri 3/14/03
2		Develop Requirements	15 days	Mon 3/17/03	Fri 4/4/03
3		Design Network	30 days	Mon 4/7/03	Fri 5/16/03
4		Select Equipment	25 days	Mon 5/19/03	Mon 6/23/03
5		Plan Cutover	12 days	Tue 6/24/03	Thu 7/10/03
6		Order/Receive Equipment	18 days	Tue 6/24/03	Fri 7/18/03
7		Order/Install WAN Circuits	10 days	Tue 6/24/03	Tue 7/8/03
8		Install Premises Wiring	20 days	Tue 6/24/03	Tue 7/22/03
9		Install Equipment	25 days	Wed 7/23/03	Tue 8/26/03
10		Cutover Preparation	5 days	Wed 8/27/03	Wed 9/3/03
11	◆	Project Cutover	0 days	Wed 9/3/03	Wed 9/3/03
12		Post-Cutover Activities	20 days	Thu 9/4/03	Wed 10/1/03

Example B–5. Initial activity listing.

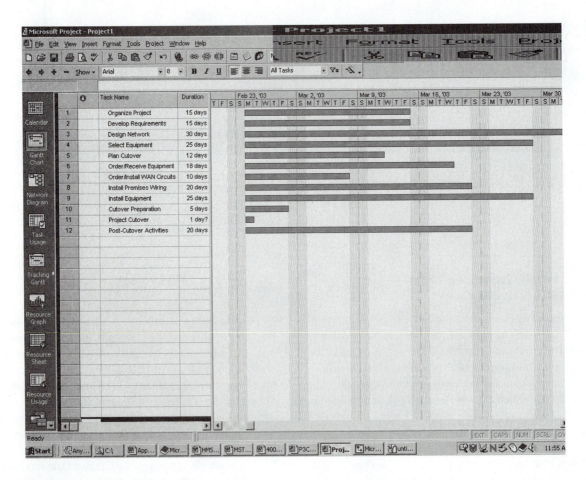

Example B–6. Activity listing with durations.

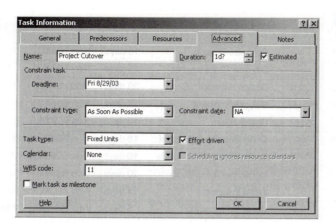

Example B–7. Deadline information for project cutover milestone.

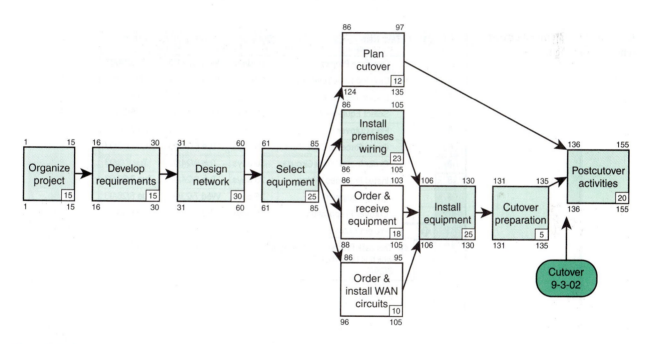

Example B–8. Chapter 14 project network diagram.

Step 5: Establishing Task Relationships

The project network diagram provided in Chapter 14 (Example B–8) was used to enter the task dependency information (Predecessors column) shown in Example B–9.

   Note: Once the activity dependency information was entered in Example B–9, a warning indicator message was generated (Example B–10), which shows that the project cutover milestone activity will be completed after its

deadline date. This was triggered by the deadline information that was entered in Example B–7.

Step 6: Creating a Project Schedule

Once task duration and task dependency information has been entered into the MS-Project Entry table, MS-Project automatically makes a calculation to provide a preliminary schedule. The preliminary forward pass schedule

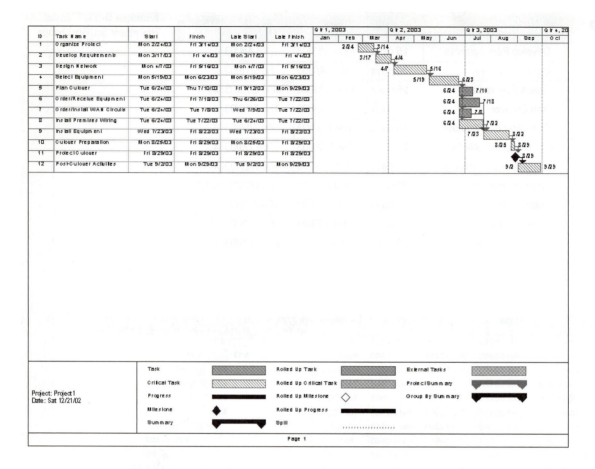

ID	Task Name	Start	Finish	Late Start	Late Finish
1	Organize Project	Mon 2/24/03	Fri 3/14/03	Mon 2/24/03	Fri 3/14/03
2	Develop Requirements	Mon 3/17/03	Fri 4/4/03	Mon 3/17/03	Fri 4/4/03
3	Design Network	Mon 4/7/03	Fri 5/16/03	Mon 4/7/03	Fri 5/16/03
4	Select Equipment	Mon 5/19/03	Mon 6/23/03	Mon 5/19/03	Mon 6/23/03
5	Plan Cutover	Tue 6/24/03	Thu 7/10/03	Fri 9/12/03	Mon 9/29/03
6	Order/Receive Equipment	Tue 6/24/03	Fri 7/18/03	Thu 6/26/03	Tue 7/22/03
7	Order/Install WAN Circuits	Tue 6/24/03	Tue 7/8/03	Wed 7/9/03	Tue 7/22/03
8	Install Premises Wiring	Tue 6/24/03	Tue 7/22/03	Tue 6/24/03	Tue 7/22/03
9	Install Equipment	Wed 7/23/03	Fri 8/22/03	Wed 7/23/03	Fri 8/22/03
10	Cutover Preparation	Mon 8/25/03	Fri 8/29/03	Mon 8/25/03	Fri 8/29/03
11	Project Cutover	Fri 8/29/03	Fri 8/29/03	Fri 8/29/03	Fri 8/29/03
12	Post-Cutover Activities	Tue 9/2/03	Mon 9/29/03	Tue 9/2/03	Mon 9/29/03

Project: Project1
Date: Sat 12/21/02

Task		Rolled Up Task		External Tasks	
Critical Task		Rolled Up Critical Task		Project Summary	
Progress		Rolled Up Milestone		Group By Summary	
Milestone		Rolled Up Progress			
Summary		Split			

Page 1

Example B–16. MS-Project final schedule report.

process of developing this information is relatively simple, and developing multiple "what if" scenarios can be done quickly and accurately with a few keystrokes. MS-Project is a real world CPM tool with Manual CPM being used only to develop conceptual skills or when rough estimates are needed quickly. When manual methods are used, simplifying assumptions must be made in the network diagram.

A finished report of the final schedule can be generated and printed from Schedule/Gantt Chart View by: 1) selecting Print Preview on the standard toolbar and 2) selecting the Print option in the Print Preview window. Example B–16 provides a final schedule report example.

CLOSING COMMENTS

A project that requires hours using manual CPM calculations can literally be done in minutes by using MS-Project software—depending upon the typing and project man-

agement skills of the individual using the software. Reworking an existing solution to create a better schedule takes just seconds with MS-Project, but it would require a complete "do over" when manual calculations are used. However, using MS-Project without understanding CPM concepts is the equivalent to driving a car without having any training. Part 3 of the text is intended to provide the CPM and project management background required to effectively use project management software.

Appendix B addressed only eight of the ten steps listed under "Building A Plan" in the in MS-Project example section. The remaining steps are part of the cost management elements that are also included in MS-Project. Cost management elements are more complex than those that have been addressed in Appendix B. They require good understanding—or access to someone who has a good understanding—of the technical requirements. In addition, it is not uncommon for other cost management tools to be used.

C

JOB DESCRIPTIONS AND PERFORMANCE APPRAISALS

INTRODUCTION

Performance appraisals are facts of life in well run busineses. They provide the opportunity for: 1) managers to give subordinates feedback regarding the manager's evaluation of their job performance and 2) subordinates to provide feedback to their managers regarding their job accomplishments and the manager's evaluation. From a business perspective, job performance results should have a direct bearing on salary administration decisions, and raises should be commensurate with performance assessments.

Two sources exist for defining an employee's job (managers or nonmanagers) more specifically than reading management texts or initiating a dialog with management: 1) job descriptions and 2) performance appraisals—documentation that is maintained for employee hiring and evaluation purposes. Well run businesses maintain job descriptions for the different positions held by its employees, and these job descriptions are used to let prospective employees know what their job responsibilities are and what qualifications are

required for the position. In addition, employees are evaluated periodically (usually annually) by using a performance appraisal process that informs employees of their job performance. Job descriptions are job specific and may cover multiple positions within a business, but performance evaluations are documents that are specifically developed for each employee.

Performance appraisals are employee specific documents that contain the objectives that will be used to establish the performance rating given to an employee.

JOB DESCRIPTIONS

It is important for employees who are hired for a job to understand what the job involves—an understanding that would include a description of the skills and background that would qualify someone for the position. This information is documented in job descriptions that are maintained in human resource department files and developed by the managers who head the department where the job exists. A job description provides an overview of a person's responsibilities, the person's role in the business organization, and the educational background requirements for the position. The accuracy and completeness of any given job description will be a reflection of the managerial effectiveness of both the human resources department and the department where the job exists.

Job descriptions provide a standard format for identifying the key characteristics of any given position. The difference between a job description prepared for a middle level manager and an entry level clerical position will be in the information used to describe position requirements.

Salary administration specialists who work closely with department managers develop internal job descriptions that identify the position attributes required to effectively perform position duties. Internal job description attributes are matched against attributes maintained in external salary databases to set fair pay scales for internal positions and provide a basis for developing internal performance evaluation information. An external salary database will normally be the reference source that determines the specific attributes used to define internal position requirements. The process of comparing internal positions to an external position database is an example of benchmarking, and an external standard is being used to ensure equitable salary treatment of employees.

In the real world, telecommunications managers will find that different views regarding the role and value of job descriptions and performance appraisals exist. Development of job descriptions and performance appraisals is a difficult task, but it is the responsibility of managers to make sure that both exist and are used.

Developing Job Descriptions

Describing job position responsibilities is a difficult and time consuming effort. However, no easier way has been developed to provide a fair and equitable evaluation of a position's requirements. The more complex and demanding a position is, the more difficult it will be to document its characteristics and attributes.

If formal job descriptions are not available and a formal appraisal process is not utilized, the employee (manager or nonmanager) is at a disadvantage. It would be analogous to taking a course test without knowing what information will be covered on the test, such as being prepared for an English composition test and finding that it is a test on organic chemistry. Test takers expect to know the topics covered on a test so they can study for the

test in advance and receive a good grade. In the same way, employees (and managers are employees) expect to know what their job responsibilities are so they can prepare for any tests (performance evaluations) that may be given.

From a human resource perspective, a mechanism is needed to pay employees fairly for the jobs they perform. Job description databases currently exist for thousands of jobs involving a wide range of activities. These activities range from simple, repetitive, clerical tasks to complex, managerial, and technical tasks that have no precedents within the department. Job descriptions contained in these external databases range from those for a customer service filing clerk to those for a chief executive officer. A cross reference exists between these job descriptions and the salaries paid to individuals who hold these positions, and the attribute and characteristic information on job descriptions is used to match salary levels to different positions.

The human resource department's role—in conjunction with the department manager(s)—is to develop internal job descriptions that can be compared to the external database so that equitable salaries can be provided to employees. Common attributes used for cross referencing internal job positions to the external salary database are:

1. instruction
2. control
3. guidance
4. planning
5. decision making
6. problem complexity
7. contacts
8. education

Job Description Preparation Guidelines

Example C–1 provides a set of guidelines for using these attributes when developing a job description. The job description (Example C–2) described in the next section is an example of how the guidelines are applied. The following discussion summarizes the eight attributes listed in Example C–1.

INSTRUCTION. The instruction attribute describes the amount of instruction provided to the position for setting goals, priorities, schedules, and deadlines, and the sequence of activities carried out by the position. This can range from having well-defined procedures that cover

Criterion	Ref	Comments
Position responsibilities		**Describe four to eight critical responsibilities or duties of the position in terms of broad responsibilities rather than specific tasks.**
1. Instruction		**Describe the level of detail of instruction required or given to the position.**
	N/A	Not applicable.
	1	Follows well-defined procedures to perform position responsibilities. When procedures do not exist, detailed instruction is provided.
	2	Requires minimal supervision to perform position responsibilities. Receives instruction for nonstandard situations. May instruct clerical or professional entry level personnel.
	3	Normally works independently using established guidelines and does not require instruction for difficult problems. Establishes new procedures and may instruct other professionals about existing and new work procedures.
	4	Receives direction only on major departures from existing procedures and policies. Uses established guidelines for work performed within the functional unit, for contacts made with other internal departments, and for contacts with outside personnel.
	5	Establishes or makes significant contributions to policy information and provides guidance on major policy departures. Provides policy interpretation advice when major departures from policy are involved.
2. Control		**Describe the nature and frequency of control exercised over the various projects, activities, and tasks performed by the position.**
	N/A	Not applicable.
	1	Activities and tasks are reviewed on a daily, weekly, and monthly basis.
	2	Approved projects or activities are reviewed at key points or when they are completed. Most projects or activities are completed in less than one year.
	3	Some projects or activities are reviewed on an exception basis during the year. Projects or activities are normally reviewed on an annual or fiscal basis and may require longer than one year to complete.
	4	Most projects or activities are long term in nature and are reviewed on an interim basis. Results may be evident only after a time period greater than one year.
3. Guidance		**Describe the degree of supervision or guidance necessary to satisfactorily perform the technical or departmental responsibilities of the position.**
	N/A	Not applicable.
	1	Requires day to day guidance in major technical and departmental job responsibility areas.
	2	Requires some unsolicited guidance in major technical and departmental job responsibility areas.
	3	Requires little solicited guidance in technical and departmental job responsibility areas. Solicits guidance, when required.
	4	Operates independently in technical and departmental job responsibility areas. Finds guidance sources within the company when unusual situations are encountered.
	5	Operates independently in technical and departmental job responsibility areas. When guidance is required, the guidance sources are primarily from outside the company.
4. Planning		**Describe the extent to which the position requires the planning of work and the nature of the planning that is required.**
	N/A	Not applicable.
	1	Carries out preplanned activities and may assist in developing these plans.
	2	Develops action plans based on strategic plan needs. Has responsibility for coordinating, implementing, and evaluating action plan results.

Example C–1. Job description preparation guidelines.

Criterion	Ref	Comments
	3	Participates in the establishment of strategic plans. Identifies and selects the action plans needed to meet strategic plan requirements. Commits the necessary financial and personnel resources to complete the action plan.
	4	Defines company business objectives and formulates the appropriate strategies to achieve these objectives.
5. Decision Making		**Describe the extent and nature of the position's contribution to the decision making process.**
	N/A	Not applicable
	1	Decision making is limited to determining how specified tasks will be completed within specified time frames. May perform analytical tasks to assist in the decision-making process.
	2	Determines the work priorities of multiple assignments that must be completed by the position holder. Decisions include the creation of time schedules for assignment tasks to meet specified deadlines.
	3	Allocates resources within defined levels to meet key action plan objectives and allocates assignments to meet action plan deadlines.
	4	Determines and approves the level of resources required to implement action plans developed to meet key business, departmental, and company objectives.
6. Problem Complexity		**Describe the extent to which the problems encountered are routine or are complex and require innovation.**
	N/A	Not applicable.
	1	Problems are normally limited to areas of departmental or technical responsibility and have well defined precedents. Solutions require a minimal amount of innovation.
	2	Problems are normally limited to areas of departmental or technical responsibility and frequently require innovation to solve. Solutions impact the department.
	3	Problems are normally complex but are limited to areas of departmental or technical responsibility. Solutions require a high level of technical innovation and normally affect the department only.
	4	Problems are normally complex and do not have precedents. Solutions require a high degree of innovation to solve, both in terms of technical and organizational issues. Solutions impact departmental, divisional, and company objectives.
	5	Problems normally involve intangible elements and impact key business, departmental, and company objectives. Precedents do not normally exist and innovative thinking must be employed to minimize adverse strategic consequences.
7. Contacts		**Describe 1) the degree to which the position requires contact with individuals of high power or authority (internal or external) and 2) the purpose of that contact and the level of importance of that contact to the company.**
	N/A	Not applicable.
	1	Contacts are primarily to provide routine information.
	2	Contacts are primarily to provide guidance or information about matters of limited complexity.
	3	Contacts are primarily for the purpose of providing advice on departmental or technical matters. Position may also operate independently in these complex areas.
	4	Most contacts are with high power and authority sources. The contact is to assist in the establishment of plans or the selection of alternative actions. Position negotiates and commits action on behalf of the company.
	5	Most contacts are with high power and authority sources regarding complex issues of major company importance. The contacts involve significant independent action.
8. Education		**Describe any special education or training that is considered essential for carrying out position responsibilities. This description may include formal degree programs, technical training, or certification tests.**

Example C–1. Job description preparation guidelines. (continued) every aspect of the position to instances where the position must establish corporate policies where no precedent exists in the organization.

CONTROL. The control attribute describes the nature and frequency of control exercised over the projects, activities, and tasks performed by the position. Control can range from having multiple reviews during the day to having reviews that are done on an interim basis—perhaps annually, at a fiscal calendar time—or when the project is completed.

GUIDANCE. The guidance attribute describes the degree of supervision or guidance required to satisfactorily perform the technical or operational responsibilities of the position holder. This can range from requiring unsolicited guidance on a day to day basis for simple tasks to cases where the position holder is expected to operate independently and use innovative techniques to carry out responsibilities.

PLANNING. The planning attribute describes the extent to which the position requires the planning of work requirements and the nature of this planning. Planning can range from carrying out preplanned activities and tasks, to positions where the person is expected to define business objectives and formulate the appropriate strategies for achieving these objectives.

DECISION MAKING. The decision-making attribute describes the extent and nature of the person's contribution to the decision-making process. Decision making may be limited to determining how specific tasks will be completed during specified time frames to being responsible for defining action plans that meet key business, departmental, and company strategies.

PROBLEM COMPLEXITY. The problem complexity attribute describes the extent to which problems that are encountered by the employee are routine or complex (which requires innovation). Problems can range from those that are limited to relatively simple functional ones or technical ones that have well-defined precedents to those that are complex and have no precedents. The latter problem type will require a high level of innovation on the part of the employee. Problems can range from those that affect the department only to those that have a major impact on divisional or corporate objectives.

CONTACTS. The contact attribute describes: 1) the degree to which the position requires contact with individuals of high power or authority—both internal or external to the company organization—and 2) the purpose of that contact and its importance to the company. Contact can be limited to individuals within the department or used for providing routine information to high power upper management personnel for the purpose of negotiating key policy issues.

If the internal job descriptions accurately portray the different attributes required to effectively perform a job, the appropriate pay levels can be selected from the external database and used as the basis for compensating employees. The process of developing internal job descriptions is a difficult, time-consuming process that requires close coordination between human resources personnel skilled in salary administration and departmental management personnel who understand job requirements and can translate them into accurate job descriptions that can be used to establish pay scales.

Voice Communications Manager Job Description Example

The preceding table has set the stage for addressing the question, "What do telecommunications managers do?" This section will apply the job description preparation guidelines to a hypothetical voice communications manager position (Example C–2) to provide the reader with one view of managerial duties.

Job descriptions contain two basic types of information: 1) a listing of critical responsibilities or duties of the position and 2) a description of the characteristics associated with the position. While this text is not intended to be a course in developing human resources documentation, the inclusion of this information is intended to highlight the managerial role in supporting employee administration activities. The wording in the job description should also provide an insight to how managerial duties are defined in a business.

Disclaimer: Example C–2 provides an example of a generic job description for a voice communications manager position. However, the primary responsibility for initiating the job description creation process is assigned to the human resources department, and they will determine the format and structure that is used. The content will depend upon the corporate policy and the need to meet internal and external legal requirements. Example C–2 is intended for use as a teaching tool to provide an insight to the responsibilities of a managerial position.

POSITION RESPONSIBILITIES: DESCRIBE FOUR TO EIGHT CRITICAL RESPONSIBILITIES OR DUTIES OF THE POSITION IN TERMS OF BROAD RESPONSIBILITIES RATHER THAN SPECIFIC TASKS.

1. Responsible for managing the voice communications department, providing voice communication support for corporate departments, and providing consulting services to operating divisions.
2. Interview and select job applicants for the voice communications department, conduct performance reviews, and identify employee development needs.
3. Monitor existing WAN service costs and identify new cost savings opportunities.
4. Identify new voice-based applications (e.g., voice mail and voice response) through the ongoing evaluation of emerging technology.
5. Assist corporate departments with identifying cost savings opportunities, including the identification of individual telephone usage abuse.
6. Manage voice communication projects, including carrying out feasibility studies, performing cost/benefit analyses, and recommending specific vendor products to division management.

INSTRUCTION: DESCRIBE THE DETAIL OF INSTRUCTION REQUIRED OR GIVEN TO THE POSITION.

Receives direction only on major departures from existing policy or for special policies to be followed involving division management. Receives little unsolicited instruction concerning project management, administration, planning, or personnel supervision.

CONTROL: DESCRIBE THE NATURE AND FREQUENCY OF CONTROL EXERCISED OVER THE VARIOUS PRODUCTS, ACTIVITIES, AND TASKS PERFORMED BY THE POSITION.

Many tasks are project oriented and fall within the annual fiscal cycle. Tasks in this category are reviewed on an exception basis. Other ongoing tasks are also reviewed annually or on an interim basis.

GUIDANCE: DESCRIBE THE DEGREE OF SUPERVISION OR GUIDANCE NECESSARY TO SATISFACTORILY PERFORM THE TECHNICAL OR DEPARTMENTAL RESPONSIBILITIES ASSOCIATED WITH THE POSITION.

Although some unsolicited guidance may be provided by the telecommunications director about enterprise objectives, minimal supervision or guidance is normally solicited on matters of a technical or functional nature. Sources of technical guidance are normally external to the enterprise, e.g., vendors, professional organizations, peer external managers, etc.

PLANNING: DESCRIBE THE EXTENT TO WHICH THE POSITION REQUIRES THE PLANNING OF WORK AND THE NATURE OF THE PLANNING THAT IS REQUIRED.

Develops and coordinates self-initiated projects to meet divisional and department objectives. Plans projects and assigns manpower (subordinates, vendors, etc.) to accomplish project objectives. Helps formulate departmental strategies by recommending specific action plans and projects.

DECISION MAKING: DESCRIBE THE EXTENT OF THE POSITION'S CONTRIBUTION TO THE DECISION-MAKING PROCESS.

Develops and recommends action plans to meet key objectives. Establishes project priorities and assigns personnel resources. Controls project budgets.

PROBLEM COMPLEXITY: DESCRIBE THE EXTENT TO WHICH THE PROBLEMS ENCOUNTERED ARE ROUTINE OR ARE COMPLEX AND REQUIRE INNOVATION.

The problems addressed are technically and financially complex and require finding technical solutions to business problems. Many alternatives must be evaluated and problems are frequently encountered that require untried applications or innovative solutions.

Example C–2a. Job description: Voice communications manager. (Page 1 of 2)

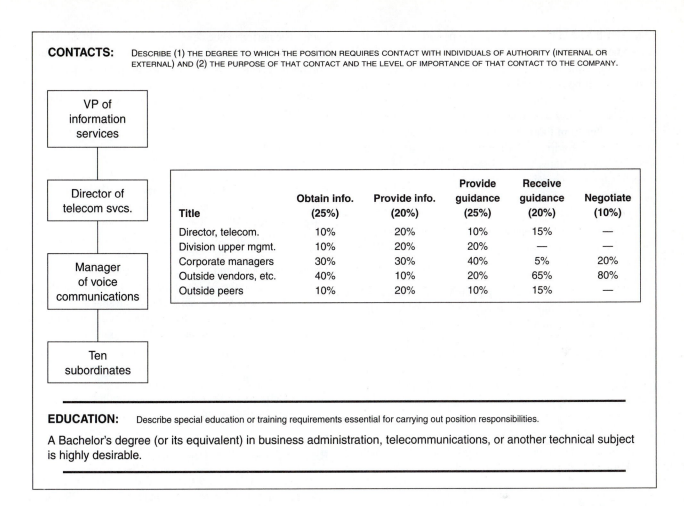

CONTACTS: Describe (1) the degree to which the position requires contact with individuals of authority (internal or external) and (2) the purpose of that contact and the level of importance of that contact to the company.

VP of information services

Director of telecom svcs.

Manager of voice communications

Ten subordinates

Title	Obtain info. (25%)	Provide info. (20%)	Provide guidance (25%)	Receive guidance (20%)	Negotiate (10%)
Director, telecom.	10%	20%	10%	15%	—
Division upper mgmt.	10%	20%	20%	—	—
Corporate managers	30%	30%	40%	5%	20%
Outside vendors, etc.	40%	10%	20%	65%	80%
Outside peers	10%	20%	10%	15%	—

EDUCATION: Describe special education or training requirements essential for carrying out position responsibilities.

A Bachelor's degree (or its equivalent) in business administration, telecommunications, or another technical subject is highly desirable.

Example C–2b. Job description: Voice communications manager. (Page 2 of 2)

If Example C–2 were compared to a job description for an entry level clerical task, major differences noted would be in the open-ended nature of the manager's attributes compared to the clerks' attributes. This is not surprising because one of the requirements associated with managerial positions is to have significant freedom (and accountability) in how tasks are performed.

The contacts attribute shows that the voice communications manager is expected to have significant amount of contact externally (vendors and peers), which has significant implications. The implications are that the manager will be acting as a representative of the enterprise and will act professionally and responsibly in all dealings with external personnel. If the Example C–1 guidelines are examined while reviewing the Example C–2 job description, you should have a good understanding of the managerial role.

THE PERFORMANCE APPRAISAL PROCESS

Every employee's work performance—regardless of where they work—will be evaluated formally or informally. A primary concern of employers is to ensure that their employees are productive. The responsibility for employee productivity is delegated to management. Employee work performance provides the basis for salary increases and promotions, and an effective performance appraisal system will accurately and equitably allocate rewards to employees based on their performance.

A good appraisal system is an objective system in which the tasks assigned to employees have measurable outcomes that are used to define different performance levels. An appraisal process identifies the projects, activities, and tasks that an individual is assigned during a given time period, and at the end of the time period provides an assessment of how well the individual employee has done while completing them. A hypothetical Performance System (PS) will be described and used to illustrate the performance appraisal process.

The attributes used during the performance appraisal process differ from those used to create a job description. While the job description's primary use is to ensure that internal salary structures are consistent with those used by other businesses, appraisal attributes focus on an individual's job accomplishments and also identify specific skills that are required by the position. The appraisal process focus is twofold: 1) provide employees with feedback regarding their performance and 2) provide employees with feedback on how they can improve themselves and obtain the necessary skills to advance within the business's hierarchy.

From an employee perspective, the appraisal process is usually a more sensitive area than a job description because performance appraisal documents are employee specific, but the same job description may be used for several employees. Effective managers are able to communicate areas that need improvement to an employee in a way that is positive and nonthreatening. Done constructively, employees will see performance appraisals as a positive process that encourages them to participate; otherwise, it will be seen as a fear, uncertainty, and doubt (FUD) factor activity by the employee—in which personal involvement is to be avoided, if possible.

Performance Appraisal Cycle Overview

Figure C–1 provides a conceptual diagram for the performance appraisal process that would take place on an annual cycle. The performance development system (PDS) would refer to all of the activities that take place during an annual appraisal cycle and would have two primary elements:

1. the development of a performance requirements (PR) document
2. the development of a performance appraisal (PA) document

The basic steps shown in Figure C–1 are: 1) define the employee's PR at the start of the cycle, 2) the employee works on the PR tasks during the year, 3) add appraisal information to the PR at the end of the evaluation cycle to create the PA document. During the documentation phase, both a PR and a PA are developed concurrently. The PR is for the future year and the PA is for the current year.

At the time the PA is completed, a new PR is also established for the next year. Therefore, in an annual cycle, the appraisal process generates two documents concurrently: a 1) PA for the current year and 2) a PR for the next year.

The PDS process will be described in two stages:

1. The development of PR
2. An example of a PR and PA for a hypothetical network operations manager

Employee Performance Requirements (PR) Document

Example C–3 provides a table that describes the general information categories for creating an employee PR document. This information will be used in the following section to create a PR document for a network operations manager, which will be updated at the end of the perfor-

Figure C–1.
Performance appraisal cycle.

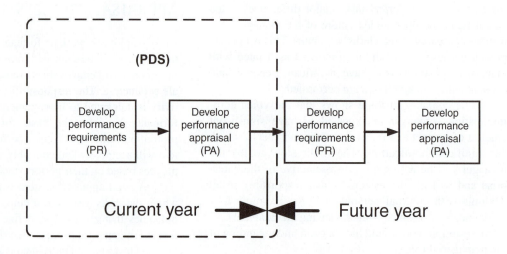

mance measurement cycle to create a performance appraisal (PA) document.

The primary responsibility for establishing a PR falls upon the direct manager of the employee. To simplify the process, a generic word processing template is used. The template is filled in with employee-specific information to create the employee's PR.

PR Templates

A standard word processing template for developing a managerial PR is shown in Example C–4. Comparison of the preparation guidelines (Example C–3) and the managerial template (Example C–4) shows that four of the five accountabilities (I, II, IV, and V) have been placed on the Example C–4 template.

The Example C–4 manager PR template is based on selecting the appropriate information from the Example C–3 guidelines and adding boilerplate information. *Boilerplate*, in a PR context, refers to including requirements that have been standardized for a job description category. The boilerplate approach minimizes the need for an employee or manager to repetitively write in standard information. Example C–4 contains minimal boilerplate information and could be the starting point for most managerial positions, regardless of how complex position responsibilities are. (When using templates for assessing employees they manage, managers would customize employee templates with the appropriate boilerplate information.)

PR Cycle

Evaluating managerial performance without identifying the managerial scope of the position (job description) or jointly setting performance goals is likely to be an unsatisfactory process for both the appraiser and the employee being appraised. Figure C–2 summarizes the desired interaction between the appraiser and the employee during the PR process that takes place at the beginning of the PDS cycle (refer to Figure C–1). The PR cycle consists of establishing the PR document that will be used as input during the PA cycle process at the end of the appraisal cycle.

As shown in Figure C–2, the manager initiates the PR process by creating a PR template that will be sent via e-mail to the employee for whom the PR is being prepared. If this is the first time the employee is being evaluated, the manager would create the template by using an electronic cutting and pasting process from an existing PR document to the new one, and customizing it for the employee. After it has been received and reviewed by the employee, the manager would set up a meeting to create

a final version that will become the basis for evaluating the employee's performance at the end of the performance cycle.

The Example C–4 template is the initial input used by the manager's manager when creating a PR. It becomes the basis for the employee's PR once the initial template is created for the individual employee.

PA Cycle

The PA cycle takes place at the end of the PDS Cycle (Figure C–1) and is created by adding results information to the PR established in the beginning of the PDS Cycle. Figure C–3 shows the steps taken during the PA Cycle.

At the end of the PDS cycle, the manager updates the PR to show the employee's performance while completing the goals/tasks/projects that were part of the initial PR. This becomes the preliminary PA. The manager sends the preliminary PA to the employee for additional comments/information. A meeting is scheduled to review the PA and reach agreement on the final PA that will be placed in the employee's file.

In practice, the next performance cycle's PR (Figure C–2) would be developed concurrently while the current cycle's PA (Figure C–3) is being developed.

The following will illustrate the application of the PDS cycle information to a hypothetical network operations manager. A PR will be developed and modified at the end of the PDS cycle to become the manager's completed PA.

PDS Example

In our example, the director of telecommunications will prepare a PR for a network operations manager, and the PR will be modified at the end of the appraisal cycle to become the network operation manager's PA. The examples will follow the process illustrated in Figures C–1, C–2, and C–3. Examples C–5 and C–6 are the end results of the PDS process that created a PA and PR.

Disclaimer: Examples C–5 and C–6 will describe a format and approach for completing a performance appraisal process. However, establishing a formal appraisal system in a real world company is a human resources department responsibility. The format and structure they use varies widely, depending on the constraints of corporate policy and the need to meet external legal requirements. The text example is intended for use as a teaching tool only to acquaint students with the need for and the general nature of an employee performance process, and to provide a focus for discussing the topic: "What do managers do?"

Information	Description
Employee-specific information	Employee-specific information includes the employee's name and position title, the appraising manager's/supervisor's name and title, the time period covered by the PDR, and the date the PDR is prepared.
Job description	A brief statement describing the employee's position and the role it has in supporting department objectives.
Accountabilities/ratings	Accountabilities are major appraisal categories, and a boilerplate description is provided on the PDR form: • Accountability I: Managerial administrative duties • Accountability II: Managerial departmental duties • Accountability III: Nonmanagerial administrative duties • Accountability IV: Projects, activities, and tasks* • Accountability V: Process skills* * Completed by managerial and nonmanagerial personnel Accountability-level ratings are required for Accountabilities I, II, and III. Individual goal ratings are used for the IV and V categories.
Goals/ratings	Goals are lower-level categories within the accountabilities categories. Some goals require a rating, which is indicated in the PDR boilerplate information. Discretionary goals that are inserted provide an opportunity for comments to be made by the employee and the appraiser, but don't require a separate rating because they will be included in the associated accomplishment or boilerplate goal rating.
Accountability/goal ratings	Accountabilities and goals receive one of three ratings: • Exceeds expectations • Meets expectations • Does not meet expectations
Overall rating categories	Three overall rating categories are provided at the end of the PDR form:* • Overall accountability/goal accomplishment (I, II, III, & IV) • Overall process skill performance (V) • Overall performance (summary of I, II, III, IV, & V) Five rating categories are available for use with the overall ratings:* • Outstanding • Above average • Effective • Needs improvement • Unsatisfactory *The appraiser is required to convert the three-level rating applied at the accomplishment/goal levels into a five-level rating structure.
Sign off	A place is provided for the employee to acknowledge the rating provided by the appraiser at the end of the appraisal process.

Boilerplate: Standard language, such as that used in preprinted forms and documents.

Example C–3. General PR guidelines.

Network Operations Manager PR

The director of telecommunications created the PR document shown in Example C–5 as a starting point for the performance appraisal process. The information contained under the job description and the various goals of Accountabilities I, II, IV, and V were extracted from the previous appraisal period's PA document used by the director for appraising the network operations manager. The specific goals shown in Example C–5 will be the primary focus of discussions between the director and the manager when they agree on a final version of the Example C–5 PR.

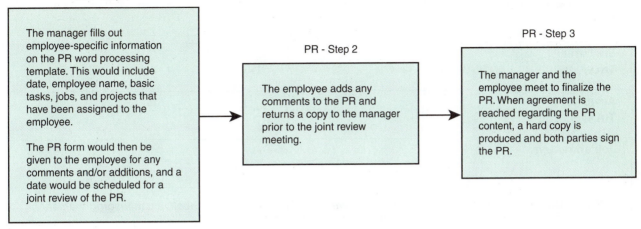

Figure C–2. Three-step performance requirements preparation process.

Examination of the Example C–5 PR shows that considerable effort has been put into developing the goals for the network operations manager (there are over twenty-five goals in the PR). The initial job statement establishes the context for the PR goals by summarizing the manager's job responsibilities. Examination of specific PR goals shows many are boilerplate items that will also be included in future network operations manager PRs. The PR includes soft goals—goals that will generate comments regarding the managerial style used by the manager, and hard goals—goals for which successful completion will be based on the existence of a measurable product, project, or other accomplishment.

Generally, PRs are longer and more complex for higher level managerial positions or for highly technical positions. Positions that perform routine functions will be short and simple and will contain many boilerplate goals that are also used for other employees who do the same job. PRs for employees who perform complex jobs are likely to have goals that relate only to that individual's PR. Examination of the Example C–5 PR reveals that many goals will apply only to the network operation manager's position. In addition, the nature of the goal statements leaves room for adding ad hoc results that will not be known until unplanned events take place during the year. For example, goal IV.C.1 states the following goal: "Provide ongoing support to branch locations accessing PDQ-Net services." The director and manager would add any new branch support requirements into the end-of-cycle PA.

The Example C–5 PR would have been developed at the start of the business's appraisal cycle, and the Example C–6 PA would be completed at the start of the next appraisal cycle. An organization that uses a standard fiscal calendar of January through December would typically begin its planning/appraisal cycle during July of the prior year and would complete it by October. For our PR example, it will be assumed that the appraisal period is coordinated with the organization's financial planning cycle and that the appraisal period will be between June 30 of the current year and July 1 of the next year.

Once the director has completed an initial version of the PR, it is sent to the manager so that the manager can make change recommendations, if desired. The director would have provided a time schedule for the three-step process shown in Figure C–3, and the manager would return the electronic PR before the meeting in which both parties will discuss the document and finalize the PR goals.

At the step 3 meeting, an agreement would be reached on the final PR, both parties would sign copies of the document and keep signed copies, and a signed copy would be forwarded to human resources. The PR document is put on hold until the end of the appraisal period, although discussions may take place between the director and manager, if needed.

We will assume that the director and the manager have agreed on the contents of the Example C–5 PR and have signed the appropriate copies. The next section will discuss how the PR is modified and evolves into a PA.

> If disagreement exists regarding the assignment of goals on the PR, the PR form provides a disclaimer statement at the end of the form that can be completed by the employee being appraised.

DATE PREPARED: **PERIOD COVERED:**	
EMPLOYEE: **TITLE:**	
APPRAISER: **TITLE:**	
JOB STATEMENT:	

ACCOUNTABILITY I: *To perform the administrative functions required for effectively managing the general operations of a department.*

STATUS: **RATING:**

GOALS:

ACCOUNTABILITY II: *To effectively manage the telecommunications department by providing PDQ Company customers with appropriate products and services needed to meet internal and external business needs.*

STATUS: **RATING:**

GOALS:

ACCOUNTABILITY IV: *To provide PDQ Company customers with appropriate products and services needed to meet internal and external business needs.*

STATUS: **RATING:**
Refer to individual goal comments.

GOALS:

Example C–4.   Manager PR template. (Page 1 of 2)

ACCOUNTABILITY V: PROCESS SKILLS PERFORMANCE

Reviews the manner in which accountabilities and goals were accomplished. This measurement typically provides a subjective indication of how others (management, peers, and end users) perceive an individual's performance.

OVERALL ACCOUNTABILITY/GOAL ACCOMPLISHMENT RATING:
(Refer to detailed performance appraisal)

OVERALL PROCESS SKILL PERFORMANCE RATING:
(Refer to detailed performance appraisal)

OVERALL PERFORMANCE RATING:

❏ *I have participated in this review, discussed its contents with my supervisor, and agree with the assessment of my performance.*

❏ I have participated in this review, discussed its contents with my supervisor, and disagree significantly. Attached is a separate page that states those items with which I disagree.

EMPLOYEE SIGNATURE: _____ DATE: _____

MANAGER SIGNATURE: _____ DATE: _____

COPIES SHOULD BE GIVEN TO EMPLOYEE, MANAGER, AND HUMAN RESOURCES

Example C–4. Manager PR template. (Page 2 of 2)

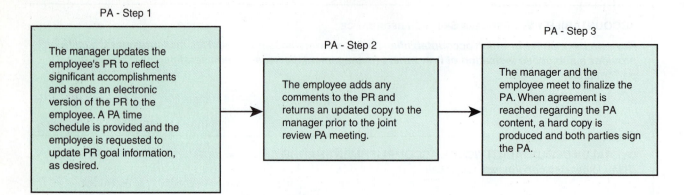

PA - Step 1

The manager updates the employee's PR to reflect significant accomplishments and sends an electronic version of the PR to the employee. A PA time schedule is provided and the employee is requested to update PR goal information, as desired.

PA - Step 2

The employee adds any comments to the PR and returns an updated copy to the manager prior to the joint review PA meeting.

PA - Step 3

The manager and the employee meet to finalize the PA. When agreement is reached regarding the PA content, a hard copy is produced and both parties sign the PA.

Figure C–3. Three step performance appraisal preparation process.

Network Operations Manager PA

In our managerial appraisal example, it is now the middle of July and it is time to begin the appraisal phase (Figure C–3) of the evaluation process that started on June 30 of the prior year.

As was the case for the PR process, the appraiser (director) initiated the PA process and established a time schedule. Example C–6 shows the completed PA, which consists of the initial PR with comments that were added by both the appraiser (the director) and the individual being appraised (the manager of network operations). Initials (Director = AEN; Manager = IMG) are used to identify the source of comments on the PA.

The Example C–5 PR changes into a PA (Example C–6) as soon as the director enters Figure C–3 step 1 information. The director adds the rating information after the manager has returned the PA (step 2 in Figure C–3), and this rating information becomes the focus for discussions at the step 3 meeting. (The rating categories used in the Example C–6 PA were provided in the Example C–5 PR.) Three rating scales are listed on the PA:

Exceeds expectations

Meets expectations

Does not meet expectations

To complicate matters, the organization's rating system uses five ratings, and the three summary ratings provided at the end of the PA must use the organization rating system:

Outstanding

Above average

Effective

Needs improvement

Unsatisfactory

If no surprises emerge at the step 3 meeting—and they should not if there is a good level of communication between the director and the manager—the PA results are finalized and copies are signed. If resolution cannot be reached on the final ratings, a follow-up meeting can be scheduled or the disagreement can be formally noted on the form, which provides the opportunity for employees to state their disagreement and attach any documents to the appraisal.

Performance Appraisal Summary

The preceding PR/PA discussion can be use in two ways:

1. as a reference guide for evaluating the performance of others or being personally evaluated

2. as a discussion forum for reviewing the accountabilities and goals in Example C–6 to identify the different roles that telecommunications managers may fill within a business enterprise

The reality is that any significant managerial role has many responsibilities. Some of them are accountabilities that are implicit in nature, where the final measurement of a manager's performance will be based on his or her boss's opinion. The performance appraisal in Example C–6 provided a reasonable—if somewhat complex—insight into the role of a manager. It has intentionally been provided with a great amount of detail, and any real-world application of this approach would be based on organizational requirements and individual operating styles.

> Managers who use informal (undocumented) job descriptions and appraisal processes are typically either 1) extremely benevolent raters of performance or 2) extremely critical raters. In the former case, everyone receives good ratings; in the latter case, no one does.

DATE PREPARED: 6-23-02
PERIOD COVERED: 6-30-02 to 7-1-03

EMPLOYEE: I. M. Grate
TITLE: Manager, Network Operations

APPRAISER: A. E. Neumann
TITLE: Director, Telecommunications

JOB STATEMENT: Responsible for managing the Network Operations department and providing telephone system, LAN, WAN, and internetwork (PDQ-Net) services at the PDQ headquarters location. Provide internetwork services to 25 remote locations, 532 external customers, and maintain the corporate network control center in a 24 × 7 operating environment.

ACCOUNTABILITY I: *To perform the administrative functions required for effectively managing the general operations of a department.*

STATUS: **RATING:**

GOALS:

I.A. To oversee and support the human resource activities required for meeting network operations department employee needs. To facilitate employee appraisal and development activities and provide for organization succession requirements.

I.B. To ensure that the department's housekeeping is in conformance with headquarters housekeeping standards.

I.C. To develop a capital expenditure, manpower, and expense forecasts in conformance with corporate requirements for the network operations department, and to operate within these forecasts except for management-approved exceptions.

I.D. To participate in the ongoing management of the network operations department and to participate in the identification, evaluation, and implementation of short- and long-term business opportunities within the department and division.

I.E. To ensure that the quality concepts are implemented in the network operations department and manage the network operations department in a manner consistent with corporate policy.

ACCOUNTABILITY II: *To effectively manage the telecommunications department by providing PDQ Company customers with appropriate products and services needed to meet internal and external business needs.*

STATUS: **RATING:**

GOALS:

II.A. To manage the network operations department so that strategic, tactical, and operational plans are prepared to meet current networking and communications consulting needs.

II.B. To manage the network operations department, both in organizational structure and in products and technologies, so that future business and technical needs of the user can be met.

II.B.1. Provide PDQ headquarters personnel with telephone, LAN, WAN, and PDQ-Net services.

II.C. To assist in the development of policies and standards to enhance current operation and/or reduce costs within the network operations department and enhance operations within PDQ Company corporate and branch functions.

Example C–5a.   Performance requirements example. (Page 1 of 3)

ACCOUNTABILITY IV: *To provide PDQ Company customers with appropriate products and services needed to meet internal and external business needs.*
STATUS: **RATING:** *Refer to individual goal comments.*
GOALS: **IV.A. ENTERPRISE PROJECTS** **IV.A.1.** To support ongoing PDQ-Net expansion activities carried out by the telecommunications development department.
IV.A.2. Provide PDQ customers with access to the PDQ customer service home page applications.
IV.B. CORPORATE PROJECTS **IV.B.1.** Add additional capacity to the headquarters PBX system.
IV.C. BRANCH PROJECTS **IV.C.1.** Provide ongoing support to branch locations accessing PDQ-Net services.
IV.D. OTHER PROJECTS **I.V.D.1.** Select and implement a new e-mail application for PDQ LANs.
ACCOUNTABILITY V: PROCESS SKILLS PERFORMANCE *Reviews the manner in which accountabilities and goals were accomplished. This measurement typically provides a subjective indication of how others (management, peers and end-users) perceive an individual's performance.*
V.A. INTERPERSONAL SKILLS: *Skills typically requiring face-to-face interaction with people.*
STATUS: **RATING:**
V.A.1. Interpersonal relations: The ability to interact professionally with all levels inside and outside the corporation in order to maintain and enhance effective business relationships.
V.A.2. Communication skills: The ability to present ideas in a clear, organized, and logical manner, both verbally and in writing, to all levels inside and outside of the corporation. The ability to listen and accept the ideas of others.
V.A.3. Teamwork: The ability to work effectively and professionally with other employees when serving as a member of a team, committee, or special group effort. The willingness to provide extra effort where needed to make the team successful.
V.A.4. Leadership: The ability to demonstrate flexibility, delegate effectively, and accept responsibility for the actions taken in support of department and/or divisional goals.
V.B. PROFESSIONAL SKILLS: *Business skills that are not related to a specific job.*
STATUS: **RATING:**
V.B.1. Flexibility: The ability to coordinate multiple projects without deterioration in quantity and quality. To accept ideas from many sources, evaluate them, make changes based on new inputs, and be responsive to the needs of the user.
V.B.2. Project management: The ability to build clear realistic plans for projects and activities, provide contingency arrangements by anticipating problems and solutions, and sharing plans with those who require information to participate in the project.
V.B.3. Organization skills: The ability to deal with work according to its appropriate priority of importance. To arrange work effectively and maintain a perspective between the overall picture and the picture details.

Example C–5b.   Performance requirements example. (Page 2 of 3)

V.B.4. Influencing skills: The ability to sell ideas effectively and anticipate and resolve conflict.

V.B.5. Innovative contribution: The ability to contribute, develop, and carry out new ideas and methods that enhance the activities or business of the department, division, or end-customer.

V.B.6. Initiative: The ability to achieve objectives when presented with extraordinary workload, environmental barriers, unforeseen or numerous changes, and the ability to go beyond the objectives independently to achieve results beneficial to the department, division, or end customer.

V.C. TECHNICAL SKILLS: *Skills involving job related knowledge and training for task achievements.*

STATUS: **RATING:**

V.C.1. Business awareness: To possess a clear understanding of the services provided by the division, as well as an understanding of the organization structure, key business goals, objectives, and issues.

V.C.2. Technical skills: The ability to demonstrate an in-depth understanding of terminology, process, and theoretical aspects of the position while maintaining a "state of the art" knowledge of the professional area.

V.C.3. Problem solving: The ability to find and deal with the essence of complex problems by asking appropriate questions, discussing problems and solutions, forecast accurately, initiate follow up, and revise solutions as appropriate.

OVERALL ACCOUNTABILITY/GOAL ACCOMPLISHMENT RATING:
(Refer to detailed performance appraisal)

OVERALL PROCESS SKILL PERFORMANCE RATING:
(Refer to detailed performance appraisal)

OVERALL PERFORMANCE RATING:

❏ *I have participated in this review, discussed its contents with my supervisor, and agree with the assessment of my performance.*

I have participated in this review, discussed its contents with my supervisor, and disagree significantly. Attached is a separate page that states those items with which I disagree.

EMPLOYEE SIGNATURE: _____   DATE: _____

MANAGER SIGNATURE: _____   DATE: _____

COPIES SHOULD BE GIVEN TO EMPLOYEE, MANAGER, AND HUMAN RESOURCES

Example C–5c.   Performance requirements example. (Page 3 of 3)

DATE PREPARED: 7-15-03
PERIOD COVERED: 6-30-02 to 7-1-03

EMPLOYEE: I. M. Grate
TITLE: Manager, Network Operations

APPRAISER: A. E. Neumann
TITLE: Director, Telecommunications

JOB STATEMENT: Responsible for managing the Network Operations department and providing telephone system, LAN, WAN, and internetwork (PDQ-Net) services at the PDQ headquarters location. Provide internetwork services to 25 remote locations, 532 external customers, and maintain the corporate network control center under a 24 × 7 operating environment.

ACCOUNTABILITY I: *To perform the administrative functions required for effectively managing the general operations of a department.*

STATUS: *Ongoing*   **RATING:** *Exceeds Expectations*

GOALS:

I.A. To oversee and support the human resource activities required for meeting network operations department employee needs. To facilitate employee appraisal and development activities and provide for organization succession requirements.

IMG note: Directly conducted 12 performance development/appraisal reviews and facilitated 15 reviews conducted by three operations supervisors.

I.B. To ensure that the department's housekeeping is in conformance with headquarters housekeeping standards.

AEN note: The PDQ network control center is a showcase that is on display for employees, customers, and supplies. We average two tour requests per week from the sales department to demonstrate the PDQ-Net's operation for prospective customers.

I.C. To develop a capital expenditure, manpower, and expense forecasts in conformance with corporate requirements for the network operations department, and to operate within these forecasts except for management-approved exceptions.

IMG Note: The network operations department year 2003 BVA performance was 2% lower than the original budget estimate.

I.D. To participate in the ongoing management of the network operations department and to participate in the identification, evaluation, and implementation of short- and long-term business opportunities within the department and division.

I.E. To ensure that the quality concepts are implemented in the network operations department and manage the network operations department in a manner consistent with corporate policy.

IMG note: The corporate internetwork logged a 99.8% uptime record while adding two more branch locations to the internetwork. This was an improvement of 6.8% over last year's operating performance.

AEN note: Network operations personnel have been extremely active in the corporate quality program and eight department members have received corporate quality awards during the past year.

Example C–6a. Completed PA example. (Page 1 of 4)

ACCOUNTABILITY II: *To effectively manage the telecommunications department by providing PDQ Company customers with appropriate products and services needed to meet internal and external business needs.*

STATUS: *Ongoing*   **RATING:** *Exceeds Expectations*

AEN note: The Los Angeles distribution center was opened on 9-11-02 and cut over onto PDQ-Net without incident. The distribution center manager, Joe Smith, wrote a letter complimenting the network operations personnel who had installed the network equipment and coordinated the network cutover activity. I have consistently received positive feedback from PDQ locations regarding the level of support received from the PDQ-Net NCC.

GOALS:

II.A. To manage the network operations department so that strategic, tactical, and operational plans are prepared to meet current networking and communications consulting needs.

IMG note: During the last year, we implemented new routers throughout PDQ-Net in an emergency mode without any service disruptions to internal or external customers. These new routers were needed to handle the increased needs created by the addition of external customers to PDQ-Net at a rate 20% higher than originally forecast by sales.

II.B. To manage the network operations department, both in organizational structure and in products and technologies, so that future business and technical needs of the user can be met.

II.B.1. Provide PDQ headquarters personnel with telephone, LAN, WAN, and PDQ-Net services.

IMG note: MAC services were provided for 369 telephone system users and 433 LAN users.

AEN note: Help Desk department statistics indicate that the LAN uptime was effectively 100% (99.98%) and the telephone services were accessible at a 100% level. Online survey forms indicate a high level of satisfaction with telephone and LAN service support functions.

II.C. To assist in the development of policies and standards to enhance current operation and/or reduce costs within the Network Operations department and enhance operations within PDQ Company corporate and branch functions.

ACCOUNTABILITY IV: *To provide PDQ Company customers with appropriate products and services needed to meet internal and external business needs.*

STATUS: **RATING:**
Refer to individual goal comments.

GOALS:

IV.A. ENTERPRISE PROJECTS

IV.A.1. To support ongoing PDQ-Net expansion activities carried out by the telecommunications development department.

IMG note: Three new hub locations were added to PDQ-Net and network operations assumed operational responsibility for them on 11-1-02.

Network operations, in coordination with the Telecommunications Development department, added two smaller PDQ locations to PDQ-Net during 2002.

IV.A.2. Provide PDQ customers with access to the PDQ customer service home page applications.

IV.B. CORPORATE PROJECTS

IV.B.1. Add additional capacity to the headquarters PBX system.

IMG note: The headquarters PBX system was upgraded to provide the capacity for adding 100 more users and the voice messaging software was upgraded to the next release level to provide telephone access to PDQ home page information. Completed August 2002.

AEN note: The project was cutover during the July 4 weekend without disrupting headquarters telephone services.

Example C–6b.   Completed PA example. (Page 2 of 4)

IV.C. BRANCH PROJECTS

IV.C.1. Provide ongoing support to branch locations accessing PDQ-Net services.

IMG note: Supported local LAN personnel in the Denver distribution center for a major upgrade to their LAN. This included sending technical support personnel to assist in the design and installation of the LAN network management center.

IV.D. OTHER PROJECTS

IV.D.1. Select and implement a new e-mail application for PDQ LANs.

IMG note: Currently working with the Telecommunications Development department to identify an alternative e-mail application to resolve ongoing operating problems experienced with the existing application. Final recommendations will be completed 10-18-03.

ACCOUNTABILITY V: PROCESS SKILLS PERFORMANCE

Reviews the manner in which accountabilities and goals were accomplished. This measurement typically provides a subjective indication of how others (management, peers, and end-users) perceive an individual's performance.

V.A. INTERPERSONAL SKILLS: *Skills typically requiring face-to-face interaction with people.*

STATUS: *Ongoing*   **RATING:** *Exceeds Expectations*

V.A.1. Interpersonal relations: The ability to interact professionally with all levels inside and outside the corporation to maintain and enhance effective business relationships.

IMG note: Participated in many meetings with PDQ branch and PDQ customers to identify PDQ-Net requirements and obtain feedback for the network operations department's activities.

V.A.2. Communication skills: The ability to present ideas in a clear, organized, and logical manner, both verbally and in writing, to all levels inside and outside of the corporation. The ability to listen and accept the ideas of others.

IMG note: Currently taking a college level professional writing course to improve my report writing skills.

V.A.3. Teamwork: The ability to work effectively and professionally with other employees when serving as a member of a team, committee, or special group effort. The willingness to provide extra effort where needed to make the team successful.

IMG note: I consistently volunteer for technical and nontechnical work groups that are formed in an ongoing basis to run headquarters social events and to establish employee communication forums.

V.A.4. Leadership: The ability to demonstrate flexibility, delegate effectively, and accept responsibility for the actions taken in support of department and/or divisional goals.

AEN note: During 2002, Ivan promoted two supervisors from the network operations group and one of his former supervisors was promoted to LAN Manager, Chicago branch. Ivan has demonstrated an ability to develop personnel by facilitating their formal education process and by providing appropriate on-the-job training opportunities.

V.B. PROFESSIONAL SKILLS: *Business skills that are not related to a specific job.*

STATUS: *Ongoing*   **RATING:** *Exceeds Expectations*

AEN note: The network operations department has seen many changes during the last year and has expanded rapidly to handle new PDQ-Net customers. Ivan has handled the change environment in an outstanding manner, including the hiring and training of new employees, developing supervisors, and implementing a wide range of operational projects.

V.B.1. Flexibility: The ability to coordinate multiple projects without deterioration in quantity and quality. To accept ideas from many sources, evaluate them, make changes based on new inputs, and to be responsive to the needs of the user.

Example C–6c.   Completed PA example. (Page 3 of 4)

V.B.2. Project management: The ability to build clear realistic plans for projects and activities, provide contingency arrangements by anticipating problems and solutions, and share plans with those who require information to participate in the project.

IMG note: The network operations department completed 23 large projects and 123 minor projects to permanently correct PDQ-Net operating problems. All projects were completed on time and within budget.

V.B.3. Organization skills: The ability to deal with work according to its appropriate priority of importance. To arrange work effectively and maintain a perspective between the overall picture and the picture details.

V.B.4. Influencing skills: The ability to sell ideas effectively and anticipate and resolve conflict.

V.B.5. Innovative contribution: The ability to contribute, develop, and carry out new ideas and methods that enhance the activities or business of the department, division, or end customer.

IMG note: Implemented new NCC procedures that reduced the need for 3rd shift coverage by one technician.

V.B.6. Initiative: The ability to achieve objectives when presented with extraordinary workload, environmental barriers, unforeseen or numerous changes, and the ability to go beyond the objectives independently to achieve results beneficial to the department, division, or end customer.

V.C. TECHNICAL SKILLS: *Skills involving job-related knowledge and training for task achievements.*
STATUS: *Ongoing* **RATING:** *Meets Expectations*

V.C.1. Business awareness: To possess a clear understanding of the services provided by the division, as well as an understanding of the organization structure, key business goals, objectives, and issues.

AEN note: Ivan has evolved from a technical background and needs to improve his understanding of the business functions and the business planning process. Based on last year's appraisal, Ivan has enrolled in an MBA program that will require approximately 4 years to complete in the evening program.

V.C.2. Technical skills: The ability to demonstrate an in-depth understanding of terminology, process, and theoretical aspects of the position while maintaining a "state of the art" knowledge of the professional area.

AEN note: Ivan's technical background was heavily data communications-oriented (LANs and internetworking). He is working on improving his knowledge regarding the technical and administrative aspects of telephone systems and has attended numerous professional and vendor meetings on these topics.

V.C.3. Problem solving: The ability to find and deal with the essence of complex problems by asking appropriate questions, discussing problems and solutions, forecast accurately, initiate follow up, and revise solutions, as appropriate.

OVERALL ACCOUNTABILITY/GOAL ACCOMPLISHMENT RATING: *Outstanding*
(Refer to detailed performance appraisal)

OVERALL PROCESS SKILL PERFORMANCE RATING: *Above Average*
(Refer to detailed performance appraisal)

OVERALL PERFORMANCE RATING: *Above Average*

❏ *I have participated in this review, discussed its contents with my supervisor, and agree with the assessment of my performance.*

❏ I have participated in this review, discussed its contents with my supervisor, and disagree significantly. Attached is a separate page that states those items with which I disagree.

EMPLOYEE SIGNATURE: _____ DATE: _____

MANAGER SIGNATURE: _____ DATE: _____

COPIES SHOULD BE GIVEN TO EMPLOYEE, MANAGER, AND HUMAN RESOURCES

Example C–6d. Completed PA example. (Page 4 of 4)

D

PRESENT VALUE OF $1

Present Value of $1.00

(a.k.a. DCF) Factors

Years	1%	3%	4%	5%	6%	7%	8%	9%	10%	11%	12%	13%	14%	15%	18%	20%
1	0.9901	0.9709	0.9615	0.9524	0.9434	0.9346	0.9259	0.9174	0.9091	0.9009	0.8929	0.8850	0.8772	0.8696	0.8475	0.8333
2	0.9803	0.9426	0.9246	0.9070	0.8900	0.8734	0.8573	0.8417	0.8264	0.8116	0.7972	0.7831	0.7695	0.7561	0.7182	0.6944
3	0.9706	0.9151	0.8890	0.8638	0.8396	0.8163	0.7938	0.7722	0.7513	0.7312	0.7118	0.6931	0.6750	0.6575	0.6086	0.5787
4	0.9610	0.8885	0.8548	0.8227	0.7921	0.7629	0.7350	0.7084	0.6830	0.6587	0.6355	0.6133	0.5921	0.5718	0.5158	0.4823
5	0.9515	0.8626	0.8219	0.7835	0.7473	0.7130	0.6806	0.6499	0.6209	0.5935	0.5674	0.5428	0.5194	0.4972	0.4371	0.4019
6	0.9420	0.8375	0.7903	0.7462	0.7050	0.6663	0.6302	0.5963	0.5645	0.5346	0.5066	0.4803	0.4556	0.4323	0.3704	0.3349
7	0.9327	0.8131	0.7599	0.7107	0.6651	0.6227	0.5835	0.5470	0.5132	0.4817	0.4523	0.4251	0.3996	0.3759	0.3139	0.2791
8	0.9235	0.7894	0.7307	0.6768	0.6274	0.5820	0.5403	0.5019	0.4665	0.4339	0.4039	0.3762	0.3506	0.3269	0.2660	0.2326
9	0.9143	0.7664	0.7026	0.6446	0.5919	0.5439	0.5002	0.4604	0.4241	0.3909	0.3606	0.3329	0.3075	0.2843	0.2255	0.1938
10	0.9053	0.7441	0.6756	0.6139	0.5584	0.5083	0.4632	0.4224	0.3855	0.3522	0.3220	0.2946	0.2697	0.2472	0.1911	0.1615

This table shows the present value (PV) of $1 received at a future time (FV). To use the table, select the interest rate from the top row and read down the column to the appropriate number of years. The PV factor is the intersection of the Year row and Interest rate column, that is, the NPV of $1 received 10 years in the future discounted at 10% = $0.3855, i.e. FV = $1.000, NPV = $0.3855

Excel Function: NPV(interest, value1, value2, . . .) Excel functions were used to calculate the values in this table.
where Value 1 = FV of Year 1, Value2 = Future Value of Year 2, etc.
e.g., NPV of $1 in Year 7 @ 7% = NPV(.07,0,0,0,0,0,0,1) = $0.6227
e.g., @ i = 12%, FV1 = 235; FV2 = 250, FV3 = 679: NPV(.12,235,250,679) = $892.42

BIBLIOGRAPHY

ACCOUNTING

Needles, Belverd E., Jr., Marian Powers, Sherry K. Mills, and Henry R. Anderson. *Principles of Accounting,* 7th Ed. Boston: Houghton Mifflin Company, 1999.

BENCHMARKING

Camp, Robert C. *Benchmarking: The Search for Industry Best Practices that Lead to Superior Performance.* Milwaukee: American Society for Quality Control Press, 1989.

FORECASTING

Makridakis, Spyros, Steven C. Wheelwright, and Rob J. Hyndman. *Forecasting: Methods and Applications,* 3rd ed. New York: John Wiley & Sons, 1998.

MANAGEMENT

Katz, Robert L. "Skills of an Effective Administrator," *Harvard Business Review* 52, 5 (1974): 90–102.

Plunkett, Warren R. and Raymond F. Attner. *Introduction to Management,* 5th ed. Belmont, CA: Wadsworth Publishing Company, 1994.

Robbins, Stephen P., and Mary Coulter. *Management*, 5th ed. Upper Saddle River, NJ: Prentice Hall, 1996.

PLANNING

Boar, Bernard H. *Practical Steps for Aligning Information Technology with Business Strategies.* New York: John Wiley and Sons, 1994.

DeThomas, Arthur R., and William B. Fredenberger *Writing a Convincing Business Plan.* Hauppauge, NY: Barron's Educational Series, 1995.

Keen, Peter G. W. *Competing in Time: Using Telecommunications for Competitive Advantage.* Cambridge, MA: Ballinger Publishing, 1986.

Nolan, Richard L. *Managing the Data Resource Function,* 2nd ed. New York: West Publishing Company, 1982.

Oppenheimer, Priscilla. *Top Down Network Design.* Indianapolis: Cisco Press, Macmillan Technical Publishing, 1999.

PROJECT MANAGEMENT

Green, James Harry. *The Irwin Handbook of Telecommunications Management,* 3rd ed. New York: McGraw Hill, 2001.

Green, James Harry. *Telecommunications Projects Made Easy.* Gilroy, TX: Telecom Books, 1997.

Kliem, Ralph L., and Irwin S. Ludin. *Project Management Practitioner's Handbook.* New York: AMACOM, 1998.

Nicholas, John M. *Managing Business & Engineering Projects: Concepts and Implementation.* Upper Saddle River, NJ: Prentice Hall, 1990.

Wysocki, Robert K., Robert Beck, Jr., and David B. Crane. *Effective Project Management.* New York: John Wiley & Sons, 1995.

TELECOMMUNICATIONS

Amato, Vito. *Cisco Networking Essentials. Vol. 1.* Indianapolis: Cisco Press, 2000.

Amato, Vito. *Cisco Networking Essentials. Vol. 2.* Indianapolis: Cisco Press, 2000.

Forouzan, Behrouz. *Introduction to Data Communications and Networking,* 2nd ed. New York: WCB/McGraw Hill, 2001.

Forouzan, Behrouz. *TCP/IP Protocol Suite.* New York: McGraw Hill, 2000.

Graham, Buck. *TCP/IP Addressing: Designing and Optimizing Your IP Addressing Scheme.* San Diego: Academic Press, 1997.

Green, James Harry. *The Irwin Handbook of Telecommunications,* 4th ed. New York: McGraw Hill, 2000.

Green, James Harry. *The Irwin Handbook of Telecommunications Management,* 3rd ed. New York: McGraw Hill, 2001.

PC SOFTWARE APPLICATION INFORMATION

Freedman, Allan. *The Computer Desktop Encyclopedia*. The Computer Language Company, Inc. 1981–2001.

Microsoft® Encanta Reference Suite 2000. © 2000. Microsoft Corporation.

Rubin, Charles. *Running Microsoft Word 2000*. Redmond, WA: Microsoft Press, 1999.

Walkenbach, John. *Microsoft Excel 2000 Bible*. New York: IDG Books, 2000.

PROBLEM SOLVING AND DECISION MAKING

Kepner, Charles H., and Benjamin B. Tregoe. *The Rational Manager*. New York: McGraw Hill, 1965.

GLOSSARY

accountabilities Appraisal categories used on an employee performance appraisal form to identify major responsibilities and set performance standards.

accounting The activity, practice, or profession of maintaining and checking the financial records of an individual or business and preparing forms and reports for tax or other financial purposes. Accounting is used for measuring the operating performance of a business enterprise.

accounting management One of five X.700 standard areas, which provide a conceptual framework for managing network investments. Accounting management provides a budget management tool to identify the cost of running a network, and the accounting information can be used to control costs and develop chargebacks for network customers.

acquisition Refers to the purchase, lease, or rental of telecommunications products and services.

acquistion accounting The accounting practices associated with acquiring telecommunications products and services—more specifically, understanding the differences between fixed and current assets and the accounting procedures used to expense them.

activity duration The time required to complete a project activity.

activity task A generic term referring to the work elements that comprise a project activity (node).

administrative project Nontechnology projects associated with a manager's business management responsibilities. These include budget preparation, preparation of employee appraisals and development plans, organizational design, management of other managers, and projects assigned by upper management. While most administrative projects are repetitive activities, ad hoc projects are typically open-ended and undefined projects for which the manager is expected to identify the requirements and "get the job done."

administrative services department The (telecommunications) administrative services department maintains the system and network equipment inventory databases, pays the bills for outside services, and issues monthly reports to users of telecommunications services.

administrative services manager A generic telecommunications management position that has the responsibility for maintaining department databases, editing and paying bills, providing administrative services to telecommunications end users, and maintaining directory services.

advanced research projects agency network (ARPANET) The research network, funded by the U.S. Department of Defense in 1969, that pioneered packet switching technologies. TCP/IP protocols were initially developed as part of ARPANET, and ARPANET evolved into today's InternetWorld Wide Web (WWW) network infrastructure.

American Telephone & Telegraph (AT&T) AT&T was founded in 1885 and acquired the original Bell Telephone Company in 1885. By 1934, AT&T (the Bell System) controlled over 80% of the U.S. local telephone company market and was the sole provider of long distance calling services. The 1984 divestiture split the Bell System and implemented a plan for the eventual deregulation of the U.S. telephone industry.

annual actual expense estimate Annual expense estimates of current year expenses. Used to calculate the next year's forecast.

annual operating cost The expenses incurred from owning a telecommunications asset (typically systems and networks). It includes maintenance, depreciation, inflation, and other overhead costs required to use the asset.

annual planning cycle The annual financial budgeting cycle undertaken by businesses to develop revenues and expense forecasts (budgets) for future time periods.

ANSI/TIA/EIA (ANSI/TIA/EIA T568A) The structured premises cabling standard used to install cabling in business and commercial buildings.

appraisal process An employee performance evaluation process, during which an employee's performance goals are established at the beginning of an appraisal cycle and the results are measured against the goals. Employee development plans are included in the appraisal process, which forms the basis for salary administration and promotion decisions.

asset depreciation The accounting process used to recover the costs associated with purchasing a fixed asset. The depreciation process (amortization) is regulated by the Internal Revenue Service (IRS) and is based on the premise that a fixed asset's purchase price should be recovered during the functional life of the asset (usually five years for hardware).

asset obsolescence A phrase used to indicate that a fixed asset has reached the end of its useful life. This may be due to wear and tear (functional obsolescence) or technological obsolescence, which means that the asset cannot operate effectively within the current technology environment because of technical incompatibility.

AT&T Information Systems (ATTIS) The postdivestiture business that replaced Western Electric as the manufacturer of communications equipment.

attitude In a telecommunications management context, attitude refers to a willingness to work with others, support business objectives, and do what is necessary to achieve business success. In a personal context, it refers to the opinions an individual has of humanity, the world, and life in general. Both contexts are interrelated.

authentication In a networking environment, authentication is when a network user's name and password are compared to a listing of authorized users and, if the system finds a match, access is granted.

automatic call distributor (ACD) ACD systems are a type of telephone system used by call centers that handle large volumes of incoming customer calls—frequently in an 800-number customer service environment. ACDs distribute incoming calls to telephone agents and are used to balance call workloads equitably, measure answering service levels, and provide statistics that can be used to manage a call center environment more effectively.

backward pass The CPM calculation process that identifies the late start (LS) and late finish (LF) values for project network activity nodes.

batch processing The practice of grouping computer transactions and processing them in a single pass against their master files to update master file information. Batch processing was used to maximize the use of mainframe computer resources.

Bell Operating Companies The twenty-two Bell Operating Companies (BOCs) that were part of the original Bell System. The BOCs provided local telephone services to customers in their geographic area and were the regulated interface into the AT&T Long Lines long distance telephone network.

Bell System The predivestiture Bell System consisted of AT&T Long Lines, Western Electric, Bell Laboratories, and twenty-two Bell Operating Companies. The Bell System dominated the U.S. telecommunications industry from the early 1900s to January 1, 1984, when it was split up in accordance with Modified Final Judgment provisions.

Bell Telephone Company The original company formed by Alexander Graham Bell in 1877 to provide telephone services under the patents granted to him. AT&T purchased the Bell Telephone Company in 1885.

benchmarking As used in business organizations, benchmarking involves comparing internal operations or practices with those in other companies or departments to identify potential operational weakness. The use of an external standard provides a level of objectivity that is not possible if performance standards are internally generated.

board of directors In a corporate business organization, the board of directors is directly accountable to the stockholders for the operating results of the business. It typically consists of several officers of the corporation and a number of outside directors. The management board (upper management) of the corporation is selected by the board of directors and is directly accountable to them.

boilerplate Stock or formulaic language that is used repetitively in legal forms or other standardized documents.

bona fide managers Management personnel who have a manager title and have direct supervisory responsibility for subordinates (as opposed to individuals who have a manager title and do not have any direct reports).

bottom-up planning In bottom-up planning, the tasks and subtasks are identified first and then grouped into macrolevel planning activities.

budget variance Deviations found when budgets (financial plans) are compared to actual financial performance (variance = budget − actual). When negative variances are generated (meaning that budgets are overspent), corrective action may be required.

budget *v.* actual (BVA)   The managerial control philosophy based on establishing a financial plan (the budget) for income and expense elements and measuring operational performance (the actuals) by comparing budget and actual information. A monthly BVA report would be the vehicle for managing expenses and income projects.

budget *v.* actual cash drawer   An analogy used in the text, where the budget dollars in a BVA report are considered similar to the cash found in the cash drawer of a mom and pop business. In this analogy, the department manager would accord the budget dollars the same attention that the proprietors of a mom and pop business would.

business communication content   The detailed information contained in a business communication: the issues, topics, recommendations, or questions addressed in the communication. While of major importance to the individual preparing the communication, it will be read by the reader only if the format and style warrant serious consideration.

business communication format   The organization of the business communication—how it looks. The appearance is the most important aspect of a business communication because it will determine whether the intended audience will accept or reject the message, depending upon its appearance. From an upper management perspective, a sloppy message is viewed as incompetence on the part of the originator.

business communication style   The basic organization of the information contained in a business communication, including the grammar and information presentation structure. The desired business style includes elements of readability, conciseness, directness, and unambiguousness.

business communication system   The use of communication technology to support business operations.

business English   A style of speaking and writing that is direct, easy to understand, concise, unambiguous, timely, and free of jargon. Basic grammar applies, but the focus is on communicating information efficiently and effectively.

business management   The managerial responsibilities associated with managing a department or other functional unit that is part of a business.

business management skills   Management skills needed to operate a department within the context of a given business. These management skills include people management skills, business skills, accounting skills, and interorganization communication skills.

business planning process   Refers to the top-down planning approach, where business objectives are formulated in a long-range strategic plan. These strategic business objectives become the basis for developing plans for different departments within the business. The strategic business and departmental plans continue through a business planning process; a tactical phase converts concepts into budgets and an operational phase implements the budgets created during the tactical planning process.

business profitability   The focus on the key objective of a business enterprise—to provide a fair return on investments made by the stockholders of a corporation, where profit = revenues − expenses. All managerial personnel are accountable for meeting the profitability expectations of stockholders.

business unit plan   A business unit is a general reference to a business entity, defined in terms of customers, products, and structure. Large corporations may consist of multiple business units that develop plans based on their individual operating environments.

business writing   Communications written for an upper management readership that conforms to a business enterprise's format and style standards.

bypass   During the postdivestiture period, bypass referred to the practice of a long distance customer bypassing the local telephone company office and connecting directly to a long distance provider's network. It was a major concern for telephone companies because it eliminated the revenues they obtained from long distance calling subsidies.

cabling model   A cabling model is used in the text to estimate the backbone and horizontal cabling length requirements in a premises cabling system. The model is intended for use as a preliminary planning model and is not a substitute for the detailed planning needed to identify actual cabling needs.

call detail record (CDR)   CDRs are computer records generated by PBX systems to keep track of all calls made on the system (intercommunications, local, and long distance calls). The CDR information includes calling number, called number, calendar date, time of day, and length of calls. CDR software generates call cost information by user extension (SMDR).

capital expenditures   The costs associated with owning and operating fixed assets. The expenditure for the purchase or expansion of a long-term asset.

Carterfone   The Carter Electronics Corporation of Dallas, Texas, sued AT&T for the right to attach its private radio system to the public network by using its Carterfone product. The FCC ruled in favor of the suit and the decision opened the door for the attachment of non-Bell devices into the Bell System Network.

cash drawer management   A reference to a simple cash-based environment, in which the financial status of a business can be ascertained by looking at the cash drawer balance. A solvent business would have a positive cash balance, but an insolvent business would have a zero cash balance and IOUs. The BVA reporting concept is a modern equivalent, where a positive variance is analogous to a positive cash balance in a cash drawer management environment and a negative variance is analogous to a negative cash balance.

Catch-22   A situation described in Joseph Heller's satire, *Catch-22*, where following the rules prevents someone from solving the problem that the rules are written to solve.

centralized business   In centralized businesses, the decision making is concentrated in upper management functions and lower management is given the responsibility for implementing the decisions.

Centrex telephone system   A telephone system that uses telephone company CO call processing equipment to provide telephone system services to customer locations. It is an alternative to the Private Branch Exchange (PBX) telephone system.

chain of command   The managerial hierarchy that exists between the lowest managerial position and every position on the way to the top managerial position in a business. The chain of command is used to pass formal communication between managerial levels to ensure that all managerial goals are aligned with top management goals.

chargebacks   Costs incurred by the business and charged back to the user. For telecommunications departments, this means putting in a system (see *chargeback system*) so the business can allocate telecommunications costs to user departments.

chargeback system   In telecommunications, used to identify the resources consumed by end users and to allocate the cost of these resources back into a department's operating budget.

common carrier   A company that provides telecommunications services to the general public, for example, a telephone company or long distance network service provider.

common cost data   The basic accounting parameters used in the text for the Life Cycle Analysis/Net Present Value (LCA/NPV) financial model used to identify the costs of owning and operating fixed assets. In a business, these parameters would be established by the accounting department.

common sense   Frequently has a negative connotation, such as "he or she doesn't have common sense." The reality is that common sense is normally acquired through experience. Individuals who have experience use common sense (good practices) to perform an activity. Individuals who have fewer skills but who use common sense (experience) will frequently outperform more intelligent, more knowledgeable individuals who don't use common sense.

compound document   An electronic document constructed from two or more applications by using Object Linking and Embedding (OLE) to insert documents, art, or other information from one application into another.

computer   A general purpose machine that processes data according to a set of instructions that is stored internally—either temporarily or permanently. The computer and all equipment attached to it are called *hardware*, and the instructions that tell hardware what to do are called *software*. Computers may be centralized computers (mainframes) or distributed computers (personal computers [PCs]).

conceptual skills   The term, used in Robert Katz's 1974 *Harvard Business Review* article, that allows an individual to intuitively understand "the whole and its parts."

configuration management   One of five X.700 standard areas. Provides a conceptual framework for managing network investments. It utilizes information stored in a database called the management information database (MIB) to initialize networks during planned or unplanned startups. The MIB information contains a detailed inventory of network elements, including data links, hardware, and software.

content   Refer to *business communication content*.

controllable expenses   Budget expenses that must be authorized by the budget manager for payment. (As opposed to noncontrollable expenses, which are paid without the budget manager's authorization.)

critical path (CP)   The longest path, from the beginning to the end, through a project network diagram. It represents the shortest time that a project can be completed for a given set of project activity durations.

critical path method (CPM)   A network-based project management approach that assumes activity (project network node) duration estimates are reliable and can be used to provide project duration estimates.

current performance   An assessment for the current appraisal period. It indicates actual operational performance as opposed to the potential for future advancement. From an appraisal perspective, strong current performance with strong future potential is the basis for being considered a candidate for promotion opportunities.

customer premises equipment (CPE)   A term used during the 1984 Bell System Divestiture to identify equipment located in telephone customer locations. CPE was deregulated under the terms of the divestiture settlement.

customer satisfaction   Good customer satisfaction occurs when a customer perceives that the product or service received meets or exceeds expectations. Using customer satisfaction as a definition of good performance requires a performance standard developed from a customer's perspective.

decentralized business   Refers to where the concentration of decision making is in a business. In decentralized businesses, decision making is largely delegated to lower management levels, and relatively few areas are reserved for upper management. Lower management levels make many decisions and also implement them.

decision making process   A general process for evaluating options and selecting the best one. A good decision-making process will include an assesment of mandatory and optional requirements.

decision points   Refers to the various management checkpoints provided in a project plan to periodically assess the project's ongoing viability and present assessment information to business management. The purpose of these decision points is to ensure that the original justification for a project has not been negated by changes in the business or technology environment.

deliverable   The tangible results generated by a managerial or technical project, especially the supporting documentation used to define and manage different project activities.

department management   The management of business departments, such as accounting, manufacturing, finance, purchasing, marketing, sales, telecommunications, and research.

department manager   A manager in charge of a departmental management area.

departmental structure   In business design, the practice of organizing departments based on their functions. An extension of the "division of labor" philosophy used to develop the efficient use of highly skilled personnel. The structure was developed in 1911, when managerial knowledge was formalized.

departmental team   Teams headed up by a designated manager (as compared to teams for which there is no designated manager, and managerial authority is a shared responsibility).

development manager   A generic telecommunications management position. This manager has the responsibility for the technical design and implementation of major telecommunications technology projects and for the development of the operating documentation that will be used to maintain and operate the installed systems and networks.

digital communication   The use of binary signals to encode communication transmissions.

direct attachment device (DAA)   An interface device that was required when non-Bell equipment was connected to the Bell System network. DAAs were intended to isolate the long-distance calling network from potential problems caused by using non-Bell equipment.

direct expenses   A term used in chargeback systems to identify expenses for which the direct user of the service can be identified. Direct expenses are charged back to the individual who uses the service.

disaster planning   A (business) disaster is any event that causes the disruption of normal business activities. *Disaster planning* is the activity of planning for the prevention of business disasters (see *disaster prevention*) and quickly recovering from any business disasters caused by telecommunications service outages (see *disaster recovery*).

disaster prevention   Elements include those activities that are initiated to prevent the occurrence of a business disaster by protecting critical resources from intentional or unintentional damage.

disaster recovery   Elements include those activities that help to resume normal business operation when a disruption has taken place. Disaster recovery procedures should address short-term and long-term outage conditions.

division of labor   Taking jobs and breaking them down into simple tasks, then assigning tasks, instead of the whole job, to employees. An automobile manufacturing assembly line of the 1950s is an example of *division of labor*.

division structure   In business design, the division structure was used to implement departmental business structures based on a product, geographic location, or customer focus. This limited the size of the business and avoided some of the problems associated with large businesses.

downsizing   Reducing the size of a business by cutting back on staffing levels.

drill down   A term used to describe the process of beginning at top-level, broad information elements and searching "down" through the layers of lower level information that supports the top level conclusions. Drilling down is common practice while searching for files or information on the Internet, where high level gopher menus and WWW pages are frequently very general but become more specific at each lower level.

dumb terminals A display terminal that does not have computer processing capability. It is normally used in a computer environment, where the terminal operation is entirely dependent on the main computer for any application processing.

early finish (EF) The earliest time that work on a network project activity can be completed.

early start (ES) The earliest time that work on a network project activity can begin, based on the time requirements of its predecessor activities.

EIA/TIA 568 Standard The premises cabling system standard established by the Electronics Industry Association and Telecommunications Industry Association (EIA/TIA) for selecting, designing, and implementing cabling systems in commercial locations. The standard has been adopted by the American National Standards Institute (ANSI) and is now referred to as ANSI/TIA/EIA-T568-A.

800-service The direct distance dialing (DDD) service introduced in the 1970s. Allowed the called party to be billed for the cost of the call. See *inbound wide area telecommunications services (INWATS)*.

electronic commerce (e-commerce) Doing business online, typically via Web facilities. It is also called e-business, e-retailing, and I-commerce. E-commerce implies that goods and services can be purchased online.

electronic mail e-mail The transmission of memos and messages over a network. Mail is sent to a simulated mailbox on the network mail server or host computer until it is interrogated and deleted.

enabling skills Enabling skills are the basic education skills (reading, writing, and mathematics), higher education skills (communication, business, technology, and learning), and PC skills that allow an individual to learn new skills quickly and develop creative solutions for different problem situations.

enterprise A commercial company or firm; organized business activities aimed specifically at growth and profit.

enterprise planning In large businesses that consist of multiple business units, the enterprise plan would define the role of each business unit with respect to the main business. In smaller companies, the business unit plan may also be the enterprise plan.

enterprise telecommunications plan A telecommunications technology plan that identifies the various technology elements (telephone systems, LANs, WANs, and internetworks) for a business. It should identify the business benefits to be gained from the plan and the costs associated with acquiring and operating it.

equal access The 1984 divestiture provision that required divested Bell telephone companies to provide telephone company customers with equal access to all long distance network providers by January 1, 1986. (Prior to the divestiture, Bell telephone companies provided access to Bell System (AT&T) network services only.

escalation procedures The use of a trigger mechanism—typically a time duration—to ensure that network or system problems are not buried in an unsolved status. Different levels of support are identified, ranging from simple problem solving procedures to highly complex problem solving procedures. The escalation proceeds from simple to the highly complex levels. A three level procedure is commonly used: level 1 = problem login and standardized help procedures, level 2 = technical support assistance, and level 3 = engineering support assistance.

estimating factor Used in the text to estimate telecommunications equipment and cabling requirements based on staffing levels. While the estimating factors used in the text are "guesstimate" factors, the use of realistic estimates will generate very reliable estimates for planning purposes.

exception management (managing by exception) Refers to the practice of reviewing information or activities and ranking them according to importance for follow up. The exception process would start at the top of the list (highest priority) and use the available time to address high priority items.

expense code Detailed expense categories used to identify expenses such as salaries, outside services, overtime, and office equipment rental. BVA reporting occurs at the expense code level.

external customer Refers to telecommunications customers who are not employees of the business that provides telecommunications services.

facilitator Someone who aids or assists in a process by encouraging people to find their own solutions to problems or tasks.

facilities management An external service provider assumes ownership of a business enterprise's infrastructure and personnel resources to operate them for the exclusive use of the original owner. It is considered a form of outsourcing.

fault management One of five X.700 standard areas. Provides a conceptual framework for managing network investments. Fault management is concerned with: 1) monitoring network operations to identify actual or potential problems, 2) isolating the problem source from the network, 3) repairing or replacing the faulty element, and 4) restoring the network to its original condition.

Fayol, Henri A pioneer in developing general administrative theories that emerged in the early 1900s to describe aspects of good management. He is best known for providing the foundation theories on which the POLC Model of management is based.

Federal Communications Commission (FCC) The U.S. regulatory agency created by the Communications Act of 1934. Regulates interstate and international wire, radio, and other broadcast transmissions, including telephone, telegraph, and telecommunications.

50%/50% manager A manager who has a balance of management skills and technology skills. The 50/50 manager has strong overall skills gained through education, training, and experience. These skills represent a 50% managerial skills (business and technology management) and 50% technology skills (technical telecommunications).

final schedule A project activity schedule that provides a single start and finish date for each activity (see *technical schedule*).

fitness for purpose A term in the Uniform Commercial Code (UCC) stating that "new equipment is warranted to fulfill the purpose for which it was manufactured but not for any other purposes that were not intended."

fixed asset cost The cost required to purchase a fixed asset. The costs assigned to fixed assets are dictated by the Internal Revenue Service (IRS) and are generally referred to as all the expenses required for purchasing a fixed asset and making it usable. This may include training and facility modifications.

fixed assets An accounting term that refers to things owned by a business and used to support business activities. Fixed assets have an operating life of more than one year compared to "current assets," which are disposable items that have an operating life of less than one year.

float (slack) The amount of time that a project activity can be delayed beyond its ES date without delaying the project.

forecast factors Used to calculate expenses that are affected by staffing levels or service rates (see *RateFF* and *StaffFF*).

forecasting Predicting future events. In telecommunications, expense forecasting is used to establish budgets for the BVA process and is an important managerial activity.

format Refer to *business communication format*.

forward pass The CPM calculation process that identifies the ES and EF values for project network activity nodes.

future potential An assessment of an employee's or manager's potential for promotion into a more responsible position. The employee appraisal process should identify those skills needed for promotion and should recommend the means for obtaining the necessary skills.

Gantt Chart A chart that shows individual parts of a project as bars against a horizontal time scale. Gantt charts are used as a project planning tool for developing schedules and were developed in the early 1900s by Henry L. Gantt, a classical management theorist.

glass house The name given to large mainframe computer data centers, which typically contained one or more mainframes. Early data centers were often constructed with floor to ceiling windows that gave visitors an unobstructed view of the data processing environment.

graphical user interface (GUI) A graphics-based user interface that incorporates icons, pull down menus, and a mouse. The GUI has become the standard way that most people use to interact with a computer.

hacker A person who uses computer expertise to gain unauthorized access to a computer system that belongs to another, either to learn about the system or to examine its data.

help desk department A telecommunications department set up to provide a single point of contact (SPOC) for users of telecommunications services.

help desk manager A generic telecommunications management position. This manager has the responsibility to provide an SPOC to users of telecommunications systems and network services. The help desk department is a customer service department and is expected to act as an ombudsmen for the end user community. The help desk department typically maintains an incident reporting system (IRS) that documents user problems and their solutions.

hierarchy of needs A management theory developed by Abraham Maslow, a human resources theorist, to identify the different motivation methods that can be used with employees.

hot site A location that contains computer and communications equipment that is maintained in a standby mode to serve as an emergency backup if a business's facility or information technology infrastructure is not available because it failed or was destroyed.

human skills The term used in Robert Katz's 1974 *Harvard Business Review* article to refer to influence skills—the ability to effectively influence, motivate, direct, or supervise others. Unlike technical skills, human skills are measured by the results that are achieved (not by testing).

inbound wide area telecommunications services (IN-WATS) The DDD service introduced in the 1970s that allowed the called party to be billed for the cost of the call. (See *800-service*).

incident reporting system (IRS) A manual or computerized system used to log end user inquiries and to identify the root cause for the inquiries. User incidents would typically consist of information requests and problem reports.

incremental budgeting The budgeting practice of accepting past revenue and expense history as an operating base and concentrating on changes (plus or minus) to that base. The alternative approach is zero based budgeting (ZBB).

inflation factor Used in the text's LCA/NPV financial model to estimate the impact of inflation on future year expenses.

insourcing The term *insourcing* was established as an antonym for *outsourcing*, which arrived on the business scene during the 1980s. *Insourcing* refers to the use of internal personnel to do functions that could be outsourced.

interexchange carrier (IXC) An organization that provides interstate (long distance) communications services within the U.S. Includes AT&T, MCI WorldCom, Sprint, and more than 700 other organizations.

internal customers Telecommunications customers who are employees of the business that provides telecommunications services.

International Standards Organization (ISO) An organization founded in 1946. Sets international standards for all technology fields except electrical and electronics, which is governed by the older International Electrotechnical Commission (IEC). Communications standards were initially developed by an ISO committee, the CCITT (Consultative Committee for International Telephony and Telegraphy). Today, standards are a responsibility handled by the ITU (International Telecommunications Union).

International Telecommunications Union (ITU) An international organization originally founded in 1865 as the International Telegraph Union for the purpose of coordinating the development of European telegraph standards. Today, the ITU engages in worldwide standards and is a specialized agency of the United Nations. It replaced the OSI CCITT as the focal point for the development of worldwide communications standards.

Internet The underlying technical network infrastructure that links computer networks all over the world by satellite and telephone, connecting users with service networks such as e-mail and the World Wide Web. The Internet's underlying technology was developed as part of the ARPANET project.

internetwork The network connectivity infrastructure that links wide area networks (WANs) and local area networks (LANs) to computers and computer communication processors to provide a seamless, any-to-any communication environment.

job description An official, written description of the responsibilities and requirements of a specific job that an employee does.

knowledge A general awareness or possession of information, facts, ideas, truths, or principles.

late finish (LF) The latest time at which an activity can be completed without causing a delay in project completion.

late start (LS) The latest time that that work on a network project activity can start and still complete the project on time.

layered writing style Refers to structuring business communications in a modular style, where each document section begins with a summary of what is covered, then describes the supporting details and their relevance to the documentation objective, and concludes by summarizing the main points. From a top level perspective, the document should begin by stating its purpose and end by stating what is being requested (next steps). The objective of a layered writing style is to provide a document that: 1) identifies its relevance to the reader at the beginning, 2) provides a format that allows the reader to quickly select areas of interest, 3) effectively highlights key areas for which decisions are required, and 4) clearly identifies the next steps needed to address any issues raised in the document.

leader Leaders are people who guide or direct others by showing them the correct way to do things or influencing behavior. Ideally, managers should be leaders, but this is not always the case.

lease A legal contract that allows the exclusive possession or use of another's property for a specified period of time and for specified payments. In general, longer term leases offer more favorable rates than short term leases. Leasing time periods are longer than rental agreements, which may be viewed as a form of short-term leasing at higher cost but with shorter time commitments.

leveraging expenses   The technique of incurring expenses in one expense category to provide major savings opportunities in a different expense category. For example, a $10,000 a year expense may be added in the telecommunications budget to offset a personnel savings of $100,000 in a customer service department.

life cycle analysis (LCA)   The concept of examining all the costs incurred by a fixed asset (telecommunications equipment) or services over the asset's functional life. These costs would include the initial purchase or lease costs and any operating costs. Evaluation of an asset's life cycle costs provides a more accurate cost picture than looking at initial costs and ongoing operating costs separately.

life cycle costs   See *life cycle analysis*.

line conditioning   A technical process of modifying the electrical characteristics of analog communications lines, in the early computer communications era, to improve operating speeds and reduce errors. *Conditioned lines* were expensive and were limited to point-to-point communications applications.

local area network (LAN)   A communications network that serves users within a physical location. It is made up of servers, workstations, and a network operating system and normally has a communications link to access remote WANs or LANs.

local exchange carrier (LEC)   An organization that provides local telephone service within the U.S., which includes the RBOCs, large companies such as GTE, and more than a thousand smaller and rural telephone companies (approximately 1,300 in total). An LEC provides service from the customer premises to its local exchange (CO) within a local geographic area.

macroplanning   A planning framework customized to incorporate key checkpoints as part of the process.

mainframe computer   In the mid-1960s, all computers were called mainframes, because the term referred to a main CPU cabinet housed in a glass house. Today, it refers to a powerful computer system.

management   Organizing and controlling the affairs of a business; the skillful handling or use of resources.

management board   The top level managers in a business who have the responsibility for carrying out daily operations. Sometimes also referred to as upper management, which typically consists of the president or chief executive officer (CEO) and the managers who report to the management board.

management style   The leadership style that a manager uses when dealing with others. Two extremes are: 1) an employee-oriented style and 2) a production-oriented or results-oriented style.

manager   Someone responsible for directing and controlling the work and personnel in a business, or a particular department within a business.

manager of managers   A manager who has primary responsibility for managing other managers (as opposed to managers who have only direct supervisory responsibility for department personnel).

manager profitability strategies   The managerial strategy of initiating activities that reduce expenses and increase revenues and, thereby, contribute directly to business profitability objectives.

managerial role   The basic managerial requirements associated with a management position. These include controlling the affairs of a business to meet enterprise objectives and skillfully handling the people, time, and money (PTM) resources used to achieve those objectives.

managerial scoring system   A concept: a dollar is the managerial unit of performance, and upper management acts as the scorekeeper. A manager must have the appropriate dollar score in various expense and revenue activities that are evaluated from an upper management perspective.

managerial success   While managerial success is largely a matter of personal perspective, long-term success in a business will be based on scoring well in the organization's managerial scoring system.

managerial toolset   The set of skills needed to operate successfully as a telecommunications manager, including enabling skills, business management skills, and technology management skills, coupled with the appropriate experience so that the manager (a craftsperson) is able to manage a telecommunications department.

mandatory requirements   A term used in the text's decision making model to indicate that an option must successfully meet a (mandatory) requirement or it will be rejected.

matrix structure   In business design, it refers to modifying the business structure to assign departmental personnel to projects. Individuals may work on one or more projects while carrying out department activities. The matrix structure has been used extensively in the aircraft industry.

merchantability A term in the Uniform Commercial Code (UCC), stating that "new equipment must conform to generally accepted industry standards."

microplanning A planning framework that can be applied to many different situations. Consists of generic, fundamental elements. The POLC Model planning process is an example of a microplanning approach.

milestone Used to identify key points within a project and provide a checkpoint to ensure the completion of internal or external events. A CPM milestone activity is assigned an activity duration of zero.

mom and pop concept A concept based on the precorporate, proprietorship business environment, where the basic simplicity of the operation allowed the family-based (mom and pop) proprietors to quickly assess their operational status and initiate required actions. The success or failure of a mom and pop operation rested directly on the proprietors, and the current status of the business could be evaluated by using cash drawer management. Within this text, the corporate department organization is, conceptually, a mom and pop operation. The department manager is directly accountable for results.

move, add, or change (MAC) Terminology that originated in the regulated telecommunications environment. It referred to moving, adding, or modifying telephone equipment for customers. Today the term may be applied to any communications device.

National Science Foundation's network (NSFNET) The initial title given to ARPANET when it officially changed from a military network project to a commercial network. NSFNET evolved into the Internet.

natural monopoly The concept of designating private companies as regulated monopolies to control the cost and quality of utility-type services to the public.

network architecture Refers to the overall design infrastructure used in a telecommunications network (LAN, WAN, or internetwork) and includes standards for the hardware, software, access methods, and protocols required to ensure interoperability of connected devices.

network management entity (NME) X.700 terminology used to identify the software interface between proprietary network elements and the central network management manager.

network management manager (NMM) X.700 terminology used to identify the common central resource that manages a multiprotocol, multivendor network environment based on the X.700 architecture.

network management system (NMS) The product used to manage network resources. The X.700 Standard provides an International Standards Organization (ISO) standard that describes a nonproprietary network management system architecture.

1984 divestiture The implementation of the 1984 Modified Final Judgment. It is also referred to as the *Bell System Divestiture*.

1984 Modified Final Judgment The 1984 Modified Final Judgment issued by the Justice Department found AT&T (the Bell System) guilty of antitrust violations and resulted in a split of the Bell System. The twenty-two Bell Operating Companies were formed into seven Regional Bell Operating Companies (RBOCs) and divested from AT&T as separate businesses. AT&T Long Lines and Western Electric were initially split into separate operating entities (ATTCOM and American Bell Corporation, respectively) that were still owned by AT&T, and Bell Labs also remained with AT&T under a different operating charter.

1982 Consent Decree The agreement, between the Justice Department and AT&T, that resulted in the 1984 divestiture of the Bell System. In the consent decree, AT&T agreed to break up the Bell System in return for the Justice Department's dropping of all antitrust charges against AT&T.

ninety-ninety rule of projects A whimsical observation that 90% of a project's benefits can be derived by expending 10% of a project's total investment cost, while the remaining 10% of the project's benefits requires the expenditure of the remaining 90% of the project's total investment cost. (A reaffirmation of the law of diminishing returns, which states that once the initial benefits have been realized, subsequent benefits do not rise in proportion to the additional effort or investment necessary to produce them.)

noncontrollable expense A budget expense that is automatically paid without the budget manager's authorization. Noncontrollable expenses consist of costs that are allocated to a department budget by the accounting department. They include the overhead costs for running the business or to cover the costs of internal departments dedicated to providing services to other internal departments (e.g., personnel).

operating costs In a business management context, refers to any budgets established to maintain department operation. In the technology management context, refers to the costs incurred while operating fixed assets (such as telecommunications equipment) after they have been implemented.

operational plan   The final budget used to implement business and technology strategies. The primary emphasis in executing an *operational plan* is to complete all objectives on time and within budget.

operational planning   Implementation planning associated with executing a tactical budget plan. Operating plans have limited flexibility for changing the time or budget resources provided by the tactical plan, and the primary focus is on ensuring that operating results are accomplished within the time and budget constraints of the tactical plan (see *strategic planning* and *tactical planning*).

operations management   The different departments needed to support and operate the business telecommunications infrastructure (LANs, WANs, internetworks, and telephone systems, etc.) in a business. Typical operations management departments include operations, administrative services, and help desk.

operations manager   A generic telecommunications management position. Operations managers have the responsibility for operating existing systems and networks to provide service to an enterprise's employees and customers. Operations departments often operate 24×7, thus, they require a high level of technical competence.

optional requirements   Decision factors that are subjective in nature, i.e., where a relative importance can be assigned between them by using a weighting system that provides higher weights to more important attributes. A scoring system is used so that decision options that contain multiple attributes can be compared to each other. A higher score means that an alternative is more desirable.

optional requirements rating   Ratings assigned to attributes used for decision making. The ratings are normally on a relative scale ranging from 1 to 10, where 10 is the highest value and 1 is the lowest value assigned.

optional requirements score   Optional requirements used for decision making are assigned importance/ desirability weights ranging from 1 to 10. Ten is the highest weight and 1 is the lowest weight used. Attribute score = optional requirements rating × optional requirements weight.

organization breadth   The horizontal dimension of organization charts—the number of departments at the same level. The horizontal dimension is largest at lower levels. Organization breadth affects span of control.

organization depth   The vertical dimension of organization charts—the number of levels in an organization from the top to the bottom. Organization depth impacts chain of command communications.

organization design   The development of a business structure that establishes communication and authority roles of the individuals who are members of the organization.

other charges and expenses (OCC)   Term originated in the regulated communications environment. It referred to costs associated with moving, adding, or changing (MAC) telephone equipment for customers. Today, the term may be applied to the costs associated with MAC charges for any communication device.

outsourcing   The use of external personnel or services to perform functions that historically (pre-1980s) had been performed by internal personnel.

overhead expense   The general operating expenses incurred to run a business that cannot be allocated to a single department budget. They are shared costs that are typically allocated across the departments or products that benefit from them.

Palo Alto Research Center (PARC)   Located in Palo Alto, California. PARC originated many computer-based technologies, including PCs, GUIs, and Ethernet LANs.

people, time, and money (PTM)   The basic managerial resources provided to a manager by a business. Managerial performance will be determined by the degree to which these basic resources are used effectively and efficiently.

performance appraisal   A periodic (typically annual) evaluation of employee performance by supervisors to determine the effectiveness of the way a person does his or her job. Performance appraisals become the basis for employee development and promotion plans, and for salary administration activities.

performance management   One of five X.700 standard areas that provide a conceptual framework for managing network investments. Performance management elements monitor network operations to identify substandard performance, peak load conditions, and network response times. It stores performance-related information in the management information base (MIB) for capacity planning activities.

personal computer (PC)   PCs are desktop computers that evolved from large, mainframe computer systems that occupied many square feet of floor space. Originally falling within the category of microcomputers, PCs were viewed as being stand-alone systems intended for use by a single individual. The power and capability of today's notebook PCs are many times greater than those of their early mainframe computer parents.

personal computer (PC) desktop applications
Software applications that are currently available in a typical suite of office applications provide productivity tools for improving personal performance. Software that is very useful for telecommunications management personnel include word processing, spreadsheet, presentation graphics, networking graphics, and project management applications.

personal computer (PC) skills   Within the context of this text, it refers to the effective use of PC software, including the operating system, word processing, spreadsheet, presentations graphics, networking graphics, and project management applications.

plain old telephone system service (POTS)   Refers to the precomputer, analog-based voice telephone network. In the U.S., most of the remaining analog lines are the ones from your house or office to the telephone company's CO.

planning   Working something out, in detail, *before it is begun*. Provides documentation that is used to measure operating performance (Plan *v.* actual).

planning horizon   Refers to the number of planning periods in the future used to generate a plan. The planning period is typically a year, but shorter time periods may be used.

planning manager   A generic telecommunications management position. Planning managers have the responsibility for strategic capacity planning, technology assessment, and budget preparation activities. In smaller organizations, individual telecommunications managers fill the planning role.

POLC (control)   A POLC Model element. Ensures that actual operating performance meets the plan standards established at the beginning of the management activity.

POLC goals   A POLC Model element. States the desired managerial outcome in terms of measurable results. POLC goals will be the basis for management plans and the assessment of success or failure of the final results.

POLC (lead)   A POLC Model element. Ensures that all POLC Model elements are carried out effectively and efficiently to meet POLC goals.

POLC Model   A management process method based on the works of Henri Fayol, a general administrative theorist whose works were published during the early 1900s. POLC refers to the planning, organizing, leading, and controlling activities that are used by managers to effectively and efficiently meet managerial objectives.

POLC (organize)   A POLC Model element. Identifies and assigns the appropriate resources (people, time, and money) so that POLC goals can be achieved.

POLC (plan)   A POLC Model element. Develops a plan that becomes the baseline measurement for managerial control activities. The plan identifies the required resources (organize), managerial elements (lead), and control mechanism (control) used.

Postal, Telephone, and Telegraph (PTT) Agency   The governmental agency responsible for combined postal, telegraph, and telephone services in many countries outside of the U.S. The 1984 Bell System Divestiture in the U.S. triggered a worldwide movement toward making all communication services competitive. The process used by PTTs to move their regulated products and services into a competitive environment is sometimes referred to as "liberalization."

potential problem analysis (PPA)   A decision-making technique that examines selected problem solutions and decisions in an open-ended manner (thinking "outside the box") to identify any potential problems with implementing the solution or decision.

practical forecasting   A term used in the text for differentiating the telecommunications expense forecasting procedures from the more theoretical forecasting techniques that are commonly used.

pragmatic expense forecasting model   The specific spreadsheet-driven forecasting model used in Chapter 16 to generate department and telecommunications expense forecasts.

predecessor activity   In a project network diagram, it refers to activities that precede another activity. The "tail" of the activity arrows is attached to predecessor activities.

preliminary screening   Used in the text's acquisition decision-making process to conduct a preliminary estimate of a vendor's response to a bid request and determine if it is competitive compared to other bids that have been received. The purpose of the preliminary screening is to minimize the work effort in the acquisition assessment process by quickly eliminating noncompetitive bids and focusing on viable bids.

premises cabling system   The technical connectivity medium and equipment used to interconnect communication devices in a location (premises) and in a multilocation campus environment.

present value (PV)   PV factors are used to convert future period currency values to the current time so that effects of interest rates are removed when comparing revenues and expenses from different time periods.

Private Branch Exchange (PBX) telephone system
Telephone equipment that allowed a large number of people in a single company location to have intercom services and access to outside long distance calling services. The call processing unit and all supporting equipment is installed at a customer's locations. A Centrex telephone system is an alternative type of telephone system.

problem analysis process   A standard approach for examining problems to identify the most likely solution for correcting it. Most problem analysis processes are based on the scientific method.

productivity   The rate at which a company produces goods or services in relation to the amount of materials and number of employees needed for the production process.

productivity tool   An activity or function that improves the internal operating performance of a business enterprise—it allows more to be done with fewer resources.

profit center   In general, an organizational unit or activity of a company for which income and expenses are reported independently. In this text, it is used to describe the accountability a department manager has for the smallest profit center operating unit: the department.

program evaluation and review technique (PERT)   A network-based project management approach that assumes that activity (project network node) duration estimates are unreliable. PERT uses statistical means to provide a best-guess project duration estimate.

project   A sequence of interrelated activities that have a common goal and must be completed by a specific time, within an assigned budget, and according to a set of specifications.

project accounting   The project management role of managing project budgets. Similar to the role provided by an accounting department in a business to ensure that financial resources are monitored and controlled.

project activity   A project work package that is shown as a node in a project network diagram. Activities have interdependencies with each other and require time and work resources to complete.

project administration   Project administration activities support a project manager's efforts in planning, monitoring, controlling, and reporting project performance.

project attributes   Refers to the basic information elements used to describe a project during the feasibility process. A general project description, the sequence of project activities, a project schedule, and the budgetary resource requirements. Project attributes will change as project steps are carried out.

project contract administration   An internal contact for authorizing work activities and change orders, and to ensure that contract terms are followed by both the contractor and the client.

project duration   The time required to complete a project.

project event   Major occurrences that take place on a project schedule. They are names given to project activities or tasks and are completed within a specified time duration.

project life cycle   The phases of a project, from its conceptual beginnings until it is implemented as an operational system, network, or product (see *project life cycle model*).

project life cycle model   The six step model used in the text as a basis for explaining project management activities. The six step sequence consists of: organizing the project, developing a detailed project plan, developing a detailed project design, acquiring project components, implementing the detailed design, and completing postcutover activities.

project management   The activities needed to ensure that an administrative or technology project meets its objectives and will be implemented on time and within budget.

project management skills   The managerial skills needed to ensure that an administrative or technology project meets its objectives on time and within budget.

project manager   The individual assigned primary responsibility for completing a project on time and within budget. In self-directed project teams, the responsibilities are shared among team members.

project milestone   A significant project point on a project schedule used to define project progress. Unlike an event, it is a point in time and is assigned a time duration of zero.

project network diagram   A graphic display of the major work activities that make up a project. Nodes represent activities and tasks that may have a hierarchical relationship to each other.

project node   An activity node shown on a project network diagram.

project risk   Refers to the likelihood of a project being completed on time and within budget. High risk projects are unlikely to meet initial time and cost estimates. This risk should be identified and the appropriate checkpoints should be provided during the project to assess the viability of continuing. Risk assessment elements include project size, experience of the project team, and the project's structure (see structured and unstructured projects).

project task   A detailed work element used to subdivide project activities into a work breakdown structure (WBS) format.

project team functions The various roles performed by a project management team, including planning and control, project engineering, project accounting, project contract administration, and support of end user functions.

project technical administration The technical role that must be performed by the project management team when a telecommunications system or network is being developed and implemented. This role is sometimes referred to as "project engineering."

protocol Rules governing the transmission and reception of computerized data.

Public Utility Commission (PUC) A government-regulated company that provides an essential public service such as water, gas, electricity, or telephone services.

Pulse Code Modulation (PCM) A technique for converting analog signals into a digital format. Digitized voice signals provide major advantages in cost and quality compared to analog transmissions.

purchase Buying something by using money or its equivalent. A purchase results in the transfer of ownership from a seller to a buyer and, in a business, results in the creation of a fixed asset.

qualitative forecasting The use of expert opinion to develop forecasts.

quantitative forecasting The use of historical data and statistical models to estimate future information. Quantitative forecasting is the most commonly used forecasting technique.

rate forecast factor (RateFF) The rate adjustment factor applied to current year data to allow for next year's rate changes.

reengineering The business management theory that advocates reorganizing a business on the basis of the market value that each department adds to the products produced by the business, and carrying out this process periodically.

Regional Holding Companies (RHCs) The post-AT&T divestiture organization that resulted when the twenty-two Bell Operating Companies were reorganized into seven Regional Holding Companies.

rent A regular payment made to an owner in return for the right to use equipment or property. Rental agreements are short-term variations of leasing agreements. Leasing agreements offer lower rates but contractually obligate lessees to longer time periods.

request for information (RFI) The practice of requesting information about a supplier's qualifications and product offerings. May be initiated by a phone call or by requesting a response to detailed requirements information. RFI information does not place legal obligations on either the requestor or the vendor.

request for proposal (RFP) A set of specifications, issued by a prospective buyer that defines the performance requirements the selected product(s) must meet. RFPs may be formal or informal. A formal RFP is a legal contract between the buyer and supplier. RFPs request product pricing information that remains in effect for some time period so that the buyer can compare alternatives and obtain the internal approvals for accepting an RFP bid.

request for quotation (RFQ) A document used to obtain formal price quotes from a supplier of products or services for standard products. A description of the product is sufficient to uniquely identify it. Purchasing organizations frequently use RFQs to purchase commodity-type products—products that are widely used and widely available.

rightsizing A phrase used in business in conjunction with reengineering efforts to indicate that an organizational assessment will be used to ensure that the functions performed and size of the operating units are in balance.

salary administration The corporate policies and practices used to allocate promotions and pay raises.

scientific management A title used to describe the early works of classical management theorists during the early 1900s, when management principles and documentation were becoming established. Frederick Taylor published a book titled *Principles of Scientific Management* in 1911, and is credited with beginning the modern management era. He helped develop the existing body of management theory and principles.

security management One of five X.700 standard areas. Provides a conceptual framework for managing network investments. Provides procedures to protect the network technology investment and the confidentiality of the information that can be accessed through the network. Security management provides guidelines for managing network access through an authentication process, assigning authorization based on individual user access rights, and maintaining a history of unauthorized attempts to access the network.

self-directed team Project teams are resources dedicated to individual projects. Self-directed project teams operate without an assigned project manager, and team members are responsible for assuming the accountability for managing the project and meeting project objectives.

7-Layer OSI Model   An ISO standard for worldwide communication. Defines a framework for implementing protocols in seven layers by defining the interface requirements between the protocol layers. The model provides multivendor interoperability by allowing equipment manufacturers to use proprietary protocols within the layer, as long as they adhere to the OSI interface standards.

shared expenses   A term used in chargeback systems to identify expenses for which the direct user of the service cannot be identified. Shared expenses are charged among the users of a service through some acceptable allocation scheme.

skill   The ability to do something well, usually gained through experience and training.

span of control   The number of subordinates who report to a manager. In classical management teachings, the recommended span of control was seven. In practice, the number of direct reports depends on the specific environment.

special weapons and tactics (SWAT) project team   SWAT teams are specialized project teams whose responsibility is to start projects, establish the project management infrastructure needed to execute the project, and turn over the newly created project management infrastructure to a project team that will implement the project.

staff forecast factor (StaffFF)   A term used in the text to identify the staffing adjustment factor applied to current year data to allow for next year's staffing changes.

station message detail record (SMDR)   SMDR records are computer records generated by PBX systems to keep track of all calls made on the system (intercommunications, local, and long distance calls). The SMDR information includes calling number, called number, calendar date, time of day, and length of calls. SMDR software generates call cost information by user extension.

stockholder   Someone who owns one or more shares of a company's stock and to whom all company managerial personnel are ultimately accountable. Stockholders are the owners of corporations in the current business environment, and corporations are the dominant form of business organization.

straight line deprecation   A common depreciation method where expense recovery is based on allowing an asset to be depreciated equally during each year of its asset life.

strategic planning   Plans developed with a planning horizon of more than three years before it will be implemented. Strategic plans are typically conceptual in nature, and financial considerations are based on educated estimates (see *tactical planning* and *operational planning*).

strategic resource   A business function or activity that is used to expand the existing revenues (sales) within a business.

structured projects   Projects whose activities are clearly understood and whose interrelationships (sequences) are known. Structured projects have been implemented previously so that there is a high level of confidence in being able to execute them on schedule and within budget (see *unstructured projects*).

style   Refer to *business communication style*.

successor activity   In a project network diagram, activities that follow another activity. The heads of activity arrows are attached to successor activities.

supervision   An overseeing activity. Someone monitors the activities of others to ensure that a task or activity is being carried out correctly.

system integration   A consulting service. The service provider custom designs a system or network made up of standard products and services for a client.

tactical planning   Plans developed with a planning horizon of between one and three years before they will be implemented. Tactical plans are finance-oriented plans that emphasize developing budgets that provide the resources needed to implement their objectives (see *strategic planning* and *operational planning*.)

tasks   The elements that make up an activity. Typically, a group of tasks must be accomplished in a specified sequence to complete an activity, and the time required is the activity duration time.

tax effect   When conducting cost *v.* benefit analysis for business purposes, tax credits may exist. Their impact is generically referred to as the "tax effect." The complexity and changing rules associated with determining tax effects is best delegated to accounting personnel who are skilled in this area.

team structure   In business design, it refers to modifying the departmental structure to assign departmental personnel to teams that have very specific goals and objectives to perform. In a team structure, the activities normally performed by managers become the responsibility of team members.

technical schedule   A CPM project activity schedule showing both the forward pass and backward pass schedule results.

technical skills   The term used in Robert Katz's 1974 *Harvard Business Review* article to refer to subject matter skills—skills for which some form of testing is the basis for judging skill levels.

technology management   The management responsibilities associated with the selection, design, development, implementation, and operation processes used to effectively and efficiently implement telecommunications technologies.

technology projects   Involve the acquisition of telecommunications equipment and services. Technical specialists typically implement technology projects, which are large projects that require the application of project management skills to coordinate multiple activities and ensure the project's completion on time and within budget.

telecommunications   The science and technology of transmitting information electronically by means of wires or radio signals with integrated encoding and decoding equipment.

Telecommunications Act of 1996   Follow-up legislation to the Justice Department's 1984 Modified Final Judgment ruling. The 1996 act redefined the role of the FCC and continued the trend toward the total deregulation of all telecommunications services—including local telephone services.

telecommunications project life cycle model   Developed in the text to provide a mechanism for estimating telecommunications technology equipment and cost requirements in a business. Elements included in the model are equipment and cabling requirements and the analysis of the associated costs in a financial LCA/NPV format.

telecommunications seven step acquisition model   Developed in the text to document the process for acquiring telecommunications products and services. Contains some of the elements found in the telecommunications planning model.

telegraph   A method of long distance communications that uses coded electric impulses transmitted through wires.

telephone system   The equipment used in businesses to provide voice communication between employees and the external business environment. Telephone system equipment may be located on the business premises (PBX Systems) or in the telephone CO (Centrex Systems).

telephony   The science of converting sound into electrical signals, transmitting it within cables or via radio, and reconverting it back into sound. It refers to the use of telephones for communicating over a network.

terms and conditions   A section contained in the RFP that identifies the legal and operating terms an RFP bidder must agree to prior to being accepted as a qualified bidder.

three stage business process model   A generic model used to describe business processes: 1) purchase labor, material, and services, 2) produce goods and services, and 3) sell goods and services. On a flowchart, item 1 provides input to item 2 and item 2 is the input to item 3.

three views of telecommunications   Telecommunications can be viewed by upper management in three ways: 1) a cost to be minimized, 2) a productivity tool for improving internal organizational efficiency, or 3) a strategic asset for increasing revenues. Ideally, an organization should support all three viewpoints concurrently.

top-down planning   Starts with a framework and adds detail to establish a plan. Top-down planning requires the identification of broad objectives and developing the detailed plans needed to achieve the broad objectives.

Transmission Control Protocol/Internet Protocol (TCP/IP)   A suite of computer communication protocols developed as part of the ARPANET project. TCP/IP protocols provide the communications infrastructure for the Internet. TCP/IP is the dominant internetworking protocol for private networks.

Uniform Commercial Code (UCC)   A body of law that applies to all new equipment purchases in the U.S.—except for the state of Louisiana. It provides a level of buyer protection for purchases of new equipment by stating merchantability and fitness for purpose requirements that must be met by new equipment.

universal service   The Bell System vision that drove the implementation of U.S. telephone services for most of the twentieth century. Simplistically stated, it had the objective of providing high quality, cost effective telephone service to all households and businesses in the U.S.

unstructured projects   Projects that have activities that are not clearly understood. Their interrelationship (sequence) is dependent upon the knowledge gained while the project is underway. Research projects are examples of unstructured projects because a successor activity frequently requires the completion of a predecessor activity before the successor tasks can be defined. The schedule and cost of unstructured projects is difficult to assess in advance and the risk of not meeting initial schedules or budget limits is high.

upper management   The top layer of management in a business enterprise, reports to the president or chief executive officer. Upper managers are also referred to collectively as "the management board," which has a primary responsibility to the company's stockholders (owners) for achieving business profitability objectives.

variance (budget variances)   Variances are calculated based on the equation: variance = budget − actual. A key managerial tool for measuring fiscal and managerial performance.

VisiCalc   The original personal computer-based spreadsheet software program. Many consider VisiCalc to be the "killer" application responsible for driving the subsequent development of PCs as a replacement for mainframe computing.

vision statement   A document stating the managerial principles that will be used to manage a business or department. Vision statements consist of philosophies that are general in nature and applicable to any planning period.

Web browser   A computer software application that allows a user to search for information on the World Wide Web (WWW).

wide area network (WAN)   The long distance network infrastructure used to provide communication between different locations. WAN services are primarily furnished by common carriers.

Work Breakdown Structure (WBS)   The WBS is a hierarchical listing of activities and tasks that defines the work effort needed to complete a project. Major work segment groupings are shown as activities (nodes) of a project network diagram.

World Wide Web (WWW)   The information infrastructure supported by the Internet; the network that links computer networks all over the world by satellite and telephone. The WWW is the large set of linked documents and other files located on computers connected through the Internet.

X.700   A set of standards issued by the International Standards Organization (ISO). Provides a network management framework for managing communication. The X.700 standard provides standards in five areas: 1) fault management, 2) configuration management, 3) performance management, 4) security management, and 5) accounting management. It also describes a "manager/agent" network management architecture that uses a network management manager (NMM) to control proprietary network components with network management entity (NME) software as an interface between the NMM and the proprietary component.

Zero Based Budgeting (ZBB)   The budgeting process of starting out with a zero base and completely justifying every expense by identifying "decision packages" of minibudgets for each product and/or service generated by a department. Each decision package is reviewed during each budget cycle and is ranked by value against all other decision packages. Only packages of higher importance will be approved.

INDEX

Business style outline, 99
Business unit coordination, 161–163
Business unit plans, 108
Business writing, 12, 97–102
BVA reports. *See* Budget *versus* actual (BVA) reports
Bypassing, 38

Cable length estimation model, 193–199
Cabling. *See also* Premises cabling
    backbone, 197–198, 208, 513, 514
    horizontal, 198–199, 208, 513, 514
    multifloor, 199
    structured system worksheet, 209
Calculator, in Excel, 597–598
Calculators, mechanical, 273
Calendar (2003), 357, 376, 388
Calendar (2004), 313, 320, 357
Call detail reporting (CDR) systems, 438
Capital appropriation budgets, 282
Capital dollars, 183
Capital expenditure budgets, 72, 183–184
Capital expenditures, and fixed assets, 510
Carroll, Lewis, 110
Carter Electronics, 31
Carterfone, 31–32, 36
Case studies
    acquisition management, 565–588
    evaluating acquisition options, 553–559
    financial planning, 202, 204–211
    operations management, 475–491
    PBX telephone system acquisition (HealthProd),
        553–559
    PBX telephone system acquisition (TransProd),
        566–587
    PBX telephone system project planning, 306–323, 351–361
    performance appraisal project, 286–289
    project management, 366–393, 612–622
    telecommunications planning, 225–266
Cash drawer management, 414, 458
Cash payment, as acquisition payment option, 502–503, 525
Catalysts, 135, 589
Catch-22, telecommunications, 86–87, 91–92
Catch-22 (Heller), 86
Catholic Church, 117
CDR (call detail reporting) systems, 438
Cells, in Excel, 595
Cellular radio, 42
Census Bureau, 43
Centralization, 73–74, 120, 164, 165
Centrex telephone systems, 32–33, 438
Cerebral skills, 88, 133–134
Certified Public Accountants (CPAs), 458
Chain of command, 162, 163, 171

Change, adapting to, 78–79
Change drivers
    business, 34–38
    defined, 27
    regulatory, 30–34
    telecommunications, 29–30
    World Wide Web, 38–39
Chargeback systems
    accounting management, 413
    administrative services department, 406
    basic charge calculation worksheet, 444
    call detail reporting systems, 438
    cost allocation concepts, 436–438
    defined, 73
    direct *versus* shared chargebacks, 437
    as managerial tool, 466
    managing operating expenses, 414
    shared chargebacks, 437–438
    telephone expense, 439–442, 469–471
Charts, organization. *See* Organization charts
Checkpoints, in project management, 280
Chronologies
    telecommunications, 29–30
    telephony transmission media, 41, 42
Chrysler Corporation, 36
Classical management theorists, 118–119, 121, 164, 168
Closed systems, 121
Coaxial cable, 42
Coke, discovery of, 8
Combination strategy, 124
Command, chain of, 162, 163, 171
Command, unity of, 120, 166–167
Commercial Building Telecommunications Cabling
        Standard. *See* ANSI/TIA/EIA 568-A Standard
Commodity type products, 529
Common carrier services, outsourcing of, 508
Common cost data table, 201
Common sense, 476
Communication
    basics, 27–29
    binary, 40
    business, 12, 18, 96–102
    department, 403
    digital, 41
    and enterprise planning, 112
    impact of computers on, 164
    international regulatory issues, 5
    with upper management, 11–12, 76–78
Commuting needs example, 189, 192, 193
Competitive bidding, 516
Composite management model, 121–122
Compound documents
    defined, 592

Development department, 174, 403, 502, 522
Development manager job description, 56
Digital communication, 41
Direct distance dialing (DDD), 6
Direct expenses, 439, 440
Direction, unit of, 120
Directors, board of, 67, 68
Directory services, 406
Disaster planning, 406–407, 462
Disaster prevention, 462–464
Disaster recovery, 464–465
Disasters
    defined, 406–407, 462
    short term *versus* long term, 464
Discipline, in management, 120
Discretionary budget cuts, 72
Divisional organization structure, 169, 170
Divisional plans, 108
Division of labor, 118, 120, 154, 159, 167
Documentation
    acquisition evaluation, 549–550, 551
    job design and documentation, 401
    management, 577–583, 584–587
    PBX telephone system project example, 319–323
    presentation, 582–583, 584–587
    for projects, 351
    purchase, 525, 529–531
Document views, in Microsoft Word, 593
Downsizing, 72–73, 74
Draco, 96
DTE (Data Terminating Equipment), 28
Dumb terminals, 36, 44, 45
DuPont Company, 274, 294

E. I. DuPont Company, 274, 294
Early finish (EF), 295–296, 299, 318, 603
Early start (ES), 295–296, 299, 603
Earthquake damage, 463
Eastman Kodak Company, 507
Eckert, Presper, 43
Eckert-Mauchly Computer Corporation, 43
E-commerce, 13, 27, 38, 71, 164
EDI (Electronic Data Interchange), 38
Education attribute, in job descriptions, 626, 629
Education skills, basic, 16–17
EF. *See* Early finish (EF)
Egyptian pyramids, 117
EIA (Electronics Industry Association). *See* ANSI/TIA/EIA
    568-A Standard
800-services, 5–6, 36, 439
800-services project example, 74–75
Electricity outages, 463
Electronic adding machines, 43

Electronic commerce. *See* E-commerce
Electronic Data Interchange (EDI), 38
Electronic mail, 91, 95
Electronic Numerical Integrator And Calculator (ENIAC), 43
Electronics Industry Association (EIA). *See* ANSI/TIA/EIA
    568-A Standard
Elephant and blind men fable, 26
E-mail, 91, 95
Employee development, 402, 460
Employee hiring, 401–402
Employee motivation, 167
Employee-oriented leadership, 135–136
Employee training, 156, 402
Empowerment, 164
Enabling skills, 15, 16, 89, 130. *See also specific skills*
ENIAC (Electronic Numerical Integrator And Calculator), 43
Enterprise organization, 172–173
Enterprise planning, 107–127. *See also* Planning
    advantages, 111–112
    business-level telecommunications planning, 124
    business planning *versus* annual planning, 115–116
    defined, 108–109, 124
    disadvantages, 112
    enterprise level business planning, 122–124
    and management theory, 117–122
    planning process, 112–115
    and POLC Model, 110–111
    process overview, 109, 423
    quotations, 110
    rationale for, 109–112
Enterprise plans, 108
Equal access provision (long distance services), 33
Equations
    budget *versus* actual, 112, 146, 429, 465
    depreciation, 201, 511
    early finish, 299, 603
    early start, 299, 603
    float time, 299
    floor space annual cost, 546
    future year costs, 201
    inflation factor, 201, 546
    late finish, 299, 603
    late start, 299, 603
    managerial performance, 157
    power and air conditioning annual cost, 546
    profitability, 12, 465
    salvage value, 201, 546
    straight line depreciation, 546
    total asset cost, 546
Equipment failure, 462–463
Equipment installation and repair contracts, 506–507
Equipment purchase contracts, 504–505
Equipment rooms, 513, 514

Morse, Samuel F. B., 4, 10, 40
Morse code, 40
Mosaic (Web browser), 38
Motivation, employee, 167
MS-Excel. *See* Microsoft Excel
MS-PowerPoint. *See* Microsoft PowerPoint
MS-Project. *See* Microsoft Project
MS-Visio. *See* Microsoft Visio
MS-Word. *See* Microsoft Word
Multibusiness plans, 108
Munsterberg, Hugo, 120

National accounts, 528–529
National Science Foundation Network (NSFNET), 37, 38
Natural monopolies, telegraph and telephone services as, 29
Needs hierarchy, 120, 121
Net present value. *See* Life cycle analysis/net present value
    standard financial model
NETWORKDAY function, in Excel, 319
Network diagrams. *See* Project network diagrams
Networking case study. *See* Project management case study
Network management entity (NME), 410
Network management manager (NMM), 409–410
Network management star topology, 514
Network management system (NMS), 408
Network operations managers
    performance appraisal example, 636, 640–643
    performance requirements example, 632–633, 637–639
New York Stock Exchange (NYSE), 462
1984 Bell System Divestiture, 31, 32, 37, 506
1984 Modified Final Judgment, 6
1982 Consent Decree, 32. *See also* 1984 Bell System
    Divestiture
90-90 rule of projects, 350
NME (network management entity), 410
NMM (network management manager), 409–410
NMS (network management system), 408
Noncontrollable expenses, 415, 428, 431
Normal expenses, 510
Normal view, in Microsoft Word, 593
Norming stage, 344
NSFNET (National Science Foundation Network), 37, 38
NYSE (New York Stock Exchange), 462

Object Linking and Embedding (OLE), 592, 593–594
Obsolescence, 6–7, 10, 510–511
OLE (Object Linking and Embedding), 592, 593–594
Open pair wires, 41, 42
Open System Interconnect (OSI) Model. *See* 7-Layer Open
    System Interconnect (OSI) model
Open systems, 121
OpenView product line, 408
Operating budgets, 72, 423

annual adjustments, 485–486, 487
    for departments, 145, 459
    jury of opinion, 147, 427
    model, 427–428
    practical, 428–430
    reliability, 428
    revenue, 145
    telephone expense example, 445–446
    theoretical, 426–428
    tools, 147
Formalization, in organization design and structure, 163
Formal leaders, 155
Format, in business communications, 12, 77, 97, 98
Forming stage, 344
Formulas, in Excel, 595–596
Forward pass
    activity dates, 300–301
    calculation, 299
    schedule, 301, 302, 303, 312, 314, 321, 376, 377
Functional obsolescence, 510
Functional organization structure, 168–169
Functional plans, 108
Functional support, in project teams, 346
Functional teams, 342–343
Future needs, anticipating, 111
Future year costs equation, 201

Gantt, Henry L., 118–119, 147–148, 273, 294
Gantt charts, 118–119, 147–148, 273, 294
Gantt Chart view, in Microsoft Project, 612–613, 618, 619,
    621, 622
Gantt Chart Wizard, in Microsoft Project, 618–620
General administrative theorists, 119, 121
General Motors (GM), 35, 36, 159
Gerstner, Louis, 110
Gilbreth, Frank, 118
Gilbreth, Lillian, 118
Gilman, George F., 456
Glass houses, 29, 43
GM (General Motors), 35, 36, 159
Goals
    identifying, 110–111, 112–113
    as POLC Model element, 9, 59, 60, 111, 288
Gordian knots, 18
Government bureaucracies, 350
Graduation project example, 296–299
Graphical user interface (GUI), 45, 94
Graphics, in business writing, 99, 100
Great Atlantic and Pacific Tea Company (A & P), 456
Great Wall of China, 117
Grid pattern selection, in cable length estimation model,
    193–196
Grocery store chains, 456, 458

Growth strategy, 123
Guesses, in forecasting, 427
Guidance attribute, in job descriptions, 625, 627, 628
Guided media, in transmission system, 28
GUI (graphical user interface), 45, 94

Hackers, protecting against, 464
Hartford, George Huntington, 456
Harvard Business Review, 87, 132–133
HealthProd Corporation case studies
    PBX telephone system acquisitions case study, 553–559
    project management, 366–393, 612–622
Heller, Joseph, 86
Help desk, 174, 400, 403, 404–405
Help desk manager job description, 56
Hesse, Hermann, 86
Hewlett Packard, 408
Hierarchical organization structure, 161–162
Hierarchical star topology, 514
Hierarchy of needs, 120, 121
Higher education skills, 17, 91–92
High frequency radio telephones, 42
Hiring, employee, 401–402
Hollerith, Herman, 43
Hollerith cards, 43
Horizontal cabling
    ABC Company case study, 208
    in cable length estimation model, 198–199
    in premises cabling standard, 513, 514
Horizontal dimension, of business structures, 167
Hot sites, in disaster prevention and recovery, 462, 464
Human resources department, 627, 631
Human resources theorists, 119–121
Human skills, 87, 133, 134

IBM. *See* International Business Machine Corporation (IBM)
IEEE (Institute of Electrical and Electronics Engineers), 45
Inbound wide area telecommunications services (INWATS),
    5–6, 36, 439
Incentive pay, 118
Incident reporting system (IRS), 404–405, 424, 461
Incidents, defined, 403
Incremental budgeting, 144–145
Individual interests, subordination of, 120
Industrial psychology, 120
Industrial Revolution
    and business management, 8, 154
    and managerial role, 14, 50, 58, 117
    organization design and structure, 159
Inflation factor, 200, 201, 546
Influencing skills, 87, 133, 134
Informal leaders, 155
Information gathering, in forecasting, 427

Twisted pair cables, 42
Typing skills, 17, 94

UCC (Uniform Commercial Code), 504–505
Unguided media, in transmission system, 28
Uniform Commercial Code (UCC), 504–505
Uninterruptible power source (UPS), 463
Unit of direction, 120
Unity of command, 120, 166–167
UNIVersal Automatic Computer (UNIVAC), 43
Universal service, 26, 30, 31
Upper management
    as business communication audience, 96, 97
    business management views, 18
    communicating with, 11–12, 76–78
    and customer satisfaction, 75
    and expenses, 72–75
    functions, 10
    managerial characteristics, 70–76
    performance standards, 70
    and planning, 75–76
    reading criteria, 97–98
    and revenues, 71–72
    as score keepers, 67–68
    telecommunications views, 5, 68–70, 398, 399
UPS (uninterruptible power source), 463
U.S. Navy Special Projects Office, 274, 294

Vandalism, 463–464
Variance reports. *See* Budget *versus* actual (BVA) reports
Variances. *See* Budget variances
Vendors
    acquisition specifications, 498–499
    documentation, in acquisition process, 549–550, 551
    evaluating, 499, 534–535
    information about, 528
    major, 185
    preferred, 534
    in purchase order process, 501
    selecting, 499, 528–529, 535, 553
    types, 7
Vertical dimension, of business structures, 166–167
VisiCalc, 18, 93–94, 594–595. *See also* Microsoft Excel
Visio. *See* Microsoft Visio
Vision statements, 114, 115–116. *See also* Enterprise planning
Voice communications manager job description, 627–629
Voice networks, 36, 40–43

Walker, Morgan R., 294
WANs. *See* Wide area networks (WANs)
Warranties, implicit, 505
Water damage, 463

WATS (wide area telecommunications services), 5–6, 36, 439
WBS. *See* Work breakdown structure (WBS)
The Wealth of Nations (Smith), 118, 159
Web browsers, 38, 95
Weber, Max, 119
Weights, for optional requirements, 140
Western Electric, 32
Wide area networks (WANs)
    ABC Company case study, 207, 208, 210
    development, 45
    estimating basic requirements, 199
    PetroProd case study, 236, 242, 243, 247, 248, 249
    as technology planning element, 185–186
    worksheet, 210
Wide area telecommunications services (WATS), 5–6, 36, 439
Wiring closets, 513, 514
Word. *See* Microsoft Word
Word processing. *See also* Microsoft Word
    and administrative projects, 289
    advantages, 17, 94
    for preliminary project plans, 356
    for project administrative plans, 369
Work areas, in premises cabling standard, 513, 514
Workbooks, in Excel, 595
Work breakdown structure (WBS), 304–305
    HealthProd Corporation case study, 372–374, 384–386
    PBX telephone system project example, 306, 308–310, 357–359
Work calendar information, in Microsoft Project, 614, 615
WORKDAY function, in Excel, 319, 603–605, 606
Worksheets
    acquisition evaluation, 551
    chargeback system basic charge calculation, 444
    financial planning calculations, 208–211
    internetwork, 210
    Microsoft Excel, 595–596
    physical network, 209
    structured cabling system, 209
    telecommunications planning, 199–200
    telephone system, 210
    wide area network worksheet, 210
    workstation/server equipment, 209
Workstation requirements, 192, 209
Work teams, 171–172, 342–343
World Wide Web (WWW), 27, 37, 38–39
Writing skills, 16, 91. *See also* Business writing
WWW (World Wide Web), 27, 37, 38–39

X. 700 Network Management Standard, 407–413, 423–424
Xerox Corporation, 45, 112, 138
Year-to-date (YTD) actual expenses analysis, 442

Zero based budgeting (ZBB), 145, 509